D0448771

INTERNATIONAL
AND
INTERCULTURAL
COMMUNICATION

A TAXONOMY OF
CONCEPTS IN COMMUNICATION
by Reed H. Blake and Edwin O. Haroldsen

COMMUNICATIONS AND MEDIA
Constructing a Cross Discipline
by George N. Gordon

ETHICS AND THE PRESS
Readings in Mass Media Morality
Edited by John C. Merrill and Ralph D. Barney

DRAMA IN LIFE
The Uses of Communication in Society
Edited by James E. Combs and Michael W. Mansfield

INTERNATIONAL AND INTERCULTURAL COMMUNICATION
Edited by Heinz-Dietrich Fischer and John C. Merrill

Humanistic Studies in | H | S | *The Communication Arts*
| C | A |

INTERNATIONAL AND INTERCULTURAL COMMUNICATION

Edited, with introductory notes
and suggested readings
by HEINZ-DIETRICH FISCHER, Ph.D.
and JOHN CALHOUN MERRILL, Ph.D.

COMMUNICATION ARTS BOOKS

HASTINGS HOUSE PUBLISHERS • NEW YORK

To

ERIKA J. FISCHER

and

DOROTHY J. MERRILL

Copyright © 1976, 1970 by Hastings House, Publishers, Inc.

First published, June 1970
Second printing, June 1974

Second Edition, Revised and Enlarged, September 1976

LIBRARY OF CONGRESS CATALOGING IN PUBLICATION DATA

Fischer, Heinz Dietrich, 1937–   comp.
    International and intercultural communication.

    (Communication arts books)
    First published in 1970 under title: International communication.
        Bibliography: p.   Includes index.
        1. Mass media—Addresses, essays, lectures. 2. Intercultural communication—Addresses, essays, lectures. 3. Propaganda, International—Addresses, essays, lectures. I. Merrill, John Calhoun, 1924–   II. Title.
    P91.F5   1976   070   76-17806
    ISBN 0-8083-3402-0   ISBN 0-8038-3403-9 pbk.

Published simultaneously in Canada
by Saunders of Toronto Ltd., Don Mills, Ontario

Designed by Al Lichtenberg
Printed in the United States of America

CONTENTS

v

PREFACE TO THE SECOND EDITION

WE ARE PLEASED to be able to bring out this new and completely revised and updated edition of *International Communication,* and we believe that it will, even better than the first edition of 1970, serve the purposes of the teacher, researcher, theoretician, and practitioner in the broad field of *international and intercultural communication.* The reader will note many changes in the book, especially a new attempt to select articles which have more "lasting" value than many of the earlier "quickly dated" pieces which appeared in the first edition. Also, many more original and previously unpublished articles are included. The generally positive reaction to the first edition of the book, however, has encouraged us to leave the basic structure of this reader.

International and intercultural communication is perhaps more important today—to both scholars and to practicing journalists—than ever before, and we have tried to design this book to reflect the main areas of concern. Even though communication among nations and cultures has received great and increasing emphasis in the last few decades, it is certainly nothing new—being as old as the history of men and nations. In most of the Biblical writings we find an emphasis on communication among nations and cultures, and the teachings of Christ and the practical actions of St. Paul add force to the early concern with spreading information across national borders. Missionaries, it might be noted, became some of the very first serious "professionals" in the spreading of messages among people of different countries, languages, and races.

In the European Middle Ages the songs of the Troubadours not only entertained the nobility but carried information of all kinds across the continent. Postmasters became another group which gathered, exchanged and distributed news. Songs and slogans of military troops and adventures of all kinds influenced the opinions and attitudes in conquered countries. And it should be observed that the first real newspapers of the early 17th century were largely international papers because their contents came from nearly all over the then-known world. One of these pioneer newspapers of 1609 exemplified in its long title a certain internationalism. The full name of this famous German "Aviso" was (in translation): *Relation of what has happened in Germany and*

Italy, Spain, the Netherlands, England, France, Hungary, Austria, Sweden, Poland, and in all the provinces, in East and West Indies, etc.

During the days of the Romans and during the Middle Ages the Latin language had the function of a *lingua franca* all over Europe, and so communication—especially between well-educated people—from country to country was rather easy. But the more Latin was pushed back and step by step replaced by various Romanic, Germanic or Slavic languages, the more complicated became the written communication among various European countries. Added to this problem was a growing censorship of publications by absolute monarchs.

The importance of international/intercultural communication to a person's general education and to society generally was recognized early. Caspar von Stieler mentions in his *Zeitungs Lust und Nutz* (Hamburg 1695), the world's oldest book about the meaning and function of the press, how important it is to be well-informed about international affairs. And many of the early newspapers covered foreign affairs much better than domestic events because a strong censorship prevented them from giving emphasis to domestic news. It is only since the Glorious Revolution in England and the French Revolution a hundred years later that significant changes have occurred in press freedom and expansion.

It has largely been during the last couple or three decades that the whole realm of international communication has been opened wide for exploration. Of course, the realm was "discovered" and stressed to some degree very much earlier. August Ludwig Schlözer of Germany's Göttingen University, for example, was one of the first academics to treat the press in his history lectures. In 1777 he observed the contents and functions of news from different parts of the world and gave some critical comments on his discoveries.

During the 19th century it became quite common for historians in their lectures and writings to touch on the development of important periodicals. In the United States, for example, in 1879 David R. McAnally had a course at the University of Missouri entitled "History of Journalism," dealing with practical daily newspaper life and emphasizing not only the *New York Herald* but also London's *Spectator* and *The Times*. This was perhaps the first course in comparative journalism offered in any university.

It has been in the present century, however, that emphasis has been given to international communication, both in writings and university courses. Journalistic activities of other nations have increasingly come under the scholar's scrutiny. One of the first published works in this respect was the German *Handbuch der Auslandspresse 1918* (Handbook of the Foreign Press 1918). It was prepared by the Foreign Department of the government's War Press Office and described the main newspapers of thirteen foreign countries. Emil Dovifat of Berlin University, one of the pioneers of research about the international press, started in 1931 a *Handbuch der Weltpresse* (Handbook of the World Press), which had several later updated editions.

Dean Walter Williams of the University of Missouri, founder of the world's oldest school of journalism there (1908), organized so-called Press Congresses of the World in San Francisco (1915), Honolulu (1921) and Geneva (1926). Williams, Karl d'Ester (Germany) and Hideo Ono (Japan) belonged to the small group of journalism educators who very early recognized the need for breaking out of the provincial and nationalistic straight-jacket in which education for journalism was then confined. In addition to Walter Williams of the University of Missouri, another professor of the same institution was one of the earliest writers to deal with foreign journalism. He was Eugene Webster Sharp who made such early studies in this area as "International News Communications: The Submarine Cable and Wireless as News Carriers" (1927), and "The Censorship and Press Laws of Sixty Countries" (1933).

Perhaps the first book to present a survey of the international press was Robert Desmond's *The Press and World Affairs* (1937) which he wrote as a Ph.D. dissertation at the London School of Economics. About this same time motion pictures and radio broadcasting had become very important in national and international and intercultural communication. John E. Harley's book *World-wide Influence of the Cinema* (Los Angeles, 1941) was one of the early studies on the multicultural function of movies. Paul F. Lazarsfeld was one of the first authors to stress the propagandistic functions of radio broadcasting across national borders; his "Radio and International Cooperation as a Problem of Psychological Research" (*Journal of Consulting Psychology*, Jan.–Feb., 1946) was one of the first studies in this area. He and some of his colleagues continued their work in this area and discovered many interesting things about the role of broadcasting in international propaganda.

The development of television since the 1950's revolutionized the cross-national relations and opened new and dramatic channels for global information. In close connection with television development is the use of communication satellites for various purposes. UNESCO's book *Communications in the Space Age—The Use of Satellites by the Mass Media* (Paris, 1968) shows some of the ways the traditional media can use this marvelous technical aid.

It can probably be said safely that it was in the late 1940's and early 1950's that the study of international communications really became important. Articles and books began to be seen more often in the 1940's, but it was not until the 1950's that the literature of international communications exploded around the world. A serious study of cross-cultural communications began at about the same time. This literature was still rather general, uneven and fragmented, to be sure, but it began to be taken seriously. A new area of concern in journalism had arrived—accompanied, of course, by a parallel interest in international communication in such fields as sociology and political science. An ever-increasing number of bright young scholars have become interested in the international ramifications of communication and have brought their individual talents to bear on the subject. Psychologists, social psychologists and sociologists have studied the communication process across national and cultural boundaries from the perspective of the individual person and of the entire social system. Political scientists have become concerned about the impact of communication on internal national politics and development, as well as on international relations. Behavioral scientists generally, taking a broad eclectic approach, have plumbed, with greatly improved research sophistication, the complex relationships between communication and human and social behavior.

One of the purposes of this book is to indicate, in a survey manner to be sure, the broad and varied aspects of the area of international communication. So far as we know, this is the first book which presents a collection of readings specifically related to international communication. In it we have tried to present articles and portions of books and theses which relate to a dozen important aspects of this area. There are many more areas and sub-areas, of course, which are not dealt with in this volume. We have tried to present readings in this book which stress the overall *international* concern and not specific national concerns; this has not been easy, and an occasional article may appear which the reader might feel presents a "national" emphasis. When this happens, however, we have felt that the article reflects an idea or concept which the reader, with a minimum of imagination, can *internationalize*.

We have tried to design a book which will be useful in a number of courses and will be of some interest to the general—especially the general *academic*—reader. Many of the articles have never been published before; however, some of them are reprints—occasionally with considerable editing or rewriting to make them more appropriate for this book. And, in line with the expanded scope of the book, we have new articles here on *intercultural* communication.

In conclusion, we wish to thank the many persons who have assisted us, with encouragement and actual help, in bringing out this book. And there have been many such persons, both in and out of the United States and West Germany. Especially are we grateful to the individual authors and publishers who have given us permission to use portions of their material and have aided us in numerous ways. Some book reviewers from different countries have made useful suggestions for changes of this new edition of the book. We have tried to provide—for the many teachers, scholars, practitioners and others engaged in the study of, and endeavors in, international communication—a compact and concise book which will serve as a catalyst to discussion and further research. If this book has, even in a small way, served to this end, we are more than satisfied.

Heinz-Dietrich Fischer,
University of Bochum (Germany)
John Calhoun Merrill,
University of Missouri (U.S.A.)

INTRODUCTION TO THE SECOND EDITION

In his Introduction to the first edition of this book (then titled *International Communication*), A. William Bluem of Syracuse University made a number of trenchant points, two of which remain in memory six years after I first read them.

First, Bluem noted, correctly and cleverly, that better communications between nations and "international understanding," as we currently use the term, do not necessarily increase international amity. On the contrary, much historical evidence indicates that, as different cultures get to know one another, the greater the chances that hostilities will break out between them. (This point is also made in passing by L. John Martin, a more pacific citizen than Bluem was or I am, in his third article in this volume.) America has not yet fought a war with Tibet! Our major enemies have been the British, the Spanish, ourselves, the Germans and the modern Japanese. Enough said?

Second, Bluem also observed, with too little emphasis, I think, that the most effective low entropy, non-redundant method of communication between nations is warfare. By extenuation, therefore, the most perfect communication device perfected to date is the nuclear bomb. This hard truth responds directly to gnostic urges of social ameliorists who vainly attempt to engineer human behavior to that hoped-for point where their neatly drawn models of communication processes are supposed to stop looking pretty and parsimonious and suddenly start to work.

Many aspects of life have changed in the years between the first and second editions of this book—some bad, some good and some irrelevant. Dr. Bluem is gone, having kept an early appointment with the spectre W. C. Fields called "the man in the white nightgown." A mere fraction of the original *International Communication* now remains between these covers, the lion's share of it having been updated, re-written and sensitively re-edited to face as bravely its Goliath-like topic in 1976 as it did in 1970.

Most important, the world itself has made giant strides in these half dozen years—in what direction I am not sure, although I might challenge the final essayist in these pages with the observation that they *may* well be heading irrefutably and directly *backwards* through the corridors of history. We are living today with the travails of detente, although we must not call it "detente" any longer, with a holy war in the oil-soaked terrain of the Near East, and a South East Asia that is being unified and pacified with karate-like efficiency. Communist Chinese now sit at the United Nations. UNESCO seems somehow to be turning into an ideological and political forum for persuasion, of quite the antithesis of its education, scientific and cultural orientation for years. (In truth, I hardly know whether Robert P. Knight's fine article on page 377 is a proud record of UNESCO's accomplishments or its obituary. And neither does he.)

Bluem's points, however, maintain their integrity, and so do his original rationales for the importance and timeliness of this anthology that remains, as it should, quite a mixed bag. Drs. Fischer and Merrill have, for this second time, set themselves to integrate a multi-faceted set of problems, the general nature of which indicate many of the difficulties presently facing the student of international communications.

Semantically, for instance, I wish I understood what an "authoritarian press" is. To me, it may be many things, including any journal edited by A. M. Rosenthal or Al Goldstein. To various authors in this volume, I am certain that it has many other meanings. Is one writer's statistical terrain compatible with another's when measuring things like television coverage given certain topics in certain countries? How I wish the University of Missouri would outlaw the use of the word "elite" among its professors in describing certain consumers of mass media, especially since the people around the world who (I assume) constitute this non-class must be extremely variegated, more unlike one another than similar.

These dissonances, cognitive or otherwise, are probably inevitable consequences of constructing a creature as large and protean as this new edition of *International and Intercultural Communication*. More significant is the fact that the range of the volume covers the skin of the entire globe in time and distance, and voices are heard that usually remain mute in more ethnocentric books on this often bewildering topic. Coming at the reader from a multitude of directions, Merrill and Fischer have managed to juxtapose philosophy, politics, economics and the mundane practice of the communication arts, one with the other, in almost an awesome manner with a freshness and contemporary insistency that has left me bemoaning my personal inadequacies as an insignificant intellectual vector, impotently bound by culture and time.

Awe is, I suppose, what the real message of *International and Intercultural Communication* turns out to be, and what Dr. Bluem was indeed writing about in his original Introduction. To face squarely the life-or-death intensity and exquisite complexity of the many problems that assault one page after page in this volume requires men and women of character and gut. In no subdiscipline of the study of communications is it easier or more tempting to hide in mommy's arms or pull the blankets over one's head than where matters of intercultural relations are concerned. In this domain, we are faced with the problems of "us" versus "them," the human race's seemingly inevitable proclivity to pursue barbarism (no matter how clever its technology or civil its prosody) and the straight news that we have presently outfoxed the deadly mushroom cloud merely by redefining warfare and lately turning diplomacy into a facet of advertising and public relations. (For details of this latter stunt, see pages 283–316.

None of this is pleasant, positive or particularly uplifting for one to consider. But I believe that a realistic reader on international communication cannot indulge for long in pleasant, positive and uplifting comforts. If it does, it is a fraud. Drs. Fischer and Merrill have edited an honest book about the puzzling condition of communications on our planet as we enter the last quarter of the present century. No escape hatch exists for the "ands" and "what ifs?" the reader will almost certainly conjure up as he studies these essays. The answer, if there is one, to the severe problems they raise will, I believe, emerge from the humanistic tradition that all of us—even the least educated and those most remotely placed on the globe—share with one another despite and because of our differences.

We all want to survive. We want our children to survive. Wars may indeed begin in the minds of men, as Julian Huxley wrote for UNESCO, but they may at least be blunted in our time by the words and pictures and music and dramas and dances that are hurled from place to place by the modern mass media of communication. If so, the next quarter century may well record some progress in the way nations live with one another—not perfection, not swords into plowshares—simply progress. May one reasonably ask for more than this?

George N. Gordon, Ph.D.
Hofstra University

June, 1976.

INTRODUCTION TO THE FIRST EDITION

Despite sometimes overwhelming evidence to the contrary, men of good intentions refuse to relinquish their hope that a system of free and open communication on a global scale will one day bring peace, justice and prosperity to all. Such a faith is not easily held, for its realization is threatened not by any failure in technological or institutional progress, but by the very nature of man. Those who believe that the mere *capacity* to communicate is sufficient to deter men from killing one another must come to grips with the haunting question of whether man really wants to communicate with his fellow beings. And beyond this lies an even more threatening possibility—that such notions as "world-community" are now being re-stated in such gross and simplistic terms as to render our traditional concepts of liberty and freedom meaningless.

Those who seriously regard the expansion of capabilities for international communications as a positive step forward might pause to consider whether the opening of new channels, the widespread battle to increase literacy, and the massive increase in application of the new electromechanical media guarantee that men and nations will be more favorably disposed to seek either understanding or peace. We are agonizingly aware that many nations which have the capability of making their intentions known to those with whom they have differences still persist in the use of armed force to settle matters. Note that the communicative option we call "war" has been employed among and within nations on this planet over fifty times since the arrival of the ultimate weapon in 1945 made "all future war unthinkable." Small wonder that there is growing impatience with the tenuous faith of those who feel that calm and logical appraisal of communicative systems will ultimately point the way toward reason, international sanity, and peace on earth.

Even if he can resist the forces of pessimism, the man of good will may still find it difficult to associate his aims and aspirations with those of certain of his fellow beings who have also discovered serious deficiencies in man's ability to live with, let alone communicate with, his fellow man. Rampant among us are the Global Villagers, the Computer-Technocrats and the Woodstock Nationals, all of whom have long since abandoned any hope that knowledge—at least in any of its linear, analytical and embarrassingly factual forms—will solve whatever issue they regard as paramount for this season. The more passionate among them will quickly reduce such phrases as "international understanding" to the level of other folk-song-and-cinema clichés like "war is hell," "love is all," and "heaven is near"—all of which are sure-fire hits among the sentimental young, who somehow feel that they have made a startlingly new discovery about the human condition. Their concern is natural, and might even be regarded as a hopeful sign in the battle for sanity were it not for the fact that they are ultimately used only for profit by purveyors of sentimentality in its cheapest and most stultifying forms. All who share real concern for the destiny of mankind must now consider whether such self-professed allies may not be our worst enemies.

Somewhere between the global village of savage innocence and the computer-driven world of total technological "achievement" lies a shell-pocked middle ground where some kind of stand for man's ability to defend himself must be made. The accomplishments here are seldom colorful, shocking or exciting, but it is only on such ground that communicators, students of communication, and all who believe in the intelligent use of public media may elect to stand. Something more than vague feelings of universal brotherhood—and something more than technological super-organization—is essential if we are to prevail.

In this work, two dedicated scholars of communication engage in the difficult and continuing task of mapping that ground. The work of Drs. Heinz-Dietrich Fischer and John Calhoun Merrill is a welcome addition to the literature of the communication arts.

A. William Bluem, Ph.D.
Professor
S.I. Newhouse Communications Center
Syracuse University

I

COMMUNICATION
SYSTEMS
AND CONCEPTS

Heinz-Dietrich Fischer
FORMS AND FUNCTIONS OF
   SUPRANATIONAL COMMUNICATION

John C. Merrill
A CONCEPTUAL OVERVIEW OF WORLD JOURNALISM

W. Phillips Davison
THE ROLE OF COMMUNICATION IN DEMOCRACIES

Chanchal Sarkar
JOURNALISTS' ORGANIZATIONS IN SOCIALIST SOCIETY

Yevgeny Prokhorov
THE MARXIST PRESS CONCEPT

1

COMMUNICATION SYSTEMS

AND CONCEPTS

JOURNALISTIC concepts, in their broadest sense, vary widely throughout the world. One would expect the role or function of the media of mass communication to differ significantly between, say, a Communist nation and a Capitalist nation. And, indeed, this is the case. But, it should be noted that even within so-called ideological contexts—between Yugoslavia and the Soviet Union, for example, or between West Germany and the United States—there are significant differences.

In addition, within any *one* press system there is growing debate about basic communication purpose or concept; many press systems appear to be changing rather rapidly, thus bringing about interesting dialogue concerning a redefinition of basic journalistic concepts. The mid-20th century emphasis on the press' responsibility to society, not only in controlled press systems but also in liberation press systems, is a case in point. Many observers are struck by the fact that a universal trend is growing to consider social stability and national progress more important than free discourse in a pluralistic press system.

The function of mass communication, not only within particular press systems but also among national press systems, is receiving increasing attention. In a way, this is a primary concern in any book related to *international* communication, and Heinz-Dietrich Fischer's opening article of this chapter discusses both the roles and functions of supranational communication. John Merrill follows this discussion with a more philosophically oriented treatise on authoritarianism and libertarianism in press systems around the world.

Following these two articles, W. Phillips Davison of Columbia University discusses the role of mass communication in libertarian democracies and points out interesting implications for *international* communication. Offsetting to some extent Davison's article is the next one in this section by Chanchal Sarkar, director of the Press Institute of India and noted press investigator, who gives many enlightening insights into the theory and practice of socialist press systems. And finally, in this section, is a fascinating article by a Russian scholar, Yevgeny Prokhorov, who clearly presents the conceptual foundation of the Soviet press system.

Certainly the reader will recognize that other press systems exist in addition to those in Communist and libertarian-democratic nations. These systems, usually called "authoritarian," combine the characteristics of both the Communist and "free" concepts, even though the organization or structure may differ somewhat. It is interesting to speculate on the broad global trends of ideologically based press theory: toward more free and open systems, or toward more controlled and "responsible" systems?

* * * *

RELATED READING

Brucker, Herbert. *Communication Is Power*. New York: Oxford University Press, 1973.

Buzek, Antony. *How the Communist Press Works*. New York: Frederick A. Praeger, 1964.

Commission on Freedom of the Press. *A Free and Responsible Press*. Chicago: University of Chicago Press, 1947.

Davison, W. Phillips. *International Political Communication*. New York: Frederick A. Praeger, 1965.

General Council of the Press. *The Press and the People*. London: General Council of the Press, 1954.

Schulte, Henry F. *The Spanish Press, 1470–1966: Print, Power, and Politics*. Urbana: University of Illinois Press, 1968.

Siebert, Fred S., Theodore Peterson and Wilbur Schramm. *Four Theories of the Press*. Urbana: University of Illinois Press, 1963.

Markham, James W. *Voices of the Red Giants: Communication in Russia and China*. Ames: The Iowa State University Press, 1967.

Merrill, J. C. *The Imperative of Freedom*. New York: Hastings House, 1974.

———, and Ralph L. Lowenstein, *Media, Messages, and Men*. New York: David McKay, 1971.

Wright, Charles R. *Mass Communication: A Sociological Perspective*. New York: Random House, 1959.

Yu, Frederick T. C. *Mass Persuasion in Communist China*. New York: Frederick A. Praeger, 1964.

Heinz-Dietrich Fischer:

Forms and Functions of Supranational Communication

GEORGE N. GORDON has said that "various forms of communication between living organisms had doubtless reached heights of sophistication long before even primitive speech (or noise) was invented." [1] The dialogue between different people and countries is as old as the history of man and nations. At least three basic elements of expression and communication have been available as "raw material" in all epochs of history: [2] the word,[3] the picture (drawing),[4] and the sound (noise).[5] And the earliest mode of communication with a larger group of people was probably speech.

Houston Peterson says that "we can be sure that tens of thousands of years ago there were individuals who cast spells over their fellows with the magic of words. At first it was not words so much as the rhythm, the sounds, the incantation that was a part of ritual. Chiefs, priests, medicine men . . . must have risen to power through skill in speech as well as skill in arms. They must have addressed themselves, in hope or in terror, to the mysterious forces of nature and to the spirits of dead relatives. Then, as now, stirring words helped to hurry men to hunt or to battle, and afterward the defeat or the victory would be relived with those who had remained behind. Perhaps the first formal orations were delivered at the graves of heroes." [6] Political and religious aims may well have been merged in those early speeches.

As a consequence of these basic possibilities of expression we find that since earliest times there have been forms of propaganda of different kinds,[7] both political and religious. Besides good examples of political propaganda of the early cultures,[8] we have several parts in the Holy Bible which show how and why peoples communicated with each other and what the content of their communication was. Especially the Old Testament is largely composed of speeches and sermons—good examples of communication between different cultures. And in the New Testament we have of the earliest instructions in this respect. Among Jesus of Nazareth's last words on earth were those exhorting his disciples to "go . . . and teach all nations" (St. Matthew, 28) or to "go . . . into all the world, and preach the gospel to every creature" (St. Mark, 16).

▶ This is a revised original article done for this book by Dr. Heinz-Dietrich Fischer, Professor of Journalism and Mass Communication Research, Ruhr-University Bochum (Federal Republic of Germany). Short portions of the article were presented at a guest lecture by the author before a class in international communications at the School of Journalism, University of Iowa, Iowa City, March 19, 1969.

In the Ancient World the Hebrews, Greeks and Romans developed new forms of political propaganda by using—for example—heroic titles, coins,[9] specific symbols, or gigantic constructions of architecture. Flags, beacon fires and other instruments were the early transmission belts for information within or outside of the empires.[10] In many ways Greeks and Romans tried to keep contact with their neighbouring countries by using various forms of written or unwritten communication. It is said that the famous 'Acta Diurna,' founded by Julius Caesar and one of the forerunners of modern information media, was distributed nearly all over the Roman Empire.[11] In addition to political propaganda, later on religion became one of the most important parts of cross-cultural communication.

Missionaries especially became real communicators between people of different countries, languages, and races. They tried to replace the old concept of the *Imperium Romanum* by popularizing the basic ideas of Augustines' book *De civitate dei* (written 413–426 A.D.) all over Europe. The different missionary activities [12] of the Church were centralized in 1622 by constituting the famous "Congregatio de Propaganda fide," which became the first propagandistic headquarters for the then known world.[13] The "propaganda fide" was one of the reactions of the Catholic church to the Reformation and a result of the Thirty Years War (1618–1648), when the Protestants developed a press policy and several journalistic activities, especially from Sweden. In this war—which was indeed a world war of that time—different forms of political and religious propaganda were practised and had effects in many countries.[14]

Since the Middle Ages, Latin as the *lingua franca* of Europe was pushed back step by step and replaced by various national languages. These languages became the main vehicle of communication for the European colonial powers in many parts of the world—especially for the English, Spanish, Portuguese, and French. This development, together with the growth of the press, was one of the most remarkable communication revolutions of all the times. These transplantations of communication systems around the globe had the result that an evolutionary process took place, merging the traditional form of communication of the newly conquered countries with those of the conquerers.[15] The English "Glorious Revolution" (1688/89) and especially the French Revolution (1789) were not only the starting points for political and social reforms of all kinds, but also the impulses for the growth of general freedom of communication.[16] The idea of free expression of ideas among the people of the home country and across the national borders never died since that time, although Napoleon Bonaparte tried to get control of public opinion for making his own imperialistic propaganda throughout great parts of Europe.[17] A French scholar made the observation that this "revolutionary period which we consider to begin about 1770 and to end about 1850, witnessed the development of newspapers into 'mass communication media' in the entire Western world," [18] because newspapers from then on became available for bigger groups than ever before. In connection with this remark one has to mention the growing importance of hymns, songs and arts as forms of journalistic expression following the Revolution in France [19] and during the Belgian Revolution of 1830, [20] spreading from country to country.

During the 19th Century one concept dominated in nearly all of the important nations and often became a mighty force and a kind of myth: *public opinion*. [21] And also mass movements can be found all over Europe as a communication factor with steadily growing importance: demonstrations, public festivities, world exhibitions, congresses, etc. With the growth of modern political forces, more and more slogans, rumors and whispering campaigns have received importance in international communication. [22] The middle of the 19th Century ushered in the so-called newsagency-epoch, [23] and it was also the time when numerous foreign correspondents spread all over the world. [24] A permanent activity in international communication since 1864 came from the different supranational communication institutions of the Socialists (Socialist International). [25]

A real bundle of international communication activities with highly propagandistic appeal was developed during and since World War I, and certain propaganda techniques were used by all nations which took part in the war. [26] During the late phase of the war a new medium was used for propagandistic purposes: the Motion Picture, which was first used as a propaganda instrument by the German War Press Department. [27] After the foundation of the League of Nations, Geneva became one of the most important communication centers of the world, [28] but the global information policy of the League was not too successful. [29] Much more activity in international communication showed, for example, the Communist International (Comintern), which was founded by Lenin in March, 1919. [30] Since the early 1920's various movements of Fascism became more and more popular in several parts of Europe with a certain international propagandistic function. [31]

At the same time radio broadcasting made its first steps to become an influential instrument for national and international communication. Especially the short-wave radio, already in its very early stage of development, was discovered for its supranational communication value. During the 1930's radio broadcasting became the most intensive vehicle for message transmissions in nearly all parts of the world. [32] The instrument was used extensively by the leading political powers, and Hitler was fascinated by the various possibilities of this medium. Journalistic and propagandistic instruments and techniques were used by nearly every nation during World War II as psychological weapons. To some extent the war was also a propaganda war, mainly led by radio broadcasting. [33] A very important instrument of international communication during and after the war became the newsreels with a rather high level of output. [34]

After 1945 a couple of organizations were established for promoting international understanding by developing the process of international communication—for example, UNESCO and the I.P.I. The communist-ruled countries established in 1947 in Bucharest (Rumania) the COMINFORM

(Communist Information Bureau), which was the headquarters of the propaganda activities of the World's Communism until its liquidation in April, 1956.[35]

Along with all these mainly political institutions there were also established some international religious organizations for propagandizing the ideas of the various churches in the modern world. For example, the World Council of Churches in Geneva established a special Department of Communication. In April, 1954, the "Trans World Radio" system of several protestant churches was begun.[36] A much longer tradition in world-wide religious radio broadcasting was "Radio Vaticana" (founded 1931), which transmits in about 30 languages of the world.[37] Great emphasis to the problem of global communication possibilities was given by the Second Vatican Council which concluded a special Decree on the Instruments of Social Communication ("Inter mirifica") on December 12, 1963. According to No. 18 of "Inter mirifica"[38] it was planned that a so-called "World Day of Social Communication Media" annually should be arranged by Catholics around the world. The first of these World Communication Days was declared by Pope Paul VI for May 7, 1967,[39] and a second was arranged for May 26, 1968.[40] A special declaration on "The Church and the Media of Mass Communication" was also presented to the Fourth General Assembly of the Ecumenical Council of Churches, held in Uppsala, Sweden in July, 1968. This declaration "was approved and recommended by the Assembly in its essential features. Compared with the Vatican Council's Decree on the Instruments of Social Communication ("Inter mirifica") it shows some correspondence in principle, emphasizing, however, different conditions of communication activities in various countries."[41]

As was mentioned earlier, "international broadcasting grew as the totalitarian countries began to propagandize their neighbors—frequently with the ultimate objective of conquering them—and the democratic countries began international services in response to the dictators' broadcasts. During World War II, the propaganda services of the German Reich and the British Broadcasting Corporation competed for acceptance in Europe and throughout the world . . . Just as World War I stimulated the development of radio, so the electronic advances of World War II contributed to the emergence of television which soon became the dominant electronic medium."[42] Besides radio broadcasting, which had been a real medium "without barriers"[43] for a long time, in the 1950's and especially in the 1960's television became *the* communication instrument for national and international purposes *par excellence*. Across-the-border telecasting operations became quite common, and across-the-Atlantic transmissions were possible after launching the first satellite (Telstar-1) in July, 1962. Since that time the term of "Communication in Space Age" became a synonym for this most modern form of communication facilities.[44] Doubtless the "Age of Television"[45] or the Space Age later in communication history will be considered a *communication revolution* because it will have many expected and unexpected influences on how people and nations communicate with each other.

So far this brief discussion has dealt with the evolution of different forms of communication. As could be demonstrated, sometimes various forms together result in a new kind of expression, but not all of these forms can be called media or even mass media. To give a systematic overview on the various areas of communication research—both in national or international context—it is necessary to present this listing [46] which includes all the possible means and forms:

- *Original Communication:*
    1. Signals (Symbols, Flags, Signs)
    2. Word and Sound (Speech, Device, Slogan, Rumor)
    3. Arrangement (Assembly, Ceremony, Demonstration)

- *Intermediatorial Communication:*
    4. Press (Pamphlet, Leaflet, Newspaper, Magazine)
    5. Picture (Drawing, Cartoon, Poster, Photo)
    6. Broadcasting (Radio, Television)
    7. Film (Documentary Film, Newsreel, Movie)
    8. Stage and Literature (Political Theater, Cabaret, Political Literature, Political Song).

This overview makes clear that, for example, forms of original communication in certain cases can be merged with those of intermediatorial: *i.e.*, if slogans, symbols, signs, etc., are brought to a larger audience by press or film, or if speeches or demonstrations are transmitted by broadcasting.

Some of these media, forms and subgroups are more, and some are less, predestined for international dialogues between people and nations, but at first we must, in this context, distinguish some basic questions. Our literature and oral discourse today often is using two terms for research activities in worldwide or regional communications: some people use "intercultural communication"; others prefer "international communication"; a third group of researchers is using both of them without making any distinctions. But in reality there exist two different meanings [47] which Gerhard Maletzke has defined as follows:

> *Intercultural Communication* is the process of the exchange of thoughts and meanings between people of differing cultures.
> *International Communication* is the communications process between different countries or nations across frontiers.

If one accepts these definitions, he might say: International and intercultural communication *may* be the very same, but not necessarily. Often there exists inter*national* communication between people of the same culture (often using even the same language), but separated from each other by national borders. On the other hand it is also possible to find inter*cultural* communication within one country if people of different cultures (and often with different languages—minority groups) communicate with each other. Sometimes the terms "supranational" or "comparative" communication are used as well, and there seems to be no real consensus in the use of terminology.

Hamid Mowlana seems to be a little too pessimistic when he said at a convention of communication researchers: "Although we are more able to cover International Communication systematically, I don't believe there is promise in trying to conquer it as a whole." [48] But Mowlana is quite right with his remark that for the individual researcher "there will have to be some form of specialization within the field." And in another context, Mowlana says: "The primary emphasis is on an introduction to the activities focused on the phenomena of international communication. After an examination of the range and definition of phenomena, an attempt is made to lay a foundation for an identification and critical evaluation of major approaches, theories, concepts, and propositions with particular attention being paid to problems of analytical integration within the field of study and to problems of interdisciplinary contributions and coherence." [49]

James W. Markham belongs to the group of researchers which looks to the past as a first step toward understanding the international communication situation of our time: "As for communications law and history, these subjects can adapt certain obvious international comparative approaches. Mass Communication systems everywhere and in past times are usually more closely related to political and legal systems of nation-states than to other aspects of the society. The student's explorations on the history of American journalism is more effectively conducted in the context of the development of world communications." [50]

Touching on the time factor in communication history, this brings up the question: Which of the journalistic concepts of our time is most-accepted in great parts of the world? The slogans of the libertarian theory of the function of the mass media have been the "self-righting process" and the "free market place of ideas," but "several types of limitation on the freedom [of communication] have been universally accepted as being consistent with libertarian principles." [51] It seems that Lenin's formula of 1901 is the best-known conception and is accepted not only by the communist countries but also by some communist-oriented groups in other nations. According to Lenin, the mass media have to be not only "a collective propagandist and collective agitator, but also a collective organizer." [52] There are, of course, several other conceptions of communication, but these two seem to be the ones which received acceptance in great parts of the world, whatever people in different countries may understand by those terms.

In any case, the main problem is what kind of content is preferred by the various media in national and international communication. Henk Prakke describes three functions of all communication as (1) information, (2) comment and (3) entertainment.[53] Information or innovation has to be the basic function from where all communication starts.[54] The comment function contains the opinionated analysis of information.[55] Entertainment in a general sense is described by William Stephenson as "Communication-pleasure."[56] Ralph Lowenstein tried to make a grouping of the "Elements of Emphasis" which he calls (a) News-information, (b) Interpretation-comment, and (c) Entertainment.:[57]

Books: 1. Interpretation, 2. Entertainment, 3. News.
Magazines: 1. Interpretation, 2. Enterainment, 3. News.
Newspapers: 1. News, 2. Interpretation, 3. Entertainment.
Radio: 1. Entertainment, 2. News, 3. Interpretation.
Movies: 1. Entertainment, 2. Interpretation, 3. News.
Television: 1. Entertainment, 2. News, 3. Interpretation.

One would have to prove if this ranking could be similar or very different in the cases of international communication. But it can be said, for example, that "information is circulated internationally in three forms: as raw material, as semifinished goods, and as finished product,"[58] and most of the research deals with the flow of news among countries. It is rather difficult to speak in general terms about cross-national effects of opinion expression of all kinds, but we know something about biasing and stereotyping in an international context, sometimes referred to by the expression "how nations see each other"[59] or "public opinion" in various countries.[60] Some forms of entertainment, especially sports events, have been brought to an international audience mainly by television.[61]

Very much still has to be done in this nearly unlimited area of research. Besides the books and articles dealing with the flow of news, such research has been undertaken in the fields of national and international attitudes and reactions to certain events. We do not know enough yet to make final decisions about the real corresponding functions in the international process. Therefore a meeting of experts on mass communication and society, organized by UNESCO and held in Montreal from 21 to 30 June 1969, touched upon these problems. Among the discussed topics were:[62] "The present status of the social sciences and their ability to deal with the study of human values and behavioural patterns; the interdisciplinary nature of mass communication research: the difficulties involved in comparative and cross-national research owing to the differing conditions obtaining in various societies and owing also to the fact that social research is often embedded in cultural values; the lack of co-ordinated effort in mass communication research; the need to study the impact of technology within a given social context; the special characteristics of communication in developing countries and the relative importance of human channels of communication in such societies; the problems of communication between countries including economic and political barriers; the effects of mass media on youth and the presentation of violence; and the rôle of mass media in achieving international understanding."

The participants of the UNESCO meeting were generally agreed on the need for quantitative as well as qualitative research, including research of an interdisciplinary nature, on a number of topics singled out for particular attention by the experts. Hereafter are given some relevant statements to research in the international communication field: [63]

". . . (c) One of the priority areas for research is the study of the rôle of mass media in conveying information and in helping to form attitudes about other people and other countries. While the media have the potential for improving and extending international understanding, intercultural communication does not necessarily or automatically lead to better international understanding. On the contrary, the opinion was expressed that what has come to be known as the "free flow of information" at the present time is often in fact a "one-way" flow rather than a true exchange of information. In these circumstances the need for "cultural privacy" tends to be asserted, and it is considered necessary to protect the cultural integrity of a nation against erosive influences from outside. However, the meeting recognized the dangers inherent in blocking any free flow of communication, and felt the whole subject was worthy of deeper inquiry.

(d) Appropriate to such concerns is the study of the value system of journalists and other communicators and their perceptions of their rôle in society. The meeting recognized the need for extensive investigation into the social, economic, political, legal and organizational factors determining the nature and degree of the flow of media messages across national boundaries and the implications thereof. It was also felt that research was needed on the rôle of mass communication in creating national stereotypes. Such inquiry would include not only the informational media but also popular cultural outlets such as comics, films and popular fiction. Assessments of media content might be made to arrive at "cultural indicators" in each of the countries as a way of gaining a better comprehension of each culture and thus improving the potential for communication.

(e) News transmission as such—both at the national and the international levels—deserves particular attention. The coverage not only of events but also of issues should be carefully studied in order to discover possible biases and their sources, over-emphasis on sensationalism, neglect of background and context. The news values of media practitioners should also be studied. Methodological approaches to these problems need to be worked out. . . ."

The participants of the meeting felt that the international exchange of mass media content and other popular cultural artifacts in general, and particularly those which affect the developing nations, involves not only the possible displacement or modification of certain cultural values, but also the problem of mutual comprehensibility. Therefore, mass communication research is needed into the perceptual patterns peculiar to cultural and ethnic groups, which should be taken into account if international exchange of materials is not to give rise to misunderstandings.

A first step to realize free flow of information between the countries and the "blocs" in east and west was undertaken at the Helsinki 'Conference on Security and Co-operation in Europe' (CSCE) including Canada, Turkey and the United States of America. The final act, signed by the conference members on August 1, 1975, is a massive document, the substance of which is divided among the subjects of three "baskets": (1) politico-military, (2) economic, scientific and cultural, and (3) humanitarian and other fields. In the so-called "third basket" the CSCE document mentions under point two ("information") a general declaration on the freedom of information for and in the mass media of all kinds and better working conditions for journalists [64]—i.e. foreign correspondents. It remains to be seen how these declamatoric demands really will change the job facilities for accredited journalists in foreign countries.[65]

In this connection also the question may be raised as to how the foreign correspondents understand their roles: as journalists or and as quasi-diplomats like the correspondents of *The Times* (London) for a long time.[66] But the communication researcher has also to observe "the ways in which both governments and private individuals and groups influence directly or indirectly those attitudes and opinions which bear directly on other governments' foreign policy decisions".[67] W. Phillips Davison pleads for what he calls "World public opinion", and he writes: "For international or world public opinion to develop as a political force, three requirements must be satisfied: People in several countries must give their attention to a given issue; they must have sufficient means of interacting so that common and mutually reinforcing attitudes can form; and there must be some mechanism through which shared attitudes can be translated into action. . . ."[68]

It will be a rather difficult and far way to realize these or similar research projects, but it gives at least arguments for a discussion on it. The British researcher Colin Cherry posed the question, if World Communication is a threat or a promise, and he confessed that this "cannot be answered in simple yes-no terms, for it is a value question." Cherry writes about a self-discovered problem: "Perhaps our greatest difficulty is to avoid the images of communication media—radio, telephone, television, books, newspapers, railways and roads . . . that naturally arise in our minds in the affluent Western countries. It is utterly useless . . . to theorize or speculate about the future of world communication in terms of these Western images alone, as though 'Western man' were 'the world.' One of the most unfortunate results of the fact that the bulk of the technology (both electronic and transport) has been created within the affluent countries, is that it can lead us to imagine the future solely in terms of such images. . . ."[69]

There are many chances to broaden the field of research in international communication questions,[70] although much has already been done in this direction. So it is hardly understandable that a general statement like this was made: "Discussions of the status of international communication, its limitations and its place in communication curricula and research have been lacking. Theoretical considerations have been ignored, underplayed or dismissed as highly speculative ventures. . . ."[71]

NOTES

[1] George N. Gordon, *The Languages of Communication: A Logical and Psychological Examination*, New York: Hastings House, 1969, p. 237.

[2] Cf. Hanns Buchli, *6000 Jahre Werbung: Geschichte der Wirtschaftswerbung und der Propaganda*, Vol. 1: Altertum und Mittclalter, Berlin: Walter de Gruyter & Co., 1962, pp. 49 ff.

[3] Cf. Lutz Mackensen, *Auf den Spuren des Wortes*, Hamburg: Verlag Nannen, 1964.

[4] Cf. Lancelot Hogben, *From Cave Painting to Comic Strip*, New York: Chanticleer Press, 1949.

[5] Cf. John Robinson Pierce, *Symbols, Signals and Noise: The Nature and Process of Communication*, New York: Harper & Row, 1961.

[6] Houston Peterson (ed.), *A Treasury of the World's Great Speeches*, New York: Simon and Schuster, 1967, p. 1.

[7] Cf. Alfred Sturminger, *3000 Jahre politische Propaganda*, Vienna—Munich: Verlag Herold, 1960.

[8] Cf. Yigael Yadin, "Communication in ancient Israel," *Gazette* (Leiden), Vol. 7/No. 1 (1961), pp. 158–162. See also Fumio Yamamoto, "Reporting in ancient Japan," *Gazette* (Leiden), Vol. 2/No. 1 (1956), pp. 29–52.

[9] Cf. Carol Humphrey Sutherland, *Coinage in Roman Imperial Policy* 31 B.C.–A.D. 68, London: Methuen, 1951.

[10] Cf. Wolfgang Riepl, *Das Nachrichtenwesen des Altertums mit besonderer Berücksichtigung auf die Römer*, Leipzig—Berlin: Verlag von B. G. Teubner, 1913.

[11] Cf. J(oseph) Vic(tor) Le Clerc, *Des journaux chez les Romains*, Paris: Firmin Didot Frères, 1838.

[12] Cf. Adolf von Harnack, *Die Mission und die Ausbreitung des Christentums in den ersten drei Jahrhunderten* (2 Vols.), Leipzig: Hinrichsche Buchhandlung, 1915.

[13] Cf. *Collectanea S. Congregationis de Propaganda Fide seu Decreta Instructiones Rescripta pro Apostolicis Missionibus*, Vol. 1, Ann. 1622–1866, Nos. 1–1299. Rome: Ex Typographia Polyglotta, S.C. de Propaganda Fide, MCMVII.

[14] Cf. Elmer Adolf Beller, *Propaganda in Germany During the Thirty Years' War*, Princeton/N.J.: Princeton University Press, 1940. See also: Göran Rystad, *Kriegsnachrichten und Propaganda während des dreißigjährigen Krieges*, Lund/Sweden: C. W. K. Gleerup, 1960.

[15] See among others: Livingston Rowe Schnyler, *The Liberty of the Press in the American Colonies Before the Revolutionary War*, New York: T. Whittacker, 1905.

[16] Cf. Wilhelm Bauer, *Die öffentliche Meinung in der Weltgeschichte*, Wildpark-Potsdam: Akademische Verlagsgesellschaft Athenaion, 1930, p. 211 ff.

[17] Cf. Robert B. Holtman, *Napoleonic Propaganda*, Baton Rouge: Louisiana State University Press, 1950. See also: Robert B. Holtman, "Thought Control in Napoleon's Satellite Countries," *Gazette* (Leiden), Vol. 4/No. 3 (1958), pp. 209–218.

[18] Jacques Godechot, "The Origin of Mass Communication Media," *Gazette* (Leiden), Vol. 8/No. 2 (1962), p. 81.

[19] Cf. C(onstant) Pierre, *Les Hymnes et Chansons de la Révolution*, Paris: Impr. nationale, Champion, 1904. See also: Cornwell B. Rogers, "Songs—colorful propaganda of the French Revolution," *Public Opinion Quarterly* (Princeton, N.J.) Vol. 11/No. 3 (Fall 1947), pp. 436–444. Cf. also: David L. Dowd, "Art as national propaganda in the French Revolution," *Public Opinion Quarterly* (Princeton, N.J.) Vol. 25/No. 3 (Fall 1951), pp. 532–546.

[20] Cf. Theo Luykx, *Politieke Geschiedenis van Belgie van 1789 tot heden*, Brussels—Amsterdam: Elsevier, 1964, pp. 44 ff.

[21] Cf. Frederick C. Irion, *Public Opinion and Propaganda*, New York: Crowell, 1950.

[22] Cf. Emil Dovifat, *Handbuch der Publizistik* (3 Vols.), Berlin: Walter de Gruyter & Co., 1968 f.

[23] Cf. Kent Cooper, *Barriers Down: The Story of the News Agency Epoch*, New York: Farrar & Rinehart, 1942.

[24] Cf. John Hohenberg, *Foreign Correspondence: The Great Reporters and their Times*, New York: Columbia University Press, 1964.

[25] Cf. Julius Braunthal, *Geschichte der Internationale* (2 Vols.), Hannover: Verlag J. H. W. Dietz Nachf., 1961–1963.

[26] Cf. Harold D(wight) Lasswell, *Propaganda Technique in the World War*, New York: Alfred A. Knopf, 1927. See also: James R. Mock and Cedric Larson, *Words that won the war. The story of the Committee on Public Information 1917–1919*, Princeton/N.J.: Princeton University Press, 1939.

[27] Cf. Georges Sadoul, *Histoire du cinéma mondiale des origines à nos jours*, (5th ed.), Paris: Flammarion, 1959.

[28] Albin E. Johnson, "Geneva now world's propaganda center," *Editor & Publisher* (New York), Vol. 60/April 21, 1928, p. 94.

[29] Cf. Dell G. Hitchner, "The Failure of the League: Lesson in Public Relations," *Public Opinion Quarterly* (Princeton, N. J.), Vol. 8/Spring 1944, pp. 61–71.

[30] Cf. Franz Borkenau, *The Communist International*, London: Faber & Faber, 1938.

[31] Cf. Ernst Nolte, *Die faschistischen Bewegungen. Die Krise des liberalen Systems und die Entwicklung der Faschismen*, Munich: Deutscher Taschenbuch Verlag, 1966. See also: Theodor W. Adorno, "Freudian Theory and the Pattern of Fascist Propaganda," in: Géza Róheim (ed.), *Psychoanalysis and the Social Sciences*, Vol. 3, New York: International Universities Press, 1951, pp. 279–300.

[32] Hans-Joachim Weinbrenner, "Grenzenloser Rundfunk," in: Kurt Wagenführ (ed.), *Jahrbuch Welt-Rundfunk*, Vol. 1:1937/38, Berlin—Heidelberg: Vowinckel, 1938. See also: John D. Tomlinson, *International control of radio-communications*, Ann Arbor/Michigan—Geneva: Edwards, 1945.

[33] Thomas O. Beachcroft, *Calling all Nations*, London: British Broadcasting Corporation, 1942. See also: John Hargrave, *Words Win Wars, Propaganda the Mightiest Weapon of All*, London, 1940; Charles J. Rolo, *Radio Goes to War*, London: Faber, 1943; Daniel Lerner, *Sykewar, Psychological Warfare against Germany*, New York: Library of Policy Sciences, 1949.

[34] See Peter Baechlin and Maurice Muller-Strauss, *La Presse Filmée dans le Monde*, Paris: UNESCO, 1951.

[35] Cf. F. Bowen Evans, *Worldwide Communist Propaganda Activities*, New York: Macmillan, 1955. See also: Denis Healey, "The Cominform and World Communism," *International Affairs* (London/England), Vol. 24/July 1948, pp. 339–349.

[36] Karl Heinz Hochwald, "Trans World Radio und Evangeliums-Rundfunk," *Communicatio Socialis* (Emsdetten), Vol. 2/No. 1 (1969), pp. 56 ff.

[37] Cf. UNESCO, *World Communications: Press—Radio—Television—Film*, 4th ed., New York—Paris: UNESCO Publications Center, 1964, pp. 295 ff.

[38] Cf. John W. Mole OMI, "The Communications Decree of the Second Vatican Council charter of the communications apostolate," *Social Justice Review* (St. Louis/Missouri), Vol. 59/1966, pp. 274–350.

[39] Pope Paul VI, "Nuntius Radiotelevisificus Universis catholicis Christifidelibus, ob diem recto instrumentorum communicationis socialis usui provehendo per totum orbem terrarum dicatam," *Communicatio Socialis* (Emsdetten), Vol. 1/No. 1 (1968), pp. 53–57 (French and German version).

[40] Text in: *Communicatio Socialis* (Emsdetten), Vol. 1/No. 4 (1968), pp. 343–346 (French and German version).

[41] Heinz Melzer, "Publizistik im Spiegel von Konzilsdekret und Uppsala-Erklärung," *Communicatio Socialis* (Emsdetten), Vol. 1/No. 4 (1968), p. 295 (summary).

[42] Burton Paulu, *Radio and Television Broadcasting on the European Continent*, Minneapolis: University of Minnesota Press, 1967, p. 4.

[43] Cf. George A. Codding Jr., *Broadcasting Without Barriers*, Paris: UNESCO, 1959.

[44] See: UNESCO, *Communication in Space Age. The Use of Satellites by the Mass Media*, Paris:

UNESCO, 1968. Cf. also: Wilson P. Dizard, *Television: A World View*, Syracuse/N.Y.: Syracuse University Press, 1966. See also: François Pigé, *La Télévision dans le Monde—Organisation Administrative et Financière*, Paris: Societé Nationale des Enterprises de Presse, 1962.

[45] Cf. Leo Bogart, *The Age of Television* (2nd ed.), New York: F. Unger, 1958.

[46] Cf. *Studium der Publizistik*: Münster/Germany: Institut für Publizistik an der Westfälischen Wilhelms-Universität, 1961, p. 5.

[47] Gerhard Maletzke, "Intercultural and International Communication," in chapter 8 of this book.

[48] Hamid Mowlana, *International Communication: A Probe into Methods and Approaches*, paper presented to the National Conference on the Teaching of International Communication, Racine/Wisconsin, March 27–30, 1969, p. 3.

[49] *Ibid.*, p. 8.

[50] James W. Markham, *International Communication Orientations for Professional Education*, paper presented at the Convention of the AEJ, International Communication Division, Lawrence/Kansas, August, 1968, p. 8.

[51] Fred S(eaton) Siebert, "The Libertarian Theory of the Press," in: Siebert, Theodore Peterson, and Wilbur Schramm, *Four Theories of the Press*, Urbana: University of Illinois Press, 1963, p. 70 and p. 54.

[52] Vladimir Ilych Lenin, *Collected Works*, Vol. 4. New York: International Publishers, 1927, p. 114.

[53] Cf. Henk Prakke et al., *Kommunikation der Gesellschaft. Einführung in die funktionale Publizistik*, Münster/Germany: Verlag Regensberg, 1968, pp. 65 ff.; cf. also Henk Prakke, "Publicistics—An European Approach to Communications", in chapter 9 of this book.

[54] Cf. Wilbur Schramm, "Information Theory and Mass Communication," *Journalism Quarterly* (Iowa City/Iowa), Vol. 32 (1955), pp. 131–146.

[55] Cf. Charles E. Osgood, George J. Suci and Percy H. Tannenbaum, *The Measurement of Meaning*, Urbana/Illinois: University of Illinois Press, 1957.

[56] Cf. William Stephenson, *The Play Theory of Mass Communication*, Chicago and London: The University of Chicago Press, 1967.

[57] Ralph L. Lowenstein, *The Elements of Mass Communication*, paper presented to his "Mass Media and Society" Course, School of Journalism, University of Missouri, Columbia, Spring 1969.

[58] Llewelyn White and Robert D. Leigh, "Merchants of Words and Images," in Charles S. Steinberg (ed.), *Mass Media and Communication*, New York: Hastings House, 1966, p. 351.

[59] Cf. W. Buchanan and H. Cantril, *How Nations See Each Other*, Urbana: University of Illinois Press, 1953.

[60] Cf. Bruce L. Smith and Chitra M. Smith, *International Communication and Political Opinion*, Princeton: Princeton University Press, 1956, pp. 5–21.

[61] Cf. H.-D. Fischer, "The Contribution of Eurovision and Intervision to Global Television" in chapter 7 of this book.

[62] UNESCO, "Mass Media in Society—The need of Research," *Reports and Papers on Mass Communication*, No. 59, Paris: UNESCO, 1970, p. 25.

[63] *Ibid.*, p. 26 f.

[64] Cf. Her Majesty's Stationary Office (ed.): *Conference on Security and Co-operation in Europe*. Final Act, London 1975.

[65] On the main problems of foreign correspondents cf.—among others—Alfred C. Lugert, Auslandskorrespondenten im internationalen Kommunikationssystem. *Eine Kommunikator-Studie*, Munich: Verlag Dokumentation, 1974.

[66] Cf. Heinz-Dietrich Fischer: *Die grossen Zeitungen. Porträts der Weltpresse*, Munich: Deutscher Taschenbuch Verlag, 1966, p. 83.

[67] Cf. Arthur S. Hoffman, *International Communication and the New Diplomacy*, Bloomington: Indiana University Press, 1968, p. 3.

[68] W. Phillips Davison, "International and World Public Opinion", in: Ithiel de Sola Pool et al. (ed.): *Handbook of Communication*, Chicago: Rand McNally College Publishing Company, 1973, p. 874.

[69] Colin Cherry, *World Communication: Threat or Promise?* A Socio-Technical Approach, London-New York-Sydney-Toronto: John Wiley & Sons, Ltd., 1971, p. 201.

[70] Cf. for such suggestions Heinz-Dietrich Fischer, "Internationale Publizistik und Kommunika-

tion. Ein Aufriß von Forschungasansätzen und Problembereichen," *Publizistik* (Konstanz), Vol. 17/No. 3–4 (July–December 1972), p. 265.

[71] Hanno Hardt, "International Communication Studies: A Critique", in: James W. Markham (ed.), *International Communication as a Field of Study*, Iowa City: University of Iowa Publications Department, 1970, p. 66.

John C. Merrill:

A Conceptual Overview of World Journalism

A NATION'S press or media system is closely tied to the political system. Although quite obvious—perhaps even a truism—this fact makes it possible to analyze the media system of a society by focusing on the philosophy and structure of government. Since there are many concepts and types of political arrangements, there are many corresponding or related concepts of journalistic relationships to government. Journalism's relationship to government in a very real sense determines its basic function or purpose in the society. Since the total society is influenced most significantly by its political system, this means that journalism relates well to, or functions properly in, a society only if it is compatible with its political philosophy.

When we ask how political theories may be classified, we are also asking how journalistic theories may be classified. And certainly there are many conceptual typologies or models which can be, and have been, suggested for governmental and journalistic systems. In this chapter several old ones and several new ones are discussed.

Regardless of how many typologies may be suggested, there are perhaps only two *approaches* to government-press classification. They might be called (1) the "Pigeon-Hole" Approach, and (2) the "Progression" Approach. The first tends toward typologies which place government and/or media systems rather snugly in one or another category in a kind of static, "immediate slice of time" way. Actually, however, pigeon-hole classification does imply the potential for change and for category-overlap, but this aspect is minimized. It should also be noted that a dichotomous classification system, such as the one which is discussed first in this chapter (authoritarian/libertarian), is really a kind of continuum or spectrum dichotomy, with possible movement implied on the continuum. However, such models are normally descriptive of a place on a scale, therefore making for a kind of pigeon-hole mode of classification. . . .

Media Relationship to Government

A media system reflects the political philosophy in which it functions. That is basic. A nation's journalism cannot exceed the limits permitted by the society; on the other hand, it cannot lag very far behind. Journalism is largely

▶ This article is a truncated version of Chapter 1 ("Political Theories and the Press") which appeared in Dr. Merrill's *Imperative of Freedom* (Hastings House, 1974).

determined by its politico-social context, and when it functions basically in accord with this national ideology it is considered—or *should* be, I maintain—socially responsible in a macroscopic sense. Many persons disagree with this, and have, as will be noted a little later, postulated a *separate* theory of "social responsibility."

Certainly there are many ways to think about media or journalistic relationships to government. These could be developed into "theories." We could talk about harmonic versus disharmonic theories; about functional versus conflict theories; about adversary versus supportive theories; about monistic versus pluralistic theories; about self-deterministic versus governmental (or "other-directive") theories; about laissez-faire versus control theories. And when we begin considering these, and there are many other ways to label them, we begin to see that they are really parts of broader or more inclusive theories.

We can also consider journalism's relationship to government in other ways, for example, as: (1) An Equal Contender, (2) A Cooperating Servant, or (3) A Forced Slave. In the first case, the press units are independent of government and each other; there is competition among them; each is a self-developed-and-managed entity. In the second case the press units in a sense form a partnership with government but would cooperate with government voluntarily; government and the "social interest" would be considered synonymous and would motivate the press system into this partnership or cooperative relationship. And in the third case, the press system as a Forced Slave would be subservient to government, would cooperate involuntarily with government out of coercion by the governmental Power Elite.

Out of all the possible symbiotic relationships of government and media systems, a basic dichotomy always seems to emerge. It presents a simple Aristotelian way of looking at differences, and in spite of its dualistic oversimplification and generalized structuring of reality, it is probably still the best way to consider either press theories or political theories.

The Basic A-L Dichotomy

Before analyzing various models describing some of the complexities of government-press theories, it might be useful to discuss briefly the basic "two-valued" typology which underlies all such models. It can be called the "A-L Model" and structures press systems (and political systems) in a dichotomous manner: as either *authoritarian* or as *libertarian*. Actually this A-L model of government-press theories is part "pigeon-hole" and part "continuum" in approach, for the person using these labels normally recognizes varying *degrees* of authoritarianism and libertarianism. Nevertheless, the basic tendency here is to consider various philosophies of government and press as either authoritarian or libertarian.

Press systems, as well as nations and individual persons, tend to be either authoritarian or libertarian. They are all somewhat schizophrenic, of course, but the basic inclination of each is toward either a well-structured, disciplined world-view with explicit patterns of behavior or toward an open, experimental, self-determined, autonomous, non-restrictive society with a minimum of rules and controls. Governments are designed on the philosophical foundation of one or the other of these two orientations. In reality, neither governments nor persons are that simple; authoritarians are open and flexible in many spheres of their activities and thinking, and libertarians are more dogmatic and inflexible than is generally assumed. Nevertheless, governments and persons appear to incline in one or the other of two directions. This is also true of the journalistic systems of the world.

Press systems are conveniently labelled authoritarian or libertarian depending on the degree of their self-determinism. The authoritarian system is the one in which the journalistic media have little or no autonomy in the sense of determining their own editorial policies and activities; the libertarian system is the one in which the media are editorially autonomous and operate in an open, competitive atmosphere.

Obviously there are weaknesses in such a dualistic typology, and perhaps it would be somewhat better to use terms like "authoritarian tending" and "libertarian tending" in describing government-press systems. Some persons, however, would not be satisfied with any such classification, for they maintain that it is impossible to make meaningful statements about freedom in one country as compared to freedom in another. Freedom, they say, means different things in different societies. Such relativistic concepts would make talk about "freedom" in the Soviet Union, for example, meaningless when compared to "freedom" in the United States.

Although it is undoubtedly true that meanings assigned to "freedom" vary in various parts of the world (even among Americans), I cannot agree that there is no validity in describing one country as having a *freer* press than another country. No good reason exists why freedom (of the press, for instance) cannot have a rather pure meaning that can be universalized or applied to the journalistic system of *any* nation. Such factors as how much criticism of government is permitted in a particular country, how many restrictive press laws are found in a country and their frequency of use can be applied universally to get at freedom. Ralph Lowenstein, in his exhaustive PICA studies, has provided a detailed discussion of how this can be done. [1]

In other words, *extra*-press restrictions and controls do indeed vary from country to country; and in this sense (a very legitimate one) press freedom can take on a universal core meaning and comparative statements can validly be made about "press freedom" in countries with disparate governmental philosophies and structures. Press freedom is fundamentally freedom from outside control. The central concept of such freedom used throughout this book—and

---

[1] Ralph L. Lowenstein, "PICA: Measuring World Press Freedom" (Univ. of Missouri: Freedom of Information Center Pub. No. 666, August 1966). For a far more exhaustive explanation of PICA, see Lowenstein, "Measuring World Press Freedom as a Political Indicator" (Unpublished Ph.D. dissertation, Univ. of Missouri, August 1967).

probably by most Americans—is press *autonomy*. This autonomy would apply most directly to the individual *media units* of the press, although it does (and should) apply to the individual journalist as well. Maximum journalistic autonomy is the imperative for authentic journalism.

The main thesis of this book is that American (and Western) journalism generally is now in a twilight zone between libertarianism and authoritarianism, and powerful forces, both external and internal, are pushing it rapidly into the snugness of authortarianism. But while saying this, I must admit that we in the United States still have a basically libertarian press when compared to many other press systems of the world. Assuming that there is this basic philosophical dichotomy (A-L) existing among the various national political and press systems, let us look briefly at the two orientations:

Authoritarian Orientation. Authoritarianism is appealing; it has a beguiling quality, a neat and disciplined aura, a lure for orderly minds who desire structure, logical progression, and institutional stability. It is a giant invisible sociological magnet which pulls unceasingly at men and nations. Authoritarianism implies an "authority" and basically it is extremely difficult and painful, if not impossible, for the mass of men to be without an authority to direct and lead them. Even for journalists, who thereotically should appreciate and savor the benefits of freedom, self-authority or autonomy is very often a traumatic and unpleasant option. It appears there is a more natural tendency to escape from freedom than to escape from authority. Commitment to freedom and willingness to accept responsibility for the consequences of exercising this freedom is not a dominant philosophical stance today, even though Existentialism has shown that there is a rather large group of devotees to personal autonomy.

It may well be that the philosophical base for authoritarianism can be traced back at least to Plato, the first great proponent of "law and order" and advocate of submission to an *aristocracy of the best*. According to Karl Popper, Plato recognized one ultimate standard: the interest of the State. Everything that furthers this interest, believed Plato, is "good and virtuous and just" and everything that threatens it is bad, wicked and unjust. For Plato, actions that serve the State interest would be moral: actions that endanger it, immoral. So, for Plato, the Moral Code would be strictly utilitarian—a kind of Statist Utilitarianism, where *the criterion of morality is the interest of the State.*[2]

It appears that in recent times there are many national leaders (American presidents included) who have this Platonic notion about morality—about journalistic ethics and responsibility to the State. In fact, it may be said that all forms of political authoritarianism are built on the rationale set forth by Plato: that citizens must submit to the dictates of the rulers of the State who know what is best for the State and who morally can (and must) impinge on the freedoms of citizens in the interest of the State.

[2] Karl R. Popper, *The Open Society and Its Enemies* (Princeton: Princeton University Press, 1930). See chapters 6, 7, and 8 on Plato.

In journalism, some manifestations of this can be seen in the increased emphasis on press councils, and other *extra*-press proscriptions and normative "help" given to the mass media. Increasingly media autonomy is being made to appear irresponsible and the old concepts espoused by Plato so long ago are returning to infect us with their anti-democratic and elitist "wisdom"—concepts which do, admittedly, have a very strong appeal to the multitudes who recognize the comfort in being directed "massmen" and also to intellectuals who are titillated by the deterministic ideas of Freudians, Marxists and Skinnerians.

Many important thinkers since Plato have contributed to the development of the closed, authoritarian, elitist political philosophy. A desire for strong government, a fear of the masses, an inclination to personal arrogance based on felt superiority, a respect for power, a hatred for anarchy, a love for social stability and national objectives commonly sought—all of these are strong forces pulling men away from freedom.

Consistent with such a philosophy, the information media must, of course, be thought of as contributing to social harmony and stability. Certain things the populace should know; other things—harmful things to society—the people should not know. The power elite will either directly operate the mass media, or will control them or dictate their actions, leading to a monolithic journalism of conformity and harmony. The goal is political and social equilibrium brought about by a submission to authority. And this is true whether the country is an authoritarian nation of the right or of the left. Although there are some notable differences between a Communist authoritarian regime and a right-wing one in terms of organization and procedures, they are "basically alike," as Carl Friedrich and Zbigniew Brzezinski contend (1965) in their superb book on totalitarian dictatorship.[3] Friedrich Hayek also demonstrates in *The Road to Serfdom* (1944) that there is no real difference in the basic philosophy of rightists and leftists: both advocate statism and control and both subscribe to a philosophy of political and intellectual arrogance where a small elite group has a deep-rooted suspicion of the masses.

Power, as Lord Acton states, does tend to corrupt. Power is also active and insistent; it must intervene—it must direct, supervise, set standards, define responsibility, eliminate nonconformists and eccentrics, and it must generally make the society march to its unified and regular drumbeat. Alexander Solzhenitsyn was talking about literature in his Nobel Prize lecture (1972), but he could have just as well have been referring to journalism. He said:

> Woe to that nation whose literature is disturbed by the intervention of power. Because that is not just a violation against "freedom of print." It is the closing down of the heart of the nation, a slashing to pieces of its memory.[4]

[3] See especially Chapter 11 ("Propaganda and Monopoly in Mass Communication") in Carl J. Friedrich and Zbigniew K. Brzezinski, *Totalitarian Dictatorship and Autocracy* (New York: Frederick A. Praeger, 1965).
[4] Quoted in John Hohenberg, *Free Press, Free People: The Best Cause* (New York: The Free Press, 1973), p. 511.

But this "freedom to print" that Solzhenitsyn sees as being at the "heart of the nation" is seen by authoritarians as potentially bad because it permits error to circulate in the society, damaging the social struture and impairing the achieving of social goals. Herbert Marcuse, one of the revolutionary "gurus" of recent years and an example of the Platonic elitists who are always grasping for social control, has been an influential guide for those who are escaping from freedom. Here is what one recent writer says of Marcuse and his idea of freedom:

> Freedom of speech is not an overriding good, for to allow freedom of speech in the present society is to assist in the propagation of error. . . . The truth is carried by the revolutionary minorities, such as Marcuse, and the majority have to be liberated by being reeducated into the truth by this minority, who are entitled to suppress rival and harmful opinions.[5]

People like Marcuse and a whole line of elitists and social engineers before him have a basic suspicion of the masses. People in general are looked upon as not intellectually capable, psychologically rigged, or educationally competent to make crucial decisions for themselves. The masses, in fact, are seen as frightened and frustrated when they are called on to excercise power and, if they do try, pose a great danger to the whole society. Special people must rule—people interested and competent, people dedicated to accumulating and wielding power, people who are ready and willing "to suppress rival and harmful opinions," as Marcuse might put it.

The authoritarian maintains that people in general desire leadership; they like simple, straightforward, easy solutions and actions; they want decisions made for them. Eric Hoffer points out in many of his writings that authoritarianism tries to reduce greatly the variety of aims, motives, interests, human types and, above all, "the categories and units of power." And this being the case, the "defeated individual, no matter how outstanding, can find no redress."[6]

Persons, of course, as well as regimes, are complex and multi-faceted; but in spite of this there does seem to be a general tendency in each political system and individual person: toward authoritarianism. We have looked at some of the characteristics of authoritarianism; now let us turn to its opposite in the basic A-L dichotomy: libertarianism.

Libertarian Orientation. This philosophical stance is as old, and maybe older, than authoritarianism. It has many roots, and Christians and Jews might even trace it back to the Garden of Eden. Undoubtedly "freedom lovers" have always existed, but it was not until the seventeenth and eighteenth centuries that the libertarian orientation took on a philosophical significance and began to have an impact on the press and public expression. John Milton with his

[5] Alasdair MacIntyre, *Herbert Marcuse: An Exposition and a Polemic* (New York: The Viking Press, 1970), p. 103.
[6] Nicholas Capaldi, *Clear and Present Danger* (New York: Pegasus, 1969), p. 269.

"self-righting process" and John Locke with his stress on "popular sovereignty" were seventeenth century pioneers in England, followed by Thomas Jefferson in eighteenth-century America; it was Jefferson who clearly expressed the necessary relationship between a free (even if it seemed irresponsible to him) press and good, sound democratic government. John Stuart Mill in nineteenth-century England added further philosophical status to the concept of press libertarianism.

These men, and innumerable others, propounded a philosophy which was considerably different from authoritarianism. Unlike disciples of Plato, and later Hegel, they basically trusted the "common man" and believed that all kinds of information and ideas should be made public. They despised secrecy; they rebelled against prior censorship and felt that free criticism was essential to personal, as well as national, happiness and growth. They were fundamentally "domocrats" and not autocrats, aristocrats, or some other variety of elitists. Of course, there are certain flaws in this generalization—for all of these men would draw the line of freedom at some point—but they determined to keep the idea of expression tied to the concept of personal and press autonomy just as tightly as possible.

A national libertarian orientation is one in which the leadership relates closely with the followship. There is a trust in the citizens, a belief that the majority—even if not always right—should be taken seriously and generally comes closest to the truth and makes sound decisions. This trust of the people is related to the mass media in that it is the media that can best inform the people so they can know enough to intelligently elect their representatives, direct them, and change them when necessary. Many students of the press today erroneously (in my view) see this concept as imposing a responsibility or obligation on the press which, if not fulfilled, will negate or cancel out the press's right to freedom.

Actually, there is a theoretical *assumption* in libertarian theory that a free and unhampered press will serve, at least to a large degree, this idealistic function of adequately informing a democratic people. But in libertarian theory there is no *obligation* on the press that it do so. This would, of course, contradict the principle of press freedom. In spite of many criticisms which can be hurled at a free and autonomous press for avowed "errors" and "excesses" and the like, it is probably safe to say that in the United States, for example, the people are very well informed about the issues of the day, the activities of their elected representatives, and the strengths and weaknesses of their political (and other) institutions.

In a libertarian society—even in one which has compromised many of its freedoms—there is considerable stress on divorcing government from journalism as much as possible. As Franklin Littell has pointed out in his cogent little essay on social pathology, the "existence of strong centers of thought and discipline separate from the state" is especially important to the lover of liberty.[7]

---

[7] Franklin H. Littell, *Wild Tongues* (London: Collier-Macmillan, Ltd., 1969), p. 88.

This is why libertarian journalists have always—until perhaps recently—shuddered at the thought of government meddling in the affairs of the press, setting goals and standards, and the like.

Unlike authoritarianism, libertarianism is a philosophy, revered by non-elitists and democrats—by those who feel that much can be learned from being exposed to ideas and opinions with which they disagree. This concept is basic in libertarian theory. It has, of course, been well expressed by such persons as Milton, Mill, Locke and Jefferson, but here is how a contemporary writer has expressed this symbiosis of free expression and democracy:

> Democracy is based on a profound insight into human nature, the realization that all men are sinful, all are imperfect, all are prejudiced, and none knows the whole truth. That is why we need liberty and why we have an obligation to hear all men. Liberty gives us a chance to learn from other people, to become aware of our own limitations, and to correct our bias. Even when we disagree with other people we like to think that they speak from good motives, and while we realize that all men are limited, we do not let our selves imagine that any man is bad. Democracy is a political system for people who are not too sure that they are right.[8]

It must be admitted that there is, in libertarian press theory, what must be considered a kind of built-in paradox. And it is this paradox which really is at the root of so much of the controversy going on today about press freedom and responsibility. The paradox arises from: (1) the basic philosophical assumption that a democratic people need information upon which to base their decisions, and (2) the basic free press principle built into the First Amendment of the U.S. Constitution (and into constitutions of other nations).

Quite naturally there are many citizens who look at the mass media, or certain of them, and see weaknesses in the way they are informing the public. So, the natural inclination is to evolve such a principle as this: if the press, or any unit of the press, fails to provide the kind of service the citizenry is entitled to in a democracy, it must forfeit its freedom. However worthy or unworthy such a rationale may be, it clearly points out the paradox mentioned above. For quite simply, the press is free and autonomous or it is not; and, of course, if it is regulated, controlled or directed from without (even in the name of "democratic utilitarianism"), it has ceased being free and autonomous.

Often the paradox is expressed in other terms; for example, some libertarians refer to two strains of freedom—*positive* and *negative* freedom. Positive freedom is the freedom to achieve some good (generally attributed to Rousseau), whereas negative freedom (usually attributed to Hobbes and Locke) is the freedom from restraint.[9] Many would say that "positive" freedom is responsible

---

[8] E. E. Schattschneider, *Two Hundred Million Americans in Search of a Government* (New York: Holt, Rinehart and Winston, Inc., 1969), p. 53.
[9] For a good discussion of this question, see Isaiah Berlin, *Two Concepts of Liberty* (Oxford: Clarendon Press, 1958).

freedom and "negative" freedom is not responsible. I have always found this positive-negative dualism troublesome, for it would appear that if a person were not free of restraint, he would not have the freedom to achieve some good (of his own choice). Therefore, it would seem that the heart of the concept of freedom is really what is called "negative" freedom. If one is *free from restraint*, he is automatically free to achieve some good (if he elects to).

This "negative" freedom, then, implies the freedom to act autonomously. And presumably, when one acts autonomously, he at least *thinks* he is acting for *some good*. On the other hand, what is referred to as "positive" freedom smacks too much of the authoritarian concept of freedom, which grants the people the "freedom" to carry out what some elite has decided to be "good." It is little wonder that Rousseau, to whom this positive freedom concept is attributed, is so often considered an authoritarian. It is true that a slave is "free" in the sense that he is free from making choices for himself and, therefore, can provide pre-determined social *good*. But, as Sydney Harris has put it, "People who live in despotic or dictatorial societies have no true security—even though the despot or the state may provide everything they need—because they lack the freedom to make choices." [10] . . . .

The "Four Theories" Typology

In 1956 three professors of communication—Fred S. Siebert, Theodore Peterson and Wilbur Schramm—brought out their *Four Theories of the Press* which went a long way in establishing such a typology in the minds of journalism educators and students. The little volume (in paperback since 1963) [11] has become standard reading in journalism departments and schools and has done much to legitimize the fourth "theory"—social responsibility. Almost every article and book dealing with philosophical bases for journalism has alluded to this book, commented on it or quoted from it. Its impact has unquestionably been great in spite of what I believe are significant weaknesses.

Siebert, Peterson and Schramm discuss journalism philosophy by presenting four theories ("concepts" might have been a more realistic term): 1) the authoritarian theory, 2) the libertarian theory, 3) the communist theory, and 4) the social responsibility theory. Very briefly, here are the main characteristics of each of these theories:

<u>Authoritarian</u>. The state, as the highest expression of institutionalized structure, supersedes the individual and makes it possible for the individual to acquire and develop a stable and harmonious life. Mass communication, then, supports the state and the government in power so that the total society may advance and the state may be viable and attain its objectives. The state (the "elite"

---

[10] *The Authentic Person: Dealing with Dilemma* (Niles, Ill.: Argus Communiations, 1972), p. 29.
[11] *Four Theories of the Press* (Urbana: Univ. of Illinois Press, 1963). Cf. for a good discussion of the four concepts (and a defense of the social responsibility theory): William L. Rivers in Chapter 2 of Rivers and Schramm, *Responsibility in Mass Communications*, revised ed. (New York: Harper & Row, 1969).

that runs the state) directs the citizenry, which is not considered competent and interested enough to make critical political decisions. One man or an elite group is placed in a leadership role. As the group or person controls society generally, it (or he) also controls the mass media since they are recognized as vital instruments of social control.

The mass media, under authoritarianism, are educators and propagandists by which the power elite exercises social control. Generally the media are privately owned, although the leader or his "elite group" may own units in the total communication system. A basic assumption: a person engaged in journalism is so engaged as a special privilege granted by the national leadership. He, therefore, owes an obligation to the leadership. This press concept has formed, and now forms, the basis for many media systems of the world. The mass media, under authoritarianism, have only as much freedom as the national leadership at any particular time is willing to permit.

Libertarian. The "libertarian" press concept is generally traced back to England and the American colonies of the seventeenth century. Giving rise to the libertarian press theory was the philosophy that looked upon man as a rational animal with inherent natural rights. One of these rights was the right to pursue truth, and potential interferers (kings, governors, *et al*) would (or should) be restrained. Exponents of this press movement during the seventeenth century, and the 200 years which followed, included Milton, Locke, Erskine, Jefferson, and John Stuart Mill. Individual liberties were stressed by these philosophers, along with a basic trust in the people to take intelligent decisions (generally) *if* a climate of free expression existed.

In theory, a libertarian press functions to present the truth, however splintered it may be in a pluralism of voices. It is impossible to do this if it is controlled by some authority outside itself. Through the years many new ideas have been grafted onto early press libertarianism; many of them will be discussed later in this book. One of these, for example, is the general acceptance of a kind of obligation to keep the public abreast of governmental activities, of being a kind of "fourth branch of government" supplementing the executive, legislative and judicial branches. This is actually a rather recent concept, having been grafted on to the original libertarian theory. There is a basic faith, shown by libertarian advocates, that a free press—working in a *laissez faire*, unfettered situation—will naturally result in a pluralism of information and viewpoints necessary in a democratic society.

Communist. The communist theory of the press arose, along with the theory of communism itself, in the first quarter of the present century. Karl Marx was its father, drawing heavily on the ideas of his fellow German, Georg W. F. Hegel. The mass media in a communist society, said Marx, were to function basically to perpetuate and expand the socialist system. Transmission of social policy, not searching for the truth, was to be the main rationale for existence of a communist media system.

Mass media, under this theory, are instruments of government and integral parts of the State. They are owned and operated by the State and directed by the Communist Party or its agencies. Criticism is permitted in the media (i.e., criticism of failure to achieve goals), but criticism of basic ideology is forbidden. Communist theory, like that of authoritarianism, is based on the premise that the masses are too fickle and too ignorant and unconcerned with government to be entrusted with governmental responsibilities. Thus, the media have no real concern with giving them much information about governmental activities or leaders. Mass media are to do what is best for the state and party; and what is best determined by the elite leadership of State and Party. Whatever the media do to contribute to communism and the Socialist State is moral; whatever is done to harm or hinder the growth of communism is immoral.

Social Responsibility. This concept, a product of mid-twentieth century America, is said by its proponents to have its root in libertarian theory. But it goes beyond the libertarian theory, in that it places more emphasis on the press's responsibility to society than on the press's freedom. It is seen as a higher level, theoretically, than libertarianism—a kind of moral and intellectual evolutionary trip from discredited "old" libertarianism to a "new" or perfected libertarianism where things are forced to work as they really should have worked under libertarian theory. The explainers and defenders of this 'theory" maintain that they are libertarians, but socially responsible libertarians, contrasted presumably with other libertarians who (if their views and actions do not agree with those of the "new" libertarians) are not socially responsible.

This fourth theory of the press has been drawn largely from a report published in 1947 by the Hutchins Commission.[12] Emerging from the Commission's publications and solidified in the literature of journalism by *Four Theories of the Press*, this new theory maintains that the importance of the press in modern society makes it absolutely necessary that an obligation of social responsibility be imposed on the media of mass communication. . . .

[12] See Commission on Freedom of the Press, A *Free and Responsible Press* (Chicago: Univ. of Chicago Press, 1947).

W. Phillips Davison:

The Role of Communication in Democracies

DOMESTIC practices affecting communications in any state held to determine both the nature of the messages from and about that state that go abroad and the impact that ideas from other countries have on its internal politics. The role of communication in democracies is a particularly complicated one, and imposes a number of limitations on the ways that democratic spokesmen can seek to influence foreign nations. It also causes difficulties for people in other countries when they try to evaluate the significance of news from democracies; and it produces a curious blend of susceptibility and invulnerability to messages from abroad on the part of citizens of democratic states.

Many of the characteristics that we associate with democracy depend on free access of all groups in a population to the channels of communication, both as senders and as receivers. These characteristics include nonviolent competition for political power among various groups within the nation (and the existence of machinery for the orderly transfer of power from one group to another), the ability of those outside the government to influence its actions, and the reliance of the government more on suasion and less on force to accomplish its domestic policies. Because of their political significance, the communication media in democracies are under constant pressure, on the one side from groups seeking preferential access, and on the other from those who feel themselves disadvantaged or who want to maintain freedom of access for all.

Democracies are also characterized by a respect for the individual, who is allowed wide latitude to seek full personal development according to his own inclinations, to pursue his own happiness, and to participate actively in a variety of groups. Satisfaction of personal desires likewise depends in large measure on access to information of many types and on freedom to communicate. Nevertheless, complete freedom for any individual can never be assured, since it may restrict the freedom of others or may conflict with strongly held group values. How much latitude each individual can be allowed is a problem with which democratic theorists have struggled since classical times; they agree only that individual freedom should be as great as possible.

Communications and the Functioning of Competing Groups

Since competing groups in a democracy have such diverse political interests, a far greater variety of media is necessary to satisfy their internal and external requirements than is the case in states where only one political point of view is permitted. Officials familiar with communications in India, for instance, have noted that, in proportion to population, much more varied information sources are required than is the case in a totalitarian country such as Communist China. Democratic states that have succumbed to totalitarianism, as Italy did in 1922 and Germany in 1933, witnessed a marked decline in the number of newspapers, magazines, and other information media that previously spoke for nongovernmental points of view. When the German press was "coordinated" after 1933, the same serial publication, by then under Nazi influence, recorded a similar decrease in the number of German newspapers, but this time explained that it was undesirable to have so many political points of view expressed, because this interfered with the formation of a single national will.

Recent trends toward the consolidation of the mass media in industrialized democracies have led to fears that in these countries, too, the media will no longer be able to give adequate expression to all principal points of view.

Perhaps equally important is the fact that many large media are hospitable to a broad range of opinions in their news coverage, even if they have become hesitant in expressing their own opinion.

Opportunities for competing groups to make use of communication channels are never perfect; some groups are better served than others. Nevertheless, most democracies have facilities for the dissemination of a wide range of information and attitudes, usually excluding material that is repugnant to moral values held by the overwhelming majority. This variety of expression enables individuals to nourish their own points of view by finding support for them in the stream of communications; it makes it possible for those with similar attitudes to learn about each other and to get in touch with each other; and it thus facilitates the growth of public opinion, the formation of new political groupings, and the modification of the programs of existing groups.

A democracy is, however, more than a network of contending groups. It is itself a larger group, and as such requires a communication network that will help ensure internal cohesion, reinforce democratic values, and assist in the formation of a national public opinion on vital issues. Plato's observation that democracy was possible only in small states may have been related to the fact that in his day effective communication via the mass media was not possible, and that a sufficient exchange of ideas through person-to-person channels could not be achieved throughout a large realm.[1]

---

[1] Winston L. Brembeck and William S. Howell, *Persuasion: A Means of Social Control* (New York: Prentice-Hall, 1952), p. 9.

Popular Influences on Government

Channels of communication from the citizenry to the government make it possible for those outside the governmental structure to influence official actions and policies. In democracies one channel is established constitutionally, in that all citizens are, in theory at least, assured of access to their representatives in the legislature. This channel is supplemented, and indeed usually overshadowed, by other mechanisms through which the citizen can influence officials: the public media, pressure groups, lobbies, communications to administrative agencies, and public opinion. Public-opinion polls offer a relatively new device through which popular views on a large range of issues can be made known to policy-makers.

It is characteristic of political communications in democracies that a large proportion of them are of a critical nature. Indeed, criticism is an important component in the working definition of news used by the mass media. When some institution or government agency is functioning as it should, this ordinarily remains unreported; a malfunction, however, usually merits headlines. The 999 honest government officials receive little attention; the one who proves to be corrupt may be at the center of the news for days.

Public opinion, especially, is likely to crystallize around an actual or potential grievance and to oppose something: corruption, segregation, integration, or inflation. Government officials may act or may be restrained from acting on an issue when they anticipate that their behavior is likely to mobilize a hostile public opinion.[2] This is not to say that public opinion does not also form around positive issues—better schools, a chicken in every pot, and so on. Many such examples could be cited, but they tend to be less noticeable than those that represent opposition.

The prevalence of critical communication in a democracy is often deplored. Nevertheless, criticism of things as they are, or as they might be, is vital to the functioning of a democratic order. Without them, organizations and opinions advocating change could not take shape, and an orderly transition of power from one government to another would be impossible. Even successful maintenance of an existing administration would be difficult unless malfunctions in need of correction were highlighted. While a certain ratio between expressions of approval and disapproval is necessary for stability, a preponderance of critical communications appears to be necessary to the functioning of a democracy, even when the opinions of a majority favor things substantially as they are. Whether attention given to real or imagined malfunctioning is justified on the basis of newsworthiness or for some other reason, information media are playing a necessary role when they give an opportunity for critical voices to be heard. The status quo, if it is to be stable, must continuously be tested against possible alternatives.

[2] David B. Truman, *The Governmental Process* (New York: Alfred A. Knopf, 1951), pp. 448–49, 511–12.

Not all citizens in any democracy take an intelligent or continuous interest in the affairs of government; the circle of those interested in public affairs, and informed about them, may be relatively small. Political scientists sometimes differentiate among the general public, the "attentive public," and policy and opinion elites. The elites take the most active interest in governmental affairs, and the attentive public, which constitutes the audience for discussion among the elites, is sometimes mobilized to act with regard to one or another political issue. The general public, which may include far more than half the population, rarely communicates to policy-makers.

The dangers inherent in this situation have been noted. Without adequate citizen participation in the affairs of government, it is difficult for a democracy to find a solid basis for policy.[3] The nation may be dominated by demagogues or by selfish minorities, or its stability may be threatened as important elements become aware of their interests and power, and demand special privileges. When any group combines political interest and activity with selfishness and ignorance, the results can be disastrous, unless its influence is countered by other groups.

Governmental Dependence on Suasion

It is axiomatic that, in a democracy, laws cannot be enforced unless they enjoy the support, or at least the acquiescence, of a large majority. Indeed, the degree of compliance with some laws has been documented statistically, and it can be shown that enforcement agencies usually have to concern themselves with only a limited segment of the population.[4] If more than a small minority resists compliance, a law is likely to become a dead letter. Although most decisions are made by a few men, these usually decide on a given course of action only if they feel fairly certain that the public will support them. For they will hold power only as long as a sufficient number of citizens approve of the way it is being exercised.[5]

Communications from a government, like other communications, are subject to serious limitations when it comes to changing strongly held individual attitudes, but they are particularly important as a means of encouraging pro-government groups and rallying public opinion behind specific measures. Indeed, an official in a democracy who is unable to reach the public through the mass media and must rely on personal or official channels is deprived of a large measure of his influence.

Government information programs in a democracy often give rise to fears that democratic processes will be weakened. Yet there are also grave dangers in not maintaining facilities that enable a government to present its case and ap-

[3] Lester Markel, "What We Don't Know Will Hurt Us," The New York Times Magazine, April 9, 1961.
[4] Floyd H. Allport, "The J-Curve Hypothesis of Conforming Behavior," Journal of Social Psychology, May 1934, pp. 141–83.
[5] Michael Balfour, States and Mind (London: Cresset Press, 1953), p. 119.

peal for support. As with so many problems of democracy, the solution appears to lie in a proper balance—in this case between government publicity and private criticism.

Controversy Over Access to the Media

Because communications play such an important role in the functioning of groups that compete for power in a democracy, one feature of democratic life is pressure on the part of some groups for preferential access to the media of public communication, and counterpressure from others that seek greater access for themselves or for all members of the society.

The most obvious group seeking preferential access to the media is government. Indeed, many of the earliest newspapers served as official organs. The first newspaper to appear in France, Renaudot's *Gazette,* was founded with the assistance of the court, and Louis XIV himself frequently wrote for it. In most countries of Europe during the eighteenth and much of the nineteenth centuries, media expressing views contrary to those of the government were either suppressed or were subject to serious disabilities. As soon as formal government controls are removed from communication media, most governments attempt to secure preferential access to them by other means. Most states maintained similar bodies for influencing the mass media, although they were not always so well organized, and controversy has continued up to the present time about the extent to which government ought to try to influence the press and the means it should use.

Private interests, no less than governments, seek preferential access to the media of communication. In many democracies, labor and business, as well as political, religious, and social groups, support extensive public-relations programs, one of the principal purposes of which is to influence the content of the mass media. In addition, certain organs, although not officially spokesmen for economic interest groups, are believed to enjoy hidden subsidies or otherwise to be dominated by a particular point of view. Thus, the pre-Hitler *Frankfurter Zeitung,* one of the great newspapers of Europe, was considered to represent the views of a liberal industrial group that supported it.

As a matter of practice, no democracy has found a way of ensuring that communication facilities are open to all groups equally. Nevertheless, various formulas for equalizing access have been developed, and these are reflected in the laws and customs of each democracy. Many countries provide for the control of broadcasting by mixed commissions, representing both public and private bodies. Persons or groups who feel that they have been unfairly treated in the press are entitled under the laws of some states to demand space for a reply. A number of countries discourage press-radio combinations or limit the right of publishers to be involved in other businesses also.

The degree to which wide access to the public media can or should be assured by law and the extent to which preferential access of any group should be discouraged are both highly controversial questions. Certainly no one solution

is the only correct one. Democracy can function (assuming its other requirements are fulfilled) as long as competing groups and interests are assured adequate use of communication media to satisfy their internal and external
requirements, even though all do not have complete equality of access. A
degree of preferential access for some groups is far less dangerous than the
complete exclusion of others. If a government can suppress media serving other
groups contending for political power, and pre-empt a major share of the communication spectrum for itself, then the threat of tyranny is imminent. Alter-
natively, if opposition groups enjoy a vastly preferred position, and no government is able to mobilize a favorable public opinion, then anarchy or instability
is assured. American concern about the threat posed by government domination of communication channels may be explained in part by the fact that the
ability of governmental leaders to reach their supporters, put their case before
the country, and rally public opinion has never been seriously in doubt. Other
democracies, in which political communications are primarily along tribal
lines or are fragmented among splinter parties or social groups, may require a
far higher degree of preferential access to the communication system on the
part of government if stability is to be assured.

In states that have not yet become nations, or where the practice of democracy has only recently been attempted, the temptation for the government
to impose restrictions on the media is particularly strong. The Director of the
Institute of the Science of the Press at Amsterdam University has reported a
large number of inquiries from emerging countries asking whether there are
ways that irresponsible attacks and other misuses of press freedom can be curtailed without destroying the basically democratic character of the state. To all
these inquiries he has replied that there have been many attempts to combine
such restrictions with democracy but that none on record in European history
has succeeded, and has concluded that "there is really no middle ground between press freedom and unchecked tyranny."

The cure for an irresponsible, divisive press appears to lie less in imposing
restrictions than in encouraging a responsible, national press as a counterweight
and ensuring that the government has adequate facilities for reaching the public.

Implications for International Communication

A democratic form of government implies freedom of two-way international communication as well as domestic freedom of information. Many of
the groups that contend and interact in a democracy require ideas and information from abroad if they are to form and function, and individuals no less
frequently seek information from other countries to satisfy personal needs. Any
person who wishes to take an intelligent interest in the foreign policy of his own
nation must have access to foreign news and opinions. If the democratic process is to function, the right of individuals to incoming information must be assured.

When it comes to the right of private individuals and organizations to transmit communications to foreign audiences, the requirements of democracy are less clear. Perhaps a democratic state could exist without allowing private communication to other countries as long as domestic freedom of communication and freedom for incoming information were assured. Foreign commerce, missionary activity, and travel would be ruled out except under government auspices, but domestic groups and individuals could still obtain all the information they required, and the internal democratic process might be able to function. This is, however, pure speculation, since in practice all democracies allow private citizens a wide range of opportunity to communicate with citizens of other countries. Furthermore, if all democracies restricted the *outflow* of information, this would mean that for each the range of *incoming* information would be greatly narrowed, a situation that might be expected to lead to the gradual undermining of democracy everywhere.

The hospitality of democracies to ideas from abroad means that democratic governments can be influenced indirectly by international communications that are given attention by important domestic groups. Dictatorships, by way of contrast, seek to exclude some categories of foreign ideas and are far less responsive to pressures from their own population. Consequently, a government in a totalitarian country, while it may be affected directly by diplomatic communications and propaganda from abroad, is less likely to be responsive to domestic pressures generated by ideas from outside the country. Although democracies do, in fact, attempt to influence mass opinion in dictatorships through propaganda, the paucity of upward communication channels in the latter makes it more difficult to affect their policies in this way.

Most democracies permit, and even encourage, a wide range of activities on the part of foreign publicists. In the United States, foreign advertisers, representatives of religious groups, and cultural salesmen of all kinds are usually welcomed. Foreign political spokesmen also are likely to be well received when they state their aims openly, and when they do not attempt to exert a direct influence on elections, legislation, or other political processes that are regarded as the prerogatives of citizens only.

Communications from abroad, if they are to have an effect, must find users among the population of the receiving country. Furthermore, if these ideas are to be politically influential, the users ordinarily must be organized in some way—in political parties, industrial enterprises, or groups sharing a public opinion. In economically developed democracies, the range of interests represented by organized groups is very wide; therefore, a great variety of domestic organizations are in the market for ideas they can use to achieve their purposes. In view of the intense competition for the attention of people in industrialized democracies, however, any communication from abroad that does not fill an important need is likely to be submerged in the sea of competing domestic and international communications.

Another set of implications for international communication arises from the fact that democracies impose few restrictions on messages that leave the country. Anything that is publicly said or done in a democracy may become known abroad. Foreign newsmen are accepted as a matter of course, and are permitted a wide latitude in their activities. Critical communications, which are necessary for the functioning of the democratic order, are especially likely to find their way into international channels and to be given wide currency by hostile media.

Furthermore, because democratic states allow freedom for outbound communications, the information about these states that reaches foreign audiences is likely to contain contradictions and inconsistencies. Just as the numerous domestic groups competing for power and influence require different kinds of incoming information for their own functioning, they also will have different things to say to other peoples, and their actions that become known abroad will reflect the divergences in their values and goals. Communications from or about a democracy are likely to highlight the contradictions implicit in a pluralistic society.

Chanchal Sarkar:

Journalists' Organizations in Socialist Society

I SHOULD explain why I have chosen the subject that I have. I strongly believe there is a great deal of ignorance and misunderstanding in India about the Press and other mass media in socialist countries. This leads to a bagful of wrong conceptions. Very often the Press in sophisticated and developed countries with a long tradition of public awareness is glibly called "backward", "unfree", "controlled" and so on.

Objectives

The mass media are part of the environment in which we live, part of the air we breathe. If we don't understand the way the media work, we don't understand the political system. Equally, if we don't understand the political system, we cannot understand the mass media. In a socialist system, particularly, the two are of a piece. We will never be able to evaluate our own mass media, their objectives and purpose, virtues and weaknesses until we examine the fundamentals of the organisation and the objectives of mass media under other systems.

My impressions and professional estimate of the mass media in the socialist countries of Europe are formed out of several visits, contacts, friendships and exchanges over the past five years.

Firstly, I have been impressed by the organisation. The organisation of journalists' associations, their foresightful planning, their training schemes, welfare efforts and cadre building. Much co-ordination and central thought go into the institutions and into shaping the human material responsible for manning the mass media in socialist countries. Although the word journalists' *union* sometimes appears in their titles I am going to use the word *association*. This is to distinguish them from trade unions which they are not. Quite often journalists in the socialist countries of Europe are members of trade unions as well.

Journalists' associations in countries like the Soviet Union, Poland, Hungary, Czechoslovakia, Rumania and the German Democratic Republic have done a great deal for the spread of the media and for the conditions of work in them. Many of the welfare facilities that journalists enjoy—medical at-

▶ Reprinted by permission from *Vidura* (New Delhi), Vol. 12, No. 3, June–Aug. 1975. Chanchal Sarkar is Director of the Press Institute of India and a prolific writer on press problems.

tention, housing, holiday homes and so on—are due to the efforts of the associations. Training in most of the countries I have mentioned is their responsibility. Other activities include consultation on all important legal measures; professional groupings for skill and knowledge; fund raising; international links and co-operation; diversification of activities to draw in greater income; a wide spectrum of publications. The work of the associations is solid and purposeful. It provides a strong base for the operation of the media.

It is important to understand that the journalists' associations in socialist countries combine the work of proprietors', editors' and working journalists' bodies and they also straddle people in all the media. This is a basic difference from the organisations of media professionals in non-socialist countries. Because they cover all the interests in the media, they are able to push hard for a group sense, for a professional approach in which all the sections of the profession and industry can combine. There are also some specialist media institutions, but they supplement the functions of the basic journalists' associations.

The Pattern

Within their many-sided activities it is possible to see a pattern. There is special concern for the young, catching them early and training them. Things are so arranged that all the problems, possible solutions and new proposals are thoroughly discussed at several levels starting with the districts before they are adopted for action. Training, it is thought, is not for beginners only but just as much for the established journalist cadres. The word "cadre" occurs repeatedly and it is very important to understand its significance. Much long-term planning goes into the programme of the associations. Sometimes they begin to set the stage from ten, even fifteen years ahead. Finally, there is great concern for those members who are ill and for those who have retired, the pensioners.

One way of appreciating how much thought has gone into the organisation of the associations is to trace the commonness of structure that runs through them, irrespective of country. Each journalists' body has a general Congress, a Central Committee, a Presidium and a Secretariat. Other countries could be said to have the same "general body" meetings, 'executive committees' and 'secretariats'. There are likenesses indeed but the structures, as we see them in the socialist countries are very similar to each other. This means that cooperation among them is much easier, whether on a bilateral basis or within the socialist community as a whole. There is the same concern for district organisation, the same set-up of professional "clubs", as they are called, and of correspondence courses. Some countries like Yugoslavia, Czechoslovakia and the Soviet Union have a federal system of government and that, too, with its regional nuances is visible in the organisation of the journalists' associations.

Earlier I said that, to understand the organisation of journalism and journalists in the socialist world, it is important to know where the mass media figure in the scheme of things. Here is one view that might help towards an understanding:

"In communist society, propaganda and agitation are an integral part of one of the most important aspects of the official activities of the State and the Party. They embrace the entire social life and activities—from the sciences through education, press and entertainment to sport—using a much wider range of media than merely the media of mass communication in the western conception. Different also is their place among the social institutions and the significance attached to them.

"It is therefore not possible to deal with them in western terms and values; they must be treated as phenomena specific to the communist society."

Lenin assigned to the media a most important place and all the major theoreticians, policy makers and activists of the socialist world have always accepted this as axiomatic and built on it.

Long ago, in 1901; in his book 'What is to be done!' Lenin wrote: "A newspaper is not only a collective propapandist and collective agitator, but also a collective organiser. In this respect it can be compared to the scaffolding erected around a building under construction; it marks the contours of the structure and facilitates communication between the builders, permitting them to distribute the work and to view the common results achieved by their organised labour".

Re-education

He spelt things out in greater detail: "Our first and main means for increasing the self-discipline of the working people and for passing from the old, good-for-nothing methods of work, or methods for shirking work, in capitalist society, must be the press, revealing shortcomings in the economic life of each labour commune, ruthlessly branding these shortcomings, frankly laying bare all the ulcers of our economic life, and thus appealing to the public of the working people for curing these ulcers." Lenin continued: "We must convert—and we shall convert—the press from an organ for purveying sensations, from a mere apparatus for communicating political news, from an organ of struggle against bourgeois lying—into an instrument for the economic re-education of the masses, into an instrument for telling the masses how to organise work in a new way."

Almost seventy years later, in 1969, President Tito said of the Yugoslav Press: "Naturally, our press is free, there is no censorship in our country and we have no intention of introducing it. This means that every article published in our papers, broadcast or telecast by our radio and television, need not necessarily express the official attitudes of the Government and of the country's leading organs. Naturally, our journalists must act along the line of the League of Communists and the development programme of our socialist society in general. This means that they have to explain the problems of our development and make a constructive contribution to their resolution. And, irrespective of occasional vagueness and dilemmas, they have an opportunity to penetrate into the substance of the matter and adopt correct views."

This is how the Statute of the Federation of Yugoslav Journalists describes the function and status of journalists: "A journalist is a socio-political worker who, by carrying out his activity publicly, through the written or spoken word, cartoon, photograph and film, takes part in the construction and development of the socialist society and strives for the fulfilment of the rights of the working people to self-government and for the establishment of humane relations among people. He is thus contributing to the development of socialist consciousness and to the forming of the socialist public opinion on all social phenomena and on concrete policies in various walks of life."

Philosophy

In any Communist State the Communist Party, whatever may be its name, sometimes the Socialist Unity Party or, the League of Communists, or the Workers Unity Party is paramount and the Party is deeply interested in the editorial framework of the major papers and the directive focus in all the other media. This is because there is a special Communist philosophy about the mass media—the composite view of its utility and function which I have outlined. A professor at the Karl Marx University in Leipzig—the sole faculty where the mass media people of the German Democratic Republic are trained-told me that the Party takes the ultimate decisions about the media. From the University he and his colleagues prepared papers for consideration by the Party's Central Committee, sometimes confidential papers, but it was the Party that finally decided. The Secretaries-General of the journalists' associations are, at times, members of the Communist Party. They may not always have been journalists. Sometimes even editors may not have started out as journalists but their acceptance by the Communist Party is most necessary. They must be politically trusted.

What is enormously important to understand is that this is the operative scheme in a socialist country, conceived, with care and forethought—and consistently implemented. Without appreciation of this frame and the meshing of the mass media into the apparatus of the Socialist State, the role and the significance of the media in the socialist world will never be grasped and there will always be unreal misunderstanding and irrelevant prejudice.

Integral Part

It is about time that the set-up was understood. Throughout the socialist countries there are powerful presses. In the Soviet Union there are 8,000 newspapers and magazines. The daily circulation of newspapers there is 85 million copies compared to 64 million in the United States. In the German Democratic Republic there are over 6,500 members of the Journalists' Association more than there are journalists in India. Between the years 1966 and 1971 the five main papers of the Soviet Union *Pravda, Izvestia, Selskaya Zhizn, Trud* and *Komsomolskaya Pravda* received over eight million letters from their readers. In 1971 Czechoslovakia had 3.18 million television receivers and 3.8 million radio sets. The Netherlands, with a slightly smaller population, had about the same spread 3.2 million television sets and 3.7 million radios. In other words the socialist systems are thriving systems and very important ones.

The mass media are an integral part of the socialist scheme of things. So there is a bedrock of effort to see that journalists are made aware of their role, because it is one which has to be learnt and understood. In the training, therefore, there is always an ideological stream and there is much discussion about the place and the responsibility of a journalist in a socialist society. Training, it is important to emphasise again, is not only at the beginner's level. There are, in the socialist countries, the Higher Party Schools to which editors of important papers or the top people in the other media might be invited, sometimes when they are at the height of their responsibility and influence. They may be at a Higher Party School for three or four years before they return to their papers or to some other paper or medium. The associations are regular in organising discussions on the ideological aspect of a jouralists' work and these discussions continue side by side with the professional and technical discussions which are also organised very systematically.

Here are some more details of the journalistic situation in the socialist countries of Europe.

The Soviet Union has more than 150,000 journalists and 52,000 members of its Journalists' Association. Membership in Russia is conferred, not automatic. Poland has 3,725 journalists in Warsaw alone. Prague has 2,300 journalists living in the city, 1,000 in Bratislava, and 4,300 in all Czechoslovakia. The GDR has more than 8,000 journalists. Yugoslavia has 5,500 Union members and about 2,000 nonmembers. Hungary's 3,600 journalists include about 350 pensioners.

Besides the regular papers which can be compared with their counterparts in other countries there are many factory papers published from factories or collectives. And there are large numbers of people who write voluntarily for newspapers. "People's correspondents" they are called. In the Soviet Union their number is estimated at six million. In the German Democratic Republic each newspaper has over 2,000 people's correspondents and the same stream runs through all the other socialist countries. This was very much a part of what Lenin had in mind. In fact he said that for every five permanent professional staff there ought to be 500 to 5,000 nonprofessional contributors.

Journalists' Associations in the socialist countries are run by well-organised secretaries with well defined departments. The secretaries are on top of their work and are extremely well informed. The associations in these countries are also very competently coordinated by the International Organisation of Journalists which has its headquarters in Prague. Some of the departmental heads of the IOJ were, previously, important figures in the journalists' associations of the individual countries. In fact Hungary, Poland, the GDR and so on always have high level representation in the secretariat of the IOJ. The present secretary for professional questions at the IOJ used to be the secretary of the Rumanian Journalists' Association; the immediate past Secretary-General of the Polish Journalists' Association also used to be at the Prague headquarters of the IOJ.

The International Organisation of Journalists is an international body with consultative status in UNESCO and, in its programmes, it works in association with international organisations like WHO, ILO, etc. There are committees for cooperation with the IOJ in many countries, like France, and Japan, for instance, which do not have their mass media organised along socialist lines. The IOJ is 30 years old in 1975.

The structure of the associations in the socialist countries closely resemble each other. They each have a general body which is often called a Congress which meets every few years. In some countries it is after five years, in some it is after three. It is the Congress which elects the Board of Directors or Central Committee or whatever it is.

The Secretariat is the executive body. There is a President who is not always full time. Not in Poland, for instance, or Hungary, or Rumania or even the Soviet Union. In the GDR he is. There are Vice-Presidents and a senior executive, often called the Secretary-General, or something, or something akin to that. Below him there could be secretaries to look after the various departments one in charge of each if there are four or five broad divisions. Some associations prefer to divide their work between a large number of departments, other prefer a more reined-in supervision.

Anyway, the main departments often are: Organisation, Finance and Economy, Training, and International. Sometimes, as in the Soviet Union, all the departments are grouped under two main ones, the Creative and the International.

At its meeting every few years the Congress elects a body that can number about 70 in Poland or 60 in Czechoslovakia or about 80 or 90 in the GDR. This is the central committee. The Presidium also has a manageable number. There are 13 in the Yugoslav Praesidium, 20 to 24 in the GDR and 15 in Czechoslovakia. On various visits I have been given different numbers, so I tend to think that the number varies from time to time according to needs or else the Secretariat members are sometimes not included in the reckoning. . . .

Problems

The Central Committee meets every three or four months and the Presidium once a month, on the average. The Central Committee discusses some of the main problems which face journalists at the time. A few years ago, for instance, in the GDR, I was told that some of the principal subjects for discussion at Central Committee meetings had been: Role of women in journalism and of women journalists; Planning and Management of Editorial Offices; District journalist; and Economic Journalism. There is a planned effort to have the main problems discussed at several levels; in the districts, in the Presidium, in the Central Committee and, finally, in the Congress. There is a line that runs through these discussions and the Secretariat acts as the link between the central body and the districts. In fact the work of the Association is described often as that of pushing through resolutions of the Unions in the districts. It is the Association's task to bring about exchange of opinions, co-ordination of the different sections. organisation of conferences at a national level and, as I have stressed, training. The districts, moreover, have the same organisation in miniature. There is, therefore, a continuous two-way communication between the smallest unit and the central bodies.

For all the widespread activity that the associations undertake, for all their many programmes, they need money. There is, of course, the subscription from members. This varies but is not high. Pensioners pay very little and juniors often pay less than seniors. But subscription income is scarcely enough. There is other funding. Some Associations get funds from bodies like a National Front. There are grants from the Ministry of Culture and the Ministry of Foreign Affairs. There are separate payments from the editorial houses of newspapers or from radio and television for training establishments. In Yugoslavia, the newspapers, radio and TV pay a special subsidy to the Federation of Journalists calculated per head.

Even all this would not be enough and so the associations have diversified their activities, they have gone into several enterprises to supplement their funds. . . .

In the office of the Union of Journalists of the USSR I was told that the principal task of the association, its main programme, was to train and improve the journalist cadres. This is now part of the credo of all the associations in Socialist Europe, it seems to me, because training occupies a large part of the effort, the staff and the money that they put in.

Time and again it is the Journalists' Association that makes itself responsible for the training of journalists. Even where there are universities, very big and distinguished universities with large journalism faculties, the Associations are involved and co-operate closely.

Varsity Courses

All kinds of courses are organised, from full-time ones, for several years to correspondence courses for those who either live away from university centres or are at work already. There are release courses to which offices send their staff for a week, say, after two weeks of work. There are refresher courses and the Associations are trying to organise things so that every journalist, after two or three years of work, comes back to base for a month or so. In the Soviet Union today they do so after every five years.

There are, of course, detailed courses for those who have specialised in something like the coal industry or oil. Then there are vacation courses, not only for people of the country but also for foreigners. The Polish Association, for instance, holds classes in the holiday season and journalists come from the GDR to learn Polish. The Association themselves run courses for journalists wishing to learn foreign languages.

I don't want to go into great detail about the courses except to show how seriously some universities take them. Take Moscow University. There are 105 professors and teachers in the Journalism Department, 25 scientific workers and 150 technical personnel. This is what the Dean of the Faculty told me in the summer of 1973. The course is six years long. There are 2,500 students, 1,000 by day who are full-time, and 1,500 by night. There are also 1,200 who do the correspondence course. About 30 weeks of the total course period is spent in practical work, the equivalent more or less, of a school year.

In the GDR I found that the students of Karl Marx University go to work in provincial papers during the vacations and also for their practical training periods. Some times the papers they go to will be the ones they will work for when they graduate. The Russians see to it that the students, for their practical attachments, have spells in different parts of the country, in the Tundra, in Siberia, in Tashkent and so on so that they get to know aspects of their vast land.

Foreign Students

In Moscow there are sometimes as many as 142 foreign students from a whole range of countries. Here is the composition in the summer of 1973 when I was last there: Salvador, Costa Rica, Peru, Colombia, Venezuela; Uganda, Nigeria, Tanzania, Malagasy, Ruanda, Sierra Leone; Egypt, Morocco, Algeria, Iraq, Jordan; India, the Democratic Republic of Vietnam, Mongolia, Bangaldesh; France, Poland, Hungary, Bulgaria, Canada and the U.S. Moscow University has laboratories and studios for television and radio as well as for the Press and for photography.

In the Soviet Union there are 24 universities which teach journalism and six Higher Party Schools which I mentioned in the first lecture, schools to which some of the senior most people in the mass media are invited for three or four years. There are also special institutions for training in radio and television.

The Karl Marx Universities in Leipzig in the GDR has 5 professors, 15 dozents and 35 senior assistants, and, before long, they had predicted there would be about 80 to 100 teachers. Maybe this has already come about. I last visited the university in September 1974 but there was a major conference on and I could not check the changes since my earlier visit.

I keep harping on the interest of the associations in training because, without a trained corps of journalists, there can never be mass media of any quality in a country. Almost each association—and, of course, the bigger universities—run correspondence courses, mainly for working journalists. The GDR Association runs a three-year combined course, combined meaning that the students are also at work in papers and are released for a period. Many of those who take the course are factory journalists, people from the other mass media and also journalists working in regular papers. For such courses, which cost about 750 marks, the office where the student works pays 300 marks, the Association pays 400 and the student himself only 50 marks.

The International Organisation of Journalists is also keenly interested in training, particularly for overseas people. It operates through the national associations. For instance, the Budapest international journalism school is run by the Association of Hungarian Journalists, the one in Berlin is run by the GDR Association. More and more there is a demand for courses to be held overseas. And so the IOJ, either itself or through the national associations, has held courses and seminars in Ghana, Algeria, Syria, Iraq and so on. Courses have been requested in Hanoi and the Budapest school has held special courses for Radio and TV people from North Vietnam.

Besides these training ventures, the Yugoslav Association of Journalists has helped to found the Press Institute in Belgrade which does research in mass media and also trains and holds symposia.

The IOJ has set up a special editorial centre for agricultural journalists in Sofia, Bulgaria, and is planning other training centres in Prague and Havana.

In all the socialist countries there is a comprehensive form of social welfare available to every citizen. This covers education, health, employment, pensions and so on. What the associations do is, therefore, additional and selective. And they do a lot.

Poland has a social section in the association which looks after social welfare and it has been able to get some special concessions from the State. Journalists, for instance, are now allowed to retire five years *before* others, at the age of 60 for men and 55 for women. They have done more: after fifteen years of service journalists are entitled to six weeks leave a year. They get higher pensions and enjoy a higher emeritus status.

Medical Care

These efforts have been motivated by surveys which show that the life of the journalist is full of stress and the average expectancy of life is not more than 50 years. All the associations are trying to mitigate this. There is an attempt to have special, comprehensive check-ups for journalists every two years. By persuasion, of course, not compulsion. In Czechoslovakia the association has been able to get 100 seats in spas for journalists especially those who suffer from cardio-vascular diseases. In fact, the emphasis in medical benefits for journalists is on preventive medicine.

Then holidays. The Hungarian Association has eight holiday homes and week-end houses in all parts of the country, by the lakeside, in the mountains, in the Great Plains and so on. I have visited one, the home in Tihany beside Lake Balaton, and can vouch that they are very beautiful places. I have also stayed in the Interpress Hotel which is also set on the same vast lake. It is a very pleasant hotel. A few miles away is the place where Rabindranath Tagore convalesced and planted a tree which has now grown to overhang his statue. It is part of Tagore Avenue and Dr. Zakir Husain also planted a sapling there a few years ago.

Journalists working in Budpest have told me that the association's holiday homes are cheap. They and their families can have a very economic holiday, they said.

The holiday home idea is of course fairly old in the Soviet Union and has now been taken up by all the socialist countries. I have already mentioned the Interpress Hotel in Hungary on Lake Balaton which is an international hotel but run by the Hungary Association. There is also one in Varna in Bulgaria.

Housing

Some of the associations have been able to do something special for city housing. The Hungarian association has tried the ownership flat idea but it has gone ahead somewhat slowly. The idea of ownership houses or flats in holiday resorts for journalists has been given up there. In other countries there is a general effort to provide houses for citizens, but there still is a shortage, I noticed, in Czechoslovakia and in Hungary where 50 flats for journalists are being built in Budapest now. The most significant progress seems to have been in the GDR where in Berlin I have seen new flats put up quickly with prefabricated material. Not elegant but adequate and inexpensive.

The East German rate of pension for journalists amounts to 90% of the salary of the ten best years. This must give the journalists a great sense of security and contentment.

I have said that the associations are doing something over and above what the State does. In Hungary, for instance, the association has set up a medical clinic in its building and some of Budapest's best doctors come and give free consultations. In the Soviet Union there is special help given by the association to journalists who have been ill for a long time and missed work. The Poles have a Widows' Fund and a fund for needy journalists. Several countries have special arrangements to send the children of the members to holiday resorts.

There are special concessions for travel in most countries. The attitude towards special benefits or privileges is somewhat different in Yugoslavia where the journalists' association claims little besides travel concessions. The Yugoslav view is that no group should have special privileges.

The International Organisation of Journalists has naturally been greatly interested in the question of social welfare for journalists. It has carried out an extensive and thorough survey of their economic and social condition. I was given a preliminary draft of the findings when I visited the offices of the IOJ in

Prague last October. Both UNESCO and ILO have shown interest in the survey and the ILO has offered the IOJ the use of its computers for processing it. The IOJ also has a proposal for a sanatorium at Karlovy Vary in Czechoslovakia. . . .

Trade Journals

Correspondence courses, run by the associations and also by some universities, are an important part of the work of the associations and are used by a great many people. There are also the many voluntary correspondents or peoples' correspondents. I mentioned that in the USSR there are some six million people from all walks of life, including those in fields and factories who write voluntarily for newspapers. The associations consider it their duty to help train these correspondents. The voluntary correspondents represent a reserve of journalists and in the Soviet Union the association runs a special magazine for correspondents in the provinces and villages, for workers and peasants. The circulation of this magazine, I was told in Moscow in the summer of 1973, was about a million. In the German Democratic Republic there are about 620 factory newspapers and a lot of attention is given to training the peoples' correspondents. There are more than 40 dailies in the GDR and each of them aims to have between 2000 to 2500 peoples' correspondents. A paper like the *Neues Deutschland* would, of course, have more.

Then there are the clubs for the young people. I have had these described to me in the Soviet Union and in Hungary. In the Soviet Union they are run by Moscow University (and presumably by other universities as well). Some of the students take lectures and practical sessions and young people come to attend the minicourses to know what journalism is all about. In Hungary senior journalists, including one who was for long a correspondent in India, take these sessions with young people. This is the process through which there is a continuous search for talent among the young and also the process by which the young are attracted to journalism.

International Links

Then there are international links. The international sections of the associations are very important. They have a fairly large staff who are multilingual and they also use interpreters. Sometimes there are trained interpreters as in the Soviet Union where the Journalists' Association arranges for them through Intourist. Elsewhere they are taken from the language departments of the universities and the students themselves enjoy these assignments greatly, partly because they get good practice and also because they earn some money. In Hungary and Poland I have had very good student interpreters who have made my visits especially worthwhile and pleasant. Some of them are interested in journalism and the international section of the association often has its eyes on them.

There are bilateral agreements among the socialist countries for exchange. Agreements with nonsocialist countries too. Delegations always seem to be visiting these countries. There is an agreement between the associations of Hungary, Poland and Czechoslovakia and the Press Institute of India for an annual exchange of visits. This month, February 1975, we expect a senior journalist each from these three countries who will come to study and write about Indian agriculture and India's nuclear effort. In the summer we shall send two Indian journalists to Poland, Hungary and Czechoslovakia. Visits between the journalists of the socialist countries and those from the nonsocialist are increasing every year. So are professional meetings as one can notice from the professional magazines of the non-socialist countries.

The Soviet Union's Association has signed agreements of co-operation with the Syndicate of Egyptian Journalists and other agreements were in preparation with Syria, Iraq, India and the Democratic Republic of Somaliland. Some of them, I presume, have been signed already.

The International School for Journalists in Budapest, run by the Hungarian Association on behalf of the IOJ, has run 18 courses already. The Budapest school and the one in East Berlin have already had over 500 students pass through them. Budapest has received students from India, Bangladesh, Ghana, Egypt, Iraq, Tanzania, Ethiopia, Venezuela, Chile, Pakistan, Afghanistan and so on. These are only a sample. There have been students from many other underdeveloped countries, showing the deep and purposeful interest that the journalists' associations in the socialist countries and the IOJ are taking in the journalists from the poorer part of the world. Quite often they have gone into the underdeveloped world themselves. In 1973, for instance, the Budapest school held a seminar in Accra in co-operation with UNESCO. The GDR association has agreements with journalists' organisations in 28 countries for the exchange of delegations, etc. So thorough is the approach of these associations that, in the international section of the Czechoslovak Association of Journalists, I found a card index of all the foreign journalists who had visited the Association and could identify the Indians who had been there.

My brief, and perhaps somewhat desultory, survey of the work of journalists' organisations in the socialist countries of Europe is done not just to assemble and spread out information. It is done really to generate self questioning and self criticism among our own organizations be they of working journalists, editors or proprietors. Are we really doing anything like what we should do for our journalism and journalists? That is the question I hope our organisations will ask.

Take, for instance, training. Again and again I repeat that this is among the most important activities of the associations in the socialist countries. Training as we have seen goes on at all levels and for all kinds of journalists, part time, full time, beginners, the experienced, factory correspondents, working journalists in centres away from universities or union headquarters. I keep returning to the description of the Russian Association defining its prime objective as being that of improving the cadres. Have we really attempted much in this field?

India's Efforts

Take the international interest that the associations and the IOJ show. They have turned their attention specially to Africa and the Arab lands and their programmes of collaboration and training are going on with quiet but unremitting purposefulness. A sub-continental country like India also has important regional interests as well as political interest in its own system and way of life. Yet are we doing much for journalism and journalists of even our neighbouring countries-Bangladesh, Nepal, Sri Lanka, and Afghanistan for instance? And a little further away, of Thailand, Burma or Malaysia? Moving a little nearer, what are we doing for Bhutan, for even the hill areas of our own country? I am talking only about efforts we should be making for journalists or potential journalists of those regions.

Consider the journalists' clubs. There are, today, some attempts to set up economic writers forums and some organisations for science writers but the professional clubs of the socialist countries represent a very well-organised way of furthering professional skill.

Nothing can be done without money. It is interesting to see how the associations in the socialist countries are diversifying their activities to rake in more funds through advertising agencies, publishing houses, balls, football matches, and so on all the money to be used to increase the activity of the association. We, too, have from time to time floated souvenirs and charity performances but have we really been able to do anything systematically? Have we been able to even raise a widows and orphans fund?

In social welfare the achievements of the socialist associations are solid. It is no good saying that those are welfare states where the basic services are taken care of by public funds. That may be so but the associations have not left it to the State alone. They have gone beyond the State's contribution, supplemented it, humanised it and improved upon it. We have scarcely begun. I should also say that in many countries, nonsocialist as well as socialist, some of the special funds like those for widows and orphans started before the State took a hand in social welfare. The widows and orphans fund of the British unions, for instance, is very old.

What about the health homes, the holiday resorts, the hotels run by the associations, the places where the children of the journalists can go for a break? Now and again we hear of some sporadic arrangements or attempts by some press club or association in an Indian city. There is inflation today and our railway fares have gone up sharply. But were these things even begun when the fares were cheap?

It is also important for us to learn from the nature and organisation of ideological discussions and discussions about the basic problems of journalism and journalists. Only through these can there be some consensus of approach and an understanding of the role of mass media people in society. The way in which the discussions are organised, the different layers of discussions, the consultative role of the associations before any changes are proposed by the government, by the legislature or anyone else—these are notable achievements.

I have been deeply impressed by the work and functioning of the journalists' associations. So much so that, in the last five years, I have several times gone back to their offices and institutions to take in as many details as I could.

I have envied them their purposefulness, their foresight and their comprehensive approach. Simultaneously they are working to have journalists better educated and trained as well as to have them better housed, rested and medically cared for. Without fuss or fanfare they have established cordial collaborative relations with like-minded bodies within the same discipline—Press Research Centres, Public Opinion Institutes, Sociological Research Bureaus.

The associations waste little time in internecine rivalry and warfare. They are anxious to attract the best people from the younger generation into the mass media. And they are not grim—there's an experimental theatre in the Budapest Association, there's good wine in the Bucharest's Callea Victoria where the Rumanian Association is housed. The restaurant in the Belgrade Association serves one of the best meals I have had in Europe.

Of course there must be weaknesses, things to criticise, things they could do better or in a more relaxed fashion. But I feel that we should first attempt something, pool the resources of our own institutions, get much more going and then perhaps we could afford to be critical.

*   *   *   *

REFERENCES

Most of the material in the text is taken from conversations; so the following list is to be treated as ancillary:

Buzek, Antony. *How the Communist Press Works*, Pall Mal Press Ltd., London, 1964.
Democratic Journalist (Periodical), International Organization of Journalists, Prague.
Facts about the IOJ, International Organization of Journalists, Prague, 1973.
Bulletin (Periodical), Federation of Yugoslav Journalists, Belgrade, 1969.
Lenin about the Press, International Organization of Journalists, Prague, 1972.
UNESCO Statistical Handbook, 1972, UNESCO, New York, 1972.
Vidura (Periodical), Press Institute of India, Vol. 10, No. 1, February 1973.

Yevgeny Prokhorov:

The Marxist Press Concept

IN THEIR EFFORTS to discredit Leninism, denigrate the ideals of socialism, and sow doubt regarding the historical gains of the Soviet people, anticommunists have had recourse to every kind of hypocritical falsification. In this connection, one cannot bypass the numerous fabrications coming from the apologists of capitalism in respect to freedom of the press in socialist society.

As far back as the early years of the present century Lenin explained the actual causes of this ceaseless speculation with high-sounding words. Later, after the triumph of the October Revolution, he wrote outright that capitalism "will raise against us the banner of freedom." This prediction has been justified. As pointed out by the American sociologist Scott Nearing, in their search for a slogan that can become a motto and serve as self-publicity, the Western leaders of today have resorted to a whole series of epithets such as "civilized," "Christian," and "Western," which they then discard because of their ineffectiveness and lack of conviction. They have made the word "freedom" their ultimate choice, seeing in it a most inspiring, all-embracing and convincing paean to the Western way of life.

The manipulations practiced by the opponents of Marxism, with their skill in social demagogy, are not so innocuous. Even honest and intelligent people sometimes succumb to the spate of phrases coming from their pens, proving incapable of seeing through their thoroughly false and hypocritical content. That is why it would not be out of place to recall some of the propositions of Marxism concerning the problem of political freedoms in general, and freedom of the press in particular.

From the Marxist point of view, freedom means the possibility of action within the framework of a realized necessity. Necessity, within the framework of history, means the sum of definite patterns that are independent of man's consciousness and make their way through a mass of happenstance. However, within the bounds of society, certain people operate who are endowed with a heightened consciousness and will-power and set themselves definite aims; here laws find effect, not directly or in a mechanical way, but through human behavior. Such action may be in harmony with necessity or law, or it may conflict with them. Ultimately the laws always achieve their ends.

▶ This article appeared originally in *Zhurnalist* (Moscow), No. 3, 1970, under the title of "The True Meaning of Freedom of the Press." It is reprinted here from *Reprints from the Soviet Press* (X:13, June 29, 1970) by permission of Compass Publications, Inc., 101 Old Mamaroneck Rd., Box 3B-6, White Plains, N.Y. 10605.

"The idea of determinism," Lenin wrote, "which postulates that human acts are objectively necessitated and rejects the absurd myth of free will, in no way destroys man's reason or conscience, or appraisal of his actions. Quite the contrary, only the determinist view makes a strict and correct appraisal possible instead of attributing everything to free will."

It is clear that the progressive forces, which are guided by the laws of functioning and development of society, are acting freely when they advance the communist ideal and fight for its achievement. But what about the forces of reaction? Their actions are an obstacle to the free development of society, an obstacle with which mankind is coping and which it will surely overcome.

It is common knowledge that the slogan "freedom of the press" was advanced by the bourgeoisie at a time when, heading the "third estate, it was at grips with feudalism" in an attempt to enjoy at least equal rights with its opponents, who had monopolized the publcation of books and other sources of spreading information. The call for a "free market of ideas" was distinctly a class demand, expressing the interests of a definite group in society which at the time was performing the historically progressive role of fighter against domination by the feudal section. The slogan "freedom of the press" was directly contraposed to the authoritarian view that the press should reflect the viewpoint of the feudal and clerical upper crust and enjoy exclusive rights of distribution.

As Lenin wrote, the "freedom of press" slogan became a great world slogan at the close of the Middle Ages and remained so up to the nineteenth century. Why? because it expressed the ideas of the progressive bourgeoisie, i.e., its struggle against kings and priests, feudal lords and landowners.

As soon as the bourgeoisie had completed its progressive mission, and turned reactionary, with another class—the proletariat—becoming the standard-bearer of further social progress, the slogan of freedom of the press lost all meaning to the bourgeoisie. Having taken over state power and established its economic domination, the bourgeoisie had now acquired full freedom in the economic and political sense, a freedom it now exploited for its own selfish aims.

To achieve those ends, the bourgeoisie did its utmost imperceptively to deceive the public; it was now necessary to turn a revolutionary slogan into a dead letter, a principle that would permit conditions of enjoyment of that freedom which would be juridically to the advantage of the reactionary forces alone. In the grip of bourgeois constitutions and bourgeois legislation, genuine freedom of the press turned into a juridical fiction.

Wherever capitalism reigns, freedom of the press means freedom to buy up newspapers, writers, and "public opinion"—in the interests of the bourgeoisie. This cannot be denied; it is a fact no one will ever be able to disprove. Lenin often emphasized this with the summary: "In actual fact this is not freedom."

Freedom of the press has now become the slogan of the proletariat and its class organizations. Such is the irony of history: once advanced by the bourgeoisie and now taken over by its grave-diggers, it has turned against its originators. Adopted by the proletariat and the masses it leads, the slogan has once more become truly meaningful. That is because the forces which are advancing it today are backed by the truth of history, for they express the interests of all social development and, according to the logic of the struggle, must win freedom of the press for themselves, something that in part can already be achieved within the framework of bourgeois society.

However, the form and the degree to which the constitutional and juridical freedom of journalism, as instituted by the bourgeoisie, can be used do not in any way depend on the democratic character or love of freedom in the Establishment; they depend on the strength and the insistence of the progressive forces, the Communist and Workers' Parties, in winning and defending the freedom of their press. The circumstances mentioned by Marx and Engels that the progressive press is reestablished after every defeat is not an argument in favor of the bourgeoisie's tolerance of the Marxist press, but proof that history cannot be turned back and that the adherents of progress in a number of countries have been strong enough to have won the right to their own press. This is not yet genuine freedom but a police brand, within the framework of the bourgeois state—a freedom which must be constantly defended. The experience of the Communist Parties has shown that where the forces of reaction do not enjoy an overwhelming advantage over the forces of progress, the conditions arise for the emergence of a kind of "free market of ideas," free both for the bourgeois and the progressive and communist press.

This is a kind of freedom whose meaning was explained by Lenin to anarchistically minded individualists and certain "Communists" in the following words:

"Calm yourselves, gentlemen! . . . Everyone is free to write and say whatever he likes, without any restrictions. . . . Freedom of speech and the press must be complete. But then freedom of association also must be complete. I am bound to accord you, in the name of free speech, the full right to shout, lie, and write to your heart's content. But you are bound to grant me, in the name of freedom of association, the right to enter into, or withdraw from, association with people advocationg this or that view."

Does this mean that a "model" of freedom proposed by Lenin in a concrete historical situation has a general and universal nature and can be brought into the conditions of a victorious socialist revolution?

A clear and unambiguous reply to this question was given by Lenin himself in the following words: "Earlier on we said that if we took power, we intended to close down the bourgeois newspapers. To tolerate the existence of these papers is to cease being a socialist. Those who say, 'Reopen the bourgeois newspapers,' fail to understand that we are moving at full speed toward socialism. After all, tsarist newspapers were closed down after the overthrow of tsarism. Now we have thrown off the bourgeois yoke. . . . We must go forward, to a new society, and take the same attitude toward the bourgeois newspapers as we did to the ultrareactionary papers in February and March."

The winning of state power by the Bolsheviks and the transition to the construction of a socialist society created an entirely new socioeconomic situation, so that the slogan of freedom of the press had of necessity to assume a new character: absolutely unrestricted freedom was granted to that press which follows the channel of sociohistorical necessity, fully and objectively depicts the "history of the times," grudges no effort in helping the construction of socialism, and wages a struggle against the ideological and psychological influence of the bourgeoisie.

The Marxist concept of press freedom in the framework of the socialist system calls for complete freedom to be granted to communist journalism, and for the liquidation of the bourgeois press. That is done in the name of genuine freedom, and to prevent the bourgeois press from misleading the masses, waging propaganda that is hostile to socialism and communism, and opposing historical progress and the development of society along the road toward communism.

That was why Lenin wrote: "Until classes are abolished, all arguments about freedom and equality should be accompanied by the questions: Freedom for which class, and for what purpose? Equality between which classes, and in what respects? Any direct or indirect, witting or unwitting evasion of these questions inevitably turns into a defense of the interests of the bourgeoisie, the interests of capital, the interests of the exploiters."

The Bolsheviks did not immediately suppress the bourgeois newspapers. A number of state measures taken immediately following the Revolution meant, as Lenin later said, "that the proletariat, when it won state power, had in view the most gradual transition possible to the new social and economic relations— not the suppression of the private press but its subordination to a certain amount of state guidance, its direction into the channel of state capitalism."

However, historical conditions developed in such a way that the bourgeoisie did not accept these conditions and declared war on the proletariat. The Soviets had to take urgent measures: a decree on the press ordered the suppression of bourgeois newspapers for libeling the Soviets and calling for action against them.

While the building of a socialist society in the USSR was proceeding within the framework of a single-Party system—inasmuch as the Communist Party did not have any allied Parties that were also advancing the ideals of scientific communism and were prepared to fight for them—the building of socialism in a number of other European countries is proceeding under vastly different conditions. The Parties existing within the framework of national fronts recognizing the leadership of the Communist Parties and conducting a joint struggle with them for the construction of a socialist society bring out their own publications just as freely as the Communist Parties do. They are free, inasmuch as they promote social and historical progress and the achievement of socialist ideals, this being registered in the legislation of the countries of socialism.

Lenin began to elaborate in detail his concept of freedom of the press under socialism as far back as 1905, in his article "Party Organization and Party Literature." This concept leaves no room for bourgeois influence in the sphere of journalism. "Emerging from the captivity of feudal censorship," Lenin wrote, "we have no desire to become, and shall not become, prisoners of bourgeois-shopkeeper literary relations. We want to establish, and we shall establish, a free press, free not simply from the police, but also from capital, from careerism, and what is more, free from bourgeois-anarchist individualism."

When the Russian proletariat was still attacking the strongholds of tsarism, Lenin was working on a concept which, in linking together the ideas of constitutional and juridical freedom and sociohistorical freedom, showed that genuine freedom for journalism meant the kind of freedom which pursued the aim of social and historical progress, freedom for journalism in its struggle for the triumph of communist ideals: "It will be a free literature, because the ideas of socialism and sympathy with the working people, and not greed or careerism, will bring ever new forces to its ranks. . . . It will be a free literature, enriching the revolutionary thought of mankind with the experience and the living work of the socialist proletariat. . . ."

Free journalism is one that is guided by the communist ideal evolved by a genuinely scientific theory of society, a journalism that leads people forward to great aims and helps to achieve them, a journalism that develops the doctrine on the foundation of a profound study of the phenomena, processes, and trends of the times.

Proceeding from that concept, Lenin formulated the principles along which journalism should function in a socialist society. Anyone familiar with that concept will easily understand why, in August, 1921, Lenin so sharply and passionately attacked the proposal to grant "freedom of the press" to all, monarchists and anarchists included. This proposal was made by G. Myasnikov, to whom Lenin replied with a letter in which he flatly declared that, as presented, this was a "non-Party, antiproletarian slogan of 'freedom of the press'."

Yet this slogan seemed to have been advanced from the purest of motives: "Outrageous abuses are rife in this country; freedom of the press will expose them. . . ." In his class analysis of Myasnikov's proposal, Lenin drew the following conclusion: (Right now) "freedom of the press will strengthen the world bourgeoisie. That is a fact. Freedom of the press will not help to purge the Communist Party in Russia of a number of its weaknesses, mistakes, misfortunes and maladies (it cannot be denied that we do suffer from a spate of these), because this is not what the world bourgeoisie wants. But freedom of the press will be a weapon in the hands of the world bourgeoisie." To grant freedom to the bourgeoisie "means making things easier for the enemy, hence helping the class enemy."

To pose the question as Myasnikov once did means "from a general class assessment, i.e., from the point of view of an assessment of the relations between all classes, backsliding into an appraisal that is sentimentally philistine."

Our Party, which give daily guidance to our mass media, is firmly and unswervingly guided by the Leninist concept of freedom of the press. The Central Committee Theses for the Centenary of the Birth of Lenin emphasize that Lenin himself linked the achievement of genuine freedom first and foremost with the liberation of labor from the yoke of capital, and with the working people getting rid of exploitation and their spiritual yoke. The political freedoms of speech, the press, association and the like were always regarded by Lenin from the class standpoint, as conditions for the socialist ideology, all of which preclude "freedom" of antisocialist propaganda and "freedom" of organization of counterrevolutionary forces.

Freedom of the press means a journalism that serves social progress, the lofty and objectively genuine ideals of humanity as revealed and formulated by Marxist theory. No matter how hard our foes—ranging from rabid anti-Communists to "reformers" of Marxism from the ranks of the revisionists—try to denigrate the Soviet press, all their strivings are doomed to failure. The history and practice of the Soviet press have on countless occasions disproved the hollowness of such claims.

At the same time, it should not be forgotten that the principle of freedom, like any other principle inherent in the Marxist press, is not a fair-weather call but a working tool. A journalist's activities are genuinely free—and that is something that bourgeois theorists and bourgeois pressmen are incapable of understanding and accepting—when he comes out as a Party journalist in every newspaper article, in every broadcast and every telecast he produces. That means approaching every fact of social life and the activities of every man with the yardstick and criteria provided by Marxist scientific methodology. Consequently, we must have a good knowledge of that methodology, and the deeper the journalist's knowledge of Marxist theory and the more precisely and consistently he applies that theory in his daily practice, the freer he is. One cannot but recall in this connection what Engels wrote in his *Anti-Dühring*: "Freedom of the will therefore means nothing but the capacity to make decisions with knowledge of the subject. Therefore the freer a man's judgment is in relation to a definite question, the greater is the necessity with which the content of this judgment will be determined: while the uncertainty, founded on ignorance, which seems to make an arbitrary choice among many possible different and conflicting decisions shows precisely by this that it is not free . . ."

Is it not clear from all this that voluntarist calls are nothing but manifestations of "non-freedom?" Yet we still hear "free" judgments emanating from dabblers in the field of journalism, who do not delve into the phenomena and processes of life (and are incapable of doing so because of their lack of training for serious analysis) but visit collective farms or factories in search of "facts" with which to lard their prefabricated schemes of "ever-ready" articles or news items.

The journalist's creative freedom does not imply merely a rich vocabulary or well-turned sentences. Such skill is hardly worth much unless it is backed by a flexible and complete knowledge of the material and the methods used in its study, a skill that ultimately leads to the free emergence of conclusions and proposals, and only effective and proper conclusions and proposals at that.

To be a journalist working for a free press is not so much cause for pride as the consciousness of one's responsibilities and duties. The Soviet journalist enjoys full freedom of criticism, i.e., freedom to wage a struggle against everything that hinders our advance, criticism of shortcomings, diseases, bad practices and abuses. That kind of criticism is not only a possibility but a duty, a law of Party life, as is emphasized in the Central Committee Theses for the Centenary of the Birth of Lenin. Positive criticism, criticism grounded in principle, yields results of tremendous importance.

It is to be regretted that criticism and self-criticism do not always and everywhere get fitting coverage in our press. There are officials who would like to see our newspapers publish the kind of criticism that is to their liking. This pernicious practice has often been condemned by the Central Committee of the CPSU. Suppression of criticism is detrimental to freedom of the press, and must be combated for one's freedom to unfold. Any journalist who "freely" turns a blind eye to anything that calls for critical analysis is simply evading his immediate duty.

The development of our free press also includes greater effectiveness of action in that press, so that no criticism may go unanswered. Not everything has been done here either. Sociological studies have shown that not all criticism in the press produces results.

The Soviet press is a tribune of the people, a democratic institution. For many newspapers, the reader has become Author No. I. However, as sometimes happens and as is borne out by sociological studies, the letters, signals, requests or opinions coming in from readers fail to find their way into the pages of local newspapers. Yet the stream of these incoming letters keeps growing, imperatively posing the question of how our readers can be "given the floor" and how a dialogue, and even polemics where necessary, can be conducted with the readership.

Discussions on a broad range of problems of interest to society; an exchange of views on drafts of important Party and state documents; a clash of opinions and proposals as voiced in letters to the editors written by working people—all these have become a norm in our social life and a law of Soviet journalism, expressing its freedom and giving it substance.

Freedom of Soviet journalism is a principle that presupposes a clear realization of the duties imposed on every journalist if he wishes fittingly and effectively to implement the freedoms he has been provided with—the freedom of creativity, freedom to study and explore our reality, freedom of criticism, and freedom of democratic discussion of those problems of social life that have matured.

For the first time in history, genuine freedom of the press is being achieved in socialist socity. Soviet journalism, which expresses the interests of society, operates from Party positions and thereby embodies the truth of history—a manifestation of "the freedom being there" as Marx once said.

2

THE WORLD'S MEDIA

Leo Bogart
MASS MEDIA TODAY AND TOMORROW

Erich Follath
AN INTERNATIONAL COMPARISON OF BROADCASTING
    SYSTEMS

Wilson Dizard
TELEVISION'S GLOBAL NETWORKS

John C. Merrill
GLOBAL PATTERNS OF ELITE DAILY JOURNALISM

Heinz-Dietrich Fischer
PERIODICALS AND THE INTERNATIONAL
    COMMUNICATION SYSTEM

Unesco
FILM AS A UNIVERSAL MASS MEDIUM

2

THE WORLD'S MEDIA

I F one hopes to keep abreast of the developments in, and growth of, the world's media of mass communication, he will become very frustrated. The global media situation is, of course, changing very rapidly, and even organizations like UNESCO find it impossible to describe the situation while it is still fresh and valid. This unfortunate state of affairs, however, should not dissuade persons and groups from trying to provide periodically an overview of the media situation in various parts of the world.

In this section we attempt to provide articles which give both a general survey of the world's media systems and also some specific looks at various of the world's media—e.g., radio, television, newspapers, magazines, and film.

The first article, by Leo Bogart, surveys the contemporary media scene and does some projecting into the future. This is followed by a new and fascinating look at broadcasting in five countries (the U.S., Britain, France, the USSR, and the People's Republic of China), written by Erich Follath, editor of Germany's *Stern* magazine. Wilson Dizard, of the USIA, next gives some insights into world-wide television. John Merrill and Heinz-Dietrich Fischer present articles which, respectively, deal with elite daily newspapers and periodicals in the international communication system. The final article in the chapter, by UNESCO, takes a look at film in international communication.

*   *   *   *

RELATED READING

Annuaire de la presse française et etrangere et du monde politique: Annuaire international de la Presse. Paris: Chambre Syndicale des Editeurs d'Annuaires. (annual).

Cherry, Colin. *World Communication: Threat or Promise?* New York: Wiley-Interscience, 1971.

Codding, George A. *Broadcasting Without Barriers.* Paris, Unesco, 1959.

Dizard, Wilson P. *Television: A World View.* Syracuse, N.Y.: Syracuse University Press, 1966.

Dovifat, Emil (ed.) *Handbuch der Publizistik.* 3 vols. Berlin: Walter de Rruyter & Co., 1968–69.

Editor & Publisher International Year Book. New York. (annual).

Europa Year Book. London: Europa Publications, Ltd. (annual).

Fischer, Heinz-Dietrich/et al.: *Innere Pressefreiheit in Europa. Komparative Studie zur Situation in England, Frankreich, Schweden.* Baden-Baden (Germany): Nomos Verlagsgesellschaft, 1975.

Fischer, Heinz-Dietrich. *Die grossen Zeitungen: Porträts der Weltpresse.* Munich: Deutscher Taschenbuch Verlag, 1966.

Haley, William J. *Broadcasting as an International Force.* Nottingham, England: Nottingham University, 1951.

Handbuch der Weltpresse, edited by the Institut für Publizistik der Universität Münster, 2 Vols., Cologne-Opladen: Westdeutscher Verlag, 1970.

Hans-Bredow-Institut (ed.). *Internationales Handbuch fur Rundfunk und Fernsehen.* Hamburg: Verlag Hans-Bredow Institut für Rundfunk und Fernsehen, 1957 ff (annually).

IOJ. *The Media Today and Tomorrow.* Prague: International Organization of Journalists, 1974.

Merrill, J. C. *The Elite Press: Great Newspapers of the World.* New York: Pitman, 1968.

———, Carter Bryan and Marvin Alisky. *The Foreign Press: A Survey of the World's Journalism.* Baton Rouge: Louisiana State University Press, 1970.

Manvell, Roger (ed.). *The International Encyclopedia of Film.* New York: Crown, 1972.

Olson, K. E. *The History Makers: The Press in Europe from its Beginnings through 1965.* Baton Rouge: Louisiana State University Press, 1966.

Paulu, Burton. *Radio and Television Broadcasting on the European Continent.* Minneapolis: University of Minnesota Press, 1967.

Peterson, Theodore. *Magazines in the Twentieth Century.* Urbana: University of Illinois Press, 1964.

Pulling, Martin. *International Television.* London: British Broadcasting Corp., 1963.

UNESCO. *World Communications.* New York: Unesco Press, 1975.

Wells, Alan, ed. *Mass Communications: A World View.* Palo Alto, Cal.: National Press Books, 1974.

Leo Bogart:

Mass Media Today and Tomorrow

THE MASS MEDIA, as we know them today, are on the threshold of a major technical revolution, with consequences perhaps even farther-reaching than those which accompanied the rise of radio in the 1920's and '30's and of television in the 1940's and '50's. Although some media organizations have begun to prepare themselves for the events to come, most of the planning has been on the technical side, with thus far little consideration of the consequences for the content and character of mass communication.

The mass media in America and Western Europe compete strongly for audience interest and advertising revenues. This creates a tendency to think in immediate terms and perhaps inhibits long-range speculation. This paper will raise some of the problems that the mass media face in the rest of this century, without suggesting solutions. Its thesis is that present knowledge of media and their audiences is quite inadequate to permit the kind of intelligent planning which is required to master the new technology, and that now is the time to face up to the problems which will soon be upon us. . . .

Since the rate of invention grows as the existing base of technology expands, the changes in the next third century will be even more dramatic than those of the last third. In that last third century we have had our communications capacities enlarged by web offset and color gravure printing, photocopying, teletypesetting, talking motion pictures and television (both first black and white and then in color), miniaturized and printed circuitry, communications satellites, audio and video tape recording, microphotography, and electronic data processing. Although the mass media which existed earlier have bent and changed under the pressure of these inventions, they have not vanished. As we try to read the future, it seems reasonable to expect that today's media will continue to exist, but also that their form, function and content will undergo radical modifications. . . .

In our developed world we can foresee a steady rise in education; in the specialization of interests; in work productivity; in income; in leisure time. All these forces point to an accelerating demand for information of all kinds, for culture, for entertainment and pastimes to fill leisure.

▶ This is a shortened version (1975) of an article ("Mass Media in the Year 2000") appearing in *Gazette* (Holland) in 1967 (Vol. 13/No. 3) by Dr. Bogart, Vice President and General Manager of the Bureau of Advertising of the American Newspaper Publishers Association. The editors believe the article as pertinent today as in 1967. Reprinted by permission.

The great cities of the world will continue to expand in size and to absorb an increasing proportion of the growing number of people. Along with the social and psychological problems of a changing, mobile population come the material problems of urban congestion, the choking of transportation networks, the degeneration of the architectual landscape. The resulting changes in the quality of life will profoundly affect the traditional role of the mass media as expressions of a community's identity and spirit.

International press services and space satellite broadcasting are symptomatic of the growing worldwide interconnections in mass communications. If we want to be optimists we might predict that in the shadow of nuclear destruction, international politics will rely more heavily on communications and less on military power. If the future were to take this happy course, it would surely change the function of the mass media as a force for national cohesion, and expand their potential as the principal means of creating a common vocabulary of ideas among all men.

The development of mass media will be profoundly influenced by the global confrontation of rival political forces and by the widening gap between what the eminent poet and athlete Mao Tse-tung calls the 'city' and the 'country'—the industrialized nations with a firm hold on the emerging technology and the agrarian nations for which this technology represents largely rumors and receding hopes.

The worldwide explosion of population (which shows no serious signs of abatement and cannot be stopped except by emergency measures) will in twenty years outstrip mankind's existing food supply capacities. How, in the case of famine, can we fail to foresee continuing political tensions and upheavals—quite apart from those directly inspired by ideology? How can there fail to be a continuing material and psychological dependence on the technically advanced countries by the impoverished peoples?

The gap between rich and poor nations will for some time to come cause new and old mass media systems to coexist at sharply different levels of technology—just as today there are nations which have no television and even a few without indigenous mass media of any kind.

Parallel to the divergence in outlook between the advanced and backward countries is the growing difference within the advanced countries between the technical elite and the untrained mass, between those who feel a sense of participation and control over the changing course of society and those who think of themselves merely as consumers. The continuing contradictions, variations and antagonisms within human society will in themselves insure the continued existence of parallel mass media systems—primitive and advanced—on both the local and international levels for many years to come.

What Do We Know about Media?

How much can our existing knowledge of communications help us to understand what is about to happen? There are only a handful of generalizations from mass media research which might provide some relevant insights:

1. Communication is a selective process which operates at a number of levels. We choose the programs and periodicals that interest us. We remember those messages that interest or concern us most, among all those we see and hear and read. But there is also selection in the earliest stages of sensory perception. For instance, when we open a newspaper page, the eye's focus is actually attracted to the items which have the greatest meaning for a reader. For the psychologist, attention may be defined as the elimination of unwanted information. Today, the mounting flow of information creates a mass immunity to unwanted messages. Too often this 'perceptual defense' serves to shut out information which is really useful. In every advanced country, opinion polls continually reveal the spectacle of massive public ignorance on matters which are widely disseminated by all news media every day. The greatest challenge before the publisher or broadcaster is to make people aware of the important realities they would prefer to avoid because they are either unpleasant or dull.

2. Communication via print is at the user's speed and to his specifications, whereas in time-bound broadcast communication the communicator controls the pace of transmission. For this reason, print is a more efficient informational medium than broadcasting for people of higher intellectual skills.

3. Media experience reflects the life cycle. As children mature they use media in different ways. Their reliance on informational media, as distinct from broadcast entertainment, reflects not only the direct influence and requirements of school assignments, but the fact that maturity carries with it a greater diversity of roles and interests.

4. When people are confronted with a choice of mass media content, they will generally take the easier way. They prefer to get communications through minimum effort. They prefer simpler to more complex and demanding content. They will normally prefer entertainment to information.

5. Exposure to mass media for entertainment appears to be largely a matter of pastime activity. For example, there is remarkably little elasticity in the amount of time people spend with television. Changes in programming or in the number of program choices available do not strongly affect the total time spent viewing. When newspapers disappear, the circulation of the survivors does not go up proportionately, but other forms of reading matter may serve as substitutes.

6. The mass media have expanded to fill the hours of leisure. Radio and even television have also become companions during the workday. Although television has taken over a great deal of time, its growth has coincided with an increased exposure to print (most of it in different forms than before) and with continuing substantial exposure to radio (especially at times and places formerly beyond reach of the mass media).

7. The mass media (except for the movies) have historically tended to represent increasingly individual experiences for their audiences. When few peo-

ple knew how to read, they read to others. With universal literacy, reading has become entirely a private matter, except in the case of parents reading to young children. With the transistor, radio—once the family entertainment center— has become portable, personal and intimate. This is now becoming true of television as sets become smaller and mobile and as more families acquire more than one set. In the United States, nearly a fourth of the families already have more than one set and the proportion will grow as color comes along. This means more differentiation of program interests and selections. At the same time there is an increased range of choice as the number of broadcasting stations and publications continues to grow. In the future no industrial nation will be able to survive with only one national television channel or radio program, any more than it could with only a single newspaper.

8. Items of media content reinforce each other. They also reinforce direct personal experience. Media enrich and create new life interests. But on the other hand, people turn to the media to rehearse or review experiences in which they have personally participated. The theatergoer turns the next morning to a review of the play in the newspaper. The football enthusiast wants to read the press report or the radio commentary of a game he has seen. By the same token, people who have heard a broadcast of an event have more interest in reading about it. Media support rather than detract from each other.

9. Tastes can be molded. Public tastes reflect what is familiar. People learn to accept and value the media content and style to which they have become accustomed. Those who control mass media content therefore bear a responsibility for shaping the tastes they seek to satisfy. By the inherent nature of their role, media operators are sensitive to public taste, even when they are firm advocates of a fixed position. Regardless of the political system under which they operate they customarily seek to expand their audiences and their influence.

10. The world of the media no longer mirrors the world of real events. It helps create it. The mass media, especially television, have given broad masses of people the illusion that they are eyewitnessing—and thus in a sense participating—in great affairs. A few centuries ago, the doings of king and ministers moved from the sphere of fantasy, rumor and occasional proclamations to become a matter of daily chronicling in the court calendar and so on to daily comment in the press. These powerful figures no longer seemed quite so grand and superhuman as they became less remote. With the coming of motion pictures, radio and television in this century, new power was added to the illusion of knowing the mighty, and the media define the roles appropriate for politics and public life. But, paradoxically, these media created a whole new class of public personalities, the 'stars' who were invested with precisely the attributes of glamor and power which belonged to the monarchs of the past.

Generalizations like the ten just listed are useful in understanding the habits of audiences for the media of today. However, they offer but slender guidance for understanding audience behavior in the year 2000.

The Five Areas of Technical Change

The technology of communication is being transformed in five areas: in assembling information, storing it, retrieving it, compressing it, and reacting to it.

1. In the graphic arts, we are getting higher quality color reproduction by a combination of graphic techniques within the same production sequence. Telecommunication makes possible decentralized production and printing at great speed and with simultaneous operations at separated places. Computerized typesetting and photocomposition, already a reality, will be more broadly used to expedite and reduce the effort required to transmit information from its source to its users.

2. Electronic recording instruments, in combination with the computer, make it possible to store aural or visual communications, transmitted at extremely high speed, for rediffusion or play-back at the option, and to the specifications, of the individual recipient. This is true not only of communication through the alphabetic symbols of print, but of the direct reproduction of sound and sight which we now experience through radio, cinema and television. The familiar tape recorder, already adapted from audio to video, is but the forerunner of far more sophisticated home recording systems that permit information to be stored and played back to suit individual specifications, needs and tastes.

3. Microphotography has given us the economical visual storage of miniaturized records which can be classified, punch-coded, retrieved through the computer, and rapidly enlarged and reproduced. This is already revolutionizing librarianship, business record-keeping and a host of other activities which require the rapid assembly of related information drawn from varied sources. New processes now make it possible to achieve microfilm quality without developing film chemically. Electrostatic reproduction, in combination with improved data recording mechanisms, provides the means for widely dispersed facsimile reproduction of the conventional forms of print media, giving substance to the old idea of a newspaper produced in the home.

4. We have vastly increased facilities for transmitting huge flows of information. Thirty million words, the equivalent of 108,000 typed pages, can be transmitted in an hour through a television scanning system. Space satellites using solar energy will make it possible for vast quantities of messages to go directly from transmitters to home receivers in any part of the world. The internationalization of the broadcast media will proceed apace, inhibited largely by language and by localized tastes. Throughout the world, radio and television become more and more universally accessible; more homes are linked through the telephone into communication centrals which ultimately will be put to

diversified uses, as in the United States has already happened with community cable antenna TV systems. Lasers permit complex messages to be transmitted along hitherto unexploited reaches of the energy spectrum; through holography they allow us to reconstruct three-dimensional images, reduced or magnified in size. The hologram may replace microfilm for information storage, and could permit the transmission of 2,000 typewritten pages a second.

These complex systems of processing communication raise new problems of information cataloguing and retrieval. Eventually these problems will be solved by indexing information successively in terms of cross-reference points which permit progressively finer expositions of detail. The translation of such machinery from the laboratory to the stage of a mass communications system is obviously limited by the fact that greater complexity requires great expansion in the band of electronic frequencies required. But this obstacle too will be overcome.

5. We will soon have the means to make mass communication a two-way process. Through a home or office console unit, tied to a computer, an individual can feed back questions, demands and other reactions to his communications source. He can control not only the flow of information but the by-products of information. In most countries the public is already accustomed to this kind of feedback in the form of opinion and marketing research. We see it in American pay-television systems, in which people pick the programs they want and pay accordingly. We see it in automated vending and mail ordering of merchandise. Already there exists in prototype the push-button in which the consumer selects the items he wants by remote control and has them assembled and packaged for delivery. It is only another step to link the home and the warehouse directly. In short, computerized selective access to goods as well as to information may represent a public utility as generally available in civilized society as water or electricity, metered and paid by the same kinds of accounting devices.

The home information system of the future may have its visual center in a large mirror on the wall, a mirror which at our command will present an illuminated reproduction of any kind of information we want. This information may take the form of written language—letters and words as they now appear on the daily newspaper or magazine page. We can summon up these messages to our command by predesignated codes which will yield the particular kind of information we are interested in. Through another system of controls (perhaps using an electronic pencil) we might get pictures to illustrate the words which interest us, just as we might be able to get the full story if the headline is intriguing. A news article about a speech by a public figure could give way to a photograph of the occasion—and in either case we could instantly get a facsimile copy. Another control might bring us the sound of the speaker's voice or the filmed visual record.

Today a few pennies can buy a newspaper or magazine, or hours of radio or television. The systems just described would be prohibitively expensive to install and operate in today's economy, and with today's information needs. And yet can anyone doubt that the time is not distant when they will represent reasonable and economical methods?

The Changing Function of Media

The sharp distinction between broadcast and print media, as we now know it, is likely to be dimmed and perhaps even to disappear in the world of the near future. This sharp distinction rests on two essential differences:

1. The differences between the visible, tactile, permanent record of a print communication and the intangible, evanescent, impermanent nature of broadcast messages. This distinction will disappear as the mechanisms for home recording of broadcasts become more simple, inexpensive and widespread.

2. The distinction between space and time media in the degree of control which the recipient exercises over the flow of information.

The great advantage of symbolic communication through print is that it may be skimmed or scanned and then dipped into selectively for the information that the reader wants to absorb in greater depth. The reader of a newspaper or magazine, like the reader entering a public library, is simultaneously engaged in two different processes of handling information.

1. He has certain expectations and wishes which he can fulfill by turning immediately to the probable source of what he is interested in. In the library he may go immediately to the shelves which deal with books on a certain subject or by a certain author. In the newspaper he can turn immediately to the pages which carry the stock market quotations, the sports results or the motion picture reviews.

2. But in either case the great advantage of having an open visual display in a storehouse of information is the opportunity for chance discovery of unanticipated treasures which arouse interest and further investigation. The browser in the library finds books on subjects that he had not thought of reading about. The reader of a newspaper or magazine encounters articles on subjects which he could not possibly have expected in advance. We very quickly filter out, from all the information which confronts us visually, the particular bits which arouse our interest and encourage us to further pursuit. This kind of skimming cannot take place with the same efficiency in a time-bound medium. We can flick the radio dial until we come upon the particular kind of music we want to hear or until we hear a station that speaks our language. But to hear a program which we anticipate with pleasure, we must inform ourselves in advance and adjust our time schedule to that of the broadcaster. . . .

As we increase our technical capacity to manipulate mass communications selectively for our individual purposes, its borderline with private communication becomes more and more indistinct. The essence of mass communication is that it makes possible the wide diffusion of identical messages, but this characteristic is lost as each recipient determines the particular form and sequence of the messages he receives.

The telephone is a private instrument. But we use the telephone as a mass medium when we call a number to get a recorded announcement of the exact time or the weather forecast or a report on traffic conditions. When the housewife calls the butcher to ask the price of lamb chops she is using it as a private medium. But she does not merely get information from the butcher; she can use the system to order what she wants; communication works both ways. And soon, as the existing telephone system becomes more complex, ordering, record-keeping and billing can be handled more efficiently, though also more impersonally, without the presence of a human being at the other end of the line.

The creation of a twilight zone between private and public communications can hardly mean an end to the mass media as we know them. But today's mass media are unlikely to keep their present form and function in the world of the future. The content of existing media may undergo drastic change, just as (in the United States at least) fiction has been almost eliminated from general magazines and drama has almost disappeared from radio as a result of less than two decades of television. We can best assume that for a long time to come there will continue to be diverse systems of media operating in competition with each other at different stages of technological sophistication, subject to different kinds of regulation and financial support. . . .

Erich Follath:

An International Comparison of Broadcasting Systems

IT IS a difficult, boundless and indeed unprofitable undertaking to want to give a survey of all the broadcasting systems of the world. Analogous to the political systems in West and East, in the Third World and the Fourth World, they have organizational structures which are exemplified by a few models to which other countries have adapted themselves or which they have emulated, as well as a large number of more or less interesting combinations of the models. But even if only a few typical broadcasting systems are singled out, as in this article, there is the danger that in the end control mechanisms and organizational forms will be merely descriptively strung together. In a comparable study therefore, the political-historical conditions in the individual countries and their appreciation should not be overshadowed by the role of the means of communication.[1] For mass media such as radio and television do not stand above society but are concretely incorporated in the political and social conflicts of society.

It is difficult to clearly typify the different broadcasting systems in the westernized democracies—in Western Europe alone nearly all combinations are represented, from those financed purely by advertising to public and state organized broadcasting. They are united in the claim of wanting to safeguard "reasonable access to the communications media for all rival groups and interests"[2]: This very "free access" is considered as a basic element of democracy. For only when it is safeguarded can "the struggle for public opinion take place, which represents an essential component not only of election campaigns but also in the battle for each national decision-making authority in the constitutional state."[3]

Broadcasting in the U.S.A.

Mass communication in the USA is, as a general principle, run on a private enterprise basis.[4] Radio and television are financed by advertising and, therefore, like the other media, are subject to the laws of free enterprise and to competing for the largest possible public.

Even in the early days of radio, the programs of the American broadcasting establishment were stamped to a large degree by the advertising economy. With the broadcasting acts of 1927 and 1934 ("Radio Act" and "Com-

▶ This is an original article done for this revised edition by Dr. Erich Follath, editor of the weekly German *Stern Magazine* of Hamburg.

munications Act") which, with slight alterations, still apply today, the organization of broadcasting based on private enterprise was legalized; at the same time the government was given the right to set up a commission for licensing and control of broadcasting. The controlling body commissioned by the government is the "Federal Communications Commission" (FCC) which is responsible for radio, television and the whole of radio communication both official and private. The seven members of the commission are appointed for seven years by the President of the USA with the agreement of the Senate.

The FCC had very little influence over the programs of the broadcasting stations, their financing and the concentration on the market which was soon to appear. Firms and advertising agencies not only bought broadcasting time for short advertisements, they also financed as "sponsors" of complete programs and determined their content. For these programs—and with them the advertisements—to reach the widest possible audience, they had to be attractive to the public; characteristic of the "golden age of the radio" in the 1940s were variety shows with popular stars, at the same time the quality of the news reporting also improved considerably. Although after the Second World War the radio audience still continued to increase at first, the radio soon had to look for new openings, now being in a situation of having to compete with television. The significance of the broadcasting networks diminished as the sponsors, desiring supra-regional advertising, changed over to television. The radio stations retained—for the time being—the very lucrative local advertising market; the proportion of pure entertainment programs continued to increase.

Then at the beginning of the 1950s television finally came into its own. The three national networks, the "Columbia Broadcasting System" (CBS), the "National Broadcasting Co." (NBC) and the "American Broadcasting Co." (ABC), secured for themselves the lion's share of the great sum of money which began to flow in after 1952. These three networks are the most important connecting link between the 600 or so television stations and the advertising economy. Ninety per cent of the financially and legally independent transmitting stations are connected to one of the program companies by a long-term purchasing contract. The transmitting stations give the networks transmission time and then take over their completed programs—paid for by the advertising firms—with advertisements included, for transmission. In return, the transmitting stations receive a share of the advertising proceeds for these programs. The high risk of loss and the considerable expense of program production prevent the transmitting stations from producing their own programs and then offering them to the agents to sponsor. In any case "The Big Three" have already taken care of the best transmitting hours of the day: They secure option time for themselves during the attractive evening hours. Taking these popular television hours as a measure, the network concentration had in 1959 already obtained 77.8 per cent of the entire transmission time of the commercial establishments. The Congress report of 1963 comments on this situation thus: "As holders of transmission licenses the stations, through their link to the program companies, have practically relinquished to them their responsibility for the production and selection of programs." [5]

Apart from the national television networks there are also some regional networks and one—sometimes known as the "Second Program"—non-commercial education television program (ETV). The teaching and educational programs of the ETV stations are all produced by the central program company "National Education Television," and are financed from public money as are charities. Attempts to launch a Pay TV failed. Households in areas without local television transmitters are increasingly being provided with cable television systems.

The disadvantages of the American broadcasting system are obvious: the lowering of standards of the programs caused by the nature of the advertising economy which always has to produce the highest possible figures of sets switched on. Sometimes topical political information is also neglected as a result of this: In 1966 the president of the CBS news resigned because the advertised live transmission of a Congress debate on Vietnam was cancelled at the last minute and entertainment shows were shown instead. But much more crucial is the concentration of the power of the three networks which is virtually uncontrolled by the public. Of particular importance here is the fact that CBS, NBC and ABC have further interests beyond television: as multi media concerns they have a share in the production of records, radios and television sets. Although cross connections between the different mass media in the form of capital involvement ("cross-channel") are limited by the FCC, the great power of the media giants has become a harmful influence on the independent press. Because of the concentration of advertising there remain only a few states in the USA today with competetive independent daily papers.

Broadcasting in Britain

The British broadcasting system has been admired by other countries, copied and praised as a model as no other in the world.[6] It was considered—and is still considered—as independent of the government, critical and even as "the fourth power in the state": a journalistically incorruptible body of control opposite the politicians which above all always took the ruling party firmly to task. Referring to those responsible for broadcasting, the following remark of the former BBC general-director, Sir Hugh Greene, characterizes their own appreciation of their position: "In view of their far-reaching influence radio and television are too powerful to entrust their control to any politician or even businessman." [7] Two public bodies—the "British Broadcasting Corporation (BBC)" and the "Independent Broadcasting Authority (IBA)"—are authorized to transmit radio and television programs in Great Britain.

The BBC, which was originally founded as a commercial company from elements within the radio industry and only after five years was transformed by Royal Charter into a public corporation, today transmits two national television programs and four national radio programs; it is also involved with 20 radio stations in local broadcasting. The BBC programs and its establishment are financed entirely from licenses, advertising is not permitted. An administrative council of 12 governors is responsible for the whole broadcasting operation, the administration, equipment and installations of the BBC. The governors, appointed for five years by the Queen on the recommendation of Parliament, do not represent party interests; they are public personalities and are chosen purely because of their professional qualifications. They appoint a Director-General from among themselves, who as head of the executive has auxiliary forces in the form of the General Advisory Council and other organizations which examine and discuss with him the program and financial side of the establishment.

However, neither the financial nor the political independence of British broadcasting is laid down by law. On the contrary: the documents under which the BBC began its work gave the government almost every conceivable authoritative power over the establishment. The government could at any time remove a disliked governor and replace him by someone more flexible. The Postmaster General, comparable to the present Minister for Post and Telecommunications, could revoke the transmitting license of the BBC if at any time he believed the establishment had failed in its duties. He could also veto any program and order the broadcasting of any government program. Today there are little formal changes in these stipulations. The government has the right of final control over broadcasting in every respect—from the possibility of withdrawing the licence to the veto of programs and the absolute financial control practiced by Parliament.

At first glance it is amazing that in these conditions the BBC has not developed into a subsidiary government department. Indeed the English governments have without exception restrained from employing the numerous formal possibilities of preventing the establishment from reporting critically. However it is not only due to the traditional British sense of fair play that politicians regard their powers as "major reserve powers", but also to political reason: The continually changing majority ratio between the two main parties, between Labour and Conservative, contributed to the fact that no government dared to interfere decisively in the programmes. Tomorrow the opposition could act in exactly the same way. If an attempt to apply political pressure was nevertheless made, as during the Suez crisis in 1956, the board of governors and strong General-Directors at its head resisted the coercive measures.

Those responsible for the BBC have always interpreted the freedom of British broadcasting in two ways: as freedom in the face of political—and as freedom in the face of commercial obligation. Since 1954 the BBC has been up against commercial competition in the field of television. Without public pressure, without any recognizable interest from wider spheres of industry and without political support from the leaders of the ruling conservative party, a small group of well organized conservative backbenchers, who were personally and materially connected with a handful of big industrialists, managed to introduce the commercial television channel. The Independent Television Authority was known as a public service to which, like the BBC, public control was allotted. But right from the beginning the ITA acted merely as a holding organisation which rarely produced its own programs. It transmitted the programs produced by a series of private enterprises which work on a regional basis and at the moment broadcast 15 different programs. Their income is drawn from the sale of advertising time. They must pay a part of this over to the controlling holding organization and the Treasury. Any form of direct influence on the program—as is usual with the American sponsor system—is prohibited, at least theoretically.

However, the dilemma soon appeared in the publicly controlled commercial television too of, on the one hand, wanting to fulfil a public demand and, on the other hand, having to be a profit orientated enterprise. Although ITV had to dedicate a fixed proportion of its broadcasting time to "serious" programs, it soon snatched away most viewers from the BBC. The commercial entertainment was less demanding and was always shown during the main broadcasting hours. In order to even roughly retain a balance of popularity with the viewers the BBC had to adapt accordingly. Not only the loss of program independence but also the increasingly dwindling political independence of the establishment was caused fundamentally by the part-commercialization of British broadcasting, to which since 1972 the possibilities for the newly named "Independent Broadcasting Authority" of making local commercial radio were also added.

Regardless of their political position political groupings of all kinds begin to call to mind the means of power due to them under the broadcasting act. In a strange "grand coalition," Left and Right are united in their mistrust and their reservations against the BBC; according to their political position one side proclaims the "unfairness" of the reporting on Northern Ireland and even the "propagation of anarchy," and the other the "bondage to the establishment" and the "Byzantine command structure." Dependence on license financing and political pressure led to highly superfluous new controlling bodies such as the "Broadcasting Council".[8] Even the character of the establishment is no longer tabu: Alternative models such as the division of the BBC into various independent blocks or a part-commercialisation by the withdrawal of license financing are under discussion.

Broadcasting in France

The "principal function" of broadcasting in England is often said to be the government control; the principal function of French broadcasting could be said to be the transmission of the actions of the Paris government. Radio and television in France are traditionally state-organized and the Gaullist governments always looked upon this as a matter of course. Three former Ministers of Information: "How can a country be governed when the government has no television monopoly?" (Malraux) "Broadcasting is by its nature dependent on the state." (Frey) "In view of the effective monopoly which the opposition has of the press, television must form a reasonable counterbalance." (Peyrefitte).

This conception of broadcasting was not without influence on the type of program offered; in France there were hardly any critical political magazines as in England. One of the reasons why television only slowly became popular: it presented itself as "garrulous, dreary and problem avoiding" [9] (so the former subordinate ORTF Director Thibau observed). Despite a few attempts at reform and mostly marginal changes the strictly controlled, centralized "Organisation de Radiodiffusion-Télévision Française (ORTF)" in Paris remained far more a sub-department of the Gaullist party than an independent journalistic establishment. The state structure and continuity of the party in power favored the filling of key positions with people trusted as conforming to the government without any regard to their professional qualifications. But even before General de Gaulle discovered television as a medium in election campaigns, Gaullist Ministers of Information "colonized" the ORTF according to their own ideas, interfered in the program whenever they thought it necessary and dismissed disliked colleagues. The party political broadcasts before general elections became a further controversial issue of French television. Even when the time was divided up, as in 1967, there were differences as to the ratio: The Gaullists claimed half of the entire time although they had only managed to collect a little more than a third of the votes during the previous election. Even more at the center of criticism than such strange ratios was de Gaulle's way of addressing the nation on television ("Français, Française, aidez-moi"), especially when there was no possibility for the opposition to reply after such dramatic appeals. [10] The French have summed up this form of influencing voters in the word "Telecracy".

In January 1975 French broadcasting was entirely re-organized. After only three days of discussion the Paris Parliament dissolved the ORTF in August 1974 and decided, against the votes of the Left, on a new broadcasting statute. This provided for the creation of seven individual autonomous corporations: four independently working program companies which are also independent of each other (radio, TV 1, TV 2, TV 3), a national production company, an "Etablissement public de Diffusion" (broadcasting firm) and an "Institut de l'Audiovisuel" responsible for archive work and research.

The administrative council of each program company consists of six members: two representatives of the state, one parliamentarian, one representative of the press and one of the employees and one "personality of cultural life." The company presidents are appointed by the Council of Ministers in Paris and they themselves have the task of filling vacancies in the direction. A "Délégation parlementerie pour la Radiodiffusion-Télévision Française" is responsible for the supervision of the management, this has to deliver a report to Parliament once a year. The program may be financed up to a maximum of 25 per cent by advertising. However, the broadcasting of advertisements is limited to certain times of the day and they have no influence over the programs. The license money is distributed to the individual corporations by the government after approval of the Parliament—the lion's share going towards the budget of the individual companies. There is no exact distribution ratio, but it is being considered whether the "quality" of the programs, determined by a commission and viewers' opinion poll, can be used as a criterion.

The occasional euphoria over the re-organization of broadcasting in France is quickly sobered. The very vaguely formulated law changed virtually nothing in the national structure. Broadcasting was neither decentralized to any considerable extent nor does the division prove to be expense saving. Once again the journalists were the ones to suffer from the financial difficulties: mass redundancies led to numerous strikes among broadcasting employees. In whatever way the organization of radio and television is restructured in the future, one thing is certain: the state and the party in power will not give up their influence on the programs. This is made possible by the impenetrable communications market which the Gaullists have built up for themselves in recent years: they not only have a financial share in the commercial radio stations on the periphery of the country ("Radio Luxemburg," "Radio Monte Carlo"), but are also closely connected both personally and materially with the French media giant, Hachette, which practically has a monopoly of cassette television programs. France's strong left-wing opposition, which after coming to power today could use French broadcasting to their own advantage as the Gaullists and the Republicans do, believes that Giscard wants to secure his influence on the media on a long-term basis through a progressive commercialization of television.

*   *   *   *

If the claim of the basic Western broadcasting systems of granting all social groups free access to the media is considered, a common problem arises. The pluralistic representational and control principle, represented in very different ways by the commercial American, the public British and the state French broadcasting systems, raises problems in the reporting on social and political marginal groups. Such groups which are not represented within a pluralistic principle have necessarily only slim chances of escaping from their minority situation by way of the "established" means of mass communication.

So the problem of such a media structure lies in having to hobble after the progressive condition of society and being unable to adequately reflect it. The more radio and television, in Western countries as well, are adapted to the political system and become pure reflections of the political majority, the greater is the danger that their effect will only be conservative and standard-lowering, that they will merely preserve what already exists and that they will neglect the role of the norm propagator which inquires after alternatives to existing conditions. However, mechanisms are conceivable which, as in England, do not exactly avoid the dangers, but contribute towards reducing then.

Broadcasting in the USSR.

The function of the mass media in Western countries—information, control by the government, criticism and participation in the forming of public opinion—cannot be compared with the Soviet interpretation. It is not the information or entertainment value of the media that is most important in the eyes of the leaders of the USSR [11], but the chance of using them as instruments to control and educate. The Party, which is known as the *avant garde* of the masses and, as a result, strictly controls broadcasting as a decisive instrument in carrying out its policy, functions as the original bearer of public opinion: "Every attempt to withdraw the means of mass communication from the control of the Party means in fact an attempt to hinder the development of the socialist conscience and to ideologically disorientate the masses. Therefore in the overall development of technical means of communication the policy of the Party is directed towards safeguarding its function in the process of shaping the socialist conscience in our society." [12] Radio and television should have the same aims, all their functions are to be subordinate to a collective function: to follow the government's interpretation of Marxist-Leninism and to make this clear to the masses.

The developing Soviet Communist Party had already defined the interest in the activity and function of the media long before radio and television took on a propagandistic character. In 1920 a department was set up in the central committee of the Party for propaganda and the stirring of public opinion. Although this department has been re-organized several times it still retains today its controlling function. The state Moscow committee for radio and television is responsible for the audio-visual media, this was transformed in July, 1970, into a state committee for the different republics of the union. Top Party officials fill many of the important positions within the media. Sergej Lapin, head of the state committee, is also a member of the first Soviet and holder of the Lenin Order.

The 500 radio stations of the country reach nearly every Soviet citizen. The Moscow broadcasting centre transmits four different radio programs for internal use; the first program with its mixture of political information, commentaries and music exercises a kind of controlling function within the country and can also be received over the radio diffusion exchange throughout the country. Here instruments similar to loud-speakers are connected to a radio nodal point and work without electricity. Soviet television has made a great leap forward in the past few years. Today 70 per cent of the Soviet population are reached through 131 television centres, 150 high performance and 1,115 smaller transmitting stations. The first of the four Moscow programs—three of them being used predominantly for educational television and repeats—is transmitted by satellite as far as Middle Asia and Siberia. There are local stations in remote districts, however their own programs are being increasingly repressed.

An essential characteristic which distinguishes Soviet from Western mass communication is the complementary function of the various media in the USSR. Radio, television, newspapers and magazines are meant to be an orchestra in the propaganda system: the different instruments are meant to form a unity, there is no competition among the media. But this does not mean that the priority enjoyed by individual media cannot be altered. It was not until the middle of the 1950s that radio was considered equal in importance to the press and was promoted accordingly, and television did not reach this stage until 1960.

Programs and their language became more informal; the second radio programme, "Majak," introduced in 1964, which transmitted information with music in magazine form, was able to survive largely due to the popularity soon achieved by the new form of broadcasting, and this against strong reproaches from powerful orthodox Party members who claimed that it simulated "objectivity hostile to the classless society," and that "it had been developed according to the principles of foreign broadcasting." As recent listener and viewer opinion polls showed, the quiz and entertainment programs are most popular with the Soviet media consumers as with their western "colleagues." The more "educational," weighty and serious a program is, the smaller is its audience.

It can no longer be denied that Soviet broadcasting is prepared to adopt compromises and new forms in the presentation of its programs; and even less so that these tendencies then have their limits where Marxist-Leninist party lines could be touched upon. Party leader Brezhnev in 1968, referring to the "Prague Spring": "To grant extensive freedom of the press means to allow journalists unreasonable influence on policy when they are in no way responsible for political decisions."

Broadcasting in China

In the People's Republic of China [13] the unity of the state theory and the communication theory is emphasized even more plainly than in the Soviet Union: "No task of broadcasting can be independent of the political situation of the time." (Chou Yang). Radio occupies the very top position in Chinese means of communication. Described by Mao Tse-tung as the "most important instrument of the dictatorship of the proletariat" and by the *Renmin Ribao* (chief Party daily) as a "significant weapon in the class war," the radio network in China has undergone a rapid development. In 1967, during the cultural revolution, it became the most important means of informing the masses and a decisive factor in mass mobilization. In the framework of general decentralization the broadcasting stations rose rapidly, above all the closing of the region bordering on the Soviet frontier was hastened.

The radio diffusion exchange which had been intensively developed since 1951 played an important role in this achievement: mass radio campaigns helped not only to produce at an early stage a clear picture of the enemy (in connection with the Korean war-against the USA) and to facilitate the settlement with the enemy within the country (in the struggle against the counterrevolutionaries), but also to propagate "the good example" in endless repeats and always with an educational emphasis—the model commune, the model school, the model university. Through the collective ownership of these loud-speaker instruments and their location (in factories, collective farms, places for spending leisure time) community listening was ensured as a radio form. Next to the radio diffusion system the "listening together system" plays an important role: certain propagandists instruct their listeners on the most important news. These communication mediators are present in factories, offices and schools and so reach almost the whole population. This very obligation, direct or indirect, of having to take part in a "radio listening group" and the early regionalization into local Party-controlled media forms illustrates a basic characteristic of the Chinese broadcasting system: the direct connection between the maker of the program and the recipient is meant to bridge the gap between the mass medium and face-to-face communication.

The supreme power in broadcasting lies with the state; the organizational "nerve-center" of broadcasting is in Peking where the "office for broadcasting affairs"—one of the 22 offices of the state council—which is directly subordinated to the Politbureau. supervises the entire running of the broadcasting and programs. At the moment (1976) there are 127 regional broadcasting centers, some of which have up to seven transmitters. The regional and local stations serve basically as transmitting stations for relaying the central program from Radio Peking; news, like all other important political programs, has to be relayed unchanged. The broadcasting center transmits four programs altogether. Television, which at the moment operates over 28 transmitters, has not yet developed beyond the early stages and is used mainly for teaching purposes at universities.

Analagous to the good relationship between the Soviet Union and China there was a high degree of agreement in questions of media until the middle or even the end of the 1950s. The Chinese orientated themselves according to the Soviet example and were praised by Moscow for their efforts. But soon afterwards the Soviet communications policy began to be called "revisionist" in Peking and this strong criticism was directed towards President Liu Shao-chi, the "Chinese Khrushchev" who had fallen out of favor. Two examples: Liu, similar to the Soviets, was of the opinion that journalism was "a special position" which necessitated a special ability and education, in other words specialists. According to Mao Tse-tung such an attitude is reprehensible: "It is quite clear that the control of the press by so-called specialists advocated by the Chinese Khrushchev means it will be controlled by a minority, this in turn means that it will be controlled by the *bourgeoisie*." [14] Academically educated Soviet journalists were compared with so-called "bare foot journalists" who had been "educated by the masses" and had also had to work on the land. The discrepancy of these attitudes is even clearer in the question of whether the wishes of the consumer should be respected. Liu: "You serve the readers. When they say your papers are good, then you have worked well." This sentence was condemned in the cultural revolution as a "bourgeois slogan." As long as Chinese society is still divided up into classes the mass media may not be regulated by public taste: they should not serve but should educate, mobilize and organize.

The achievements of the Chinese communication system are considerable. Like a huge clasp it has contributed substantially to the cohesion of the state and has also definitely strengthened the unity of the nation. The price for the success of the Chinese formula for communication consists in what seems in western eyes to be equal to a relinquishing of individuality and personal freedom—the obligation to volunteer which prevents the recipient from establishing himself in neutral or unpolitical groups, the obligation of not being able to escape the omnipresent radio network, the obligation of having to take part in an organized feedback. Here two factors must be considered. First of all, there has never in Chinese history been personal freedom comparable to that of Western systems, so the average Chinese citizen and radio listener probably is not aware of this lack; then the feedback system is far from being only a propaganda trick of the Chinese Party leadership, it is also reflected in impulses which "run from the bottom to the top."

NOTES

[1] Some summaries are recommendable: Eckert, Gerhard: *Das Fernsehen in den Ländern Westeuropas.* Gütersloh: Bertelsmann, 1965; Emery, Walter B.: *National and International Systems of Broadcasting: Their History, Operation and Control.* Michigan State Univ. Press, 1969. But these books are only descriptive surveys. The author tried a comparative study: Erich Follath: *Ein internationaler Vergleich von Rundfunksystemen. Die Interdependenz von Rundfunkpolitik und Gesamtpolitik in Großbritannien, Frankreich, der Sowjetunion, der VR China und Indien.* Diss. Stuttgart-Hohenheim, 1974.

[2] See W. Phillips Davison: *The Role of Communication in Democracies,* in Chapter 1 of this book.

[3] See Gottfried Eisermann: "Soziologie in der Politik," in: *Die Lehre von der Gesellschaft,* Stuttgart 1969, p. 357.

[4] Basic literature for the American broadcasting system: *The Television Broadcasting Industry,* Report of the Antitrust Subcommittee of the Committee on the Judiciary, 85th Congress, 1st Session, House Report No. 607 (Celler-Report), US-Government Printing Office, Washington, 1957; *Television Network Program Procurement,* Report of the Committee on Interstate and Foreign Commerce, 88th Congress, 1st Session, House Report No. 281, US Government Printing Office, Washington 1963. Helmut Arndt: "Das kommerzielle Fernsehen in den USA," in: Prokop: *Massenkommunikationsforschung,* Vol. 1. Frankfurt: Fischer 1972. Lichty, Lawrence W. and Malachi C. Topping: *American Broadcasting: A Source Book on the History of Radio and Television.* New York: Hastings House, Publishers, 1975.

[5] See *Television Network Programme Procurement,* p. 106.

[6] Basic literature for the British broadcasting system: Briggs, Asa: *The History of Broadcasting in the United Kingdom.* Vol. 1 (1961), Vol. 2 (1965), Vol. 3 (1970), London: Oxford University Press. Paulu, Burton: *British Broadcasting in Transition.* London: MacMillan, 1961. Wilson, H. H.: *Pressure Group: The Campaign for Commercial Television.* London: Secker & Warburg, 1961.

[7] See Greene, Hugh C.: *The Conscience of the Programme Director.* London, BBC-Papers, 1965.

[8] See *The Guardian,* 10.4.1972, p. 3.

[9] Basic literature for the French broadcasting system: Frédéric, Claude: *Libérer l'ORTF.* Paris: Du Seuil, 1968. Louis, Roger: *L'ORTF. Un combat.* Paris: Editions du Seuil, 1968. Thibau, Jacques: *Une télévision pour tous les francais.* du Seuil, 1970.

[10] Just like he did in the election campaign 1967. See Follath, p. 154.

[11] Basic literature for the Soviet broadcasting system: Hopkins, Mark W.: *Mass Media in the Soviet Union*. New York: Western Publishing Company, Pegasus, 1970. Koschwitz, Hansjürgen: *Pressepolitik und Parteijournalismus in der UdSSR und derv VR China*. Düsseldorf: Bertelsmann Univ., 1971. Roth, Paul: "Das sowjetische Fernsehen 1930–1959 and 1960–1972," in: *Rundfunk und Fernshen* (Hamburg), Nr. 3/1972 and Nr. 2/3/1973.

[12] See Stoljarow, Vitali: "Lenin zur Rolle der Kommunikation und der Kommunikationsmittel im Prozeß der Bewußtseinsbildung," in: *Deutsche Zeitschrift für Philosophie* (Ostberlin), 1970.

[13] Basic literature for the Chinese broadcasting system: Liu, Alan P. L.: *Communications and National Integration in Communist China*. Berkeley: University of California Press, 1972. Liu, Alan P. L.: *Radio Broadcasting in Communist China:* Cambridge: M.I.T., 1964. Markham, James W.: *Voices of the Red Giants. Communications in Russia and China*. Ames: The Iowa State Univ. Press, 1967. Yu, Frederic T. C.: *Mass Persuasion in Communist China*. London: Pall Mall Press, 1964.

[14] See *Peking Review*, Nr. 37/1968.

Wilson P. Dizard:

Television's Global Networks

AT THE BBC's new London studios there is a small room with a futuristic sign on its door. The sign reads: International Control Room. Here BBC engineers can exchange programs with over two dozen other television systems in Europe and North America. Soon, with the development of world-wide communications satellite facilities, they will be able to provide BBC viewers with programs for fifty countries. Within a decade this will extend to a hundred or more countries.

The BBC's international control room is a working symbol of the next major development in world television—the formation of regional and intercontinental networks. Such links are an old story in Europe where the pacesetting Eurovision network has been in operation for over a decade. Intervision, a Soviet-sponsored network, links eight East European countries. Fiscal, political, and geographical barriers have decreed a slower pace for similar networks in other parts of the world. Despite these difficulties, regional networks will play a key role in television's development in Latin America, the Middle East, and the Far East. In each of these areas, the first steps toward forming electronic links between national television systems have already been taken. Africa has, understandably, lagged behind in plans for regional telecasting, but even here the managers of that continent's national television systems talk confidently of TV links among themselves and with the rest of the world.

In any event, it is already clear that by the early 1970's regional and intercontinental network links will be available to a billion or more viewers in over sixty countries throughout the globe. The prospects of simultaneous sight-and-sound transmissions on such an unprecedented scale has political, economic, and cultural implications for all countries, and for American world leadership in particular. What we say about ourselves on these new links, and what is said about us by others, can seriously influence the image the world has of our national character and our international role. A closer look at the present development of these networks and their future prospects is therefore in order.

The earliest TV transmissions to cross national frontiers came from the United States. In the late 1940's, television stations in U.S. cities bordering Mexico and Canada began attracting large audiences across the border. By the

▶ From: *Television: A World View,* by Wilson P. Dizard. Copyright © 1966 by Syracuse University Press, Syracuse, N.Y. Reprinted by permission of the publisher.

early 1950's, the process became reciprocal as Canadian and Mexican television entrepreneurs began building stations with an eye on nearby U.S. audiences.

This across-the-border TV eavesdropping is now common in other parts of the world. In Europe, the largest audiences of the commercial stations in Luxembourg and Monte Carlo are nearby French, German, Belgian, and Italian viewers. Belgian and German programs have larger audiences in parts of the Netherlands than does the state-controlled Dutch station. In the Mediterranean area, the low-lying littoral provides excellent transmission conditions for long-distance telecasting Viewers in Greece and in North Africa tuned into Italian television for years before television became a reality in their own countries. Cairo television is readily available to viewers in Lebanon, Israel, and Jordan.

In a number of cases, this factor of geographical proximity has been used to beam programs directly across borders for political purposes. The best-known example of this is in Germany where the West and East Germans conduct an elaborate, expensive form of electronic warfare aimed at attracting each other's television audiences. A similar, small example of directed Communist television programs was reported in 1963 when a Soviet station in the Arctic instituted programs in Norwegian design to attract audiences in northern Norway. A similar effort has been reported in Korea where North Korean Communist authorities have directed part of their programming efforts toward nearby South Korean viewers.

These across-the-border telecasting operations, whether random or intentional, are a small part of the new international character of television. The major emphasis is on binational, regional, and intercontinental agreements to connect television systems at all levels.

The first formal exchange of television programs on an international scale took place on August 27, 1950, between Great Britain and France. With British equipment, the inaugural program was sent from Calais to Dover. A major problem at the time was the incompatibility of British and French equipment, due largely to differences in television tube line counts. BBC and Radiodiffusion Télévision Française engineers successfully developed converter systems to a point where in July, 1952, formal bilateral exchanges of programs between the two countries were inaugurated. It is doubtful that even the most enthusiastic supporters of the exchange realized that they were taking the first practical step toward forming a link which, in little more than ten years, would reach form the Urals through Europe and across the Atlantic to California.

The initial Franco-British television exchanges were not simply an exercise in technical virtuosity or hands-across-the-Channel camaraderie. They were part of a pattern, planned several years earlier, for strengthening European cooperation in the television and radio fields. The result was the Eurovision international network whose parent organization was, and still is, the European Broadcasting Union.

Eurovision is a massive test case of the opportunities, and the limitations, involved in developing regional and intercontinental networks. It is doubtful that any area of the world will come close to European accomplishments in this field for a long time. Europe had the advantages of a relatively small geographical area, high technical competence, cultural compatibility, and, above all, a strong impulse toward regional unity at many levels. Eurovision was nurtured in the dynamics of postwar European regional cooperation, and in turn it has contributed to this movement through a unique sight-and-sound ability to dramatize it.

Eurovision's success in regional transmissions led the Communist nations to attempt a similar venture within their own borders. The result was Intervision which is—technically, at least—Eurovision's opposite number in Eastern Europe and the Soviet Union. The technical achievements of Intervision are, in fact, considerable. It is geographically the most widespread single land network, stretching from East Berlin to the Urals, with the prospect of being extended to Vladivostok on the Pacific Ocean within a few years. This latter achievement would involve a linear distance of over nine thousand miles. Intervision does not, however, service as many individual stations or as large an audience as its Western European counterpart.

There is no doubt that Europe, both East and West, has a long lead in regional network television. Geography, politics, and financial considerations are all formidable obstacles to the development of similar networks in other parts of the world. Despite these barriers, however, such regional links will become a reality on every continent within the next decade.

If current plans develop, Asia will have a regional network by 1970. This planning effort is being carried out largely under Japanese leadership. Japanese television broadcasters and equipment manufacturers are fully aware of the long-range financial benefits of their participation in television's development in the Far East. Supporting this is the Japanese government's desire to re-establish its political and economic influence in Southeast Asia—influences which are still checked by local memories of Japanese military occupation during World War II. Television offers the Japanese a uniquely effective medium for further strengthening their role as a political and economic power in the Far East.

Japanese efforts to play a leading role in Far Eastern radio and television date from the formation of the Asian Broadcasters Conference in 1957. The conference was, to a large degree, a Japanese creation. All of its early meetings, in 1957, 1958, and 1960, were held in Tokyo, where delegates were appropriately impressed by the fact that Japan has the most advanced radio and television systems in Asia. At its 1962 meeting in Kuala Lumpur, the conference voted to establish itself as the Asian Broadcasting Union. The new union came into formal being in July, 1964. It is modeled, in form and spirit, on the European Broadcasting Union. Headquartered in Tokyo, its membership includes the broadcasting systems of most major nations in the Far East, South Asia, and the Middle East.[1]

Although it is still in its formative stages, the new Asia Broadcasting Union will undoubtedly be quickly involved in a plan for regional television networks during tte next few years. The initial impetus for such a plan is, of course, Japanese. In 1961, a group of Japanese equipment manufacturers and broadcasters formed a corporation known as Asiavision to explore the possibilities of directly linking the Japanese television network with other Far Eastern systems. Asiavision began as a wholly-owned subsidiary of Fuji-TV, one of the large commercial Japanese networks. Its board of directors included officials of major electronics firms. Basically it was a commercial combine, designed to explore the prospects of expanding television equipment and broadcasting sales throughout Southeast Asia.[2]

According to its original prospectus, the Asiavision link would run from Japan to Okinawa and the Philippines, crossing over to the Asian mainland via Saigon, and then on to Laos, Cambodia, Thailand, Burma, Pakistan, and India. Korean television would also be included in the network. The technical problems involved in such a link are formidable but not insoluble. Japanese engineers have plans to span the overwater segment between southern Japan and Okinawa by microwave circuits. The other overwater distances are comparable in the technical hurdles they present. More formidable, technically, is the fact that several countries, notably Cambodia, Laos, and Burma, do not have television systems. These gaps preclude any direct regional telecasting for years to come. In its early stages, Asiavision will have to restrict itself to exchanges of taped and filmed program material.

Japanese broadcasters have already had a taste of some of the political difficulties involved in their attempts to play a leading role in Asian television. Japanese offers to assist in the development of television in the Philippines have been treated warily, despite the fact that a number of stations there have been hard pressed financially in recent years. Another example of such cautiousness took place in Formosa in 1962. Fuji-TV, sponsor of Asiavision, had signed an agreement with the Chinese government in Formosa to build a television system on commercial terms generally regarded as favorable to both sides. Among other concessions, the Japanese planned to advertise Japanese products on Taiwan television and to provide a fixed amount of Japanese programing. In

---

[1] Eleven such organizations are ABU charter members: Australian Broadcasting Commission, Broadcasting Corporation of China (Taiwan), All India Radio, Japan Broadcasting Corporation (NHK), Korean Broadcasting System, Radiodiffusion National Lao, Radio Malaysia, New Zealand Broadcasting Corporation, Radio Pakistan, Philippine Broadcasting Service, and the UAR Broadcasting Corporation (Cairo).

[2] It would, however, be wrong to dismiss the proposed Asiavision network simply as a Japanese commercial venture. Its organizers have an awareness of its potential political effect. One of them declared, in a 1962 Tokyo interview with the author, that Asiavision "was something like your American Peace Corps."

April, 1962, the Chinese parliament passed a resolution which in effect vetoed these provisions in the contract. The issue became a political one between the Japanese and Chinese foreign offices. It was settled eventually, but not without leaving a legacy of doubt about the speed with which an Asian television network might be formed.

There is no doubt that such a regional network will become a reality eventually, or that the Japanese will play a leading role in its formation. However, it is probable that the network will develop slowly, first through the exchange of filmed and taped programs, and then through limited binational microwave connections which will one day be extended to other countries in the region, probably under the auspices of the Asian Broadcasting Union.[3]

Similar political and economic difficulties have inhibited realistic planning for regional telecasting in the Middle East and Africa. The idea of a network linking Arab television systems has been discussed since television was introduced into the area in the late fifties. However, political differences within the Arab bloc have militated against any practical implementation of what would undoubtedly be an important step toward dramatizing Arab unity. The strongest force behind a regional network, if it should materialize, would be the UAR's Gamal Abdel Nasser, who has already developed Egyptian television into the best of its kind in the region. Paradoxically, the first practical move toward an Arab network has been made by an American firm, the American Broadcasting Company. In October, 1963, ABC International announced the formation of an "Arab Middle Eastern Network" consisting of TV stations in Syria, Lebanon, Kuwait, Iraq, and Jordan. The "network" is primarily a program and advertising sales arrangement, linked to ABC International's affiliations with these stations. There is, however, some significance to the fact that the network's organizing meeting in Beirut drew almost five hundred businessmen, advertisers, government officials, and station representatives.[4]

The prospects for regional television links are perhaps dimmest in Africa. It will probably be a decade before African countries move beyond bilateral program exchange arrangements to a multinational regional network.

The most practical planning in regional television outside of Europe has taken place in Latin America. Three Central American countries are already linked directly in a small-scale version of a larger regional network that will eventually stretch from the Mexican-U.S. border south seven thousand miles to the tip of South America. The first "live" program exchanges between Latin American countries took place in 1961 when Argentinian television carried news reports of the Organization of American States conference at Punta del

---

[3] Not the least of the problems facing the proposed Asian network would be the admission of the Chinese Communists into its activities. The Chinese Reds, who already have considerable television experience, are well aware of the propaganda potential of a link with other Asian television systems.

[4] *Variety*, October 2, 1963.

Este in neighboring Uruguay. A year earlier, telecommunications experts from Latin American nations, meeting in Mexico City, agreed in principle to the idea of planning a continental network.

Since that time, the international network idea has been kept alive largely by the Mexicans. It was not, however, until the Central American network began operations in 1964 that any practical moves were made to realize the plan. The network is known as CATVN—Central American Television Network. (The participants are Nicaragua, Costa Rica, Guatemala, Panama, Honduras, and El Salvador.) It was originally set up in 1960, largely under the guidance of the international division of the American Broadcasting Company of New York. As with its "Arab network" efforts in the Middle East, ABC International organized CATVN primarily as a commercial advertising and program sales organization.

It would, however, be incorrect to dismiss CATVN as a sales promotion gimmick. In fact, the nations involved have growing political and economic ties that make a television link part of a logical pattern of regional interdependence. In 1963, five of the six CATVN countries—all except Panama—formed a Central American Free Trade Area, somewhat on the model of the European Common Market. Trade barriers were eliminated on more than half the commerce between the member countries, with further reductions scheduled in 1965. A regional bank has been established as another effort to raise economic levels well above the current per capita income of 250 dollars a year. Whether it is reporting a sports event or a regional political conference, television has a role to play in the new efforts of Central American nations to strengthen each other politically and economically.

Plans are currently underway to extend "live" interconnections between CATVN's members. The success of this "subregional network" will undoubtedly have an important influence in encouraging other Latin American nations to move forward with their much-discussed plans for a network spanning the entire continent.

The next step beyond regional television networks is, of course, intercontinental television linking all areas of the world. Most speculation about worldwide television broadcasts has emphasized the role of space communications satellites (comsats). However, comsats may, in fact, play a relatively minor role in such a system. It may be more practical, financially and technically, to base the system on interlocking regional networks connected by land cable or microwave systems. TV networks in Europe, Africa, and Asia could be linked in this manner. One comsat over the Atlantic or Pacific could connect the Western Hemisphere with this Eurasian system. (The two American continents would be joined either by microwave relays or a comsat system operating on a north-south axis.) The potential role of regional networks in a global system was demonstrated at the time of President Kennedy's death. Only two communications satellites—one each over the Atlantic and Pacific—were needed in an international network that involved twenty-six countries on four continents and a viewing audience of over three hundred million persons.

There will, however, be few similar events that will enlist such worldwide interest as to justify global coverage. Most television exchanges between regional networks will involve areas with common cultural or political interests. Thus, U.S. television will probably concentrate most heavily on program exchanges with Europe and Latin America. The two regional networks in divided Europe will undoubtedly develop a more active exchange schedule.

A number of proposals for a world television network organization have been put forward in recent years. Most of these have come from American sources. In 1962, several U.S. television officials proposed that American and European broadcasters take the lead in this field. However, none of the proposals have been acted upon. [5] It will probably be several years before any active planning for world television network arrangements is begun. The chief reason, of course, is that technical achievement of such a network, through comsat and surface connections, is five to eight years in the future. In the interim, however, there will be a steady increase in the number of bilateral regional television exchanges, notably in the North Atlantic area. For the rest of the world, the question of intercontinental television may depend largely on the pace of regional network developments.

In summary, regional television networks will become a reality in all parts of the world within the next decade. The model for such arrangements will be the ten-year-old European network which has demonstrated both the opportunities and the pitfalls involved in international telecasting. A world-wide television system will be formed by the combination of communications satellites and interlocked regional networks.

The United States has, of course, an important stake in these developments. Increasingly, television is taking over Hollywood's role as the chief purveyor of the American image abroad. The America that foreign viewers see on their living room screens is already a major factor in the shaping of their attitudes toward us. Equally important is the part that international television can play in defining and clarifying, as no other medium can, the realities of the rest of the world beyond their own borders. Using this gift in ways that strengthen the prospects for a democratic world order will be increasingly important for American leadership in the future.

[5] The proposals were made at the special European Broadcasting Union meeting held in New York shortly after the launching of the first Telstar communications satellite in 1962. There were some indications at the time that the European members of EBU resented the manner in which the Americans presented their proposals without first consulting privately with their EBU associates. See *Variety*, October 10, 1962.

John C. Merrill:

Global Patterns of Elite Daily Journalism

ALTHOUGH the elite press of the world may be considered as a kind of intellectual journalistic "community," it is clearly an uneven, multi-faceted one. A seriousness of tone and purpose and a high readership among influential persons are about the only common denominators of the elite press. Its membership, because of differences in language, economic stability, degree of freedom and basic philosophy, is splintered and fragmented and suffers from too little rapport and theoretical consensus. Thus, the world's elite press is heterogeneous and pluralistic in spite of its commonalities of seriousness, general civility and influence. Struggling against great obstacles everywhere but with renewed hope and vigor, it is developing unevenly throughout the world. It falls roughly into at least three major patterns.

The first pattern is primarily *political or ideological.* Elite papers tend toward separation from government or they tend toward integration with government. While the free elite see themselves as *independent agents,* standing aloof from, and unaffected by, government, the authoritarian elite envision themselves as *partners in government,* cooperative agents of their government bent on carrying forth the socio-political system of their people.

Both groups of elite papers are dedicated to their philosophies and take their responsibilities, as they see them, quite seriously. It should be noted, however, that such a binary classification of the world's elite is too simple in reality and that all papers everywhere are free to varying degrees and restricted to varying degrees, although the character of freedom and restraint may differ significantly.

Many students of the press place considerable emphasis on "social responsibility" in determining the elite status of a newspaper. To what degree is the paper socially responsible? The answer to this question, to many, will largely determine the quality or eliteness of a newspaper. In the United States and other Western democracies, "social responsibility" is thought of generally in terms of non-authoritarianism or freedom from governmental control—coupled with some sense of "doing the right thing at the right time." In other words, "social responsibility" is the press utopia into which only libertarian-oriented newspapers may pass. This, however, seems much too simple a theory and is

▶ Written for this book as a modified version of an article appearing in *Journalism Quarterly,* Vol. 45, No. 1 (Spring 1968). Revised in 1976.

unsatisfactory in the modern world of fragmented and pluralistic serious journalism.

It is this writer's contention that *all* conscientious and serious newspapers—regardless of what nation or political ideology they may represent—are "socially responsible." This idea was put forth in a paper in early 1965 and met with considerable objection from some quarters; however, it was also embraced by a surprisingly large number of persons who had previously failed to challenge the concept of press social responsibility being connected only to a libertarian press. [1]

Why cannot the authoritarian press or the communistic press (if there is really any difference) claim to be socially responsible also? In fact, in certain respects, a newspaper would be more "responsible" if some type of governmental supervision existed; indeed, reporters could be kept from nosing about in "critical" areas during "critical" times. And, as the Russians are quick to point out, the amount of sensational material could be controlled in the press, or eliminated altogether. Government activities could always be supported and public policy could be pushed on all occasions. The press could be more educational in the sense that more news of art exhibits, concerts, national progress and the like could be stressed. In short, the press would eliminate the "negative" and stress the "positive." Then, with one voice the press of the nation would be responsible to its society; and the definition of "responsible" would be functional—defined and carried out in the context of the existing government and social structure. This, of course, may seem unreasonable or even "treasonable" in the Western democracies, but its unreasonableness is unrealistic when projected onto the screen of international journalism.

So it would seem logical to believe that all newspapers (of any political system) which reflect the philosophy of their governmental system and try to present serious, educational reading fare are not only responsible to their society but are members of the elite press—or they are climbing into that select fraternity.

Assuming that a nation's socio-political philosophy determines its press system, and undoubtedly it does, then it follows that the nation's leading and most prestigious papers are socially responsible and form the elite. For example, the Marxist or Communist press system considers itself socially responsible, and certainly it is to its own social system. A capitalistic press, operating in a pluralistic and competitive context, would be socially *irresponsible* if suddenly transplanted into the Communist society.

The same thing might be said of the so-called "authoritarian" press system, exemplified by Spain. A critical press such as found in the United States, a press which by its pluralistic nature would tend to undermine national policy and disrupt national harmony, would be anathema in a nation like Spain.

[1] John C. Merrill, "The Press and Social Responsibility," (University of Missouri: Freedom of Information Center Publication No. 001, March 1965).

Spanish newspapers, the most serious like *ABC* and *Ya* of Madrid and *La Vanguardia Española* of Barcelona, are exceptionally responsible to Spanish society; and, it should be added, they supply a surprising diversity of orientations and viewpoints within the confines of the national policy.[2] In other words, the elite press of a nation, even one under considerable government control, will still prove its eliteness through its subtleties, skillful restraint and capacity to make the most of the situation in which it finds itself. In many ways, it takes more journalistic ability and acumen—as well as courage—to put out an elite newspaper in a country such as Spain than in a country like Britain or Sweden.

A second important pattern among the world's elite, and one that is even more ragged than the political one just mentioned, is that of *economic diversity*.

This pattern, of course, is related to the political context, but actually is quite different. For example, one elite paper in a libertarian nation can run into dire financial difficulties while another in the same country prospers and grows. An elite paper is not determined by how much property it owns or the profit it makes. Elite papers throughout the world exemplify a wide range of economic development and prosperity, but their overriding concern with serious news and views and their desire to influence opinion leaders manifests itself quite apart from such differences in economic health.

Naturally, there is a point below which an elite paper (or any paper) may not fall and keep up its desired level of quality. Certainly, it must have the facilities to do good printing. It must be able to pay enough to get conscientious, well-educated staff members. It must be able to receive a variety of services from news agencies, as well as to collect much national and world news with its own correspondents. It must, therefore, either have a rather sizable circulation, or it must develop a special elite readership which will offset a small circulation. Although some elite papers like *Asahi* of Japan and *Pravda* of the Soviet Union have tremendous circulations, most of the world's elite have only modest ones.[3]

The elite newspaper (especially in a libertarian nation) runs the risk of lowering its quality when it makes a bid for larger readership—at least unless it does it very slowly. For it is the popular or mass press that is after the big circulations; the elite press is after readers of discernment and influence. Unfortunately for international rationality, the public—as Leo Rosten has said— "chooses the frivolous as against the serious, the lurid as against the tragic, the

---

[2] The Monarchist *ABC* and the Catholic *Ya*, for example, often carry outspoken criticisms of municipal officials and are taken seriously in Spanish ministerial circles. *ABC*, *Ya* and *La Vanguardia* (Barcelona) have circulations of about 100,000 each, but the total daily circulation of the country is not much more than 600,000—about one copy of a paper to every 50 Spaniards.

[3] Most elite papers of the world are small—under 300,000 daily circulations. The largest are found in the USSR, Red China and Japan where *Pravda*, *People's Daily* and *Asahi* have circulations exceeding two million. A few other elite dailies, like the New York *Times* and Italy's *Corriere della Sera*, have circulations of more than 500,000.

trivial as against fact, the diverting as against the significant." Rosten points out that very few people in any society "have reasonably good taste or care deeply about ideas" and that even fewer appear to be "equipped—by temperament and capacity, rather than education—to handle ideas with both skill and pleasure." [4]

Most elite newspapers realize that their readership will probably be small, but they know that it is usually potent, sapient and prestigious. It should be mentioned, however, that there are some few elite papers—in nations such as Sweden where the whole public is literate and uncommonly serious—which manage to be rational and serious and at the same time furnish all types of reading material.

The third pattern of the elite press is *geographical*. And this, of course, is closely related to national development. Most of the elite are published in developed or modern countries, although there are a few that represent the developing (modernizing) or transitional nations. Europe and North America are the principal homes of the elite newspapers. This is not surprising since these two continents are the most industrialized, the most technological and most literate of all the continents. As the economic bases become stabilized, and literate and well-educated populations of other continents grow, the evenness of dispersion of the elite press throughout the world should improve significantly. Presently, however, elite newspapers are scattered about the earth in a very uneven fashion. This pattern of clusters and vast gaps greatly hinders the total impact of serious, concerned journalism in the world as a whole. It might be well to look more closely at this geographical pattern of the world's elite press.

Asia, with the exception of China, Japan and India, is virtually without an elite press. Of the three, Japan stands out for its great progress in quality journalism—and popular journalism, too, for that matter, *Asahi* is without a doubt the best quality daily in Japan and shows that an elite paper can, with editorial flexibility and sagacity, develop a large circulation within a free-market press system. *Pravda* and its counterpart in Peking, *Jen-min Jih-pao* of course, have fewer problems building circulation since Communist party members and many others find that they *need* to have these daily journals of guidance and news.

In India, the problems of the elite papers are much more acute than in either the USSR, China or Japan. There are many reasons for this, but the chief is probably the problem of too many languages. At present the major elite papers of India are published in English, understood only by the educated mainly found in a few of the large cities. And, even within the English-reading public, the circulation of the English elite press is segmented since there are three very important elite dailies in the country—*The Statesman* of Calcutta, *The Hindu* of Madras and *The Times of India* of Bombay and Delhi. The vernacular languages of India, of which Hindi is the official one, have not caught

[4] Leo Rosten, "The Intellectual and the Mass Media," *Daedalus*, Spring 1960, pp. 333–46.

on as press languages—although there are a few well-written-and-edited papers in some of them, but with little or no national or international prestige. To the language problem facing the development of the Indian elite press must be added these (generally applicable throughout Southeast Asia): low literacy rate, underdeveloped educational system, scarcity of training facilities and trained journalists, and old and inadequate printing equipment. One other barrier to the further development of elite newspaper journalism in India is the increasing authoritarianism of the government.

In Africa, outside Egypt in the extreme northeast and the Republic of South Africa in the far south, there is no significant elite press; [5] and even in these two republics considerable government sensitivity has hindered development of a truly *quality* press. Egypt, with its nationalized newspapers, would—from a Western viewpoint—have to take second place to South Africa as a nation with a pluralistic press. In South Africa, for example, in spite of government sensitivity to what it feels are press "excesses," the papers—especially those in English—show clearly that "the searchlights of inquiry and criticism are still able to shine, only slightly filtered, and to concentrate on those dark areas where a regime is most sensitive." [6] Without a doubt, South Africa has the freest newspapers on the continent, and within the English-language press are papers which are the equal in quality and tone to the elite of most nations of the world.

Johannesburg's morning *Rand Daily Mail* is a good example. It has consistently presented facts and opinion which have irritated the government, and has given its readers healthy portions of national and foreign news. Although most Afrikaans-language papers present a rather narrow pro-government picture, an important exception is *Die Burger* of Cape Town, committed generally to the policies of the Nationalist Party but often refreshingly independent and deviationist.[7] It is also interesting that in South Africa, the freest papers—generally the English-language ones—have the largest circulations. For instance, the Johannesburg *Star* (about 170,000), has a circulation of almost double the combined circulations of the city's two Afrikaans papers—the *Transvaler* and the *Vaderland*.

The Egyptian press, although long being well-developed for the African context, has slowly but increasingly become a state-controlled press. In spite of this nationalization (or "people's press"), a few of the highly regarded old dailies of Cairo still provide their Arab readership with substantial amounts of serious

[5] In most parts of Africa the problems of establishing some sort of stable government while various factions are vying for political power hamper the development of any type of viable press, much less an elite press. Aside from political unrest, other problems face newspapers of the new African states: financial instability, unskilled journalists, a multiplicity of languages, high illiteracy, unsettled political direction, and a widespread absence of native national leadership.

[6] Tertius Myburgh, "The South African Press: Hope in an Unhappy Land," *Nieman Reports*, 20: 1 (March 1966), p. 6.

[7] *Ibid.*, p. 4.

journalism. For example, *Al Ahram* gives a good (for Egypt) selection of news and features and keeps its cosmopolitan tone.

In the neighboring Middle East the press systems are mainly transitional—caught between the severe problems of many parts of Asia on one side and of Africa on the other. One hindrance to elite press development in this area is that these nations cannot decide whether to have their press systems (and governments) veer toward libertarianism and competition or toward authoritarianism and state planning. Governments throughout the region are generally suspicious of the press and sensitive to its criticism. Also the persistent military, terrorist, and propaganda activities in the Middle East have certainly harmed the growth of elite journalism there.

Latin America, in spite of awesome economic and literacy problems, has somehow managed to develop a rather sizable group of elite newspapers. Without a doubt, this region of the world has a far more-advanced press in all respects than is generally found in Asia and Africa. One obvious explanation for this is the fact that Spanish is the almost common language of the press of Latin America,[8] whereas in both Asia and Africa the polyglot of languages and dialects makes the development of newspapers of substantial influence and circulation extremely difficult, if not impossible.

Many Latin American dailies meet the demands of serious readers for percipient journalism; almost every major nation south of the United States has at least one journal which is in, or aspires to, the elite press. Argentina has its *La Nación* and *La Prensa*, Chile its *Mercurio*, Peru its *Comercio*, Columbia its *Tiempo* and Mexico its outstanding trio—*Excélsior, Novedades* and *El Universal*. These and many other serious dailies of Latin America do an outstanding job of providing large proportions of scientific and humanistic news and views, with much emphasis on foreign affairs. Perhaps the Latin American serious press, like its ancestral press of Iberia, places undue stress on philosophical, theological and literary discussion; but this is simply an intellectual Latin proclivity and the elite press does well to serve it. This philosophical proclivity to serious, intellectual journalism in Latin America appears unable, however, to hold its own with increasing social and political instability in the region. More and more government control of the press, along with economic problems, has stymied elite journalism.

In Oceania, Australia alone has a press which includes newspapers of the elite type. Barriers to press growth in this sprawling island region are mainly 1) small population, 2) technological underdevelopment, 3) scarcity of trained journalists and 4) geographical isolation from the main stream of international

---

[8] Brazil, with its Portuguese-language press sitting like an island in a sea of Spanish, has developed an extremely vigorous and qualitative press—especially in its two largest cities, Rio and Sao Paulo. Several dailies are outstanding, with *O Estado de S. Paulo* and *O Globo* of Rio undoubtedly the best.

concerns. In Australia several papers might be included among the elite and several others are aspirants. *The Age* of Melbourne is usually considered the most serious and influential. Even a paper like the same city's *Herald*, which is an afternoon journal which does not avoid appealing to all classes, furnishes some 500,000 readers a substantial diet of serious material every day. Its economic coverage and its weekly book page are especially laudable. *The Australian*, with main offices in Sydney, is developing into a truly national daily and a first-rate journal in every respect.

In North America (above the Mexican border) the elite press thrives. The *Globe and Mail* of Toronto, with a circulation of some 230,000, is Canada's only truly national daily. It is also generally considered the best of the country's dailies. Montreal's evening *La Presse*, a comprehensive afternoon daily with an exceptionally fine weekend edition, is the largest French-language daily in the Western hemisphere. In Winnipeg, Manitoba, the *Free Press* provides excellent international coverage and provides one of the most thoughtful editorial pages in North America.

Although there are elite and near-elite papers in every major section of the United States, most of them are concentrated along the East Coast and in the Middle West. In the East are such sophisticated dailies as the New York *Times*, the Washington *Post*, the *Christian Science Monitor*, the Baltimore *Sun* and the Miami *Herald*. In the Middle West a few of the leaders among the elite are the St. Louis *Post-Dispatch*, the Minneapolis *Tribune* and the Kansas City *Star*. In Kentucky, there is the Louisville *Courier-Journal*; in Georgia, the Atlanta *Constitution*. Quality papers of national and international prestige tend to fade out in the Plains and Mountain area of the West, with the Denver *Post* ruling a vast empire from its strategic position. Along the West Coast, there are the Los Angeles *Times* (probably the fastest-improving U.S. daily) and the Portland *Oregonian*.

If the press of North America is well-developed and the elite papers numerous, the press of Europe (Western Europe) might be said to be *over*-developed and the elite papers *very* numerous. From Scandinavia to Spain, and from Britain to Russia, elite dailies (and weeklies) spread their serious journalism into every corner of the continent and, increasingly, into distant lands. The elite dailies of Europe are probably the most erudite and knowledgeable in the world, providing insights which Quincy Howe (former editor of *Atlas*) has said are available nowhere else.[9] European papers, says Howe, "speak with authority," and it is not only a matter "of Germans reporting on Germany, French on France and British on Britain," but also "of Germans writing about the French, the French writing about the British, and the British writing about the Germans."[10]

[9] Quincey Howe, "What Americans Can Learn from the Foreign Press," Guild Memorial Lecture (Minneapolis: University of Minnesota School of Journalism, 1963).
[10] *Ibid.*

All types of quality papers are to be found in Europe. There are the free elite of most western Europe—led by the super-serious *Neue Zürcher Zeitung* of Switzerland, *Le Monde* of France, the *Times* and the *Guardian* of Britain and *Frankfurter Allgemeine* of West Germany. There are the authoritarian elite of Spain such as *ABC and La Vanguardia Española,* and the Communist elite such as *Pravda* and *Izvestia* of Russia and *Borba* and *Politika* of Yugoslavia. There are the dailies of Scandinavia such as Oslo's *Aftenposten,* Copenhagen's *Berlingske Tindende,* and Stockholm's *Dagens Nyheter* that combine a rather flashy typographical dress with a heavy diet of serious news and views. There are also such dailies as *Die Welt* of Hamburg and *Corriere della Sera* of Milan which are able to combine a "modern" demeanor with a solid seriousness. And, of course, there is the stolid drabness of ultra-seriousness to be found in a very special kind of prestige daily, *Osservatore Romano* of Vatican City. The European elite press offers the reader a wide selection of packaging and political orientation; there is a paper whose journalistic style and philosophy—as well as size, layout and typographical tone—appeal to any kind of serious newspaper reader.

It is interesting to note that in the areas of the world where daily journalism is most advanced and there are many elite papers, there are also the largest numbers of journalism schools and institutes, and training programs of one type or another. This concern with, or emphasis on, journalism education, of course, is coupled with a high development of education generally. In the underdeveloped nations, such as are common in Asia and Africa, the little emphasis on journalistic training which has been begun is still concerned chiefly with the technical aspects of journalism: typesetting, printing, newsprint acquisition and the overcoming of basic economic handicaps. On the other hand, in the more advanced nations where the elite is strongest, these elemental problems are secondary in journalism education, and concern with editorial quality, ethical standards and social responsibility comes in for more consideration.

This non-technical and non-economic emphasis or approach inevitably results in a higher quality journalism. The seriousness and size of a country's elite press undoubtedly reflects the nation's general development and cultural level, and it is reassuring to know that among the thousands of daily papers of the world, there are conscientious and intelligent journals dedicated to serious discourse and bounded together by invisible cords of pride into a fraternity of prestige and excellence. These journals represent the tiny "saving remnant" of the world's newspapers. But their number appears not to be increasing in proportion to population and general circulation increase.

So, even though elite journalism offers some hope for rational dialog in the world, there is no real cause for optimism in today's climate of increasing press control, status quo journalism, and "conveyor belt" newspaper production of newspapers aimed at the enlarging masses of literate persons with low journalistic expectations. This is reflected in increased space given inane "features" and sensational pap on one hand and growing fascination with sophisticated gadgetry of production and the accompanying depersonalization on the other.

It is a difficult time for newspapers wanting to rise above the dreary mediocrity of print journalism. The decline of independent, personalized, and creative journalism aiming above the "lowest common denominator" portends the slow death of the elite press during the late 1970s and 1980s. A reaction could, of course, set in against this trend toward sensational and superficial newspapers, but the steady increase of "viewing" and "listening" audiences for journalism indicates that such a reaction is an unlikely one.

Heinz-Dietrich Fischer:

Periodicals and the International Communication System

FORERUNNERS of what we call today "magazines" or "periodicals" were annual or semiannual publications mainly printed in Germany. As early as 1588 Michael von Aitzing published every six months the *Messrelation* containing information about the fairs of Frankfurt.[1] In 1634 Johann Philipp Abelin established in Frankfurt the famous *Theatrum Europaeum*,[2] and from 1659 on the *Diarium Europaeum* came out as a historical and political collection of European affairs.[3] Johann Rist founded in 1663 a monthly publication under the title *Monatsgespräche*, in Wedel near Hamburg.[4]

However, "France can be considered the mother of magazines"[5] because the first real magazine with varied contents was established January 5, 1665, in Paris by Denys de Sallo under the name *Journal de Sçavans*.[6] This periodical, which has appeared with short interruptions until our present times, from its very first day of publication did not use Latin, as did the other publications, but the French language and was mainly oriented in philology, history, and sciences in an international scope. Soon after the foundation of this French magazine an imitation was established in England under the name *Philosophical Transactions*, edited by Henry Oldenbourg, Secretary of the Royal Society. A similar project was started in 1668 in Italy, when Francesco Nazzari founded at Rome the *Giornale de' Letterati* which contained also book reviews on sciences and languages.[7] These and some other early periodicals had readers throughout great parts of Europe, because they were mainly oriented to well-educated people.

A big influence on the development of magazines in several European countries were the literary and moralistic periodicals from England. Daniel Defoe issued in 1704 *The Review* as the earliest example of this kind of magazine, which was "a cross between a newspaper and a magazine."[8] And especially Joseph Addison and Richard Steele's *Tatler* (founded 1709) and the famous *Spectator* (founded 1711) were the pioneers of these magazines aimed at broader audience than the mainly scientific-oriented periodicals.[9] The history of the *American Magazine* and the *General Magazine* started in 1741.[10]

▶ This is a revised original article done for this book by Dr. Heinz-Dietrich Fischer, Professor of Journalism and Mass Communication Research, Ruhr-University Bochum (Federal Republic of Germany).

During the 18th Century in most European countries magazines were—with a few exceptions—mainly made for and read by people in their own countries, although they had sometimes more liberty in expressing certain feelings than censorship and absolutism permitted to the newspapers. But in reality magazines did not have more freedom than the rest of the press, because "the Tudors in England, the Bourbons in France, the Hapsburgs in Spain—in fact practically all western Europe—utilized the basic principles of authoritarianism as the theoretical foundation for their systems in press control." [11]

Before we continue our discussion on the development of magazines in an international context we have to make clear what a magazine really is, because there is some confusion about this term: "A periodical (or magazine) possesses periodicity: it is issued at intervals more or less regular. The term appears to have been first applied, as an adjective, to the essay type of journal as distinguished from the general magazine; but by the end of the eighteenth century it was being used to designate all regularly issued publications excepting, perhaps, newspapers." [12]

In great parts of Europe the French term *journal* or its Italian equivalent *giornale* were dominating for some time, and even the English adopted the French term and Anglosized it. Nearly a century after the foundation of the *Journal de Sçavans* synonyms for the term "journal" came up in the Germanic-speaking countries. The German word *Zeitschrift* was probably first used in 1751,[13] and later on similar expressions came up in the Netherlands or in Scandinavian countries.

"The term *magazine*," says Frank Luther Mott, "has undergone some change since it was first applied to publications. The first such application seems to have been in the title of *Gentleman's Magazine*, founded in London in 1731 . . . Alexander Pope . . . defined magazines, in 1743, as 'upstart collections' of dullness, folly, and so on. Thus the term, as taken over from the meaning of *magazine as storehouse* . . . came to be accepted as designating the whole class of *Gentleman's* imitators." [14] Finally, Frank Luther Mott makes an attempt at a definition: "While the word *magazine* is . . . to be defined as a bound pamphlet issued more or less regularly and containing a variety of reading matter, it must be observed also that it has a strong connotation of entertainment." [15] There is also the term *review*, but it is much more loosely used today than it was during the 19th century. The only other more neutral-sounding term would be *periodical*, because it is "perhaps the most concise word . . . , but *magazines*" is "the more popular and meaningful term" for "all types of serial publications," says Mott.[16]

So the term "magazine" from here on will be used in a very general sense, and it will be necessary to try to give a typology in a later paragraph. Especially since the early 19th century most of the old universal-oriented magazines with subscribers in several countries have died, because this century has been mainly the age of newspapers. The magazines, more and more, became mouthpieces of elite groups for the exchange of literary ideas or political opinions. But this trend toward specialization did not go so far that there were no magazines with international standards. For example, in the 19th century there were England's *Westminster Review* (founded 1824) [17] or the *Contemporary Review* (1866). Among the British historical and scientific magazines the *Economist* (1843) or the *English Historical Review* (1887) are outstanding examples. In Austria, the *Wiener Literaturzeitung* [18] (1813), and in Germany the *Hallische Jahrbücher* [19] (1838) had European readership. The revolution of 1848 was disastrous to the periodical press in Germany and very few journals survived it. Among the best-known German journals of the 19th century were the *Historische Zeitschrift* (founded 1859), [20] the *Deutsche Rundschau* (1874) [21] and the *Neue Rundschau* (1889). In the United States *The Atlantic Monthly* began its distinguished literary career in 1857. Three prominent New York weeklies were *Harper's Weekly* (1857), the *Nation* (1865) and *Outlook* (1870). By 1870 there were, for example, around 1200 periodicals in the U.S.A., close to 2400 in 1880 and nearly 3000 in 1890. [22]

The 19th century had also produced a vast flood of cheap popular magazines for light reading, like the *Penny Magazine* (1832) in England which had imitators in several countries. But these popular magazines rarely were distributed internationally. But the *English Illustrated Magazine* (1884) may perhaps be considered the parent of illustrated periodicals going to many parts of the world, where printing presses were available for the reproduction of pictures of various kinds.

Since the beginning of the 20th century a couple of new forms of magazines have arisen, a great number of them concerned with very specific problems of certain professions or sciences and not aiming at a larger audience. In pre-World-War I times in nearly all of the important countries political magazines were founded, sometimes subsidized by the governments because of their importance in foreign affairs. [23] After World War I, the world situation of magazines had changed in some respects. The Bolshevik revolution produced a great upheaval and was responsible for an enormous output of periodicals of all kinds. And also in countries outside of the Soviet Union there was increasing demand for the development of magazines which were different from those of the pre-war era.

Symptomatic of a group of mainly cultural oriented periodicals were such like the Spanish *Revista hispano-americana de Ciencias, Letras y Artes* (1921), the Swiss *Schweizerische Monatshefte* (1921), the Italian *La Cultura* (1922), the German *Deutsche Vierteljahresschrift* (1923), the French *Chronique des lettres françaises* (1923), or the Portuguese *Lusitania* (1924). [24] In Russia, the literary magazine *Novy Mir* (1925) published important works of the leading authors and made them known in other countries. [25] In February, 1922, the *Reader's Digest* [26] was founded as a magazine, which "started a new trend in size, contents, approach." And in 1923, *Time* [27] followed; it was "curt, clear, complete" [28] like no other periodical before. On the other hand, there arose a number of abstract journals, particularly in the fields of science, medicine, and technology.

The 1920's and 1930's have also been the times for the establishing of important political magazines in several countries. In Germany *Die Weltbühne*, of the later Nobel prize winner Carl von Ossietzky, had growing importance among some groups of intellectuals.[29] In England, *The New Statesman* (founded 1913), in the United States *Newsweek* (1933) and *U.S. News and World Report* (1933), were very successful. In 1936, Time, Inc. launched a weekly picture magazine under the title *Life*, which made a great success and had some imitators, chief of which was the fortnightly *Look* (1937).[30] In the Soviet Union, periodicals like the satirical *Krokodil* (1922), *Literaturnaja Gaseta* (1929) and especially the prime theoretical journal *Kommunist* (1924)[31] were "designed for both home and foreign consumption."[32] During World War II, the German minister of propaganda, Joseph Goebbels, established a weekly under the title *Das Reich* which was mainly a Nazi propaganda instrument for foreign countries.[33] After the war in many countries of the world magazines with a certain international appeal have been founded and the periodical press of the world became "extremely varied in scope, quality and general purpose. Magazines and journals range from the popular 'illustrateds' of many nations (e.g. *Stern* of Hamburg, Germany)[34] to the ultraserious journals of comment and news (e.g. *Swiss Review of World Affairs* of Zurich). There are also well-written quality 'humor' or 'satire' magazines of the *New Yorker* type such as Britain's *Punch* and Italy's *Il Borghese* and offbeat varieties such as the Soviet Union's *Krokodil*."[35]

Without any doubt, the periodicals with a large circulation for home and domestic distribution are the news magazines of all kinds, sometimes having special international editions. Among these news magazines, the American examples of this group have the highest circulations: the leading one is *Time* with around six million copies, followed by *Newsweek* (2.5 million), *U.S. News and World Report* (1,950,000), *Der Spiegel* of Germany[36] (1,068,000), and the French *L'Expresse*[37] (843,000). Much smaller circulations among the news magazines have *Elseviers Weekblad* of The Netherlands (121,000); *Tiempo*, Mexico (19,000); *Shukan Asahi*, Japan (16,000); *Reporter Kenya* (8,000); and India's *Link*, Argentina's *Veritas*, and Turkey's *Akis*.[38]

Especially *Time* magazine, with its various editions, is an excellent example of an international-oriented and global-distributed magazine, shown by the following listing form 1974/75:[39]

	Circulation
United States Edition	4,250,000
Asia Edition	190,000
Atlantic Edition	450,000
Canada Edition	510,000
Latin American Edition	115,000
South Pacific Edition	160,000

More impressive than even *Time* is the situation of the U.S. magazine with the world's largest circulation, *Reader's Digest*, which is also *the* international magazine. Sixteen years after its foundation, in 1938, the magazine started a special edition for England, followed by the first foreign language edition (Spanish) for Latin America in 1940. Two years later (1942) an edition in Portuguese was founded; in 1943 followed editions in Swedish and Arabic, and after World War II French, German and a couple of other editions were started. In 1958 *Reader's Digest* was published in 13 languages in 30 different editions for distribution in over 100 countries. It was published in various English editions for the United States, Great Britain, Canada, Australia, New Zealand, and other countries of the British Commonwealth. It was also published in different French-language editions for France, Belgium, Switzerland, and Canada. The remaining editions were in Spanish, Portuguese, Swedish, Finnish, Danish, Norwegian, German, Italian, Japanese, Dutch and Arabic. Even the German edition was circulated in 58 countries, the Italian in 86, the Spanish in 71, and even the small Dutch edition in 56 lands.

The total circulation of the *Reader's Digest* international editions, including a special Overseas Military Edition, in 1958 was 8.8 million copies per month. "Each of the foreign editions has in its title the words 'selections from' or 'the best from' the *Reader's Digest* or an equivalent phrase. Every article appearing in any of these editions has first appeared in a recent or past issue of the *Digest* in the United States; but not every article published in the parent magazine is republished abroad." [40] This flexibility in contents is one of the advantages and secrets of this magazine to stay in touch with a global audience. Wood says in this respect: The foreign editors "and their staffs are citizen and residents of the country where the given edition has its chief circulation. They know national characteristics, sentiment, interests, customs, circumstances . . . Translating is done with extreme care, not only to transfer the sense and spirit of the article accurately from one language to another, but also to render the whole in the usage peculiar to the countries where the edition will be read." [41]

In 1968 the *Reader's Digest* appeared in 13 languages and 30 different basic editions and 51 regional editions with a total circulation of more than 28 million copies per month, among this around 17 million for the United States. [42] See page 104 for an overview on the different titles of *Reader's Digest*. [43]

But the gigantic success of *Reader's Digest* has not been without any complaints, especially from Canadians: "Some publishers and members of the intelligentsia feared that the superior technical resources of American magazines and their wealth in a war-impoverished world could lead only to American cultural imperialism, and there were cries against 'Coca-Colonization' and the spread of 'a Reader's Digest culture.' Even at home there were instances of protest, as when Senator Joseph Guffey of Pennsylvania called the *Reader's Digest* a 'world cartel' and spoke of an antitrust suit, which, however, did not come about. The majority of foreign readers seemed to share little of his concern, for circulations of American magazines abroad continued to rise." [44]

PUBLICATION	LANGUAGE	BASIC EDITIONS	CIRC.
Reader's Digest	English	8	20,977,000
Sélection du Reader's Digest	French	4	1,405,000
Selecciones del Reader's Digest	Spanish	6	1,395,000
Seleçôes do Reader's Digest	Portuguese	1	350,000
Das Beste aus Reader's Digest	German	2	1,395,000
Het Beste uit Reader's Digest	Dutch/Flemish	2	380,000
Selezione dal Reader's Digest	Italian	1	675,000
Valitut Palat koonnut Reader's Digest	Finnish	1	165,000
Det Bedste fra Reader's Digest	Danish	1	175,000
Det Beste fra Reader's Digest	Norwegian	1	200,000
Det Bästa ur Reader's Digest	Swedish	1	355,000
リーダーズ ダイジェスト Reader's Digest	Japanese	1	500,000
讀者文摘 Reader's Digest	Chinese	1	150,000
13 Publications in 13 Languages		30	28,122,000

Besides the giants among the world's magazines in respect of their circulations there exists a small but rather influential group of elitist magazines with a certain orientation toward foreign affairs. Magazines like *Aussen-Politik* (Germany), *Chronique de Politique Etrangère* (Belgium), *Chronology of International Events* (Great Britain), *Estudos Políticos* (Spain), *International Politikk* (Norway), *Internationale Spectator* (The Netherlands), *Relazioni Internazionali* (Italy), *Foreign Affairs* (U.S.A.) or *Kommunist* (Soviet Union) and *Hung-chi* (Red Flag) (Red China) are—more or less—theoretical discussion organs.[45] Readers of these kinds of magazines can be found in elitist groups of many countries, although the circulations of these periodicals generally are rather small. This example also demonstrates very clearly why magazines are not always necessarily mass media in the common sense because of their very limited audience group.[46]

If the German term *Weltblatt* can be defined as the "internationally distributed daily press with a permanent world-wide resonance," [47] this brings up the question if there can be found a similar expression for stressing the international reputation of magazines. It is rather difficult to do this because even weeklies are sometimes regarded as newspapers by reason of their newspaper format. In reality, the weeklies are crosses between newspapers and magazines, and there are certain reasons to group them as magazines on account of the contents. John C. Merrill has separated them from the daily press without grouping them as newspapers or as magazines: "In addition to the elite daily papers," he writes, "it should be remembered that many excellent elite weekly papers exist in a number of countries (most of them in Europe) which reinforce the international concern and reasonableness of the elite dailies. No one should minimize the extremely high-type journalism of such papers as the London *Observer* and *Sunday Times*, the *National Observer* of the United States, *Weltwoche* of Zurich, *Embros* of Athens, *Le Canard Enchâiné* of Paris, *Die Zeit* of Hamburg, *Christ und Welt* of Stuttgart, *Rheinischer Merkur* of Cologne, *Jeune Afrique* of Tunis, and *The Nation* of Rangoon." [48]

In magazines we have in the world at large a much broader spectrum of varieties than is true in newspapers which are to a certain extent much more easily groupable. Roland E. Wolseley is quite right when he says that "the breadth of the magazine field is not always realized," [49] because some directories do not contain all groups. This general uncertainty as to how to define magazines broadly makes it difficult to give a useful typology of them. Wolseley presents some magazine typologies made by other authors. [50] His own opinion is that broadly magazines today fall into two groups: (1) The consumer or general interest, and (2) the specialized, and he breaks these groups into some 13 subdivisions. [51] A large variety of groups is given by a world guide to periodicals [52] and another catalogue divides the magazines into 21 groups, most of them containing several subdivisions. [53] If one looks at these typologies critically, he discovers that there are numerous overlappings in most of them—if they are given many subgroups. Because of the mistakes made by subordination, it seems to be useful to have only a few main groups, and so Wolseley's grouping is a good example. More than a decade ago Walter Hagemann tried to describe the phenomenon of magazines by the tripartite grouping as follows: [54]

1) *Trade magazines* which are helpful for the individuals by fulfilling of their professions.
2) *Class and Group magazines* which promote the integration process of the various social groups of society.
3) *Spare-time magazines* which help the readers from all of the different professions, classes and organizations to busy themselves in their leisure time.

Magazines from all of these three groups can be objects of international communication. Trade magazines of all kinds are often subscribed to by members of certain professions in a number of countries. Class and group magazines are read by sympathizers abroad. And sparetime magazines, which include as a subgroup the large number of entertainment periodicals, are also distributed across national borders.

Although there is not an exact number of the world's magazines available, one is able to determine some points for a general orientation. It can be estimated from UNESCO information that at least some 45,000 periodicals can be found in the world.[55] If one subtracts from this number around 7,000 daily newspapers found by a German research team,[56] there remains around 38,000 magazines of all kinds. It can be estimated that the great majority of the world's magazines belong to the first and second of Hagemann's groups, dealing with trade, class and group magazines. The third category possibly has a smaller number by titles, but the total circulation of these magazines seems to be higher than that of the other groups together.

Last but not least, the wide variety of magazines around the world can be well summarized by this UNESCO description of 1959: "A periodical other than a newspaper of general interest is a publication which appears under the same title at regular or irregular intervals, but more than once a year and over an indefinite period, and whose content varies widely, ranging from information of a general nature to specialized trade, technical and professional subjects."[57]

In the past years UNESCO seems to have discovered that it is not easy to handle with the two terms only: "newspaper" and "periodical." So in a recently published book UNESCO uses three types among press and it gives this definition:[58]

a) *"Daily newspapers* are defined as newspapers of general interest published at least four times a week; they may include printed or roneotyped bulletins".

b) *"Non-daily newspapers* are newspapers of general interest published three times a week or less; Sunday or week-end editions of daily newspapers are included in this category".

c) *"Periodicals* are publications of general issue, other than general interest newspapers, containing either general or specialized information; weekly news magazines are included in this category".

It's easy to find out that there is still a certain danger of overlapping between these three not too well separated from each other categories. So UNESCO itself could not solve all the problems by completing a press statistics according to its three categories. Since the categories two and three are quite unclear UNESCO for most of the countries of the world did only give complete informations on category two, although this contains a great lot of what we could call "magazines". In any case it might be of interest to present here a complete listing of the press situation in around 200 countries resp. territories of the world:[59]

Country	Population	Area Sp. km	The Press					
			Dailies			Non-dailies		
			total number	total circulation	copies per 1 000 people	total number	total circulation	copies per 1 000 people
Afghanistan	17 480 000	647 497	18	101 000	6	2	7 500	0 4
Albania	2 230 000	28 748	2	130 000	58	10	140 000	63
Algeria	15 270 000	2 381 741	4	275 000	18	8	160 000	10
American Samoa	29 000	197	1	3 000	103	2	7 500	259
Andorra	20 000	453	-	-	-	1	5 000	-
Angola	5 430 000	1 246 700	4	66 000	12	15	-	-
Antigua	60 000	442	-	-	-	1	4 000	66
Argentia	23 552 000	2 776 889	180	4 250 000	180	63	-	-
Australia	12 552 000	7 686 810	58	4 028 000	321	502	-	-
Austria	7 490 000	83 849	31	2 460 000	328	125	-	-
Bahama Islands	190 000	11 405	3	30 000	158	5	50 000	262
Bahrain	220 000	598	-	-	-	3	4 500	29
Bangladesh	60 670 000	142 776	25	-	-	-	-	-
Barbados	240 000	430	1	24 000	100	2	17 000	71
Belgium	9 726 000	30 513	55	2 450 000	-	107	-	-
Belize	124 000	22 965	1	3 000	24	4	11 500	93
Bermuda	54 000	53	1	13 600	252	3	29 000	537
Bhutan	854 000	47 000	-	-	-	3	1 620	2
Bolivia	5 190 000	1 098 581	16	169 000	33	13	-	-
Botswana	690 000	600 372	2	13 500	20	2	9 000	13
Brazil	98 850 000	8 511 965	261	3 498 000	35	730	-	-
British Solomon Islands	170 000	29 785	-	-	-	5	6 400	38
Brunei	140 000	5 765	-	-	-	3	30 500	218
Bulgaria	8 580 000	110 912	13	1 765 000	206	33	919 700	107
Burma	27 584 000	687 033	8	230 000	8	133	1 285 680	47
Burundi	3 620 000	27 834	1	300	0 08	3	47 000	13
Cameroon	5 840 000	475 442	2	17 000	3	4	19 000	3
Canada	21 850 000	9 976 139	121	5 117 700	234	1 031	5 800 000	265
Canal Zone	45 000	1 432	-	-	-	-	-	-
Cape Verde Islands	246 000	4 033	-	-	-	2	-	-
Cayman Islands	10 000	259	-	-	-	1	3 750	375
Central African Republic	1 640 000	622 984	1	500	0 3	-	-	-
Chad	3 800 000	1 284 000	1	-	-	6	9 000	-
Chile	8 992 000	756 945	46	-	-	-	-	-
China (People's Republic. of)	787 180 000	9 561 000	(1 908)	-	-	-	-	-
Columbia	22 490 000	1 138 914	36	2 369 400	105	16	218 000	10
Comoro Islands	271 000	2 171	-	-	-	3	1 100	-
Congo (People's Republic of)	980 000	342 000	3	ca. 50 000	-	12	12 000	12
Cook Islands	25 000	234	1	750	30	21	21 000	-
Costa Rica	1 840 000	50 700	5	130 000	71	7	-	-
Cuba	8 660 000	114 524	16	924 500	107	-	-	-
Cyprus	650 000	9 251	12	80 000	123	21	137 000	211
Czechoslovakia	14 500 000	127 869	27	4 059 100	280	105	852 000	59

Country	Population	Area Sp. km	The Press Dailies			Non-dailies		
			total number	total circulation	copies per 1 000 people	total number	total circulation	copies per 1 000 people
Dahomey	2 760 000	112 622	1	1 500	0 5	2	1 700	0 6
Denmark	4 966 000	43 069	53	1 808 000	364	-	-	-
Dominica	72 000	751	-	-	-	3	6 500	90
Dominican Republic	4 300 000	48 734	5	150 000	35	30	-	-
Ecuador	6 510 000	238 561	22	283 300	43	17	19 200	3
Egypt (Arab Republic of)	34 840 000	1 001 449	14	712 231	20	20	703 661	20
El Salvador	3 534 000	21 393	12	267 000	76	12	-	-
Equatorial Guinea	290 000	28 051	1	1 000	1	1	-	-
Ethiopia	25 250 000	1 221 900	3	39 000	2	2	-	-
Faeroe Islands	41 000	1 399	-	-	-	7	20 000	488
Falkland Islands	2 000	11 961	-	-	-	2	1 400	700
Fiji	540 000	18 272	1	16 000	30	8	-	-
Finland	4 630 000	337 009	60	1 970 000	425	173	-	-
France	51 720 000	547 026	106	12 066 800	233	934	26 429 400	511
French Guiana	51 000	91 000	1	2 000	39	2	2 000	39
French Polynesia	121 000	4 000	4	-	-	-	-	-
French Territory of the Afars and the Issas	97 000	22 000	-	-	-	1	2 300	24
Gabon	500 000	267 667	1	700	1	1	5 000	10
Gambia	375 000	11 295	-	-	-	11	7 500	20
German Democratic Republic	17 040 000	107 771	40	7 235 710	425	612	1 970 000	116
Germany (Federal Republic of) and West Berlin	59 600 000	247 973	1 093	19 701 000	330	93	4 918 000	82
Ghana	8 858 000	283 537	3	270 000	30	39	680 000	77
Gibraltar	27 000	6	2	6 100	226	2	4 200	155
Gilbert and Ellice Islands	57 000	886	-	-	-	3	2 800	49
Greece	8 957 000	131 944	104	-	-	557	-	-
Greenland	50 000	2 175 600	-	-	-	22	-	-
Grenada	96 000	344	1	3 000	31	1	10 000	10
Guadeloupe	332 000	1 779	1	4 500	14	-	-	-
Guam	100 000	549	2	17 000	170	7	-	-
Guatemala	5 350 000	108 889	8	143 000	27	38	-	-
Guinea	4 010 000	245 857	1	5 000	1	1	-	-
Guyana	784 000	214 969	4	82 000	104	6	29 000	37
Haiti	5 070 000	27 750	6	35 000	7	6	8 000	2
Holy See	1 000	0 44	1	30 000	-	7	75 000	-
Honduras	2 582 000	112 088	8	114 000	44	95	-	-
Hong Kong	4 089 000	1 034	81	1 500 000	367	36	-	-
Hungary	10 400 000	93 030	27	2 250 670	216	80	4 278 920	411
Iceland	214 000	103 000	5	94 000	439	49	-	-
India	563 490 000	3 268 090	821	9 096 000	-	4 102	5 771 000	-
Indonesia	121 198 000	1 904 345	120	1 200 000	10	-	-	-
Iran	30 480 000	1 648 000	39	750 000	25	78	150 000	5
Iraq	10 070 000	434 924	7	-	-	15	-	. -
Ireland	3 010 000	70 283	7	702 477	233	50	1 420 761	472

Country	Population	Area Sp. km	Dailies total number	Dailies total circulation	Dailies copies per 1 000 people	Non-dailies total number	Non-dailies total circulation	Non-dailies copies per 1 000 people
Israel	2 998 000	20 700	24	550 000	183	101	-	-
Italy	54 350 000	301 225	78	7 700 000	142	119	-	-
Ivory Coast	4 420 000	322 463	2	26 000	6	2	38 000	9
Jamaica	1 900 000	10 962	2	130 759	69	14	363 500	191
Japan	105 611 000	372 077	172	55 845 000	539	800	-	-
Jordan	2 470 000	97 740	4	58 000	23	7	48 000	19
Kenya	12 070 000	582 644	3	119 000	10	12	-	-
Khmer Republic	6 701 000	181 035	3	-	-	-	-	-
Korea (Democratic People's Republic of)	14 281 000	120 538	6	-	-	30	-	-
Korea (Republic of)	31 920 000	98 477	42	4 400 000	138	105	2 764 000	86
Kuwait	910 000	16 000	6	40 000	44	11	50 000	55
Laos	110 000	236 800	6	8 000	2	-	-	-
Lebanon	2 873 000	10 400	52	-	-	46	-	-
Lesotho	950 000	30 355	-	-	-	2	-	-
Liberia	1 571 000	111 370	1	7 000	5	4	7 100	5
Libyan Arab Republic	2 080 000	1 759 540	7	35 000	17	10	50 000	24
Liechtenstein	21 000	157	1	5 516	263	2	6 850	326
Luxembourg	350 000	2 586	6	158 000	451	1	-	-
Macau	321 000	16	6	-	-	-	-	-
Madagascar	6 750 000	587 041	13	103 300	15	19	111 500	17
Malawi	4 670 000	118 484	-	-	-	3	23 000	5
Malaysia (Federation of)	12 324 000	332 633	40	950 000	77	20	216 000	17
Maldives	110 000	298	1	155	1	-	-	-
Mali	5 260 000	1 240 000	2	3 350	0 6	-	-	-
Malta	325 000	316	6	-	-	4	-	-
Martinique	341 000	1 102	2	28 000	82	8	-	-
Mauritania	1 200 000	1 030 700	1	300	0 2	2	-	-
Mauritius and Dependencies	836 000	2 045	12	14 500	17	14	6 000	7
Mexico	52 640 000	1 972 546	200	-	-	288	-	-
Monaco	24 000	1	-	-	-	2	-	-
Mongolia	1 283 000	1 565 000	1	100 000	78	30	-	-
Montserrat	12 000	98	-	-	-	1	-	-
Morocco	15 830 000	446 550	6	-	-	52	251 000	16
Mozambique	7 376 000	783 030	6	60 000	8	7	-	-
Namibia	574 000	824 292	3	7 500	13	2	-	-
Nauru	7 000	21	1	950	136	-	-	-
Nepal	11 470 000	140 797	30	39 000	3	41	4 400	0 3
Netherlands	13 330 000	40 844	95	4 100 000	307	138	1 055 061	79
Netherlands Antilles	230 000	961	5	33 000	143	7	19 000	83
New Caledonia	107 000	19 000	1	7 000	65	10	7 500	70
New Hebrides	84 000	14 763	-	-	-	5	5 700	68
New Zealand	2 910 000	268 675	40	1 067 000	367	103	-	-
Nicaragua	1 990 000	130 000	4	76 600	38	-	-	-
Niger	4 210 000	1 267 000	1	2 000	0 5	1	2 000	0 5

Country	Population	Area Sp. km	The Press					
			Dailies			Non-dailies		
			total number	total circulation	copies per 1 000 people	total number	total circulation	copies per 1 000 people
Nigeria	55 074 000	923 768	11	ca.200 000	–	ca. 15	–	–
Niue	5 000	259	–	–	–	1	800	160
Norfolk Island	2 000	36	–	–	–	1	850	426
Norway	3 940 000	324 219	79	1 541 000	391	80	327 000	83
Oman	680 000	212 457	–	–	–	1	–	–
Pacific Islands	107 000	1 779	–	–	–	6	4 400	41
Pakistan	56 040 000	801 408	98	–	–	436	–	–
Panama	1 520 000	75 650	7	130 000	86	11	–	–
Papua New Guinea	2 481 000	461 691	1	14 000	6	1	4 500	2
Paraguay	2 470 000	406 752	4	75 000	30	–	–	–
Peru	14 460 000	1 285 216	56	–	–	320	–	–
Philippines	39 040 000	300 000	19	650 000	17	143	1 028 735	26
Poland	32 749 000	312 677	44	7 553 000	231	42	1 896 000	58
Portugal	9 630 000	92 082	33	–	–	645	2 361 000	245
Portuguese Guinea	563 000	36 125	1	500	1	1	500	1
Portuguese Timor	614 000	14 925	–	–	–	2	–	–
Puerto Rico	2 757 000	8 897	3	246 000	89	10	–	–
Qatar	81 000	22 014	–	–	–	2	1 500	18
Reunion	470 000	2 510	2	28 000	60	11	63 000	134
Rhodesia	5 690 000	389 361	4	83 000	15	10	–	–
Romania	20 470 000	237 500	57	3 537 877	173	19	661 733	32
Rwanda	3 828 000	26 338	–	–	–	1	8 000	2
San Marino	19 000	61	–	–	–	5	6 000	316
St Helena and Dependencies	5 000	314	–	–	–	2	1 800	360
St Kitts-Nevis and Anguilla	62 000	357	1	1 200	19	2	–	–
St Lucia	103 000	616	–	–	–	3	–	–
St Pierre and Miquelon	5 000	242	–	–	–	1	–	–
St Vincent	90 000	388	–	–	–	1	15 000	167
Saô Tomé and Principe	70 000	964	–	–	–	2	–	–
Saudi Arabia	7 965 000	2 149 690	5	55 000	7	5	38 000	5
Senegal	4 022 000	196 192	1	20 000	5	4	40 000	10
Seychelles	53 000	376	2	2 550	48	3	2 675	50
Sierra Leone	2 600 000	71 740	2	15 000	6	13	ca. 20 000	–
Sikkim	200 000	7 107	–	–	–	1	–	–
Singapore	2 150 000	581	10	414 696	193	11	400 000	186
Somalia	2 940 000	637 657	1	4 450	2	2	2 500	0 8
South Africa (Republic of)	22 990 000	1 221 037	21	1 075 000	47	130	–	–
Spain	34 360 000	504 750	115	3 396 000	99	121	3 851 000	112
Spanish Sahara	50 000	266 000	–	–	–	1	3 000	60
Sri Lanka	12 760 000	65 610	17	612 000	48	17	1 058 000	83
Sudan	16 490 000	2 505 813	4	–	–	12	–	–
Surinam	406 000	163 265	3	20 000	49	2	2 000	5
Swaziland	430 000	17 363	–	–	–	2	–	–

Country	Population	Area Sp. km	The Press Dailies			The Press Non-dailies		
			total number	total circulation	copies per 1 000 people	total number	total circulation	copies per 1 000 people
Sweden	8 120 000	449 750	108	4 183 500	515	53	367 400	45
Switzerland	6 320 000	41 288	98	2 466 414	390	173	900 000	142
Syria	6 660 000	185 180	5	60 000	9	12	-	-
Tanzania	14 000 000	939 703	7	61 000	4	23	213 000	15
Thailand	35 335 000	514 000	35	849 999	24	32	250 000	7
Togo	2 022 000	56 000	3	13 000	6	4	-	-
Tokelau Islands	2 000	10	-	-	-	-	-	-
Tonga	90 000	699	-	-	-	2	3 800	42
Trinidad and Tobago	1 040 000	5 128	3	145 000	139	7	-	-
Tunisia	5 137 000	164 150	4	107 000	21	7	59 000	11
Turkey	37 010 000	780 756	432	-	-	661	-	-
Turks and Caicos Islands	6 000	430	-	-	-	1	1 600	267
Uganda	10 460 000	236 036	7	90 000	9	26	133 000	13
Union of Soviet Socialist Republics	245 090 000	22 402 200	639	81 633 000	333	8 055	59 083 000	241
United Arab Emirates	200 000	83 600	-	-	-	2	-	-
United Kingdom	55 790 000	244 044	109	24 356 000	437	1 163	37 459 000	671
United States of America	208 840 000	9 363 353	1 761	65 510 000	314	10 100	79 834 000	382
Upper Volta	5 491 000	274 200	1	2 000	0 3	3	6 000	1
Uruguay	2 960 000	177 508	29	795 000	269	-	-	-
Venezuela	10 970 000	912 050	42	997 660	91	21	-	-
Vietnam (Democratic Republic of)	21 154 000	158 750	50	-	-	-	-	-
Vietnam (Republic of)	18 810 000	173 809	56	95 000	5	32	250 000	-
Virgin Islands (UK)	11 000	153	-	-	-	1	2 000	182
Virgin Islands (USA)	65 000	344	3	14 000	215	2	11 300	174
Western Samoa	143 000	2 842	-	-	-	3	50 000	350
Yemen (Arab Republic of)	6 060 000	195 000	3	-	-	1	-	-
Yemen (People's Democratic Republic of)	1 510 000	287 683	4	29 000	19	5	-	-
Yugoslavia	20 770 000	255 804	25	1 853 000	89	1 493	6 630 000	319
Zaire	22 480 000	2 345 409	6	-	-	12	-	-
Zambia	4 520 000	752 614	2	60 000	13	13	150 000	33

With these statistics one only gets a certain impression of the structure of the daily and periodical non-daily press. The difficulties of giving an exact typology of the sub-categories of the magazine press were already described by Merrill et al. in 1970: "The international publication pattern runs on through the periodical spectrum into the purely entertainment magazines, confessions, hobbies, comics, offbeat 'art' journals, and romance and adventure journals. Thus the world reader in most every country has a wide assortment of periodicals to choose from if he desires to supplement his newspaper reading." [60] Because of language barriers, political and ideological frontiers etc. only a rather small number of periodicals can be declared as *international magazines*. But already it does not happen too often that editors and publishers call their magazine an internationally read periodical if only one or very few copies are distributed to other countries.

One has no reliable information about the fluctuation on the magazine market in the different countries, but in general one thing can be stated as UNESCO also found out: "Regarded statistically over the past ten years, the press in most countries seems just to be holding its position; in some, there are now more newspapers and/or more readers; in others, there is no progress. . . . However, it should be noted that many countries have considerable numbers of newspapers appearing once or several times a week, and even larger numbers of periodicals—both general and specialized—which may have quite sizable readerships. Perhaps the main role of the press will come to be one of analysis and in-depth coverage of the news events which radio and television can now report almost instantaneously. . . . Newspapers, like periodicals and books, have become increasingly expensive to produce (and hence to buy) because of rises in production and, especially, newsprint costs and the loss of advertising revenue to other media. . . ".[61]

NOTES

[1] Cf. Felix Stieve, *Über die ältesten halbjährigen Zeitungen oder Messerelationen und insbesondere über deren Begründer Freiherrn Michael von Aitzing*, Munich: Bayer. Akademie der Wissensch., 1881.

[2] Cf. Hermann Bingel, *Das Theatrum Europaeum, ein Beitrag zur Publizistik des 17. und 18. Jahrhunderts*, Ph.D. dissertation, University of Munich 1909, Berlin: Ebering, 1909.

[3] Wilmont Haacke, *Die Zeitschrift—Schrift der Zeit*, Essen/Germany: Stamm-Verlag, 1961, p. 257.

[4] Cf. Alfred Jericke, *Johann Rists Monatsgespräche*, Ph.D. dissertation University of Leipzig, 1923, Berlin—Leipzig: de Gruyter, 1928.

[5] Roland E. Wolseley, *Understanding Magazines* (2nd ed.), Ames/Iowa: The Iowa State University Press, 1966, p. 24.

[6] Cf. Betty Trebelle Morgan, *Histoire du Journal des Sçavans. Depuis 1665 jusqu'en 1701*, Paris: La Presse Universitaires de France, 1929.

[7] Joachim Kirchner, *Das Deutsche Zeitschriftenwesen. Seine Geschichte und seine Probleme*, Vol. 1, 2nd ed., Wiesbaden/Germany: Otto Harrassowitz, 1958, p. 16 ff.

[8] Roland E. Wolseley. *Understanding Magazines*, p. 24.

[9] Cf. Günter Graf, *Der Spectator von Addison und Steele als publizistische Erscheinung*, Unpublished Ph.D. dissertation, University of Münster/Germany, 1952.

[10] Cf. Frank Luther Mott, *A History of American Magazines, 1741–1850*, Cambridge, Massachusetts: The Belknap Press of Harvard University Press, 1957.

[11] Fred S(eaton) Siebert, "The Authoritarian Theory of the Press" in: Fred S. Siebert, Theodore Peterson, and Wilbur Schramm, *Four Theories of the Press*, Urbana, Illinois: University of Illinois Press, 1963, p. 9.

[12] Frank Luther Mott, *A History of American Magazines, 1741–1850*, pp. 5 ff.

[13] Cf. Hansjürgen Koschwitz, "Der früheste Beleg für das Wort 'Zeitschrift,' " in: *Publizistik* (Konstanz/Germany), Vol. 13/No. 1 (January–March 1968), pp. 41 ff.

[14] Frank Luther Mott, *A History of American Magazines, 1741–1850*, pp. 6 ff.

[15] *Ibid.*, p. 7.

[16] *Ibid.*, p. 9.

[17] G. L. Nesbitt, *Benthamite Reviewing. The First Twelve Years of the Westminster Review, 1824–1836*, New York: Columbia Univ. Press, 1935.

[18] Cf. Hermann Anders, *Die Wiener literarischen Zeitschriften von 1800–1815 und ihre Auseinandersetzung mit der deutschen Klassik und Romantik*, Ph.D. dissertation, University of Vienna, 1930.

[19] Cf. Else von Eck, *Die Literaturkritik in den Hallischen und Deutschen Jahrbüchern, 1838–42*, Berlin: Ebering, 1926.

[20] Cf. Theodor Schieder (ed.), *Hundert Jahre Historische Zeitschrift, 1859–1959*, Munich: R. Oldenbourg, 1959.

[21] Cf. Wilmont Haacke, *Julius Rodenberg und die Deutsche Rundschau*, Heidelberg: Kurt Vowinckel, 1950.

[22] F(rank) L(uther) M(ot)t, "Periodicals—United States," in: *Encyclopaedia Britannica*, 15th ed., Vol. 17. Chicago—London—Toronto: Encyclopaedia Britannica, Ltd., 1956, p. 516.

[23] Cf. Wilmont Haacke, *Die politische Zeitschrift, 1665–1965*, Stuttgart/Germany: K. F. Koehler Verlag, 1968.

[24] C.T.H.W. and F.L.K., "Periodicals" in: *Encyclopaedia Britannica, op. cit.*, pp. 512 ff.

[25] James W. Markham, *Voices of the Red Giants: Communications in Russia and China*, Ames, Iowa: The Iowa State University Press, 1967, p. 229.

[26] Cf. J. Bainbridge, *Little Wonder: or the Reader's Digest and How it Grew*, New York: Reynal and Hitchcock, 1946.

[27] Cf. Uwe Magnus, *Time und Newsweek: Darstellung und Analyse*, Hannover: Verlag für Literatur und Zeitgeschehen, 1967.

[28] William H(oward) Taft, *American Journalism History: An Outline*, Columbia, Mo.—Los Angeles: Lucas Brothers Publishers, 1968, p. 59.

[29] Cf. Alf Enseling, *Die Weltbühne—Organ der intellektuellen Linken*, Münster/Germany: Verlag C. J. Fahle, 1962.

[30] F(rank) L(uther) M(ot)t, "Periodicals—United States," *op. cit.*, p. 517.

[31] Foundation figures from: Karl-Marx-Universität (ed.), *Die sowjetische Presse in Dokumenten*, Leipzig: Fakultät für Journalistik, 1963, p. 531.

[32] James W. Markham, *Voices of the Red Giants*, p. 225.

[33] Cf. Carin Kessemeier, *Der Leitartikler Goebbels in den NS-Organen 'Der Angriff' und 'Das Reich*,' Münster/Germany: Verlag C. J. Fahle, 1967.

[34] Cf. Sherilyn C. Bennion, "Mass Magazine Phenomenon: the German 'Illustrierte,' " in: *Journalism Quarterly* (Iowa City, Iowa), Vol. 38/No. 3 (Summer 1961), pp. 360–362.

[35] John C. Merrill, Carter R. Bryam and Marvin Alisky, *The Foreign Press, A Survey of the World's Journalism*, 2nd ed., Baton Rouge, Louisiana: Louisiana State University Press, 1970, p. 12.

[36] Cf. Dieter Just, *Der Spiegel: Arbeitsweise, Inhalt, Wirrung*, Hannover/Germany: Verlag für Literatur und Zeitgeschehen, 1967.

[37] Cf. Uwe Magnus, "L'Express als publizistische Opposition in der V. Republik," in: *Publizistik* (Bremen), Vol. 10/No. 4 (1965), pp. 534 ff.

[38] Circulations from: Willy Stamm, *Leitfaden für Presse und Werbung 1975*, Essen, Germany: Stamm-Verlag, 1975.

[39] Willy Stamm, *Leitfaden für Presse und Werbung*, 27th and 28th ed., Essen, Germany: Stamm-Verlag, 1974, p. 5/175; 1975, p. 5/158.

[40] James Playsted Wood, *Of Lasting Interest: The Story of The Reader's Digest*, Garden City, New York: Doubleday & Company, Inc., 1958, pp. 169 ff.

[41] *Ibid.*, p. 173 ff.

[42] Verlag Das Beste (ed.), *Die Geschichte des "Reader's Digest,"* Stuttgart/Germany: Verlag Das Beste GmbH., 1968, p. 7.

[43] Compiled from: *Reader's Digest International Editions Advertising Rates 1969* and: Verlag Das Beste (ed.), *Die Internationalen Ausgaben von Reader's Digest. Anzeigenpreisliste 1969*, Düsseldorf, Germany: Verlag Das Beste GmbH., Anzeigendirektion, 1969. Cf. also: *World-Wide Circulation of Reader's Digest (based on single issue sales)*, 1968.

[44] Theodore Peterson, *Magazines in the Twentieth Century*, Urbana, Illinois: University of Illinois Press, 1964, p. 111.

[45] Cf. Golo Mann and Harry Pross, *Aussenpolitik*, Frankfurt/Main: Fischer Bücherei KG, 1958, p. 350. See also: James W. Markham, *Voices of the Red Giants*, pp. 225 and 397.

[46] Cf. Henk Prakke et al., *Kommunikation der Gesellschaft. Einführung in die funktionale Publizistik*, Münster, Germany: Verlag Regensberg, 1968, p. 84.

[47] Heinz-Dietrich Fischer, "Weltblatt—Weltpresse," in: Kurt Koszyk and Karl Hugo Pruys (eds.),

dtv-Wörterbuch zur Publizistik, 3rd ed., Munich: Deutscher Taschenbuch Verlag, 1973, p. 379.

[48] John C(alhoun) Merrill, *The Elite Press: Great Newspapers of the World*, New York—Toronto—London: Pitman Publishing Corporation, 1968, p. 53.

[49] Roland E. Wolseley, *Understanding Magazines*, p. 7.

[50] *Ibid.*, pp. 8 ff.

[51] *Ibid.*, pp. 9 ff.

[52] Cf. Karl-Otto Saur, *Internationale Bibliographie der Fachzeitschriften. World Guide to Periodicals*, 3 Vols., 5th ed. Munich: Verlag Dokumentation, 1967.

[53] Cf. Willv Stamm, *Leitfaden für Presse und Werbung 1969*, pp. 3/1 ff.

[54] Walter Hagemann, *Die Deutsche Zeitschrift der Gegenwart*, Münster, Germany: Verlag C. J. Fahle Gembh, 1957, p. 9; cf. also the discussions of Heinz-Dietrich Fischer, "Die Zeitschrift im Kommunikationssystem", in: H.-D. Fischer (ed.):*Deutsche Zeitschriften des 17. bis 20. Jahrhunderts*, Munich: Verlag Dokumentation, 1973, pp. 11–27.

[55] See John C. Merrill, Carter R. Bryan and Marvin Alisky, *The Foreign Press*, 1st ed., Baton Rouge, Louisiana: Louisiana State University Press, 1964, p. 6.

[56] Cf. Henk Prakke et al. (eds.), *Handbuch der Weltpresse*, (2 Vols.), Cologne-Opladen: Westdeutscher Verlag, 1970.

[57] UNESCO, *Statistics of Newspapers and Other Periodicals*, Paris: UNESCO, 1959, p. 15.

[58] UNESCO, *World Communications*. A 200-country survey of press, radio, television and film, Paris—Epping (England)—New York: Unesco Press, Gower Press Ltd., Unipub, 1975, p. VIII.

[59] Compiled by the author of this article from *ibid.*, pp. 37–507.

[60] John C. Merrill, Carter R. Bryan, and Marvin Alisky, *The Foreign Press*, 2nd ed., p. 13.

[61] UNESCO, *World Communication*, 5th ed., p. 3.

UNESCO:

Film as a Universal Mass Medium

THE WORLD FILM PATTERN in the seventies is markedly different from the pattern for the other media. Some 50 countries are regularly producing feature-length entertainment films (in all, around 4000 a year) and the rest of the world depends on them for supply. Eight countries in Africa have recently produced their first feature-length films. Other countries are regularly producing documentary and educational films only. In all countries except those of Eastern Europe, the USSR, Cuba, the People's Republic of China and the Democratic People's Republic of Korea, film production, distribution and exhibition are run by private commercial enterprises. In a dozen or so countries (nine in Western Europe), the State, for cultural and economic reasons, gives financial and other concrete assistance to private commercial production.

The two largest producing countries, each making around 400 feature films a year, are Asian—India and Japan (in 1965, Japan produced nearly 900 and was by far the largest producer ever of feature films). Four Asian countries (the Republic of Korea, the Democratic People's Republic of Korea, the Philippines and Hong Kong) produce between 100 and 200, three others more than 50, and seven from 5 to 30 each. No figures are available for the People's Republic of China later than 1964 when the number of feature films produced was reported to have been well over 400. Asian feature films are produced essentially for domestic exhibition; most Asian countries have large numbers of cinemas and high cinema attendances, although attendances, as in almost all countries in the world, are small in relation to the total population and are predominantly urban. Only a small number of films produced in Asia reach audiences outside the continent—these are shown in Europe and North America, usually in a limited number of cinemas specializing in foreign films.

The three largest feature-film producing countries outside Asia, producing between 200 and 300 films a year, are Italy, the USA and the USSR; in the USA production which had dropped from 400 to 140 in 1961 had risen to 280 in 1971. Next in output, producing between 100 and 200, come France, the Federal Republic of Germany, Greece, Spain and Turkey in Europe and, in

▶ From: UNESCO, *World Communications. A 200-country survey of press, radio, television and film.* Paris: Unesco Press and Epping, England: Gower Press, 1975, pp. 32–34. Reprinted by permission of Unesco and Gower Press Ltd. The statistics at the end of the article are compiled from the same source (pp. 37–507) by Mrs. Ingrid Dickhut, Ruhr-University Bochum (Federal Republic of Germany).

Central America, Mexico. Then come the UK (90), Egypt (60), Brazil (50) and Czechoslovakia (50). Besides the countries in Asia already referred to, 12 countries including Argentina produce between 10 and 30, while another ten, including two Spanish-speaking countries, produce around 5. Half of the 28 countries producing less than 30 films have languages peculiar to themselves, which means that, except for occasional outstanding ones, their films are rarely shown in other countries.

In all, 17 Asian countries produce more than half the world's feature-length entertainment films. Twenty-four European countries and the USSR produce about a third. The rest are produced by ten countries, notably the USA, Mexico, Egypt and Brazil.

The world distribution pattern is largely determined by language (and has been since the coming of sound). Dubbing or subtitling is expensive and is now obligatory in a number of countries for films which are widely released. Cultural affinities, as well as political and commerical ties, also affect the pattern. Thus, Chinese-language films are distributed in many Asian countries which have large Chinese populations, but other Asian-language films are largely confined to their country of origin. American films are the most widely distributed foreign films in most Asian countries. Indeed, English-language films, and predominantly those of American origin, occupy a very large part of screen time in almost all countries except the USSR, the countries of Eastern Europe, the People's Republic of China, India and a few others. The distribution of the great majority of Russian-language films is limited to the USSR and other countries with similar economic, social and cultural systems. The USSR imports around 100 films a year from a wide range of countries. The 20 or so Spanish-language countries receive Spanish-language films from the three countries regularly producing them—Mexico, Spain and Argentina. Arabic-speaking countries are almost entirely dependent on Egypt, although in the coming years Algeria, Morocco and Tunisia, together with Lebanon, may increase the supply. The Spanish- and Arabic-speaking countries, because of Latin cultural affinities and other ties and contacts, import a number of French and Italian films. Similar considerations of language and colonial history affect the import of films in the different countries of Africa. The USA imports films from many countries, notably the UK, France, and Italy, but often only for distribution to the increasing number of small, specialized cinemas. To enhance the possibilities of wider international distribution and hence to offset costs, and occasionally for artistic reasons also, producers in several larger film-making countries are increasingly resorting to coproduction with enterprises in other countries; the major coproducers, in some cases to the extent of almost half their total production, are France, Italy, Spain and the UK, particularly with the USA.

The vast majority of feature-length films produced in almost all countries are dramatized fictional films designed for showing in public cinemas where people pay to be entertained. Other kinds of films—newsreels, documentaries, and even short entertainment films such as animated cartoons—have almost disappeared from the public screens in most countries. But thousands of documentary and educational films are produced every year, not only in countries where feature films are produced but in many others as well. They are produced for television or for showing in schools and other educational institutions. In many countries where there is commercial feature-film production by private enterprise, and also in some countries where there is none, there are government film services and autonomous public film boards producing and distributing such films and even exhibiting them by means of mobile units in schools, community halls, libraries, museums, etc. These films are seen by tens of thousands of small audiences of schoolchildren and students of all kinds, industrial workers and farmers, scientists, doctors and other professional workers and by general community audiences seeking information and instruction. Many of the films are diffused by television organizations during hours devoted to educational programmes. It seems likely that it will be via television in different forms rather than by means of film projectors installed in schools, etc. that the use of films for educational and instructional purposes will be extended and developed to its full potential. Exchanges and coproduction of educational films are developing. In these various ways, the film continues to be used deliberately to spread information, education and culture and to promote understanding between peoples. Films made to entertain people will continue to have powerful influences on how they think and feel, and on their knowledge of and attitudes towards other peoples.

The number of cinemas, cinema seats and annual cinema attendances in Asia are increasing whereas in most of the rest of the world they now seem to be more or less stable at much lower figures than ten years ago. Even so, in seven Western European countries, the number of cinemas ranges from 1000 in Greece to over 10,000 in Italy, and in five Eastern European countries from 2800 in Poland to over 6000 in Romania. In the USSR, the number of cinemas and halls in which films are regularly shown has increased by 50% to 147,000, and attendances by 30%.

It may be of some additional interest to give here a complete statistical overview on the international situation of films and cinemas around the world (as of 1975):

Country	Cinemas (fixed)	Total seating capacity	Seats per 1 000 people	Country	Cinemas (fixed)	Total seating capacity	Seats per 1 000 people
Afghanistan	24	12 000	0.6	Dahomey	6	9 000	3
Albania	93	23 700	11	Denmark	350	138 200	28
Algeria	640	218 758	14	Dominica	3	1 500	21
American Samoa	5	1 800	62	Dominican Republic	73	43 000	10
Andorra	7	2 900	145	Ecuador	164	114 600	18
Angola	35	28 000	5	Egypt (Arab Republic of)	246*	219 626	6
Antigua	2	1 700	28	El Salvador	57	57 000	16
Argentia	1 637	733 100	31	Equatorial Guinea	11	6 300	22
Australia	1 100*	800 000*	64	Ethiopia	30	26 138	1
Austria	835	276 500	37	Faeroe Islands	9	1 292	31
Bahama Islands	5	4 100	22	Falkland Islands	2	500	250
Bahrain	9	9 845	45	Fiji	35	17 470	32
Bangladesh	-	-	-	Finland	318	97 000	21
Barbados	6	4 700	20	France	4 237	2 012 017	39
Belgium	740	400 000	41	French Guiana	9	3 400	66
Belize	8	4 500	36	French Polynesia	10	4 000	33
Bermuda	4	2 215	41	French Territory of the Afars and the Issas	8	6 700	69
Bhutan	3	1 500	2	Gabon	2	1 700	3
Bolivia	120*	66 000	13	Gambia	15	-	-
Botswana	11	3 000	4	German Democratic Republic	1 197	354 964	21
Brazil	3 194	1 911 200	19	Germany (Fed.Rep.of) and West Berlin	3 171	1 279 861	21
British Solomon Islands	1	600	3	Ghana	13	14 400	2
Brunei	8	8 390	60	Gibraltar	3	2 394	89
Bulgaria	3 106	707 100	82	Gilbert and Ellice Islands	2	1 600	28
Burma	452	364 800	13	Greece	1 034	135 300 000	-
Burundi	2	600	0.17	Greenland	47	7 000	140
Cameroon	38	20 000	3	Grenada	3	3 000	31
Canada	1 156	665 996	30	Guadeloupe	20	-	-
Canal Zone	9	4 800	107	Guam	25	8 500	85
Cape Verde Islands	6	2 700	11	Guatemala	105	75 400	14
Cayman Islands	7*	-	-	Guinea	28	10 000	2
Central African Republic	8	2 000	1	Guyana	50	375 000	48
Chad	9	6 000	2	Haiti	20	12 300	2
Chile	360	245 749	27	Holy See	-	-	-
China (People's Republic of)	-	-	-	Honduras	60*	-	-
Columbia	378	291 757	13	Hong Kong	97	118 355	29
Comoro Islands	4	1 300	5	Hungary	3 755	595 239	57
Congo (People's Republic of)	24	6 500	7	Iceland	25	9 541	44
Cook Islands	12	5 000	200	India	4 716	3 066 000	5
Costa Rica	132	-	-	Indonesia	490	-	-
Cuba	428	-	-	Iran	437	282 000	9
Cyprus	150	88 000	135	Iraq	24	-	-
Czechoslovakia	3 469	992 765	68	Ireland	-	-	-

Country	Cinemas (fixed)	Total seating capacity	Seats per 1 000 people	Country	Cinemas (fixed)	Total seating capacity	Seats per 1 000 people
Israel	252	177 000	59	Niger	4	3 800	0.9
Italy	10 719	-	-	Nigeria	183	36 800	0.7
Ivory Coast	88*	80 000*	18	Niue	1	120	24
Jamaica	42	39 400	21	Norfolk Island	1	100	50
Japan	2 673	1 249 000	12	Norway	450	145 000	37
Jordan	39	22 000	9	Oman	-	-	-
Kenya	32	18 800	2	Pacific Islands	19	4 500	42
Khmer Republic	59	28 800	4	Pakistan	578	300 000	5
Korea (Democratic People's Republic of)	-	-	-	Panama	23	28 400	19
Korea (Republic of)	793	473 100	15	Papua New Guinea	13	7 305	3
Kuwait	7	12 000	13	Paraguay	61*	-	-
Laos	16	8 200	3	Peru	276	-	-
Lebanon	170	86 640	30	Philippines	951	-	-
Lesotho	1	-	-	Poland	2 465	576 445	18
Liberia	8	-	-	Portugal	485	273 300	28
Libyan Arab Republic	28	19 100	9	Portugese Guinea	4	1 500	3
Liechtenstein	3	700	33	Portuguese Timor	1	600	0.9
Luxembourg	37	-	-	Puerto Rico	168	-	-
Macau	12	12 600	39	Qatar	2	3 300	41
Madagascar	43	15 000	2	Reunion	20	7 000	15
Malawi	13	5 335	1	Rhodesia	90	51 443*	9*
Malaysia (Federation of)	550	385 000	31	Romania	6 244	-	-
Maldives	2	823	7	Rwanda	4	800	0.2
Mali	19	17 100	3	San Marino	9	-	-
Malta	40	24 847	76	St Helena and Dependencies	1	650	130
Martinique	38	15 300	45	St Kitts-Nevis and Anguilla	2	1 000	16
Mauritania	-	-	-	St Lucia	9	9 500	92
Mauritius and Dependencies	53	52 000	62	St Pierre and Miquelon	3	900	180
Mexico	1 765	1 496 000	28	St Vincent	-	-	-
Monaco	2	1 051	44	São Tomé and Principe	1	1 000	14
Mongolia	60	-	-	Saudi Arabia	-	-	-
Montserrat	1	200	17	Senegal	87	50 415	13
Morocco	260	150 000	9	Seychelles	2	546	10
Mozambique	22	22 000	3	Sierra Leone	10	5 500	2
Namibia	17	6 600	11	Sikkim	-	-	-
Nauru	3	1 000	143	Singapore	75	62 916	29
Nepal	10	-	-	Somalia	26	23 000	8
Netherlands	321	187 774	14	South Africa (Republic of)	685	498 000	22
Netherlands Antilles	11	7 000	30	Spain	6 064	4 444 000	129
New Caledonia	4	3 000	28	Spanish Sahara	4	1 768	35
New Hebrides	5	3 000	36	Sri Lanka	303	128 544	10
New Zealand	239	143 969	49	Sudan	52	84 000	5
Nicaragua	104	60 000	30	Surinam	26	-	-

Country	Cinemas (fixed)	Total seating capacity	Seats per 1 000 people	Country	Cinemas (fixed)	Total seating capacity	Seats per 1 000 people
Swaziland	2	800	2	United Kingdom	1 482	1 381 261	25
Sweden	1 334	–	–	United States of America	14 300*	10 000 000	48
Switzerland	554	204 000	32	Upper Volta	6	2 000	0.3
Syria	70	–	–	Uruguay	180	124 700	42
Tanzania	36	14 500	1	Venezuela	429	544 400	49
Thailand	392	422 216	12	Vietnam (Democratic Republic of)	–	–	–
Togo	4	2 000	1	Vietnam (Republic of)	143	91 000	5
Tokelau Islands	–	–	–	Virgin Islands (UK)	1	328	30
Tonga	5	3 600	40	Virgin Islands (USA)	5	2 700	42
Trinidad and Tobago	66	42 100	40	Western Samoa	13	4 500	31
Tunisia	104	44 800	9	Yemen (Arab Republic of)	–	–	–
Turkey	700*	–	–	Yemen (People's Democratic Republic of	–	–	–
Turks and Caicos Islands	1	200	33	Yugoslavia	1 393	479 950	23
Uganda	17	16 000	1	Zaïre	57	17 000	0.8
Union of Soviet Socialist Republics	147 200	–·	–	Zambia	29	13 359	3
United Arab Emirates	–	–	–				

*) Australia: Including drive-ins.
   Bolivia: In 1963.
   Cayman Islands: Including 1 drive-in.
   Egypt (Arab Republic of):   Including 93 open for only six months of the year.
   Honduras: Data for 1960.
   Ivory Coast: Including outdoor and mobile cinemas.
   Paraguay: In the city of Asunción.
   Rhodesia: For 80 cinemas only.
   Turkey: In the larger towns only.
   United States of America: Including 4600 drive-ins.

3

PROBLEMS OF FREEDOM AND RESPONSIBILITY

John C. Merrill
FREEDOM OF THE PRESS: CHANGING CONCEPT?

Ralph L. Lowenstein
PRESS FREEDOM AS A BAROMETER OF POLITICAL
    DEMOCRACY

Raymond B. Nixon
FACTORS RELATED TO FREEDOM IN NATIONAL
    PRESS SYSTEMS

Heinz-Dietrich Fischer
PRESS COUNCILS THROUGHOUT THE WORLD—
    AN EMPIRICAL APPROACH

3

PROBLEMS OF FREEDOM
AND RESPONSIBILITY

THE whole subject of freedom and responsibility in communication has become one of the main preoccupations of writers, teachers and politicians throughout the world. Although it is difficult to generalize about global trends, there are numerous indications that restrictions on the press are increasing with each passing year.

One of the main problems, of course, in any consideration of freedom of information is the problem of differing national concepts. Freedom of the press in Russia, for instance, certainly means something quite different from what it means in the United States. And, even between such countries as Sweden and the United States there are differing concepts. Therefore, it is very difficult to study such a thing as "press freedom" without falling into the trap of using one's own country as the point of departure—or as the standard for evaluating press freedom in other countries.

In the first article of this chapter, John Merrill contends that the concept of press freedom, even in the "libertarian" countries, is undergoing a rather rapid change—more and more conforming to authoritarian notions of national security, social responsibility and the like. Ralph Lowenstein, in the second article, presents his PICA index for studying press freedom around the world and shows linkages to a nation's political situation. Unlike many scholars of international communication, Dr. Lowenstein, of the University of Missouri, believes press freedom can be measured rather accurately and presents what is probably the first systematic device for carrying out this complex task.

The third article, by Dr. Raymond Nixon, professor emeritus of journalism at the University of Minnesota, provides what was one of the first studies of cultural and socio-economic factors in a nation and how they are related to press freedom. Concluding the chapter is an article, never published before, by Heinze-Dietrich Fischer on the development, theory, and practice of press councils throughout the world. It should be noted that in all of these articles freedom and responsibility of the press rear their heads simultaneously. Does one lose at the expense of the other, or can they coexist harmoniously? That is a big and unresolved question, fraught as it is with semantic difficulties.

*   *   *   *

RELATED READING

Brucker, Herbert. *Freedom of Information.* New York: Macmillan, 1969.

Bruns, Viktor and Kurt Häntzschel. *Die Pressgesetze des Erdballs.* (10 vols). Berlin: Stilke, 1928–1931.

Chafee, Zechariah, Jr. *Government and Mass Communications.* (2 vols). Chicago: University of Chicago Press, 1947.

Eek, Hinding. *Freedom of Information as a Project of International Legislation: A Study of International Law in the Making.* Uppsala: Lundequistska Bokhandeln, 1953.

Hocking, William E. *Freedom of the Press: A Framework of Principle.* Chicago: University of Chicago Press, 1947.

Hulteng, John L. *The Messenger's Motives: Ethical Problems of the News Media.* Englewood Cliffs, N.J.: Prentice-Hall, 1976.

Knight, Robert P. *The Concept of Freedom of the Press in the Americas.* Unpublished Ph.D. dissertation, University of Missouri, 1968.

Lowenstein, Ralph L. *Measuring World Press Freedom as a Political Indicator.* Unpublished Ph.D. dissertation, University of Missouri, 1967.

Löffler, Martin and Jean Louis Hébarre. *Form and Function of Internal Control of the Press.* Munich: C. H. Beck'sche Verlagsbuchhandlung, 1968.

Merrill, J. C. *The Imperative of Freedom.* New York: Hastings House, 1974.

———, and R. Barney, eds. *Ethics and the Press.* New York: Hastings House, 1975.

Rivers, Wm. L., and W. Schramm. *Responsibility in Mass Communication,* 2nd ed., New York: Harper & Row, 1969.

Siebert, Fred, Theodore Peterson and Wilbur Schramm, *Four Theories of the Press.* Urbana: University of Illinois Press, 1956.

Terrou, Fernand and Lucien Solal. *Legislation for Press, Film, and Radio.* Paris: UNESCO, 1951.

Wiggins, James Russell. *Freedom or Secrecy.* New York: Oxford, 1964.

John C. Merrill:

Freedom of the Press: Changing Concept?

. . . . Quite simply, there are two main ways to consider freedom of the press: (1) as media autonomy with journalistic self-determinism, and (2) as media adjustment to social or political desires. In other words, one can look at press freedom as media-determinism of the content of mass communications or as public (a kind of people's lobby or majority desire) determinism of media content. The latter view of press freedom (really a pseudo-view) is in its ascendancy and unless it is contested vigorously and constantly by journalists of the Free World, by 1984 the journalism-of-social-adjustment will have triumphed and the editors and publishers, news directors and various media managers will have turned into passive "secretaries for the public" (or for various public pressure groups and lobbies) who will provide the various audiences only with what they want, what pleases them, what reinforces their prejudices and what enhances their social position.

But how, some readers will ask, is this bad? Is it not the "democratic" way? Should not the mass media messages be produced by a kind of public "will"? What is really wrong with news media pleasing outside groups and not necessarily themselves with their message-selection, content and emphasis? Is not anything else merely dictatorial on the part of the media persons?

These are common questions with some rational justification, and lie at the very heart of the problem the Western World faces with the concept of "press freedom." They are questions which are inciting the social responsibility apologists and the social functionalists who are always looking for accommodation, adjustment, stability and social harmony.

The basic question, however, that should be asked is this: Just what does the Social Responsibility devotee mean by the term "social responsible press," and who (or what group) will determine what is socially responsible journalism? And, if the answer is, as it often has been, *that the determination of socially responsible journalism will, of course, be left strictly to the media people themselves, then the question is closed, the debate is over: for this is exactly what we already have in a libertarian, laissez-faire, self-deterministic media system that the Social Responsibility people are trying to discredit and change.*

There are those among us, and they are growing in number very rapidly,

▶ This is a shortened version of Ch. 3 from Dr. Merrill's *The Imperative of Freedom* (Hastings House, 1974).

who extol harmony over dissonance, adaptation over competition and friction, social stability and viability over social disharmony and contention. And they are wise enough to see that the communications media play a large part in social conflict theory—that is to say that *free* or *autonomous* media play a large part in this theory, and since this disturbs them they have set about to change the whole meaning of press freedom so that autonomous journalism will be considered irresponsible whereas "socially controlled" journalism will be both "free and responsible."

It is interesting that these persons recognize that it is not yet quite the time to drop the term "free" from their catechism, and so they plunge ahead brainwashing others (even themselves, evidently) into believing that a press can be both "free" and "responsible" in some kind of collective, monolithic or commonly-accepted way. This, of course, is a myth and a logical contradiction: if a newspaper, for example, must be "socially responsible" according to some *outside* standard, then quite logically, its editorial freedom is curtailed. It need not accept this-or-that as its responsibility if it is an autonomous and freely acting agent. This is what is interesting about such journalistic clichés as the press "being a fourth branch of government" or a "watchdog on government"; a free press (or units thereof) has no reason to consider itself either of these. Press units of a free journalistic system are *whatever* they want to be; they might even decide to be government supporters and apologists. So be it.

Egalitarianism and Libertarianism

One of the factors which has accelerated a change in the press freedom concept has been the rise of the idea of egalitarianism. It grew rapidly in the latter part of the nineteenth century and has been gaining great momentum in the last generation. Equality—especially equality in social or public institutions—has been the modern watchword, not only in sociology but in various schools of psychology and philosophy. In one sense, egalitarianism has supplanted in the late nineteenth and twentieth centuries the libertarian impulse which was dominant in the late eighteenth and early nineteenth centuries. At least it would appear so on the surface, although as Robert Waelder has observed, this does not mean that people are really becoming more equal; rather, he says, "more realistically it means that such an intellectual climate is conducive to a new elite of intellectuals who are assuming a kind of priestly power.[1] In other words, the very people who do the most talking about equality and equal journalistic rights for all the people, not just the journalists, are the ones who thrust themselves into a kind of position of arrogance and omniscience where they feel they can say with exactitude what the press should and should not do.

All of this is, of course, understandable. If one is for the fuzzy concept of

---

[1] Robert Waedler, *Progress and Revolution: A Study of the Issues of Our Age* (New York: International Universities Press, Inc., 1970), p. 53.

equality, then he must at least make the proper noises to show that he is against any preferred position for journalists who largely control the contents of our mass media. John Doe, the audience member, is envisioned as "equal" to the editor of the newspaper and his voice should be listened to in respect to the newspaper's content and positions; his ideas and information should be considered for publication equally with those of the journalists, and his freedom of access to the press should be equal to the editor's freedom of editorial self-determinism.[2] Forgotten or ignored is the fact that the editor cannot practice editorial self-determinism if he must provide "journalistically equal" members of the public access to his paper's columns.

Egalitarianism, of course, is a curious and even an impossible concept. Like "social responsibility" or "loyalty" it sounds good, but falls to pieces on analysis. And, in journalism, it is ridiculous. We do not have, we never have had, nor will we ever have, an egalitarian press. Even if every citizen had an equal amount of money with which to get into the media business, we would not have any egalitarian press. For there are innumerable other factors which would militate against it. For example, equally wealthy (or equally poor) people would not have the same temperament, or education, or motivation, or talents—or even *opportunity*—to go into journalism.

The word "opportunity" should be noted in the above list; usually it is felt that money automatically provides journalistic opportunity, but it is not that simple. You can have the money—and even the education, ability and motivation—to start a newspaper, but the opportunity may not be present; for example, the community in which you wish to live and work cannot support another newspaper. You are therefore not really journalistically equal to the person who can (and does) start a newspaper. And, even if you were to start one, too, it is a fact that one of the newspapers would have a larger circulation than the other, that one would sell more advertising, that one would have better writers, that one would deal more forcefully with the issues or that one would have more pages than the other every day. Journalistic egalitarianism is only a term, full of noble connotations, but signifying nothing.

Let us assume that "press freedom" is equally available and a rightful commodity of all citizens. Just how would it work? Would every citizen have *equal* access to the press? Would I get fifty words of my side of the question into Newspaper A and every other person with opinions on the matter get an equal fifty words into Newspaper A? And would they all appear on the front page? And would they all have equivalent headlines? And would these "equal" messages get equally into all other media?

A more interesting, but relevant question, would be: Just who would make

[2] See Jerome A. Barron, "Access to the Press—a New First Amendment Right," *Harvard Law Review* (June, 1967); Cf. Barron, "Access to the Press: A New Concept of the First Amendment," *Seminar* (March 1969); Dennis E. Brown and John C. Merrill, "Regulatory Pluralism in the Press?" *Seminar* (March 1969); Mary E. Trapp, "Americans Need Access to Today's Mass Media," *Communication: Journalism Education Today* (Vol. 5, Summer 1972).

the decisions as to whose messages got in and what place and emphasis each would get? In other words, who would decide *what* would be given "equal" treatment and *how* it would be done? An arbiter of some kind, presumably. Someone who was qualified (thereby "unequal"?) to make such egalitarian decisions. But, I might ask, are not all persons equally qualified? Why permit some special person to make such important decisions—especially since we are not satisfied to permit editors to make them? Of course, what all this amounts to is a contradiction which might be called the Paradox of Equality. Always there must be decision makers, arbiters, or what you will; they are *more equal* than others, as the old saying goes.

Egalitarianism in journalism is a concept best discarded before it does irremedial harm to freedom and common sense. *Freedom is impossible where egalitarianism is enthroned, and egalitarianism is impossible where freedom is permitted.* Where freedom operates, superior persons and journalistic media are going to emerge, thrive and dominate; where a kind of egalitarianism is enforced, outstanding journalists and media find no real incentive or motivation for individualistic achievement and content themselves with taking orders and keeping out of trouble.

Pluralism and Press Freedom

Another assumption of libertarianism, one which has grown up in the twentieth century, is that a free press must be pluralistic. This assumption, like the one that a free press must be egalitarian, has given birth to much criticism of a press system such as that of the United States. If, for example, the media system is not as "pluralistic" (the term is usually not defined) as certain critics might like, it is indicated as not being truly libertarian and therefore in need of revamping—or scrapping. Most critics of the American press today gather their statistics about mergers, group ownerships, chains and the like, and bemoan what they see as a loss of press pluralism. They even go further: they equate this with a failure of libertarian theory.

Several things are wrong with this kind of thinking: First, the concept of pluralism implied in the above criticism ("unit pluralism") does not assure an informed citizenry—for it is possible for four independent media to provide no greater variety of news and views than two media belonging to the same owner. Secondly, and more important, the contention that pluralism (of any kind) is necessary in a libertarian system is fallacious.

It is amazing how many people—even journalists and so-called communication scholars—use "pluralism" without ever really analyzing its meaning or meanings. Normally they have some vague concept of pluralism as having to do with "great" numbers of media, or a "wide diversity" of ownerships of the media. How great or how wide, they cannot really say. But they have a quantitative concept and generally seem to equate *number of units and ownerships* with diversity and number of different stories and points of view. Yet they have no real basis for this equation. A good example of this kind of assumption is Bryce Rucker's *The First Freedom* in which he presents certain statistics which show a steady growth of newspaper chains and cities with non-competitive dailies.[3] He then bemoans the demise of pluralism and the passing away of libertarianism.

Rucker's thesis is far too broad to be supported by his basic assumption—this basic assumption being that *numbers* of media determine diversity of information and viewpoints. Even if this were proved true (and it has not been), one could still question the tie-in with libertarianism. It should be noted that if we are playing the "numbers game" with pluralism, then we should be able to assume that in an advanced, well-developed closed society—such as the Soviet Union—there is a great pluralism of viewpoints and information *since there are a large number of media*. But we cannot assume this; also we must admit that a large number of media units can present very few viewpoints—even if they are under varied ownerships as in Sweden. Perhaps we should, however, recognize the corollary to what has just been said: a few media units can present a very great pluralism of information and viewpoints. Much research needs to be done in this area; so far we can give no clear-cut conclusions.

The only way to really get at pluralism (the significant type: *message* pluralism) is to conduct thorough—and continuing—content analyses. The stress, then, must be on *content*, not on *numbers* of media or ownerships. Unfortunately, the myth persists that press pluralism is shrinking in the U.S. It is, of course, *possible* that it is, but those who say it is have absolutely no evidence on which to base their conclusion. Only content analysis (searching for variety of information and viewpoints) of the total messages today as compared to the total message content at an earlier time can give evidence of shrinking—or expanding—pluralism. As yet, nobody has systematically tackled this difficult task. . . .

One's thinking about press pluralism would become a little clearer if he had a systematic framework in which to consider the term. Of course, there are obviously many ways to define pluralism, but one typology which has been useful to me and my students is presented below—giving three *types* and three *levels* of pluralism:

(1) *Message Pluralism.* Here the emphasis is on the diversity of messages to which a person is able to expose himself. And it should be realized that this is not the same as the diversity (or number) of media units to which a person may expose himself. The way to get at this is through content analysis, and through this procedure only.

(2) *Media ("Unit") Pluralism.* This kind of pluralism is the one which is

---

[3] See Bryce Rucker, *The First Freedom* (Carbondale: Southern Illinois University Press, 1968). Cf. a book by the same title by Morris Ernst (New York: Macmillan, 1946) in which he, like Rucker, contends that pluralism is dying and that "our nation has been put to sleep under the blanket of laissez faire" (p. 41). He adds the prediction, however, that "the public will finally wake up to its mental starvation" (p. 245). In spite of their many statistics related to numbers of media and their many opinions about the state of our media system, neither author actually shows that Americans are being mentally starved and are getting less (or even less varied) information than previously.

usually considered and used by those who would indict our press system for loss of pluralism. Here the quantity of, or diversity of ownerships of, media units is the important consideration. It is assumed here that the more units you have (or the more ownerships), the more viewpoints and stories you will have. This, of course, is not necessarily true.

(3) *Communicator Pluralism.* The emphasis here is on the number and diversity of message-encoders or message-senders. And the assumption is usually that the wider the diversity of communicator "types" and the greater the number of communicators (using the mass media), the greater will be the diversity of information and opinions. This, of course, is not necessarily true, but it would appear to be more valid than the "Unit" Pluralism assumption. The only way to get at this type of pluralism in a sound methodological way would be to study the communicators (their backgrounds, education, religion, etc.) and then study the messages they send, and then see what correlation exists between the diversity of backgrounds and the diversity of messages they communicate.

Of the three types of pluralism briefly discussed above, the most significant one, in my view, is Type I (Message Pluralism). The only way to study it is through content analysis, and this must be thorough and continuing. One must look for the diversity of opinions and information in a certain universe of messages at a particular time for comparison with similar analyses at other times and in other universes. Types 2 and 3 *may* contribute to Message Pluralism, but they may not.

Now, let us consider briefly the *levels* of pluralism:

(1) *System Pluralism.* This level is the one many writers emphasize and, if it is "good" (many media or diversity of messages), it is held up as something very commendable; there are a great many bits of information and viewpoints available in the *total media sytem* (e.g. in the media system of the United States).

(2) *Community Pluralism.* This level brings the concept of pluralism closer to home, limits it to a smaller geographical or social community—such as a region, state or city. The question of importance here: How much diversity is present at the *local* level? To many persons the System Pluralism is really unimportant when compared to this local Community Pluralism. For example, they will say that the fact that certain viewpoints (or stories) are published in a few newspapers in California is really insignificant if people in the Midwest do not have these items in *their* local media. What counts, then, at this level is that items and viewpoints be available in the media of a specific *locality*.

(3) *Individual (Audience Member) Pluralism.* This, I maintain, is the ideal *level* of pluralism just as Message Pluralism is the ideal *type* of pluralism. At this level, pluralism is related to that information which *gets to the individual citizen* and is not what is available somewhere in the media of a country or a community. In other words, at this level—the perception level of the audience—the amount and diversity of information which the person actually ex-

poses himself to (or assimilates) is the only important consideration. The way to study this level would be to study the individual citizen, trying to ascertain through recall studies, interviews, etc. what he was *getting* from the pluralism of messages revolving about him. . . .

Libertarian "Press Freedom"

In discussing press freedom within the libertarian context of the West, four ways of considering such freedom suggest themselves. Each one might be considered a different *spectrum* which could be briefly described as (1) the potency or non-potency of government control, (2) the political extremes in governmental philosophy, (3) philosophical or psychological inclination, and (4) governmental and private ownership of journalistic enterprises.

Spectrum 1. At one end of this spectrum is anarchy and at the other total government control. The person who believes in press freedom (at least in the way it is extolled in this book) has a tendency toward anarchy. He rebels against government control—at least very much government control—and wants himself and his social unit (for the journalist: his medium) to be under little or no government compulsion or direction. He would agree with Thoreau, who virtually proclaimed himself an anarchist, that "that government is best which governs not at all." [4] So, on this spectrum "Press Freedom" would be well toward the *anarchy* end and far away from the *government control* end.

Spectrum 2. As has been pointed out earlier in this book, both authoritarianism on the right and on the left tend to stifle freedom of the press and to dissipate media or journalistic autonomy. Therefore, the ideal spot for a free press on a Communism/Fascism spectrum would be in the center. Most journalists (at least in the Western libertarian world) would agree with this if they were using *journalistic autonomy* as the key to their concept. A free press had better attempt to follow a path about half-way between the tempting and ever-beckoning poles of Communism and Fascism. [5] Truly the middle-way here is more compatible with journalistic autonomy and media self-determinism. Both extremes are areas where the press would have to submit itself to an elite, persons or groups, who would dictate to the press and determine its actions in line with their own interests and socio-political philosophies.

Spectrum 3. This is probably a more controversial spectrum than the others for its poles are the semantically difficult terms, Liberalism and Conservatism. A free press, here, is midway between these two poles—the same as it was midway between Communism and Fascism. Although Liberalism, as has been discussed earlier, has the more favorable connotation, the pragmatic Liberal or Liberal government can be just as authoritarian or elitist as can the prag-

[4] H. D. Thoreau, "Civil Disobedience" in M. Meltzer (ed.), *Thoreau: People, Principles, and Politics* (New York: Hill and Wang, 1963), p. 36.

[5] "Fascism" is probably a misnomer here, since unlike "Communism" it has specific reference to a national political ideology (Italy in the 1930's and 1940's). Perhaps "right-wing authoritarianism" would be a better term.

matic Conservative or Conservative government. In fact, it is quite possible that today's Liberal is tomorrow's Conservative—at least in the sense of wanting to conserve his brand of li liberalism. At the extremes, Liberals and Conservatives are arrogant, self-righteous, heavy-handed, dictatorial, and opposed to criticism and open discussion. They know what is best for the society and will enforce their will if they get the chance. The Free Press or the autonomous journalist had best steer a middle course between them so as not to get entangled in the ideological nets thrown far out by the clever ideologues of both groups.

Spectrum 4. It is my opinion that capitalism more than socialism expands the opportunities of personal and media autonomy, competition and the clash of ideas. Therefore, the Free Press finds its most compatible home on this spectrum far toward the capitalistic end. Capitalistic societies have certainly contributed more to personal and journalistic autonomy than any other societies in the world. Capitalism engenders individualists, persons who like to compete. Socialism engenders conformists, persons who like to adapt and move along together. Alexis de Tocqueville, writing in 1848, expressed well the danger to freedom found in socialism. He referred to "democracy" (which he contrasted to *socialism*) as an individualist institution standing in irreconcilable conflict with socialism. He wrote, in part:

> Democracy extends the sphere of individual freedom; socialism restricts it. Democracy attaches all possible value to each man; socialism makes each man a mere agency, a mere number. Democracy and socialism have nothing in common but one word: equality. But notice the difference; while democracy seeks equality in liberty, socialism seeks equality in restraint and servitude.[6]

From Freedom to Responsibility

Books and articles tracing the development of freedom of the press (freedom of expression and other related freedoms) abound and there is no need here to examine this subject in great detail. There are many fine sources for the person interested in the historical landmarks of press freedom during its evolution.[7] The literature of press freedom is sprinkled with outstanding writers; one can start with John Milton and his *Areopagitica* in 1644 (licensing impractical, impairing the search for truth; truth arises from the free and open encounter of ideas—his "self-righting process") and proceed through the eighteenth century where John Locke extolled man's natural rights and his rationality and postulated that free expression was a natural right.

---

[6] "Discours prononcé à l'assemblée constituante le 12 septembre 1848 sur la question du droit au travail," *Oeuvres complètes d'Alexis de Tocqueville* (1866), IX., 546.

[7] For a good discussion of the landmarks of press freedom during its evolution, see Ch. 2 ("Freedom of Speech and Press") in Carl L. Becker, *Freedom and Responsibility in the American Way of Life* (New York: Vintage Books, 1960). Cf. William E. Hocking, *Freedom of the Press: A Framework of Princple* (Chicago: Univ. of Chicago Press, 1947).

Also in the eighteenth century was Voltaire, probably the best known defender of freedom of expression at this time, who accepted the biblical injunction that the "truth shall make you free" but recognized the problem: one had to be free to know the truth. And there was also Adam Smith who proposed his famous concept of *laissez faire* in 1776; the government should keep hands off and let the various business enterprises make their own way in the market place (and this would include the press). In America about this same time, Thomas Jefferson was expressing strong faith in the rationality of man, as Locke had done, and was advocating a minimum of government interference in everyday affairs. For Jefferson, the free and autonomous press was essential for public enlightenment and as a safeguard of personal iberties.

Another great American spokesman for press freedom was John Adams, who advised journalists in 1765 that they should not "suffer themselves to be wheedled out of their liberty by any pretences of politeness, delicacy, or decency." These, said John Adams, were simply three different names for "hypocrisy, chicanery, and cowardice." [8]

And back in England there was Jeremy Bentham (1748–1832), viewing every law as a restriction of freedom and urging that laws be minimized. He saw society as composed of atomistic individuals pursuing their own happiness. To him, a realization of individual self-interest (of which the best judge is the individual himself) must occur in an atmosphere of freedom. Freedom of the press he defended mainly on the grounds that publicity is necessary to good government, that publicity is the best way to secure and keep public confidence in government.

A close associate of Bentham, James Mill (1773–1836) thought the "middle rank" of society the "most wise" and "most virtuous." He advocated freedom of the press because it made known the conduct of the individuals who were elected to wield power in government, and unless information about their activities was made public the officials might serve their own interests.[9] James' son, John Stuart Mill (1806–1873) solidified his father's ideas on freedom in the nineteenth century and his famous tract "On Liberty" justified free expression on Utilitarian principles. He pointed out that liberty was the right of a *mature* person, and that for the good of society, man mut not be restrained. He insisted that intelligence atrophies and initiative dies from overzealous direction by government. One might wonder what might happen to the intelligence and initiative of an "immature" person when directed by government.

It will be noted that up until the present century, the emphasis in the discussions of press freedom and freedom of expression generally was on *laissez-faire*, on government separation from the press, on personal and media autonomy, on the elimination of licensing and on the "free" marketplace of ideas individually determined by the various media. In the twentieth century this

---

[8] Reuven Frank, "The First Amendment Includes Television," *Nieman Reports* (Dec. 1971), p. 8.
[9] E. M. Zashin, *Civil Disobedience and Democracy* (New York: The Free Press, 1972), p. 25.

began to change, and Oliver Wendell Holmes (1841–1935), in a very real sense, set the stage for the new trend toward limited freedom with his "clear and present danger" concept and his implication that the government should be allowed to protect itself. (One is reminded of the statement of President John Kennedy's Pentagon spokesman, Arthur Sylvester, in the early 1960's that the government has a right to lie to protect itself.)

Continuing this trend toward "social responsibility" or limited freedom have been such men as Walter Lippmann, Walter Berns, Robert Hutchins and Jerome Barron who have cautioned the press to be more responsible and to operate in certain ways in order to warrant or deserve its freedom. These are the elitists who would prescribe what the press should do to keep its freedom and whose impact has been great in the recent trend toward such pressure groups and media arbiters as press councils. The broadcast media, of course, have from the beginning operated under the "responsibility" doctrine instead of the "freedom" doctrine; although many broadcasters are agitating for equal freedom with the print media, they are likely to get nowhere as long as the trend continues toward responsibility and away from freedom or autonomy. In fact, what is more likely is that the print media will find themselves one day operating under some type of FPC (Federal Press Commission) in much the same way that the broadcast media operate under the FCC (Federal Communications Commission). . . .

It is very easy to confuse democracy and even responsibility in journalism with "giving the people what they want." But this is a false concept—or at least an erroneous application of the democratic principle, for journalism is something more than a mere public utility that produces a stable, physical staple such as water or electricity. It is at least a quasi-*art*, a creative enterprise whereby individual talents go into its production. Journalism (at least, free journalism) is something other than a fountain which pours forth a predictable and consistent product at the beck-and-call of the consumers.[10]

But many of the attacks on the free press are coming from these "populist" critics as well as from the Platonic elitists. Actually, however, the "populists" are no more than elitists themselves, for they know very well that some group of people's "representatives" must speak and act in the name of the people. These representatives thus become "elitists" and solidify their position as time goes on. But "Give the people what they want" is a fine-sounding slogan, having a more democratic ring to it than "Give the people what our elite group of intellectuals want them to have." Good as it may sound, this kind of public or consensus journalism is the journalism of slave-journalists. It is debilitating to the authentic journalist who wants more than to be at the beck and call of so-called "public opinion."

So, we can see that there is a disposition in many quarters today to

---

[10] See Sydney J. Harris, *The Authentic Person* (Niles, Ill.: Argus Communications, 1972), esp. Chs. 3 and 4.

"redefine" freedom of the press, to divorce it from independent editorial determinism by the media and to place it somewhere else with a shifted emphasis on
the press's obligations rather than on its freedoms. This redefining, whether it
comes from politicians or from intellectuals in nonpolitical situations, is limiting the concept and making it into something else. Abraham Lincoln in his
statement that a nation cannot exist "half slave and half free" pointed out the
fallacy of trying to tamper with the definition of freedom. If freedom of the
press is to have any real meaning—the kind that has to do with autonomy—
then it means freedom from outside (non-journalistic) forces and nothing
more. . . .

Ralph L. Lowenstein:

Press Freedom as a Barometer of Political Democracy

JOURNALISTS in democracies are usually concerned with the degree of "press freedom" that they enjoy. They are concerned not simply because this freedom involves their ability to produce the product from which they earn their livelihood, but because they believe press freedom is inextricably bound up with political freedom.

Though sometimes overlooked by political scientists, the press plays perhaps the most important role in the modern political system. It can be an avenue for freedom, or a tool for suppression. Russell H. Fitzgibbon, who has measured democratization in the 20 republics of Latin America every five years since 1945, found a stronger relationship between "free and competitive elections" and "freedom of the press" than between "free and competitive elections" and any of the remaining 13 political, social and economic criteria in his survey.[1] Other political scientists have made similar findings, though these have largely gone unreported except in the learned journals.

Press freedom, then, is of vital importance to society and should not be the concern simply of those who have a financial stake in the press. Axel Springer, West German publisher, put it succinctly when he said:

> A society of free men comes into being on the basis of free elections, and the free expression of opinion. We recognize a tyranny not only by the fact that its subjects are denied free elections, but also by the fact that they are denied a free press.[2]

Although the press in the newly-developing nations is burdened with the additional task of mobilizing the people toward national development goals, its political role should be much the same as the press in the West. Lucian W. Pye has written:

---

[1] Russell H. Fitzgibbon and Kenneth F. Johnson, "Measurement of Latin American Political Change," *American Political Science Review*, 55:3 (September 1961), p. 525.
[2] Axel Springer, "Deutsche Press Zwischen Konzentration und Subvention," *Kieler Vortrage*, 48 (1967), p. 4.

▶ This is an original article done for this book by Ralph L. Lowenstein, School of Journalism, University of Missouri. Portions of this article were adapted from two monographs on world press freedom written by Dr. Lowenstein and published by the Freedom of Information Center, University of Missouri.

Even in the most weak and unstable country the mass media must still retain to some degree one of their most basic functions: that of serving as an inspector general to the entire political system so as to provide the necessary public criticism to ensure some degree of political integrity among the power holders.[3]

It would seem to follow, then, that an accurate rating system for press freedom, if applied to every independent nation in the world at regular intervals, would enable journalists and social scientists to:

1) Establish the precise position of any nation at any given time on a "free-controlled" political continuum.
2) Predict the political direction in which a nation is heading.
3) Find needed data for correlations between press freedom and other social, economic, and political phenomena.

Two major weaknesses of various rating systems used in the past are that they have not used a standard set of criteria for each country judged and they have not considered factors other than those of obvious government interference. Annual surveys of world press freedom reported by the Associated Press, International Press Institute (and a survey of the Western Hemisphere by the Inter American Press Association) do not pretend to be any more than general ratings. They are based on round-up reports, primarily of government interference that has occurred in the countries mentioned. Countries listed in several of the surveys one year are not always mentioned in the next. Many countries are never listed.

Wire service surveys have been criticized because they are concerned primarily with countries where foreign correspondents have experienced difficulties.[4] The IAPA survey, concerned only with the Americas, often condenses its report on a particular country to one sentence: "There is freedom of the press."[5]

In 1963, Arthur S. Banks and Robert B. Textor sorted 99 countries into four categories with respect to degree of press freedom.[6] But since their ratings were based only upon the AP's year-end censorship reports for 1961 and 1962 and an IPI survey published in 1959, their results are open to all the criticisms already mentioned.

Up until the middle 1960's, the most significant rating system attempted

---

[3] Lucian W. Pye, "Communication, Institution Building, and the Reach of Authority," in Daniel Lerner and Wilbur Schramm (eds.), *Communication and Change in the Developing Countries* (Honolulu: East-West Center Press, 1967), p. 37.
[4] Raymond B. Nixon, "Freedom in the World's Press: A Fresh Appraisal with New Data," *Journalism Quarterly* (Winter 1965), p. 11.
[5] "Report of Inter American Press Association Committee on Freedom of the Press, Document 5." Unpublished report, mimeographed, March 19, 1960.
[6] *A Cross-Polity Survey* (Cambridge: The M.I.T. Press, 1963), Computer Printout pars. 50–52.

was that of Raymond B. Nixon, who published his first set of results classifying 85 countries in 1960.[7] After refining his methodology and scale slightly, he made another survey during 1963–64 in which he classified 117 countries. These results were published in 1965.[8] Only three men, including Nixon, were involved in classifying the countries in the first survey. In the second survey, there were four permanent judges and a fifth judge who was a specialist in one country or a group of countries. The fifth member of the panel of judges therefore varied. This panel of judges classified each country according to each member's own evaluation of the situation in the given country. Most of the final ratings represented a complete agreement; the remainder represented a consensus.[9] Nixon's studies were limited to print media only, and whereas his system was a device for *classifying*, it was not a device for *measuring*, since there was an absence of uniform and complete criteria for determining the degree of press freedom in each country.

In 1966, the Freedom of Information Center of the School of Journalism, University of Missouri, undertook a worldwide survey of press freedom, directed by the writer. In pursuing this project, the Center hoped to show that it could provide not only an index, but perhaps a predictor, of political change in the nations of the world. The Center started with this definition of a "free" and "controlled" press:

A completely free press is one in which newspapers, periodicals, news agencies, books, radio and television have absolute independence and critical ability, except for minimal libel and obscenity laws. The press has no concentrated ownership, marginal economic units or organized self-regulation.

A completely controlled press is one with no independence or critical ability. Under it, newspapers, periodicals, books, news agencies, radio and television are completely controlled directly and indirectly by government, self-regulatory bodies or concentrated ownership.

The following factors were selected for measuring press freedom on the basis of their overall inclusiveness and comparability: [10]

1. Legal controls on the press, not including libel and obscenity laws (but including laws involving official censorship, contempt, forced corrections and retractions, suspension, privacy, security, incitement to riot, etc.).

---

[7] Raymond B. Nixon, "Factors Related to Freedom in National Press Systems," *Journalism Quarterly* (Winter 1960), pp. 13–28.
[8] Nixon, "Freedom in the World's Press . . . ," p. 6.
[9] *Ibid.*.
[10] For further details about the selection of these factors and the methodology of the survey in which they were employed, see Ralph L. Lowenstein, "PICA: Measuring World Press Freedom," Freedom of Information Center Publication No. 166, University of Missouri, August 1966; and Ralph L. Lowenstein, "World Press Freedom, 1966," Freedom of Information Center Publication No. 181, University of Missouri, May 1967. Detailed tables on individual factor scores in 94 different countries can be found in Ralph L. Lowenstein, "Measuring World Press Freedom as a Political Indicator," Unpublished Ph.D. dissertation, University of Missouri, 1967.

2. Extra-legal controls (threats, violence, imprisonment, confiscation, etc.).

3. Libel laws.

4. Organized self-regulation (press councils, courts of honor).

5. News and editorial personnel (all media) subject to government licensing, certification and appointment.

6. Favoritism in release of government news.

7. Media allowed to utilize services of foreign news agencies.

8. Government control over domestic news agencies.

9. Print media subject to government licensing.

10. Government control of circulation and distribution, not including postal service.

11. Degree of press criticism of local and regional governments and officials within country.

12. Degree of press criticism of national government and national officials within country.

13. Government or "government party" ownership of media (including radio, television and domestic news agencies).

14. Publications of opposition political parties banned.

15. Broadcasting and press units owned by networks and chains (concentrated ownership).

16. Government control of newsprint.

17. Government control of foreign exchange and/or purchase of press equipment.

18. Government subsidies and/or bribes to press and newsmen.

19. Government loans to media.

20. Media dependency on government advertising.

21. Tax rate on press (either higher or lower) as compared to other businesses.

22. Pressure from labor unions (to influence editorial policy, to suspend publication).

23. Number of marginal (economically insecure) press units.

In a questionnaire sent to "judges" throughout the world, each factor was followed by a five-point verbal scale, usually ranging from "none" to "all" or from "none" to "complete." In the scoring, all 23 factors were given equal weight. There was provision for each judge to score each factor "don't know" or "not applicable."

Factors 3 and 4 and Factors 14 through 23 were eliminated for any country in which most or all of the media were state owned. These factors simply did not appear to be applicable to the press in such countries. Although the Press Independence and Critical Ability (PICA) survey conducted by the Freedom of Information Center did not utilize special factors for communist nations, there are such factors that could give a better definition between the press systems of the various communist countries. The following criteria were suggested to this writer by Prof. Georges H. Mond of the University of Paris and by Leo Gruliow, editor of *The Current Digest of Soviet Press:* 1) public access to foreign publications; 2) extent of jamming of foreign broadcasts; 3) relative rigidity of the press hierarchy (the degree to which lower-level and local media are policed by central media); 4) the weight ascribed by the authorities to readers' preferences, as demonstrated by market demand, when paper supplies are being allocated among media; 5) the right to demand retraction of unfounded press accusations or criticisms; 6) restriction of public access to files of periodicals and to books published in the past; 7) penalties for transmission of manuscripts from person to person; 8) the range of aesthetic diversity permitted in theater, fiction, journals of the arts and television; 9) publication of information which does not conform to the current policy of the party; 10) publication of commentaries criticizing governmental decisions and administrative measures.

The PICA survey also made no attempt to measure "responsibility" of the press. The word "responsibility" is so subjective as to defy definition or measurement. In fact, a press system that could score at the very top of the PICA scale would probably be a completely "irresponsible" press and would exist in a country that few individuals would care to live in. PICA was attempting to measure nations on a scale ranging from "absolute" freedom to "absolute" control, though it expected no country to reach either extreme.

In addition, PICA made no attempt to measure "stability." The stability of a country, it was felt, would become apparent if future measurements were conducted. The position of the United States, for example, would probably change only a fraction between measurements. But some of the more mercurial Latin American countries could be high on the scale during one measurement and very low during the next.

Some criteria for measurement were not used in the PICA survey because they were considered less meaningful in practice, too difficult to assess or not pertinent enough to press freedom *within* a country by natives of that country. Some of these were: constitutional guarantees of press freedom, access to government records, treatment of foreign correspondents, the flow of foreign publications into a country, advertising influence as a press control and foreign ownership of press units.

Finally, there were three highly unusual and perhaps unique characteristics of the judging in the PICA survey. They were:

1. PICA attempted to use both native and non-native judges to rate a particular country. If the native judges differed from the non-natives (mostly American foreign correspondents) by more than 6 per cent of the total points possible on the scale, the native scores were discarded and only the non-natives used.

2. PICA essentially used a different set of judges for each country.

No person in the world is intimately familiar with the press systems of the more than 100 independent nations of the world; individual sets of judges were therefore necessary. For the most part, these included native newsmen in the country and foreign correspondents then living in the country. The overwhelming majority of the non-native judges was composed of Americans with news experience in the United States. It was believed that they would be judging each country by the American standard of press freedom.

  3. PICA is what has been referred to as a "consensus index" rather than a poll based on a sample. The Center hoped to receive a minimum of four questionnaires (two native and two non-native) from each country. To attain this goal, the Center carefully selected its judges. They were reliable and experienced men and women, representing quality newspapers, periodicals, broadcast units, news agencies and universities throughout the world.

Exactly 1,003 questionnaires were mailed out between September, 1966, and March, 1967. Each judge was asked to score the nation on the basis of conditions in 1966 only. A total of 571 questionnaires, or 56.9 per cent, was returned. About 44 per cent of them came from native judges in 85 different countries. The remaining 56 per cent came from non-native judges.

On the basis of the questionnaires returned, the Center was able to assign a PICA score to 94 of the 115 independent nations of the world with populations of more than 1 million. The maximum score a country could receive was plus-4 and the lowest score a minus-4. Table I shows how this nine-point scale was divided into seven different classifications. It also shows the results of the PICA survey for 1966. The intermediate zone was called "transitional" because this writer hypothesized at the time of the survey that those countries falling into this zone would not be stationary, but would be in the process of moving toward more freedom or more control, and that such countries would be more likely to exhibit political change than countries falling in the other categories.

Of the 115 independent nations considered, 55 had "free" press systems. This represents some 1.5 billion people. A total of 29 countries had "controlled" press systems, representing 1.3 billion people; this was largely due to the Soviet Union's 230 million people and Communist China's 760 million people falling into this category. Ten countries, representing about 434 million people, were in the "transitional" zone.

According to the PICA survey, 45.2 per cent of earth's population was free in 1966, 39.2 per cent was not free and 13 per cent was somewhere in between, at least on the basis of their press systems. The 21 countries not ranked represented only 2.6 per cent of the world's population. Thirteen of those unrated countries were in Africa, four in the Middle East, two in Asia and two in the Western Hemisphere. All but the two in the Western Hemisphere have non-complex press systems and would have been simple to score and classify.

TABLE I

DISTRIBUTION OF INDEPENDENT NATIONS INTO
SEVEN CLASSIFICATIONS OF PRESS FREEDOM
ACCORDING TO PICA SURVEY, 1966

FREE—HIGH DEGREE
(2.51 to 4.00)

* Australia	* Denmark	* The Netherlands	* Philippines	* United
* Belgium	* Finland	* Norway	* Sweden	States
* Canada	* Guatemala	* Peru	* Switzerland	Uruguay
Costa Rica				* Venezuela

FREE—MODERATE CONTROLS
(1.51 to 2.50)

* Austria	Ecuador	Honduras	Jamaica	* Panama
* Bolivia	* El Salvador	* Ireland	* Japan	* Singapore
* Colombia	* France	(Erie)	* Malaysia	Turkey
* Cyprus	* West Germany	* Israel	* New Zealand	* United Kingdom

FREE—MANY CONTROLS
(0.51 to 1.50)

Argentina	* China	Kenya	Morocco	Thailand
* Brazil	(Taiwan)	Lebanon	* Rhodesia	Uganda
Ceylon	Dominican	Malawi	* South Africa	Zambia
* Chile	Rep.	* Mexico	Tanzania	
	* Greece			
	* India			

TRANSITIONAL
(−0.50 to 0.50)

* Burma	* Ghana	South	Nigeria	South
Congo	Indonesia	Korea	* Pakistan	Vietnam
(Kin.)		Laos		Yugoslavia

CONTROLLED—LOW DEGREE
(−0.51 to −1.50)

Afghanistan	Iran	Jordan	Portugal	* Tunisia
Cambodia	Iraq	* Nepal	Spain	

CONTROLLED—MEDIUM DEGREE
(−1.51 to −2.50)

Cameroon	Hungary	* Syria
Haiti	Senegal	U.A.R.

TABLE I (continued)

CONTROLLED—HIGH DEGREE				
(−2.51 to −4.00)				
Albania	Chad	Czechoslovakia	North	U.S.S.R.
Algeria	China	Ethiopia	Korea	Upper Volta
Bulgaria	(Mainland)	East	Poland	
	Cuba	Germany	Rumania	

UNRANKED				
(Insufficient Information)				
Burundi	Ivory Coast	Mali	Rwanda	Sudan
Cent. Afr.	Liberia	Mongolia	Saudi	Togo
Rep.	Libya	Nicaragua	Arabia	North
Dahomey	Malagasy	Niger	Sierra Leone	Vietnam
Guinea	Rep.	Paraguay	Somalia	Yemen

* Represents agreement between native and non-native scores; these scores were within 6 per cent of each other and were averaged to give country this placement on scale. Countries without asterisks represent, except in very few instances, assessments of non-native judges only; this indicates that native and non-native scores differed by more than 6 per cent, or no native scores were received.

But in many of them there are few native newsmen and no foreign correspondents.

A look at the distribution of countries, by regions, into the seven classifications (see Table II) shows the Western Hemisphere to have the highest degree of press freedom of all five regions. More than 96 per cent of the population of the Western Hemisphere lived under free press conditions in 1966.

Europe is greatly polarized, with 13 of its 25 nations falling into the top two levels and 7 in the bottom level. But because of the size of Russia, 55.3 per cent of the population of Europe lived under controlled press conditions and only 41.8 per cent was subject to a free press.[11]

In the Middle East, not one country could be ranked in the top level of press freedom, and the four unranked countries would surely have fallen into the controlled division if measured completely. This means that 72 per cent of the population is exposed to a controlled press, making the Middle East the most oppressive region of the world in regard to press freedom.

In Africa, the melancholy fact is that no country in that vast continent fell into either one of the top two levels of press freedom. Although almost half of the 28 nations in Africa (North African countries were classified with the Middle East) were unranked in the survey, they represented only 17.7 per cent of Africa's population, and there is little doubt that almost all of them would

[11] A study of Czechoslovakia in 1968 probably would show that step-by-step liberalization of the press preceded or paralleled political liberalization up until the time of the five-nation invasion of that country in August, 1968.

TABLE **II**

DISTRIBUTION OF INDEPENDENT NATIONS ON PICA SCALE
FOR EACH REGION OF THE WORLD, 1966

	West. Hem. (23) *	Europe (25)	Middle East (17)	Africa (28)	Asia (22)
FREE— High Degree	7	7			2
FREE— Moderate Controls	7	6	3		4
FREE— Many Controls	5	1	2	7	4
TRANSITIONAL		1		3	6
CONTROLLED— Low Degree		2	5		2
CONTROLLED— Medium Degree	1	1	2	2	
CONTROLLED— High Degree	1	7	1	3	2
Unranked	2		4	13	2

* Number of nations (with population more than one million) in region.

fall into the "transitional" or "controlled" areas. Only 26.5 per cent of Africa's population had a free press system, and fully 37 per cent was in the transitional area, hanging somewhere between freedom and control.

Asia had more countries in the "transitional" area than did any other section of the world, but this represented only 18.4 per cent of Asia's population. India, with a population of more than 471 million, fell into the free area, somewhat offsetting the weight of Communist China at the bottom of the scale.

Only one country outside of Asia and Africa fell into the "transitional" area—Yugoslavia.

The select 16 nations in the highest category of press freedom were all within a few percentage points of each other. The PICA scores for those nations ranged from 2.53 to 3.06, with even the highest scoring nations (Norway, Switzerland and The Netherlands) almost one full point below the maximum plus-4 of "absolute freedom." Several communist countries (North Korea and Albania) were about one-half point from the other end of the continuum, indicating that a very high degree of control is more attainable than a very high degree of freedom.

There were several surprising aspects to the top category. One was that Guatemala and Venezuela were able to climb these heights. Guatemala, especially, had been on and off the Inter American Press Association's blacklist in prior years and even in 1966 had left-wing guerrillas in the hills. Even so, the score supported written reports that there had been a high degree of press freedom—for both leftists and rightists—since the inauguration of civilian President Julio Cesar Mendez Montenegro in mid-1966.

Another surprising aspect was that Japan, England and New Zealand did not make the top category. Japan received a minus score only on the factor of concentrated ownership, but received consistently mediocre scores on many other factors. England received high scores on a number of factors, but negative scores on almost an equal number, notably libel laws, organized self-regulation, concentrated ownership, government control of foreign exchange and number of marginal press units. New Zealand received relatively poor scores on libel laws, local and regional criticism, and national criticism.

In general, the PICA findings agreed very closely with the results of Nixon and Banks and Textor. But like any tool of this nature, however, some of the specific findings had to be considered in the light of other conditions. India's press, for example, rates considerably higher in degree of criticism than its overall score would indicate. This would indicate that the press is overcoming a number of economic controls and disadvantages to pursue its role of vigorous criticism. On the other hand, South Africa and Rhodesia display characteristics of press freedom, while denying huge segments of the population access to the press or opportunities for democratic participation.

In addition to the specific findings regarding regions of the world and individual nations, the PICA survey indicated:

1) Press freedom can be measured and probably with a good degree of accuracy. [12]

2) The standards for judging press freedom are very similar in most countries of the world. In 77 countries, both native and non-native judges returned PICA questionnaires. In 57 per cent of those countries, the scores of the native judges were in substantial agreement with the scores of non-native judges.

3) No nation will long remain half free, either in relation to its press or in relation to its politics. Those countries in the intermediate or "transitional" zone are likely to show more press and political change than countries in other zones.

This third indication is worth looking at more closely, especially in respect to political occurrences that have taken place since the conclusion of the PICA survey. If one agrees that press freedom is closely bound up with democracy, in

---

[12] Using a slightly different methodology, PICA was updated in 1967. However, fewer countries were rated during the second survey. See "World Press Freedom, 1967," Freedom of Information Center Publication No. 201, University of Missouri, May 1968.

the Western sense, then one must pay special attention to the predictive capacity of a system for measuring press freedom. No one can look at the seven levels of the PICA survey without being struck by the fact that most of those countries lying within the top two levels and the bottom three levels are relatively stable political systems, while most of those in the third ("Free—Many Controls") and fourth ("Transitional") levels are relatively unstable.

The original hypothesis when the PICA results were published in 1967 was that those countries in the Transitional zone were likely to undergo sharp political change in the near future. But it is now apparent that the third level will bear close watching, also. Journalists interested in international communications could help political scientists by keeping a close lookout for subtle (and overt) press controls that may be instituted in nations falling within these two levels. Such controls are likely to presage political changes within the country, and the sweep of these political changes is likely to be in direct ratio to the severity of the press controls instituted.

The third level is the danger zone, the warning light of the press freedom (and democracy) scale. Many of the countries at this level were sitting on the edge of a volcano in 1966. Some of them were sitting quite solidly on the edge, in no immediate danger of falling into the crater, but they were still on the edge. Some might have inched slightly away from the edge and, hopefully, are moving toward greater democracy and political stability. But some are leaning the other way. Argentina and Brazil are in this category, and the slide toward political and economic chaos in those countries is supposedly being prevented only by the strong hand of the military. Other countries in this zone have maintained long-time stability by one-party governments (Taiwan, Kenya and Mexico, to mention only three), a delicate political balance (Lebanon) or outright subjugation of a majority within the political entity (South Africa and Rhodesia). Greece was rated in this third category late in 1966. In April, 1967, the military coup occurred, eliminating both press freedom and democracy at the same time. The colonels were overthrown in 1974 in another military coup, but this time Greece was aimed in the direction of greater press freedom. Not surprisingly, a rebirth of political democracy has accompanied this return to competitive, open journalism.

Greece is the only country in this third zone that has shown significant improvement during the ten years since the original Freedom of Information study. The Latin American countries, in the maelstrom of massive social and political problems, have doubtlessly dropped lower. And so have the African countries in this category as the oppressiveness of one-party or one-man rule hardens.

The most shocking loss to the free press systems of the world was the "temporary" eclipse of press freedom in India in the mid-1970s. Barring *coups d'état* similar to the most recent in Greece, "temporary" losses such as this have a way of becoming permanent. Those countries in the third level of the PICA survey rest uneasily.

Those in the fourth (or Transitional) zone leave no question about their instability. They are in the caldron already, more likely than not to be undergoing extreme civil strife. The swaying between press freedom and press control is a good indicator of the political chaos or uncertainty existing within most of these countries.

In 1966 the Congo (Kinshasa) was emerging, under military control, out of deep civil strife, Ghana was attempting to restore democracy after the Nkrumah years, Indonesia was only recently rid of Sukarno, South Korea was facing the increasing authoritarianism of a strongman leader, Laos was in the middle of an undeclared civil war, Nigeria was on the verge of a major tribal war, the two parts of Pakistan rumbled under Ayub Khan and South Vietnam was engaged in a civil war. Changes have occurred in many of these countries since 1966. Bangladesh won its freedom, and then lost its freedom, including freedom of the press. South Vietnam and Laos have become highly controlled systems. Maintaining any semblance of a critical press has become a difficult and dangerous job in Nigeria and South Korea, to mention only two.

Yugoslavia has the type of stability that would not warrant its being in this category. It was at this level, however, because it had oddly come to rest at this half-way house between freedom and control, between the Soviet Communist system and the Western free press system. It is the exception to the hypothesis, and is unlikely to move very much in either direction in the near future.

If we even look at the highest category of press freedom we are struck by the presence of the Philippines there in 1966—and its obvious absence today. Martial law that extinguished most other freedoms also snuffed out freedom of the press.

In 1966 only about half the population of the world lived in nations having relatively free press systems. Ten years later, we can say that this figure has diminished tragically. Perhaps three-quarters of the population of the world now lives under systems that are neither politically nor journalistically free.

Press freedom is an excellent political indicator, although it might indicate facts that we would rather not hear. However, PICA was a far better indicator than predictor, since frequent measurements are necessary if one is to predict political motion and direction.

If PICA brought one message that bears repeating, it is this: the institution of even seemingly minor controls on the press almost always harbingers a diminution of political freedom.

Raymond B. Nixon:

Factors Related to Freedom in National Press Systems

IN HIS ESSAY on "The Challenge to Communication Research," [1] Wilbur Schramm makes this observation:

> If one looks at a book like *World Communications,* or at twenty articles in the *Journalism Quarterly* on twenty countries and their press, it is perfectly apparent that the literacy of each country, the gross national product, the distribution of wealth and population, and other elements are instrumentally related in some way to the pattern by which press systems have developed. But exactly how? A cross-country study of some of these variables in relation to communication systems would be revealing.

The same thought must have occurred to many other students of comparative journalism. For it long has been apparent, as Schramm suggests, that a particular kind of press or political system can develop only to the extent that certain variables—socioeconomic, cultural and otherwise—make it possible.

Yet it also has been obvious until recently that the data were inadequate to enable any large-scale comparative studies of these variables to be made. For example, until the United Nations and Unesco publications of the '50s began to appear, comparable data were lacking for most countries on even such basic factors as literacy and per capita income; the statistics still leave much to be desired. And this is to say nothing of the kinds of survey research data that require elaborate and costly field studies by qualified scholars and interviewers within each country. The paucity of data could explain why comparative analyses of communication systems have been so few, and why theory has been so slow to develop.

Happily, both the data and the theory of comparative journalism have been greatly enriched during the last 18 months by two new books. The first of these to appear was Daniel Lerner's *The Passing of Traditional Society.* In this extraordinary work, a brilliant social scientist develops a theory that clearly

[1] In Ralph O. Nafziger and David M. White (eds.), *Introduction to Mass Communications Research* (Baton Rouge: Louisiana State University Press, 1958), p. 17.

▶ This article, prepared by Dr. Nixon especially for this book in 1969, is basically adapted from an article by the same title which appeared in *Journalism Quarterly*, Vol. 37, No. 1 (Winter), 1960, pp. 13–28. Reprinted here, with certain changes by the author, by permission of Dr. Nixon, School of Journalism, University of Minnesota, and of *Journalism Quarterly*.

shows the vital functions performed by the press and other mass media in the transition from "traditional" to "modern" ways of life. A few months later came the International Press Institute's *The Press in Authoritarian Countries*, a volume completing a series of surveys in which journalists and scholars have collaborated to appraise the kinds and degrees of press control in all major countries of the world today. This is a body of new data that assumes even greater importance in the light of Lerner's analysis.

It is when appraisals like those of the IPI are compared with the kinds of data analyzed by Lerner that we begin to glimpse a partial answer to the question of *how* and *why* one press system rather than another develops. There is nothing new, of course, in being able to say that a "free press system" like that of the United States usually is found only in countries with a high rate of literacy and per capita income. But it is new to have sufficient material for determining whether these cultural and socioeconomic factors are related to press freedom and control in a definite and systematic way.

The writer undertook the present study to test the hypothesis that such relationship does exist. Accordingly, he arrayed the most recent UN and Unesco data related to national press systems alongside the information on press freedom reported by the IPI and a kindred organization, the Inter-American Press Association. The data were cross-checked with other sources for accuracy.

The results are striking, as the accompanying chart will show. And they become even more meaningful when the relevant aspects of Lerner's theory are kept in mind.

The uniqueness of the Lerner theory for journalism lies in the dynamic role that it ascribes to the mass media in the emergence and maintenance of modern society. Earlier analyses of UN and Unesco data had shown the fundamental importance of literacy. For example, Golden had found that literacy correlated at .87 with industrialization and at .84 with per capita income.[2] But this is a static relationship, bearing only indirectly upon the press and political systems. Lerner puts these cultural and socioeconomic factors into an overall theory of modernization that also includes *media* and *political* participation.

Lerner derived his hypothesis from history. Viewing the development of Western democracies, he saw that their modernization has exhibited "certain components and sequences whose relevance is global. Everywhere, for example, urbanization [to which he subsumes industrialization] has tended to increase literacy; rising literacy has tended to increase media exposure; increasing media exposure has 'gone with' wider economic participation (per capita income) and political participation (voting)." This, in the older democracies, is a "historic fact."

By cross-checking the first (1951) edition of Unesco's *World Com-*

[2] H. H. Golden, "Literacy and Social Change in Underdeveloped Countries," in *Rural Society*, 20:1–7 (1955).

munications with other UN and Unesco sources, Lerner obtained comparable data on 54 countries. From these he developed indices for the first four factors in his "model of modernization":

1) *Urbanization*—the proportion of a country's inhabitants living in cities over 50,000;

2) *Literacy*—the proportion of adults (*i.e.*, persons over 15) able to read in one language;

3) *Media participation*—the proportion buying newspapers, owning radios and attending movies (all combined into one index number);

4) *Political participation*—the average proportion voting in the last four national elections.

The multiple correlation coefficients of these four variables were found to be: Urbanization, .61; literacy, .91; media participation, .84; of correlation between the variable named and the three remaining variables.[3]

But this demonstration of systematic relationships among these four variables is merely the prelude to Lerner's chief contribution: the addition of the personality variable of *empathy*. Empathy, to use his simplified definition, is "the capacity to see oneself in the other fellow's situation"; it is the skill of "imagining oneself in another's shoes." He identified the more empathic individuals among 1,357 survey interviewees in six Middle Eastern countries by using the "latent structure analysis" technique of Paul F. Lazarsfeld in analyzing their responses to nine projective questions. These included such questions as: If you were made "head of the government" (or "editor of a newspaper," or "put in charge of a radio station"), "what are some of the things you would do?"

Lerner found that the more empathic individuals have more "mobile personalities"; this enables them to express opinions on a wider range of subjects. It is by providing people with vicarious or "psychic mobility" that the mass media accelerate the development of empathy and thus perform an indispensable service:

> Audiences and constituencies are composed of participant individuals. People "participate" in the public life of their country by having opinions about many matters which, in the isolation of traditional society, did not concern them. Participant persons have opinions on a variety of issues and situations which they may never have experienced directly— such as what the government should do about irrigation, how the Algerian revolt should be settled. . . . By having and expressing opinions on such matters a person participates in the network of public communication.
>
> The media teach people participation of this sort by depicting for

---

[3] Daniel Lerner, *The Passing of Traditional Society* (Glencoe, Ill.: The Free Press, 1958), pp. 46, 63.

them new and strange situations and by familiarizing them with a range of opinions among which they can choose. Some people learn better than others, the variations reflecting their skill in empathy.[4]

Lerner concludes that "a communication system is both index and agent of change in a total social system. This avoids the genetic problem of causality, about which we can only speculate, in order to stress correlation hypotheses which can be tested. On this view, once the modernizing process is started, chicken and egg in fact 'cause' each other to develop."

It is worth noting, however, that media participation comes *third* in Lerner's "typology of modernization." Thus, it follows urbanism and literacy, but precedes political participation and high empathy—two qualities characteristic of those societies where political democracy and press freedom have flourished.

The basic procedure used in this study—that of arranging related data on different countries in parallel columns for comparison—was so simple that little explanation seems necessary. However, since one of these variables represents a classification of qualitative appraisals by "experts" on the press, it is necessary to explain the method of classification so that the reader may judge its validity.

The UN and Unesco publications were the starting point, as they were for Lerner. Examination of these sources to the middle of 1959 indicated that reasonably comparable data could be obtained on 85 countries and territories for three variables related to national press systems:

> *Per capital national income*—defined by the United Nations as the average income per inhabitant "accruing to factors of production supplied by normal residents of the given country before deduction of direct taxation."
>
> *Percentage of adults (persons 15 years and older) illiterate*—illiteracy being defined by Unesco as "inability to read and write in any language."
>
> *Daily newspaper circulation*—a daily being "any newspaper published more than four times a week."

The dates selected for each variable were the latest for which comparable statistics on the largest countries could be found.

It was decided to use daily newspaper circulation, rather than a general index of "media participation" like Lerner's, partly because circulation figures were available for a larger number of countries. But further reflection revealed a much sounder reason: Since broadcasting systems in most countries outside the Western Hemisphere are either owned by the government or operated by a government-controlled monopoly, the conditions affecting press freedom relate primarily to the printed media.

[4] Lerner, *op. cit.*, p. 412.

The main problem of methods arose in trying to bring together "modern, precise research procedures and the more traditional broad approaches of historical . . . and journalistic appraisal." In the first place, before setting up a continuum with *freedom* at one end and *control* at the other, it was necessary to define the two terms and the various points of classification between. Secondly, a method was required for quantifying the various degrees of freedom so that this factor could be correlated statistically with other variables.

The author began by accepting the IPI's definition of an "authoritarian regime" as one characterized by "a permanent censorship or a constant and general control of the press," either by the government or the political group in power. A "free press system," by contrast, is one marked by the *absence* of such a permanent censorship or constant and general control; it is one in which private owners and independent journalists are free to supply news and opinion to the general public under statutes of libel and decency which are applicable to everyone and not capable of arbitrary and discriminatory interpretation by the ruling power. In other words, the chief criterion is the degree of control normally exercised by any official agency which has the power to interfere with the dissemination and discussion of news.

It immediately became apparent that a classification of countries according to their constitutional guarantees or statutes regarding press freedom would be of little help in determining the actual situation. Most countries have constitutions or laws that pay lip service to the principle of freedom of expression and the press, but their practices frequently are something quite different. It therefore was decided to base the classification primarily upon the situation as reported by IPI-IAPA observers and analysts.

On the basis of the two major IPI surveys (1 and 2 in the sources listed in the chart), a five-way classification was set up:

F   Free press system; normally no major government controls.

F—   Free press, but with less stability and/or more controls than F.

I   Intermediate; some characteristics of free press, but with varying kinds and degrees of authoritarian control.

A—   Authoritarian, but with less rigid press controls than A.

A   Authoritarian press system; strong controls over all mass media.

Since journalists in the Communist countries object strongly to having their particular type of government and party controls classified as "authoritarian," a sixth category of "C" was created for the Communist systems, with "C—" designating countries in which there is substantial evidence of less rigidity in enforcement.

The writer did not wish to depend upon his own unaided judgment in classifying qualitative data. He was aware that he might have been influenced by impressions received over the last three years on personal visits to some 45 of the countries and territories under study. He therefore submitted his own classification to two other judges, one in Europe and one in the United States. Both are journalists and scholars whose principal area of research is comparative journalism.

The two judges together raised questions about seven of the 85 classifications. In each case it was a question only of moving a particular country from one position to an adjoining position on the scale; in no case did either judge suggest that an "F" or "F—" country should be classified as "A" or "A—", or the reverse. In the four cases where both judges disagreed with the writer, the classification was changed to agree with the majority opinion.

But to what extent had two or more judges been influenced by the same biases? How would a person who had to rely entirely on available documentary sources classify the same countries?

A graduate student (Kenneth A. Gompertz) was assigned to work on this problem. For information, he searched not only the IPI and IAPA sources but also the New York *Times* and *Editor & Publisher*. In the period since the founding of the IPI in 1951, he found reports related to press freedom in 101 countries. When he eliminated those countries on which information was incomplete or fragmentary, 61 countries remained.

The press controls reported in these 61 countries were classifiable into 10 different categories. Three of these eventually were dropped because of inconsistency of pattern or infrequency of occurrence. One of the categories that had to be discarded, as might be suspected, was a classification on the basis of legal guarantees. The seven categories that appeared to establish a "typology" were:

1) Control through punitive action, legal and extra-legal, other than that covered by statutes against libel and obscenity. This includes civil and criminal action, arrests, detention, jail sentences, fines and deportation. Such action was recorded only if it discriminated against the journalist, such as through the law of *desacato* ("disrespect toward authority") found in most South American countries. Such a law typifies public security measures used to control journalists considered "dangerous to public order."

2) Control of publication's existence or very life through such action as a) seizure of newspapers, b) restriction of newsprint and other supplies, and c) permission to publish only under favorable government disposition.

3) Control of official news through governmental attitude toward official news releases (*i.e.*, that such news must be published without change) or through limited access to governmental news.

4) Control of newspaper personnel, either by direct approval or by appointment of staffs or punishment or censure.

5) Control through official censorship, either through overt cen-

sorship organs or by police or police-like actions. The existence of an office of censorship was considered control through threat even in cases where relatively little activity was reported.

6) Control of periodical content or format, ranging all the way from complete planning and policy control to pressures exerted to restrict ideological "wandering."

7) Control of periodical distribution, either directly or indirectly.

The 61 countries were "scored" on each of these controls. The resulting rank data were subjected to a Guttman-scale type of analysis to find out whether the different kinds of restriction did, indeed, cumulate.[5] This scalogram analysis produced a "model of press control" with eight types, ranging from 0 controls to 7 (Table 1).

In the listing above, the types of control are presented in the order in which they tend to cumulate. Thus a country which has control 7 (distribution) typically will have most if not all of the other controls. Again, a country with restriction 4 (control of personnel) will tend to have the controls which appear to the right of it in Table 1, but not controls 5, 6 or 7.

When the independent ratings obtained by this method for the 61 countries were compared with the classifications of these countries by the three judges, a statistical correlation of .94 was found; the correlation with the final ratings of these countries in the chart was .96.[6]

This phase of the project accomplished three things: 1) It tended to support the ratings of the three judges; 2) it pointed to the possibility of establishing an objective method for classifying types of press control; 3) it called attention (as the judges also had done) to the desirability of further shadings and qualifications in the classification scheme finally to be adopted.

For this latter reason, the five original categories on the freedom-control continuum were expanded to eight, with a ninth category possible. Thus, "F¹" was inserted between "F" and "F—" to identify five countries where the existence of a strong "free press system" was unchallenged by the judges, but where special circumstances had led to the imposition of certain controls on an emergency basis during the period studied. The "I+" symbol was added for those "Intermediate" countries where long-term tendencies since 1951 have seemed to favor press freedom, and "I—" for those in this category where the long-term development has been less favorable. Finally, a "C¹" symbol was adopted for two European Communist countries (Albania and Rumania) that had been listed for general comparison, but which could not be included among the 85 studied simply because their controls are so thorough-going as to make adequate information impossible to obtain. An "A¹" also was provided.

---

[5] For a description of the method used, see Louis H. Guttman, "The Cornell Technique for Scale and Intensity Analysis," *Educational and Psychological Measurement*, 7:248–79 (1947). The coefficient of reproducibility was .92.

[6] The coefficient is tetrachoric *r*, which provides an estimate of the product-moment correlation between the two scales.

TABLE I

MODEL OF PRESS CONTROL

Control Type	METHOD OF CONTROL						
	Distri-bution (7)	Content-Format (6)	Censor-ship (5)	Personnel (4)	Official News (3)	Seizure (2)	Criminal-Civil (1)
Type 7	x	x	x	x	x	x	x
Type 6		x	x	x	x	x	x
Type 5			x	x	x	x	x
Type 4				x	x	x	x
Type 3					x	x	x
Type 2						x	x
Type 1							x
Type 0							

An "x" indicates the presence of the control category in a governmental system.

The scale of the "freedom-control" continuum then was expressed quantitatively, for purposes of statistical analysis, as follows:

F F^1	F–	I+ I I–	C– A–	C C^1 A A^1
1	2	3	4	5

These nine categories [7] made it possible to identify qualitative differences not shown by the original classification. For purposes of correlational analysis, however, the five-point numerical scale was retained (as shown above) in order to approximate the assumption of equal intervals along the continuum. In general, it was felt that the differences in degree of control were approximately equal along the five-category scale.

Support for the decision to assign the same weight to class "C" as to class "A" systems was found in the "model of press control" shown in Table 1. When the ratings of the 61 countries forming the basis of this model were compared, both the major Communist country (the Soviet Union) and the Dominican Republic, under whose military dictatorship the press system was classified as "A," fell into Type 7. This is the scale type of category in which control of the press by governmental authority is most nearly complete.

The statistical findings of this study thus strongly support the hypothesis that there is a definite and systematic relationship between the degree of free-

---

[7] In the author's second study, made five years later, a simple nine-point numerical scale was used. See "Freedom in the World's Press: A Fresh Appraisal with New Data," *Journalism Quarterly*, 42:3–14, 118–19 (Winter 1965).

dom in a national press system and three other variables. The correlation between press freedom and each of these variables [8] is as follows:

Per capita national income	.64
Proportion of adults literate	.51
Daily newspaper circulation per 1,000 inhabitants	.63

Each of these correlation coefficients is significant at the 1% level. In other words, there is less than one chance in one hundred that the relationship could be purely coincidental.

Thus, in the world of today, wherever per capita income is high, press freedom is likely to be found—along with its necessary concomitant, political democracy. Literacy also is related to press freedom, but not so closely as per capita income.

The statistics also support what the history of the press reveals: that high newspaper circulation and press freedom tend to go together.

Discussion

In looking for specific patterns, it was noted that every country which had an annual per capita income of $600 or more in 1952–54 had then, and has today, a strong free press system. Most of these countries also have an adult illiteracy rate of only 1–2%. This top group in per capita income also embraced the 15 countries highest in daily newspaper circulation per 1,000 population, except for Japan.

Only two countries in the $600 or more annual per capita income group required the "F¹" classification, indicating the occurrence of certain emergency controls during recent years in what otherwise is a strong free press system. One of these countries was France, where recurrent economic and military crises appear to account for deviations from its normal pattern of freedom. The other was Finland, where the press probably is as free as any in Europe except for a law which makes it an offense to "endanger Finland's relations with her neighbors"—*i.e.*, the Soviet Union. But both these countries repeatedly have shown their determination to maintain freedom of expression, even under adverse circumstances.

Even when all countries with an annual per capita income of $300 or more were considered, only six had classifications other than "F, F¹ or F—." These were Spain, classified as "A"; Cuba, now "C"; and the four Communist countries of Europe that are most advanced industrially: Czechoslovakia, East Germany, Poland and the U.S.S.R. To these four might be added Hungary, whose more recent per capita income figures put it ahead of Poland.

Spain, as the IPI survey points out, is the only non-Communist country in the world today with an authoritarian system based upon "a well-established

[8] Because the data for the relationship between press freedom and the three independent variables did not meet the assumption of linearity, the correlation ration (eta—coefficient of curvilinear correlation) was used instead of product-moment *r*.)

doctrine on information." To understand its system of press controls one must remember that the country over which General Franco gained supreme power in 1936 was, like the Tsarist Russia which the Bolsheviks took over in 1917, an old-style monarchy with strong religious underpinnings. It had been touched scarcely at all by the liberalizing influences that had led to the development of democratic institutions in Western Europe and the United States. The main difference between what happened in Spain and what happened in Russia is that Franco led a "broad" revolution which kept essentially the same elements in power, whereas the Communists appealed to long-suppressed, "deep" revolutionary forces that completely overthrew the old ruling classes in what is now the Soviet Union.

Cuba's plight points up the general instability that has characterized even the richest of Latin American countries during most of their independent existence. Essentially it grows out of the fact that these countries, as colonies of Spain and Portugal down to the early part of the 19th century, likewise were isolated from the liberalizing influences that revolutionized politics, economics, religion and the press in England and elsewhere during the 17th, 18th and 19th centuries. Even the leaders of independence movements in most Latin American countries came from a relatively small class of European descent, and their ideas did not penetrate very far down into the Indian and mestizo masses. The strong middle-class support that leads both to a stable democratic government and to a strong free press has been generally lacking, except in three countries (Uruguay, Chile and Costa Rica) where a fairly homogeneous population has helped to produce a more equitable distribution of income, and one country (Mexico) which has made consistent progress in improving the general welfare over the last 30 years.

This brings us to the five communist countries of Europe that are highest in per capita income and literacy (Czechoslovakia, East Germany, Poland, the U.S.S.R. and Hungary). These five nations stand out as the most conspicuous deviations from the general rule of a close relationship between these two variables and the existence of press freedom as defined in the Western world.

The deviation shown by these Communist countries is not as difficult to explain, however, as it might at first appear. In the first place, it must be remembered that when the Communists came to power and installed their system of press controls, the adult illiteracy rate of the Russians by their own figures was between 60 and 70%, and the old Russian Empire was on the verge of economic collapse. Moreover, it was the long-suppressed aspirations of the Russian people for a more democratic political system, as well as for economic improvement, that hastened the rise of the Communists to power. It was the need to appeal to these deep revolutionary forces—quite similar to the forces that much earlier had led to revolutions in France and England—that led the Communists to include in their political apparatus a number of democratic forms, including "freedom of the press," which in turn are counterweighted by totalitarian controls that enable the party to use the press as one instrument for achieving its social goals. These goals include the elimination of illiteracy and the raising of living standards—the same goals which the Western world had been achieving gradually over a period of years by less authoritarian methods.

From conversations with journalists in seven Communist countries during the summer of 1959, the writer feels sure that some of these journalists are sincerely convinced that their system of controls does permit them press "freedom," although of quite a different type from freedom as the West defines it. The paradox of this situation has been explained by an American historian, who points out that "man can seem to be free in any society, no matter how authoritarian, as long as he accepts the postulates of the society." To this the Western democracies have added the important concept that "man can only be free in a society that is willing to allow its basic postulates to be questioned." [9]

So far the Communist leaders of the Soviet Union have not allowed their "basic postulates" to be questioned. But now that their country has attained a high degree of literacy and industrialization, there seems to be reason for believing that it may tend increasingly to follow the pattern shown by Lerner's historical "model of modernization," and thus to manifest more of the characteristics of a truly "participant society."

As for Czechoslovakia, East Germany, Poland and Hungary, they already had attained the conditions for press freedom, along with industrialization and literacy, before they fell under Communist control as a result of developments following World War II. There is impressive evidence that they would have essentially the same kind and degree of freedom today as that of the West, except for circumstances beyond their control. These circumstances can be explained only in terms of the rise of the Soviet Union to a position of great military strength.

Already there are signs of some relaxation in the extent to which the Soviet government controls the lives of its citizens, and this is spreading to the other Communist countries of Europe. The possible benefits of an extended period of peaceful coexistence with the Western democracies are implicit in Siebert's "theory of press freedom." After an exhaustive study of the development of press freedom in the Western world, Siebert advanced as a tentative law of history that "the area of freedom contracts and the enforcement of restraints increases as the stresses on the stability of government and of the structure of society increase." [10] Obversely, as the stresses on the stability of the government and the structure of society *decrease*, the area of freedom may be expected to expand.

One of the greatest dangers in any highly centralized political system with strong press controls is that the government and ruling party can use the mass

[9] John B. Wolf, "Man's Struggle for Freedom Against Authority," in *Social Science and Freedom* (Minneapolis: University of Minnesota, 1955), p. 1.
[10] In Introduction to Frederick S. Siebert, *Freedom of the Press in England, 1476–1776* (Urbana, Ill.: University of Illinois Press, 1952).

media to create whatever tensions they may regard as necessary to justify the imposition of even more rigid controls. It is no longer unusual, however, to find Communist journalists who will admit that this is one weakness of a system which they otherwise may strongly defend. In the same breath they frequently will declare that the Soviet Union today would not tolerate another dictator like Stalin. The fact that some Communists thus recognize the dangers of absolute power is one of the most hopeful signs of all.

Certainly it is in the Communist countries that still have the farthest to go along the road to literacy and high per capita income (Bulgaria, Rumania, Albania and China) that one finds the controls over the press and other institutions to be the most severe. The difference between the stern discipline of China's "great leap forward" and the more relaxed atmosphere of present-day Russia is so great, indeed, that some observers believe the Soviet Union some day may find itself closer in many respects to the United States and the democracies of Western Europe than to its great Asian ally.

But what of those European and Asian countries with a low per capita income—some also with high illiteracy—that nevertheless have made substantial progress up the ladder toward political democracy and press freedom? It is here that one finds the clue to other factors related to press freedom that deserve careful study.

One of these countries is Japan, the other the Republic of the Philippines. Without lessening in any sense the credit due the Japanese and Filipino people, it can be said that the policies of the United States have been a contributory factor in the development of their free systems. Both Japan, since regaining its sovereignty in 1952, and the Philippines, since becoming fully independent in 1946, have shown their determination to maintain press freedom. The Japanese press, however, appears to have the stronger foundation, because of Japan's higher literacy, high per capita income and huge newspaper circulation— the fifth largest per capita in the world. The foundation in the Philippines is potentially less stable, both because of the lower literacy rate and because newspaper ownership and circulation are so heavily concentrated in one city, Manila.

The most amazing country of all is India (F—), which has attained a fairly stable democracy and free press system despite a per capita income of less than $100 a year and an illiteracy rate of 75–80%. A long period of association with British democracy and press freedom must be given some credit here, as also in Ceylon (F—) and in the present and former British dependencies elsewhere in Asia and in Africa. But one cannot explain the phenomenon of India without considering the strong personal charisma of leaders like Gandhi and Nehru, and also the possible influence of the Hindu religion.

The other Asian country with a per capita income of less than $300 which can be definitely classified as having a free press system is tiny Lebanon (F—). Almost invariably its system is rated by those familiar with the area as "the freest press in the Middle East." This can be attributed in part to a favorable geographic situation, which has helped to give it a higher per capita income than all its neighbors except Israel. But it aso is probably due to a relatively long period of development as a French protectorate, and perhaps most of all to the stabilizing influence of a truce between the Christian and Moslem populations.

It is the "I" and "A" classifications that seem to be the least satisfactory. In Africa, for example, all the countries and territories except the Union of South Africa are in one sense "authoritarian," not because any totalitarian government has usurped the power, but simply because in many places there would be no communication system at all unless the government provided it. The widespread illiteracy, the multiplicity of native languages and dialects, and the lack of adequate electric power in some regions to maintain even radio communication on any widespread basis—all these tend to keep most of the newly emerging African states in a strange mixture of free and authoritarian forms. In the larger and more prosperous cities inhabited by people of European descent will be newspapers much like those of the countries from which whites have come, and enjoying much of the same freedom; for the natives, the situation may be quite different. Even the press in the Union of South Africa, where democratic institutions have been developed to the highest level, must be classified as less than free because of the pressures and suspicions created by the official policy of *Apartheid*. The best that can be said for most of the newly emerging African states is that their press is in an "intermediate" state of development; "mixed" would describe the situation better as of today.

Actually, the term "authoritarian" as used by the IPI and as adopted in this study for all except the Communist countries, covers too wide a range of non-democratic systems. It includes, at one extreme, the absolutist monarchy of Yemen, which has no daily newspapers at all and depends for mass communication mainly upon a government-owned weekly and radio station. But it also includes the more democratically inclined constitutional monarchies of Libya and Ethiopia; the military dictatorships of Spain, Latin America and other areas, varying widely in their objectives if not their methods; and the still different type of authoritarian rule represented by the more dynamic United Arab Republic.

This latter type of authoritarianism, as Lerner analyzes it, seems, like Communism, to represent "people in a hurry" to obtain more of the better things of life. The violent upheavals so frequent in the Middle East can be attributed, indeed, to the fact that the demands and expectations of the people, stimulated in part by the mass media, greatly exceed their socioeconomic and cultural capacity for achievement. But if they continue to improve their economic status and their capacity for genuine media and political participation, they too may eventually succeed in establishing the conditions that make true press freedom possible.

Heinz-Dietrich Fischer:

Press Councils Throughout the World: An Empirical Approach

THE IDEA of press self-control had been discussed in various Scandinavian countries and at least partially realized in Sweden (1916), Finland (1927) and Norway (1928) through the establishment of the very first institutions designed for such a purpose. Thereafter, such initiatives were largely forgotten. The idea experienced a renaissance as a result of the censorship and other dirigistic measures associated with war and experienced by many countries.[1] Deliberation on the subject of press self-control seems to have taken place at an early stage in Japan.[2] At about the same time, a "regulating council", which initiated various activities on the lines of such self-control, was established in the Netherlands.[3] Internationally, a U.S. Press Commission's call for a free and responsible press[4] received a warm reception.

Far more effective impulses, however, find their origin in the various postwar efforts in Great Britain aiming at rationalization and liberalization of the press. Inspired by a Press Commission set up in 1947 and completing its work in 1949, the idea of a so-called "press council" (the term had not been used previously) was systematically popularized. Although the notion of a voluntary body imposing its own discipline was already widespread publicly as well as among many journalists, clarity and agreement concerning the competency of such a council (how and against what it should be directed) was lacking. It was neither generally accepted that its role lay in protecting the interests of the press against government interference nor in limiting the power of the newspaper owner. After much bargaining the "General Council on the Press" was finally established in 1953.[5]

The British example in setting up such a council had a considerable boosting effect on many countries where similar ideas had been entertained for quite a time. This was true especially in the case of the German Federal Republic. Certain ideas concerning press self-control which found their origin in the Weimar Era were already being discussed during the allied occupation of Germany between 1945 and 1949.[6] After a lengthy tug-of-war between various interest groups, e.g. journalists and publishers, but inspired by the British example, and fears regarding proposed federal press legislation, the German press

▶ This is an original article written for this book by Dr. Heinz-Dietrich Fischer, assisted by Klaus Detlef R. Breuer, M.A. and Hans-Wolfgang Wolter, M.A., from the Ruhr-University Bochum/Germany; translated by Stefan R. Melnik, B.A.

council ("Deutscher Presserat") was set up in late 1956.[7] The countries mentioned below followed suit in relatively quick succession: Turkey (1960),[8] Austria (1961), South Korea (1961),[9] Israel (1963),[10] Denmark (1964), India (1965),[11] Canada (1972), New Zealand (1972), Sri Lanka (1973), USA (1973),[12] and Switzerland (1974, but not yet fully functional).[13]

It remains to be noted that the structure and functions of press councils vary from country to country. It can be implied from such literature as that above, that detailed analytical monographs dealing with the development of such councils from the time of their foundation are not to be found. If this is the case at a national level, excepting the annual reports published by some press councils, one cannot hope for much in the way of literature from an international or comparative point of view. A few eclectic attempts—in some cases full of mistakes—aside, it is impossible to refer to more than a relatively small number of preliminary works. As indicated above, these are of limited use.

To begin with, it can be taken for granted that before 1960, because of the small number of press councils in existence at that time, no studies beyond national horizons were undertaken. At best, the literature that was published compared press laws and legislation.[14] One of the first—and ever since most discussed—attempts to schematize the characteristics of various press systems and degrees of press freedom at a theoretical level was made by Siebert, Peterson and Schramm. In their well-known book, *Four Theories of the Press* (authoritarian, libertarian, social responsibility, and Soviet-totalitarian)—self-control is also discussed.[15]

The embedding of the concept of self-control in the realm of social responsibility clearly has its origin in the recommendations (already referred to above) of the American "Commission on the Freedom of the Press" in 1947 calling for press responsibility in the context of social responsibility. This question, among others, is also tackled in a frequently reprinted International Press Institute (IPI) publication on press councils and press codes, originally published in 1961. For instance, the IPI Director, Per Monsen, expressed his fears concerning the interpretation of the concept of press responsibility. Journalists might feel themselves compelled to support government policies unconditionally, a result of possible government pressure. It is all too easy for the latter to call many only mildly critical comments irresponsible.[16]

The first tentative attempt to work out certain similarities between press councils and their common problems was made at the time of the setting up of the Indian press council.[17] In the late sixties a study by Löffler and Hébarre, whose title seems to promise much, was published. One quickly discovers, however, that the work is purely descriptive and not always accurate and reliable. A number of countries with press councils are listed without attempting to schematize or draw a single continuous comparison.[18] A serious attempt to study the phenomenon of press councils comparatively was undertaken by the Honorary President of the International Federation of Journalists (IFJ) in Brus-

FOUR RATIONALES FOR THE MASS MEDIA

	AUTHORITARIAN	LIBERTARIAN	SOCIAL RESPONSIBILITY	SOVIET-TOTALITARIAN
Developed	In 16th and 17th century England; widely adopted and still practiced in many places	adopted by England after 1688, and in U.S.; influential elsewhere	in U.S. in the 20th century	in Soviet Union, although some of the same things were done by Nazis and Italians
Out of	philosophy of absolute power of monarch, his government, or both	writings of Milton, Locke, Mill, and general philosophy of rationalism and natural rights	writing of W. E. Hocking, Commission on Freedom of Press, and practitioners; media codes	Marxist-Leninist-Stalinist thought, with mixture of Hegel and 19th century Russian thinking
Chief purpose	to support and advance the policies of the government in power; and to service the state	to inform, entertain, sell — but chiefly to help discover truth, and to check on government	to inform, entertain, sell — but chiefly to raise conflict to the plane of discussion	to contribute to the success and continuance of the Soviet socialist system, and especially to the dictatorship of the party
Who has right to use media?	whoever gets a royal patent or similar permission	anyone with economic means to do so	everyone who has something to say	loyal and orthodox party members
How are media controlled?	government patents, guilds, licensing, sometimes censorship	by "self-righting process of truth" in "free market place of ideas," and by courts	community opinion, consumer action, professional ethics	surveillance and economic or political action of government
What forbidden?	criticism of political machinery and officials in power	defamation, obscenity, indecency, wartime sedition	serious invasion of recognized private rights and vital social interests	criticism of party objectives as distinguished from tactics
Ownership	private or public	chiefly private	private unless government has to take over to insure public service	public
Essential differences from others	instrument for effecting government policy, though not necessarily government owned	instrument for checking on government and meeting other needs of society	media must assume obligation of social responsibility; and if they do not, someone must see that they do	state-owned and closely controlled media existing solely as arm of state

sels, H. J. Bradley: in dispatching questionnaires to journalists' organizations in member countries only, however, he automatically excluded some councils from his assessment. Despite this, one can rightly say that this was *quasi* the first attempt to tackle the topic of press councils empirically.[19]

*　　*　　*　　*

A professor at the University of Missouri, seeking to answer a different set of questions concerning press liberty, developed a further empirical approach. He drew up a catalogue of criteria with the help of which the extent of press freedom could be gauged in more than a hundred countries. The professor in question, Ralph L. Lowenstein, was the author of the PICA-index (press independence and critical ability). Twenty-three criteria were used for assessing the situation in each country in question.[20] [See second article, by Lowenstein, in this chapter.] One of these criteria—related to press councils, is "Organized Self-Regulation."

A questionnaire containing questions pertaining to all 23 criteria had to be completed by insiders or nationals for each country on one hand, and independent observers on the other. Each question was answered in terms of a five-category scale. All 23 criteria were equally weighted for the purpose of evaluation. Finally, the average between the national and independent estimates was calculated for each country. Of the 115 states for which such an assessment was attempted, 94 returned enough information (and sufficient information was returned on their behalf) so as to enable a ranking according to the PICA index. The highest attainable index number was +4, the lowest, −4. Between these two extremes, absolute freedom of the press and absolute control, classification according to the following seven categories was possible:[21]

Freedom of the
World's Press

Absolute freedom	+4
(1) Free—high degree	+3
(2) Free—moderate controls	+2
(3) Free—many controls	+1
(4) Transitional	0
(5) Controlled—low degree	−1
(6) Controlled—medium degree	−2
(7) Controlled—high degree	−3
Absolute control	−4

Since Lowenstein's criteria deal with negative attributes, through which the extent of press freedom is reduced, the existence of press councils in the countries concerned helps—according to this system—to reduce rather than increase their rating. Lowenstein originally wrote that "press councils and courts of honor may indeed be institutions for raising the ethics of the press, but they also serve as a control on absolute press freedom".[22] The table that follows may help us understand to what extent the existence of organized bodies of self-control can affect the PICA index calculation of press freedom for the 19 countries whose press councils were recently the object of a broader analysis and comparative study.[23] One should note that the countries marked with an asterisk did not possess true press councils at the time of compilation for the PICA index. It is to be implied that other forms of organized self-regulation must have existed at the time, and it was these that were evaluated: [24]

Country	PARTIAL INDICES FOR ORGANIZED SELF REGULATION		Final PICA Index
	Native Estimate	Non-native Estimate	
Norway	0.00	0.00	3.06
Switzerland	1.00	1.00	3.06
The Netherlands	0.50	—	3.02
Sweden	−1.20	0.00	2.83
Canada	4.00	4.00	2.78
Finland	2.00	2.00	2.72
United States of America	2.57	0.67	2.72
Denmark	0.67	3.00	2.65
Japan	1.00	0.40	2.44
Germany (Fed. Rep.)	1.33	1.33	2.43
Great Britain	0.80	−0.50	2.37
New Zealand	4.00	—	2.24
Austria	1.33	0.50	2.10
Israel	−0.80	0.50	1.75
Turkey	1.00	1.33	1.66
Sri Lanka (Ceylon)	2.50	2.00	1.14
South Africa	2.00	1.00	1.07
India	0.57	−1.00	0.98
South Korea	−0.67	1.33	0.42

A comparison between the values obtained for organized self-regulation and those for the final index shows that all countries, with the exception of Canada, New Zealand, Sri Lanka, and South Africa clearly have lower ratings in the former than in the latter final index. In some cases, the partial indices even show negative ratings. Unfortunately, there is no room in this article to discuss the relative merits and shortcomings of Lowenstein's assessment methods. It can be said, however, that if this method is stringently re-examined, the high degree of divergence in the ratings under consideration is significant—even in the case of countries that did not possess an institutionalized press council at the time of Lowenstein's study.

If one starts from Lowenstein's premises, it may be of interest to compare those countries with press councils with respect to their position in the PICA index:

1st category: *"free-high degree"* (+2.51-+4.0)-eight countries (Canada, Denmark, Finland, the Netherlands, Norway, Sweden, Switzerland, U.S.A.);

2nd category: *"free but with moderate controls"* (+1.51-+2.50)-seven countries (Federal Republic of Germany, Great Britain, Israel, Japan, New Zealand, Austria, Turkey);

3rd category: *"free but with many controls"* (+0.51-+1.50)-three countries (India, South Africa, Sri Lanka); and

4th category: *"transitional systems"* (-0.50-+0.50)-one country (South Korea).

The other classifications in the PICA index ("controlled-low degree", "controlled-medium degree", "controlled-high degree" and "absolute control") did not apply to any of the countries with press councils. Since all 19 countries under study are categorized positively, former IPI director Ernest Meyer's comment that press councils exist exclusively in countries where they are hardly necessary seems to be a valid point for discussion.[25] However, such a narrow and myopic view hampers a differentiated analysis of different varieties of press council with various degrees of efficiency and importance in such a way that simple generalisations—without all the sufficient checks—could all too easily be attempted.

*   *   *   *

Robert P. Knight also considered the concept of press self-regulation in relation to press freedom in his study of the situation in South America.[26] Closely related to the subject of press councils as institutions in various countries, is the question as to the existence of ethical codes, which either serve as guidelines for their decisions or are otherwise referred to. Apart from the description of the codes of honor in many countries in the above-mentioned IPI publication, an American, Joe Bill Vogel, researched the topic. He studied the ethical codes adhered to by the press in 29 countries, recognizing that such codes constitute an important disciplinary instrument despite the fact that, according to his observations, higher ethical standards are hardly ever attained.[27]

For many years now, supranational organizations have attempted to work out a binding common code of honor for a number of countries. In a "Declaration on Mass Communication Media and Human Rights" issued by the Council of Europe it is said: "It is the duty of the press and other mass media to discharge their functions with a sense of responsibility towards the community and towards the individual citizens. For this purpose, it is desirable to institute (where not already done): . . . (b) a professional code of ethics for journalists

. . . . , (c) press councils empowered to investigate and even to censure instances of unprofessional conduct with a view to the exercising of self-control by the press itself." [28] UNESCO also took up these two issues, at first it put forward proposals for discussion under the heading of ethical principals for journalists,[29] later on it was followed by suggestions on mass media councils.[30]

There is wide acceptance nowadays of the need for instituting press councils and drawing up press codes. Ralph Lowenstein has altered his position somewhat since the publication of the PICA index in which the existence of press councils is poorly rated. He gives the creation of the National News Council in the U.S.A. his guarded approval. At the same time he avoids evaluating the experiment for the time being.[31]

One can discern from the following model, depicting present and possible future press structures, that Lowenstein foresees a growth in self-regulation:[32]

LOWENSTEIN PROGRESSION TYPOLOGY

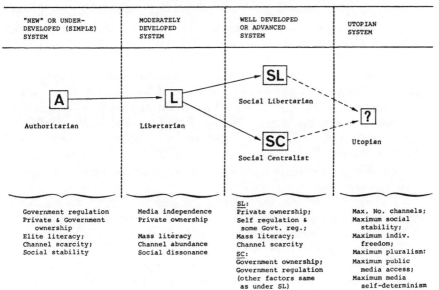

"NEW" OR UNDER-DEVELOPED (SIMPLE) SYSTEM	MODERATELY DEVELOPED SYSTEM	WELL DEVELOPED OR ADVANCED SYSTEM	UTOPIAN SYSTEM
Government regulation Private & Government ownership Elite literacy; Channel scarcity; Social stability	Media independence Private ownership Mass literacy Channel abundance Social dissonance	SL: Private ownership; Self regulation & some Govt. reg.; Mass literacy, Channel scarcity SC: Government ownership; Government regulation (other factors same as under SL)	Max. No. channels; Maximum social stability; Maximum indiv. freedom; Maximum pluralism; Maximum public media access; Maximum media self-determinism

In this model, the so-called "social libertarian" media systems in highly developed countries are characterized by their institutionalized or some other form of self-regulation. Having surveyed the literature and developments to date, and before press self-regulation or control is looked at more closely, some definitions and descriptions of the functions of a press council can be noted. Darel Vasak of the Council of Europe ascribes two basic functions of press councils: "(1) to protect the freedom of the press—it is therefore a *machinery for self-defence*; (2) to combat abuses of press freedom—it is therefore a *machinery for self-control*." [33] A press council can also be defined in the following manner: "A voluntary self-administering decision-making body for the purposes of press self-control independent of state and pressure groups." [34]

Franz Ronneberger writes that "as far as actual self-control is concerned, the media neither wish to involve society nor the state in their affairs. Rather, they wish to look after themselves. They wish their conduct with regard to the adherence to certain norms to be scrutinised constantly by a self-constituted body whose members are elected from their own ranks. Such a body's decisions are accepted as binding." [35] One of the German legal experts on questions concerning the press, Martin Löffler, describes the duties of such a body as follows: "Internal control of the press is an institution created by the press and for the press, in which journalists and publishers co-operate of their own free will and responsibility, in order to ensure the proper relationship between press on one hand and the State and society on the other, by maintaining professional ethics within and defending the freedom of the press without." [36]

*   *   *   *

These general definitions and descriptions of function, however, do not suffice for a comparative analysis of status and function of press councils. Although certain minimum criteria are offered, they prove to be too coarse for such purposes. In the study which now will be considered (already mentioned above), it was therefore necessary to start from scratch. [37] Basic information concerning press councils had to be collected through the means of a questionnaire (in German and English). It was a) sent to all known national press councils in the world; b) that apart, it was distributed amongst the press council representatives present at the "Round Table on Press Councils" held in Stockholm in September, 1974; and finally c) distributed in 14 countries by the press attachés of embassies of the German Federal Republic. The percentage return of questionnaires was relatively high as a result of this three-pronged (largely parallel) organized drive.

It proved impossible to make any reliable general assertions about national institutions describing themselves as press, media or honorary councils because of discrepant nomenclature and widely differing descriptions of function. In all cases therefore, the starting point had to be the analysis of current statutes or procedural rules. This could be used as a starting point on the basis of which further questions could be posed. The findings over the 19 analyzed institutions still proved to be so varied that it seemed hardly justifiable—theoretically or partically—to discuss press councils in an undifferentiated manner. Consequently, on the basis of criteria yet to be mentioned, the following classification into three groups was undertaken:

1. *Primary Press Councils:*
Institutions where the functions have been fully developed and realized; journalists and publishers are represented.
2. *Secondary Press Councils:*
Bodies with certain specific functions only. Not only press councils but also news and media councils are included in this category. Press councils

in which only one interest is represented (either that of journalists or of publishers).

3. *Tertiary Press Councils:*

Here institutions resembling press councils, either not fully operational to date or which have ceased to function, are included. Organizations at a pressure group level with self-control but without the aims and duties of a press council in the true sense of the term.

As can be seen from this proposed classification of press councils, similarity is not theoretically presupposed. It is based intentionally on empirically documented deviations in structure, competency and "Selbstverständnis" (press council's own understanding of its role and function). The map on the following page, indicating the location of the press councils under study here, will help to illustrate a few more points.

It can be seen that institutionalized press self-control is mainly a European phenomenon; first of all it can be found in countries with Germanic languages! Of the "primary press councils" only two—those in Israel and New Zealand—are to be found outside Europe. Both have their roots in the British example. "Secondary press councils," on the other hand, are to be found elsewhere: in North America, Africa and Asia. In these continents one also finds a few institutions belonging to the third category. It remains to be said that in the whole of Central and South America, North and Tropical Africa, and in the states of Central Asia and the Far East (with the exception of India, Sri Lanka, South Korea and Japan) there is no form of press self-control at all. The question of press self-control in communist states can hardly be raised. Their understanding of the role of the press—as a tool for the ideological purposes of the Party—differs from that of most other countries. Where the press is subject to state supervision, there can be no self-control in the sense discussed here.

Furthermore, it is possible to say that some of the above mentioned press councils were set up to serve as an alibi. Such councils exist in a *milieu* where press legislation does not guarantee all fundamental principles of freedom of the press. Organizations of this variety are to be found amongst press councils in the second and third categories. Approximately 45% of all press councils were established shortly before or during the early sixties. There were set up shortly after the end of the Second World War. The number of press council committee members differ considerably from one another e.g. South Africa only has three whereas Israel has 80.

In other respects the 19 press councils show greater similarities than one would be led to expect from the above account. For example, there seems to be a far-reaching consensus concerning the duties of such institutions: they lie in the maintaining and safeguarding of freedom of the press as well as in the surveillance and adherence to ethical rules pertaining to the press. In this, with the exception of Denmark and South Africa, journalists *and* publishers or editors share responsibility. Only in two countries—in the Netherlands and Swit-

WORLD MAP OF PRESS COUNCILS

Japan
South Korea
New Zealand
Finland
Sri Lanka
India
Sweden
Turkey
Israel
Norway
Rep. of
South Africa
Denmark
Austria
Fed. Rep. of
Germany
Switzerland
United Kingdom
The Netherlands
Canada
USA

zerland—do such bodies function without the participation or involvement of publishers, i.e. they are run exclusively by journalists.

The trend to include the potential recipient (representatives of the general public or special readers' groups) in the self-control of mass communication networks is relatively new. Such participation by the general public is not foreseen so far (for financial reasons amongst others, for instance in the German Federal Republic) everywhere, but it exists in seven of the 19 countries. The direct participation of bearers of a political mandate exists only in South Korea, Sri Lanka and India, whereas almost every press council attempts to elect one or more lawyers—mostly high court judges—above all to the position of chairman (president) or deputy chairman.

In almost half of the institutions under survey, an outsider (i.e. *not* a press council committee member) takes the initiative in involving a press council in a particular case involving a travesty of the journalistic ethos or an inroad against freedom of the press. Press councils in eight countries can also initiate action themselves should it seem necessary. Only in Japan and Switzerland can cases be dealt with exclusively as a result of the press council's own initiative. The outsider or non-committee member is explicitly given the right of complaint in over 75% of the press councils in existence. In two countries, the Netherlands and Turkey, this is restricted to those persons directly involved in a case. The Japanese newspaper organization's statutes do not allow for the possibility of the lodging of complaint by a non-committee member. Finally, in Switzerland, where—as in Japan—the press council operates internally (only for members of the organization), one suspects that there will also be no way in which public complaint can be lodged.

Generally, the decision as to whether a charge should be investigated or not depends on the following criterion: has the matter been brought to court at the same time or not? However, statutes usually allow for exceptions to the rule. There is no definite exclusion of cases which the law is also investigating, apart from in Finland and in South Africa. The question of sanctions—that is, the possibility of punishing those press organs found guilty of non-compliance to general rules and regulations—is treated in a number of different ways, ranging from a statement of position from the press council on the issue (in four countries), warnings and censure to fines and other economic measures (such as the withdrawal of advertisements as in Turkey). Expulsion of members from their professional organization is foreseen in four countries only.

A further, and in this context important, way in which a travesty of professional code can be penalized is through the publication of the rulings or decisions of the press council by the "guilty" party. Legislation ordering publication of the press council's decisions exists only in India. However, in nine countries (ten, if one includes Switzerland), the member organizations (publishing bodies) of press councils have agreed to abide by rulings requiring publication of a decision or statement. It remains to be said that in day-to-day practice this voluntary agreement is frequently circumvented. At the same time, press councils frequently complain about the missing feedback as far as their work is concerned and a general lack of information amongst the general public about their role and function.

Press councils as a rule are financially supported by their constituent organizations. This is the case in over half of the councils under study. In four countries the costs incurred through their activity are carried by a single organization. Only in India does the state carry the total running costs, whereas in Finland the state undertakes to pay 34% of the council's annual budget. Through the payment of a subscription the plaintiff can, to a certain degree, aid the financing of such a council. In South Africa and Sweden that person or body against whom a complaint is directed (and where the charge is proved) has to contribute towards the council's budget.

Ten press councils publish annual reports in various forms describing their activities over the past year. On top of this almost all institutions publish material at irregular intervals as well as non-printed circulars. The Indian press council is the only one to publish a quarterly; here one can find information not only concerning its own activities but also of those of similar institutions in other countries.

*   *   *   *

Concluding, a general definition on the basis of the above account, but one which cannot include all possible variations in competency and structure, must be made. Because of the limitations, the attempt should be looked at critically: *The concept of "press self-control" or "press council" generally applies to every recognized voluntary institution consisting of those involved in the communication process* (the communicator, i.e. journalists and publishers; the general public, e.g. individual representatives or representatives of influential and important groups in society: the recipient). *Such an institution acts as refereeing body or "court of appeal," whose members enjoy independence of state interference of political party and private economic interests, and who represent the country's press in its entirety. It defends a range of general and specific journalists' norms; deals with complaints—a result either of its own or external initiative; and autonomously imposes sanctions. Its decisions, which should neither be questioned nor cancelled, are published openly or confidentially with the aim of realizing its intentions as far as the party guilty of travesty of the set norms is concerned.*

The future of press or media councils probably will largely depend on their function as "dogs with two heads—one head barking outwards and the other inwards." [38] But this watchdog philosophy seems to be a too simple demand, because one has to raise the question: "If there is a watchdog—who watches the watchdog?" Ralph Lowenstein writes of the situation in the United States: "The press has not done a good job monitoring the N(ational) N(ews) C(ouncil). . ." [39] . One of the leading American newspapers is very critical of the activities of the NCC: "It is discouraging," an NCC official reacts, "to record one great newspaper's continuing opposition to the Council. I speak of the *New York Times*. On occasion after occasion, the *Times* has responded negatively to Council requests for information to assist in answering public complaints against that newspaper. . . ." [40]

There is almost no information available on questions like this: how are recipients of mass media (readers, viewers, listeners) in different countries thinking about the efficiency of their national press or media council? For example in Germany the "Deutsche Presserat" is not mentioned too often in press reports, and therefore it seems that it is rather unknown by great parts of the population. Only in Great Britain do we have the situation that decisions of the press council sometimes are reported on the front pages of the leading newspapers. . . . [41]

NOTES

[1] On details cf. Henk Prakke et al. (eds.): *Handbuch der Weltpresse*, Bd. 1: Die Pressesysteme der Welt, Cologne—Opladen (Germany) 1970.

[2] Cf. Susumu Ejiri: *Characteristics of the Japanese Press*, Tokio 1972, p. 139 ff.

[3] Cf. J. A. van Hamel (ed.): *Beslissingen van de Raad van Tucht der Federatie van Nederlandse Journalisten* (1948–1961), Leiden (Netherlands) 1962, pp. 3–9.

[4] Cf. Commission on Freedom of the Press: *A Free and Responsible Press*, Chicago 1947.

[5] Astrid Sunarti Susanto-Sunario: Die politischen Kräfte hinter der Entstehung des Britischen Presserates, Ph.D. dissertation (FU) Berlin 1965, p. 183 (mimeographed).

[6] Cf. Jürgen Heinrichsbauer: *Die Presseselbstkontrolle. Eine historisch-kritische Untersuchung*, Munich (1953), p. 34 ff.

[7] Cf. Alfred Frankenfeld: Der Deutsche Presserat 1956–1970. Ursprung, Funktion, Effizienz, in: Hansjürgen Koschwitz/Günter Pötter (ed.): *Publizistik als Gesellschaftswissenschaft*. Internationale Beiträge, Konstanz (Germany) 1973, pp. 277–290.

[8] Cf. Abdi Ipekci: "Self Regulation of the Turkish Press," in: *Gazette* (Leiden), Vol. X/No. 1 (1964), pp. 59–62.

[9] Cf. Korean Press Ethics Commission (ed.): *Korean Press Ethics*, Seoul 1956, p. 9 ff.

[10] Cf. Meir Ben-Gur: "The Israel Press Council," in: *I.F.J. Information* (Brussels), Vol. XIC/No. 1–2 (January–June 1965), p. 6 f; cf. also Meir Ben-Gur: The Israelic Press Council (Hebrew), Tel Aviv 1971.

[11] Cf. Gautam Adhikari: *Press Councils: The Indian Experience*, New Delhi 1971, p. 13 ff.

[12] Cf. Alfred Balk: *A Free and Responsive Press*. The Twentieth Century Task Force Report for a "National News Council," New York 1973.

[13] Cf. N.N.: "Avant la création d'un Conseil de la presse," in: *Gazette de Lausanne* (Lausanne/Switzerland) September, 2nd, 1974.

[14] Cf. the relevant titles in: Institut für Publizistik der Freien Universität Berlin (ed.): *Handbuch der Auslandspresse*, Bonn—Cologne—Opladen 1960, p. 841 ff.

[15] From: Fred S. Siebert/Theodore Peterson/Wilber Schramm: *Four Theories of the Press*, Urbana/Illinois 1963, p. 7.

[16] Cf. International Press Institute (ed.): *Press Councils and Press Codes*, 4th ed., Zurich 1966, p. 8.

[17] Cf. Chancahl Sarkar: *Press Councils and their Role*, New Dehli 1965, pp. 2–7.

[18] Cf. Martin Löffler/Jean Louis Hébarre (ed.): *Form und Funktion der Presse-Selbstkontrolle in weltweiter Sicht*, Munich 1968, pp. 7–15.

[19] Cf. H. J. Bradley: "Enquiry on Press Councils, 1971–72," in: *I.F.J. Information* (Brussels), Vol. 22/1972, pp. 3–6.

[20] Henk Prakke et al. (ed.), *op. cit.*, p. XIII.

[21] *Ibid.*, p. XVII.

[22] Ralph Lynn Lowenstein: Measuring World Press Freedom as a Political Indicator, Ph.D. dissertation University of Missouri, Columbia, Mo., 1967, p. 58 (unpublished).

[23] The following empirical dates are mainly based on Heinz-Dietrich Fischer/Klaus-Detlef R. Breuer/Hans-Wolfgang Wolter: "Komparative Status- und Funktionsanalyse nationaler 'Presseräte' in weltweiter Perspektive," Bochum 1974 (unpublished). The study was undertaken by a research grant from the German Federal Ministry of Interior Affairs, Bonn.

[24] Compiled from Ralph L. Lowenstein, *op. cit.*, pp. 330 ff.

[25] Dr. Ernest Meyer, former Director of the International Press Institute (Zurich/Switzerland) during a discussion at the "Round Table on Press Councils, Stockholm, 26–27 September 1974"; quotation according to shorthand notes by the author of this article.

[26] Cf. Robert Patrick Knight: The Concept of Freedom of the Press in the Americas. An Exploratory Study, Ph. D. dissertation University of Missouri, Columbia, Mo. 1968, p. 8 ff. (unpublished).

[27] Cf. Joe Bill Vogel: "Ethical Codes and Courts of Honor in the Press of The Free World," Ph. D. dissertaton State University of Iowa, Ames/Iowa 1961, pp. 329 ff. (unpublished).

[28] Consultative Assembly of the Council of Europe (ed.): *Resolution No. 428* (1970) containing a declaration on mass communication media and human rights, Strasbourg 1974, p. 3 f.

[29] Cf. UNESCO: *Collective Consultations on Codes of Ethics for the Mass Media*, Unesco House, Paris, 12–13 November 1973, Paris 1974, p. 1 ff. (mimeographed).

[30] Cf. J. Clement Jones: *Collective Consultations on Mass Media Councils*, Unesco House, Paris, 3–4 October 1974: Background paper on Press councils, Paris 1974 (mimeographed).

[31] Cf. Ralph L(ynn) Lowenstein: *Press Councils: Idea and Reality*, Columbia/Missouri (USA) 1973, p. 18 f.

[32] Adapted from: John C(alhoun) Merrill: *The Imperative of Freedom. A Philosophy of Journalistic Autonomy*, New York 1974, p. 41.

[33] Karel Vasak: "Introductory Report." Stockholm Round Table on Press Councils (26–27 September 1974), Strasbourg 1974, p. 2 (mimeographed).

[34] Bundesministerium des Innern: Vermerk, Referat SK III 1, Bonn, July 5, 1974, p. 1 (Manuscr.).

[35] Franz Ronneberger: Probleme publizistischer Selbstkontrolle, *Publizistik* (Konstanz), Vol. 17/No. 2 (April–July 1972), p. 179.

[36] Martin Löffler/Jean Louis Hébarre (ed.), *op. cit.* p. 28 (Short version in English).

[37] Cf. Heinz-Dietrich Fischer/Klaus Detlef R. Breuer/Hans-Wolfgang Wolter, *op. cit.*

[38] H. J. Bradley, *op. cit.*, p. 6.

[39] Ralph L. Lowenstein: *National News Council Appraised*, Freedom of Information Center Report No. 0015, Columbia, Mo. 1974, p. 6.

[40] Stanley H. Fuld: Foreword by the Chairman, in: National News Council, Inc. (ed.): *In the Public Interest. A Report by the National News Council 1973–1975*, New York 1975, p. 4.

[41] Interview of the author of this article with Mr. Henry Bate, Deputy-Chairman of the British Press Council during the "Round Table on Press Councils" at Stockholm, September 27, 1974.

4

NATIONAL DEVELOPMENT AND MASS MEDIA

Wilbur Schramm
WORLD DISTRIBUTION OF THE MASS MEDIA

John C. Merrill
MEDIA AND NATIONAL DEVELOPMENT

Leslie G. Moeller
MASS MEDIA AND NATIONAL GOALS

Ralph L. Lowenstein
USE OF FOREIGN MEDIA BY
    DEVELOPING NATIONS

John T. McNelly
MEDIA EXPOSURE IN DEVELOPING
    URBAN SOCIETIES

Peter Meyer-Dohm
INVESTMENTS IN COMMUNICATION AND THE
    DEVELOPMENT PROCESS

4

NATIONAL DEVELOPMENT

AND MASS MEDIA

S TUDENTS of the mass media would be hard to find who would deny that a
very close relationship exists between the socio-politico-economic development of a country and the degree to which its mass communication system has
advanced. Many studies have been made in the last decade which have shown
that the mass media and national development are interrelated. There does,
however, remain some doubt as to *cause*; i.e., whether mass media reach a
high degree of development in a generally highly developed society, or whether
a progressive and rapidly expanding media system brings about general national
development.

In the first article of this section, Wilbur Schramm, emeritus professor of
communications at Stanford and former director of the Communications Institute of Hawaii's East-West Center, provides a look at the way mass media are
dispersed throughout the world and thereby gives us a general developmental
media context in which to consider the following articles. The next article, by
John Merrill, summarizes many of the findings of researchers who have probed
the relationship of mass communication to national development; he also
presents a rather pessimistic model of media-political development which postulates an authoritarian-freedom-authoritarian cycle.

Leslie G. Moeller, professor emeritus of journalism at the University of
Iowa, next presents some stimulating thoughts on the importance of setting and
communicating national goals, and shows what part the mass media should
play in such planning. Next, Ralph Lowenstein discusses his "EPS development curve" and shows how many small modern nations "borrow" elite media
from foreign countries, thereby "leapfrogging" themselves (at least their own
elites) into a specialized stage of media development.

John McNelly, professor of mass communication at the University of Wisconsin, next concentrates on the kinds of research most needed in the area of
media and development, especially as it relates to urbanization processes. And,
in the final article, Peter Meyer-Dohm, German economist and rector of the

Ruhr University Bochum, deals with the impact of State investments in communications, especially books, in the development process.

*   *   *   *

RELATED READING

Doob, Leonard W. *Communication in Africa*. New Haven: Yale University Press, 1961.

Houn, Franklin W. *To Change a Nation*. Glencoe, Ill.: Free Press, 1961.

Lerner, Daniel. *The Passing of Traditional Society*. London: Collier-Macmillan Ltd., 1958.

Lerner, Daniel and W. Schramm, eds. *Communication and Change in Developing Countries*. Honolulu: East-West Center Press, 1967.

Mass Media in the Developing Countries. ("Reports and Papers on Mass Communication," No. 33), Paris: UNESCO, 1961.

Merrill, J. C. *The Elite Press: Great Newspapers of the World*. New York: Pitman, 1968.

Prakke, H. J. *Publizist und Publikum in Africa*. Cologne: Verlag Deutscher Wirtschaftsdienst, GmbH, 1962.

Pye, Lucian W. (ed.). *Communications and Political Development*. Princeton: Princeton University Press, 1963.

Rogers, E. M., and F. Floyd Shoemaker. *Communication of Innovations*. 2nd ed. New York: The Free Press, 1971.

Schramm, Wilbur. *Mass Media and National Development*. Stanford: Stanford University Press, 1964.

Sommerlad, E. Lloyd. *The Press in Developing Countries*. Sydney, Australia: Sydney University Press, 1966.

[Note other literature on this subject in notes to various articles.]

Wilbur Schramm:

World Distribution of the Mass Media

WE HAVE BEEN speaking of the transition to modern communication as though it were a certainty. And, indeed, it is a certainty, barring some unforeseen event that would reverse the direction of economic and social development. The question we are considering in these pages is not *whether* the mass media will ultimately come into wide use in the developing countries as channels of information and education, but rather whether their introduction should be *hurried* so that they can do more than they are doing at present to contribute to national development.

The mass media have a particular importance at this point in history. They are the great multipliers. Just as the machines of the Industrial Revolution are able to multiply human power with other kinds of energy, so are the communicating machines of the Communication Revolution able to multiply human messages to a degree previously unheard of.

The presence of mass media makes a significant difference in the level of information *even among people who are unable to read the printed media and do not have access to the electronic media.* The fortuitous fact about the relation of information to national development is that mass communication should be available and well developed, and its use relatively well understood, when so many new countries are trying to communicate so much so quickly to so many people.

Mass communication, throughout its entire history, has been effective in combating privilege. The significance of the development of printing in the fifteenth century was not only to swing the balance from the long centuries of spoken firsthand communication toward visual and secondhand communication on a grand scale, but, more important, to extend learning beyond a privileged handful. Almost at once, the printed media became tools of political and social change. The revolutions in Europe and North America would have been most unlikely without the printed media. The development of public schools would have been most unlikely, if not impossible, without the printed media. In the nineteenth century, new developments in mass communication reached over the heads of the specially privileged and the specially educated to offer information and education to the great masses of men. Political democracy, economic opportunity, free public education, the Industrial Revolution, and mass communication were all woven together to make a great change in human life and society on several continents. Now the new electronic developments in communication have swung the balance back toward communication in which one can see and hear the communicator. They have given the developing countries potential channels of information with which to reach fantastically large audiences, to communicate with underprivileged masses despite the literacy barrier, to teach difficult skills by "showing how" they are done, to speak almost with the effectiveness of face-to-face communication.

It may well be that mass communication (and the interpersonal communication we have learned to combine with it) are about to play a key part in the greatest social revolution of all time—the economic and social uplift of two-thirds of the world's people. We are not implying that mass communication can do it alone. Without determined national leadership, adequate population and resources, and sources of capital, the most efficient communication system in the world could not bring about economic development. But this at least we can say with confidence: if the mass media or some equally potent and rapid means of information were not available, it would be utterly impossible to think of national economic and social development in terms of the timetables that are being attached to such development today.

Let us therefore see how widely available the mass media are for such use in the developing countries. Where are the facilities adequate, and where are they in short supply, for the battle of development? What is the rate of growth of these media, and what are the conditions under which they grow or lag?

The Haves and Have-Nots

Let us not harbor any delusion that the mass media are alike in all the underdeveloped countries. Quite the contrary: there is a great and sometimes astonishing variety. The media systems are as different from each other as the countries themselves. For example, in seven African countries there is no daily press except roneotyped bulletins from a government information service, and in 15 African countries there are no daily newspapers of any kind. On the other hand, throughout Latin America the press is well developed in both large and small cities. Despite lagging national economies, a highly sophisticated daily press has emerged—one example out of many is Chile. In some underdeveloped countries—Mauritania, for example—it is necessary because of lack of printing facilities to have such periodicals as exist printed outside the country. In other underdeveloped countries, like India, the printing industry is highly developed and equipped to publish in a number of languages and a variety of technical subject matters. In some countries the whole broadcasting operation depends on an ancient transmitter held together only be loving care and constant maintenance. In some almost equally underdeveloped countries, the radio stations are shining with new equipment. The writer has been in a country where the breakdown of a single projector, and the difficulty of getting someone to repair it, eliminated for months a large part of the total capability of the country for showing educational films, and in another underdeveloped country where one educational center had been given a quarter-million dollars' worth of audiovisual equipment.

Thus there is no single pattern. But as one moves from country to country one becomes aware of a condition that is more often the rule than the exception in developing countries. This is the condition of scarcity.

We can sum up the distribution of mass communication throughout the world:

1. In every respect except film making, Latin America is somewhat further developed in communication than either Asia or Africa. This is most notably true of radio and television, but also holds in the case of newspapers: per capita circulation in South America is twice what it is in Asia, and six times as much as in Africa. The busy Asian studios out-produce those of South America, but the annual attendance per person is greater in South America than in either Asia or Africa.

2. The underdeveloped regions of the world are moving along impressively toward meeting the Unesco minima in radio. The rate of growth in radio will take both Asia and Africa over the Unesco standards within a relatively few years. South America has already passed the minimum. It seems apparent that the less-developed lands are planning to depend chiefly on radio to reach their scattered and largely illiterate populations.

3. The underdeveloped regions are lagging in newspaper development. This is probably related to the development of literacy and education; and when the growth is sufficient in those two areas, we can expect faster growth in newspaper circulation.

4. But all these differences are overshadowed by the great overall difference between the parts of the world where economic development is far along and the parts where it is not. It is the same order of difference we have noted earlier, in comparisons of life expectancy, productivity, industrialization, income, and the like, and here the discrepancies are fully as spectacular as the earlier ones. In every respect, the peoples of Africa, Asia, and Latin America are have-not people in mass communication. Latin America does very well in newspapers and radio, it is true, but is still below well-developed regions, and it lags, despite its widely used common languages, in forming news agencies. The band of scarcity is no illusion. This is what Unesco was talking about when it spoke of "a dearth of facilities over wide regions of the globe [which] prevents hundreds of millions of people from effectively enjoying freedom of information.*

The Media in the Developing Countries

Not all the differences between mass communication in the developing and the highly developed countries are quantitative ones.

One of the first things one notices about mass communication in underde-

---

* UNESCO, *Mass Media in Developing Countries*, Paris: UNESCO, 1961.

veloped countries is how the media cluster in the cities. To some extent, of course, this is true everywhere. In highly developed as well as underdeveloped countries, the newspapers, broadcasting stations, and film theaters tend to be where the concentrations of people are. But in highly developed countries, the majority of people live in urban settings; in a typical underdeveloped countries, the majority of people live in urban settings; in a typical underdeveloped country 80 per cent of the people live in rural settings. Therefore, if the media concentrate on urban centers in developing countries they are really concentrating on a *minority* of the people.

To a lesser extent, radio and films also cluster in the cities. One would expect to find the studios and transmitters in the cities, of course, but one might hope to find in the rural regions a larger proportion of the radio receivers (inasmuch as radio can cover great distances) and a larger proportion of the film attendance (inasmuch as films, like radio, can jump the literacy barrier). But actually only a little more than one in ten of India's radio receivers, to take one example, are in the villages, where the rural four-fifths of India's people live, and the bulk of cinema attendance is likewise in the cities. It is spectacular in many developing countries to see the signs of the media all but vanish at the borders of the cities. One can read the morning papers in his hotel, see the young people stroll past his window carrying transistor radios, see the advertisement for the current movie across the street; then drive out of the city to spend the day in the villages, and probably see not a single newspaper, radio receiver, or film theater all day.

Why should this be? One reason is the inordinate difficulty of circulation. The newspapers have to combat inadequate roads, washouts in the rainy season, inadequate postal services. Radio and films face a lack of electricity in the villages, and lack of technically trained personnel outside the cities to repair receivers or operate film showings. In more than one country, a well-meant plan to extend the coverage of radio has failed simply because there was no one to recharge or replace a battery in an otherwise operable receiving set.

Literacy too drops off at the edge of the cities. In the cities there are concentrations of literates, even though the overall percentage may not be very high. But a village may have no more than one or two persons able and willing to read a newspaper. Serving such minuscule audiences makes an obviously difficult circulation problem.

Money for mass media is harder to come by in subsistence economies and in the village. A villager in Burma or Malaya will be investing a sizable part of his annual cash income if he subscribes to a magazine. By the same token, a radio is a major purchase in a village. If Unesco's long-pursued goal of a five-dollar radio could be realized, it would make a considerable difference in the circulation of radio in the rural regions of developing countries.

Still another reason for impeded circulation is the language problem. The existence of Spanish (and in Brazil, Portuguese) as lingua franca may be one of the key reasons why the press has developed faster and more fully in Latin

America than in Africa or Asia. Some of the language problems facing the media in Africa and Asia are fantastic. India is the classical example: 14 states with their own languages, 72 different languages spoken by at least 100,000 persons each, a national radio system that can hardly ever broadcast nationally, national wire news services that must be translated for each of the vernacular newspapers, government agricultural and community development information that must be either decentralized or translated at each state or district level.

Low circulations make for financial difficulties. When theaters are few and admission small, a developing country finds it hard to make films. In some South Asian countries, exhibitors calculate that films must run six or seven weeks at each theater in order to make a profit. Newspapers in developing countries often face a cruel financial struggle. The Unesco conferences on development of the mass media reported that only a small percentage of the papers were in sound financial position.

Newsprint costs more outside the great cities. Because of shortages of capital and foreign exchange, the smaller papers often have trouble making long-term agreements for purchase of newsprint, and therefore may have to pay premiums on prices that are already higher than their city competition pays.

News agency costs are proportionally higher on a small daily, and, if it is a local-language daily, the cost of translation must be added to the fee for the wire service. But if there is no wire news, the paper is not doing the job it should do, and is less attractive to subscribers.

Furthermore, in some countries even the wastepaper value of a newspaper is something that purchasers or subscribers take into account. They can subtract from the price of the paper the money they receive from selling the used copy. This, too, makes life harder for the smaller paper. The less advertising it has, the fewer pages it can print, and the less it will be worth as wastepaper to the subscribers.

Suppose the paper does get its head above water. Suppose it is so successful that its circulation, after three years, rises above 10,000. This is too many papers for a flat-bed and cylinder press; another press is needed. The paper faces a staggering outlay of capital if it is to grow larger—$40,000 or so for a rotary press.

Thus, although a new paper can be started inexpensively, it finds it hard to keep going and hard to grow.

Something of a phenomenon, in view of the cost problems, is the introduction of television into so many developing countries. Television is the most costly of the media to capitalize, and it requires perhaps a wider diversity of skills than any other medium. Its receiving sets are expensive, compared with radio, and repairs are more difficult and costly. Some new nations have introduced television chiefly as an aid to their educational systems; others, apparently, because television has prestige. We do not mean to imply that the introduction of television may not be economically desirable; indeed, [in some] situations it may save money as well as contribute to the speed of development.

But in many places it contrasts oddly with the communication shortages one sees on every hand: shortages in machinery and technical personnel, raw film, newsprint, trained management and editorial personnel, and research.

Yet, despite the shortages, the machinery runs. Communication flows. One reason why the system works better than might be expected is that the common and traditional channels of communication are pressed into use to extend the new media. Not every country has a communication device so spectacular as the Yoruba talking drums, and yet almost every developing country has the custom of reading the newspaper to illiterates—in the coffee houses, the village square, the schoolhouse, or any other place where people congregate. Institutions like the bazaar, where for centuries people have exchanged information, now serve to carry information first planted by the mass media. Where the mass media cannot readily reach, the puppet shows, storytellers, poets, ballad singers, and dramatic groups carry some of the same information and persuasion. Radio listening and discussion groups are formed around some of the radio receivers. Leaders of many of these countries have learned to use very large public meetings with great skill, and, indeed, the crowd at a meeting may be more numerous than the readers of the local newspaper, or the listeners to a speech on the radio. Thus we must not think of the media in a developing country as standing by themselves. They fit into the larger communication system of the country; and the drums, the bazaars, the meetings, and the ballad singers all help to carry the word.

And yet, one comes away from a developing country worrying that the media numbers are so small, the coverage is inadequate, the rural targets are not being reached, the media are not being integrated fully enough with interpersonal organizations and communications. This is true, as we have said, in some places and some media more than others. In Asia, although there is usually too little chance to see films, there is a remarkable amount of film making. In Latin America, the press is well developed, and radio coverage is more extensive than in either Asia or Africa. But there is still not enough development of the media, not enough integration with the interpersonal channels, not skillful enough or general enough to use to let mass communication do the job it is capable of doing.

Summary

We can sum up very briefly. The less-developed countries have less-developed mass communication systems also, and less development in the services that support the growth of mass communication. Their systems are underfinanced and underequipped, and as a result the flow of information is much less than it could be. However, there is an encouraging rate of growth throughout the developing regions, both in the mass media and in their supporting services. The question is whether it is fast enough for countries in a hurry.

Perhaps the best way to evaluate these growth rates is to calculate how long it would take the underdeveloped countries on two of the less-developed continents to reach the Unesco minima—ten copies of daily newspapers, five radio receivers, two cinema seats for every 100 persons—at their 1950–62 average rate of growth. This we have calculated, * using 1962 figures as a baseline and taking the average annual growth rate through the period as the angle of projection. If they continue to grow at this rate, it then follows that

—To reach the standard of ten copies of daily newspapers for each 100 persons would take Africa until 2035, Asia until 1992;
—To reach the standard of five radio receivers for each 100 persons would take Africa until 1968, Asia until 1970;
—To reach the standard of two cinema seats for each 100 persons would take Africa until 2042, Asia until 1981.

Is that too long? Certainly it seems an inordinately long time for Africa and Asia, at least, to wait. Of course, in making the estimate we have assumed a steady rate of growth. This may not prove to be the case. It may well be that at a certain point in the growth of literacy and education, the circulation of newspapers will rise faster, or that, at a certain point in the progress of electrification, there will be a swifter growth of cinemas. It may also be that a decrease in the rate of population growth will occur and make the per capita figures look better. This we can hope for. But the picture points to the importance of radio in the decade ahead, and calls for increased efforts to speed the growth of the other media and their supporting services. Countries in a hurry can hardly be expected to be satisfied that—at the 1950–62 rate of development—Asia would not reach Unesco minima for daily newspaper circulation until nearly the end of the century, and Africa not for 70 years!

* This estimate has been made by using the same formula as for compound interest, $A = P (1 + r)^n$, in which A is the amount to be attained at a given future time, P is the present amount, r is the rate of growth compounded annually, and n is the number of years.

John C. Merrill:

Media and National Development

A NATION'S communication media develop as the nation develops. Significant changes in the scope, sophistication, and purpose of the mass media are evidences of political modification in a society. This is generally known as the "reflective theory" of media-government relationship. A country's political system (stemming from the political idology) is obviously related to the direction and speed of a country's total national development. If this basic assumption is true, and it would certainly appear to be, then media and national development join in a kind of symbiotic relationship of a complex and intriguing nature. It is this symbiotic relationship that has been consuming more and more of the time and effort of researchers and theorists in the related fields of journalism, sociology and political science since about mid-point in this century.

All kinds of questions are raised pertaining to the relationship between political ideology and communication philosophy, between political systems and communication systems, between politics and national development, and between communication and national development. This chapter will summarize some of the basic problems in this area of concern, will present many of the conclusions which have been reached by researchers, will offer some fresh insights into the media-political symbiosis, and will present and discuss a multifactor model of media and national development which is in keeping with the overall thesis of this book: that nations and press systems are becoming ever more authoritarian.

Spurred on by UNESCO and a number of potent "international outreach agencies" (e.g., the U.S.'s Agency for International Development) of the major powers, a fascination with, and emphasis on, communication and national development has ridden into academic and governmental consciousness on the crest of the post-World War II wave-of-concern with international communication generally.[1]

[1] A few of the UNESCO studies will give an idea of the emphasis in the area of communication and national development since 1950: *Radio in Fundamental Education in Undeveloped Areas* (1950); *Television, A World Survey* (1953); *Developing Mass Media in Asia* (1960); *Los Medios de Informacion en America Latina* (1961); *Mass Media in the Developing Countries* (1961), and *Developing Information Media in Africa* (1962). Since about 1962 developmental studies and works by UNESCO have seemed to disappear, to be replaced by many books and articles by communications scholars of many countries.

▶ This article is a much-shortened version of a chapter by the same title from Dr. Merrill's *The Imperative of Freedom* (Hastings House, 1974).

Scholars have made some interesting efforts to fashion meaningful theories about the role of institutionalized communication in the national developmental process, but it is obviously too early for coherent theories of communication and national development to emerge. Their time has simply not arrived, and we are still in a period of unsynthesized case studies, theoretical dialogue, and splintered speculation about this whole area of concern.

Anyone expecting startling insights into the question of media impact on national development is destined for disappointment. At best he may get a few glimmers of understanding from a hodge-podge of theorizing and uneven research done mainly in underdeveloped regions of the world.

Basic Literature

The literature on this subject is far from skimpy. In America alone, scholars such as Daniel Lerner, Lucian Pye, Karl Deutsch, Gabriel Almond, Ithiel de Sola Pool and Wilbur Schramm have produced weighty tomes related to the subject of communication and national development, and many others—such as Everett Rogers, John McNelly, William Hachten, V. M. Mishra, Hamid Mowlana, Vincent Farace and the late Paul Deutschmann have shed further light on this complex subject in books and articles. Their basic conclusions, when there are any, are very similar; and the vast amount of literature which appeared in the last several decades has been largely descriptive, correlational, and speculative—and to a rather great degree, co-terminous. [2]

Most of these studies indicate relationships among such factors as economics, religion, press freedom, industrialization, etc. Several studies, for example, have found a high correlation between the measures of economic growth and measures of communications growth—hardly a finding which would surprise anyone. Daniel Lerner, for example, noted high correlations among four factors: urbanization, literacy, media participation and political participation. Deutsch pointed out a correlation between mass communication of a country and its national spirit and action. Such correlations abound; researchers are constantly finding additional ones. A conclusion emerges: *Communication is necessary, not only for all aspects of a person's development, but also for all aspects of a nation's development.*

So, in a sense we now see that most of the work done in this area has focused on the entire national organism—on the process of *interaction*—and,

---

[2] A few books contributing to the literature of communication and national development follow: Karl Deutsch, *Nationalism and Social Communications* (1953); Elihu Katz and Paul Lazarsfeld, *Personal Influence* (1955); Daniel Lerner, *The Passing of Traditional Society* (1958); Gabriel Almond et al, *The Politics of the Developing Areas* (1960); Everett M. Rogers, *Diffusion of Innovations* (1962); Wilbur Schramm, *Mass Media and National Development* (1964); Lucian Pye (ed.), *Communications and Political Development* (1963); W. Phillips Davidson, *International Political Communication* (1965); E. Lloyd Sommerlad, *The Press in Developing Countries* (1966); H. D. Fischer and J. C. Merrill (eds.), *International Communication* (1970); V. M. Mishra, *Communication and Modernization in Urban Slums* (1972).

of course, on *inter-relationships*. What we have had, up to now, have mainly been what might be termed *Gestalt* studies—descriptive, correlational and relational profiles which try to focus on communication networks within nations, while at the same time showing how these networks function in concert with other national institutions.

Lack of Cause-Effect Studies. Notably lacking are credible *cause-effect* studies which give valid insights into the fundamental question that seems to plague us: Do the mass media bring about national development, and if so, how and to what extent?

There is an obvious reason why such a question is difficult (or impossible) to answer, and it lies in the intrinsic weakness of social science research itself: Too many human and social variables impose themselves to make for a neat experiment. How can we have a society working normally and realistically and isolate one variable (the mass media) and test its impact? We cannot really be very optimistic about this type of research.

It could be, however, that one day some researcher or Research Foundation will be able to establish a nation which will agree not to have any communications media for—say—ten years. At the same time, perhaps another nation of equal constituency would be created, but this one *with* primitive communications media from the start. Then we could sit back and happily observe the development of both countries for ten years—one nation with communications media at the outset and the other without them; but in all other ways the two nations would be operating and growing naturally. After ten years we might be able to make some valid conclusions as to the specific impact of communications media on national development.

But it is hard to imagine such an experiment developing. And even if it did, I am not convinced such a test would be meaningful for the simple reason that it would seem as unrealistic to isolate a communications system from a nation as it would be to isolate an economic system or a political system from a nation and expect it to function in *any* conceivable manner for *one* year— much less ten.

Some researchers, it is true, have studied the impact of mass media on a small social unit—for example, a village in India.[3] The natural temptation is to project these findings to a *national* context. Certainly such studies have their value, but it is doubtful that their implications for more complex nation-states are very meaningful or valid. One might just as logically study the impact of a message on *one person* and project it to a whole group of people. . . .

A Review of Basic Findings

Let us turn to a few of the principal conclusions and generalizations which have come from a rather sizable number of technical and observational studies

[3] Examples of case studies: Y. V. L. Rao, *Communication and Development: A Study of Two Indian Villages* (Minneapolis: Univ. of Minnesota Press, 1966), and William B. Ward, "Press Media in India's Agricultural Development," *Vidura* (Indian Press Institute, New Delhi), Vol. 18, No. 5, 1971.

since the end of World War II. Most of these appear to be generally accepted by most students of communication and national development, so in some cases the following statements will not be attributed to any one person.

• Mass communication is necessary to a national consciousness, spirit, and concerted national action. (Karl Deutsch).

• Social communication's structure is reflective of the structure and development of society. (W. Schramm). Communication grows and changes with society because it is something society *does;* it is the way society lives. And, it might be added, communication is a *function* of society or a *tool* of society with which society constantly fashions and repairs itself.[4]

• Communications media contribute to (a) a people's awareness of potentialities, (b) dissatisfaction and a desire to change, (c) a heightened sense of collective power among the people, (d) either stabilizing or disrupting the society, and (e) either instilling in the people realistic goals or creating extravagant expectations. (It is well to remember that communication activities contribute to these results—but it should be noted that *communication activities* are not necessarily carried on through *mass* media. For example, in early stages of development we can find rather complex networks of informal and personal pre-"mass media" communication working well.)

• Mass media provide information to a nation's people, and the more information people get, the more they are interested in political developments. (Schramm).[5]

• Communication can (a) raise the goals of the society, (b) spread news of these goals, and (c) widen the acceptance of these goals.

• Pye sees the communication process in nation-building as mainly serving an amplifying function, but also as linking the political process to the people, providing the essential bases for rationality in mass polities, and giving form and structure to the political process by reminding politicians that political acts have consequences and the populace of what the acts are and what the consequences might be.[6] This, of course, is an important function of communication in advanced or well-developed nations, as was exemplified in the United States by the great "Watergate Story" of 1973.

• Schramm says communication must be used (a) to contribute to a feel-

[4] Schramm stresses these aspects of social communication which reflect the structure and development of society: *size* of communication activities reflects the *economic* development of the society; the *controls* on communication reflect the political development of the society; the *content* of communication at any given time reflects the *value* patterns of the society, and the pattern of communication networks reflect the homogeneity of culture and geography of a society.

[5] An important consideration in Schramm's statement about information and political development is the stage of development at which the nation finds itself: this largely determines (a) the impact of the media, and (b) the kind of media most effective. Mass media, it would appear, become more and more important in speeding up modernization as the nation rises to ever-higher levels; at the very lowest level, mass media are virtually non-existent, therefore unimportant.

[6] At least two things can be concluded about the importance of the mass media to political development and functioning: (a) in small or new nations mass media are not very important in the political realm, and (b) in authoritarian or communist nations mass media are not as important to political functioning as they are in libertarian, democratic nations.

ing of nation-ness, (b) as a voice of national planning, (c) to help teach necessary skills, (d) to extend the effective market, (e) to help people look to the future, and (f) to prepare people to play their role as a nation among nations.[7]

• In transitional nations (most of the world's nations) the mass media develop almost simultaneously with the new awareness of the outside world and a new national self-consciousness.

• New nations tend to have a one-party press and have media systems of a rather highly authoritarian nature.

• Mass communications can be used either as a national stimulant or tranquilizer. (As Schramm says, the mere presence of a communication system does not necessarily contribute to national development; it depends on the *use of*, and *content of*, the media.) Programs and stories could be largely entertainment and fantasy, for example, and could actually divert attention *away from* national problems. This is exactly what Polynesian media appeared to be doing in the '70's, according to a study by Ralph Barney.[8]

• A rapidly developing mass media system—or a well-developed one, for that matter—does not necessarily contribute to a wider and more democratic political base. (Schramm: Efficient communication works as well for the dictator as for the democrat—maybe better, because the dictator is likely to have a monopoly on communication;[9] but communication development *provides the conditions* for wider democratic participation—if the political philosophy permits it.)

• More than two-thirds of the world's citizens reside in nations which are normally classified as "emerging," "underdeveloped" or "modernizing."[10]

• The press in underdeveloped nations is almost exclusively the result of

[7] See Schramm's *Mass Media and National Development* (Stanford: Stanford Univ. Press, 1964). As pertains to Schramm's admonition about media use, it should be noted that an important consideration is the *proper* use of media—or the use of the *proper media*. These techniques or media should be meaningful and understandable to people at a certain stage of national development. For example, there is little need to introduce magazines and newspapers into a society that is basically illiterate and isolated geographically. Radio or "wall newspapers" would be much more appropriate and effective.

[8] Ralph D. Barney, "The Mass Media, Their Environment and Prospects in Western Polynesia" (unpublished Ph.D. thesis, University of Missouri, summer 1971). Barney, of the journalism faculty of Brigham Young University, found that the new nations of Polynesia have a sense of cultural and racial "consciousness" but almost no national or political consciousness. At least this was true outside of a very small elite leadership group. And it should be noted that the mass media—if you can call them that—are doing little there to enhance a national consciousness; rather they are hitting their small audiences either with certain kinds of educational programs or with "escapist" entertainment.

[9] A rapidly developing media system—or a well-developed one—does not necessarily contribute to a wider and more democratic political base. Examples of the USSR, Spain, Egypt, Taiwan, Greece, the Philippines and Israel may be given. Note that all of these nations partially rationalize their press controls and lack of general freedom by pointing to internal and external dangers to their national security. Even such nations as the United States are prone to do this from time to time.

[10] W. Phillips Davison, *International Political Communication* (New York: Frederick A. Praeger, 1965), p. 130. Cf. for an excellent survey of communications in these "emerging" nations: Chapter 3 ("Traditional Societies") in Ronald C. Benge, *Communication and Identity* (London: Clive Bingley Ltd., 1972).

Western efforts and influence, says Herbert Passin; no precedent for journalists can be found in traditional (emerging) societies. Journalism develops almost simultaneously with national self-consciousness and growing awareness of the outside world. [11]

• Mass communication has brought to developing nations a "revolution of rising expectations" (in the 1950s) and since the 1960s a "revolution of rising frustrations." People of backward nations suddenly sensed through the mass media that a better life was possible; then they realized, when they began trying to get this better life, that their attempts generally were thwarted, leading to increased frustration. [12]

• Mass communication has often been overemphasized in considering impact on national development, according to Pye. "It is apparent . . . that some governments in new countries once placed excessive faith in the potentialities of modern means of mass communications. Deeper analysis shows that the press and radio can have a profound influence in changing the ways of people only if they are fully supported by the informal, social channels of communication which are intimately related to basic social processes. Rapid national development calls for the coordinated and reinforcing use of both the impersonal mass media and the more personal, face-to-face pattern of social communication." [13]

*　　*　　*　　*

Conflict and National Development

Many ways exist for considering the communications media and national development. Several have already been suggested. One way, which I have not seen before, is from the point of view of conflict in the society and communication's relation to it. It is postulated here that as individual, political and press freedom increases, social conflict also increases and as freedom diminishes, conflict decreases. Underdeveloped or *traditional* societies have very little conflict; *transitional* and early modern societies have the most, and late *modern* societies have almost none. The social "conflict cycle," then, is highly correlated to the general political cycle. Let us look a little closer at the three basic stages of development just mentioned:

(1) *Traditional Society:* Conflict (friction) is mainly within the autocratic or elite leadership group; communication, then, is of a personal nature, designed to inform the active agents in governmental military and institutional hierarchies, and to stabilize society. Since there are no true *mass* media (see

[11] Herbert Passin, in Lucian Pye (ed.), *Communications and Political Development* (Princeton: Princeton University Press, 1963), p. 98.

[12] Daniel Lerner in Pye, *op. cit.*, pp. 327–31. Cf. Ronald Benge, *Communication and Identity*— Ch. 6 ("Development and Communications").

[13] Lucian Pye in Pye, *op. cit.*, pp. 9–10. Cf. Gunnar R. Naesselund, "From Information to Communication Systems in Development," *Vidura* (New Delhi), February 1973.

Figure 1) designed to bring "the people" into a sharing of policy, conflict exists principally among competing elite *persons* who might be competing for power. Communication channels are personal and informal (*elite* media), and are used mainly to try to develop a viable and outwardly stable political system by easing tensions and supporting infant institutions. Communication's main aim is to eliminate conflict and bring social stability.

(2) *Traditional Society:* In this more highly developed society (stage of development), there is likelihood of considerable political power conflict, class conflict, party conflict and institutional conflict. Communication becomes less supportive and monolithic and increasingly becomes more competitive, ideological and pluralistic. Communication is considered a political weapon or tool—a way to gain power for some and dissipate competing and conflicting power. *Mass* media are put in use not simply for solidifying and harmonizing the society, but as propaganda (change) agents—internally and externally. Communication's main function in this stage is to help in political conflict as a means for gaining party, group or personal power.

In the later phase of this stage, libertarianism develops and the media units themselves have maximum self-determinism. Competition and pluralism grows. (See Fig. 1) Government's control decreases, individual freedom expands and governmental democracy dominates. The mass media spread their general information to medium-sized and large populations.

(3) *Modern Society:* Actually there are two main phases of development in a modern society—a kind of *early* phase where individual and media freedom is still extolled; where ideological conflict among factions, classes and parties is widespread; where the mass media *increase* dissonance and provide a catalyst for change and a pluralism of news and views to all citizens. Then there is a *later* phase flowing into authoritarianism and finally totalitarianism (see Fig. 1) where conflict is discouraged (or banned) and what little there may be is among political factions and strong leaders, and where mass media are mainly used for internal *social control* and external *propaganda*. The overall purpose of the media: to stabilize and direct society and to propagandize other societies.

Profile of a Traditional Society

It might be well to consider further these three "societies" (or developmental stages), first describing the most primitive of the stages—the *traditional* society and its inter-relationship with the mass media.

When we are talking about an "underdeveloped" or traditional society, I would postulate two things about mass media: (1) At this stage of national development there are *really no mass media* (See Fig. 1) within the nation, and (2) The Power Structure or Elite (autocrats) of the nation at this early stage *do not really want a mass media system*.

True "mass" media in this earliest stage are non-existent; only specialized or *elite* media are to be found. No mass media exist mainly because there is no mass literate audience; related to this is the fact that there is a kind of tribal isolationism, poor transportation and communication facilities, and low economic levels. At any rate, media cannot really communicate *with* (or even *to*) the masses of people. What *is* present at this stage of national development are elite lines of communication: from elite to elite within the Power Structure. So it can be reasonably said that the traditional society has *elite* media, not *mass* media.

Emphasis here is on communication of basic policy, aims, objectives, plans, etc. within a rather small select governing group—not on sharing policy material with the general populace. In fact, the leadership elite feel that mass communication is a danger—not an asset—to national growth and cohesiveness. So the elite lines of communication are set up (conferences, luncheons, meetings, workshops, etc.) at a high level on a *personal, seclusive* basis.[14] The object: to rally the elite of the nation to nation-building and loyalty to the ruling Power Structure.

Little attention is given in this developmental stage to the masses—to their participation in government, to their achieving literacy, to their "right to know" and all such things. These concerns appear at a later stage when the nation is fairly well-established, is stable, and has what is considered by the elite a viable political and economic base. But at this very early stage, the elite of the Power Structure do not feel that the nation can "afford" all the trappings of political sophistication and libertarianism.

Authoritarianism is considered not only most expedient at this point, but most rational. The general assumption: the people are unable to rule themselves in a traditional society; they do not even expect to. And, the elite are not anxious to encourage them through mass communication *to expect to*—at least not until the complex foundation of nationhood is worked out by the ruling autocracy.[15] Most of these early leaders (usually military men) are convinced that the people (the masses) want and expect strong rule imposed from the top and these leaders are determined to give it to them. The Power Structure elite, therefore, decide what will be communicated and just how fast lines of communication will be opened to wider and wider segments of the population.

The elite of the Power Structure, then, at this early stage determine the *nature* of—as well as the quality and quantity of—the communication media.[16] Therefore, if anything determines or causes national development at this stage, it is the leadership elite—using informal and specialized media. So it may be said that media in new nations are creatures of a small elite group and develop very slowly and in accordance with careful planning by the elite. As

[14] It is obvious that in many nations the *elite media* actually supplement the informal communication activities such as luncheons, conferences, fairs, etc.—not the other way around.

[15] See William A. Hachten, "Newspapers in Africa: Change or Decay?" *Seminar: A Quarterly Review for Newspapermen* (Dec. 1971) for a look at government press intervention and its harm to national development in new African nations.

[16] By "nature" of the mass media in the primitive society is meant the basic press concept: purposes, aims, objectives; "nature" in terms of guiding philosophy or theory. This is quite different from *quality* and *quantity* of the media.

the media *become mass*, the nation is passing from the traditional to the *transitional* stage. (Then, as the media pass through a mass-oriented stage into a more pluralistic or specialized stage, the nation emerges from the upper reaches of the transitional developmental stage into the final or *modern* stage. See Fig. 1)

In the earliest or traditional stage that I have been discussing, it is not really important to have *mass* support for the leadership—but it is important to control major institutions and to have *military* support. The elite set about slowly instilling in the people the national "consciousness" referred to earlier, giving them a set of common goals, and stressing cultural, racial and religious similarities. Also, it is important at this stage to provide for the people a *common enemy*. This is certainly a potent cohesion factor. A common enemy helps the people subordinate their differences and gives them a common *negative objective*. People can, as Eric Hoffer and others have pointed out, be rallied easiest when they can all be *against* something (some country, ideology, or group) [17] Concern with stressing what the people *are to be for* comes later in the transitional and modern stages of development.

Many persons from countries exemplifying this traditional stage, or even the early transitional stage which follows it, are irritated by the "advanced" nations' tendency to force their conception of *development* upon them. Development, they insist, must take into account the cultural context of a particular country, its traditions, and so forth. And, they insist with considerable justification, economic and technological growth should not be the main indicator of national "development." Chanchal Sarkar, one of India's most outstanding journalists, recommends a "new journalism of development" which would reflect and lead the public into thinking more fairly and realistically about this subject. He writes:

> In the underdeveloped countries . . . we stand at a crossroad without signposts. We are in search of a new philosophy of development in which GNP is not the king. . . . the philosophy and the strategy must aim to preserve some of the liberation freedoms, which are taken for granted in the advanced social welfare countries but which, in underdeveloped societies, have been enjoyed only by a handful of highly privileged people. [18]

The model of development which I present in this chapter (see Fig. 1) does go beyond the economic factor and postulates several factors—including libertarianism—which are important in the progression of development. Some traditional societies, especially in Africa, appear to be trying to by-pass the newspaper age and go directly into full-fledged broadcast journalism. The Brit-

[17] Eric Hoffer, *The True Believer* (New York: Mentor Books, 1958), p. 86
[18] Chanchal Sarkar, "Development and the New Journalism," *Vidura* (New Delhi), October 1972, p. 338. Cf. Edward W. Ploman, "New Trends in Communication," *Vidura*, April 1973, pp. 93–97.

MEDIA DEVELOPMENT AND NATIONAL AND POLITICAL DEVELOPMENT: A MULTI-FACTOR MODEL

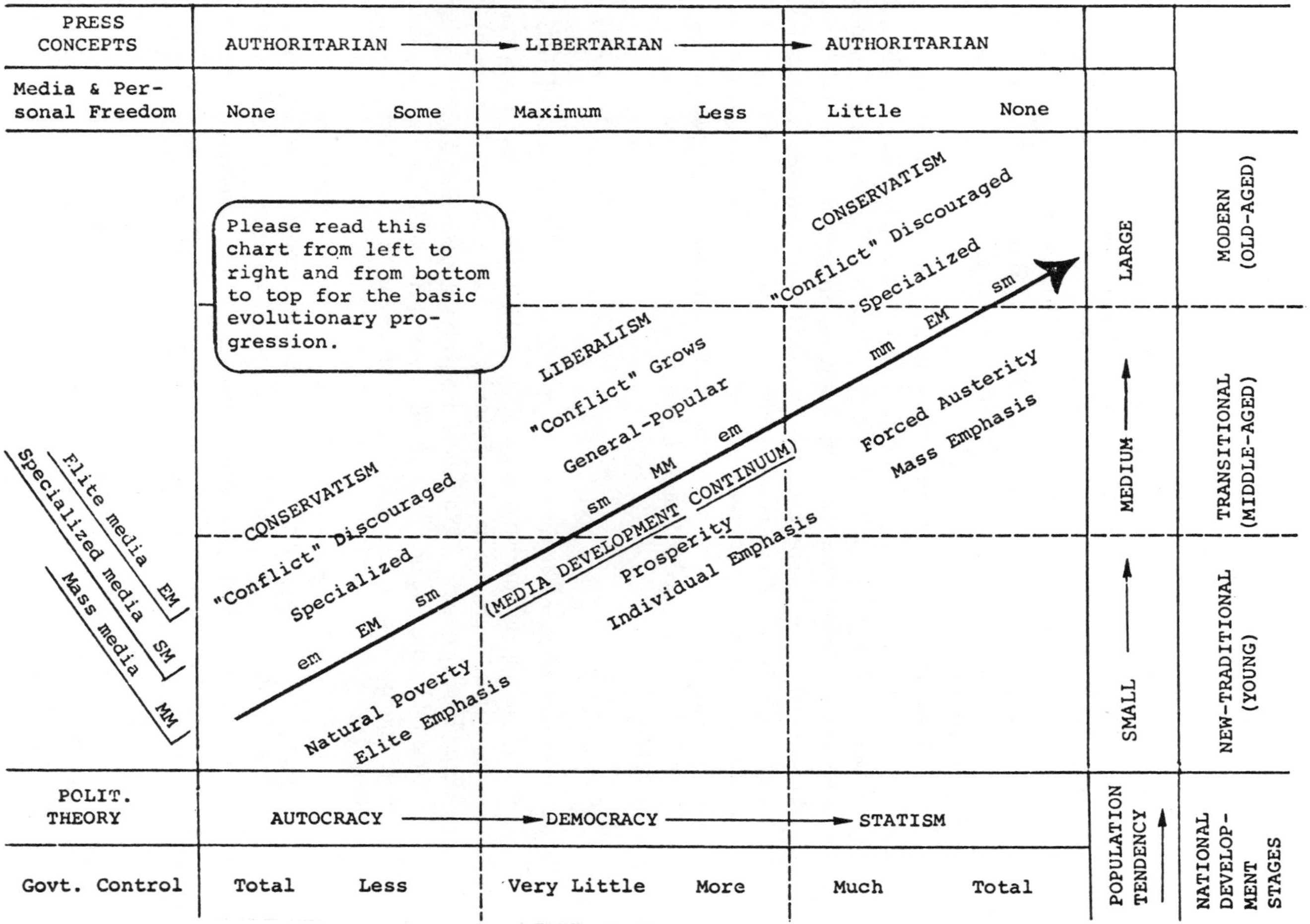

PRESS CONCEPTS	AUTHORITARIAN ⟶		LIBERTARIAN ⟶		AUTHORITARIAN ⟶	
Media & Personal Freedom	None	Some	Maximum	Less	Little	None

NATIONAL DEVELOPMENT STAGES: MODERN (OLD-AGED) — TRANSITIONAL (MIDDLE-AGED) — NEW-TRADITIONAL (YOUNG)

POPULATION TENDENCY: LARGE ⟵ MEDIUM ⟵ SMALL

Diagonal continuum labels (read from bottom to top):
- Natural poverty — Elite Emphasis — CONSERVATISM Discouraged — "Conflict" Specialized
- Individual Prosperity Emphasis — LIBERALISM Grows — "Conflict"-popular — Generalized
- (MEDIA DEVELOPMENT CONTINUUM)
- Forced Austerity — Mass Emphasis — CONSERVATISM Discouraged — "Conflict" Specialized

Media types: Elite media EM, Specialized media SM, Mass media MM (EM, em, SM, sm, MM, mm)

> Please read this chart from left to right and from bottom to top for the basic evolutionary progression.

POLIT. THEORY	AUTOCRACY ⟶		DEMOCRACY ⟶		STATISM ⟶	
Govt. Control	Total	Less	Very Little	More	Much	Total

195

ish press consultant and critic, Tom Hopkinson, quotes an official of a former French colony as saying: "We shall by-pass the newspaper age just as we shall by-pass the railway age. We shall go straight into radio and television—government-controlled, of course." [19]

Hopkinson frowns on such suggestions, believing that newspapers "are an essential part of the working of a modern democracy"; I tend to agree with him, but I do not assume that *all* traditional societies—or at least their leadership—believe that democracy is best for them. Broadcast media, controlled by the State, can certainly by-pass the imposing barrier of illiteracy and provide cybernetive information directly and effectively. Broadcasting is undoubtedly the most potent control instrument which an elite group can use to give a nation a consciousness and stability.

Apparently recognizing this, Hopkinson admits that "in the special circumstances of Africa today an unusual degree of responsibility is rightly demanded of the journalist," and that press freedom "has clearly got to mean something different from what it means in Brussels or New York." Even though I do not pretend to know what it means even in Brussels or New York, I will readily agree that in a new or traditional society it must, if it is used at all, mean something quite different from independent editorial self-determinism by the media. It is only in the next stage—the *transitional*—that government control slackens and media independence or autonomy has a real chance for viability.

Profile of a Transitional Society

A society passes slowly from the traditional stage, just discussed, into the transitional (or intermediary) stage. It is unreasonable to expect a political or media system to pick up democratic and libertarian philosophies overnight. As Aldous Huxley observes, "No people that passes abruptly from a state of subservience under the rule of a despot to the completely unfamiliar state of political independence can be said to have a fair chance of making democratic institutions work." [20]

As the society becomes more affluent, chances increase for its general progress into new philosophical frontiers of democracy and press libertarianism. Growth and decline of societal prosperity is closely related to democracy and freedom. Huxley makes this point when he says that "liberalism flourishes in an atmosphere of prosperity and declines as declining prosperity makes it necessary for the government to intervene ever more frequently and drastically in the affairs of its subjects." [21]

A very important factor in the transitional society is the natural pull toward democracy and libertarianism. Another characteristic of this society is that media tend to be general or "mass" rather than specialized and elite, although

[19] Tom Hopkinson, "Africa: Battle for Survival," WAY *Forum* (Brussels), No. 57, Dec. 1965, p. 3.
[20] Aldous Huxley, *Brave New World Revisited*, p. 31.
[21] *Ibid.*

some elite media persist and are supplemented by specialized media reaching segments of the general public.

In the early and middle phases of this transitional stage, circulations of print media are still rather small and lag behind rising literacy. This is largely due to the heritage of elitism and government control which has carried over from the traditional stage. It appears that newspapers, free of controls, can expand and grow much faster than those under government restrictions. Tarzie Vittachi, a noted Indian journalist, is prone to agree.[22] He writes:

> The failure of the newspapers of India and Ceylon to keep pace with the growth of literacy must, in substantial measure, be attributed to state controls. Indian newspaper publishers as well as working journalists have repeatedly demanded the liberalization of government controls on the import of newsprint and machinery for expansion of the press.

It can be said that the transitional stage of national development roughly corresponds to the late autocratic (authoritarian) and the early democratic (libertarian) politico-press developmental stages. See Figure 1 for a schematic picture. In a real sense, then, this transitional stage would seem to be a bridge from one form of authoritarianism across a libertarian river to another form of authoritarianism on the other side. Put another way, in this developmental stage autocracy (personal elitism) merges into democracy and then on into statism (impersonal elitism).

In its earliest phases, the transitional society is still relatively small, autocratic and controlled; in its intermediate phases it becomes larger, democratic, individualistic and pluralistic; and in its later phases it comes even larger and more complex, more mass-oriented, more conformist and more authoritarian. Emphasis begins to shift from individualism to collectivism (or at least statism): the *modern* developmental stage is just ahead.

Profile of a Modern Society

A society in the early phases of its *modern* period still retains many of the democratic and libertarian principles brought over from its transitional stage. There is still some individualism, but it is increasingly suspect. There is still some press freedom, but it is dissolved in the name of social responsibility. There is still an element of *laissez-faire* journalism, but it is increasingly being labelled as outmoded. There is still some ideological conflict and dissonance, but it is increasingly being muted. True "mass" media still exist, but they are being de-emphasized and subordinated to specialized media.

In the later phases of modern society, the tendencies above continue until the growing authoritarianism passes into totalitarianism; partial governmental

[22] Tarzie Vittachi, "Asia: A Need for Communication," WAY *Forum* (Brussels), No. 57) Dec. 1965), p. 7.

interference in media affairs becomes total interference; collectivist or statist objectives completely eliminate individual or personal objectives; conflict or social dissonance disappears; media pluralism fades away in the face of State control and domination; and a variety of concepts about responsibility to society are replaced by a single concept of social responsibility.

When the extreme phase of the *modern* stage is reached, national development has, in many respects, come full circle: from authoritarianism through libertarianism and back to authoritarianism. It is true that now the emphasis is on the total society—on the masses—whereas in the autocratic days of the traditional society the emphasis was on the few leaders of the elite. But individual freedom, press self-determinism, competition, ideological conflict and "closed" aspects of the modern society are about back to where they were in the autocratic traditional society.

Far into the final, or modern, stage of development the journalist, and all citizens for that matter, find themselves under a kind of collectivist or statist government, referred to by some writers as "mass" or "corporate." In this stage, as Karl Jaspers says, the "apparatus" dominates and "the importance of the individual leader persists, but peculiar circumstances now become decisive in the choice of leaders." According to Jaspers, "great" men pass into the background and "efficient" men come to the foreground, and the power of the masses remain effective "through the instrumentality of mass-organisations, majorities, public opinion, and the actual behaviour of vast multitudes of men." [23]

Societies (nations) can proceed ever deeper into this mass-oriented, corporate state either through revolutionary (involuntary) or evolutionary (voluntary) processes. One could say that Russia entered it through revolution, for example, and that Sweden entered it through more natural evolution. Although many might disagree with him, one long-time observer of Sweden, Roland Huntford of London's prestigious *Observer*, has contended in his book *The New Totalitarians* that Swedes have quietly and voluntarily given up their freedom and have retired into a conformist, collectivist society.

Writing of the mass media of Sweden,[24] Huntford maintains that

> To judge solely by its mass media, Sweden appears to be run by a tolerant dictatorship. Press, radio and TV show a remarkable similarity, as if guided by some Ministry of Propaganda. . . . It is virtually impossible for anybody opposing the government to get a hearing. Broadcasting has turned into a servant of the party and the State. . . . The Swedish communicators act as a corporate body, collectively following the trend of the moment. They are conformist to a fault, wanting only to promote the concensus.

[23] Karl Jaspers, *Man in the Modern Age*, p. 55.
[24] Roland Huntford, *The New Totalitarians* (New York: Stein and Day, 1972), pp. 285–93 *passim*.

A Few Conclusions

Assumptions can be made about the impact of mass media on national development, but these inferences must be drawn almost entirely from correlational studies. Little or nothing is known about cause-effect in regard to mass media and national development.

It is generally assumed that a nation's mass communication system is tied in with the nation's general progress. We note that the mass media in well-developed nations are well-developed and that media in new or traditional societies are poorly developed. We can observe also that media in a rapidly changing nation tend to be rapidly changing.

Communication is obviously necessary for a nation to grow and change, just as it is for an individual person. Communication can increase and facilitate personal freedom, but it can also increase and facilitate government control of its citizens.

Media freedom provides a good barometer to a society's general political atmosphere and democratic health.

Societies tend to develop or progress from autocracy, to democracy, to statism, with their media systems going from authoritarianism through libertarianism back to authoritarianism. This is the normal circular progression tendency of social and media development postulated in this chapter—and throughout the book.

Media systems as they naturally evolve, first discourage, then encourage, then discourage social "friction" or dissonance.

Normally media develop from (1) elite (specialized) media, to (2) mass (generalized) media, and finally to (3) elite (specialized) media, although mass and elite media coexist in the last two developmental stages.[25]

Political theory and press ideology are closely related to economic level in a society's natural progression through the developmental cycle; these, of course, are accompanied by other significant factors such as social friction, population size, type of media and age of the society.

The natural tendency of both political and journalistic development in *any* society is toward authoritarianism and state tyranny. This results in increased "social responsibility" and collective consciousness but at the price of the loss of personal and media freedom.

[25] An excellent article which discusses a three-stage theory of media growth and social change postulating development from elite media through popular (general) to specialized is Richard Maisel's "The Decline of Mass Media," *Public Opinion Quarterly* (Summer, 1973), pp. 159–70.

Leslie G. Moeller:

Mass Media and National Goals

IN THE modern world, any nation, whether developing or developed, must certainly face the need for a statement of national goals. Of course, all nations have goals, whether stated or unstated, but in today's whirling world there seems an especial desirability for having a statement of goals which has been formally proposed and openly talked about, so that a rather substantial consensus exists on behalf of the targets which have been set out.

Such a pattern of decision on goals is in a sense unavoidable, since in these times such a statement is so desperately needed. An obvious major reason is that no nation now has those unlimited resources of personnel, facilities and finance which make the attack of all goals immediately possible.

In such a situation, choices must then be made. The decision will be made that within element A, let us say, education, educational sub-phases C and E deserve priority, but that for the moment sub-phases G and K do not have priority. This could mean, for example, that providing certain phases of technological education take precedence over high competence, as distinguished from basic competence, in a second language.

Such a situation is reached, as Gerhard Colm has so effectively pointed out, when a nation, after first having no goals pattern, moves into a period of crises involving performance and achievement goals. These crises make clearer than before, as was the case, for example, in the United States after the Russians orbited Sputnik, that certain assumptions should be reexamined. As a result, there is a birth of a new consciousness of goals.[1]

In the United States, in the late 1950s, a Commission on National Goals was named by President Eisenhower, and its report, in 1960, listed goals but did not consider costs and also did not consider priorties.[2]

That further step was undertaken by a number of bodies, one of the most notable being the National Planning Association, which set up a Center for Priority Analysis. The Center considered such U.S. needs as consumer expenditures and savings, private plant and equipment, urban development, social welfare, health, education, transportation, national defense, housing, research and development, natural resources, international aid, space, agriculture,

▶ This is a shortened version of a presentation by Prof. Moeller at a Mass Communications Seminar at the Universidad Iberoamericana in Mexico City (March 11–15, 1974). Prepared for this book by Prof. Moeller, a professor emeritus of journalism at the University of Iowa.

manpower retraining, and area redevelopment; the Center also estimated costs, and matched these against estimated income.[3]

To take the next step, and to produce a statement of priorities, it is essential along the way to consider resources. What is the expectable trend of gross national product? What are the financial and other resources which are potentially and actually available?

But it is not enough today to consider only the economic and financial factors; in these times it is necessary to bring in also social and cultural and psychic and highly individual values (even moral systems). To be specific: the building of a park does not usually enhance gross national product, because the park is not "productive," but more and more we are coming to the view that the park may be highly "productive," and that this factor must be apparent in goal setting.[4]

There are, then, efforts to revise the approach to the GNP, so that it is more meaningful, and also to develop social indicators which can be quantitative measures of changes of certain crucial factors in society often thought of earlier in primarily a qualitative sense.[5]

Determining National Goals

How then do we go about determining these national goals? In many societies, and most of those with which we are here most concerned, the setting of goals can no longer be most effectively done by a centralized authority, often the executive, which proceeds essentially with only nominal consultation with elements outside the planning group and its superior authority.[6]

Instead, the process demands a quite high level of general participation, not, I will grant, achieved in many societies, if the process is to be most effective. This approach calls for the receiving of suggestions at many levels, and from citizens of all types and classes. The suggestions are then reviewed in a wide-ranging and continuing process, probably at a number of different levels.

It is unwise to have the planning done by a unit completely separate from operating agencies; most planning which is well done is carried out in close conjunction with the operating divisions of an enterprise; Norway, for example, has recently completed long range plans for civil science and technology programs with a very wide base of participation in discussion.[7] In a nation, it is perhaps acceptable from time to time to have a major group of nationally known persons carry out a special spotlighted project on the nation's goals, but on a month-to-month and year-to-year basis the planning should be done with intensive participation by the operational staffs and by many citizens.

This approach implies also that there is an ongoing review of plans so that goals and procedures and priorities are always under examination.

What results can be expected from the preparation of such a statement of national goals? What will come to pass, ideally, as a result of its completion? And why should the mass media be more than usually concerned?

First, obviously, such a statement informs the public; it provides knowledge of what the declared goals are. Such a statement also focuses attention. It spotlights the major issues of national concern. It increases interest; it raises the national level of alertness.

Well done, a goals statement can stimulate and inspire. It is interesting to consider how much the United States might have lost if it had not had its beginning in the Declaration of Independence, a most memorable statement, which still, after nearly two centuries, has great power to arouse and to motivate.

Such a statement helps tell the citizen what the problems are; perhaps he gets the message here more clearly than in any other way, unless the media are exceptionally active and alert, and it is also true that the probabilities are high that he will receive his word of the goals statement through the media.

Such a statement of goals has the potential to bring an increased ability to use relevant, or even total, resources, and to use them better. Well done, the statement could help bring out the effective—and that word is important—use of modern management techniques such as PERT (Program Evaluation and Review Technique) and PPB (Planning, Programming, and Budgeting). Such a statement also offers the opportunity for "management by objectives," permitting the setting of quantitative and qualitative targets of many kinds, at many levels, and at many stages, so that there is a logical opportunity for checking progress and fulfillment of planned targets.

Continuing reexamination is thus made much easier and more certain.

Developing a national statement of goals has the important result of bringing conflict to the surface, so that the opportunity then arises to use conflict constructively for the public interest.

In a slightly different way, the setting of national goals offers some opportunities for using constructively the not always beneficent forces of nationalism—a way of tapping resources and power which might not otherwise be used so well. A goals statement offers aid, too, in the field of international relations. If there are dealings with international financing, such as the Inter-American Development Bank, such a goal statement offers not only evidence of national concern, but of concern strong enough to result in sustained consideration and decision.[8]

In considering how the functions of the mass media are brought to bear on the planning of national goals, we may begin with the fourth of the five ideal requirements for the mass media set out by the Commission on Freedom of the Press, the so-called Hutchins Commission: "The presentation and clarification of the goals and values of the society." [9] The Commission amplifies by declaring that "the agencies of mass communication are an educational instrument, perhaps the most powerful there is; and they must assume a responsibility like that of educators in stating and clarifying the ideals toward which the community should strive."

What Are Media Functions?

Specifically, what functions of the media are most apparent?

First, of course, is the function of the disseminating of information, of providing a continuing flow of content to aid the citizen in day-to-day orientation to his environment; in John Merrill's words, "The press wields tremendous power today as a purveyor of vital information." [10] Beyond orientation for instrumental purposes, in which the news is often quickly put to use, I must mention that other informative material will also fill the important function of satisfying curiosity. "What's happening now?" is an honest, frequent, and meaningful question in society, and it deserves an answer.

An important related function is that of explanation, of interpretation, to fill the need of the citizen for a picture of how new things change his old world, of why things are changing, of what the changes will mean.

This explanatory-interpretative work might, for example, well have for its foundation as many as possible of the six elements for estimating possibilities of social change which are being used by Nestor E. Terleckyj in a study for the National Planning Association: 1. Selection and definitions of areas of concern and identification of indicators of social conditions; 2. projection of trend levels of these conditions and of resource uses; 3. distinction between fixed and discretionary activities, over time; 4. identification of discretionary activities, costs, and effects; 5. projections of resources available for discretionary activities; 6. maximum feasible output of combinations of discretionary activities which can be undertaken within the estimated resource supply. [11]

From the standpoint of achieving national goals, it is especially important that the explanation in the media anticipate worries, troubles, and malfunctions—that the explanation work to prevent dysfunction—but in such a way that the citizen is not overly dependent on the mass media to do his thinking, and that the citizen does indeed retain a capability for reaction and for comment and criticism.

A somewhat related subphase is the setting of the agenda for the society, in which the media make clear the matters which are under discussion in the society, and provide a vocabulary of discussion, so that the citizen can enter the universe of discourse and be made much more a working partner in society. This setting of the agenda is described effectively by Deutschmann, Ellingsworth, and McNelly in their study of how new technology is introduced in Latin America. [12] Media power in setting agenda is summarized by Funkhouser in the comment, "Apparently the average person takes the media's word for what the 'issues' are, whether or not he personally has any involvement or interest in them. [13]

Even more, the media can make clear a different type of agenda: the agenda which *ought* to be discussed in the society, those items which are on the horizon; these include "the intrusive event," which Nisbet has spoken of as a great change-bringer.[14] The citizen today needs to know that these elements, whether the energy crisis or some other factor, are at the least highly likely to loom large in the tomorrow. This role of expanding the mental horizon is often beset with difficulties because of attitudes toward the media; as John Lent points out in commenting on Asian newspapers, "The press role in Asia historically has been seen as the circulation and promotion of 'correct' ideas rather than the purveying of news . . . and the furnishing of a forum for competing ideas." [15]

The media aid also in the developing and in the recognizing of new leaders; since all societies face the constant urgency of renewal, this function, which can be better performed by the media than by any other element, is crucial.

The mass media should, in essence, provide much leadership constantly in the whole field of social change. They work to break citizens loose from apathy. They transmit pictures of needs. In the words of Schramm, the media weld the nation together by "keeping the *national* goals and the *national* accomplishments always before the public." [16] The media encourage and explain the process of planning. The media raise questions: for example, must this nation really be like most other nations in its targets, goals, pattern, development? Should this nation consider at least some differences in emphases?

As still another function in most nations, and this is interestingly brought out in recent work by Elihu Katz, the media have the need to build a greater faith in the quality of the society and in its functioning.[17] This function does not, of course, relieve the media from the obligation to police the society, to expose malfeasance, and to improve still further the functioning of the society.

Media Reaction to Their Responsibilities

In facing up to the immediate assignment of carrying out these functions, how do the mass media conduct themselves in their responsibilities on national goals? Obviously size is a factor; the smaller media can, usually, do less than the larger, but all can be concerned, and active also. (And I am aware as well that many have much concern with the immediate problems of press freedom, as is apparent at once from reading the trauma-laden pages of the IAPA and the IPI bulletins.)

As a beginning, the media might well look again at their often tradition-bound approaches to the treatment of news content. For example, on one major assignment, that of information, which is much more complicated than one would at first think, it is not now enough, as many people have said, merely to "cover" the news in the old sense.

We are rapidly moving past that mid-20th-century concept, and beginning to face up to the new situation: that the nature of news has changed, and that too often the media do not soon enough present what the citizen must have for adequate comprehension, and for adequate preparedness.[18]

In great part this is the case because crucial news today is often only presented as casually episodic in nature, in bits and pieces, so that "what happened today" often does not clarify, and may even distort. Such major news is now so often a matter of a "continuing situation," rather than a single one-day event or episode.

These stories, then, deserve a new kind of major investigative treatment, if the public is soundly to perceive the whole picture, rather than the incident-by-incident coverage of earlier years.[19]

The other great change has come in the content or subject matter of the new-type major news stories. Most of them are not simple in nature and the subjects may be abstruse. Consider fiscal policy, the flow of international trade, energy, balance of payments, natural resources, population change, genetic engineering, environmental control, or the changing needs of the populace for education. They are not suited for simplistic, here-it-is-in-200 words, black-or-white, good guys or bad guys treatment.

In these new approaches, much of the content will be summarizing, interpretative, and quite general or broad in nature. At the same time, the presentations must both be sufficiently local, and be seen as sufficiently applicable to the self, if they are to have an increased and an immediate impact for most members of the audience.

In helping to set the agenda for the society, the media need again to be certain that the materials are presented so that they take hold of the citizen and so that the citizen can see quickly why he should take hold of them.[20] If material is presented in this meaningful way, taking into account especially the pluralistic nature of most societies, and the great and often conflicting diversities of interests, the chances for citizen participation are greatly increased.

Presenting ideas for the possible agenda for coming years (as distinguished from now) can help the media to effectively encourage the planning process, since the presentation of actual near-future problems helps make clear the need for planning and for making the planning process work better.

The continuing emphasis on local and regional methods of feeding into national planning patterns is crucial. The media help here by working to make local planning function at a very effective and efficient level.

The program of the *Kobe Shimbun* is an example. In operating a Special Investigatory Reporting desk in a community service program for the past several years, this Japanese daily has worked directly with local communities on the formal planning of specific programs for improvement. To get more complete information for planning, reporters lived in homes of fishermen and of farmers.[21]

If one assumes that widespread citizen involvement in planning is important, the media have a crucial part in building that involvement. A case in point is the work of the *Honolulu Advertiser* in persuading, and aiding, the state of Hawaii to carry out a planning program; the Hawaiian legislature appropriated $50,000 for a planning committee, and some 250 persons made suggestions on the middle-range future and on the situation in the year 2000.[22]

In the course of building public involvement, the media have the opportunity to encourage new and additional leadership. The media can observe the work of new leaders in civic affairs, can call attention to their activities, can present their ideas, with full credit, and can help put leaders into situations that will aid further personal growth. Consultation, information providing, and general steering are other possible functions here for the media in working with these new leaders.

This close contact with affairs also spotlights the obligation of the media as watchdogs, constantly examining the process of governing at all levels, and, in this context, paying special attention to the performance of the planning process.

A part of this procedure today is inevitably the mixture between various power sectors and their functioning. I think especially of the relationship between commercial ventures, financed by private capital, and government units.

Although governments are powerful, in most nations private entities also have great resources, and their actions have an important effect upon the setting of national goals. The urgency of exchanging information, and of working closely on the inter-development of plans, is very great, and media can be of much service by helping to spotlight long range planning in the private sector. In less developed countries (LDCs), efforts with the multinational corporations are especially important, and media can aid in making local attitudes more clear so that there is a better foundation for exchanges of ideas. As Abelson has pointed out, MNCs in many cases are becoming more willing to fit their plans to the needs of LDCs, which usually are shifting toward a pattern of greater local involvement in production.[23] For example, assembly of IBM electric typewriters in Bogota, Colombia, is much more labor intensive than in the United States, by design, so that more than half the final cost of the machine is added in Colombia. LDCs are also urging MNCs to localize research and development activities.[24]

Media Involvement in Planning

I come now to an area where there is less agreement, and that is the field of very direct media involvement in the planning process itself. By direct I mean personal contact with members of planning agencies by representatives (not necessarily news gatherers) of individual media, attempting to influence the nature of the planning.[25] In instances where the media representatives for some reason, preferably through careful preparation, have high expertise and are capable advisers, the practice would appear to contribute solidly to the public welfare.

In all of this activity, the media have an opportunity to set a good example of civility. If the media are direct and clear and forceful without being shrill or strident or petty, they not only have higher promise of effectiveness in their own endeavors, but they provide a pattern through which other elements in the society will perhaps be more inclined to be relatively more rational in demands, statements, and actions.

The media contribute also by the manner in which they handle news of conflict. If such news stresses the factor of conflict, rather than the issues under discussion, a pattern found too often in most media treatment of news, the chances of workable resolution are weakened. If, instead, the media, not overlooking conflict and difference, will find more satisfying ways of presenting the major forces and elements in each situation, perhaps using the method advanced recently by Haskins, they will perform a great public service.[26]

In order effectively to work in this fashion in planning for national goals, each medium must carefully work out its own procedures for its treatment of the future.[27]

It has seemed to me to be important that each medium have an ongoing group of staff members who are charged with developing adequate plans, for the advising of management, on actions and plans needed within the medium for the adequate coverage of the future; of course this coverage would include the setting and the explanation of national goals.

As one phase of the essential effort on a medium to take continuing steps, on a conscious basis, for its part in planning national goals, it is desirable to encourage certain staff members to become specialists in crucial fields, whether these be transportation, energy, education, or agriculture. Special training for these staff members is highly desirable; I realize that in many cases these staff members must be essentially self taught, but it will indeed be possible for them to learn a great deal from reading and through discussion with available specialists.

It is also a part of the work of the mass media to prepare the public for the functioning of the mass media. In most nations the public does not fully appreciate the importance of the press, and the great services which can come from the press if it is adequately understood, encouraged and financed. Such an understanding should ideally produce solid support for the mass media in many of their activities which often are not well understood and by their nature are often opposed by certain social elements, including forces in government. Hachten's summarizing words on Africa apply in other continents as well: "Politicians and government leaders need to be eduated on the role of the press."[28]

The mass media need vigorous professional associations, which are prepared to plan for the media future, and to speak out strongly. Organizations of individual journalists are also important; I have much hope for such enterprises as the Society for Professional Journalists, which is now an international body. Individual journalists are tremendously important; media management may make policies, but only individual journalists can carry them out effectively.

Journalism schools also have their place in the work of journalism in the setting of national goals. They can urge students to obtain substantial public affairs grounding. The schools can offer basic training in planning, perhaps through simulation or role playing. Students can study problems of resistance to planning, and can be given detailed word on sources of information about planning procedures and about the areas which will be the subject of goal setting.

The schools can aid also in continuing education programs for news workers, and in intensive short courses on fields which are the subject matter for national-goal planning. For media workers not able to come to on-campus sessions, the schools can provide detailed and specific reading lists on subject matter fields important in planning.

All of these factors are important in considering how the mass media of communications can play a crucial part in the intelligent setting of goals for the nation. The media can inform, they can explain, they can stimulate. They can be very substantial contributors, not only in setting goals, but in the effective effort to reach those goals.

To do this, most mass media must greatly expand their vision of service, and their fields and patterns of action.

Given this larger vision, they can greatly help the citizens of a nation in the march toward the realization of today's vision of a better tomorrow.

NOTES

[1] Gerhard Colm, "Introduction," *Goals, Priorities and Dollars: The Next Decade*, by Leonard A. Lecht. (New York: The Free Press, 1966).

[2] *Ibid.*, p. 5.

[3] *Ibid.*, passim.

[4] For a discussion of the balancing of economic and other factors, see Ronald G. Ridker, "To Grow or Not to Grow: That's Not the Relevant Question." *Science*, Vol. 182, No. 4119 (Dec. 28, 1973), pp. 1315–8.

[5] For a more extended discussion, see Nestor E. Terleckyj, "Estimating Possibilities for Improvement in the Quality of Life in the United States, 1972–81." *Looking Ahead*, National Planning Association, 20:10 (January 1973), pp. 1–12.

[6] For a report on how the media are used in national goals programs in a low-consultative society, see Frederick T. C. Yu, "Campaigns, Communications, and Development in Communist China," in *Communication and Change in Developing Countries*, edited by Daniel Lerner and Wilbur Schramm (Honolulu: East-West Center Press, 1967), pp. 195–215.

[7] James Brian Quinn and Robert Major, "Norway: Small Country Plans Civil Science and Technology," *Science*, Vol. 183, No. 4121, (Jan. 18, 1974), pp. 172–9.

[8] An insightful treatment of the problems of Central and South America is found in an address by Sol M. Linowitz, "The Future of the Americas," *Science*, Vol. 1181. (Sept. 7, 1973), pp. 916–20.

[9] The Commission on Freedom of the Press, *A Free and Responsible Press*. (Chicago: University of Chicago Press, 1947), pp. 27–28.

[10] John C. Merrill, Carter R. Bryan, and Marvin Alisky, *The Foreign Press: A Survey of the World's Journalism* (Baton Rouge: Louisiana State University Press, 1970), p. 3.

[11] Terleckyj, *supra*.

[12] Paul J. Deutschmann, Huber Ellingsworth, and John T. McNelly, *Communication and Social Change in Latin America*. (New York: Frederick A. Praeger, 1968).

[13] G. Ray Funkhouser, "Trends in Media Coverage of the Issues of the '60s," *Journalism Quarterly*, 50:3, (Autumn 1973), pp. 533–38.

[14] Robert A. Nisbet, *Social Change and History* (London: Oxford University Press, 1969), p. 281.

[15] John A. Lent, ed., *The Asian Newspapers' Reluctant Revolution* (Ames: Iowa State University Press, 1971), p. xvi.

[16] Wilbur Schramm, *Mass Media and National Development* (Stanford: Stanford University Press, 1964), p. 44.

[17] An excellent general discussion of the functions and uses of the mass media is found in Elihu Katz, Michael Gurevitch, and Hadassah Haas, "On the Use of the Mass Media for Important Things," *American Sociological Review*, 38:2 (April 1973), pp. 164–81, based on extensive research in Israel.

[18] John Alius, "A Free Press Means Development," *IAPA News*, No. 201 (March 1971), p. 4.

[19] Max Ways, "What's Wrong with News? It Isn't New Enough," *Fortune* (October 1969), pp. 110–4, 155–61.

[20] A helpful discussion of agenda setting is found in Maxwell E. McCombs and Donald L. Shaw, "The Agenda-Setting Function of the Mass Media," *Public Opinion Quarterly*, 36:2 (Summer 1972) pp. 176–87.

[21] Hirosuke Inamoto, "In-depth analysis as aid to community," *IPI* (International Press Institute) *Report*, May 1968, pp. 8–9.

[22] George Chaplin, "The Future Is Being Shaped Today," *Bulletin of the American Society of Newspaper Editors*, No. 541 (May 1970), pp. 5, 6, 17.

[23] Philip H. Abelson, "Corporations and the Less Developed Countries," *Science*, 182 (Nov. 30, 1973), No. 4115, p. 873.

[24] *U.S. International Firms and R,D, & E in Developing Countries*, report of an ad hoc panel of the Board on Science and Technology for International Development (National Academy of Sciences, Washington, D.C.), 1973.

[25] Pertinent materials for all phases of change-persuasive activity are found in Donald N. Michael, *On Learning to Plan—and Planning to Learn* (San Francisco: Jossey-Bass, 1973) described as the first detailed and systematic examination of the social psychological resistances of individuals and groups in organizations to change.

[26] Jack C. Haskins, " 'Cloud with a Silver Lining' Approach to Violence News," *Journalism Quarterly* 50:3 (Autumn 1973), p. 549–52.

[27] This concept is developed more fully in an address, Leslie G. Moeller, "The Mass Media, and Preparation for Great Social Change," before the Communications session of the General Assembly of the World Future Society, Washington, D.C., May 14, 1971.

[28] William A. Hachten, *Muffled Drums: The News Media in Africa*, (Ames: Iowa State University Press, 1971), p. 48.

Ralph L. Lowenstein:

Use of Foreign Media by Developing Nations

IN THE normal development process, each country moves through predictable stages of media growth—from "elite" to "specialized." Large, modern nations, such as the United States, England, France, and Germany, have conformed to this formal growth pattern through natural evolution. Small developed countries—such as Switzerland, Norway, and Denmark—have made special adaptations to allow their media to grow toward the specialized stage.

THE ELITE-POPULAR-SPECIALIZED CURVE

The Elite Stage

The evolutionary media pattern through which large nations have moved and are moving begins with the "Elite Stage" (see Chart I). This stage is characterized by general illiteracy and poverty. The majority of the population is unable to read print media and unable to afford either print or electronic media.

These restrictions of illiteracy and poverty have implications beyond the individual in this society. Whole segments of the population are cut off from media exposure because rural and outlying areas are without schools, roads, and electricity. Newspapers from the capital are dependent upon overland communication for circulation. Television, and to a lesser extent radio, must be umbilically attached to a power supply to pick up a signal.

Those media that exist, therefore, are usually found in urban areas. Even there, they appeal to an urban elite of opinion leaders. Their content is informational or didactic, primarily. The media are relatively expensive to obtain, and advertising (which could ordinarily subsidize the media and thus reduce the cost to the individual) is largely lacking.

The Popular Stage

When a nation breaks through the barriers of poverty and illiteracy, circulations and audience size begin to rise dramatically. The media in this stage appeal to a heterogeneous "mass" audience, which can now read and afford print media, and pay the cost of electronic receivers. Content of the media is geared

▶ This is an original article done for this book in 1976 by Ralph L. Lowenstein, professor of journalism, University of Missouri-Columbia.

CHART I

ELITE-POPULAR-SPECIALIZED (EPS) CURVE
OF MEDIA PROGRESSION

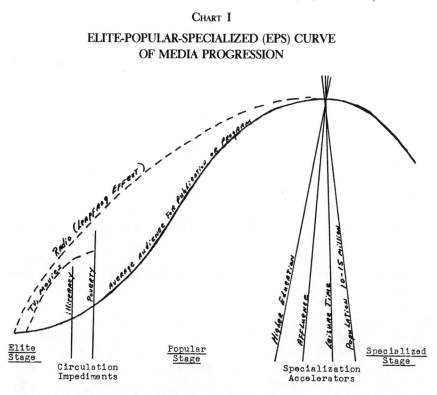

SOURCE: John C. Merrill and Ralph L. Lowenstein, *Media, Messages, and Men* (New York: David McKay Co., 1971), p. 34.

to the "lowest common denominator" in the audience. But it must be understood that the range between the "lowest common denominator" and the "highest common denominator" is not extremely great in this society. Most people in this stage have at least a grade school education; few have more than a high school education. The mass audience shares a common educational experience, and is likely to find the general fare in the mass media satisfactory.

The audience is affluent enough to be worth reaching; advertisers thus subsidize the media, making publications even more accessible to the masses.

Even in this stage, there are specialized media—but those that exist are likely to be vestiges of the Elite Stage, rather than bona fide products of a later, Specialized Stage, and media development.

It must be added here that the electronic media, at least in recent years, do not always conform to this slow progression from Elite to Popular. Radio, since the popularization of the transistor following World War II, has had a "leapfrog" effect, hopping across the barriers of both illiteracy and poverty. This has permitted radio to reach a mass audience, while other media are still in the Elite Stage.[1] Movies and television are able to leap across the barrier of illiteracy, but still are generally stopped at the poverty barrier. Both are dependent upon relatively expensive equipment; both are dependent upon external power supplies.

The Specialized Stage

The final stage of media development, the Specialized Stage, is attained in fully developed countries when there is a coalescence of four factors: 1) higher education, 2) affluence, 3) leisure time, and 4) population size of at least 10 million to 15 million. The media in this stage appeal to and are consumed by fragmented, specialized segments of the population, primarily.

Higher education assures varied professional and intellectual needs and tastes. At the same time, there is a higher degree of job specialization among the non-university educated. From all segments of the population there is a demand for specialized publications and programs appealing to a wide spectrum of interests.

An *affluent* population can afford a variety of media; their affluence also spawns more advertising with its concomitant media subsidies. In addition, the average family can afford a variety of specialized units within each medium; i.e., five magazines, four radios, three television sets, etc. This affluence assures fragmentation of the family unit as media consumers, permitting media to abandon "common denominator" content in favor of specialized content.

Leisure time is so closely related to affluence that one is reluctant to insert it as a separate factor. But the presence of this factor emphasizes that the audience must not only have the money to obtain specialized media, but the time to consume them, as well. The average American watches television more than four hours each day; the average American home has a television set on for more than six hours each day. A society must have a short working day and a long weekend to feed this sort of appetite for the media.

To enter the Specialized Stage in a normal manner, a country must have a *population* large enough to support the production and distribution of specialized media. Although this factor has never been tested methodologically, we can assume that the population *literate* in a *single language* must be in the 10–15 million range. A smaller literate population could not support a variety of specialized media even if the other three factors were present.

The United States is the only country that is now primarily in the Specialized Stage. All media, with the exception of television, are characterized by a high degree of specialization. The popularization of cable television (CATV) and the development of cassette television will vastly multiply the number of channels in this medium, permitting television to move into the Specialized Stage, also.

The Small, Modern Country

What is the plight of the modernized or modernizing country in which the factors of higher education, affluence, and leisure time are present, but the factor of minimum population size is absent? These countries may also move into the Specialized Stage by "borrowing" specialized media from a larger country. Since a variety of specialized media can be found today only in countries where English, French, Russian, and German are the dominant languages, the small, modernized nation must seek publications and programming in one of the four "technological" languages. Its small size precludes translation of such specialized material to any large degree.

If the small nation is in the mainstream of a "technological" language, this borrowing process is fairly simple to achieve. French-speaking Belgians, for example, borrow all sorts of media from France; Switzerland borrows from France and Germany; New Zealand borrows from England, Australia, Canada, and the United States. If the small, modern nation is not in the mainstream of a "technological" language, it must adopt one of the four "technological" languages as a second language if it hopes to maintain its relative technological position among the nations of the world.

Small nations—even though modern—cannot satisfy their national needs in the areas of defense, trade, higher education, medical technology, etc. without borrowing media from other countries. They must have or adopt a "technological" language in order to become borrowers. That is a fact of life in the latter half of the twentieth century.

MANIPULATION OF THE EPS PATTERN

The EPS pattern is evolutionary. It may be artificially manipulated in a "revolutionary" manner if a country has the desire and/or the money to do so. Thus, small modern nations may force themselves into the Specialized Stage by "borrowing" from other nations. Theoretically, an underdeveloped nation may manipulate the pattern by distributing radios and TV sets at government expense, by barring general interest magazines, or by subsidizing specialized media. Daniel Lerner refers to such government interference as a stochastic factor in the historical model—"social control" as opposed to "individual participation." [2]

THE UNDERDEVELOPED NATIONS

Wilbur Schramm has referred to the "band of scarcity" which stretches around the center of the earth.[3] These are the major regions of Africa, Asia, and Latin America where media of all kinds fall below the Unesco minimums. Virtually all countries in these areas have some rudimentary form of the mass media. All of the underdeveloped countries are now in the Elite Stage of media development. Eventually, if the EPS pattern is correctly predictive, they will become literate and affluent, and will move successively into the Popular and Specialized Stages, even without government manipulation.

However, no country lives in a media vacuum while this process is taking place. External print and electronic messages are swirling around the underdeveloped countries and penetrating deeply into them—sometimes by infusion, sometimes by invitation.

It can be assumed that where some media products are lacking in a developing nation, at least some portions of society seek to supplant this fare by "borrowing" media products from other nations. The questions for which we seek the answers are these: Are these external media consumed only by elites in a developing nation? Do these external media play any role in moving the nation to a higher stage in the media progression curve?

Foreign Newspapers

Two kinds of newspapers are imported by developing nations: 1) major newspapers from the former colonial power, with which the country may still have political, economic, cultural, and linguistic ties, and 2) "elite" newspapers that have tremendous international influence. [4]

In the Ivory Coast, for example, where there is only one daily newspaper (published in French), newspapers from France arrive within 24 hours of publication. These newspapers are read by the urban literate, and tend to reinforce the elites in the cultural mold of their former colonial masters. The influence of these newspapers diminishes as former colonial countries emphasize their own culture and develop an elementary press system.

The influence of the "elite" press, however, is likely to increase along with a country's development. The information or views of these newspapers are important to developing countries because the newspapers generally 1) represent countries that have massive political power, "fulcrum power," or significant influence over "fulcrum nations," * 2) represent cities that are economic and/or political capitals of their nations, 3) reflect government or major opposition views, and 4) are published in a widely understood language.

The development of fast international communication via aircraft has increased the influence of "elite" newspapers.

Foreign Magazines

Specialized periodicals—news magazines, learned journals, literary gazettes, etc.—are important sources of information for developing nations. They are publications for which there is no counterpart in underdeveloped nations, since the literate population is not large enough to support such local production. A wide range of needs, from up-to-date medical knowledge to political awareness, depends upon their importation. Like newspapers, these specialized journals are increasingly delivered by air.

Foreign Books

No proper measurement has been made of the influence of foreign books on underdeveloped nations. Specialized books have the same value to these nations as specialized periodicals. American paperbacks have found a vast market abroad, and the export of American textbooks tripled during the last three years

---

* A "fulcrum power" would be a nation like Yugoslavia or Egypt, nations not having military, economic or political strength of major world powers, but exerting strong influence over certain blocs of nations that may be able to shift toward one sphere of influence or the other.

of the 1960s.[5] Most, of course, have gone to modernized nations. But whereas these textbooks are going to universities in the modernized nations, they are probably used at the high school level and below in the developing nations, especially where a "technological" language has been adopted as the official, unifying language of the country.

Foreign Radio

Virtually every country in the world communicates with other countries via radio. How many people in other countries listen is open to question. The major communicators, according to Thomas C. Sorensen,[6] are:

Soviet Union	1,555 hours per week (67 languages)
Communist China	1,131 hours per week
Egypt	910 hours per week
Voice of America	850 hours per week (38 languages)
BBC	731 hours per week
West Germany	721 hours per week

The reaching power of these international communicators is determined by 1) the power of transmitters, especially medium wave transmitters, 2) the comprehensibility of language, and 3) the credibility of broadcasts. At present, most international programming is transmitted by shortwave. But few people in developing nations have shortwave receivers. Since the transistor radio has made radio receivers (medium wave) available to even the poor in most nations, the Voice of America is seeking to supplement its powerful shortwave transmitters with more medium wave transmitters. VOA estimates that it can now reach 70 per cent of the populated areas of the world.[7] It claims a weekly audience of between 42 million and 43 million persons.[8] One can assume that listeners to foreign broadcasts, especially in developing countries, are primarily "elites."

Foreign Records

Although American records are popular in many nations, they are rarely heard in those developing nations that have a completely different musical culture. One is curious about their linguistic influence on other nations, but one can also assume that they play no great role in media development.

Foreign Motion Pictures

Few developing nations can afford to produce a variety of quality films. But few people in developing nations have access to motion pictures, or the money to pay for admissions. Foreign films spread culture, language, and political thought. But their usage probably does not extend far beyond the urban dwellers, especially the urban elite. One could hypothesize that locally-produced films, though of a lower quality, are likely to be more attractive to the masses in a developing nation. The economic infeasibility of "dubbing" voices in foreign films for limited audiences would preclude their wide popularity. Foreign films, however, are "grafted" on to local television, increasing their circulation, and thus their utility.

Foreign Television

Because of limited reaching power and limited number of channels, there has been no significant amount of international telecasting, except on a small regional basis. International television exchange, at present, falls into two categories: 1) regional cooperative agreements and 2) importation of television film or tape for local re-broadcasting.

The regional arrangements now operating successfully are in modernized regions—"Eurovision" in Western Europe and "Intervision" in the Soviet sphere of influence. Japan has been the moving force behind a plan for "Asiavision"; the Arab nations have considered a regional network, but the plans have never gotten off the ground; and a Central American network (CATVN) has operated with limited success, although it has not accomplished its envisioned expansion to include most of Latin America.[9]

Far more significant has been the importation of film and tape for re-broadcast locally. Developing nations that have been able to establish television have been largely unable to finance quality programming. The developing nations therefore must import programming—entertainment, documentaries, even news film. U.S. networks are the largest retailers of these materials, and the cultural, political, and linguistic effects can only be imagined.[10]

Production of television programming is so expensive that even fully-developed countries are "co-producing" series in order to share the expense. England and West Germany, and Russia and Finland are only two sets of countries among the many that have moved in this direction.[11]

CONCLUSION

This quick survey of the use of foreign media in developing nations indicates that such media:

1) Play an elitist role, primarily; they provide elite materials (newspapers, magazines, motion pictures) for an elite audience, and, to a lesser extent, didactic materials (radio) for new elites.

2) Provide an important supplement for those local media that have entered the Popular Stage; this supplement includes television programming (film and tapes) and radio programming (musical records).

3) Allow elites to leapfrog into a Specialized Stage by giving them access to highly specialized material (periodicals, scholarly journals, books).

Foreign media usage does not appear to create a significant acceleration of the EPS progression within a country. Such foreign media cannot in and of themselves break down the "circulation impediments" in the Elite Stage. Nor can they significantly affect the four factors necessary for the attainment of the

Specialized Stage. A developing nation's progress through these stages of media progression depends more upon its ability to achieve meaningful economic and educational goals than upon its physical access to foreign media.

However, it must be added that developing nations must, at the very least, make it possible for their elites to leapfrog into the Specialized Stage by providing them with a "technological" language at some point in their educational careers. At the very best—perhaps reaching toward the Utopian—a developing country will attempt to break the barrier of illiteracy not only with "literacy," but with "bi-literacy." Thus, if a developing nation is not in the mainstream of a technological language—and wants to maintain its own language for a host of reasons—it must attempt to teach its youth to read and write *two* languages. This would permit a high degree of borrowing in the Popular Stage and allow a significant portion of the population to leapfrog into the Specialized Stage.

NOTES

[1] All media in a particular country need not be in the same stage at the same time. Some media lag behind the country's normal progression to a higher stage; others precede it.

[2] *The Passing of Traditional Society* (New York: The Free Press, 1958), pp. 67–68.

[3] *Mass Media and National Development* (Stanford: Stanford University Press, 1964), p. 92.

[4] See John C. Merrill, *The Elite Press: Great Newspapers of the World* (New York: Pitman Publishing Company, 1968), especially Chapter 4, "The Elite: Names and Rank," pp. 32–45.

[5] John C. Merrill and Ralph L. Lowenstein, *Media, Messages, and Men* (New York: David McKay Co., 1971), p. 58.

[6] *The Word War: The Story of American Propaganda* (New York: Harper & Row, 1968), p. 227.

[7] John W. Henderson, *The United States Information Agency* (New York: Frederick A. Praeger, 1969), p. 183.

[8] *Ibid.*, p. 184.

[9] Wilson P. Dizard, "Television's Global Networks," in Heinz-Dietrich Fischer and John C. Merrill, *International Communication* (New York: Hastings House, 1970), pp. 335–340.

[10] See Herbert I. Schiller, *Mass Communications and American Empire* (New York: Augustus M. Kelley, 1970), especially pp. 85–91.

[11] *Variety*, April 14, 1972 (Vol. 262, No. 9), p. 68.

John T. McNelly:

Media Exposure in Developing Urban Societies

AGGREGATE statistics tell us a dramatic story of the spread of the mass media—especially radio and television—across the developing world in recent years. But the country-by-country figures fail to alert us to a crucial aspect of this phenomenon: the heavy build-up of media facilities in the urban centers, as contrasted with rural areas. This confluence of media and people in the cities presents a growing challenge to development planners and to communication researchers.

Neither group has yet risen to the challenge in a concerted way. The amount of scientific inquiry into urban communication in developing countries has been notably meager. Relatively more research attention has followed the funding agencies' preoccupations with rural developmental problems. Because the media are less prominent, and sometimes completely unavailable, in rural settings, rural research has not yielded as striking evidence of media effects as might be expected to be the case in urban settings.[1]

Meanwhile the mounting pace of this urbanization is evident even to a casual visitor to cities of Asia, Africa and Latin America where freeways and forests of television antennae occupy former farm and jungle areas. Already in Latin America, the formerly rural region from which come most of the research findings cited in this paper, urbanization reached the 50 per cent mark in the past decade and is, of course, still climbing. Some observers expect the proportion of the region's population living in settlements of 2,000 or more inhabitants to rise to 80 per cent by the turn of the century, a condition already attained by Uruguay. A basic phenomenon has been the appearance of gigantic megapoli marching across vast reaches of countryside with *cinturones de miseria* (belts of misery) at their edges in the form of shantytowns. Moreover, there has appeared in the Latin-American demographic literature the phrase *urbanización del campo* (urbanization of the countryside). This refers to the spread to rural areas of urban ways of living, working and consuming (including mass media consumption) and the gradual erosion of distinctions between urban and rural, creating a totally new economic, social and political configuration of the region.[2] This "rural urbanization" phenomenon enormously increases the potential scope of the study of urbanizing processes and of the role of the media therein.

▶ Reprinted here with permission of the author from a paper presented at the East-West Communication Institute, Honolulu, Hawaii (Feb. 12–17, 1973). Dr. McNelly is professor of journalism at the University of Wisconsin, Madison.

It should not be overlooked that the hundreds of millions of persons who are now experiencing the processes of urbanization are experiencing them in drastically different ways. Urban life to some means jobs, education, a share of the luxuries of life. To many, however, including the hordes of "rural refugees" [3] in the slums, it means loneliness, confusion and bitter struggle for food and shelter. These people are prime target audiences for the kinds of media informational and educational efforts urged by the high-level International Commission on the Development of Education in its recent report, "Learning to Be," produced at the request of the United Nations Educational, Scientific and Cultural Organization (UNESCO).

Focusing on the need for self-education, on lifelong learning as contrasted with the traditional classroom teaching which is beyond the reach of many, the Commission urges the exploitation of the full arsenal of communication technology including television, audio-visual aids, video-cassettes, computers and satellite transmissions in order to achieve a global "learning society." [4]

United Nations agencies, the World Bank and other organizations have been willing to help developing countries bring the new media technology to bear on their urgent needs for out-of-school as well as in-school education. Outside assistance must be justified, however, by evidence of the effectiveness of such endeavors. [5] That means research, both to evaluate existing projects and to develop theories or hypotheses that can serve as guides in the planning of new projects. Heavy investments will be required to make the media technology optimally useful to the urban masses. Without an adequate research base, resources may be misallocated or—far more likely—not allocated at all. The latter has been the outcome up to now in many developing countries.

To the extent that media building thus far has not been merely an accidental or incidental by-product of general urbanization or industrialization processes, it appears to have been based on administrative intuition. In the past decade or so a few guiding principles have drifted in from the research fronts of the social sciences. As will become evident in some of the following discussion, however, they have tended to be speculative in nature or to stand rather tentatively on insubstantial empirical foundations.

Communication research must make major advances if it is to meet the challenge of the revolutionary technologies that are becoming available to reach urbanizing masses in the final quarter of the twentieth century. The setting of research priorities is a long-range task calling for contributions from scientists of many disciplines and cultures. Priorities tend to emerge on a continuing basis in interaction with technological innovations and administrative demands. One starting point, however, is that of unfinished business. It is in that context that the following three directions of inquiry are suggested as meriting consideration. They are not presented in order of priority or importance but in terms of a general progression from earlier to more recent unfinished business.

1. *More research is needed into the complex of relationships between media growth and other urbanization processes.*

The high correlations repeatedly found in cross-national aggregate data analyses between indices of media availability and indices of urbanization and other facets of modernization have been subject to varying interpretations. Oversimplified, one issue is whether urbanization causes media growth or whether it is the other way around. Are the media a consequence—perhaps just artifacts—of urbanization, or do they play some causal role in the process?

Daniel Lerner tackled this question in his pioneering analysis of data based on UNESCO and UN figures published in 1951 for most countries of the world. His interpretation of the data suggested that urbanization came first, followed by literacy and media growth, the latter two in close reciprocal relationship.[6]

But Schramm and Ruggels, on the basis of an analysis of data from the same and additional countries about a decade later, raised the question whether the spread of transistor radios and rapid transportation had not made urbanization less basic as a causal factor. Their analysis also raised the question whether the concept of a single pattern of media growth in relation to other development processes may not be too simple. The media, they suggested, may play different roles in different regions or cultures or at different stages of development.[7]

With respect to the first question, at least part of the answer is suggested by the broader concept of urbanization mentioned earlier as embracing not only the growth of cities but also the spread of urban ways of life into the countryside. Under this concept, the question of causality becomes less relevant: the media are viewed as being part and parcel of the urbanization process, not just as causes or effects. That is not, however, to detract from the relevance of the second question referring to the possibility of different media roles for different regions, cultures, or stages of development. That warrants further looking into. A multivariate study within the Latin American region showed that media growth, as indexed by newspaper circulation per capita, was closely involved with urbanization and other variables in a general "developmental" factor,[8] but that kind of regional study is limited by the small number of countries available for the sample. Both the global and the regional approaches are limited in how much they can reveal because the aggregate data for whole nations tell us nothing about vast and crucial differences *within* nations, particularly between the urban and rural sectors.

An approach that shows promise for probing into regional and cultural differences is that of analyzing data for political units within a single country. A recent study of data from Mexico's 50 largest cities shows that urbanization (as indexed by number of inhabitants) does not by itself predict significantly the per capita distribution of newspapers, radios or television sets, but that television sets and to some extent radios are correlated with other indicators of urbanization and modernization such as the availability of electrical facilities.[9]

With the spread of urban conveniences such as electric power and radio and television signals to the smaller cities, and gradually to rural areas, we can expect a gradual attenuation of urban-rural differences in media accessibility. But this is by no means a uniform or automatic process across regions and cultures; it happens in varying degrees and sequences as a result of policies, or lack of policies, on the part of decision-makers in governmental and private sectors. For example, a decision to construct a television transmitter with relay stations to cover an entire small country can drastically alter the pattern of diffusion of television receivers, and possibly of other urbanization processes in the bargain. One media expert has observed that television for urban areas only is apt to encourage the trend toward cities.[10] Conversely, widely-diffused or decentralized television might be used to encourage less concentrated patterns of population.

Decision-making in this field thus can have implications reaching far beyond the huge investments in media hardware. Decisions of this nature can be taken with some advance awareness of their likely consequences as researchers learn more about the reciprocal relationships between media growth and urbanization phenomena.

Media-building strategy should be based not only on considerations of the distribution of media facilities but also on how people *use* these facilities. Thus our second suggestion for communication research:

2. *More research is needed into consistent patterns of exposure to the media among populations in developing urban societies.*

By far the simplest—and, not surprisingly, the most popular—conception of media exposure patterns is that the media *supplement* rather than *complement* each other. That is to say, as new media are brought into the life of an individual or society, they simply get added onto the media already in use, rather than displacing any of them. The implication is that more media mean more media exposure. This concept provides a convenient rationale for the unplanned proliferation of new media ventures in developing countries. Government officials can take pride in acquiring the latest in media hardware, without worrying about the possibility of needless and expensive redundancy.

And this "more the better" strategy is consistent with the most commonly-accepted view of media exposure patterns among social scientists. Lerner called it the "centripetal tendency." By this he meant a tendency among those in his Middle East samples who read newspapers also to be "the heaviest consumers of movies, broadcasts, and all other media products."[11] This tendency also was reported by Deutschmann and by Rogers in separate studies of underdeveloped villages in Colombia. They found, furthermore, that measures of exposure to the various media fitted into a cumulative (Guttman) pattern. This suggested that media exposure was a unidimensional form of behavior.[12]

But it should be noted well that these findings were reported in rural settings where the media are far less accessible than they are in cities. When we move to urban settings we find different results. In Santiago, Chile, Carter and Sepulveda did find intercorrelations among use of the different media, but they failed to find any cumulative pattern of unidimensionality.[13] In Quito, Ecuador, McLeod *et al.* found no generalized pattern of media exposure whereby use of one medium necessarily implied exposure to another.[14] And in a recent study in Lima, Peru, utilizing more extensive measures of media exposure, McNelly and Molina not only found a lack of a single generalized pattern of exposure but also found, instead of unidimensionality, five separate factors to represent media exposure.[15]

On the basis of data from a national sample in the United States, Greenberg and Kumata found that for the most part exposure to any one medium was independent of exposure to a second.[16] An exception in both the U.S. and Lima studies was that exposure to newspapers was found to be associated with exposure to magazines. Data from a number of urban studies in Latin America indicate that, as in the United States, the print media tend to be used more heavily by persons of relatively high education and status, while those of lower socioeconomic position tend to make heavier use of radio—and of television when they have access to it.

There are further suggestions in these studies that television is gradually displacing radio and movies in the time budgets of urban Latin Americans, even as in the more industrialized countries.

Fast-changing media consumption habits in the developing urban societies are creating new problems and possibilities both for those who utilize the media and those who develop them. The "centripetal tendency," the idea that people can just keep adding new media to their lives without displacing old media habits, is not a valid guide to media behavior in urban Latin America, and likely will become less valid even in rural areas as more media become accessible. Making media more accessible to people will not necessarily increase their overall media exposure; it may just change their patterns of exposure. That makes life more complicated for media decision-makers.

The electronic technologies already on the scene in those places—and more yet to arrive such as audio and video cassettes and satellite receivers—present endless potential combinations and permutations of media-building priorities upon which to make decisions. The decisions made can save or waste millions of dollars and bear heavily on the success of a variety of development programs. Decisions of that kind are best made on the basis of hard evidence.

The challenge to communication research goes well beyond providing evidence on how to reach the largest audiences in the most economical ways. More fundamental questions are at issue, involving present and potential roles of the media in meeting the needs of particular segments of urbanizing populations. Some of these questions will be discussed in connection with our final suggestion for communication research:

3. *More research is needed into differential roles of the media for lower so-cioeconomic and recent migrant groups in developing urban societies.*

Here again there is a rather simple answer available. Again it is a popular one. And it is consistent with a view widely publicized among social scientists and their students. It is simply not to worry about media accessibility for all of the less educated and affluent members of a society, for they will be reached through interpersonal contacts by opinion leaders.

This approach is clearly implicit, if not always explicit, in much social science literature and in developmental programs that depend on traditional interpersonal communication channels to reach the masses. The rationale for this approach lies, of course, in the early literature on the two-step flow hypothesis (which came to be labeled variously a theory, a model, and even a doctrine): "that ideas often flow from radio and print to opinion leaders and from them to the less active sections of the population." [17] For a quarter-century the two-step flow was probably the most popular model utilized in diffusion research. [18]

Its shortcomings have been amply discussed elsewhere, [19] but one particularly concerns us here. In its conceptual vagueness, not distinguishing between *information* and *persuasion*, the two-step flow hypothesis failed to take into account the differential roles of the communication channels at different stages of the receiver's decision-making process. Much research evidence indicates that, while interpersonal channels appear to be more effective in persuading people to accept an idea or a practice, the mass media are particularly important in the earlier informational (awareness) stage. [20] So the media have a role to play not only with opinion leaders but with the general population. The point has been acknowledged by one of the early promulgators of the two-step idea, who notes that the tendency among researchers "is no longer to look at the media as competitive but, rather, as complementary by virtue of their function in various phases of an individual's decision." [21]

The informational stage is crucial to the less educated and affluent—the less active sections of a population—because they tend to have so little of it to start with. Not only do they start with less knowledge of matters like personal hygiene, child care and spacing, and local and national politics, but they ordinarily are less likely to be exposed to such information through the interpersonal communication networks to which they belong. There also is evidence to indicate that the less privileged members of a society are less likely to seek information through personal contacts with those in the know.

But scattered evidence from several studies suggests that exposure to the mass media can serve to compensate for such informational deprivation. Where media are available—as they increasingly are in urban areas—people are able to get from them information that ordinarily is lacking in their interpersonal channels. In Lima, Peru, for example, correlations between media exposure and world affairs knowledge were found to be significantly higher for people in the lower socioeconomic stratum than in the upper levels. To the extent that the less privileged were informed at all, they tended to have been informed through the media. [22]

Information gaps between the rich and the poor are unlikely to be eliminated given present differential patterns of media usage, which tend to favor the rich. But improved delivery systems for information, utilizing the new media technologies, hold possibilities for further breaking down age-old barriers to social communication.[23]

Unless additional research evidence is forthcoming, however, on which to base innovative strategies for media building and utilization, it will be all too easy for developmental planners to continue using the same old communication approaches under which the present informational inequities came into being in the first place. It seems to come naturally to planners to pour human and material resources into traditional communication programs emphasizing personal contacts to persuade people to accept pre-packaged ideas or practices. The concept of making use of modern technology to make large amounts of information and education available directly to the people so that they can *make their own decisions* seems less easy to grasp and put into operation than are elitist, manipulative, or "trickle-down" concepts of communication.

This is reflected in the budgets for new media ventures in developing countries. As one authority notes, formal educational systems in many societies are budgeted to the limits of their resources, while public service radio and television have been "the poor stepchildren." [24] The International Commission on the Development of Education points out, "For hundreds of millions of illiterate people in the world, school can no longer be of help." The Commission calls instead for more massive nontraditional educational patterns—the use of television, for example, not just to fill gaps in school programs but for its full educational potential.[25]

The new media transmission facilities now spreading over much of the earth's surface and through outer space offer revolutionary opportunities for the redistribution of information.[26] As is not uncommon in technological development, the hardware is far more advanced and sophisticated than are the plans for its social applications. Developing urban societies, with their millions of children and adults crowded together to seek more out of life than they could get where they came from, present unparalleled possibilities for investigation and action on the social uses of the media.

NOTES

[1] This is not to say that important media effects have not been found in rural settings. See Everett M. Rogers, *Modernization Among Peasants: The Impact of Communication* (New York: Holt, Rinehart and Winston), especially Chapter 5.

[2] John Friedman, "El Futuro de la Urbanizacion en America Latina: Algunas Observaciones sobre el Papel de la Perifera," en Horacio H. Godoy (ed.), *Situacion Social de America Latina en el Año 2,000*, (Lima, Peru: Instituto Peruano de Estudios del Desarrollo, 1969).

[3] Daniel Lerner, *The Passing of Traditional Society: Modernizing the Middle East* (New York: Free Press, 1958), p. 67.

[4] *Survey of International Development*, October 1972 (published by the Society for International Development, Washington, D.C.).

[5] G. Naesselund, "Public Service Programming and Development Support in National Communication Planning," paper presented before Asian Broadcasting Union, Istanbul, Turkey, September 1970. Mr. Naesselund is Director of the Department of Mass Communication of UNESCO.

[6] *Op. cit.*, p. 60.

[7] Wilbur Schramm and W. Lee Ruggels, "How Mass Media Systems Grow," in Daniel Lerner and Wilbur Schramm, *Communication and Change in the Developing Countries* (Honolulu; East-West Center Press, 1967), pp. 57–75.

[8] Paul J. Deutschmann and John T. McNelly, "Characteristics of Latin American Countries, "*American Behavioral Scientist,*" Volume 8, pp. 25–29 (September 1964).

[9] Enrique Leon-Martinez, "Urbanization and Media of Mass Communication: The Case of Mexico," unpublished paper, University of Wisconsin, 1972.

[10] Naesselund, *op. cit.*

[11] Lerner, *op. cit.*, p. 64.

[12] Paul J. Deutschmann, "The Mass Media in an Underdeveloped Village," *Journalism Quarterly*, 40:27–35 (1963); Rogers, *op. cit.*, pp. 102–103.

[13] Roy E. Carter Jr. and Orlando Sepulveda, "Some Patterns of Mass Media Use in Santiago de Chile," *Journalism Quarterly*, 41:216–24 (1964).

[14] Jack M. McLeod, Ramona R. Rush and Karl H. Friederich, "The Mass Media and Political Information in Quito, Ecuador," *Public Opinion Quarterly*, 32:575–87 (1968–69).

[15] John T. McNelly and Julio Molina R., "Communication, Stratification and International Affairs Information in a Developing Urban Society," *Journalism Quarterly*, 49:319 (1972).

[16] Bradley S. Greenberg and Hideya Kumata, "National Sample Predictors of Mass Media Use," *Journalism Quarterly*, 45:643–46 (1968).

[17] Paul F. Lazarsfeld, Bernard Berelson and Hazel Gaudet, *The People's Choice* (New York: Duell, Sloan and Pearce, 1944), p. 151.

[18] Everett M. Rogers with F. Floyd Schoemaker, *Communication of Innovations: A Cross-Cultural Approach* (New York: Free Press, 1971), p. 206.

[19] *Ibid.*, pp. 206–208; and John T. McNelly, "*Mass Communication in the Development Process*", in Heinz Dietrich Fischer and John C. Merrill (eds.), *International Communications* (New York: Hastings House, 1970), pp. 158–65.

[20] Rogers, *loc. cit.*

[21] Elihu Katz, "Communication Research and the Image of Society: Convergence of Two Traditions," in A. G. Smith (ed.), *Communication and Culture* (New York: Holt, Rinehart and Winston, 1966), pp. 555–56.

[22] McNelly and Molina, *op. cit.*

[23] Cf. P. J. Tichenor, G. A. Donohue and C. N. Olien, "Mass Media Flow and Differential Growth in Knowledge," *Public Opinion Quarterly*, 34:159–70 (1970).

[24] Naesselund, *op. cit.*

[25] *Survey of International Development*, op. cit.

[26] John T. McNelly, "Mass Media and Information Redistribution," *The Journal of Environmental Education*, 5:31–36 (1973).

Peter Meyer-Dohm:

Investments in Communication and the Development Process

1. The Problem

In an important investigation carried out on behalf of UNESCO, Robert Escarpit has made reference to the existence of "literary high- and low-pressure zones" which become apparent when production and demand for books are looked at on a global scale.[1] Many of the Third World countries, lacking a numerically-strong educated class which is both financially well-situated and in possession of political influence, belong to these literary low-pressure zones. For it is this stratum of the population which on the one hand forms the nucleus of the reading public, whose demand presupposes the production of literary material, and on the other hand forms the climate in which writers are able to develop.[2]

A recent UNESCO publication confirms this idea and the resulting "book-hunger" of the Third World.[3] In 1950 37% of all literate adults and 42% of all children going to school were to be found in Africa, Latin America and Asia (not including Japan); the contribution of these areas to world book production was 24%. Around 1970 this contribution had fallen to 19%, although the proportion of literate adults had risen to 50% and that of school-going children to 63%. At the same time it should be noted that the average circulation of books in the Third World is well below that of the industrial nations.

Obviously the production and demand for books are factors which should not be casually dismissed in educational economic analysis and communication policy analysis, in view of the fact that the demand for books and consequently for, among other things, a medium of information and further education, is a magnitude by which the efficiency of the educational system can be measured, which in turn creates, *inter alia*, the prerequisites for such a demand. It must therefore come somewhat of a surprise that this association of factors has thus far scarcely been analyzed or researched and that the formulation of educational policy is limited narrowly to the actual educational system. An attempt will thus be made in this article to set forth the investments in education and their complementarity effects within the "Kulturwirtschaft" ("cultural economy") of developing countries and thereby to broaden the perspective of educational economy.

▶ This is an original article done for this book by Dr. Peter Meyer-Dohm, full professor for economic policy and rector of the Ruhr University Bochum (Federal Republic of Germany).

2. Complementarity Effects and Derived Demand

When an attempt is made to describe the stock and structure of the strategic human capital of a national economy quantitative indicators are usually used which give information about developmentally active as well as economic, social, political, and intellectual elite groups.[4] The size and composition of the strategic human capital is thus reflected, for example, in the number of teachers, engineers, scientists and doctors; in the number of pupils of different age-groups as a percentage of the population; in the number of students; in the ratio between members of scientific and technical disciplines and those of the humanities. These indicative features and others of a similar nature are usually considered to be adequate for the purpose of formulating certain strategies, on the basis of the economic situation and the general aims of development, for the expansion of the educational system. Nevertheless, experience should have shown that it is not sufficient merely to draw up strategies for the field of instruction in the education-sector, as for instance in the fixing of proportionate periods for the individual stages of education (the planning of the education-pyramid) and a corresponding planning of outlays for physical capital (school buildings etc.). Rather should consideration be given to the fact that investments in education only develop their full productive potential when at the same time on a corresponding scale and in a balanced structure, complementary investments are planned and also carried out. In addition to this empirically verifiable proposition a short theoretical study will be necessary.

When we speak of *complementarity* in connection with investments then we mean the following relationship which Hirschman uses in the framework of his theory of development: An increase in demand for a commodity A leads not only to an increase in its price but also to an expansion of its production and thereby increased demand for another commodity B as well. If it is a question of a rigid, purely technical complementarity relationship in the manufacture of both types of goods then one talks, where B is concerned, of "derived demand." Thus, for example, an increased demand for cars leads to a derived demand for fuel. It may, on the other hand, be a looser type of complementarity relationship, which is of particular significance and relevance for the process of development. In that case we speak of "entrained wants," a concept which makes clear the way in which increased production—more precisely—increased utilization of A awakens wants which give rise to increased demand for B.[5] Between the two goods there is, however, no rigid relationship as there was in the car-fuel example; rather do we mean those numerous wants which arise from car-ownership and which extend from accessories which are not absolutely necessary through road atlases to parking facilities at tourist spots.

Complementarity means in general, quoting Hirschman: ". . . that increased production of A will lead to *pressure* for increasing the available supply of B. When B is a privately produced good or service, this pressure will lead to imports or larger domestic production of B because it will be in the *interest* of traders and producers of B to respond to the pressure." [6] Derived demand and entrained wants are thus an expression for new scarcities which, on the introduction of a product, arise in other markets and characterize a variably rigid and clear-cut relationship. From this we can also infer that, in virtue of such complementarity effects, investments can be induced in other markets or in other economic sectors.

The significance of entrained wants within the realm of education can be particularly well demonstrated by the literacy campaigns in the developing countries. The policy of increasing literacy has the aim of integrating individuals into a national (and often international) system of communication and also of increasing receptivity for information, e.g. about technical innovations, thereby hastening and facilitating the introduction of modern production techniques in agriculture and industry. A foundation is laid for the mastering of more demanding occupations and the economic productivity of the individual is altogether increased as he is made more receptive to innovation. It does not, however, by any means follow that an increase in productivity automatically takes place as a consequence of increased literacy. Rather do these primary investments in education only then reach their full maturity and obtain an appropriate return when an adequate quantity of suitable reading—and informative—material is continually made available to the new literates, so that the once-awakened abilities may be deepened and strengthened.

On the example of numerous literacy-campaigns it can be demonstrated that there exists an inadequate synchronization between the planning of primary investments in education and the planning of the complementary—or induced—investments (e.g. the provision of reading material for the subsequent encouragement of new-literates) which are necessary to cover the cost of the entrained wants which arise as a result of complementarity effects. This has led to the relapsing of a large proportion of the new literate classes into so-called secondary-illiteracy. The newly acquired knowledge fades after a short time if it is not utilized in daily life. The "printed word environment" is of fundamental importance for the success of the literacy-programme. [7] For as long as the attempt to bring literacy to society—a sufficient supply of appropriate reading-material—lags behind primary investments in the education sector, for so long will a policy of general literacy entail the risk that great numbers of secondary-illiterates will be produced, an effect which may have detrimental consequences for the social development of that society, for these are as a rule groups with increased aspirations and a greater tendency to frustration—it is unwise to actuate dormant wants and then to leave them unsatisfied. Economically, secondary-illiteracy means a waste of scarce resources.

This one example shows that the educational-economic approach, which until now limited itself to primary educational-investments and the activity of the State in the educational system, must be broadened to include the field of complementary investments within a comprehensively viewed educational and information network. The concept of the "Kulturwirtschaft" (cultural economy), may be of help at this point, for it includes, together with the educational system in its entirety, publishing and the book trade, libraries, theatres, films and museums, radio, television and the press as well as other cultural institutions.[8]

An increased demand within the education system, which leads to the latter's expansion and thereby to an increase in the numbers of those who pass through the various educational/training establishments, calls for the entrained wants, which in turn press for satisfaction in other areas of cultural economy.[9] Entrained wants for reading-material, referred to above, appear thus as demands on the press and on the publishing- and book-trades, as well as on libraries. Without doubt equally loose complementarity relationships can be established with other sectors of the cultural economy. The purport of such a concept of induced investments, when understood in this way and applied to the cultural economy, can be put as follows: namely, that the State introduces imbalances through its investments in a sector which, in most of the developing countries, is extensively controlled by itself, that is, in the education system.

These imbalances appear as scarcities in other cultural-economic sectors which are partly governed by the market and by commercial profit-seeking. In commercial terms, this means nothing else than the opportunity of sizeable profits which represent a challenge to the stationary routine of the suppliers. If the latter are entrepreneurs they respond accordingly. The basic idea is that the State exercises the pioneer function in a sector which is particularly suitable for its activity, in order to send stimulating impulses into those sectors which obey private economic laws and, step by step, to implant in them a dynamic rhythm determined by supply and demand. This strategy will have succeeded when the private economy has adapted the rules of the game and when sequences of investment are produced.

For the economics of education our deliberations mean that the criteria for the appraisal of the educational-economic situation of a national economy are to be extended by the addition of characteristics which show the degree to which the population is being provided with the products of the cultural economy in its entirety. The reference to the entirety is to be understood in the sense that at all events those products and sectors of production relevant to development are to be taken into consideration which, when lacking, result in the eventual stand-still of the development efforts. For the mass media (press, film, radio and television) standard requirements have been developed in order to be able to determine the extent of such provision within the developing countries. On the whole an extremely unsatisfactory situation is revealed. Reference to the provision of books was made at the beginning of our exposition; if one considers the per capita income together with the comparison of "high- and low-pressure zones" it becomes apparent that the low-level of book-supply is accounted for not only by the broad strata of illiterates and the relative novelty of reading for the new literate groups, but also by the lack of available purchasing power. Until now this lack has also prevented the domestic book-production from enjoying to the full the advantages of mass-production.

The statistics of book-production as an essential part of the general educational statistics are considered as a barometer of the intellectual level and of intellectual life in general. Together with statistics concerning the educational level of the population the factors which have been put forward reveal to an alarming extent an underdevelopment of human capital in the developing countries. At the same time they reveal the huge dimension of the entrained wants which can be expected in the next decades within the sphere of cultural economy.

3. Complementarity Investments as State and Private Responsibility

In as far as the whole sphere of the cultural economy, like, generally, most other spheres of the economy as well, is seen as a State responsibility (though not due to a basic political decision), we are faced with the question of the role or significance of the regulating-mechanism of the free market economic system in the developmental process. In principle the cultural economy of a free market system has a dual nature. In the market-sphere it is predominantly characterized by the profit-principle, while in the State-sphere the cultural policy responsibilities are financed via the public budget and the revenues of the cultural institutions. Every consideration of the cultural economy must take note of this dual character, and must not fail to take into account the fact that the cultural-policy measures taken by the State also concern the market. The cultural policy of the State is made apparent in the public or semi-public institutions for cultural encouragement, protection and promotion as well as in laws and decrees which contain the norm-regulations for the cultural sphere or control its support. The independent cultural-economic activity which the State develops via the public budget naturally makes itself felt in its sphere of influence, ordering and regulating in like manner. Basically, cultural policy measures which are taken by the State may be classified from an economic viewpoint as follows:

1. On the one hand the State itself appears in the position of *supplier* of cultural services. The State maintains establishments for education, for collections of cultural objects, institutions with the means for presentation and performance, and produces in individual cases learning-material (State publishing plants) or participates in cultural establishments. On the other hand, the State influences the cultural-economic supply in the market. This is done in various ways, for instance by means of special, purposeful encouragement of cultural performance by awarding culture-prizes and granting State subsidies, by means of the control of the level of proficiency (State supervision in private schools), through aid- and support-programs (subsidies for private theatres and other cultural establishments), and finally by means of the prohibition of culturally harmful productions, the limitation of sales possibilities and the coercion to

produce certain works which may be considered as culturally effective. The range of possibilities is very broad and, as the examples show, of great complexity.

2. Two groups may also be formed within the area of *demand:* on the one hand, the State itself appears as the customer for cultural-economic works, chiefly in connection with the institutions which it maintains (the demand for teachers for state schools, the procuring of books for libraries, the purchase of works of art for museums); the State also has an important part to play in its task of assigning commissions to scientific institutions and other cultural vocations. On the other hand, the State influences the demand for cultural commodities in different ways, we can think for example of the educational work of schools, of cultural propaganda, of the educational effect of exhibitions and the like.

If we now turn to the control of cultural-economic markets we can make the following general statements: The survival of cultural-economic undertakings is, if we do not take into account subsidies and external financial sources, dependent on the response of the market-demand. When a market success is obtained, i.e. the commodity is sold, the proceeds of the sale, if sufficient, cover the costs and possibly realize a profit. In the market there can only be a demand for what is available and, at least in the long run, only that can be supplied which is saleable. This approach makes clear with abstract sharpness the theory of consumers' sovereignty: since, in the last resort, consumers determine the success or failure of production through the distribution of their purchase power on the products supplied, they control the production with their wishes, which the entrepreneur takes pains to interpret. Strong objections are raised against this theory, which cannot, however, be discussed here. [10] Even if, with reference to reality, one is doubtful of the influence of consumers on production this surely cannot be completely denied; the wishes of consumers will always play the most important part in the deliberations and decisions of the profit-orientated producer or trader. His success is, after all, dependent on the right interpretation of the wishes of the consumers and also, of course, on influencing these wishes.

It is true, however, in the State school system that the "supply" is determined according to the receptivity of the pupils, but not according to their wishes. The pupils, as consumers of learning-material, are subject to a compulsory consumption which they (and their parents) are in general unable to resist. In the market there reigns, however, in principle, consumers' freedom, even if, in reality, this can be limited in various ways. Here too things may come to a "dictatorship of the supplier," namely, if he holds a monopoly.

Can we now, with reference to the developing countries, make any statements about an optimal combination of the principles of control—planning and the market—in the sphere of cultural economy? As a rule the system of education is here considered to be a State responsibility and it is reasonable to assign all cultural-economic "inputs" of the educational system (learning- and teaching-material) to State production as well, especially as a considerable gap in supply is usually found at this point. This state of affairs allows the basic question of who should undertake complementary investments in the cultural-economy, the State or the private entrepreneur, to be exemplarily clarified.

4. The Production of Learning-material and the Book-market

From the viewpoint of educational policy the provision of school- and textbooks is extremely important; this supply must be guaranteed, whereupon the question arises as to which system of publishing would be able to cope with this task. If we go back once again to Hirschman's concept of complementary-investments then the pressure of the derived demand or of the entrained wants, in as far as they are directed at a privately produced article or a private service, leads to imports or to a greater domestic production of this commodity, because it will be in the commercial interest of the traders and producers of the commodity to respond to this pressure. Without wanting to prejudice a basic political-economic decision valid for the cultural economy of all developing countries, a quantitative factor can be advanced in principle for an emphasis on State activity in this field: the very great need for books. It can be said in favor of private schoolbook production that that system of publishing is to be encouraged which, at a time of rising per capita income in the population, sees itself faced by the process of need-differentiation, something which must also assuredly take place in the book market. The more differentiated the demands for quality, the more varied must be the qualitative structure of the supply. The time is, at this stage, ripe for the efficiency and ability of private enterprise, which has shown itself until now to be the best interpreter of consumer wishes in the industrialised nations and which can better develop itself on the stable foundations of continuous schoolbook production.

In the individual developing countries one finds a broad scale from the strong intervention of State schoolbook publishing firms, on the one hand, to almost 100% provision of books through private schoolbook publishers on the other. But everywhere, where private schoolbook publishing firms are active, one finds that the difficulty of procuring books and especially the necessity of maintaining quality at lowest possible prices lead to the attempt at producing schoolbooks under State management. In view of the progressively increasing need for books in most of the developing countries a constant expansion of printing capacity is necessary. It is obvious from the situation that the State sees in this a responsibility for itself.

However, before the question of State of private schoolbook production can be conclusively answered, a look is necessary at the ways in which entrained wants in the book market may be satisfied. In the case of schoolbooks it is after all a question of a rigid demand, whereas the greater part of the remaining book production finds its sales as the result of a general need for reading material. First of all we can note that the book markets of the various developing countries display considerable differences. We shall therefore exclude from our deliberations all those countries in which, in the meantime, modern conditions have come into being in the book market. We are more interested in the book industry in the early stages of its development, when it is characterized by the production of only a small number of titles, by a relatively low average edition of individual works, and when the import of foreign books is relatively large. These characteristics hold true in most of the developing countries of Asia and Africa. Investigations of such book markets have shown that there are several factors which exert a hampering influence on the position of books and the book-trade. [11]

Illiteracy is not the only factor which limits the market; a decisive part is played, too, by the level of education and by the extent to which reading is a customary activity. Even among those who can read, one finds that a sense for the significance of books and for the value of book reading is not very widespread. Even when this feeling is present there may still be a long way to go before the purchase of a book, either because the wish for the ownership of a book is not present or because this wish cannot, owing to the lack of available money, be fulfilled. The provision of reading material is then undertaken by the libraries which again have a limited budget and whose demand is itself not a solid basis for promoting the circulation of a book. One sees here the beginnings of a vicious circle and as in the case of schoolbook production there are those who emphatically advocate State initiative in the book market and are sceptical towards any kind of participation by private entrepreneurs. In view of the partly very small production capacity of the domestic publishing trade, one also hears increasing support for an increase in book imports, not only in the developing countries but also in those countries providing development aid.

This development contains dangers, however, which cannot be disregarded. In the first instance the foreign trade situation of the developing countries ought by itself to forbid an unlimited continuation of book imports, since the foreign currency which is needed represents a serious burden on the already heavily overstrained balance of payments. There are also more basic doubts which can be raised against large-scale imports. The flood of cheap books would considerably hinder the establishment and growth of a domestic publishing trade, if not making this impossible. Foreign educational aid can, for this reason, only mean putting the developing countries in the position where they can themselves establish a publishing network which corresponds to their own needs. Undoubtedly this process will not take place without mistakes and setbacks, but the way of trial and error appears to be the most appropriate for stimulating the productive capacity of the developing countries.

Moreover, the significance of domestic book production for the establishment and stabilization of a domestic literary culture is not to be underestimated. It is not the xenophobia of the Middle Ages nor a kind of national-cultural chauvinism when the developing nations express their fear of foreign infiltration or control of their autochthonal intellectual life due to a glut of books from the West. The intellectual exchange between nations can only then be realized when all those taking part have the means at their disposal with which to express themselves in their own appropriate way. Nothing is more dangerous than the existence of "book production superpowers" who dominate the "smaller powers." This is not the least of the reasons which make the complete appeasement of the huge, still partly latent, book hunger of the developing countries by means of imports from the West appear to be unreasonable, for to some extent it is evidently a question of very special needs. Extensive educational and psychological preparatory studies are, for example, necessary in order to consolidate and further stimulate the newly aroused motive-forces and reading requirements of the new-literates with appropriate reading-material.[12] Educational aid can here only mean the encouragement of the book production inside the developing country.

If, like Hirschman, one considers the process of development to be a "chain of disequilibria,"[13] then the investments which the State makes in the educational sector appear, as has been shown, as the cause of disequilibriated situations which, if the "right" answers are provoked in cultural-economic markets, then have a positive influence on development if, for example, the book industry responds with investments which increase efficiency or capacity. As experience shows there are obstructive factors at work which adversely affect the responses which development policy hopes for. And, in view of this fact, we can again follow Hirschman in the conception of his development strategy, for the State should not only create "pressure situations" which stimulate economic activities but at the same time bring into play forces which are able to remove the disequilibria again. This can be achieved through credit aid, training programs and similar measures, but also through State stimulus in the market. However, when the State's initiative goes so far that private publishers are squeezed out of the market for schoolbooks or indeed never permitted to enter it, one is then faced with the possibility that, through this necessarily pre-eminent and also quantitatively important book production, a branch of the economy will be encouraged which might, on such a basis, more easily meet the difficulties of expansion and adaptation with which it is confronted. Competition among private publishers for State contracts is able to increase their output performance, something which could also benefit the rest of the book-market.

NOTES

[1] cf. Robert Escarpit: *Die Revolution des Buches*, (The Book Revolution), Gütersloh 1967 p. 72 ff.
[2] *ibid*. p. 74.
[3] Ronald Barker and Robert Escarpit, Eds., *The Book Hunger*, UNESCO, Paris 1973, p. 16 f.
[4] cf. Frederick Harbison/Charles A. Myers: *Education Manpower, and Economic Growth*. New York-Toronto-London, 1964, p. 15 f.

[5] cf. A. O. Hirschman: *The Strategy of Economic Development*. New Haven and London: Yale University Press. 1961, p. 67 ff.

[6] A. O. Hirschman, *op. cit.*, p. 69.

[7] cf. Curle's criticism of the UNESCO literacy-aid programs, especially of the insufficient provision of reading material. (A. Curle: *World Campaign for Universal Literacy: Comment and Proposal*. Cambridge, Mass. 1964. (Occasional Papers in Education and Development. No. 1).

[8] For the development of the concept of *Kulturwirtschaft*, which we translate in this context as "Cultural Economy," cf. P. Meyer-Dohm: "Ansatzpunkte und Bereiche kulturwirtschaftlicher Analyse" (Approaches and Scope of Cultural Economic Analysis) in: Friedrich Uhlig (ed.), *Buchhandel und Wissenschaft*, Gütersloh 1965, p. 97 ff; also H.-G. Eicke: "Kulturwirtschaft," in: *Handwörterbuch der Betriebswirtschaft*, Vol. 3., 3. Edition, Stuttgart 1960, col. 3605 ff., and also "Die kulturwirtschaftliche Unternehmung" (The Cultural-economic Enterprise) by the same author in: J. Fettel and H. Linhardt (Eds.): *Der Betrieb in der Unternehmung. Festschrift für Wilhelm Rieger*, Stuttgart 1963, p. 367 ff.

[9] This does not mean that the entrained wants which develop with the maturing of educational investments arise *only* in the sphere of cultural economy.

[10] cf. P. Meyer-Dohm: *Sozialökonomische Aspekte der Konsumfreiheit*, (Socio-economic Aspects of Consumer Freedom), Freiburg 1965, p. 62 ff.

[11] cf. Om Prakash: "The Production and Flow of Books in South East Asia," in: *Books for the Developing Countries*, Paris 1965. (Report and Papers on Mass Communication, No. 47), p. 10 ff.

[12] Of informative interest is the investigation of these conditions in various countries in the UNESCO publication: *The provision of popular reading materials*, ed. by Ch. G. Richards, Paris 1959 (Monographs on Fundamental Education).

[13] A. O. Hirschman, *op. cit.* p. 65.

5

INTERNATIONAL NEWS FLOW AND PROPAGANDA

Al Hester
INTERNATIONAL INFORMATION FLOW

Karl Erik Rosengren
INTERNATIONAL NEWS: TIME AND TYPE OF REPORT

Günter B. Krause-Ablass
THE NEED FOR INTERNATIONAL COMMUNITY SYSTEMS OF
    SATELLITE TELECOMMUNICATIONS

L. John Martin
EFFECTIVENESS OF INTERNATIONAL PROPAGANDA

Jacques Ellul
INTERNATIONAL PROPAGANDA AND MYTHS

5

INTERNATIONAL NEWS FLOW AND PROPAGANDA

NEWS appears to be flowing well among nations today. There are some parts of the world, of course, where this cannot be said, but generally the *flow* of information across borders must be considered extremely good. Many students of international communication have shifted their concern from the *flow* (a quantitative consideration) to the *type and content* (qualitative consideration) of the information. Most scholars, however, are forced to consider the two aspects—the flow and content—together, and generally this is the treatment given the two aspects in this section.

It does not take great insights to recognize that flow and content are rather closely related. When, for example, news flows poorly and spasmodically from Nation A, it may reasonably be assumed that the *quality* (and most likely even press freedom) of the communications media of that nation is not very good. Numerous studies have shown that in countries where the quality of the journalism and the degree of media development are high, there is little difficulty—technologically speaking—in getting information from other nations and sending information to other nations. In some instances, however, a rather highly developed national press system will have news *flow* problems stemming from political—not technical—restrictions.

It is hardly surprising that, with increased international news flow, we find world populations submerged under a blanket of propaganda. There is no doubt but that there is a positive correlation between the total media content and the total propaganda outpouring.

Even a casual observer of the media of mass communication cannot fail to notice that men's minds—nationally and internationally—are being subjected to a ceaseless and clever bombardment of messages. These messages are calculated to influence and control. Internationally, these propagandistic messages are either directed against real or potential enemies or at "neutral" message consumers who might be won over. In addition, of course, much of the international media effort is aimed at reinforcing "friendly" images held in other nations of the country engaged in the propaganda effort.

239

Nations use their own propaganda agencies (government-owned-and-operated) supplemented, of course, by any private or quasi-private media they have available. Many critics of the press believe that this is actually hindering world understanding and cooperation, that it is instilling suspicions and animosities among nations and thereby worsening the global psychic crisis. One of this book's editors, John Merrill, writing in *The Foreign Press* (1970), puts it this way:

> Great amounts of propaganda are in the news stream—propaganda aimed at perpetuating the psychological tug of war among nations and peoples; "exceptional" incidents which are further exaggerated by the newspapers are disseminated as important news; "eccentric" and "dangerous" people are the subject of much of the news. In short, we find that "unreal" and "alarmist" news dominates the newspaper columns. . . . Instead of being conveyors of enlightenment, the national press systems tend too often to be "press agents" for individual countries or special groups, thus doing a good job of increasing irritations and suspicions among governments and giving distorted pictures of various nations.

*   *   *   *

In the first article of this section, Al Hester of the Henry Grady School of Journalism, University of Georgia, discusses the information flow among nations—how, why, and where it flows—and the impact of such flow. In the next article, Karl Erik Rosengren, a sociologist at Sweden's University of Lund, places the whole subject of the flow of the news in a theoretical framework, surveys much of the pertinent research on the subject and points up important directions for further research.

In the third article, Günter B. Krause-Ablass, Hamburg lawyer and university lecturer at Bochum, deals with problems of satellite telecommunications and space law. This is followed by L. John Martin's (University of Maryland) discussion of the types and effectiveness of international propaganda. The noted French social and political philosopher, Jacques Ellul, in the final article, presents a fascinating glimpse of the use of propaganda and the myths surrounding it, especially in democracies.

*   *   *   *

RELATED READING

Barghoorn, F. C. *The Soviet Image of the United States: A Study of Distortion.* New York: Harcourt, Brace, 1950.

Brown, J. A. C. *Techniques of Persuasion: From Propaganda to Brainwashing.* Baltimore: Penguin Books, Inc., 1963.

Cherry, Colin. *World Communication: Threat or Promise?* New York: Wiley-Interscience, 1971.

Davison, W. Phillips. *International Political Communication.* New York: Praeger, 1965.

———. *Mass Communication and Conflict Resolution.* New York: Praeger, 1974.

Domenach, Jean-Marie. *La Propagande Politique.* Paris: Presses Universitaires de France, 1962.

Doob, L. W. *Propaganda, Its Psychology and Technique.* New York: Henry Holt, 1935.

Ellul, Jacques. *Propaganda: The Formation of Men's Attitudes.* New York: Random House (Vintage Books), 1973.

Gallaway, J. F. *The Politics and Technology of Satellite Communications.* Lexington, Mass.: D. C. Heath, 1972.

Gordon, George N. *Persuasion: The Theory and Practice of Manipulative Communication.* New York: Hastings House, 1971.

Hoffman, Arthur S. *International Communication and the New Diplomacy.* Bloomington: Indiana University Press, 1968.

Koop, Theodore F. *Weapon of Silence.* Chicago: University of Chicago Press, 1946.

Lee, John (ed.). *Diplomatic Persuaders: New Role of the Mass Media in International Relations.* New York: John Wiley and Sons, 1968.

Lippmann, Walter. *Public Opinion.* New York: Harcourt-Brace, 1922.

Lumley, F. E. *The Propaganda Menace.* New York: Century, 1933.

Manvell, Roger. *The Age of Communication.* Glasgow and London: Blackie, 1966.

Martin, L. John. *International Propaganda: Its Legal and Diplomatic Control.* Minneapolis: University of Minnesota Press, 1958.

Merrill, J. C. *The Elite Press: Great Newspapers of the World.* New York: Pitman, 1968.

Owen, Bruce M. *Telecommunications Policy Research: Report on the 1975 Conference Proceedings.* Palo Alto, Cal.: Aspen Institute, 1975.

Prosser, Michael H. (ed.). *Intercommunication Among Nations and Peoples.* New York: Harper & Row, 1973.

Qualter, T. H. *Propaganda and Psychological Warfare.* New York: Random House, 1962.

Smith, B. L., Harold Lasswell and Ralph Casey. *Propaganda, Communication and Public Opinion.* Princeton: Princeton University Press, 1946.

Unesco. *World Communications.* New York: Unesco, 1975.

Unesco. *Communication in the Space Age.* Paris: Unesco, 1968.

Whitaker, U. G., Jr. *Propaganda and International Relations.* San Francisco: Howard Chandler, 1960.

White, Llewellyn and R. D. Leigh. *Peoples Speaking to Peoples.* Chicago: University of Chicago Press, 1946.

Al Hester:

International Information Flow

AT ANY given moment an extremely complicated process of interaction is occurring between the national systems into which mankind has grouped itself. These nations or countries represent the type of system by which, according to Karl Deutsch, mankind is attempting to carry out the art of government.[1] The national systems are in a constant process of development or degeneration, as viewed over time. Some are building up, delineating their boundaries from the global environment more clearly, taking their place as nation-states in the world. Others work to preserve and conserve the national systems already achieved. And still others are disintegrating, becoming shadowy and permeable, not maintaining a clear demarcation between themselves and the 'outside'.

Yet if we could place ourselves figuratively above the earth and if we had the sensitivity to tell what is going on among mankind below, we would find generally that men have organized themselves into national systems with discernible identities. Some elements of a 'world-system' might be present, but the nation-state is still the main unit of governance at this stage of history.

But while nations have their unique and separate being with their own processes of interaction and senses of community within their systems, they are no more completely isolated than are the individuals who dwell in a great city. A constant interplay of activity brings nations as well as individuals into contact with others. Events external to the system or to an organism may have the most important consequences for it, and all living systems have provisions for receiving information concerning external events from the 'outside'.

The price a living system or organism may pay if it fails to utilize its powers of surveillance of its environment can be death or serious injury to it. Nations, just as biological organisms, must carry out this surveillance of the environment through an exchange of information if they wish to continue existence in the face of outside hazard. Informational inputs resulting from such surveys of the environment give the controllers and directors of the systems knowledge upon which to base responses appropriate to the maintenance of their system.

Information—knowledge, facts, intelligence—is the raw material which

[1] *Nationalism and Social Communication* (Rev. Ed.; Cambridge, Mass.: The M.I.T. Press, 1966), p. 4.

▶ Reprinted by permission from *Gazette* (Holland), Vol. XIX, No. 4, 1973. Dr. Hester is a member of the Henry Grady School of Journalism faculty, University of Georgia.

must be digested and interpreted and the appropriate responses correlated. Lasswell's functions of communication as a surveillance of the encironment and then correlation of response by parts of a society apply to a consideration of the relationship between nations of the world.[2] His third function of communication, passing on the cultural heritage, would seem also to apply, but to a lesser degree.

Information exchanged between national systems, then, may be processed to protect the existence of the systems, and to set policies for their governance. The forms such information may take are many. A few of them would include diplomatic messages as purveyors of information to the home government, espionage, oral communications by travellers, letters and telegrams sent in international transactions, radio and television boradcasts over international boundaries, information relayed via satellites, books, specialized publications, magazines, newspapers, items transmitted via news agencies and from foreign correspondents for publications or the electronic media.

Sometimes international information flows are direct between individuals of different nations ('summit conferences' as an example), and at other times they may pass through long chains with many relay points where the volume of the flow may be changed, as well as its content.

On occasion, information may flow directly to national decisionmakers, but at other times the incoming information may disseminate to the general population or to special or attentive publics interested in certain types of messages from the external environment. The general public or attentive publics may attempt with varying degrees of success to influence national policies in foreign affairs, based upon the information which they have received.

National systems vary greatly as to the degree to which the influence of general domestic public opinion may exist or have influence upon decisionmakers, or the degree to which attentive publics may influence governmental actions.

But from our figurative vantage point above the world, would we be able to discern any pattern to the flow of information and communication among the national systems of the world? Are there needs of national systems which determine specific patterns of information and communication between nations or is the process of information exchange a random one, with no ascertainable pattern?

It would seem logical that persons or organizations governing the in-flow or information and communication into a national system would select from the myriad messages from the outside surroundings those perceived as most useful, meaningful or rewarding to members of their own system. This process would appear to be made unconsciously at times and consciously at other times, or by different selectors.

[2] Harold Lasswell, 'The Structure and Function of Communication in Society', in *Mass Communications*, ed. by Wilbur Schramm (2nd ed.; Urbana, Ill.: University of Illinois Press, 1960), p. 118.

It seems worthwhile to study the international flow of information because such information may be in part the basis upon which national policies in foreign affairs are decided, or upon which domestic policies may in part be based. By observing what those who carry out the surveillance of the global environment select for processing into the national system we may learn much about what such systems deem important to themselves and how leaders in national systems see themselves in relation to other national systems. The direction, volume and content of international information flow is measureable, at least in part. An understanding of how national systems function and their relationship to other systems has implications for the setting of foreign policy, the chances of war or peace, and solving problems of cohesion or division among mankind.

This article is an attempt to explore the determinants of information flow among national systems and how they contribute to the voluem and direction of such flows. If we can discover what are the variables causing information flow, we may perhaps be able to predict the volume of its flow and its direction.

A Hierarchy of Nations

Basic to this discussion is the belief that the nations of mankind are at any given time arranged in hierarchies of power or 'pecking orders'. Such an order may certainly change over time, but it is necessary that nations have some perception of their place in such an order. Whether they wish to accept such a place or struggle to change it is beside the point. The point is that they perceive such an ordered relationship between their own country and other nations. Nations may be likened to individuals in a small social system such as a classroom. Class members usually have some idea of who is the largest student, the most aggressive or perhaps the pupil who is materially or intellectually at the top of the heap.

The perceptions of various nations' places in the hierarchy or 'pecking order' of national systems determine in part the types of information flow, direction and volume. The smallest boy in a classroom may have a good reason for finding out what the classroom bully is planning or doing. But the classroom bully may have little interest or concern about gathering information about the activities of the smallest boy. The same analogy might apply to nations. An inflow of information about a dominant or aggressive nation may be very vital for the survival of a small neighbor which may have to decide whether to prepare itself against attack or attempt to join in alliance with its more powerful neighbor. Yet what the smaller nation does is probably of lesser importance to the powerful nation. It would seem a reasonable speculation that a greater volume of information will flow from powerful nations to weaker nations than from weak to powerful. Of course, the very factors which have gone to make a power dominant may themselves increase the volume of information output from such a power, too. A large, more complex system might be expected to generate more invormation.

Thus not only do perceptions of dominance or weakness in the hierarchy of nations have effects upon information flow, but so do the resources and activities of the nations themselves. Factors in a nation's position in the hierarchy might include geographic size, population, economic development and its length of existence as a sovereign nation.

Another speculation is that nations perceiving threats or potential threats to their existence from other nations will want an increased flow of information concerning such threats. Not only is this true between weak-strong pairs of nations but also of nations which are of nearly equal status. Such nations might be compared to dominant roosters who must meet in challenge if only one is to be master in the chicken-yard—the nation's sphere of influence.

Yet the relationships of nations and the flows of information among them is not simply one of dominance and weakness, of strength and of power, or the lack of these qualities.

Cultural Affinities and Economic Association

Another determinant of the flow of international information may be that of cultural affinity. Going back to our classroom example, there will be individuals who wish to procure a flow of information about other individuals to which they feel a kinship, a congruence of interests or similarity of life-styles or backgrounds. The relationship between such individuals is not perceived as one of threat or of danger but of one in which a closeness and community of interest is to be cultivated. Such relationships, which might almost be called affective relationships do exist between nations as well, and measures of them might include a shared language, the amounts of migration between them, the amount of intermarriage between nationals, the amount of travel between them, and statuses and past-statuses such as mother country-colony, or patron-protege. It is hypothesized that the flow of information between countries sharing such traits would be greater than between countries having little cultural affinity.

The economic relationship between nations is also another possible determinant of information flow. Total trade between two nations, the amount of foreign aid given (if any), and the amount of business investments each nation has in the other might be measures to ascertain the extent of economic relationships. It is hypothesized that where economic relationships are strong, more information flow will be observed between nations than when only a weak economic relation prevails. The nation to which the economic linkage is most vital would seem likely to utilize more information from the other nation in the pairing.

'News' and 'Information' Conflicts

A major question may be raised by some who see a conflict between the determinants of international information flow and the definition of 'news values'. A large portion of international information flow is in the form of news transmitted by the wire services or by foreign correspondents. Journalists have been taught to select material which is of significance and interest to large numbers of people. Information which is timely, of magnitude, or which has human interest qualities or which excites the emotions is frequently the basis for many of the stories which are transmitted in international information flow. Thus the 'yard-stick' by which the newsman selects what he sends in international communication is not consciously that which is necessary, meaningful or rewarding to the national system. The journalist attempts to conceive of his audience as made up of individuals, and he writes or transmits what he believes will make them want to read or view or listen to his medium.

But when we examine the qualities which make an event international news we see that many of these qualities do in fact give needed intelligence to be used by leaders and other members of national systems. The biggest conflict between the type of information transmitted as international news and information used strictly as intelligence or knowledge by national systems is not in subject matter so much as it is in irregularity or regularity of occurrence. The movement of news from crisis areas of the world may come sporadically as such 'news storms' occur. Perhaps in days, months, or at most a few years, these news storms change with current events and move on somewhere else. It is a postulate of this article that the *basic* pattern of flow of international information, including news, between nations remains fairly set over long periods of time—say several decades. At a given time, reportage of crises may alter the pattern of the flow. This reportage may be likened to the throwing of a rock into a strongly flowing river. The rock temporarily creates ripples, but the strong flow or current continues underneath and is again visible after the ripples die.

If we attempt to measure the flow of internatonal news at only one point in time we may obtain a distorted picture of what the directions and volumes of flow usually are among the nations. It is an assumption, which is certainly testable, that a logitudinal study of the flow of information internationally will reveal discernible patterns. Such patterns may indeed change over long periods of time as relationships alter between nations, but the basic patterns will be revealed by studies over time.

*   *   *   *

Let us for a moment review the basic scheme we have proposed for studying the flow of international information. Basically we are saying that certain independent and pre-existing variables such as national rank in the power-hierarchy of nations, dominance and weakness of nations, and cultural and economic affinities are causal factors in the patterns of information flow between nations. We see the volumes of such information flow and its direction as dependent variables. We have said that contaminating variables such as temporary crisis reporting or 'news storms' may distort the perceived patterns, but that investigation over time should reveal the patterns of information flow between nations.

What follows is a somewhat more formal listing of some postulates, assumptions and hypotheses spelling out in more detail these ideas.

Postulates:

1. There is much exchange of information among national systems.
2. The national system or nation-state is the major structure within which men govern themselves at this point in time.
3. Systems or organisms must have knowledge of events in the external environment to maintain the existence of the system from outside dangers.
4. An exchange of information (including news) among nations is necessary if nations systems are to function. Such knowledge is gained and used to keep the national system functioning.
5. Information may be used directly by decision-makers or it may be the basis of public opinion which is consulted by decision-makers as they set policy.
6. There are methods by which it is possible to measure the international flow of information.

Assumptions:

1. The need for surveillance of the environment surrounding a national system is a triggering mechanism for the gathering of information to be used in national systems.
2. Citizens and leaders perceive a hierarchy of nations in the world environment—a 'pecking order'. Members of the system perceive the rank or 'place' of their nation in this hierarchy.
3. A power hierarchy of nations may also be determined by measurement of how they rank on such variables as geographic size, population, economic development.
4. Leaders of nations especially seek information about other national systems which they perceive as threats or potential threats to their own nation.
5. Professional journalists, in reporting and transmitting news, often unconsciously fulfill the same goal as in Number 4, above.
6. Reporting of international crises or 'news storms' may temporarily alter the patterns of international information flow, but the basic patterns remain and are again visible after the crisis has passed.
7. Cultural and historical affinity also may generate the flow of information between nations. Lack of such affinity retards the flow of information.
8. Economic relationships also generate the flow of information between nations. Lack of such relationships retards the flow of information.
9. Self-interest in maintaining the national system is a key to the selection of types of information from the international information flow by a given nation.

Some hypotheses:

1. More information will flow from 'high'-ranking nations in the hierarchy of national systems than will flow from those nations ranked 'low' in the hierarchy. (Ranking to be based on measures mentioned as determinants of position in the hierarchy.)
2. The volume of information flowing from a 'high'-order nation into a 'low'-order nation will be greater than that flowing in the opposite direction from the 'low'-order nation to the 'high'-order nation in the hierarchy.
3. The flow of information from Nation A, considered as a threat or potential threat by another nation, Nation B, will be greater than the flow from a nation, Nation C, not considered threatening to Nation B.
4. Information flows between nations having cultural and historical affinities will be greater than flows of information between nations not having such affinities.
5. Information flows between nations having active economic relationships will be greater than the flows between nations not having such economic ties.
6. The inflow of information from Nation A to Nation B which is economically dependent upon Nation A will be greater than the inflow of information into Nation A from Nation B.
7. The inflow of information from a mother country to a colony or former colony will be greater than the outflow of information from the colony or former colony to the mother country, unless the colony or former colony is perceived as being higher ranking in the hierarchy of nations.

Testing the Theoretical Considerations

While it is not the purpose of this article to propose a research design, something should be said about ways of testing the predictive characteristics of the theory. Several tools are available for this purpose.

Assembling information about the independent variables: Measures for placing nations within a power hierarchy can be based upon aggregate national data. Data on such measures as geographical size, population, economic wealth, industrial development and length of time of existence as a sovereign state are available over a fairly long time span. Many developmental, political science and other social science studies have already collected much data in easily accessible form.

Such information also exists in aggregate form concerning measures of cultural and historic affinity. Data on languages of nations, migrations and travel between nations, and mother country-colonial statuses are also available over considerable time periods. Aggregate data are also richly available concerning economic relationship indicators such as volume and value of trade between nations, and amounts of foreign aid and private investment.

Measurement of information flows may be accomplished in several ways. Figures are available on volume of mail sent between nations, the volume of

Some international information flow hypotheses

(Width of arrows indicates relative volume of flow)

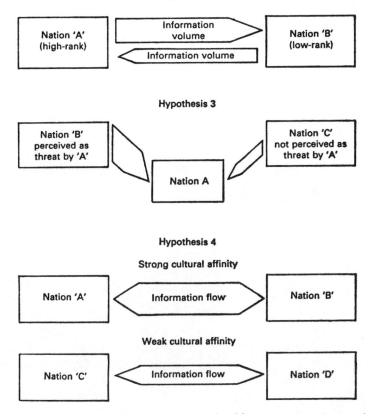

Hypothesis 2

Hypothesis 3

Hypothesis 4

Strong cultural affinity

Weak cultural affinity

international telephone calls, telegrams and cablegrams, at various points in time. Also available are data concerning the size of diplomatic missions from one country to another.

The measurement of news as an important portion of international information poses more problems, but is possible. Content analysis of the files of the wire agencies and of news appearing in newspapers, television or radio may be accomplished using sampling techniques in longitudinal studies. The magnitude of comparative studies in international news or information flow seems to point to the need for team efforts by investigators in several different nations, who would compile and share data.

Randomized sample surveys may also prove useful in determining perceptions of power hierarchies of nations, and of cultural affinities. Some work has already been done by investigators trying to gain information about perceptions of citizens concerning 'psychological distances' between nations, creation of national stereotypes, etc.[3] Some work also has been attempted to see whether correlations exist between demographic variables and the volume of news flow in specific media.[4]

[3] Malcolm S. MacLean Jr. and Luca Pinna, 'Distance and News Interest: Scarperia, Italy', *Journalism Quarterly* 35 (Spring, 1958), pp. 36–48.
[4] John David Dupree, 'International Communication: View from "A Window on the World" ', *Gazette* 17, No. 4 (1971), pp. 224–235.

Karl Erik Rosengren:

International News: Time and Type of Report

FOR several reasons, the international flow of news is an important field of research. Much work has gone into the field: some hundred papers and a couple of books. Excellent investigations concerning various aspects of the subject are Adams,[1] Cutlip,[2] Galtung & Holmboe Ruge,[3] Hart,[4] Markham,[5] Schramm,[6] to mention just a few among the papers.

Yet, there is no doubt that much remains to be done. For instance, the sampling problem must be given more attention, so that the results obtained may be generalized to a well defined universe. The units of measurement must be systematically investigated, in order to obtain reliability, validity and comparability. The interest should be focused towards the theoretical aspects of the problem to a higher degree than has been the case up to now. And the time perspective must not be neglected—as only too often it is in sociological research.

In this paper a theoretical suggestion by Himmelstrand [7] concerning the time perspective will be combined with a methodological approach used by Szalai (several types of units of measurement applied on the same material).[8]

"Time perspective" in this connection may mean at least three different things.

---

[1] J. B. Adams, "A Qualitative Analysis of Domestic and Foreign News on the AP TA Wire," *Gazette*, Vol. 10/1964, p. 285.
[2] S. M. Cutlip, "Content and Flow of AP News—From Trunk to TTS to Reader," *Journalism Quarterly*, Vol. 31/1954, p. 434.
[3] J. Galtung & M. Holmboe Ruge, "The Structure of Foreign News," *Journal of Peace Research*, Vol. 2/1965, p. 64.
[4] J. A. Hart, "Foreign News in U.S. and English Daily Newspapers: A Comparison," *Journalism Quarterly*, Vol. 43/1966, p. 444.
[5] J. W. Markham, "Foreign News in the United States and South American Press," *The Public Opinion Quarterly*, Vol. 25/1961, p. 249.
[6] W. Schramm, "Newspapers of a State As a News Network," *Journalism Quarterly*, Vol. 35/1958, p. 177.
[7] U. Himmelstrand, "Nyheter och nyheter," *Ord och bild*, Vol. 76/1967, p. 383; U. Himmelstrand, "Världen, Nigeria och Biafra. Sanningen som kom bort," *Aldus*, Stockholm 1969. (In Swedish; English edition in preparation.)
[8] Unitar Panel on Communication and Information, June 12–14, 1969: Public Information on the United Nations, *United Nations Institute for Training and Research*, New York 1969 (mimeo).

▶ This is an original article done for this book by Karl Erik Rosengren, Department of Sociology, University of Lund, Sweden, 1969.

1. Most investigations on the international flow of news are cross-sectional: how many per cent of the news hole in a paper or a collection of papers are dedicated to foreign news, to news from a given country, to foreign news belonging to a certain content category (social, political, economical news etc)? But sometimes a time perspective is introduced by combining several cross-sectional investigations, as it were, one after the other. An example of this is Mott's investigation of "Trends in Newspaper Content," showing that the foreign material in the American press was growing during the first half of the 20th century; [9] another is Schwarzlose's investigation into "Trends in U.S. Newspapers' Wire Service Resources, 1934–66," showing a decline in the papers' use of more than one major press association during the period of observation. [10] The application of a time perspective in this sense is very important and somewhat neglected; it could easily be undertaken in various ways in a country like for instance Sweden, with its very long series of official statistics, and with its State libraries containing in principle everything printed in the country since a couple of hundred years. However, it will not interest us in this paper.

2. Another use of the time perspective is met with in investigations like Cutlip's, concerning the flow of the news from trunk wire over TTS into the paper. [11] That is, the investigator asks, what happens to the news as it passes through the news machinery? An interesting—but neglected—question in this connection is the following one: what are the determining factors of the varying amount of time between event and report? Cutlip had some predecessors—White's famous gatekeeper study, for instance [12]—and more followers. His is an interesting use of the time perspective. However, it will not concern us any further in this paper.

3. The third use of a time perspective is not even as common as the other two, rare as these may be. In fact, as far as I know, only Ulf Himmelstrand has treated it at some length, and even his treatment is hardly more than an outline of an argument. However, it seems to be a rather interesting outline. In principle, it consists in asking what happens to the international flow of news about a given event or, rather, a given sequence of events (e.g., a crisis of some sort), as time passes by and new events are added to the "first" one.

In essence, Himmelstrand's approach is that of the ideal type. As something important happens and continues to happen, he says, the international

---

[9] F. L. Mott, "Trends in Newspaper Content," in W. Schramm (ed.), *Mass Communications*, 2nd ed. (Urbana: University of Illinois Press 1960).

[10] R. A. Schwarzlose, "Trends in U.S. Newspapers' Wire Service Resources, 1934–66," *Journalism Quarterly*, Vol. 43/1966, p. 627.

[11] S. M. Cutlip, *loc. cit.*

[12] D. M. White, "The Gatekeeper': A Case Study in the Selection of News," *Journalism Quarterly*, Vol. 27/1950, p. 383.

communication of news about the set of events may be seen as developing in three or four phases.[13]

In the first phase, what happens is reported: hard and hot news. The details are few, however, and the basis for commentary and interpretation brittle. Therefore, what interpretation there is, is rather sketchy and loaded with clichés and prejudice. (Sometimes, there is quite a lot of this type of comment.)

In the second phase, as the pattern of events is developing, the material grows richer, the basis for interpretation firmer. There is a possibility of correcting whatever inadequacies and inadvertencies were produced during the first phase, a possibility, however, that is not always made use of.

Instead, *the third phase* may be entered, that of reduced news value of the set of events, leading to oblivion or latency. In a possible *fourth phase*, for some reasons the news value may be rising again, and this time, with the help of their archives, the mass media may produce a better picture right from the beginning. (This possibility, of course, is not always taken care of. Instead, the media may return, as it were, to phase I again.) The phases may be of varying length for different sets of events and different media.

Himmelstrand underlines that his phases are applicable mainly to really "new" news, things happening unexpectedly and/or in remote places of the world, difficult to reach for geographical or other reasons.

Himmelstrand further suggests that news and interpretation may interact in a *circulus vitiosus* to bias the total reporting of the event by a given newspaper or group of newspapers. What interpretation is made in the first phase, is rather like a projective test of the prejudices of the commentator. In the second phase these biased interpretations direct the choice among and the play up of the various news items available by then. The biased news, in return, helps create new biased interpretations, and so on, till the third phase, that of oblivion or latency, is entered. Thus, very often the second phase is characterized not so much by "better," i.e., more unbiased interpretation, as by just more interpretation than during the first phase.

Himmelstrand illustrates his argument with data gathered from the Swedish press concerning the Nigerian civil strife in 1966, and with a comparison between the reporting of the same events by the Swedish radio and BBC.

The literature concerning the international flow of news is mostly *ad hoc*, rather poor of theoretical arguments.[14] Therefore, and because they concern a time perspective otherwise all but completely neglected, Himmelstrand's suggestions should be further looked into. Ideal type arguments as a rule are difficult to falsify. But often they may prove of great heuristic value. And in this case it so happens that data collected for quite other purposes may be marshalled in support of the argument.

In 1968, under the auspices of the United Nations, a world-wide investigation concerning news about the United Nations was carried through under

---

[13] U. Himmelstrand, *loc. cit.*
[14] For brilliant exceptions, see e.g., Galtung & Ruge, *loc. cit.*, and *Schramm, loc. cit.*

the direction of Alexander Szalai. Two preliminary reports have already been issued, and a definitive report is said to follow in the near future.[15] The investigation is a really full-scale one. A great deal of material has been collected and many interesting questions have been raised. In this paper, however, only two things will be touched upon: the unit of measurement, and the time perspective in the third sense mentioned above.

In several investigations of the international flow of news, different units of measurement have been used in the same investigation.[16] Common units are column inch, number of words, number of paragraphs, number of news items. When more than one type of unit have been used, as a rule one type has been preferred, the other being used mainly as a means of validating the measurement.

In the UN investigation, too, more than one type of unit of measurement were used: number of news items and number of characters (expressed as STP—standard typewritten pages of 2,000 characters). There is nothing very new about that. But then an innovation was introduced: the different units of measurement were not seen as measuring the same concept, as in most other investigations of this kind. Instead, the two subconcepts of *amount* and *volume* of news output were introduced, amount being operationally defined as number of news items, volume as number of STP.

When amount and volume of news output were measured and plotted over time, an interesting observation was made: "Characteristic of the broken-line volume-of-output curve is that its peaks and plateaus often lag in time behind the peaks and plateaus of the amount-of-output curve. This lag seems to be due to the fact that "flashes," "spot news" and "first reports" about critical events are in general relatively brief, but if interest in the matter persists, the newsmedia on subsequent days give relatively voluminous "follow-up" and "background" stories. Thus, the time lag of the volume-of-information output behind the amount-of-information output gives a certain measure of the commentative and interpretative effort of the mass media." [17]

The quotation, of course, sounds rather like a reformulation of Himmelstrand's phase model, and *vise versa*. But Himmelstrand presented his argument in Swedish, before the mimeographed report of Szalai's. The fact that similar results have been reached independently by two qualified researchers in the field makes them worth following up. One way of doing this is by trying to combine them in a set of testable propositions forming the outline of a verbal theory of certain aspects of the flow of news. The rest of the paper will be dedicated to an effort in this direction.

---

[15] Unitar Research Paper No. 1: Public Information on the United Nations, *United Nations Institute for Training and Research*, New York 1968 (mimeo); Unitar Panel; *op. cit.*
[16] Cf. G. A. Van Horn, "Analysis of AP News on Trunk and Wisconsin State Wires,"*Journalism Quarterly*, Vol. 29/1952, p. 426; W. Schramm, *op. cit.*; R. W. Budd, "U.S. News in the Press Down Under," *The Public Opinion Quarterly*, Vol. 28/1964, p. 39.
[17] Unitar Panel, p. 25.

Events reported in the mass media form *news*. Events may vary as to degree of *importance* and degree of *predictability*. Consequences of unpredictable events are less unpredictable than the original event. News may be *factual* and/or *interpretative* to a varying degree.

The operationalization of these basic concepts of predictability, importance, factual and interpretative news should not be too difficult. For the latter two concepts, an operationalization in the form of a code sheet for news items is already in existence.[18] For the first two, simple trichotomized ratings should be sufficient for a beginning. As the terms are understood here, it is a predictable event that a president is elected in the United States on a given day. It is an unpredictable event if, later on, he is murdered. Both are important events. A less important event is when Sweden changes her minister of agriculture. (For further refinement of the concept of importance, McNelly's operationalized concept of "meaning intensity" might be of some use. McNelly touches upon the time aspect, too.) [19]

Accepting these four basic concepts, it may be hypothesized that the more unpredictable the event, the more factual and the less interpretative its report. And the more important the event, the greater the need for interpretation. From this follows:

1. Important and predictable events will be reported at once factually and interpretatively.

2. Events that are important and unpredictable tend to be reported at first predominantly factually, then more and more interpretatively.

3. Less important events will be reported mainly factually, regardless of whether they are predictable or not.

Himmelstrand's argument may now be expressed in the terms suggested. His phase model concerns mainly events described in proposition 2, to some extent also events described in proposition 2 and followed by events described in proposition 1. Representing the two types of reporting by two curves varying over time, Himmelstrand's phase 1 may be said to last until the curve representing factual reporting has started to decline and/or the curve representing interpretative reporting has reached a given value. Phase 2 may be said to last until the curve representing interpretative reporting has started to decline. In phase 3 both curves are low, and phase 4 is marked by the sudden rise of both of them. (It may be added, that, if measured, the *quality* of both factual and interpretative reporting should rise with time.)

Szalai's argument, too, may be expressed in the simple terms suggested.

[18] B. H. Westley & M. S. MacLean, *Obform Coding Instructions*, University of Wisconsin, no date, (mimeo), quoted in: J. T. McNelly, "Coverage of the 1956 American Presidential Campaign in Britain's National Newspapers," *Gazette*, Vol. 4/1958, p. 33, note 11.
[19] J. T. McNelly, "Meaning Intensity and Interest in Foreign News Topics," *Journalism Quarterly*, Vol. 39/1962, p. 161.

His observation probably represents a mix of events described in proposition 1 and 2. In terms of the relations of the two curves his argument says: the peaks and troughs of the curve representing interpretative reporting should tend to lag after the peaks and troughs of the curve representing factual reporting. The amount of lag should co-vary (negatively) with the degree of predictability.

The whole argument, of course, presupposes that the news media report available news immediately. This is not always so. In some socialist countries, for instance, at least part of the news is not published until an authoritative interpretation is available.[20] The extent of this practice is an empirical question. In some cases, it might be more rewarding to study the lag between event and report rather than that between report and comment.

So far, little has been said about the duration and composition of the event reported as news. As far as the argument in this paper concerns, it should not matter whether *event* means one single event, clearly delimited in time and space, e.g., a murder or a nomination, or whether it means a sequential set of related sub-events like a revolution.

The theory outlined, of course, may be refined by introducing additional concepts. One that is often suggested in arguments concerning the international flow of news is *distance*, physical or psychological. (Physical distance may sometimes be used as an indicator of psychological distance.) [21] *Distance*, in combination with the concepts already introduced, could be used for instance in the following proposition: The more distant the event, the more unpredictable and the less important it seems. In combination with hypotheses suggested above, this gives us: the more distant the event, the more factual the reporting—a hypothesis that receives some support from data gathered by Adams.[22]

The fact of this support lends further credibility to the outline of a theory of one aspect of the international flow of news presented in this paper. It motivates further research along the lines suggested by the theory. One hypothesis to be tested (along with the ones already suggested) might be the following one: The greater the distance of an event, the greater the lag between its factual and interpretative reporting, degree of importance and predictability kept constant. This proposition is somewhat more complicated than those suggested earlier in this paper, but in the present writer's opinion, it should be possible to test it.

[20] I am indebted to Ole Jess Olsen, Institute for Peace and Conflict Research, Copenhagen, for reminding me of this fact.
[21] Cf. R. E. Carter & W. J. Mitofsky, "Actual and Perceived Distance in the News," *Journalism Quarterly*, Vol. 38/1961, p. 223; D. R. Bowers, "A Report on Activity by Publishers in Directing Newsrooms Decisions,"*Journalism Quarterly*, Vol. 44/1967, p. 43; G. Stanley, "Emotional Involvement and Geographical Distance," *The Journal of Social Psychology*, Vol. 75/1968, p. 165.
[22] J. B. Adams, *op. cit.*, table 3; cf. E. Östgaard, "Factors Influencing the Flow of News," *Journal of Peace Research*, Vol. 2/1965, p. 39, note 15. Östgaard has suggested in personal communication that the relationship between distance and degree of factual reporting may be curvilinear.

Günter B. Krause-Ablass:

The Need for International Community Systems of Satellite Telecommunications

THE QUANTITY of international satellite telecommunications is limited in two regards: there exists a limit to the number of advantageous positions for the orbiting of stationary telecommunications satellites as well as to the number of available frequencies for radiocommunications. These facts set the problem of distributing the limited quantity of chances of satellite telecommunications.

As far as the restriction is due to the limited number of advantageous positions of orbiting, distribution is a matter concerning the law of public order in outer space. As far as the restriction is due to the limited number of available radio frequencies, distribution is a matter concerning the international law of telecommunications. Therefore, the legal principles which concern the distribution of the chances of satellite telecommunications are a matter not only of one single legal domain but of the two interacting domains of space law and telecommunications law.

Space law

Space law does grant access to stationary positions in orbit not without legal premises. The positions for the orbiting of stationary satellites are a patrimony common to all nations. Outer space lies beyond the sovereignty of the individual states. It belongs to the common competence of all states together. It is, on the terms of international law, free for use to all nations. This principle of free and equal use is laid down in art. 1 par. 2 of the 1967 Treaty on Principles Governing the Activities of States in the Exploration and Use of Outer Space, including the Moon and Other Celestial Bodies (Space treaty). Art. 1 par. 2 of the Space treaty [1] reads as follows:

Outer space, including the moon and other celestial bodies, shall be free for exploration and use by all states without discrimination of any kind, on a basis of equality and in accordance with international law, and there shall be free access to all areas of celestial bodies.

▶ This is the revised version of a paper by Dr. Günter B. Krause-Ablaß (attorney at law of the Hamburg bar and lecturer for mass media law at the Ruhr University of Bochum) presented at the Fifteenth Colloquium on the Law of Outer Space of the International Institute of Space Law of the International Astronautical Federation, Vienna 1972, Proceedings, South Hackensack 1973, p. 81.

This principle, however, was not just originated by the Space treaty. It is a general principle of international law, and therefore it is binding even without any international treaty stipulation, and also binding upon states which did not join the Space treaty.

The international law of general principles has legal force by its own. The general principles are, on equal foot with international treaties and customary law, one of the sources of international law.[2] The international law of the general principles is the entity of the general principles of law recognized by civilized nations. There are, among the scholars of international law, different opinions about the meaning of this notion. The most accepted opinion says that the general principles are the basic legal principles which are laid down conformably in the domestic legislations of the great legal systems. This is not the place to discuss the different opinions. May it suffice to give here my personal opinion. The definition as principles recognised by the civilized nations involves the conclusion that the law of the general principles is constituted by the consent of the civilized nations. Due to the fact that the basis of the law of the general principles is confined to the consent of the nations being on the level of civilization—that is: all nations which are organized in a state recognised as a state in international law—the origin of the principles of the law of general principles must be a cultural one. The principles are those that correspond to the cultural standard of the world's society. They are those principles which the civilized nations have recognized to be necessary by virtue of the cultural standard of the world's society. Contrary to the customary law, the law of the general principles does not require practice among the conditions constituting the raising of a rule. Any act manifesting consent is appropriate to create rules of the law of the general principles. Among others, especially resolutions of the General Assembly of the United Nations' Organization are such acts.

The general principle of free use of outer space was consented to by the UN General Assembly's Resolution no. 1962 (XVIII) of 13 December 1963, constituting the Declaration of Legal Principles Governing the Activities of States in the Exploration and Use of Outer Space.[3] This Declaration is supported by universal support. Par. 2 of the Declaration reads as follows:

> Outer space and celestial bodies are free for exploration and use by all States on a basis of equality and in accordance with international law.

A reduction of the individual nations' right to use the outer space for the orbiting of telecommunications satellites results directly from the international law principle of free and equal use. This follows from the immediate implications of the principle of equality.[4] The principle of equality, in cases of conflict between the right of free use and the limited quantity of chances of use, must be reduced to the right of equal share in a system of fair distribution of all chances of use. For the use of outer space, the system of fair distribution must be a system created by the community of states and regulated in accordance with international law. The opinion denying that a restriction results directly from art. 1 par. 2 of the Space treaty [5] omits notice of these implications. It is true, however, that actually the restriction is suspended in practice. The states take their stationary positions by free choice. But this fact does not eliminate the legal rule of restriction. It is only a matter of the fact that there is, until now, no organized institution competent to accomplish the legal rule.

The principle of equality of use does not preclude every use which is of a nature to exclude others from identical use, provided that the exclusion of the others is of a mere transitory nature or of minor importance. If a flying object is located in a certain spot in outer space, no other flying object can simultaneously use this very position. In case that the exclusion of others caused thereby is of a mere transitory nature, due to the fact that the flying object is on flight and therefore moving away, or in case that the position permanently occupied by a stationary satellite is of no essential importance, the use is, nevertheless, compatible with the principle of equal use. Otherwise, there could not be any use at all of the outer space, as every use of the outer space excludes, in its very moment, all extraneous users from using that spot where in that moment the use is taking place. The principle of equal use prohibits, however, the permanent occupation of a position for stationary orbiting, which is, due to its factual characteristics, of a special advantage, e.g., for the orbiting of a stationary telecommunications satellite, if there exists only a limited number of positions likewise advantageous for an use of this kind. For, in the case of an essential limitation of the supply of advantageous positions, occupation by one nation would prevent the others from enjoying the material substance of their right of equal use of the outer space.

The right of equal use does not merely guarantee the equal legal chance of being the first one to occupy the most advantageous positions. To provide the first-comer with the right to exclude the others would be incompatible with the very nature of the principle of equality of use. Moreover, it would be in conflict with the principle that prohibits all national appropriation in outer space, provided for by art. 2 of the Space treaty of 1967. The right of equal use implies principles of public order in space limiting the freedom of use. No state can avail itself at will of the insufficient supplies of advantageous positions for stationary telecommunications satellites. They are subject to the control by all states. All states together must create an international authority invested with the competence to distribute the advantageous positions for the orbiting of the satellites. This authority, in its policy of distribution, must take into consideration not only the nowadays demands for advantageous orbiting positions in proportion to the quantity of available positions, but must take care just as much of the future development and the future demands to come from nations which accede to space activities only later on. As utilization of the advantageous space positions is at its best in the case of a cooperative system carried on by a great number of states together and therefore equality of use is the most efficient in community systems of utilization, this international space traffic authority has to distribute the best positions, by preference, to community systems of satellite telecommunications.

Telecommunications Law

The law of the general principles likewise guarantees the right of use, equal for all nations, of the international ether for the purpose of radiocommunications. Although there is no general principle prohibiting national occupation of frequency positions in the ether, the utilization of the ether is, nevertheless, subject to the common competence of regulation by all states together. This follows from the principle of equality of use. Due to the fact that the repertory of available frequencies is not sufficient for all potential demands, the right of free use of the ether is reduced likewise by the principle of equality. This principle likewise prohibits the acknowledgment of the assets of the first-comer, and it requires distribution of the frequencies by an international authority bound to the principle of fair distribution and bound to take care of the future developments as well.

In fact, the international telecommunication law provides for the organizational system of frequency distribution. International public order in the ether is subject to the regulatory competence of the International Telecommunication Union, a specialized agency in the organizational system of the United Nations and connected with the United Nations' Organization. The International Telecommunication Union (ITU) is set up by the International Telecommunication Convention. However, the authority instituted by the ITU for the task of an administrative body for public order in the ether, the International Frequency Registration Board (IFRB) at Geneva, has no distribution power. It is an authority of supervision for the self-regulating occupation of frequencies by the states.

The states are bound only by some basic principles, by the Table of Frequency Allocations of the Radio Regulations and by some special frequency plans. The Radio Regulations are an annex to the International Telecommunication Convention. Its Table of Frequency Allocations allocates frequency bands to radiocommunications services, e.g., to the broadcasting service, but it does not distribute individual frequencies to individual states. Individual distribution is provided for by some special frequency plans, specially for frequencies for broadcasting. Beyond the special frequency plans, frequencies can be occupied by the states, subject to the principles of protection of acquired frequency positions and to the provisions of procedure of the Radio Regulations. In fact, the Radio Regulations of the treaty law of the International Telecommunication Union materialize the protection of assets of the first-comer. The Radio Regulations, however, are subject to the prevailing principle of equal use, from which results the principle that the assets of the first-comer must yield to an eventual redistribution of the frequencies which would be necessary because of a changed situation in future.

The principle of fair distribution, which obligates the future development as much, because of the deficiency of a sufficient quantity of satellite telecommunications chances, prohibits the establishment, at the present time, of national satellite telecommunications systems for international radiocommunications. The right of all nations to have part in international satellite telecommunications is reduced to the right to share in an international community system of satellite telecommunications. Therefore, there need to be international organizations to carry on international community systems of satellite telecommunications, like Intelsat and Intersputnik. These organizations must grant admission to all nations willing to accede and must secure to all nations their proper share in the use of its telecommunications channels. The activity of these organizations must be strictly confined to the technical running of the system. They are by no means allowed to intervene in the contents of the news, correspondences or programs to be transmitted by the community satellite telecommunications system.

NOTES

[1] *United Nations Treaty Series*, vol. 610 p. 205; *American Journal of International Law*, 1967, p. 644.

[2] Art. 38 par. 1 lit.c of the Statute of the International Court of Justice.

[3] General Assembly Official Records, Eighteenth Session Supplement no. 15, Resolutions adopted by the General Assembly during its Eighteenth Session 17 September–17 December 1963, p. 15.

[4] Cf., for a similar problem of the German constitutional law of radio broadcasting and television, G. B. Krause-Ablaß, "Rundfunk und Fernsehen," *Staatslexikon Recht Wirtschaft Gesellschaft*, 6th ed., vol. 3, Freiburg/Germany, 1970, p. 127.

[5] A. Bueckling, in: *Recht und Staat, Festschrift für Günther Küchenhoff*, Berlin 1972, p. 775.

L. John Martin:

Effectiveness of International Propaganda

IT IS impossible even to estimate the amount of money that is being spent on international propaganda. Knowing the budgets of the propaganda agencies of individual countries would be inadequate, since their sum is only a fraction of the total amount involved. The major effort appears in the guise of numerous official activities that do not go by the name of propaganda or by one of its euphemisms. It is safe to assume that the international outlay on propaganda is in the hundreds of millions of dollars. Hardly any country is too small or too poor to invest in it. One can say this quite authoritatively without extensive investigation for one simple reason: there is no consensus either among the practitioners or among the theoreticians as to what constitutes propaganda. Definitions range from very specific types of messages transmitted through very specific types of media for very specific ends, to deeds that, often in retrospect, result, or are intended to result, in particular behavior on the part of the target. With this latitude in interpretations one can fearlessly make statements such as the above.

By any definition, the amount of money and effort that goes into what people take to be international propaganda—including the people who pay for it—is impressive. For purposes of this article, I will define *propaganda* as a persuasive communicative act of a government directed at a foreign audience. I would have liked to exclude the activities of the diplomatic corps when they are dealing with their counterparts in an official exchange; but nowadays that is difficult. In the old days, such activity was called diplomacy. Today, the target of international propaganda quite frequently is made up of government officials, and the channel or medium often is the interpersonal relationship of a cocktail party. Yes, one might say, but the message is different. A diplomatic exchange is legally, or at least diplomatically, binding. Propaganda is not. This is cold comfort. Often nowadays, diplomatic moves are publicized through the mass media, while diplomatic exchanges are repudiated without qualms.[1]

The expenditures on international propaganda are especially remarkable in view of the fact that there is very little assurance that the activity will have the desired effect; frequently there is very little indication that the propagandist

▶ From: *The Annals of the American Academy of Political and Social Sciences* (Philadelphia), Vol. 398, Nov., 1971. Reprinted here with permission of author and publisher. Dr. Martin is professor of journalism at the University of Maryland and a former research administrator in the U.S. Information Agency. He is author of *International Propaganda*.

knows what effect he desires, nor does he have any theory as to why his propaganda activity is likely to produce a particular effect. Such a theory is necessary if he is to satisfy economy-minded guardians and disbursers of the public funds, who normally insist on evidence of effectiveness. As Edward A. Suchman has pointed out, "A test of 'Does it work?' presupposes some theory as to why one might expect it to work." [2]

What will come as the greatest surprise to most people, however—not least to the propagandist himself—is that by far the largest chunk of the propaganda budget is not spent on propaganda at all. It is spent on what I shall call *facilitative communication*. This is an activity that is designed to keep lines open and to maintain contacts against the day when they will be needed for propaganda purposes. It is a ploy that is familiar to the newspaper correspondent faced with a press conference and a limited number of telephones on the premises to phone back a hot scoop. He puts an assistant on a phone to his home office and thus keeps the line open until he is ready with his story.

Facilitative communication by international propaganda agencies most frequently takes the form of radio newscasts, press releases, books, pamphlets, and periodicals of a general or technical nature, artistic and other cultural programs, exhibits, films, seminars, language classes, reference services, and personal social contacts. None of this, naturally, is engaged in or performed with any conscious, limited objective other than the generally conceded hope of creating a friendly atmosphere, or, as a psychologist might put it, a favorable *affect*.

I have made no systematic study of the content of the world's so-called international propaganda as opposed to its facilitative communication, but my educated guess is that in peacetime, between 95 and 99 percent of the communication activity that is paid for by governments—because they think that engaging in international propaganda is the "in thing" to do—is really not propaganda at all. Ironically, few governments will publicly admit that they are engaged in propaganda because of the pejorative meaning the term has acquired. They prefer such euphemisms as *information program* or *cultural activity*. But for budgetary purposes it is justified as propaganda and serious efforts are made to measure its effectiveness in terms of its persuasiveness.

TYPES OF COMMUNICATION

I have defined propaganda as a persuasive communicative act. All communication is purposive by definition,[3] but not all communication is necessarily persuasive in intent. Besides propaganda, there are other forms of persuasive communication, such as advertising, education, and political campaigning. These differ from propaganda in source, purpose (or content), and target. What they have in common is the process. They are all forms of communication. The question is, how effective are they?

There is no doubt that one human being can affect and even persuade another through communication under certain circumstances. All communication, no matter how insignificant (even a brief "Hi!") leaves a mark on the receiver. Communication specialist Wilbur Schramm likens the effect to calcareous water dripping on a stalagmite. Occasionally a drop leaves an especially large deposit, but generally it merely contributes to the imperceptible growth of the spur. There is some empirical evidence of this lasting effect. Psychologist Harold E. Burtt, for example, occasionally read passages from Sophocles to his two-year-old son in the original Greek. He did this daily for three months, then put the experiment aside until the child was eight years old, when he had the boy memorize a number of selections. He now found that it took a significantly larger number of repetitions for the child to learn passages he had never heard than it took him to learn the ones he had heard six years earlier—a clear indication of a residual effect.[4]

The question, however, is not whether communication leaves a mark—that is, whether it is purposive—but whether it is effective. Effectiveness by definition assumes a *predetermined* outcome. One cannot speak of effectiveness—that is, attaining an intended or expected objective—unless one has a prior objective in mind. This, in essence, is the connotative meaning of persuasion. Purposiveness does not have that connotation. It does not necessarily imply movement or change. Persuasiveness does.

Is persuasive communication effective, then? Generally, the answer is, "No, it less than effective." Raymond A. Bauer of the Harvard Graduate School of Business Administration has pointed out, for instance, that an advertiser seldom expects more than 2 to 5 percent of his target audience to be influenced by his message. Is this effective? It is .02 to .05 effective, but it could represent new sales of 150,000 to 400,000 if his medium is a magazine with a circulation of seven to eight million. A politician would probably be happy with a persuasive communication that was 10 to 15 percent effective, while a teacher would expect at least 70 to 80 percent effectiveness, realizing that 100 percent effectiveness is a pipe dream. There is an interesting difference between the advertiser and politician on the one hand and the educator on the other. The first two often (though perhaps not always) have very specific objectives when they engage in persuasive communication. Generally, these center in the cash register or the ballot box. The educator, on the other hand, frequently has only a vague notion of his objectives. The tests and exams used in measuring the effectiveness of his "persuasive communication" are, therefore, often attacked by those taking them as "subjective" and "unfair"—meaning that the tests do not adequately measure the effectiveness of the persuasive communication.

The propagandist has much in common with the educator. As I pointed out above, most of the time he is engaged in facilitative rather than in persuasive communication and, ironically, most of the time he does not realize it. As a result, he searches feverishly but, naturally, in vain for evidence of his effectiveness, so that he can justify his continued existence to the controllers of his budget. What he ends up with—and this is true of propagandists the world over—are some figures that attest to the effectiveness of his facilitative communication.[5] But not realizing that this differs from persuasive communication, he feels guilty and frustrated about having to present clearly inadequate data.

Yet there is a fundamental difference between the measure of the effectiveness of persuasive communication and that of facilitative communication. The former is measured from the top down. The objective is to persuade a given target, and effectiveness is approached though seldom attained. In fact, by the time it is attained the objective has changed, since objectives in international propaganda are defined and circumscribed in terms of time, space, and publics. The effectiveness of facilitative communication, on the other hand, is measured cumulatively from the bottom up. Since its objective is to open or to maintain channels of communication with a given individual, group, or public as potential future targets, effectiveness is measured incrementally, rather than decrementally as is the case with persuasive communication. One can only be more effective, not less than effective. Everyone is potentially a target and must be counted, until a specific objective involving persuasive communication specifies and delimits the target. Obviously, propagandists would just as soon their open channels were never put to the test, since that would involve decremental measurement, in which they almost invariably come out relatively poorly.

HIERARCHICAL IMPACT MODELS

Facilitative communication requires no more than exposure as evidence of effectiveness. If we think in terms of a hierarchy of impact measurement, beginning with the input of the propagandist and ending with a change in the behavior of the target, we can conceive of several intermediate points at which measurement is feasible. Besides measuring input in terms of the number of hours of broadcasting, pages, pamphlets, pictures, periodicals, projections, or what-have-you emitted by the propagandist, one might measure the number of people exposed to the input. Many communication specialists [6] say that the next step in the hierarchy of the effectiveness process is awareness, which involves a conscious knowledge of the subject. Nothing will happen unless the communication can carry the individual on to the interest stage and, possibly, an evaluation stage, which requires an understanding and a "reception" of the message. This is followed by an acceptance, trial, or yielding stage, often thought of as a stage in which attitudes are changed. I refer to this as "collimation of the receiver's cognitive world," since what happens is a realignment or reorientation of a person's attitudes, values, opinion, and behavior within his "reality world." This may be likened to a magnet passing over a piece of iron and changing the orientation of its molecular magnets; only, here the change is in the salience (that is, the psychological closeness of an object to a person) and pertinence (that is, the relative importance of objects) of the situations, objects, and people in his cognitive world.[7] A final adoption or behavioral change step is suggested by some communication specialists, which involves overt action on the part of the target. This, in my opinion, is tautological, since behavior follows from the readiness to act when the opportunity presents itself, and this is inherent in a person's attitudinal orientation.

This hierarchical model encompasses two distinct processes rather than one. The first is the process of facilitative communication that begins with input and ends with exposure. With exposure, the process has been completed. The line of communication is open and that is its sole purpose. The question of efficiency may be raised: What is the cost-per-exposure of opening and maintaining this channel of communication? But effectiveness is achieved once a single contact is made. The second process involves persuasive communication, and begins with awareness. Awareness is clearly unnecessary for facilitative communication; it is crucial for persuasive communication. The step from exposure to awareness is a quantum jump because it moves communication from the physical plane to the intellectual. It is a step that some people can never take because of intellectual or educational deficiencies. John R. Mathiason, studying the urban poor in Venezuela, found that exposing them to more mass media was futile since they had not been trained to process the information transmitted to them. "The poor of Ciudad Guayana have difficulty defining their situations," he concluded.[8]

VALUE OF FACILITATIVE COMMUNICATION

Does facilitative communication have any propaganda value? Yes, it has been shown that familiarity itself tends to create a positive feeling toward an object or subject. Numerous experiments using Chinese characters, nonsense syllables, and human photographs support the theory that repeated exposure—that is, familiarity—creates a favorable attitude toward an object. True, people will turn to a novel stimulus or situation in preference to a familiar one when they have a choice. But exploration or search for novelty correlates negatively with liking.[9] In this sense, therefore, as Marshall McLuhan would say, the medium is the message.

There are two caveats, however, in a propaganda situation as opposed to a laboratory experiment. The favorable *affect* (that is, feeling or emotion) toward the channel—say, the Voice of America—engendered by mere familiarity may be tempered or even reversed if the original attitude of the target either toward the communicator or toward his message was negative. This will be discussed in more detail. Secondly, the positive feeling is limited to those who voluntarily expose themselves to the channel, and this, in turn, raises two questions: Were these people friendly to the channel in the first place, or did they become friendly as the result of exposure? And, more importantly, when at some future date it is necessary to transmit a persuasive communication—that is, propaganda—through the channel, will those who have been linked to it by facilitative communication also be the target of the prescribed persuasive communication?

PERSUASIVE COMMUNICATION

And now, finally, we come to the pay dirt in the propaganda mine. How effective is propaganda, which by all definitions is *persuasive* communication? This question has plagued and intrigued communicators the world over, although it was not studied systematically until the twentieth century, which happens to coincide with the period of the development of social science.

Both inductive and deductive approaches have been tried.

INDUCTIVE APPROACHES

The inductive approaches are exemplified by the applied research begun by the Army's Information and Educational Division during World War II and continued by Carl I. Hovland and his colleagues in the Yale Communication and Attitude Change Program. These researchers and others who proceeded along the same lines of enquiry examined the effects of communication through controlled experiments in which they carefully subjected one variable after another to the test. Their findings have included the following:

1. *The Communicator*

A credible persuasive communicator—and, in most instances, a likeable one—has a great initial advantage over a non-credible communicator. A credible source is one that is seen to be "trustworthy" and "expert," although researchers have found it hard to disentangle the two attributes. It helps if the communicator also appears to have views in common with his audience. The initial advantage of credibility disappears a few weeks after the message is heard, the tendency being to forget who the communicator was. This is called *the sleeper effect*. Other factors, such as age and appearance, have been found to enhance a communicator's effectiveness under certain conditions. Unfortunately for the propagandist, credibility, attractiveness, and similar positive attributes are not characteristics of the communicator but are judgments of the audience.[10] In other words, the propagandist has little control over them.

2. *The Message*

The effectiveness of propaganda is increased if its message fulfills a need or an aspiration of its target and if it agrees with existing values, attitudes, opinions, beliefs, norms—or whatever one would like to call them—of the audience. It was also found that presenting only one side of an issue is more effective than presenting two sides when the audience is not well educated, already convinced, and unlikely to hear the other side; that presenting both sides of a case is more effective with those who are well educated or initially opposed, and that in general, two-sided presentations tend to inoculate against future counterpropaganda. Effectiveness of a communication is influenced by the order in which the pro and con arguments are presented, but the differential effect depends on the number of sources, how the message is introduced, what happens before or after each side is presented, and the type of audience. Fear-arousing and threatening communications have in some cases been found to be directly related, and in other cases inversely related, to effectiveness. The same is true of emotional as against national presentations. A liked message has a better chance of being remembered than a disliked one, a selected message better than one that the audience chanced onto. One fact pervades all these studies: every variable appears to interact with audience factors over which the communicator has no control.

3. The Medium

Because of the great difference in the cost of communicating through the various mass media, much emphasis has been placed by all "persuasive communicators" on determining the differential effects of the media. The findings have been very disappointing. While a cross section of the public is reached by each medium, with a small decline in magazine readership and a large one in book readership at lower educational levels, each channel—by which I mean the specific radio or TV program, newspaper, newspaper column or page, magazine, and so on—has a very distinctive audience with little overlap.[11] Given the same audience segment, researchers have found no consistent pattern of advantage in one mass medium over another. Joseph T. Klapper, in his often quoted study of the effects of the mass media, concludes that

> *All other conditions being equal, as they are in the laboratory*, face-to-face contact is more efficiently persuasive than radio, which in turn is more efficient than print. TV and films probably rank between face-to-face contact and radio, but this latter point has not been empirically demonstrated.[12]

He goes on to say that all other conditions are rarely equal in real life. This is an understatement. They can rarely be made equal even in the laboratory, as numerous studies, especially in the field of education, attest. Much depends on the communicator, and this carries over into intimate, face-to-face communication. Not only does interpersonal communication of necessity reach smaller numbers than communication through the mass media, but the impact of the communicator is more vivid and is likely to have a negative effect if he is attempting to persuade individuals on a matter involving personal values.[13]

4. The Audience

More than anything else, effectiveness of persuasive communication depends on the past history of the receiver of a message—the ground in which the seed is sown. This includes the cognitive system—the values, attitudes, beliefs, opinions—and the habitual behavior patterns of the individual, which, in turn, also depend on such idiocratic factors as age, sex, education, socioeconomic status, geographic region, and race. Equally relevant are such personality factors as need for social approval, aggressiveness, authoritarianism, high versus low need for clarity or simplicity, self-esteem, and whether the target is particularly topic-bound, appeal-bound, communicator-bound, media-bound, style-bound, or situation-bound. People, it has been found, expose themselves selectively to messages, although it is no longer believed, as it once was, that they will tend to expose themselves only to supportive communications. They will tend to perceive selectively, or, more correctly, their retention is selective, since they must have perceived a message before deciding to reject it. Finally, the pressure of group norms tends to inhibit attitude change except insofar as the group itself is changing in its values. [14]

DEDUCTIVE APPROACHES

The deductive approaches to the study of communication effects have started out with either a behavioristic or a cognitive theory of attitude formation.

Behaviorists

The behaviorists such as Leonard Doob, Burrhus F. Skinner, Caryl Bem, and Arthur and Carolyn Staats base their theories of attitude change on learning theory. Theirs is essentially a hypodermic model of attitude formation and modification, in which a communication stimulus leads to an observable opinion or behavioral response mediated by an attitude. This, in turn, is a tendency, learned through conditioning, to respond in a given way.

Cognitive Theorists

The cognitive theorists such as Leon Festinger, Fritz Heider, Charles Osgood, and Theodore Newcomb have developed consistency models that explain attitude modifications in terms of a strain toward balance in the beliefs and emotions of the individual. It is a homeostatic model in the sense that a person tries to maintain a logical consistency in the things he knows and likes. Thus, if A likes President Nixon but doesn't like his China policy, he will attempt to restore cognitive balance either by changing his attitude toward Nixon or by modifying his attitude toward China. Festinger would add that he is liable to reduce his dissonance by refusing to believe that Nixon holds those views, or by misperceiving the news, or by minimizing the importance of China, or by forgetting what the President said.

These theorists not only explain why and how attitudes are formed and modified but also try to predict the outcome of a communication effort in terms of their theories. The models occasionally lead to incongruous conclusions. As Festinger once pointed out, regardless of how much a child likes Popeye, he can't be made to like spinach. Yet balance theories tend to suggest that he can. Festinger's dissonance theory has some useful applications to the analysis of persuasive communication if one can first measure the attitudes of the target on relevant factors. Sometimes the predicted behavior fails to materialize, which has led to the suggestion that "dissonance theory is almost Freudian in its ability to explain data, no matter how they come out." [15]

There are other deductive approaches that attempt to explain why people are influenced by persuasive communication, but they tend to be extensions of the two described above. One is based on the perceptual theory of Solomon Asch and on Muzafer Sherif's assimilation-and-contrast theory, suggesting that attitude change is due to a change in pertinence, or the relative importance of objects, rather than to a change in a person's feelings about the object. Another theory is based on the functional approach of Daniel Katz, who says that a person's attitudes are tied to his need system or ego-defensiveness. Any changes in his attitude would be due to a change in his psychological need. [16]

EFFECTIVENESS OF PROPAGANDA

In both theory and practice, persuasive communication has been shown to have an effect. But this is a far cry from evidence of effectiveness. Nor is effective persuasion necessarily the same thing as effective propaganda. If we could select our audience on the basis of certain idiocratic factors—objective physical and personal characteristics peculiar to an individual, such as age, sex, race, education—we might increase by a statistically significant fraction the proportion of those influenced by a message. But we would have no control over such factors as personality and susceptibility to persuasion, existing values, beliefs and opinions or attitudes toward the objects, subjects and situations involved in the persuasive message. We can choose our communicator but not determine his image. We can select the vehicle of transmission but not the channel of reception of the target of our communication. We could maximize the effect of all these factors for a single individual, especially if we were able to subject him to intensive precommunication analysis. But there is no way that this can be done for the diverse assortment of individuals who normally make up the audience of the mass media, the vehicles most commonly used in international propaganda.

What all this boils down to is that if our persuasive communication ends up with a net positive effect, we must attribute it to luck, not science. The propagandist cannot control the direction or the intensity of impact of his message, if, indeed, he reaches his target at all.

So much for the effectiveness of persuasive communication. Propaganda, as I said earlier, differs from other forms of persuasive communication in its source, its purpose, and its target. The purpose of propaganda may be to influence a government, but it is quite conceivable that the most effective and efficient way to accomplish this is to persuade a particular segment of the population whose composition is totally different from that of the individuals who make up the government. It is further possible that the propagandist is highly effective in his persuasive communication with this segment but that his effectiveness does not carry over to the ultimate objective of his propaganda—

influencing the government. The effectiveness of propaganda may, therefore, be even less predictable and controllable than the effectiveness of mere persuasive communication.

Now, prediction and control are two key elements of effectiveness. Another element is an articulable objective. Measurement of effectiveness is, of course, impossible without a specifically stated objective, since we cannot say how well a person has succeeded unless we know what he is trying to do. Put another way, if you don't know where you are going, any road will take you there. Having an objective, the only way a person can successfully attain it is to have control of the vehicle that will take him to it. Finally, the only way he can control the vehicle is by being able to predict what will happen if he moves various knobs and levers in it.

Most of the research to date has concerned itself with moving one lever at a time, or, at most, two or three. What happens at the interface, when the impact of each factor interrelates with every other factor, the propagandist has no idea—as yet.

NOTES

[1] A recent example was the feeler by the senior United States diplomat in the United Arab Republic, Donald C. Bergus, whose suggestions to President Sadat regarding a Suez Canal solution were termed his personal views by the State Department when they backfired, *The New York Times*, June 30, 1971.

[2] Edward A. Suchman, *Evaluative Research: Principles and Practice in Public Service and Social Action Programs* (New York: Russell Sage Foundation, 1967), p. 86.

[3] Some have spoken of non-purposive communication—for instance, the reflexive "communication" of bees described by von Frisch—but admit that this is not true communication. See D. O. Hebb and W. R. Thompson, "The Social Significance of Animal Studies," in Gardner Lindzey and Elliot Aronson, eds., *The Handbook of Social Psychology*, vol. 2, 2d ed. (Reading, Mass.: Addison-Wesley, 1968), pp. 738–740.

[4] Harold E. Burtt, "An Experimental Study of Early Childhood Memory: Final Report," *Journal of Genetic Psychology* 58 (1941), pp. 435–439.

[5] I have discussed this problem with British, German, Egyptian, Indian, Polish, Czech, and French propaganda analysts, to name just a few, and found that they all faced the same dilemma we did in the United States. At the time, my analysis of the problem had not as yet crystallized in its present form.

[6] Cf. Everett M. Rogers, *Diffusion of Innovations* (New York: Free Press, 1962), pp. 76–120; William J. McGuire, "Personality and Susceptibility to Social Influence," in E. F. Borgatta and W. W. Lambert, eds., *Handbook of Personality Theory and Research* (Chicago: Rand McNally, 1968), pp. 1130–1187.

[7] Cf. Steven H. Chaffee, "Salience and Homeostasis in Communication Processes," *Journalism Quarterly* 44 (Autumn, 1967), pp. 439–444, 453. Leon Festinger has suggested that "when opinions or attitudes are changed through the momentary impact of a persuasive communication, this change, all by itself, is inherently unstable and will disappear or remain isolated unless an environmental or behavioral change can be brought about to support and maintain it" ("Behavioral Support for Opinion Change," *Public Opinion Quarterly* 28 [Fall, 1964], p. 514). I disagree. Festinger's own dissonance theory, when viewed in conjunction with Fritz Heider's balance theory, points to the probability of collimation, which requires no change in the environment, only a reorientation toward it.

[8] John R. Mathiason, "Communication Patterns and Powerlessness Among Urban Poor: Toward

the Use of Mass Communication for Rapid Social Change," in *Studies in Comparative International Development* (St. Louis, Mo.: Washington University Social Studies Institute; forthcoming.)

[9] See Robert B. Zajonc, "Attitudinal Effects of Mere Exposure," *Journal of Personality and Social Psychology—Monograph Supplement*, vol. 9, no. 2, part 2 (June, 1968).

[10] C. W. Sherif, M. Sherif, and R. E. Nebergall, *Attitude and Attitude Change* (Philadelphia: W. B. Saunders, 1965), pp. 201–202.

[11] Alfred O. Hero, *Mass Media and World Affairs* (Boston: World Peace Foundation, 1959), p. 50.

[12] Joseph T. Klapper, *The Effects of Mass Communication* (New York: Free Press, 1960), pp. 108–109.

[13] This finding emerged from a study that was done by USIA in India under my supervision. Intellectuals in India having close personal contacts with Americans were less favorably influenced toward Americans than was a matched sample of Indians without such contacts. On the other hand, they were more favorably influenced toward America as a country. *Opinions of USIS Target Groups and Other Literates in Delhi, India,* unpublished report (Washington: USIA, Research and Reference Service, September, 1966).

[14] A good general review of the literature in this field is provided in Ralph L. Rosnow and Edward J. Robinson, *Experiments in Persuasion* (New York: Academic Press, 1967).

[15] Charles A. Kiesler, Barry E. Collins, and Norman Miller, *Attitude Change* (New York: John Wiley, 1969), p. 236. This book also provides a good general review of the literature on deductive approaches to persuasive communication effects.

[16] See McGuire, op. cit., pp. 1136–1139.

Jacques Ellul:

International Propaganda and Myths

IN THE domain of external politics and the propaganda that is directed toward the outside, there is practically no more private propaganda or any diversity of propagandas. Even parties indentured to a foreign government, and thus making propaganda different from that of their own national government, direct their propaganda to the interior. But what character does this unique form of propaganda (directed to the outside) take, and what repercussions has it on a democracy that conducts it? Can it be that it really exists in the domain of information?

We have abundant proof nowadays that straight information addressed to a foreign country is entirely useless.* Where the problem is to overcome national antipathies (which exist even between friendly nations), allegiance to a different government, to a different psychological and historical world, and finally to an opposite propaganda, it is fruitless to expect anything from straight information: the bare fact (the truth) can accomplish nothing against such barriers. Facts are not believed. Other than in exceptional cases (military occupation and so on), people believe their own government over a foreign government. The latter's facts are not believed. In fact, propaganda can penetrate the consciousness of the masses of a foreign country only through the myth. It cannot operate with simple arguments pro and con. It does not address itself to already existing feelings, but must create an image to act as a motive force. This image must have an emotional character that leads to the allegiance of the entire being, without thought. That is, it must be a myth.

But then democracy takes a path that needs watching. First of all, it begins to play a game that drives man from the conscious and rational into the arms of irrational and "obscure forces"; but we already know that in this game the believer is not the master, and that forces thus unleashed are rarely brought under control again. To put it differently: mythical democratic propaganda in no way prepares its liteners for democracy, but strengthens their totalitarian tendencies, providing at best a different direction for those tendencies. We will have to come back to this. But above all we must ask ourselves what myth the

---

*We are talking here primarily of propaganda directed at the Communist countries.

▶ Reprinted from part of Chapter 5 ("Socio-Political Effects") of Ellul's *Propaganda* (New York: Knopf, 1965) by permission of the publisher. Dr. Ellul is a well-known French social and political philosopher and the author of many books and articles.

democracies should use. From experience we have seen that the democracies have used the myths of Peace, of Freedom, of Justice, and so on.

All that has now been used, and is all the more unacceptable because everybody uses these words. But the myth used by propaganda must be specific: the myth of Blood and Soil was remarkable. What specific myths are left for democracy? Either subjects that cannot possibly form the content of a myth, such as well-being or the right to vote, or democracy itself.

Contrary to what one may think, the myth of democracy is far from exhausted and can still furnish good propaganda material. The fact that Communist authoritarian regimes also have chosen democracy as the springboard of propaganda tends to prove its propagandistic value. And to the extent that democracy is presented, constructed, and organized as a myth, it can be a good subject of propaganda. Propaganda appeals to belief: it rebuilds the drive toward the lost paradise and uses man's fundamental fear. Only from this aspect does democratic propaganda have some chance of penetration into non-democratic foreign countries. But one must then consider the consequences.

The first consequence is that any operation that transforms democracy into a myth transforms the democratic ideal. Democracy was not meant to be a myth. The question arose early—in 1791 in France. And we know what, shortly after, Jacobinism made of French democracy. We must understand this: Jacobinism saved the country. It claimed to have saved the Republic, but it is clear that it only saved the Jacobin regime by destroying all that was democratic. We cannot analyze here at length the influence of the myth on the abolition of democracy during 1793–5. Let us merely say that democracy cannot be an object of faith, of belief: it is expression of opinions. There is a fundamental difference between regimes based on opinion and regimes based on belief.

To make a myth of democracy is to present the opposite of democracy. One must clearly realize that the use of ancient myths and the creation of new ones is a regression toward primitive mentality, regardless of material progress. The evocative of mystical feelings is a rejection of democratic feelings. Considerable problems arise in the United States because of such diverse myths as, for example, the Ku Klux Klan, the American Legion, or Father Divine. These are anti-democratic, but they are localized, only partial and private. The matter becomes infinitely more serious when the myth becomes public, generalized, and official, when what is an anti-mystique becomes a mystique.

Of course, we have said that such democratic propaganda is created for external use. People already subjected to totalitarian propaganda can be reached only by the myth, and even that does not change their behavior or mentality; it simply enters into the existing mold and creates new beliefs there. But looking at things this way implies two consequences.

First, we accept the fact that such external democratic propaganda should be a *weapon*, that we are dealing here with psychological warfare, and that we adjust ourselves to the enemy's train of thought; and that, proceeding from there, the people that we subject to our propaganda are not those whom we want to see become democratic but whom we want to defeat. If we actually work on such a nation with the help of the myth, we confirm it in a state of mind, in a behavior, and in a concept of life that is anti-democratic: we do not prepare it to become a democratic nation, for on the one hand we reinforce or continue the methods of its own authoritarian government; and on the other, we cannot give the people, by such means, the desire to adhere to something else in another way. We are simply asking for the same *kind* of acceptance of something else, of another form of government. Is this sufficient to make people switch allegiance? That is the democratic propaganda problem in Germany and Japan.

In the second place, such methods imply that we consider democracy an abstraction; for if we think that to cast different ideas in the mold of propaganda is sufficient to change the nature of propaganda, we make a mere theory or idea of democracy. Propaganda, whatever its content, tends to create a particular psychology and a determined behavior. Superficially there can be differences, but they are illusory. To say, for example, that Fascist propaganda, whose subject was the State, and Nazi propaganda whose subject was the race, were different from each other because of their difference in content, is to become a victim of unreal and academic distinctions. But "the democratic idea" when promulgated by means that lead to non-democratic behavior only hardens the totalitarian man in his mold.

This does not take into account that this democratic veneer and the myth of democracy as a propaganda subject are very fragile. It is, in fact, one of propaganda's essential laws that its objects always adjust themselves to its forms. In this, as in so many other domains of the modern world, the means impose their own laws. To put it differently: the objects of propaganda tend to become totalitarian because propaganda itself is totalitarian. This is exactly what I said when I spoke of the necessity to turn democracy into a myth.

Thus, such propaganda can be effective as a weapon of war, but we must realize when using it that we simultaneously destroy the possibility of building true democracy.

I have said that such propaganda was for external use, that the myth was directed to the outside. But it is not certain that one can impose such a limitation. When a government builds up the democratic image in this fashion, it cannot isolate the external and internal domains from each other. Therefore the people of the country making such propaganda must also become convinced of the excellence of this image. They must not merely know it, but also follow it. This, incidentally, sets a limit to the degree to which propaganda can lie; a democratic government cannot present to the outside world a radically inexact and mendacious picture of its policies, as can a totalitarian government.

But one must qualify this thought in two ways: on the one hand a democratic nation is itself more or less in the grip of propaganda and goes along with the idealistic image of its government because of national pride; on the other, even authoritarian governments are aware that in propaganda the truth pays, as I have said: this explains the final form of propaganda adopted by Goebbels in 1944.

From there on, the myth created for external use becomes known at home and has repercussions there; even if one does not try to influence people by making propaganda abroad, they will react indirectly. Therefore, the repercussions on a democratic population of the myth developed by its government for external use must be analyzed; these repercussions will lead primarily to the establishment of unanimity.

This is a primary and very simple consequence. A myth (an image evoking belief) can stand no dilution, no half-measures, no contradictions. One believes it or does not. The democratic myth must display this same form, incisive and coherent; it is of the same nature as other myths. In order for the myth to be effective abroad, it must not be contradicted at home. No other voice must arise at home that would reach the foreign propaganda target and destroy the myth.

Can anyone believe that it was possible to make effective propaganda, for example, toward Algeria, when it was immediately contradicted at home? How could the Algerians—or any other foreigners—take seriously a promise made by General de Gaulle in the name of France when the press immediately declared that one part of France was in disagreement with it? *

This will lead to the elimination of any opposition that would show that the people are not unanimously behind the democracy embodied by the government. Such opposition can completely destroy all effectiveness of a democratic propaganda. Besides, such propaganda is made by a government supported by a majority. The minority, though also democratic, will tend to be against such propaganda merely because it comes from the government (we saw this in France after 1945). From there on, though in accord with the idea of democracy, this minority will show itself hostile to the democratic myth. Then the government, if it wants its propaganda to be effective, will be forced to reduce the possibility of the minority's expressing itself—*i.e.*, to interfere with one of democracy's essential characteristics; we are already used to this from wartime, as with censorship. Here we are face to face with the fact discussed above: propaganda is by itself a state of war; it demands the exclusion of opposite trends and minorities—not total and official perhaps, but at least partial and indirect exclusion.

If we pursue this train of thought, another factor emerges: for the myth to have real weight, it must rest on popular belief. To put it differently: one cannot simply project a myth to the outside even by the powerful modern material means; such an image will have no force unless it is already believed. The

---

* This non-coherence, leading to the ineffectuality of the myth, was the cause—among many others—of years of unsuccessful negotiations.

myth is contagious because beliefs are contagious. It is indispensable, therefore, that democratic people also believe the democratic myth. Conversely, it is not useful that the government itself should follow suit; but the government must be sure that its propaganda abroad is identical with its propaganda at home, and understand that its foreign propaganda will be strong only if it is believed at home. (The United States understood this perfectly between 1942 and 1945.) And the more the myth will appear to be the expression of belief of the entire nation, the more effective it will be. It thus presumes unanimity.

We have seen how all propaganda develops the cult of personality. This is particularly true in a democracy. There one exalts the individual, who refuses to be anonymous, rejects the "mass," and eschews mechanization. He wants a human regime where men are human beings. He needs a government whose leaders are human beings. And propaganda must show them to him as such. It must create these personalities. To be sure, the object at this level is not idolatry, but idolatry cannot fail to follow if the propaganda is done well. Whether such idolatry is given to a man in uniform bursting with decorations, or a man in work shirt and cap, or a man wearing a business suit and soft hat makes no difference; those are simple adaptations of propaganda to the feelings of the masses. The democratic masses will reject the uniform, but idolize the soft hat if it is well presented. There can be no propaganda without a personality, a political chief. Clemenceau, Daladier, De Gaulle, Churchill, Roosevelt, MacArthur are obvious examples. And even more, Khrushchev, who, after having denounced the cult of personality, slipped into the same role, differently, but with the same ease and obeying the same necessity. The nation's unanimity is necessary. This unanimity is embodied in one personality, in whom everyone finds himself, in whom everyone hopes and projects himself, and for whom everything is possible and permissible.

This need for unanimity is accepted by some of those who have studied the problem of propaganda in democracy. It has been claimed that this unanimity indicates the transition from an old form of democracy to a new one: "massive and progressive democracy." In other words, a democracy of allegiance; a system in which all will share the same conviction. This would not be a centrifugal conviction, *i.e.*, one expressing itself in diverse forms and admitting the possibility of extreme divergences. It would be a centripetal conviction with which everything would be measured by the same yardstick; democracy would express itself in a single voice, going further than just forms—all the way to rites and liturgies. It would, on the other hand, be a democracy of participation in which the citizen would be wholly engaged; his complete life, his movements would be integrated into a given social system. And one of the authors gives as an example the Nuremberg Party Congress! What a strange example of democracy.

It is true that only such a unanimous and unitary society can produce propaganda that can be effectively carried beyond the borders. But we must ask ourselves whether such a society is still democratic. What is this democracy that no longer includes minorities and opposition? As long as democracy is merely the interplay of parties, there can be opposition; but when we hear of a massive democracy, with grandiose ceremonies in which the people participate at the prompting of the State, that signifies, first of all, a confusion between the government and the State, and indicates further that anyone who does not participate is not merely in opposition, but excludes himself from the national community expressing itself in this participation. It is a truly extraordinary transformation of the democratic structure, because there can no longer be any respect for the minority opposition to the State—an opposition that, lacking the means of propaganda—or at least any means that can compete with those of the State—can no longer make its voice heard.

The minority is heard even less because the effects of the myth, inflated by propaganda, are always the same and always antidemocratic. Anyone who participates in such a socio-political body and is imbued with the truth of the myth, necessarily becomes sectarian. Repeated so many times, being driven in so many different forms into the propagandee's subconscious, this truth, transmitted by propaganda, becomes for every participant an absolute truth, which cannot be discussed without lies and distortion. Democratic peoples are not exempt from what is vaguely called "psychoses." But such propaganda, if it is effective, predisposes people to—or even causes—these psychoses.

If the people do not believe in the myth, it cannot serve to combat totalitarian propaganda; but if the people do believe in it, they are victims of these myths, which, though democratic on the surface, have all the traits of all other myths, particularly the impossibility, in the eyes of believers, of being questioned. But this tends to eliminate all opposing truth, which is immediately called "error." Once democracy becomes the object of propaganda, it also becomes as totalitarian, authoritarian, and exclusive as dictatorship.

The enthusiasm and exaltation of a people who cling to a myth necessarily lead to intransigeance and sectarianism. The myth of democracy arose, for example, during the period of the Convention; there we had forms of massive democracy, with great ceremonies and efforts at unanimity. But was that still democracy? Are there not also changes in the mores of the United States when everything is called un-American that is not strict conformism? This term, *un-American*, so imprecise for the French, is in the United States precise to the extent that it is a result of the belief in the myth. To provoke such belief and launch a people on the road to such exaltation, without which propaganda cannot exist, really means to give a people feelings and reflexes incompatible with life in a democracy.

This is really the ultimate problem: democracy is not just a certain form of political organization or simply an ideology—it is, first of all, a certain view of life and a form of behavior. If democracy were only a form of political organization, there would be no problem; propaganda could adjust to it. This is the institutional argument: propaganda is democratic because there is no unitary State centralized by propaganda. If, then, we were merely in the presence of an ideology, there still would be no problem: propaganda can transmit any ideology (subject to the qualifications made above) and, therefore, also the democratic ideology, for example. But if democracy is a way of life, composed of tolerance, respect, degree, choice, diversity, and so on, all propaganda that acts on behavior and feelings and transforms them in depth turns man into someone who can no longer support democracy because he no longer follows democratic behavior. . . .

6

ADVERTISING AND PUBLIC RELATIONS

Braxton Pollard
INTERNATIONAL ADVERTISING: PRACTICAL
   CONSIDERATIONS

Roland L. Kramer
INTERNATIONAL ADVERTISING MEDIA

S. Watson Dunn
THE INTERNATIONAL LANGUAGE OF ADVERTISING

Barbara Baerns
INTERNATIONAL BUSINESS PUBLIC RELATIONS

6

ADVERTISING AND PUBLIC RELATIONS

I F *advertising* of any type roughly can be defined as *commercial propaganda* for all kinds of products, business, trade and industry, and is mainly an economics-oriented function, so *public relations* may be called *idealistic propaganda* for persons, groups, institutions, etc. in behalf of their public images. In certain cases, of course, elements of advertising are merged with those of public relations, and very often public relations campaigns are nothing but a series of advertisements.

Advertising is much older than the history of newspapers or magazines; in fact, it is impossible to speculate on the origins of advertising back in the mists of pre-history. Early forms of advertising (as it is generally recognized today) were already being seen in pamphlets from the 15th and 16th centuries. Since the middle of the 17th century, newspapers have carried advertisements, and from the 19th century on, commercial announcements have been an important part of the economic base of the press.

In the world's press today we find great differences in the proportions of advertising to editorial content. Nearly no, or very few, ads can be found in the state-owned press of the Communist countries. In some Western European nations there is a proportion of about 60% editorial matter to 40% advertising, and in the United States these figures are approximately reversed.

Throughout the world there are many different concepts as to what kinds of advertisements are properly found in certain kinds of newspapers and magazines. Usually this is rather vague, and patterns of advertising use vary considerably from publication to publication and from country to country. In 1957, however, there was founded an organization of leading European dailies which proposed to cooperate and to coordinate their advertising practices—named TEAM (Top European Advertising Media). It is composed today of seventeen dailies from eleven countries, and was established largely as a cooperative institution through the initiative of the Paris daily *Le Figaro* and the Amsterdam paper *Algemeen Handelsblad*. This is a fascinating example for international cooperation and strategy in the field of newspaper advertising.

Since the late 1920's paid messages for products of all kinds became an important factor in financing the numerous radio stations within the United States and in several other countries. And since TV was introduced in the United States, the same system was transplanted to this audio-visual medium. In most European countries, where the costs of radio and television broadcasting to some extent are paid by license fees, the daily times for commercials are limited to certain hours and are never found in other parts of the daily programs. Only Radio Luxembourg is a commercial radio station which can be received in nearly all parts of Europe, whether on medium or on short wave. And Radio Luxembourg not only has a program with commercials from many countries, it also serves in several languages its mainly entertaining program. In other parts of the world similar examples of an international radio program mainly on the basis of commercials may be found.

Although *public relations*, as a term, is one of our century, the activities of this concern have a much longer tradition. The key word in this field is the presentation of *images*—usually for institutions, countries or persons. Public relations activity tries to correct bad attitudes toward certain people or associations by changing the images people have, by using psychological aids of various kinds. Because public relations more and more has gained the connotation of a propagandistic institution, the PR departments today often prefer in their titles words like "information" or "promotion" or "news." Almost every national or international organization—such as the UN, NATO, SEATO, the Common Market and corporations, universities and the like—make use of extensive programs of public relations. Governments also have well-organized and often quite complex PR departments, under a wide variety of names, to look after their images.

In the section which follows, three outstanding international advertising specialists discuss various aspects of a rapidly growing emphasis. In the first article, Braxton Pollard, long-time international advertising manager for Monsanto Company, presents a fresh discussion of the practical considerations connected with successful international advertising. In the next two articles, Dr. Roland Kramer presents fundamentals of advertising abroad and surveys the fields of international advertising media, and Dr. S. Watson Dunn of the University of Illinois considers the problems of translatability of advertisements from country to country.

Finally, public relations and its many problems on the international level is handled in some depth in an original article for this book by Dr. Barbara Baerns of the faculty of Publizistik und Kommunikation at the Ruhr-University Bochum.

*　　*　　*　　*

RELATED READING

Backman, Jules. *Advertising and Competition*. New York: New Yorker University Press, 1967.

Barton, Roger. *Advertising Agency Operations and Management.* New York: McGraw-Hill, 1955.

Barton, Roger. *Media in Advertising.* New York: McGraw-Hill, 1964.

Bernays, Edward L. *Public Relations: Principles, Cases and Problems.* Homewood/Illinois: Richard D. Irwin, 1968.

Buchli, Hanns. *6000 Jahre Werbung: Geschichte der Wirtschaftswerbung und der Propaganda.* (3 Vols.), Berlin: Walter de Gruyter, 1962 ff.

Crane, Edgar. *Marketing Communications,* 2nd ed. New York: John Wiley & Sons, 1972.

Cutlip, Scott M. and Allen H. Center. *Effective Public Relations.* 3rd ed., Englewood-Cliffs/New Jersey: Prentice-Hall, Inc., 1971.

Dowd, Laurence P. *Principles of World Business.* Boston: Allyn and Bacon, Inc., 1965.

Dunn, S. Watson. *International Handbook of Advertising.* New York: McGraw-Hill, 1964.

Ellis, Nigel and Pat Bowman. *The Handbook of Public Relations.* London: Harrap, 1963.

Ettinger, Karl E. *International Handbook of Management.* New York: McGraw-Hill, 1965.

Fayerweather, John. *International Marketing.* Englewood-Cliffs/New Jersey: Prentice Hall, Inc., 1965.

Hundhausen, Carl. *Werbung um öffentliches Vertrauen: Public Relations.* Essen: Verlag Girardet, 1951.

Johnson, Malcolm M. et al. *Current Thoughts on Public Relations.* New York: M. W. Lads Publ. Co., 1968.

Oeckl, Albert. *Handbuch der Public Relations: Theorie und Praxis der Öffentlichkeitsarbeit in Deutschland und der Welt.* Munich: Süddeutscher Verlag, 1964.

Paneth, Erwin. *Die Entwicklung der Reklame vom Altertum bis zur Gegenwart: Erfolgreiche Mittel der Geschäftsreklame aus allen Zeiten und Völkern.* Munich: Verlag Oldenbourg, 1926.

Steinberg, Charles S. *The Creation of Consent: Public Relations in Practice.* New York: Hastings House, 1975.

Stephenson, Howard. *Handbook of Public Relations.* New York: McGraw-Hill Book Company, 1960.

Braxton Pollard:

International Advertising: Practical Considerations

THE real growth companies of our time no longer think in terms of domestic business and overseas business. Enterprises that would achieve their potential in today's drive for success must make decisions and develop communications on a world-wide basis. The advertising program must be truly international.

The reason for this international thinking is obvious. Today there is unmistakable evidence that the overseas market is the truly critical market for the U.S. economy. The performance of U.S. business in the international effort is increasingly determining the ability of the U.S. economy to grow and prosper.

A significant transformation has taken place. Instead of many national markets there has emerged a single global market encompassing the entire free world. Businessmen can no longer concentrate almost wholly on what was once the lucrative and uncomplicated home market.

Now, many U.S. and foreign companies, because of increasing mass production capacity, highly developed market penetration, mounting costs and strong competition—largely at home—face diminishing returns on their investments. Companies caught in this position are solving their problems only by the most critical attention to costs and to increased volume. This condition is providing a force for increased international operations and investments. So it seems apparent that the overseas market and how well companies participate, is determining largely whether their earnings will increase or decrease.

With this drive for business has come a change in the character of the advertising/marketing operation. The traditional pattern of the past for U.S. advertising/marketing management engaged in foreign business utilized a sharp distinction between domestic and international responsibilities in company organizations. This distinction was marked usually by the use of an international division, separate and apart from the management of domestic operations, with responsibility and authority for all operations outside the home country.

During the past few years a new pattern for managing foreign operations has emerged. The essence of this pattern is full and integrated management participation in global markets. This does not mean that the international system failed. The change has simply accomodated the increasing size and growing importance of world trade and the need to give equal attention to both domestic and foreign business.

▶ Written especially for this book (1976) by Braxton Pollard, former manager, International Advertising, Monsanto Company, and visiting professor, School of Journalism, University of Missouri-Columbia.

As the international company develops and progresses, it adds to its responsibilities for selling its company and its products in the home market, the responsibility for its exports and for the marketing/advertising of its growing foreign or overseas production.

Management of the global company must recognize the changing role of advertising as a communications force. Those responsible for advertising in the multinational company will be called upon to make advertising/marketing decisions on a world-wide basis.

Does international advertising differ from advertising at home? Not long ago the *Harvard Business Review* put the answer this way, "Companies that are successfully competing as world enterprises find that the factors needed for success differ from those required in domestically oriented businesses." Fundamental to success in overseas operations are basic advertising skills. All of the basics of domestic advertising that apply equally well to the international operation must come first. However, international advertising is a distinct type of advertising that calls for added skills—the ability to organize and develop international advertising/marketing programs plus the ability to adjust to foreign market conditions influenced by different and varying cultures. The successful international advertising manager must learn the art of adapting basic marketing concepts and advertising skills to fit the environments created by foreign societies and the economics that bind the nations of the world together.

With this accelerated activity by business leaders in overseas markets there is rising interest among students in the entire field of international communications. Tom Sutton, executive vice president-International, J. Walter Thompson Company, had this to say about the growth of international markets and the opportunities for young people trained for this vital segment of business:

With an increasing number of multinational manufacturers looking at marketing and advertising operations from global viewpoints, international markets will get bigger year after year after year. The greater prizes of these growing markets will attract even stiffer competition. The stakes will be high, forcing up standards everywhere. The bottleneck to expansion is unlikely to be financial resources but the lack of well-trained and experienced international marketing and advertising executives. Universities, marketing companies and advertising agencies bear the responsibility of preparing young men and women for the exciting challenges of international business of the future.

Those who would succeed in the drive for world business must not be misled by the often repeated credo that advertising to overseas markets is a highly complicated and totally different endeavor employing a high degree of hocus pocus. Generally, prospects and customers are much alike whether they are in Latin America, the Far East or in Europe. They are motivated by the same forces, have essentially the same interests and will respond in basically the same ways. They want to know something of the advertiser's ability to serve their needs and how their products or services can help them with their problems. Appeals and techniques may vary for different areas of the world but if the advertiser will study the wants, the needs and the ability to buy in each country or area and apply this knowledge to proven U. S. advertising principles, he will have a vital mass communications force for mass consumption in overseas markets.

Same Advertising Good in All Countries?

This is not to imply that the same advertisements that succeeded in the U.S. can be translated into a foreign language and made to work. This is a tempting but disastrous pitfall that must be avoided. The point here is the advertising concept; the application of a thorough knowledge of the overseas market, the people, their needs and their wants to the proven principles of U.S. advertising.

There are those who will argue that advertising campaigns that worked in one area will succeed everywhere. David Ogilvy, chairman of Ogilvy & Mather Inc., New York, has said that he can see the day coming when the head office of an agency with an international account would prepare one campaign that could be used throughout the world because evidence was mounting that one campaign that worked in one area would work everywhere. However, here is what the managing director of his British office had to say on the subject: "I think that is probably true. At the moment we have a number of campaigns that are either the same internationally or bear a remarkable resemblance. These are Hertz, American Express, Schweppes and a few others. But we have come to that by a country-by-country decision by which each country has seen a campaign produced in the United States or the United Kingdom as the case may be; and by testing it along with a lot of other things found that the campaign is the one that works best." In this case it seems significant that Hertz, American Express and Schweppes all have one thing in common; their advertising is directed toward a rather narrow and somewhat upper-class market in all areas.

Those who contend that an advertising campaign that succeeded in one country will surely succeed in any or all others, will invariably cite the case of "The Tiger in the Tank" campaign used world-wide a number of years ago. This campaign, created for one of the companies of Standard Oil, was a great success in almost every area of the world served by any of the Standard Oil companies. However, the campaign was used only after careful testing in each specific area. This case is more likely to be the exception rather than the rule; the fact that there have been few repeaters seems to substantiate this thinking.

For ten years the Monsanto Company ran a basically-the-same corporate campaign that was phenomenally successful in every country of the free world. The task of acquainting business leaders with the capabilities of a company that manufactures hundreds of products in thousands of formulations for dozens of countries in varying stages of development with different needs, represented an almost unsurmountable task for a world-wide communications program. The solution was an advertising campaign with an uncomplicated and measurable objective. It would communicate a single idea world-wide, that Monsanto was a leading and dependable source of chemicals in their country; that it was to any user's best interests to contact Monsanto locally whenever they had any problem relating to the use of chemicals or chemical technology. This campaign was used throughout the world because the advertiser was able to find a suitable common denominator that appealed to his audience everywhere; in this case, the very human side of the company embodied in the dedicated scientists at work solving problems that related to them. Each advertisement was an unmistakable part of the highly stylized series; however, all were carefully selected for the area or market in which they would appear. Each was carefully previewed with the locals of the area. All copy was adapted in the country in which the advertisement would appear.

Developing one campaign that has a chance of success world-wide is a difficult task that depends greatly on finding the right universal appeal for a common objective. Such opportunities and such campaigns are rare.

The thesis here is that if the advertiser can develop or create the great common denominator for a successful world-wide campaign he will be fortunate indeed; but before trying it, test the advertising in each area to make certain it is right and has a chance to succeed. One of the greatest mistakes committed by inexperienced international advertisers results from the exporting of solutions to problems, the practice of assuming that what worked at home will work some place else. Export the approaches to problems; but always avoid projecting the solutions. The odds are that they won't work.

The Logistics for Doing Business

With the advent of the single global market, the advertiser/marketer must be concerned with the logistics for doing business. The idea, of course, is to utilize that system or combination of systems that is competively practical and which permits the lowest cost overall operation for maximizing profits. However, in all cases, in the truly international company, decisions must be made on a world-wide basis. Management must have a single identifying characteristic; that there will be no barrier to distance or of language, or of law, or of taxation, which interferes in the process of its thinking of the world as a single market. In advertising, France or Germany, Argentina or Japan must be considered along with New England or the Middle-West as a part of a whole company communications program.

The logistic systems employed for international operations usually fall under four general headings:

(1) *The export of finished goods from the company headquarters country.* The company produces the goods in the home country; marketing (including

advertising and promotion), shipping etc., are handled either by the manufacturing company or placed in the hands of specialized independent export operators or agents. These companies or organizations usually handle this export service for a number of manufacturing companies, most often, in the same or related line of business.

Whenever feasible, companies prefer to supply foreign markets by export from their home base, resorting to other methods only when forced to by costs or other considerations. Export is the simplest form of overseas trade and the way practically all companies start their overseas planning. This logistic eliminates the risks of overseas investments, and adds to the volume of output from home plants, thus making them more efficient.

(2) *The export of components from the home country or third countries.* In some countries finished products can not be imported. However, the maker can often export some parts or supplies for use in overseas plants, especially for those manufacturing complex products such as electronic equipment, aircraft, automobiles and drugs. Because these countries find certain components required for locally-manufactured products difficult or extremely costly to produce, the importing of such products is permitted.

The two remaining systems for overseas business come under the heading of investment operations. This is the means by which a business participates in overseas trade by either full or part ownership of a plant or plants with a foreign country. These systems are:

(3) *Manufacture in another country for sale in that country.* Companies selling goods in lesser developed countries are repeatedly confronted with the choice of manufacturing within the country on a protected basis or being excluded by restrictions designed to protect those who are willing to invest and manufacture. Consequently, the company has the choice of coming in or being out completely.

(4) *Foreign plants producing for local and export markets.* This system is likely to increase as trade restrictions are reduced under international agreements and by the development of common markets. These economic communities, which represent both an opportunity and a challenge to outsiders, trade among themselves free of all tariffs and other restrictions, but with a common external tariff against all other countries. This system tends to overcome the problem of high costs in producing goods for a one-country market. As trade barriers are lowered, companies are shifting to logistic systems based on a small number of fairly large plants located at strategic points around the world.

Either the third or fourth systems for local manufacture can be achieved by: (1) full ownership, (2) through merger with an established foreign company or (3) by means of a partnership or joint venture with local foreign interests to form a third company. In such mergers or joint ventures, the home-based company seldom gains control of the operation; but there can be a number of advantages to be had from participation by nationals, particularly in the critical area of communications. Unquestionably, the investment method of operations represents the greatest growth and profit potential for the U.S. company in world trade.

Authority and Responsibility for the Advertising

Today there are three basic structures for use in handling local or international advertising for the multinational company. Each will have a different set of procedures and each may require different types of advertising agency services.

(1) *Headquarters-created advertising.* Under this method of operation, corporate headquarters maintains full responsibility and authority for plans, creativity, production, media selection, placement and budgets throughout the world. This may cover either products, services or corporate efforts. Under this plan of operation, local market management may make recommendations but only corporate headquarters can make decisions. This method of handling is more likely to be found in straight export operations where no member companies are involved.

(2) *Advertising created locally to broad guidelines; followed by periodic reviews.* This procedure represents real autonomy. The advertising is created locally to guidelines set by corporate headquarters and released with no prior corporate clearance. The question of corporate headquarters control versus local control invariably comes up in the handling of advertising for the international company. Certainly the assistance of the nationals of the country is to be encouraged as these people are likely to be able to provide invaluable guidance in making sure that the advertising conforms to the habits and the peculiarities of a particular market. However, there is inherent danger in corporate headquarters relinquishing the authority for determining policy and strategy. In going after world markets, corporate headquarters must be extremely cautious in delegating the interpretation and the presentation of the company, its ideas, its policies and the products themselves to anyone thousands of miles away.

(3) *Locally created advertising but requiring varying degrees of approval, ranging from actual clearances of copy, illustration and layout by central headquarters to simple conformity to established corporate policy and strategy.* Full clearances for advertising requires tight control, excellent communications and carefully defined authorities. Such a procedure is complex and time-consuming.

The world market for most sizable and aggressive companies is far too large, too complex and too varied in character, with local conditions too subject to change, to be served efficiently through the development and execution of centrally controlled, market-by-market advertising programs.

Planning for International Diversity

In the increasingly expanding and complex overseas activity, there is mounting evidence that the greatest success will be achieved through centralization of responsibility for advertising policy and strategy and by the creation of a uniform, distinctive and positive world-wide corporate or brand image as a guide for influencing product or service purchase; and the decentralization of responsibility for local advertising planning and operations, with the flexibility to react quickly to local changes and to utilize first-hand knowledge of the market. This procedure will be served best by the "area management" concept in which local or zone advertising managers, reporting to overall company advertising managers, will direct and supervise the local planning, the execution and the operation with local selling organizations; and with the freedom to utilize the best of local advertising skills and services.

Cultural Influences

Man's style of living dictates the manner in which he consumes, the priority of his needs and wants; so it follows that if the advertising is to succeed it must reflect a sound knowledge of each area in which it appears. Some factual knowledge of each area is relatively easy to acquire through trade reports, business surveys, banks, government offices, advertising agencies, etc. However, a thorough knowledge of each group of people the advertiser hopes to influence, their values, their feelings and their ways of living, so essential to effective communications through advertising, can be obtained only through diligent work and getting to know the people first-hand.

No one could or should try to provide a reference to which an advertiser may go when concerned with the cultural habits of a particular area or country. Likely they are varying and changing. Too much emphasis cannot be placed upon the need for understanding the shades of differences in peoples and areas and the need for critical on-the-spot study of each before preparing the advertising which is expected to stimulate a favorable response. There is no such thing as the Latin American market, the European market, the Scandinavian market. Each area, each country and even sections of countries may vary considerably in their characteristics. The successful international advertiser must learn how such locals differ, not only in language but in consumer attitudes, channels of distribution, competitive environments, market size, maturity, rate of growth and even the means by which the people get their information.

Simple violations of life styles may offend or mark the advertiser as so unknowledgeable as to be unworthy of the reader's or viewer's business. However, appeals cleverly associated with the local customs can be used to bring a favorable attitude toward the product or the company. A knowledge of the people is fundamental to good advertising communications. All good international advertising, like all good advertising at home, begins with people, not products. People buy from people.

While advertising, to be successful, must reflect a knowledge, an understanding and a sensitivity to the distinctive way of life of each area, it may in turn shape the culture of its readers or viewers. Whether it is good or bad, and aside from its direct economic effects, the cultural influences of advertising as it appears in various areas of the world, is tremendous. There would seem to be little question that cultures or life styles are influenced by ideas communicated through advertising. The way most of us think, dress and live reflect our exposure to advertising.

During the years of *Life* magazine's greatest success and *Life International* and *Life en Español* were edited and published especially for areas outside the U.S., I spent much time in Europe and Latin America. Repeatedly I was contacted by local residents with the request to try to arrange for them to receive the U. S. edition. *Life International* and *Life en Español* did an excellent editorial job of reporting events of special interest to readers outside the U. S. and both editions carried advertising directed to those readers. What I learned was that these people wanted to see U. S. advertisements. They wanted to see, and no doubt wanted to be influenced by, what people in the U. S. were buying.

The Importance of Market Research

The lack of thoroughly reliable information, even the statistical variety, around the world generally makes market research difficult. Much of the information available today in the international area is of questionable value and what is done by local research organizations may not be entirely dependable. In some cases the problem lies in lack of research skills but even when competent organizations are to be found, the work may be impeded by practical working problems. Interviewers in Latin America and even France and Italy are looked upon with extreme suspicion. Often these interviewers are thought of as government investigators trying to obtain information for tax purposes. The result is often inaccurate data relating to purchases, income, property ownership etc. As John Fayerweather, professor of International Marketing at New York University, put it:

> These circumstances require first of all a suspicious, exacting approach to foreign market data to assure that reasonable conclusions are drawn from it. Beyond that there is need for reasonable ingenuity in finding and using to the utmost the limited data that are available. For example, one company researching for a barometer of market conditions in Peruvian cities found the answer in the periodic reports of beer tax payments. Finally, the lack of firm statistical data puts a premium on personal observation. In many instances, a large portion of the market research consists of impressions of men who visit a market, talk to people and, in any way they can, pick up a "feel" for the situation. This is no work for beginners. A man must be familiar with similar markets, know what is important and what is unimportant and be able to interpret what he encounters.

While much market research may leave something to be desired, the international advertiser has information sources which isolated mean nothing, but taken collectively can provide a composite story from which the company can get a relatively good idea of the market problem and what is needed to solve it.

Where vital information is lacking, the advertiser may be forced to go into the area and gather it even if the cost is high. Much, even basic, research is yet to be done in many countries around the world. In some nations, even in the Western Hemisphere, little or no reliable information is readily available on such subjects as population and income distribution. However, progress is being made. The statistical situation is slowly improving through the combined efforts of the United Nations and various government agencies. Professional market research societies have been established in England, Holland, France, Germany, Greece, Australia and Japan. In Latin America substantial advances are taking place in Mexico, Brazil and Argentina. These advances have to be impressive since no appreciable work was done in this area prior to the end of World War II.

In general, the ultimate responsibility for market research in the international field is the same as in the domestic area. It rests with the advertiser. While all research methods and techniques should be utilized whenever possible in developing international advertising plans, nothing can be as rewarding as personal on-the-spot contacts with customers, prospects and the local advertising/marketing organization. Actual visits with these people can often provide more valuable information than bundles of correspondence and all of the research reports.

The Media for Advertising

One of the sage observations that Archie Lee, the "Mr. Coca-Cola" of D'Arcy Advertising Company (now D'Arcy, McManus, Masius) years ago used to repeat to some of us trainees was, "The power of an idea is in its circulation." If media are vital to the success of advertising ideas in the U. S. they can be even more important in the complex international area; yet the selection and the evaluation of media for much of the world outside of the U. S. is extremely difficult. In many areas the ideal medium does not exist and, except for international media published in the U. S. for foreign readership, dependable circulation and readership information is almost impossible to come by.

For the international advertiser, print media generally fall into two principal classifications: (1) International and (2) Local. The question of whether the global advertiser should use international media or local media or a combination of both seems nebulous. There can be no logical generalizations on local or international media because the use of either must be determined by the product and its market, the media available, the customs of the people and their particular environments. Obviously, the best medium is that which reaches the people the advertiser wants to influence under the most favorable circumstances and at the most economical rate.

All of the various media—magazines, newspapers, radio, television and outdoor—are available to advertisers outside the U. S. but not all of them in all areas and in the same degree of effectiveness. Each country or each area would seem to present its own media opportunities and its own problems. To examine each fully in a publication of this type would be impossible. Space will not permit; conditions change too frequently. Each would have to be considered on a day-to-day, case-by-case basis.

Periodicals published for distribution internationally are generally classified as: (1) general audience, (2) business papers, and (3) trade publications. Such leading U. S. headquartered publications as the *Reader's Digest* with editions in 13 languages, *Time International, Newsweek International* and *Vision* in the general audience field, with *Fortune, Business Week* and *International Management* in the business area have achieved astonishingly high readership and editorial influence internationally. Many may regard this as a sad commentary on the caliber of local publications. Trade publications such as *Export, El Exportador, Industrial World, El Embotellador, World Farming* and *La Hacienda* have been the pioneer media which have contributed heavily to an extensive U. S. market around the world. Edited exclusively for the overseas audience, the importance and the influence of U. S. export-type trade publications in their particular markets can hardly be overemphasized.

Nowhere in the world has the publication of trade magazines reached the proportions, the high degree of development and the importance that it has in the U. S. However, outside of the U. S., except for England, Canada, Western Germany, Switzerland, Holland, and perhaps Brazil and Argentina, there are few of importance. For the international company, newspapers are used most often for advertising items that can be bought by the consumer. However, in some areas of the world where middle management of the industrial company is a buying influence and does not read international trade publications, highly specialized industrial products or equipment are advertised in the daily newspapers. Knowing that there is nothing as dead as yesterday's newspaper, this is a discouraging commentary on the state of the foreign trade press. While this may represent the most practical solution to the local media problem, the use of local newspapers to reach large areas can be extremely costly. Checking copy and obtaining proofs for approvals in a multiplicity of markets is an almost impossible task. Considering the shortage of suitable business and trade publications around the world, it is not surprising that the U. S. press has moved in to help fill the void.

Newspapers outside of the U. S., both editorially and mechanically, run the gamut from bad to excellent. While local newspapers represent one of the best means of reaching the consumer in foreign countries their use presents some problems. Many of the newspapers in Canada, much of Europe and to some extent in Latin America, rival in scope, editorial content, advertising and general quality the best newspapers in the U. S. In lesser developed areas reproduction standards are poor. Accurate and dependable readership information is seldom available. Particularly in Latin America and on the continent of Europe, many newspapers are the organs of group opinion rather than authentic and unbiased news media as generally found in the U. S. The danger of associating a company's advertising with such a group is obvious.

Radio and television, while not developed technically or in format to the same extent as in the U. S., are strong communications forces in most areas of the world. Use of the broadcast medium is too complex and fast changing to be dealt with here. Each advertiser must evaluate the media, their availability and their value on a case-by-case, country-by-country basis as possible needs arise.

Some Basic Principles

In preparing the advertisements themselves for use around the world, the international company should be guided by a few simple principles: (1) the messages must be meaningful in terms of the experiences of the people they want to influence; (2) the advertisements must communicate something of interest to the intended reader or viewer and stimulate some action, either mental or physical, or both; (3) those advertisements that will succeed best must relate to developments that are new, that avoid association with commonplace materials or ideas that the audience has come to accept as a part of their daily lives; (4) clichés and American "advertisingese" are untranslatable. But warmth, humor and drama are universal: (5) one of the great dangers of universal campaigns is that too often the advertisements that are right, attention-getting, interesting, meaningful and stimulating for one carefully defined audience are not meaningful to another in terms of personal experience.

In presenting the advertisements for international use, the advertiser must make sure; (a) the appeal is entirely compatable with the reader's life style and environment; (b) your audience can readily understand and absorb what you are saying; (c) what you are saying and the way you are saying it does not offend the reader's or viewer's sensitivities. Above all, remember you are creating for another language so keep your words and your copy simple.

Finally, it would seem that there are four fundamental ingredients for successful international advertising: (1) sound mastery of advertising skills and techniques as demonstrated successfully in the U. S.: (2) a basic knowledge of your company, its policies, its products and their uses; (3) a thorough knowledge of the market, the people, their needs, wants, likes and dislikes; and (4) executive leadership with a worldwide perspective and a thorough and sympathetic understanding of the international field.

Roland L. Kramer:

International Advertising Media

IN THE keen competition encountered in world markets, the American foreign trader is aided, as perhaps are the businessmen of no other nation, by the sales-producing force of advertising.

Skillfully planned and directed publicity not only at home but also abroad will overcome prejudice, combat foreign competiton, establish new habits, satisfy wants, build goodwill, and thus multiply sales and lay a foundation for permanent and profitable business.

This is not to say that the businessmen of other industrial nations do not utilize advertising to good advantage. However, mass production in the United States poured such a mountain of products on the market that, in line with the purchasing power of this market, it was necessary to develop mass distribution. Thus, advertising, in all of its branches, was rapidly developed as an integral part of mass distribution.

The subject of advertising in all of its ramifications is extremely complex; and when its usefulness and application in foreign countries are considered, the most that can be attempted in chapters of this nature is to outline the highlights and sketch the principles. Details relating to the use of any one channel of advertising for any one product or service in any one country are exacting. Witness the veritable libraries of books bearing on advertising in the United States market alone.

FUNDAMENTALS OF ADVERTISING ABROAD

At the Ninth International Advertising Convention held in 1957 in New York, Arthur "Red" Motley observed the following four fundamentals of advertising abroad:

> 1. Create a *climate* at home on the part of top management. Try to have them think in terms of the domestic market and to take the same broad vision with regard to international operations. This is probably the most basic of all fundamentals.
>
> 2. Do not think of the overseas market as a poor market. Despite the fact that a certain market may be underdeveloped, there is a market with money and it is interested in quality.

▶ From: *International Marketing*, by Roland L. Kramer. Copyright © (second edition) 1964 by South Western Publishing Company, Burlingame, Calif.—New Rochelle, N.Y.—Cincinnati, Ohio—Chicago, Ill.—Dallas, Tex. Reprinted by permission of the publisher.

3. News is of prime importance so do not overdo prestige or age of company or establishment of a trade name or even the number of gold medals won at trade fairs since 1890 or 1870.

4. People are interested in real people, real situations, and in the use of a product. One of the great fundamentals is that people wish to believe that many other people just like themselves are doing the same thing; use the same equipment, the same product, the same service; have the same fine complexion, the same chic look; and can command the same means of traveling—by automobile.

While all channels of advertising may be used to promote a good corporate image by skillful public relations, there is basically the essential that the company, from top management down, is worthy of the image that is portrayed. This means top management backing and high ethical standards. The phrase "corporate image advertising" is commonly used. It refers to publicity of any and all sorts that will serve to give a good impression of the company that makes the products. In the view of Mr. Maynard, this is preliminary to advertising products. In general, business firms do both simultaneously; for instance, "The world-famous manufacturer of X product invites your consideration of its offerings."

International Advertising Copy

Domestic advertising copy, particularly for use in the publications field, is often found to be unsatisfactory for international advertising purposes. The form in which a story is to be told is said to depend upon the temperament and psychology of the people for whom it is intended. The "snappy" or jocular copy, which appeals to the American public, would not be satisfactory in a more conservative part of the world. Tradition, religion, and economic conditions may dictate the necessity of wording an appeal in such manner as to meet particular situations.

The Frenchman has quite definite ideas about advertising. He prefers a slogan. He will not be bothered with discursive texts (as in more disciplined countries like Germany). Loquaciousness is lost on him. He wants to be captivated and amused at the same time.

And he often gets what he wants. French advertising is original, sometimes brilliant. Despite this there is still a tendency to lose harmony between a brilliant conception and the final ad.

Another failing is the tendency, especially in women's magazines, to pack too many trade names into an ad. This brings about the pretense of its being a consumer ad when in reality it is a dealer's ad.[1]

With respect to Germany, the following observation is made:

[1] *Advertising Age*, Vol. 34, No. 21 (May 20, 1963), p. 56.

Advertising here, generally considered, is still about five years behind the U.S. The VW [Volkswagon] campaign may pave the way for more originality in the usual dead-serious German approach to advertising.[2] Concerning Japan the comment is:

Commercials are generally couched in very polite terms and never come right out and say, "Buy Brand X Today." Such approach is offensive to delicate Japanese sensitivities. Rather the message will attempt an interesting explanation of [the] product and at the end suggest mildly that you try the product once. The most direct ads will say "XYZ Brand Please." [3]

Finally with respect to the Arab world:

Advertising to the 30,000,000 people living in seven Arab lands was almost an unknown commodity ten years ago.

But today, it's estimated that ad budgets for the seven countries are somewhere in the neighborhood of $10,000,000 annually—with most of the money going to Arab and English-language newspapers, local radio and television, cinemas and outdoor.[4]

Illustrations

The use of illustrations in international advertising calls for a knowledge of local conditions in order that they may fit required circumstances. A picture tells a story that is understood everywhere and, particularly in countries where literacy is not high, illustrations may be of greater proportionate value than copy. Color preferences are also to be found and superstitions may sometimes eliminate entirely or may strongly recommend the use of certain subjects for copy purposes. These factors are especially significant in connection with outdoor advertising, window display cards, or other illustrations that appear before the transient public, as well as packages, magazines, and catalogs.

Certain taboos are important and the successful advertiser will take note of them. A few examples will serve to illustrate this fact. Illustrations to be used for advertising in India, for example, should never show a cow—it is a sacred animal. Advertisers in Moslem countries should not forget that the purdah (a screen hiding women from the sight of men or strangers) is not extinct. An advertiser in the Sudan showed a camel in his illustration, knowing that camels are to be found there. Unfortunately he showed a Bactrian (two-humped) camel—and Sudanese camels have but one hump! Animals used to illustrate humans are not attractive or even understandable to Arabs. Allah states that a beast is a beast and a man is a man.

The symbol of three is lucky in West Africa. In the Far East white is the color of mourning among the Chinese and blue is not very lucky, but

[2] *Ibid.*
[3] *Ibid*, p. 78.
[4] *Ibid.*, p. 96.

in the Far and Middle East and Africa red is a very lucky color. Color plays an important role in the lives of these people and all films should be produced in bright colors. In Greece and Cyprus, houses should be white with blue shutters, the national colors of Greece.[5]

Many a sale has been lost which may have taken years of build-up through polite correspondence—only to be thrown to the winds during a personal meeting when one of the parties violates a customs taboo.

The well-meaning American custom of patting a child on the head . . . is one example of a strong Oriental taboo where the head is held sacred. A careless flick of a cigarette into a hearth is also commonplace here in the United States but in Japan the hearth is regarded as sacred.

Our Hong Kong adviser tells that the Chinese do not, as a rule, send clocks as presents. Giving clocks as gifts is strictly taboo . . . since to the Chinese, clocks can be taken as a bad omen. An overseas advertiser should think twice before using a gift-giving angle in his clock promotions.

Perhaps because religion is a more all-pervading life force in the Orient than in the Occident, it is good business sense not to choose an advertising symbol which might offend the religious sensibilities of Eastern peoples.[6]

Translation

A common problem in copy work for international marketing is translation. If it is intended for a British public, it is important to render the copy in the King's English and to recognize differences in American and British spellings and colloquialisms. A more difficult problem is translating copy into a foreign tongue. Particularly in technical translations, as in export catalogs, there may be a complete absence of foreign synonyms for certain English words. Perhaps new words may be coined or a description may be phrased that will correctly convey the idea in the foreign language. Moreover, there is sometimes the question of a number of languages or dialects in a particular market. In India, for example, there are 14 languages and any nation-wide campaign— be it visual or audio—must be planned very carefully.

FIELDS OF INTERNATIONAL ADVERTISING MEDIA

A survey of international advertising media can be only general in character, since the specific conditions that currently affect any particular method or locality are constantly changing.

International advertising media may be divided into three fields: 1. Trade or industrial; 2. Consumer; 3. Professional or ethical.

[5] Bruno Kiwi, Director, Pearl and Dean Overseas Company, London, in *Export Trade* (January 26, 1959), p. 74.
[6] Noble de Roin, President, International Advertising Company, Denver, Colorado, in *Export Trade and Shipper* (May 12, 1958), p. 55. Mr. de Roin also quoted Elma Kelly, Managing Director, Cathay Limited, Hong Kong.

As recognized in domestic practice, *trade* or *industrial* advertising aims to reach distributors, seeking to induce them to stock the merchandise advertised, and commission sales representatives who solicit indent orders. *Consumer* advertising, on the other hand, seeks to induce consumers to purchase advertised products by name or brand from the store or outlet that serves the consumer. *Professional* or *ethical* advertising attempts to influence professional people to prescribe or to advise the use of the publicized produts. Medical and dental publications come to mind in this connection. Some advertising media serve exclusively the aims of one field, but in many instances the media serve exclusively the aims of one field, but in many instances the media may be useful in more than one field.

Foreign Publications. Daily newspapers are among the most effective methods of reaching the buying public in any land. There is no civilized part of the world that does not boast of its newspaper, and the effectiveness of this medium for advertising purposes may be compared favorably with its position in the United States. Indeed, newspapers may afford a greater relative value for advertising purposes abroad than in this country. When the literacy of a people is low, the consuming population for most goods is confined largely to those highest in the economic and social scale. These are generally literate and read the dailies that are published locally. It therefore follows that an advertisement in the newspapers will reach almost the entire effective buying public.

Magazines, weekly or monthly, published abroad are also to be considered by the international advertiser. These may have a wide circulation throughout a country, and in some instances, as in the case of feminine interests, they may provide the only means of special appeal. The use of magazines is important to make United States trademarks and United States products known and to reach distributors or sales representatives who may not be covered by United States trade magazines. Generally, however, magazines in foreign countries are confined in their circulation to a certain locality where they may be of considerable, although restricted, advertising value. One or two examples will serve to illustrate these problems.

Advertising in the Benelux countries introduces problems that are not likely to be anticipated by the uninformed. According to a Belgian, Dan E. G. Rosseels, Advertising Manager of the Belgian editions of *Libelle, Goed Nieuws-Bonnes Nouvelles,* and *Panorama,* a common mistake in advertising in Belgium is to consider that country as French-speaking, whereas 55 percent of the population speaks Flemish.

In the African (Rhodesia and Nyasaland) markets, the white press reaches only a small group of educated Africans.

The advertising value of foreign newspapers and magazines depends, in large measure, on the nature of the product that is advertised. From this standpoint, these advertising media must be carefully studied in order to prevent unnecessary waste of funds.

Problems in Using Foreign Publications. Several serious difficulties may confront advertisers in most foreign publications. It is generally considered that in many foreign countries advertising is behind in its development, when compared with American advertising. This is not true of all publications or of all countries, but the export advertiser is likely to find a different appreciation of advertising abroad from that at home.

Some of the difficult problems that may be encountered are:

1. Difficulty of ascertaining circulation figures. There is seldom to be found abroad any complement of the ABC (Audit Bureau of Circulation) in the United States. Reliable circulation figures for all or a certain number of publications are obtained through ABC or a foreign equivalent in the United Kingdom and the Dominions (Canada, Australia, New Zealand, South Africa, India), Norway, Sweden, Denmark, Argentina, Puerto Rico, Mexico, Venezuela, and Dominican Republic. There is a slow growth abroad in appreciating the value of independent audits of circulation. Therefore, the circulation claims of foreign newspapers and magazines may or may not be accurate.

2. Ascertaining class and sex of readers.

3. Accurate analysis of the purchasing power of readers may also be difficult.

4. Political views of newspapers in foreign countries are often pronounced and the class of readers, for example, liberal, radical, progressive, and labor, may be determined from this attitude. The editorial views of some newspapers may eliminate them from consideration for advertising purposes by American exporters, particularly when these views are un-American or anti-American. In times when the national interest of the United States may not be concerned, however, anti-American editorials may not necessarily be taken seriously.

5. Ascertaining rates and space. The one-price system is an American institution and has yet to win approval throughout the world. There may be alternate haggling and bargaining in dealing with publishers abroad. Sometimes so-called "American" advertising rates are higher than for local advertisers. The higher American rate is claimed to be due to the inclusion of an allowance for the publisher representative's commission, in addition to an advertising agency commission. The United States representatives of international publications advertising and foreign editors should be considered part of overhead.

6. Lack of uniformity of column width and page size, which results in greater production expense for the advertiser.

In addition to the national press, there are newspapers and magazines of other nationalities published in foreign countries. Some United States papers are published abroad, for example, *European Herald Tribune*. Such media may possess a wide appeal when it is considered that publications in English are read by the British, by the Americans, and by many educated local residents.

Direct-Mail Advertising

Direct-mail advertising, in its accepted sense, consists of all forms of publicity sent by an advertiser to prospective customers with the intention and hope of influencing or consummating a sale. In its most extended use by an exporting manufacturer or export house, it provides a flexible counterpart of publication advertising.

Direct-mail advertising is most effective when purchases may be made locally or where inquiries may be addressed to a local dealer or sales office. Direct-mail advertising consists principally of various forms of printed matter transmitted through the mails, for example, letters, catalogs, house organs, booklets, and a large number of miscellaneous forms such as calendars and blotters, which are so well-known in the United States.

Circularization. Circular letters, either individual or in series, are used extensively in international marketing as part of the advertising program.

Export Catalogs. Another direct-mail piece of advertising is the export catalog. An export catalog should provide the sales force necessary to sway a prospect into attention, then consideration, conviction, and finally action. It has to tell its own story and answer all manner of questions or objections that might be raised and otherwise go unchallenged. The catalog cannot argue and convince as does the salesman—it tells its story and then closes its cover.

Motion Pictures (Cinema)

International theater screen advertising is gaining increased recognition as a major, effective and growing medium.[7]

In countries too small to support quality magazines and newspapers, cinema advertising enjoys considerable success. Many theaters in small countries sell commercial film time. In certain areas, however, audiences have grumbled about the quality of cinema advertising, and some governments (Brazil for example) have issued decrees banning them.[8]

It is often thought that theater advertising is restricted only to the showing of "spot" commercials on the theater screen. However, in many world markets, in addition to showing spot commercials we find that they are also running soft-sell short subjects, and newsreels containing paid-for news items such as the opening of a cient's store or similar promotional activity. Ever growing in importance is the use of theatres for merchandising. This includes giving out samples, distributing redeemable coupons and also lobby displays. The last three activities are generally tied in with conventional spot commercials on the screen.

---

[7] International Advertising Association, *International Advertiser*, Vol. 1. No. 1 (June, 1960), p. 10.

[8] *Advertising Age, op. cit.*, p. 93.

Cinema advertising is world-wide. The latest estimate is that there are 140 markets in which theater advertising plays an important role. As such markets grow in importance, an organization devoted exclusively to handling cinema advertising usually is formed. These theater advertising factors are grouped together into two world-wide organizations. The oldest is the *International Screen Advertising Services* with headquarters in London, England. This organization has more than 21 large theater advertising concerns as members and through them theater commercials can be booked in more than 100 world markets.

The second world organization is the *International Screen Publicity Association*. These two organizations cooperate each year in holding the International Advertising Film Festival. Films are designed to take advantage of the large screen and generally tend toward a softer sell with emphasis on amusement values. This is out of respect to the "captive" nature of their audiences.

There are two main types of theater advertising: individual placement and package plans. Individual placement means that one orders a *specific* commercial exhibited in a specific theater for a specific time period. Package purchases involve either a number of theaters on a set circuit or the use of an entertainment vehicle such as a sportsreel, newsreel or revista short subject to encapsulate the commercial. Once spliced into such a short subject, the advertising film remains part of it during all its bookings.

Commercial Fairs and Exhibits

Commercial fairs and exhibits, held at regular intervals in many foreign cities, afford the exporter a novel method of publicity. Such events are more common and are more largely attended than are those in the United States, and in many instances they have attained a high reputation. By engaging space at a fair, distributing literature, and providing demonstrations, it may be possible to obtain good distribution connections abroad.

Among the various private and old established fairs are the Leipzig sample fairs that date from the Middle Ages. The International Sample Fair at Lyon, first held in 1419, annually attracts worldwide attention, and the same is true of the sample fair that has been held at Frankfort-on-Main since the year 1219. Of recent origin is the British Industries Fair that is held annually at London, Birmingham, and Glasgow. The Canadian National Exhibition held each year at Toronto is also wide in scope.

In recent years, as sales efforts have become more direct, American concerns have taken more interest in these events as exhibitors. Formerly they were visited almost exclusively by import buyers who found a wide display of foreign products.

Outdoor Advertising

"Outdoor advertising is one of the major advertising media throughout the world. The tremendous increase in the daily use of the automobile in many countries found corresponding increases in the importance of the outdoor medium." [9]

Outdoor advertising relates to billboards, electric or illuminated signs, and posters. As is true of every method of advertising when used abroad, it will be found that conditions vary widely throughout the world.

Aside from billboards, which are growing in number and effectiveness, located at heavily traveled points and in sporting areas, in a few countries some stores have painted advertisements which are colorful and attractive on walls, doors or metal store front closures.

A new type of display made from thousands of oversized, vari-colored sequins has made its appearance in a few countries. Usually this sign is limited to trade-marks, trade names, or simple designs. If properly located, this display has a glittering, live brilliance which attracts the eye even from a distance.

Some companies have made good use of small, permanent, all-weather enameled metal signs. Sometimes the product trademark or company name could be illustrated without the need for text matter; thus the sign was purchased in bulk for universal distribution. Frequently such signs were purchased and distributed from abroad at a considerable saving. However, companies and their foreign representatives were unanimous in their opinion that the placing of the sign must be done by the manufacturer or his own representative. . . .

The judicious distribution at sporting events of eye shades and fans with advertising messages is effective for some products, as are wall or wallet calendars. However, these are so acceptable that the advertiser must be prepared to meet a demand of astronomical proportions.

Bus cards are good, especially for products usually bought by the bus riders. However, most buses are overcrowded; therefore interior cards are of doubtful value. The outside cards are more visible and the preferred position, those on the back of the bus.

Specific consideration should be given to permanent metal signs in areas where heat, humidity, or other severe weather conditions would make other types of outdoor signs impractical. Under the most favorable conditions, outdoor advertising is managed with the same ease and it produces the same results as in the United States. In many places, however, centralized ownership of outdoor advertising facilities is lacking, rates are not fixed, and municipal ordinances may hinder their employment. Long-range home office supervision is out of the question and branch house, dealer, or agency control over outdoor advertising of all kinds is essential.

Light standards are also equipped in some countries for carrying advertisements. It is true, however, that electric signs, including neon, are nowhere as widely to be found as in the United States; and it is generally admitted that no country has succeeded quite so well in effectively concealing landscapes behind

[9] International Advertising Association, *Code of Standards of Advertising Practice* (New York, 1961), p. 103.

billboards. One American company is fortunate in having a name that lends itself to ingenious Spanish advertising by means of illuminated electric signs. Admiral uses a step by step flashing message in Spanish. The first flash reveals MIRA (Spanish for look!); then follows ADMIRA (Spanish for admire!); finally, the complete name is shown ADMIRAL.

Radio

In recent years, radio advertising has attracted wide and increasing attention and American advertisers have been prompt in investigating possibilities of the radio for promoting foreign sales.

Radio advertising in international marketing is conducted almost entirely through local broadcasting stations abroad. These stations are either government owned and controlled (generally accepting no advertising) or they are independent. Many of them broadcast both long- and shortwave. Radio chains have been slow in developing in the various countries.

Radio advertising has shown vast drawing power, particularly for promoting the sale of consumer goods. This is of special value in advertising in countries with low literacy ratios, but with purchasing power for the advertised product. The number of radio listeners in an overseas area, such as Latin America, cannot be accurately determined from the estimated number of radio-receiving sets because of the installation of loud speakers at public squares, markets, cafes, drug and department stores, beaches, hotels, and amusement resorts.

Television

Television, the newcomer to the advertising media field (having been introduced in the United States as recently as 1947), is arousing the same interest abroad that it has in this country. Progress of installing television transmitting stations in foreign countries was slow due to the great expense of the equipment.

Three systems of controlling television are in effect throughout the world today:

1. The multiple enterprise system used in the United States and in Latin America.
2. The monopolistic system used, for example, in Belgium and France.
3. The combination system such as used in Italy and Great Britain.

Multiple Enterprise System. Under this system numerous broadcasting stations are permitted to operate; and they operate for commercial profit. This system is the plan used in the United States.

Monopolistic system. No commercial broadcasting is permitted under the monopolistic system. In France, for example, television is controlled by Radiodiffusion Tèlèvision Français (RTF). "General programs are varied in scope and content, including drama, films, newsreels, sports, panel shows, and Eurovision." The last named, Eurovision, was pioneered by RTF and BBC (British Broadcasting Company) television and consists of a network linking eight European countries—the United Kingdom, Switzerland, the Netherlands, Italy, German Federal Republic, France, Denmark, and Belgium.

Combination System. Under this system, used in Great Britain and in Italy, "prior to 1955, British TV viewers on a particular night were treated to a one and one-half hour program called, 'The Development of the Lung Fish.' Viewers were either left gasping for breath or irrevocably opposed to 'culture' in such large doses." In 1955, the Independent Television Authority (ITA) was formed and was placed under the control of the Postmaster General. All television facilities are owned, in the name of the government, by the Postmaster General who grants concessions to four private program contractors. These contractors now command 70 to 90 percent of the television audience and obtain revenue from commercials. Advertisers do not control nor sponsor programs. The commercials are sold adjacent to or within the programs.

Italy permits no live commercials; but film commercials are permitted for two and one-fourth minutes, of which only 20 seconds may be used for actual selling. The remaining one minute and fifty-five seconds must show anything considered to be quality entertainment.

S. Watson Dunn:

The International Language of Advertising

WHEN the marketing executives of Standard Oil of New Jersey tried to convince their marketing counterparts in the various Standard Oil subsidiaries, affiliates, and joint ventures in Europe that they should adopt the now famous "Tiger in your tank" campaign in each of these markets, they were told, quite emphatically I understand, that the campaign—fine as it was for the United States—just would not work in these countries. The Europeans, however, were finally persuaded to give the campaign a try, and the result is a classic success story of how to internationalize advertising. Last summer I asked the head of McCann-Erickson's Paris office why so many European businessmen had resisted the campaign, and he said many still feel you have to be a native to know how to persuade people of a given country.

Let me cite another instance before we try to decide what we mean by the "international language of advertising." Approximately a year ago Kraft Foods beamed by means of satellite a closed circuit telecast originating in New York to the company's annual international management conference in Burgenstock, Switzerland. This was part of Kraft's continuing plan, according to its present, William Beers, to find out how to use international commercial television to create an international image for the company and its products. There are, of course, a few language problems to be considered, but this is not, according to Kraft officials, as much of a problem as it might seem, because the commercials depend heavily on the visual to get their story across. Even though some of the products are regional in appeal, some, such as processed cheese, for example, are sufficiently international that they could be promoted almost anywhere in the world.

After considering these and many other examples, after supervising a series of research studies in Europe and the Middle East, and after talking at some length with many of the older and more experienced international marketers, I have come to the conclusion that we are moving quite rapidly toward an international language of advertising. It is my contention that we are building an international language of symbols, some of which are pictorial—for example, illustrations of certain "international types" of people and logotypes like that of IBM—and some of which are word symbols understandable in any language—

for example, "OK" and "marketing." It is quite possible in fact that international advertising reaches more people than any other type of message emanating from a foreign source, that Mrs. Popapopoulis in Athens or Señora Gomez in Argentina is more likely to see or hear some foreign advertising message than she is to see or hear some message from U.S. Information Agency or its counterpart in some other country. Although reliable data on international investments by advertisers are hard to come by, it is fairly clear that the top three or four U.S. advertisers spend more in foreign advertising and promotion than the U.S.I.A. has to spend on all its various operations outside the United States.

This is not to say that basic differences in cultures are lacking. In fact, I suspect that one must have a pretty good knowledge of cultural differences to be able to use international advertising effectively. Our cultural anthropologists have studied and reported on many of these differences. Edward Hall, for example, has related many of them to the problem of communication in his book, *The Silent Language*. [1] He points out that a common way for an Iranian male to communicate his manliness is to throw a temper tantrum—for example, the famous ones of Mossadegh a few years ago. Most Americans think it shows you have a low opinion of a person if you keep him waiting to see you when he has an appointment. On the other hand, many Latin Americans find it surprising that Americans should feel offended at what seems to them such a minor occurrence. Or consider how the broad humor of the Old West offends many Orientals who prefer humor in its more subtle forms.

The various *prototype* campaigns represent a recognition that there is a sort of international creative approach that works in a variety of markets. When he prepares such a campaign, the American advertiser is saying to marketing people in his foreign subsidiaries, or his licensees or distributors, that a layout or a copy theme which worked in the United States is pretty likely to work there too, provided there is a good translation of the verbal material and there is some checking to see that the ad does not violate any foreign taboos. Some companies, for example, Coca Cola and Remington Rand, appear to have had considerable success with prototype material. Some have run into resistance on the part of local marketing people, and some U.S. companies just do not bother to prepare prototype material at all.

Findings in Case and Field Studies

During these new few years many an advertiser will face the problem of determining to what extent he should internationalize his advertising. In an effort to throw some light on this complicated question and to gain certain information as a guide for planning our field studies, I conducted, in 1964–1965, a series of case studies of the foreign campaigns of thirty large international advertisers. [2] Most of these were U.S. corporations and most focused on a cam-

---

[1] Edward T. Hall, *The Silent Language* (New York: Doubleday & Co., 1959).
[2] "Case Study Approach in Cross-Cultural Research," *Journal of Marketing Research* Vol. III (February 1966), pp. 13–24.

paign in one western European country and one underdeveloped country. We were trying to find out under what conditions sophisticated and experienced marketers were using domestic campaigns abroad. We found that one criterion was the type of product advertised. For example, six out of seven food companies we studied made only minimal effort to internationalize their promotion. It was felt by the executives concerned that food preferences and eating habits varied so much from one market to another that common appeals or ads were fruitless. On the other hand advertisers of patent medicines tended to use much the same approach in all markets—the prevention of disease or the relief of discomfort. However, in a few cases they had to change certain symbols. For example, Vicks promoted its Vaporub for the relief of cold discomfort in children in a wide variety of countries. In the Arab countries the company substituted illustrations of little boys for those of little girls since the health of a little boy is a matter of somewhat more importance there than that of a little girl. We found also that international advertising and marketing experts used certain marketing criteria to determine the transferability of campaigns: What is the competition doing? They used certain cultural criteria: Are there any real cultural or psychological barriers to acceptance of this campaign in that market? And they used media considerations: Are the media for which we designed this campaign in the U.S. available also in the new market?

We followed up these case studies with a series of field tests in France and Egypt. [3] We ended up with some very convincing evidence that the language of advertising is indeed more international than many people seem to suspect. We were trying to find out under what conditions an American advertisement would be successful in a foreign market. The five products we chose were all low-priced convenience items, and all the ads had been run in at least one American magazine. We used three variations of the illustrative material and two of the headlines and copy—all of them consistent with the original creative platform. One of the illustrations was the original as used in an American magazine, one replicated this illustration with French models and another with Egyptian models. One version of the copy and headlines consisted of an idiomatic translation into French and Arabic. The other was composed from the original by a professional copywriter of the country. The audiences consisted of a good sample of middle and upper middle class consumers in the largest city in each country and we used three measures of effectiveness for each ad. All of us who worked on the study were somewhat surprised to find how little difference there was in the effectiveness of the various versions—regardless of which measure of effectiveness you used. There was little evidence indeed to support the fact that in a case such as this you needed a local model or that you needed to attribute the message to a local—as compared with a foreign—source and only limited evidence that the message started from scratch was more effec-

---

[3] See Final Report, Group Psychology Branch, Office of Naval Research, Contract Nonr 1202 (24), "Study of the Influence of Certain Cultural and Content Variables on the Effectiveness of Persuasive Communications in the International Field."

tive than a good, refined translation from the U.S. original. The skill with which the material was translated was more influential in the case of France than of Egypt. I should point out, though, that the type of products chosen were ones we knew were used internationally, and the appeals featured in the ads violated no cultural or other taboos in these countries.

I should point out, too, that the audience was not a mass audience but was instead an urban, middle class one. Some people maintain that there is within each country an audience which looks for foreign symbols, foreign clothes, and foreign movies and that it prides itself on being distinct from the mass audience, so perhaps our audiences were too atypical. However, I am inclined to suspect that we have, within each country, many international audiences, one tuned to sports, another to music, another to food, and so forth. In general, the study raised as many questions as it answered. For example, why were the Egyptians more influenced by *all* versions than the French? Would the results have been different if the respondents had seen different brands of the same product instead of different products? If we had had a measure of the self-confidence or the expertise or the sophistication of these respondents would the results have been different?

Implications of Research Findings

I would like now to explore some of the implications of the developments I have been discussing—for business, for government, and for society in general.

First of all, there is the implication that some of these days you will be able to avoid the waste of starting over again when a campaign is transferred to a foreign market. And what a saving this could be! Think how scarce really good creative concepts are. And how much we need to get full use from a really good one. Think how much better it would be if we could use the original—or at least a good part of it—to communicate in another market. This implies, though, that the creative people or whoever works with them will know enough about foreign communication and culture to make needed changes but will still have the know-how and the guts to insist that foreign advertisers keep what is worth keeping.

Furthermore creative people have to be just as careful with the visual aspects of this advertising language as with the more obvious verbal pitfalls.

For example, a series of television commercials integrating white and colored persons was prepared in France for use in the United States by an American advertiser. Sometime after the commercials were in production the head of the Paris office of the American agency involved noted that one of the stars was not an American Negro, as planned, but was instead a Negro from French Africa with just enough difference in facial features to be noticeable. It was decided to recast the commercial.

I do not mean to imply that we can forget what we know and practice regarding market segmentation. Rather the developments I have been discussing mean that segmentation along national lines may become less important, that the differences between national and foreign markets will diminish, and that our markets will be segmented along more sophisticated, more meaningful demographic or perhaps even psychological lines.

This internationalization also implies that we may see a great spurt in the growth of truly international agencies and media. Although much is made these days of the fact that American agencies are establishing a multitude of offices abroad—frequently through purchase of a sizable stock interest in an ongoing agency—the fact is that a good many of these are American in name only. Many of these are native agencies with an American name and perhaps an American or two on the staff. I doubt that these need ever become truly American or even that they need have many American employees, but I think it is quite possible that their point of view might become more multinational, less parochial and nationalistic.

I would like to look also at some of the implications in fields other than advertising. For example, the field of economic growth. This is a fashionable topic these days, but most people who talk about it as applied to the underdeveloped areas worry mainly about how to increase agricultural or manufacturing output. However, I for one suspect that advertising can contribute a good deal to these economies just as it has to ours in the United States and to those of western Europe. We know that even in the days when the United States was truly one of the underdeveloped areas of the world, promotion played an important part in supporting the struggling media, in helping innovators with a real product advantage gain product acceptance, in informing consumers of product development. A lot of us have followed with interest the change in the Soviet party line since 1957 when advertising became for the first time quite respectable. Last year *Pravda* included the following:

> The more goods and products in the shops—the greater the need for advertising, for providing customers with systematic qualified information on the quality and features of one or another commodity and on where it can be bought.

The largest department store in Moscow, GUM, spends six million rubles a year ($5,400,000 at current exchange rates) on advertising and has a staff of fifty to handle print and broadcast advertising, window displays, commercials broadcast in the store, leaflets to be distributed on the counters and posters inside and outside the store. Moscow television currently carries five to ten minutes of advertising three or four times a week. We can hardly say that Russia is supporting advertising for sentimental reasons since encouraging it involved an embarrassing change in government policy. Instead we must conclude that there is substantial evidence that it contributes to that country's economic growth—even though it is a socialist economy.

Perhaps a more obvious implication of these developments lies in the field of propaganda. Arthur Meyerhoff in his *Strategy of Persuasion* insisted the United States has made a serious mistake in not "applying our sales techniques to selling ourselves and our ideas to other countries." [4] There are of course big differences between selling soap and selling our foreign policy, but there are also certain similarities. If U.S. marketers can find out how to communicate effectively with the various nations of the world, it seems highly advisable that the government use what is known to get its story across also. It is interesting to note that the new director of the U.S.I.A. is already at work exploring how advertising measurement methods can be used to test the effectiveness of some of the organization's communications program. A series of meetings devoted to this topic were held recently, and selected specialists in advertising research were invited to participate.

Most Americans are a bit wary of propaganda—even the name has a bad connotation. In addition we are inclined to be sensitive about being the big nation of the world and to worry about throwing our weight around. Consequently, the evidence is that our government's programs have been heavy on information but light on persuasion. However, if we learn how to communicate across national borders should not we share it with our government?

We should also consider the other side of the coin—the possible negative aspects of internationalizing our language. We may look back twenty years from now and wish we had not been quite so successful in our internationalizing efforts. Perhaps when we find out how to use this international language, how to apply this common denominator of persuasion, we may at the same time level some of the values and the customs that make one region so different from another. Perhaps we shall no longer be able to say about some of those charming spots in western Europe, "*Vive la différence.*" Many of them will undoubtedly retain their basic charm, but there is bound to be a certain lessening of the differences that give a country or region its basic character. If the people of Germany respond so readily to the language of the Beatles—whatever it is—and the people of Vietnam quicken to Batman, how can we avoid a certain lessening of differences in values and in customs from country to country?

Suggestions for Utilizing International Language in Advertising

Some advertisers are making out fairly well these days in using this international language of advertising. Many are not doing so well. What needs to be done?

First of all, I think we must find out a lot more about it than we know now. We must have research. Doesn't it seem strange that we have so little research evidence in the area of advertising where we are least at home and where the pitfalls are the greatest—in the international field? Most of you can probably put your hands on studies of almost any market I could name in the

---

[4] Arthur E. Meyerhoff, *The Strategy of Persuasion* (New York: Coward-McCann, Inc., 1965) p. 15.

United States—and even if you couldn't find research evidence, you could probably make out pretty well without it. But think how different the situation is in the international field. Now I realize the problems one may run into in international research—for example, the cost, the scarcity of trained personnel, the difficulty of getting cooperation from audiences, and so on. However, these are often overestimated. At any rate they are certainly not insurmountable.

I would like to repeat a proposal I made at the Stockholm meetings of the International Advertising Association in 1963. At that time I suggested that the leading international agencies, advertisers, and media cooperate in the establishment of an international advertising research organization. More specifically I would like to suggest that we have this organization set up several international advertising experiment stations in major cities of the world—for example, New York, London, Paris, Frankfurt, and Tokyo. Campaigns from various clients and various countries would be tested simultaneously in these areas. Some evidence could be gained fairly quickly regarding the effectiveness of alternative creative or media or even overall promotional strategies. Comparisons could be made among countries and even among groups within a particular country. We have come a long way in the use of the experimental approach in advertising—note, for example, the Milwaukee Advertising Laboratory and the experimental work of Du Pont and of Ford Motor Company. My predecessor at the University of Illinois, C. H. Sandage, has for some years advocated a U.S. advertising experiment station. Why not put the same idea into effect on an international scale?

My second suggestion is that we get busy educating people for the international advertising field. There is a notion in certain firms that a person who can operate effectively in this country can do just as well in the international field. I am not at all certain this is true when I observe some of the failures in international advertising and marketing. I am proposing that we try to train people to be international communicators just as we train foreign service officers for our government and international lawyers for our big law firms. It is true that certain people have better personalities and more aptitude for the international field than others, but all can profit from the right kind of training.

What kind of education do we need to provide? I think we can benefit from the experience of the successful advertising education programs around our American universities. Emphasis would be placed on a strong liberal arts base with considerable stress on languages and social science. The international adman should know psychology, cultural anthropology, economics, and marketing. However, he should also know something of the philosophy and practice of advertising with particular emphasis on problem solving and decision making in the international field. How much more efficient it is to provide university training in these areas than to expect on-the-job training to prepare people properly.

A good deal of attention is paid these days to the problem of attracting bright, young college graduates to the business field. A lot of these students believe that the horizons in government or teaching are less confining than business and that the pay there is after all satisfactory for their needs. A program geared to international horizons just might attract students who feel that business as a whole—and particularly advertising—is a little too shallow to challenge the best that they have to offer. To work though, such a program would need a lot more support than the advertising industry has so far been willing to give to advertising education. It would need moral as well as financial support. Recently the "Adwoman of the Year," Jo Foxworth of Calkins and Holden, pointed out in a speech that "there is a particular piece of arrogance in the ad business which holds that advertising can not be learned in school . . . that it can be learned only on Madison Avenue by a process of osmosis." Miss Foxworth could not be more correct. The interesting thing is that this situation does not hold in such other creative areas as art and music or in such other business areas as accounting or business law. There it is taken for granted that a person must undergo certain training before starting his professional career.

Third, I would suggest that advertising campaigns be planned on a multinational basis. When you collect the planning facts, when you work out the media and the creative strategy, expect that it will be applied to many markets, not just to one. Assume that the segmenting is along demographic lines—age, sex, and the like—or along user lines—heavy vs. light—and that it may or may not follow national boundaries.

And, finally, I would suggest that we accept the fact that the United States is not the only country where advertising talent—creative, research or any other kind—abounds. A few years ago we could say that the *word* was in the U.S. and if you wanted to learn how to communicate through advertising you had better get your feet wet on Madison Avenue. But take a look at some of the graphics they are using in Western Europe and Japan. Or look at some of the cinema commercials from France or Italy. We can learn a lot from them—not only on how to communicate with their country, but also how to communicate in our own country. Some of these foreign advertising examples represent the language of advertising at its creative best.

There are many more questions I might raise, but I had better not because I am not sure I can propose even tentative answers. What, for example, is the role of the verbal versus the visual in communicating in a foreign area? Is a television campaign more international than one in print? These are among the questions I would like to leave to you.

Barbara Baerns:

International Business Public Relations

BUSINESS public relations traditionally had its origins in the United States towards the end of the nineteenth and beginning of the twentieth centuries. The context was seen to be one of advancing industrialization and urbanization, the result of rapid technological development, and of increasing non-transparency of large-scale enterprise and production processes, combined with more outspoken articulation of employees' interests and literary and political "muckraking campaigns" through which the misuse of economic power was harshly criticized.[1] Bearing these trends in mind, various authors could explain why a number of former journalists employed by private enterprise earned a reputation for themselves between 1888 and 1917 for defending industrial interests against public criticism. They worked either independently or as the salaried personnel of the firms concerned, in so-called literary bureaus, news or publicity bureaus or departments, and thus helped to establish what was thought to be a "new" profession in the communications field.

In this connection, in the literature under consideration, one's attention is especially focused upon the example of Ivy L. Lee, who until 1903 worked as a Wall Street reporter for the New York *World.* Lee in his subsequent occupation, it seems, was not satisfied simply in being the mouthpiece of the business enterprises he assisted (Anthracite Coal Corporation George F. Baer and Associates, Pennsylvania Railroad and Standard Oil (Rockefeller)). He also impressed upon his clients the need for publicizing their conduct of business as well as scrutinizing and adjusting their policies with the interests of the general public in mind. Only in such ways could a better climate and more sympathetic press coverage be achieved.[2] This aspect, adjusting private to general interests as a precondition for public expression of aims and policies, was seized upon by the second generation of American pioneers in public relations; they argued that it was the most essential aspect of their job.[3] Further attempts to define public relations in such a way that advertising on the one hand and propaganda (explained as one-sided indoctrination) on the other were excluded, finally led to definitions where the term was almost a synonym for two-way-communication.[4] The term "public relations," for the phenomenon we are looking at, was first used, according to Cutlip and Center, by the Association of American Railroads in their Yearbook of Railway Literature.[5]

▶ This is an original article written for this book (1976) by Dr. Barbara Baerns, Ruhr University Bochum (German Federal Republic). Translated into English by Stefan R. Melnik, B.A.

Business PR—an American Invention?

Not only American authors but also those of other nationalities see the history of business public relations in its beginnings as being particular to the United States.[6] Haacke, however, in the case of Germany, rightly points out—and thus helps to correct this picture—that industrial public relations is not as new as it seems. Already in the mid-nineteenth century, he writes, the Rhineland industrialist, Gustav Mevissen, inspired by the renowned writer and commentator on economic affairs, Friedrich List, made the suggestion that criticism of share-holding corporations should be countered (and thus weakened) by the maximum of publicity possible.[7] Mevissen's aim, in his own words, was "neither the disclosure of current business transactions nor the monthly publication of income and expenditure, which in most cases do not allow one to predict final performance with any certainty, but the publication of a detailed annual report describing the company's overall situation." [8] In support of his arguments he referred to the example of the railway companies of that time, whose practices in this respect he thought worth following.

At about the same time in Germany, to bring a further example, Alfred Krupp was also considering ways and means of developing an image for his industrial enterprise at home and abroad. In a letter to his financial advisor, Albert Pieper, dated 27th November, 1866, he wrote: "We think . . . it is time that authoritative reports concerning factory matters in accordance with the facts should be propagated on a regular basis through newspapers which serve to enlighten the public. We can supply the material for this purpose and should qualified experts at times be unavailable, it is our wish to contact respectable newspaper editors ourselves." [9]

As can be discerned from later Krupp documents it proved impossible for Alfred Krupp to find an assistant with the qualifications required for such work. However, his son, Friedrich Alfred Krupp, commissioned Adolf Lauter in 1893 with the setting up of a news bureau. This department officially became an integral part of the firm's organization plan in 1901 and a year later published its first report in which press information activities ("propaganda"), press documentation and protocol were described.[10]

These examples taken from German industrial history serve to emphasize the point that reliance hitherto on American public relations literature has led to the overlooking or disregard of a historical question which should have been quite obvious: Did public relations activities arise on the behalf of industrial enterprise outside the United States and independently of the American example as a result of similar social, political and economic changes, which created a need for and encouraged new techniques in communication? This will remain an open question until comparable monographs describing national developments are available.

Contemporary International Public Relations

In one of his recent publications Bernays is of the opinion that for each country public relations means something different.[11] As with the historical perspective which we have dealt with above, this argument concerning the current situation can also be refuted, despite the lack of individual studies, through a comparison of a) the growth of membership; b) the aims; and c) the function and role of such activities as various national public relations organizations see them. The existence of such organizations is itself an indicator of a general trend. National public relations organizations, as opposed to smaller professional bodies organized according to industrial branches, are a post-1945 development. Such large scale organizations, are now fairly common.[12] Their members for the most part are freelance or independent public relations consultants or the salaried staff of public relations departments in business or industrial enterprise, in public institutions, and in associations and federations representing various interests. The strongest contingent of public relations experts usually comes from the field of industry and commerce.

A non-standardized questionnaire was sent to the 15 European national public relations organizations, of which 60% (9 countries) were answered and returned. These could be included in the analysis (see Table 1). Apart from that, data concerning public relations organizations in the USA, Canada, Chile, Malaysia and Egypt were used (see Table 2).

From the relevant data available it was possible to reconstruct the growth

Table 1 : European Public Relations Organisations

Country	Name of Organisation	Seat of Organisation	Year of Foundation	Objectives A* B** C***	Means of Finance	No. of Members in 1975
Great Britain	The Institute of Public Relations	London	1948	A B C	Membership Subscriptions	3.610
Norway	Norsk Public Relations Klubb/ until 1973: Norsk Public Relations Forening	Oslo	1950	A B · C	Membership Subs. Income from Further Education Courses	200
France	Association Française des Relations Publiques/ until 1955: La Maison de Verre	Paris	1952	A B C	Membership Subs.	1.200
Ireland	Public Relations Institute of Ireland	Dublin	1953	A B	Membership Subs.	-
Belgium	Centre Belge des Relations Publiques/Belgisch Centrum voor Public Relations	Brussels	1953	A B C	Membership Subs. Donations from Industry	500
Italy	Federazione Italiana Relazioni Pubbliche	Rome	1954 1970 2nd Establishment	A B C	Membership Subs.	434
German Fed. Republic	Deutsche Public Relations Gesellschaft	Cologne	1958	A B C	Membership Subs.	712
Denmark	Dansk Public Relations Klub	Copenhagen	1961	A B	Membership Subs.	125
Spain	Agrupacion Española de Relationes Publicas	Barcelona	1965	A C	Membership Subs. Donations from Industry	560

* A : The objective to unite those engaged in the profession and thus to establish a common platform for discussion.

** B : The objective to promote high standards of public relations practice through provision of educational opportunities.

*** C : The objective to describe for the public the functions of public relations and of those who practice it.

Table 2 : Non-European Public Relations Organisations

Country	Name of Organisation	Seat of Organisation	Year of Foundation	Objectives A* B** C***	Means of Finance	No. of Members in 1975
USA	Public Relations Society of America	New York	1947	A B C	Membership Subscriptions	7.300
Canada	The Canadian Public Relations Society/La Société Canadienne des Relations Publiques	Ottawa	1948	A B C	Membership Subs.	1.100
Chile	Instituto Chileno de Relaciones Publicas	Santiago	1959	A C	Membership Subs.	270
Malaysia	Institut Perhubungan Raya Malaysia	Kuala Lumpur	1962	A B C	Membership Subs. Income from Further Education Courses	220
Arab Republic of Egypt	The Arab Public Relations Society	Cairo	1965	B C	Membership Subs. Donations	500

* A : The objective to unite those engaged in the profession and thus to establish a common platform for discussion.

** B : The objective to promote high standards of public relations practice through provision of educational opportunities.

***C : The objective to describe for the public the functions of public relations and of those who practice it.

of membership numbers in various national organisations (see Figure below). The following conclusions could be drawn: In the three countries—the USA, Great Britain and Canada—where between 1947 and 1948 the first national public relations organizations were established, membership numbers increased

Figure: Growth of Membership Numbers of National Public Relations Organisations between 1947 and 1975

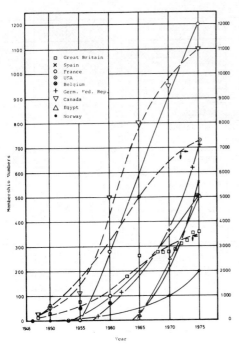

Explanatory comments:

1. Trends have been demonstrated more clearly by a smooth curve which compensates for minor fluctuations in the positions of the points derived from available data.

2. If figures for membership numbers in the year of foundation were unavailable, zero was taken as the starting point.

constantly until 1965/1970. The increase is less rapid after this period, and it possibly attains its final level in the foreseeable future. In every other country where such professional organizations were established at later dates, the first stage has not yet been superseded. If one can draw any conclusions from the first group's experience, France and Belgium may be the next countries where the trend levels off.

Similarly, the main objectives of public relations organizations correspond to a large degree. They can be generalized as follows:

• the objective to unite those engaged in the profession and thus to establish a common platform for discussion;

• the objective to promote high standards of public relations practice through provision of educational opportunities; and

• the objective to describe for the public the functions of public relations and of those who practice it.

In all countries under consideration, public relations organizations publish a periodical to help achieve such objectives (see Table 3). Two publications appear on a regular basis in the United States. Such a periodical is being planned in Chile. Six, as far as content is concerned, reach beyond the scope of a circular and can be described as professional journals. The circulation figures for three of these—*Public Relations Journal*, USA; *PR-magazin*, German Federal Republic; and *The Arab Public Relations Journal*, Arab Republic of

Table 3 : Periodicals Published by National Public Relations Organisations

Country	Publisher of Periodical	Name of Periodical	Frequency of Publication Per Year	Circulation	Content A[1] B[2] C[3]
Great Britain	The Institute of Public Relations	PUBLIC RELATIONS (until December 1951: Pro Fide)	4 x	–	(A) (B) (C)
Norway	Norsk Public Relations Klubb	ExPRessen	6 x	350	A B
France	Association Française des Relations Publiques	LA MAISON DE VERRE	6 x	1.500	A B
Ireland	Public Relations Institute of Ireland	Circular	irregular	–	(A)
Belgium	Centre Belge des Relations Publiques/ Belgisch Centrum voor Public Relations	NEWSLETTER	4 x	500	A B C
Italy	Federazione Italiana Relazioni Pubbliche	Circular	6 x	440	(A)
German Fed. Republic	Verlag Rommerskirchen in Cooperation with Deutsche Public Relations Gesellschaft	PR-magazin	6 x**	1.000***	A B C
Denmark	Dansk Public Relations Klub	PRspektiv	6 x	125	A B C
Spain	Agrupacion Española de Relationes Publicas	HOYAS INFORMAS	12 x	600	A B
USA	Public Relations Society of America	PUBLIC RELATIONS JOURNAL / PRSA National Newsletter	12 x / 12 x	10.000 / 7.300	A B C / A B
Canada	The Canadian Public Relations Society/ La Société Canadienne des Relations Publiques	Circular	4 x	1.100	(A)
Arab Republic of Egypt	The Arab Public Relations Society	THE ARAB PUBLIC RELATIONS JOURNAL	4 x	5.000	A B C
Malaysia	Institut Perhubungan Raya Malaysia	PERHUBUNGAN	4 x	200	A B
Chile	Instituto Chileno de Relaciones Publicas (being planned)		–	–	–

1) A : News on organisation's activities
2) B : Current public relations news
3) C : Discussion and analysis of theoretical questions

* The figures in brackets are reconstructions which could not be checked.
** Monthly publication between January and June, 1975, (incl.). Publication was on a quarterly basis until the end of 1974.
*** Publications on special subjects are printed in an edition of 5.000 to 7.500 copies (information from the publisher dated 1st December, 1975).

Egypt—indicate that there is a larger (presumably professional) public for such literature than the membership figures would allow one to infer.

Although not expressly said in one case, basic and further training courses play a significant role in the activities of all public relations organizations. All organize basic and advanced courses on the techniques, principles and aims of the profession on a regular basis, with the exception of Italy and Denmark where they are held at irregular intervals. On top of this—in Norway, France, the German Federal Republic, Great Britain, the USA and Egypt—such organizations cooperate to a limited extent with universities and other institutions of higher education in working out courses on public relations. Complete officially recognized university or advanced courses on the subject exist in France, Spain and the USA.

Questions concerning the functions and aims of public relations as professional organizations see them were orientated on the definition in its present stage of development indicated above. They took as their premise the contention that—leaving the term "public relations" aside—the concept is qualitatively new and that, as far as existing forms of persuasive communication are concerned, it can and should be kept distinct from advertising and propaganda. (See Table 4). The answers given by each organization unmistakably show (disregarding an exception, where the US organization pleads for close cooperation between the two) the importance that is attached to differentiation between advertising and public relations. As for the status of product publicity—in our opinion advertising by non-conventional means—there seems to be uncertainty

Table 4 : Public Relations Definitions of National Public Relations Organisations

Country	"Public relations and advertising should be kept distinct"	"Product publicity can be assimilated to public relations"	"Public relations is two-way communication"
Great Britain	0	0	+
Norway	+	+	+
France	+	0	+
Ireland	0	0	0
Belgium	+	+	+
Italy	+	+	+
German Fed. Republic	+	±	+
Denmark	+	−	+
Spain	0	0	0
USA	−	+	+
Canada	+	±	+
Arab Republic of Egypt	+	−	+
Malaysia	+	+	+
Chile	+	+	+

+ yes
± undecided
− no
0 no reply

and disagreement: six organizations accepted it as being part of the range of public relations activities; two were against inclusion; two were undecided; and four did not answer at all. The Canadian Public Relations Society, for instance, shows its own indecision confronted by this problem when it says that it does "not normally promote (product publicity) although some practitioners of public relations wear more than 'one hat' ". On the other hand, there seems to be a general consensus in maintaining that public relations is not a one-sided process (propaganda) but a form of two-way (reciprocal) communication. The relevant thesis was universally supported without further comment.

Industrial and Commercial PR in Socialist States

To the extent of our knowledge, socialist states have largely been excluded from studies on the subject. It is regarded as being a phenomenon of the "free world." Cutlip and Center, for instance, write that ". . . public relations grows best in a climate characterized by three dominant elements: 1. a stable and democratic government; 2. a political and economic system that allows the development of private enterprise and encourages competition in many fields of endeavor; 3. the existence of prosperous and thoroughly independent media, over which the government has a minimum of control." [13] Marxist authors agree, but completely reverse the premises. [14] A closer look at the facts will help to correct the picture that public relations is practiced only in systems based on private enterprise.

The Ministerial Council of the German Democratic Republic (GDR) finalized and published "Principles for public relations activities (*Öffentlichkeitsarbeit*) including those of press consultants in government, local government and business enterprise" on 6th December, 1967, which foresaw that under the responsibility of state authorities and economic enterprise public relations offices would organize and coordinate public relations work in areas of state activity. [15] The principles were refined and approved by the VIIIth Party Conference of the East German Socialist Unity Party (*Sozialistische Einheitspartei Deutschlands*) held between the 15th and 19th June, 1971, which proclaimed the beginning of developed socialism. Willi Stoph, at that time chairman of the Ministerial Council of the GDR, said in a speech outlining the future five-year economic plan that "effective channels of information and public relations are crucial to effective leadership. It is important to work closely with the press, radio and television. State officials should address workers-collectives more frequently and give more time and attention to press, radio and television in order to explain State measures and decisions; describe exemplary initiatives in socialist competition; and answer the questions of the working population convincingly. The authorities of State and economy must supply the delegates of the people's representatives with concrete and lucid information which will help them to make decisions competently, discuss resolutions with the working population and organize the implementation and control of policies." [16]

The periodical, *Neue Deutsche Presse*, the organ of the Journalist Association of the GDR, has given space since December 1971, to discussion between experts on the topic of public relations. Worth noting is the fact that public relations is characterized as a function of leadership, even though its individual features and aspects, as they are described, hardly differ at all from those of Western industrial nations. Experts employed in this field, for the most part journalists themselves, have been integrated into the association. Generally, they are members of special subgroups (*Sektionen für Öffentlichkeitsarbeit*) devoted to the discussion of problems centering on public relations. [17]

This development is by no means confined to the GDR and independent of other East European developments. The USSR, for instance, had already sent delegates to the first world congress organized by the International Public Relations Association held in Brussels in 1955. [18] Bulgaria, Czechoslovakia, Poland and Yugoslavia use public relations techniques, at least in foreign trade. [19] A detailed draft plan for integrating public relations methods was drawn up in the early '70s in Rumania inspired by a Hungarian study published in 1968 which recommended public relations as a useful tool for the economic sector. [20] As a result of the discussion initiated by the Faculty of Foreign Economics at the Academy of Economic Science in Bucharest, a study was published in 1973 in which the two authors, Mircea Cora and Liviu Mureșan, describe public relations as follows: [It is] "a relatively new field of activity. Public relations has been practiced for a few decades now by enterprise, institutions and organizations in industrialized countries. In the last few years it has also been practiced in socialist countries. The essence of public relations consists of maintaining contact with diverse sections of the public, with influential leaders in enterprise, institutions and organizations, with representatives of the media, local officials, etc., with the aim of winning sympathy, understanding and support at home as well as abroad. . . ." [21] Press legislation was passed in Rumania on 1st April, 1974, foreseeing (in Article 60) the employment of press officers for central state authorities, and other executive committees. Such officials would be responsible for maintaining constant and close contact with the media. [22]

Public Relations as Two-Way Communication?

Critical comparisons between business public relations norms and reality have only been attempted and presented at a descriptive level. In this way Scharf went about comparing 18 American and German publications on the subject, and through analysis of the texts ascertained that they oriented themselves on the neo-liberal ideology of the market economy, the concept of social partnership and that of the harmonization of different interests. Most public relations authors, he writes, unjustly accept the premise that public relations activities are able to represent the general interest and indeed do so. [23] Empirical studies examining the central claim that public relations is a form of two-way communication have hardly been undertaken at all. Specifically referring to the relationship between public relations and the press, initial studies have been made, which can be used as a basis for further research.

In late 1974 and early 1975 Aronoff undertook an attitude survey of 48 journalists on the editorial staff of a newspaper based in Austin (Texas), the *American Statesman*, and on a sample of 25 public relations practitioners and public information officers throughout Texas.[24] These individuals were presented with statements concerning public relations and asked to indicate their agreement or disagreement with them (see Table 5). According to Aronoff's results journalists' attitudes towards public relations tended to be negative and differed considerably from the attitudes held by public relations practitioners towards their own profession, even though a majority of the former agreed with the statement that "Public relations and the press are partners in the dissemination of information."

Journalists in the German Federal Republic share the opinions of their counterparts in the USA that public relations is normally publicity disguised as news; that public relations practitioners all too frequently attempt to deceive the press; and that they do not help reporters by giving them exact, complete and current information. Such similarities are drawn from the results of a survey carried out by the journal *PR-magazin*, in September, 1975, which, to a large extent, adopted Aronoff's questionnaire.[25] It must be noted, however, that there are dissimilarities in sample size and procedure (see Table 6).

Controversial opinions concerning the role of industrial press information offices have also been discussed in the German Democratic Republic. Looking at the *Neue Deutsche Presse*, one finds that journalists have complained that public relations restricts the scope of news coverage on economic enterprise and thus constitutes an attack on socialist press freedom.[26]

The flow of information from business enterprise to the press, with a view to answering the question as to whether public relations information regulates news coverage, or whether it constitutes contribution to a form of dialogue with the public through the press, is at present being investigated by the author together with students at the Ruhr-University in Bochum (Federal Republic of Germany). For the purpose of this pilot study all written and verbal information distributed to the press by one internationally renowned German industrial enterprise in 1974, at first, was collected, and compared with the news coverage on the firm in various daily newspapers with high circulation figures. In the case under consideration, the hypothesis that public relations information channels news coverage will be verified, at least as far as local and regional newspapers are concerned. Journalists seem to abandon investigation with the result that the flow of information becomes a one-sided process. It is necessary, however, to undertake more case studies of this kind, also on an international basis, in order to draw any general conclusions.

Table 5: Attitudes Concerning Public Relations
Activities Maintained by Journalists
and Public Relations Practitioners
(Survey in the USA 1974/1975*)

S t a t e m e n t s	J** P***	Agree %	Dis- agree %	No Opin- ion %
Public relations and the press are partners in the dissemination of information.	J P	59 89	39 9	2 2
Practitioners help reporters obtain accurate, complete and timely news.	J P	48 91	44 7	8 2
Practitioners are necessary to the production of the daily newspaper as we know it.	J P	40 74	54 10	6 16
Practitioners too frequently insist on promoting products, services and other activities which do not legitimately deserve promotion.	J P	91 65	4 24	5 11
Practitioners have cluttered our channels of communication with pseudo-events and phony phrases that confuse public issues.	J P	78 42	16 52	6 6
Practitioners often act as obstructionists, keeping reporters from the people they really should be seeing.	J P	82 38	12 56	6 6
Public relations material is usually publicity disguised as news.	J P	84 29	6 54	10 17
Practitioners too often try to deceive the press by attaching too much importance to a trivial uneventful happening.	J P	89 33	4 56	7 11
Public relations is a profession equal in status to journalism.	J P	10 76	79 16	11 8
Practitioners understand such journalistic problems as meeting deadlines, attracting reader interest and making the best use of space.	J P	39 89	50 4	11 7

*   Questioned: 48 journalists working for 'American
Statesman', Austin, Texas and
25 public relations professionals or
press information officers from
Texas.

**   J(ournalists)

*** P(ublic Relations Practitioners)

Table 6: Attitudes Concerning Public Relations
Activities Maintained by Journalists
and Public Relations Practitioners
(Survey in the GFR, September, 1975*)

Statements	J** P***	Agree %	Disagree %	No Opinion %
Public relations and the press are partners in the dissemination of information.	J P	80 86,6	20 6,6	– 6,6
Practitioners help reporters obtain accurate, complete and timely news.	J P	10 93,3	80 6,6	10 –
Practitioners are necessary to the production of the daily newspaper as we know it.	J P	80 60	20 33,3	– 6,6
Practitioners too frequently insist on promoting products, services and other activities which do not legitimately deserve promotion.	J P	40 60	20 26,6	40 13,3
Practitioners have cluttered our channels of communication with pseudo-events and phony phrases that confuse public issues.	J P	20 26,6	40 73,3	40 –
Practitioners often act as obstructionists, keeping reporters from the people they really should be seeing.	J P	20 13,3	40 80	40 6,6
Public relations material is usually publicity disguised as news.	J P	60 26,6	40 66,6	– 6,6
Practitioners too often try to deceive the press by attaching too much importance to a trivial uneventful happening.	J P	60 53,3	20 46,6	20 –
Public relations is a profession equal in status to journalism.	J P	40 33,3	60 53,3	– 13,3
Practitioners understand such journalistic problems as meeting deadlines, attracting reader interest and making the best use of space.	J P	80 53,3	– 26,6	20 20

* 103 readers of the journal 'PR-magazin' completed and returned questionnaires. Of these,
25 were journalists and
78 public relations professionals or press information officers.

** J(ournalists)
*** P(ublic Relations Practitioners)

NOTES

[1] See, for example, Edward L. Bernays, "American Public Relations. A Short History", *Gazette* (Leiden, 1956, No. 2), pp. 69–77; and Scott M. Cutlip and Allen H. Center, *Effective Public Relations*. (Englewood Cliffs, New York: Prentice Hall, 1971). See also Charles S. Steinberg, *The Creation of Consent: Public Relations in Practice*. (New York: Hastings House, Publishers, 1975).

[2] Bernays, *loc. cit.*, p. 70; Cutlip and Center, *loc. cit.*, pp. 74–79.

[3] Edward L. Bernays, author of the first conducted book dealing with this subject (published in 1923) and who conducted the first course on public relations at New York University in the same year, writes as follows: ". . . Public relations concerns itself with the relations of a unit, an organization or individual with the publics on which it depends for viability. Public relations advice covers adjustment to the public, information to the public and persuasion of the public to accept the service or product. . . . Effective public relations establishes a coincidence between the principal and the publics on which the principal depends, to the highest degree of adjustment. . . ." Edward L. Bernays, "Ten Essentials of Public Relations", ZV + ZV—*Das Organ für Presse und Werbung* (Bonn-Bad Godesberg, 1972, No. 12), p. 560.

[4] cf. "Public relations is the planned effort to influence opinion and action through socially responsible performance based on mutually satisfactory two-way communication," in Cutlip and Center, *loc. cit.*, p. 2. A summary of American public relations definitions can, for instance, be found in Wilfried Scharf, "Public Relations in der Bundesrepublik Deutschland. Ein kritischer Überblick über die gegenwärtig maßgebenden Ansichten," *Publizistik* (Konstanz, 1971, No. 2), pp. 163–180.

[5] Cutlip and Center, *loc. cit.*, p. 81.

[6] cf. Scharf, *loc. cit.*, pp. 163–165; and S. Sreenivas Rao, "Dimensions of Public Relations", *Communicator* (New Dehli, 1975, No. 7), pp. 47–59; esp. pp. 54 onwards.

[7] Wilmont Haacke, " 'public relations'—oder das Vertrauen der Öffentlichkeit", *Aus Politik und Zeitgeschichte* (supplement to the weekly, DAS PARLAMENT, 29th November, 1969, No. B 48/69), p. 5.

[8] Haacke, *loc. cit.*, p. 6.

[9] Wilhelm Berdrow, *Alfred Krupp Briefe 1826–1887* (commissioned by the family and the firm Krupp, Berlin: Reimar Hobbing, 1928), p. 225.

[10] The Krupp Archive, communiqué dated 8th December, 1975.

[11] Edward L. Bernays, *Biographie einer Idee* (German edition, Düsseldorf and Vienna: Econ, 1967), p. 7.

[12] At the time of publication there were 49 national public relations organizations in the following countries: Argentina, Australia, Belgium, Brazil, Canada, Chile, Republic of China, Columbia, Denmark, Ecuador, Finland, France, Federal Republic of Germany, Ghana, Great Britain, Greece, Hong Kong, Republic of India, Iran, Ireland, Israel, Italy, Japan, Kenya, Lebanon, Malaysia, Mexico, The Netherlands, The Netherlands Antilles, New Zealand, Nigeria, Norway, Republic of Panama, Paraguay, Peru, The Philippines, Portugal, The Arab Republic of Egypt, Rhodesia, Republic of Singapore, Spain, Republic of South Africa, Sweden, Switzerland, Tanzania, United States of America, Uruguay, Venezuela, Zambia. Not all are organized in one of the following regional supranational associations: the European Centre of Public Relations (CERP) with its seat in Brussels, Belgium; Inter-American Federation of Public Relations (FIARP) with its seat in Caracas, Venezuela; and the Pan Pacific Public Relations Federation (PPPRF) with its seat in Honolulu, Hawaii. The International Public Relations Association (IPRA) with its seat in Geneva, Switzerland, was set up in 1955. IPRA had approximately 420 members from the above mentioned states in 1975. The association obtained consultative status at the United Nations on 15th May, 1974.

[13] Cutlip and Center, *loc. cit.*, p. 637 onwards.

[14] (Authors' Collective), Manipulation. Die staatsmonopolistiche Bewußtseinsindustrie (Berlin: Dietz, 1968), p. 191 onwards.

[15] "Welche Anforderungen werden an den Pressereferenten gestellt?", "*Neue Deutsche Presse*", *Zeitschrift für Presse, Funk und Fernsehen*. Organ des Verbandes der Deutschen Journalisten (Berlin, 1971, No. 24), p. 9.

[16] Willi Stoph, "Bericht zur Direktive des VIII. Parteitages der SED zum Fünfjahresplan für die Entwicklung der Volkswirtschaft der DDR in den Jahren 1971 bis 1975 (Protokoll der Verhandlungen des VIII. Parteitages der Sozialistischen Einheitspartei Deutschlands 15. bis 19. Juni 1971 in der Werner-Seelenbinder-Halle zu Berlin, 2 volumes, Berlin: Dietz 1971), Volume 2 (4. und 5. Verhandlungstag), pp. 6–58; esp. p. 55.

[17] "Enge Partnerschaft Pressereferent—Redaktion. NDP-Gespräch: Der Beitrag des VDJ zur weiteren Verbesserung der Öffentlichkeitsarbeit", *Neue Deutsche Presse, loc. cit.*, (1971, No. 23), pp. 2–4.

[18] Cutlip and Center, *loc. cit.*, p. 456.

[19] Author's information from the embassies in the German Federal Republic of the countries mentioned; inquiry: 29th August, 1975.

[20] Joszef Lipot, *Public Relations a Gyakovlatban* (Budapest: KDJ, 1968); author's interview with Dr. Mircea Coraş at the Rumanian Embassy in the GFR (Trade Department), Cologne, 26th November, 1975.

[21] Mircea Coraş and Liviu Mureşan, *Relatiile Publice Internationale in Activitatea de Comert Exterior* (Bucharest: Aromar, 1973). A Translation of p. 14 et seq. was kindly given by Dr. Mircea Coraş.

[22] *Buletinul Oficial* (Bucharest, 1st April, 1975); interview with Dr. Mircea Coraş, Cologne, 26th November 1975.

[23] Scharf, *loc. cit.*, p. 176.

[24] Craig Aronoff, "Newspapermen and Practitioners Differ Widely on PR Role", *Public Relations Journal* (New York, 1975, No. 8), p. 24 et seq.

[25] "Raue PR-Sitten in Texas? Und bei uns?", *PR-magazin* (Remagen-Rolandseck, 1975, No. 7), p. 23; "Umfrageergebnis: PR-Leute besser als ihr Ruf", *PR-magazin* (1975, No. 8), p. 54.

[26] Rolf Liebold, "Industriepressestellen—Partner oder Zensoren?", *Neue Deutsche Presse* (Berlin, 1972, No. 6), p. 6 et seq.

7

SUPRANATIONAL COMMUNICATION EFFORTS

Wilson Dizard
TOWARD A WIRED WORLD

Heinz-Dietrich Fischer
THE CONTRIBUTION OF EUROVISION AND INTERVISION
TO GLOBAL TELEVISION

Kurt Koszyk
THE DEVELOPMENT OF THE INTERNATIONAL PRESS
INSTITUTE

Robert P. Knight
UNESCO'S ROLE IN WORLD COMMUNICATION

Mary A. Gardner
THE EVOLUTION OF THE INTER AMERICAN PRESS
ASSOCIATION

7

SUPRANATIONAL COMMUNICATION EFFORTS

ALTHOUGH some attention had been given to international cooperation in information exchange in the 1930's—and even earlier with the news agencies—it was really only after World War II that any systematic, organized efforts were made toward improving supranational communication. Naturally, as improved technology, e.g. in transportation, brought the world closer together, peoples found themselves more interested in communicating with other peoples. The organizations and technical developments which arose in the 1940's, 1950's and 1960's were inevitable results of this "one worldism" and have contributed greatly to our present concern with, and attention to, the problems of peoples in widely diverse and separated parts of the world.

Dr. Wilson Dizard, of the United States Information Agency, in the first article of this section surveys the growing linkages of the world through cable systems facilitating international radio and TV signals. Dr. Heinz-Dietrich Fischer next discusses the contributions of Eurovision and Intervision to worldwide television.

Dr. Kurt Koszyk of Dortmund, one of Germany's leading journalism researchers, then traces the evolution and achievements of the International Press Institute. The next article, by Dr. Robert P. Knight of the University of Missouri, surveys UNESCO's activities in international communication. A brief history of another type of international (but not world-wide) organization—the Inter American Press Association—written by Dr. Mary Gardner of Michigan State University, a Latin American scholar, closes the section.

*   *   *   *

RELATED READING

Barber, R. B. B. *Eurovision as an Expression of International Cooperation in Western Europe.* Unpublished Ph.D. dissertation, Northwestern University, Evanston, Ill., 1963.

Codding, George A. *The International Telecommunication Union: An Experiment in International Cooperation.* Leiden, The Netherlands: Brill, 1952.

Cooper, Kent. *Barriers Down: The Story of the News Agency Epoch.* New York: Farrar and Rhinehart, 1942.

Emery, Walter B. *Five European Broadcasting Systems.* Journalism Monographs, 1. Austin, Texas: Association for Education in Journalism, 1966.

European Broadcasting Union. *Monographs* (occasional). Geneva.

Evans, F. Bowen. *Worldwide Communist Propaganda Activities.* New York: Macmillan, 1955.

Gardner, Mary A. *The Inter American Press Association: Its Fight for Freedom of the Press, 1926–1960.* Austin: Univ. of Texas Press, 1967.

IAPA. *Press of the Americas* (New York). Usually monthly; English, Spanish.

IOJ. *Facts About the IOJ.* Prague: International Organization of Journalists, 1973.

IPI. *IPI Report* (Zurich, Switzerland). Monthly; in English, German, French.

Kruglak, Theodore E. *The Two Faces of TASS.* New York: McGraw-Hill Paperbacks, 1963.

Kurta, Henryk. "The UNESCO Informational Department and the International Exchange of Information," in: *International Review of Journalism* (Warsaw, Poland), Vol. 1/No. 1 (1966), pp. 71–80.

Morris, Joe Alex. *Deadline Every Minute: The Story of the United Press.* Garden City, N.Y.: Doubleday and Co., 1957.

Nolte, Ernst. *Die faschistischen Bewegungen.* Munich: Deutscher Taschenbuch Verlag, 1966.

Storey, Graham. *Reuters Century, 1851–1951.* London: Parrish, 1951.

UNESCO. *World Communications: Press-Radio-Film-Television.* New York and Paris, 1975.

White, Llewellyn and Robert D. Leigh. *Peoples Speaking to Peoples.* Chicago: University of Chicago Press, 1946.

Wilson Dizard:

Toward a Wired World

WIRED CITY . . . wired nation . . . wired world. The progression may seem a natural one to those who have high hopes for cable's future as a large-capacity, multi-service information utility. Realistically, this kind of wired world is a long way off. There is, however, a growing interest in, and experimentation with, cable systems overseas.

For the present this interest centers largely in Western Europe and Japan. Cable is on the communications agenda of every Western European country, with several of them already involved in experimental systems. The Japanese, with typical thoroughness, are developing an innovative prototype full-service system near Osaka, building upon their experience with over nine thousand small cable operations over the past twenty years.

In this survey, we will examine European and Japanese developments, in terms of both hardware and software, followed by a look at the special circumstances in Canada which make that country's cable experience especially interesting to Americans concerned with public-service applications of the technology.

The European experience with the "wired city" concept is an old one, dating back almost a century. Budapest had an extensive closed-circuit audio system, providing news and entertainment over telephone lines in the 1880s. Similar systems operated in French and British cities early in the century. They were closed down in the face of government decisions to invest in centralized over-the-air broadcasting. The recent development of high-capacity cable technology has revived European interest in "wired city" systems as supplements to, and perhaps replacements for, over-the-air radio and television services.

It would be misleading to suggest that this is going to happen quickly. Interest in cable communications abroad has generally followed the same pattern as in this country and Canada. This involved, initially, the use of cable as a re-transmitter of over-the-air television in isolated areas. As in this country, initial re-transmission development was followed by euphoric plans for capitalizing on cable's wider potential, particularly in urban areas. It soon became apparent that there were some harsh political and economic realities involved in mesh-

▶ From: *Cable Handbook, 1975–1976* (Mary Louise Hollowell, ed.), Communications Press Inc., Washington, D.C., 1975. Reprinted here by permission of author and publisher, Publi-Cable, Inc. Dr. Dizard is Chief of Planning and Operational Policy, U.S. Information Agency, Washington, D.C.

ing the new technology's promises against the entrenched claims of the over-the-air broadcasters and other telecommunications interests. Europeans are facing these realities now. They have not yet experienced the shake-out exercise the U.S. industry is now going through, primarily because most of their cable plans are still on paper or in the experimental stage.

The current shake-out in the U.S. cable industry has tended to have a sobering effect on the Europeans. They are watching us and the Canadians carefully for clues on how (and perhaps whether) we manage the shift from re-transmission of over-the-air broadcasts to large-scale origination of entertainment programs and specialized broadband communications services. There are no systems in Europe comparable to those in New York City and San Diego with their relatively strong subscriber bases and their experience in program origination. On another scale, there are no European systems that have done the pioneering community programming one finds in such U.S. systems as those in Reading, Pennsylvania and Rockford, Illinois.

The Europeans are also well aware that there is another major difference between the American cable experience and theirs. It is, of course, the fact that, whatever the final outcome of the current debate on government oversight of cable systems, U.S. cable will continue to be primarily a commercial venture, with marketplace economics determining size, location, and program services. Given Europe's tradition of tight control of national communications systems, its approach to cable development will be different.

The question is: How different? The Europeans and Japanese are well aware that cable can be a multi-purpose communications delivery system, not simply an extension of existing broadcasting. As in the United States and Canada, cable's potential ability to provide a broad spectrum of specialized local services intrigues them. European telecommunications ministries and radio-TV authorities are conditioned to dealing with a small number of broadcasting outlets, generally under central control. The prospects of hundreds of local cable systems, each with its own pattern of services (some in competition with over-the-air broadcast services) is a novel one, with basic political, economic and social implications.

If it is clear that the Europeans will not adopt the American pattern (diffused commercial control, with minimal government regulation), it is also clear that they cannot fit cable into the old broadcasting pattern of government ownership and centralized control. The mix will be a different one, probably involving greater commercial participation in the development and ownership of cable systems, with a larger measure of local autonomy for cable services.

The evidence for this projection is, admittedly, scattered. European cable systems are still largely small re-transmission operations. They are heavily concentrated in bi-lingual countries (Belgium, Switzerland, etc.,) where they provide alternative broadcast services for ethnic minorities. The long-term pattern for European cable will emerge—as in the United States—when systems move into urban areas with a schedule of viable origination services. At this level, the

Europeans face the same problems as their American counterparts. The financing of such a capital-intensive technology is, of course, one such shared problem. But the basic question is determining the mix of program services which will attract sufficient audiences, and funds, for large urban systems. If the United States, with over six hundred systems originating local services, has not found the answers, we are not behind the Europeans.

The Europeans have begun to look at the problem more intently, however. Their approaches are different from ours, but they offer—both in philosophy and techniques—some useful lessons for us to ponder and perhaps, to adapt to American conditions.

GREAT BRITAIN

Britain is a useful starting-off point since conditions affecting cable developments there are closer to the American experience than is the case with other European countries.

As in this country, there is a long-standing private enterprise factor in the cable picture. This is generally not true anywhere else in Europe, with the exception of Belgium. Wired distribution of radio and television signals has a history in Britain dating back to the Nineteen Twenties. The technology generally has involved only simple paired wires. However, there are a number of prosperous, cable-distribution companies which have the experience and the desire to begin large-scale high-capacity cable program origination and distribution. For the present, the companies are limited largely to re-transmission of existing over-the-air radio and television signals. At the end of 1972, there were 1,300 operating cable licenses for systems serving nearly 2.2 million households.

A second fact familiar to Americans is that Britain has an extensive commercial television system. Since 1955, this system has prospered as a supplement to the TV services of the British Broadcasting Corporation. (More recently, supplementary commercial radio service has also been inaugurated.) Any proposals for originating cable services in Britain have to reckon with the opposition of strongly-entrenched broadcasting organizations. It is a situation with which the American cable industry has also had some experience.

Finally, there is the national government faced with the decisions on weighing the claims of old-line broadcasting organizations for protection against a competing technology whose services could drastically re-arrange the national audience pattern.

The government has moved cautiously in making its decisions. The cable distribution firms have concentrated their efforts on breaking down opposition to the idea of program origination. In 1972, the government agreed to a limited experiment of local cable TV services in five areas—Bristol, Greenwich, Sheffield, Swindon and Wellinborough. The licenses limited origination programming to those "specially designed to appeal to the local communities in the areas served." No advertising or sponsored programs were permitted. Despite these commercial handicaps, cable firms in each of the licensed areas were prepared to underwrite local programming in the interests of demonstrating the wider range of cable possibilities.

At the same time, the cable distributors mounted a large-scale campaign in favor of changing the technology's limited status. Their proposal, issued in March, 1973, is entitled "Britain's Television: a plan for consumer choice." It argued for a phased expansion of both over-the-air broadcasting and cable-system origination services. The report claimed that four million households could quickly be connected to existing cable lines, for a total of 30 percent of all British homes.

The campaign was intended, among other purposes, to enlist public opinion support for cable expansion. The cable operators had their sights on the fact that, at the time they issued their report, the government franchises for both BBC and commercial television were scheduled to be reviewed in 1976. It seemed to be a good opportunity to get some basic decisions about cable expansion. Their hopes were frustrated when the government decided in 1973 to postpone its decisions about television until the end of the decade. It also set up a committee, headed by Lord Annan, to examine the overall future of British broadcasting, including the cable factor.

Of more immediate interest to the cable operators, however, was a report on British communications, "The People and the Media," issued by a Labor Party study group in July 1974. The report has been dismissed in some quarters as an expression of opinion by left-wing Labor elements, although others suggest that it may have more impact following the Labor Party's second electoral victory within a year in the fall of 1974.

The report recommends that cable should be placed under public ownership as part of a national policy for an integrated telecommunications system. A Communications Council and a Public Broadcasting Commission would be set up as a "permanent institutional expression of public involvement in the communications industries."

"While we recognize the exciting possibilities of the multi-channel capacity of cable and its ability to accept cheaply originated material not up to ordinary broadcasting standards, we believe that its potential must be properly explored within the framework of national services and carefully planned experiments. Random private enterprise development with vested interests at stake cannot do the job properly. This is exactly the sort of project that the Communications Council should now be organizing and evaluating," the report says.

It came as no surprise that the British Cable Television Association, the industry trade group, disapproved of the Labor report's proposal. The industry's alternate proposal is to set up an independent Cable Television Council which would encourage cable development and license "suitable persons and organizations" to provide programming.

In a separate development, the cable industry's five program origination projects were given permission to extend their experiments until 1979. However, early in 1975, it became apparent that the projects would not continue unless the government authorized some form of revenue-producing programming, or a subsidy from local authorities.

Local origination programming will continue in the five experimental cable systems for the time being. Most of the programming on the five systems has been conventionally orthodox by American standards—community bulletin boards, discussion shows and some out-of-studio Portapak projects. There is little of the free-swinging type of controversial programming that takes place on some American access channels, a combined tribute perhaps to British reticence and to the cable companies' desire not to allow their fragile experiments to get out of hand while the final decisions on program origination are still to be made.

FRANCE

The French interest in cable (or *télédistribution,* as they like to call it) centers on two points. The first is the problem of fitting cable into the traditionally tight control all modern French governments have had in the telecommunications field.

The second interest involves programming. The French show a more active concern for the problem of cable software than is found in other European countries. There is a strong, growing video experimentation movement which draws much of its inspiration largely from U.S. and Canadian experience and adds distinctive Gallic touches of its own. Video groups, limited now largely to small closed-circuit demonstrations, look to cable as a major outlet for their work in the future.

They are not holding their breath over this prospect. French cable systems, as in most other European countries, are in their infancy. Nevertheless, there are some encouraging developments, particularly in prototype systems under joint public and private sponsorship.

Any significant expansion of cable systems will, however, have to await resolution of the question of how much local autonomy, at both the operating and programming levels, is to be accorded to cable systems. Any significant autonomy will involve modifying the long-standing French tradition of centralized government management of telecommunications outlets. This issue came to a head during the latter years of the DeGaulle government, with charges of blatant politicization of French radio and television over and above what was considered traditionally acceptable. The resultant discord—involving strikes and other disruptions—led to changes, in 1972 and 1974, in the way that the State radio-TV monopoly (ORTF) was structured. One of the incidental factors in this process was the first official recognition by the government of the role that cable systems might play in the country's communications pattern.

Previously, cable had been limited to small systems clustered largely in the northern part of the country. They were designed to retransmit ORTF programs as well as programs from nearby Belgian and German stations. By the early 1970s, there were about four hundred such systems in operation.

Two other factors contributed to the French interest in cable systems. One was the growing interest by video experimenters and audio-visual specialists in U.S. and Canadian experiments with cable program origination, particularly in the educational and community service fields. The second factor was the closer look which French businessmen and other entrepreneurs were giving to the investment possibilities of cable systems.

These circumstances led in 1972 to two official moves designed to deal with the future of cable communications in France. In March, the government issued a decree setting up a joint ORTF-Post Office company, the Societé Française de Télédistribution, with a mandate to determine cable's role in meeting national communications needs, as well as to study technical standards and to advise local authorities on planning cable systems.

This move was followed two months later by the enactment of new radio-TV broadcast legislation in which cable, for the first time, was given a specific legal basis.

Three passages in this 1972 legislation are relevant to cable. The first reaffirms that French radio and television services are a state monopoly not only for over-the-air broadcasts but also for programs transmitted by any telecommunications process.

The more significant article, however, says that exemptions from this monopoly can be granted "for the broadcasting of programs to specific publics, provided that programs concerned with education and training may be decided by the Ministries concerned." In other words, central government control over cable systems could be modified to include participation by other entities, public or private. The future development of French cable will depend on the "mix" of interests who will be permitted to participate in the development of cable systems throughout the country.

Finally, the 1972 legislation set up an Audio-Visual Council (*Haut Conseil de l'Audiovisuel*) to advise the government on the development of new audio-visual techniques, including "certain categories of exemption from the broadcasting monopoly," i.e. cable.

The stage was set for a series of cable experiments involving program origination at the local level.

In July, 1973, the government announced plans for experimental cable systems in five medium-sized towns. In each case, the experiments are being conducted by what would in the U.S. be regarded as public corporations, with both private and government (national and local) participation. The systems are scheduled to have sixteen channels, three of which must transmit the national ORTF television services.

In one of the typical experimental systems, in the northern town of Creteil, the system will be developed in stages. Cabled homes will receive the three ORTF channels free of charge. Fee payments will begin with the phasing in of additional services.

The municipality with the head start in cable programming experience is at Grenoble-Echirolle, a self-contained suburb near Grenoble which will have a population of 45,000 by the end of the decade. Since 1972, the Ministry of Culture and the municipality have sponsored an active closed-circuit VTR experiment. The test preceeded the installation of a cable system in the first section of the town to be built. Known as "Video-Gazette," it is an integral part of a Center for Permanent Education and Promotion of Socio-Cultural Activities. During its first two years, hundreds of residents have learned how to use the VTR equipment, and to experiment with program production. The emphasis is on neighborhood concerns. Half of the "video artisans" in the experiment are under twenty, and overall there are as many women as men.

ITALY

The Italian flair for doing things in a special way extends to their approaches to cable. The result could be a pattern that might make cable a major force on the Italian scene in the coming years and a pace-setting example for other European countries.

In other parts of Europe, cable systems are developing primarily as relayers of over-the-air broadcast signals. Not so in Italy. The first Italian cable system, Tele-Torino, began operations in 1967 in downtown Turin, with a schedule of its own news shows, variety and drama shows and a heavy dose of commercial advertising. The operation was short-lived. By 1973, however, there were almost two dozen cable TV operations throughout Italy, most of them devoted to transmitting videocassette programs to a small number of public receivers. The exception was a system called A-21 Telebiella, operating in a small town near Milan. Telebiella was an originating station from the start, concentrating on coverage of local events, interspersed with films.

Telebiella became the central focus of another distinctive aspect of the Italian cable scene. Other European countries have been able to keep cable system operation within strict government regulatory controls. The Telebiella cable system upset this pattern for the Italian government. When the system began full operations in 1971, it was registered in the local court under the provision in the Italian constitution which establishes the "right to free expression through the spoken and written word and any other means."

This interpretation was challenged by the national government. Charges were brought against Telebiella in January 1973 for violating the forty-year-old law which gave the government the right to assign all television operations exclusively to the state-owned broadcasting corporation, RAI-Radiotelevisione Italiana. The local judge ruled that Telebiella had not broken the law because cable transmission was not mentioned in that law.

His ruling appeared to open the way for a quick expansion of cable distribution systems throughout the country, originating their own programs. This prospect was attractive to advertising agencies and their clients, whose television access to Italian consumers is hampered by RAI's regulations limiting the number of minutes of advertising its stations will carry each evening. Cable seemed to offer a new channel for advertising-supported programming.

Plans for a number of cable systems were announced during the Spring of 1973. Eighteen cable systems in the Lombardy region agreed to form a network under the sponsorship of Telebiella. In central Italy, the city of Aquila appropriated funds for a five year period to support a cable system sponsored by a local cultural association.

These plans for independent cable systems were placed in jeopardy in May, 1973 with the issuance of new Postal Code regulations extending the State telecommunications monopoly to cable transmission. The new regulations stipulated that cable systems could be operated only through a government concession and it listed a series of penalties for illegal operation of such systems.

Once again, the courts became involved with cable. In July, 1974, the Italian Supreme Court overturned the government's cable regulations, on the basis of Constitutional provisions of freedom of speech. The result, which is perhaps unique to Italy, is a situation in which cable systems have the legal right to operate in direct competition to over-the-air broadcasters. The court did, however, give the government the right to control any future nationwide cable system.

These court decisions were reflected in definitive regulations on cable and over-the-air broadcasting issued by the Council of Ministers in November, 1974. The regulations provide that cable system service areas would be restricted geographically, with a maximum of 40,000 subscribers permitted. Interconnections are prohibited. At least half of each system's head-end programming must be produced locally, with advertising limited to five percent of transmission time. Cable franchises will be issued jointly by the central ministry of posts and telecommunications and the regional governments. A Parliamentary commission on broadcasting will have the right to issue directives for cable transmissions (to quote the Council regulations) "particularly during electoral campaigns."

Despite these restrictions, the 1974 Italian cable regulations provide a green light for the large-scale development of cable systems. It is a distinct break with the cautionary approach taken by other European countries. Although proposals for over a hundred systems were announced by the end of 1974, their promoters may be forced to moderate their plans for a quick take-off, primarily because of the depressed state of the Italian economy.

However, other indicators point to an optimistic future for Italian cable systems. Although advertising time is limited, there are strong indications that advertisers plan to take advantage of this new marketing channel. Another reason for cable's potential success is a provision in the new regulations authorizing relay of foreign television programs from Switzerland, France, Yugoslavia and Corsica. Presumably new cable systems in border areas will attract subscribers through these relay services.

A more important factor in Italian cable's future may, however, be political. Italian broadcasting has always been highly politicized, and there is little reason to doubt that this tradition will carry over into the new cable systems. The largest party, the Christian Democrats, had been generally wary of cable before the new regulations came into force because of the threat it posed to the party's centralized control of radio and television broadcasting. A 1974 reorganization of RAI, the Italian state broadcasting corporation, forced the Christian Democrats to surrender some of this control to other parties. The leftist parties, notably the Communists, originally opposed private cable systems as alleged tools for bolstering capitalism in Italy.

Now that definitive cable regulations have been laid down, all parties are taking another look at the long-range political implications of this new communications channel. The Communists have already signalled their interest in supporting cable systems. The center and rightist parties can be expected to take similar steps, either directly or through their supporters in the business world.

Whatever the outcome, the Italians have already made their mark on the international cable scene as a result of their decisions to grant cable communications some measure of autonomy from the government telecommunications monopoly.

GERMANY

The Germans are taking, literally, a broad view of the future of broadband cable communications. A two-year study is currently under way to determine the country's future information requirements, and the technical channels needed to fulfill them. The future of cable services is an important part of the study, which is being carried out by an independent commission supported by the Ministry of Post and Telecommunications and the Ministry for Research and Technology.

German experience with cable to date has been limited to retransmission systems, mainly in remote areas. However, small urban experiments are under way. Within the past year, the Post Office has developed two pilot systems in Hamburg and Nuremberg. These systems were designed primarily to provide interference-free reception of over-the-air broadcasts in areas where high-rise apartments were being built. A third system, sponsored in Bremen by the municipal television authority, has added an origination channel devoted to news and features about the local neighborhood.

Although it will center much of its attention on coaxial cable technology, the commission is also empowered to look into alternate technologies such as fiber optics, lasers and reception diodes, all of which have higher capacities than cable.

Another area of debate is the question of how to finance and manage cable systems. One German estimate is that 9,000 separate systems will be needed to service the entire country adequately.

Although the Post Office controls all telecommunications channels, such a system might be beyond its fiscal capacities. As a result, the debate in Germany tends to emphasize some form of mix between state and local governmental interests, with commercial support, in developing the systems. This would follow in the post-war tradition of decentralizing broadcasting responsibilities throughout the country.

One of the more intriguing technical prospects being considered by the Germans is the possibility of utilizing a national communications satellite to link cable systems for network services.

OTHER EUROPEAN COUNTRIES

Some of the smaller European countries have been more flexible in adapting to the prospects opened by cable technology. This has been particularly true in Belgium and Switzerland, where cable has served the particular purpose of providing distant signal importation from other countries for their ethnic minorities. Belgium is currently the most heavily cabled country in Europe, largely as a consequence of its French/Flemish linguistic split.

The most extensive urban cable systems in Europe are in Spain. Scheduled for completion during 1975 in Madrid and Barcelona, the systems are being built by the Spanish PTT and will be operated by the state broadcasting organization. Although they are intended primarily as re-transmitters of over-the-air television programs, the systems include channels set aside for cultural and entertainment programming. The initial systems in each city are scheduled to serve about 40,000 families. The government plans to authorize cable systems in other large Spanish cities within the next three years. Urban cable systems will reach about thirty percent of the population by the end of the decade if these plans are carried out.

All of the Scandinavian countries have relatively large numbers of small cable systems. All are looking into the prospects of supplementing re-transmission of TV programs with head-end origination. One interesting note: in Denmark, cable franchising is the province of the Ministry of Culture.

Another country where the cultural ministry is playing a role in cable development is The Netherlands. About one-third of all Dutch homes have some form of wired television, usually a limited master antenna system. However, larger capacity cable systems are being introduced, and with them the prospects for program origination. Experimental origination projects have been authorized by the Ministry of Culture to local foundations in six Dutch communities.

JAPAN

In their quiet way, Japanese cable groups may be doing more in 1975 to test out the "wired city" concept than any of their counterparts in Europe, Canada or the United States.

Japanese CATV systems began as conventional retransmitters of over-the-air broadcasts. They were encouraged by subsidies from NHK, the national public broadcasting network, as part of the government's goal of extending television coverage to remote areas. By the middle of 1972, over nine thousand such systems had been developed. About two-thirds of these systems were sub-sidized directly by NHK; beginning in 1969, however, NHK has concentrated on developing systems jointly with local subscribers. Quantitatively, Japan probably has more CATV systems than the rest of the world combined. In fact, most of these systems are so small—serving only a few dozen houses—that they might more properly be classified as master antenna TV systems.

The more interesting CATV story in Japan, however, is the attention given by the government and private enterprise to cable's role in an integrated national telecommunications system, in line with government decisions taken earlier in this decade to provide the infrastructure for an "information inten-sive" society.

Even before these decisions were reached, several Japanese cities had begun experimenting with a full-service cable distribution system. One of these towns, Tama, near Tokyo, with a population of 400,000, is cooperating with the national Post-Telegraph-Telephone (PTT) system in an ambitious project which is also supported by a consortium of manufacturers and broadcasting or-ganizations. The Tama system includes, besides retransmission facilities, capa-bilities for pay TV, head-end program origination, facsimile and two-way infor-mation services. A similar project is being conducted at Shimoda, a smaller city seventy miles from Tokyo. Like the Tama project, the organizers of the Shimoda scheme are building on an existing first-generation cable system, ex-panding it to full-service capability.

One of the fascinating regulations set out by the Shimoda cable propo-nents is that head-end program origination will be done without rehearsals, editing, an advance script or the use of make-up by any of the participants. Pre-sumably these rules are designed to guarantee a high degree of spontaneity (if not amateurism) in local transmission.

The most interesting Japanese "wired city" experiment, however, is lo-cated in a new town project in the Higashi Ikoma area near Osaka. The initial system at Higashi Ikoma will be a small one, involving fewer than four hundred households. Its significance lies in the innovative organizational struc-ture the Japanese have developed to examine the prospects for full-service cable systems. Higashi Ikoma is a first step towards implementing their ideas.

The key to the structure is the close partnership of private and government interests which characterizes so many areas of Japanese economic and social af-fairs. In this case, the Ministry of International Trade and Industry (MITI) is the key government agency involved. MITI has played a leading role in recent years in the effort to develop an intensive national information system. One part of this plan is the Video Information System Development, a non-profit corporation set up to implement MITI's pilot cable plans.

Cooperating in the Higashi Ikoma project will be a large number of com-puter and telecommunications firms, banks, broadcasting and advertising firms and the new-town development company.

Its sponsors describe the Video Information System as "a two-way system, enabling collection, distribution, processing and display of multi-purpose information through a combination of coaxial cables and computers, the former having capabilities of bi-directional transmission and columinous information items, and the latter with capabilities of powerful information control/processing/display."

The Higashi Ikoma project, scheduled for installation this year, is regarded as primarily a social experiment, setting standards for human needs in a post-industrial society. "The concept of efficiency born of a 'production-first principle,' evolved by an industrialized society, has now lost its dominant position," according to the project prospectus. "Instead the concept of effectiveness achieved through a welfare society must be pursued."

Following these standards, the Higashi Ikoma cable distribution system is being designed to provide a full range of twenty experimental services, ranging from conventional TV relay to computer-assisted instruction, with heavy emphasis on interactive services.

The project sounds, in fact, like the proposals for full-service cable put forward by many different groups in Europe and North America during the past decade. The difference is that the Higashi Ikoma project is actually being built through the combined efforts of public and private enterprises. There are undoubtedly some unique Japanese features about the way that they are going about it. Nevertheless, there are lessons in their approaches to developing the wired city concept that the rest of the world can study to its advantage.

CANADA

The first fact to consider here is that Canada is, per capita, the most cabled country in the world. *Over one-third of Canadian households are served by cable.* Toronto is about 70% cabled, and other large cities can boast similar records. Clearly, it would seem, Canada is a good example of what cable communications can mean for a country, particularly in urban areas.

The lesson, however, is not that clear. There are factors which make the Canadian experience a unique one. Canada may be the major proving ground for cable's potential as a high-capacity communications delivery system for a wide range of personal and community services—but it hasn't reached that point yet. In the meantime, there are important reasons why Canadian cable developments should be studied closely by Americans interested in public service applications of the technology.

The first reason is the existence of what is, by current standards, a large cable communications infrastructure. Canadians are accustomed to cable services, in both metropolitan and rural areas. The second reason is that there is a lively interest in cable program origination, encouraged by the Canadian Radio and Television Commission and other organizations. Finally, the Canadian government, at both the federal and provincial levels, is examining cable's overall role as a major communications resource, not simply as a re-transmission system.

For the present, however, Canadian cable is limited largely to the role of relayer of over-the-air broadcast signals. In this it resembles the pattern of U.S. cable—with one significant difference. The difference is that a good part of the motive power behind the development of Canadian cable systems has been the desire to improve the range and reception of U.S. television stations along the long common border. U.S. stations have always been within the signal range of large portions of the Canadian population. Cable systems have extended the signal now to a majority of the population.

The reason for this, simply, is that Canadians like United States programs, and they are willing to pay (in the order of $5 to $10 monthly) for cable systems that give them a good signal from U.S. stations. This happens despite the fact that their own Canadian Broadcasting Corporation (CBC) network is one of the best in the world, with generous government funding of about $250 million annually for its operations. (A comparative per capita figure for our own Public Broadcasting Service would be a staggering $2 *billion*.) CBC can count on an average 20% share of the television viewership. The rest is divided between Canadian commercial stations and their U.S. counterparts.

This situation affects the communications structure in both countries. About two dozen stations on the U.S. side of the border have a significant Canadian audience, either in their own signal area or by cable retransmission. A heavy share of their advertising revenue is dependent on Canadian advertisers appealing to Canadian viewers. Canadian critics are quick to document how American stations operate with a commercial eye across the border. One of their favored examples is in Pembina, North Dakota. Pembina has a population of about 200, and an ABC-affiliated television station that (in the words of one Canadian) "takes $1.5 million a year out of the Winnepeg market."

On the Canadian side, microwave and cable links have been fashioned to extend the range of U.S.-originated programs to areas hundreds of miles north of the border. As a result, Toronto cable households have a choice of sixteen U.S. and Canadian television stations.

The first cable systems in Canada date from the early 1950s, and they experienced a rapid and largely unregulated growth through the Sixties. One result of the general inattention to cable was that by 1967, U.S. corporations owned or controlled systems reaching over three-quarters of all Canadian cable subscribers. (Canadian government pressure has forced a cutback in U.S. commercial interests in these cable systems in recent years.)

All this has set off a lively political debate, with strong economic overtones. The powerful intangible in the debate is the question of national identity. For Canadians this is a two-tiered problem, involving on the one hand internal linguistic and other cultural difference and, on the other hand, the long-standing U.S. influence in Canadian life. Whatever their differences over specific aspects of their own culture, Canadians are agreed that it is not a northern version of what people think or do in California, New York or points between. They regard their general affinity for things American and their own sense of uniqueness as clearly distinguishable parts of their national makeup.

This is very much a factor in their attitudes and actions when dealing with television and with the newer cable systems. Television—direct or by cable—is the most visible and controversial form of American "cultural intrusion"—a phrase often heard in Canadian debates on the subject. This covers not only the question of direct transmissions from Stateside stations but also the *ersatz* American-style programming which originates from local stations.

More than one Canadian observer has noted wryly that the only true national programming is the twice-weekly hockey games—a Wednesday and Saturday night staple which always gets top ratings. Canadians complain that televised hockey is being "Americanized" by a trend towards the kind of mayhem-on-ice allegedly favored by U.S. hockey fans. Despite hockey's nationalistic popularity, the remainder of the top-rated shows are such shared U.S.-Canadian favorites as Archie Bunker, Walter Cronkite and NFL football.

The pressure to reduce U.S. influence on Canadian broadcasting has been steady and insistent during the past decade. The first step involved regulations which limited programming of U.S. materials to 40% of primetime offerings on Canadian stations. More recently, Canadian authorities have put into effect a series of regulations designed to reduce further U.S. content. Under one regulation, when an American network program is being shown simultaneously on both a U.S. and Canadian station, the cable systems are encouraged to carry the Canadian station. In another ruling, the cable systems are required to delete commercial advertising from programs retransmitted from American stations. Finally, there is a Parliamentary proposal for a revision in the tax regulations not to allow a business deduction for Canadian advertising carried on U.S. stations—a move that could involve a $20 million annual revenue loss for U.S. border stations.

These moves have been protested vigorously by U.S. broadcasters and their trade associations. The issue has taken on diplomatic overtones, with the filing of a formal protest by the U.S. State Department, the burden of which is that the Canadian regulations place limits on the free flow of information between the two countries.

Over and above the freedom-of-information argument, U.S. commentators have asked whether the economic moves made by the Canadians are not really primarily an exercise in marketplace control rather than a concern for cultural integrity. The Canadians answer that economics cannot be ignored, and that their media industry needs a stronger fiscal base from which to compete against the highly polished products of the American entertainment industry. They go back four decades to cite the example of the Famous Players Co., a U.S. firm which bought up Canadian movie houses to assure itself of distribution outlets for American films. One of the casualties of that move was the small but growing Canadian film industry, which has only begun to make a comeback in recent years.

At a more contemporary level, they also cite the results of a government regulation promulgated in the late Sixties that 30% of all records played on Canadian AM radio stations be Canadian in origin. The result has been a spectacular growth in the record and cassette industry, now booming along at a $100 million annual level. Economics aside, the most important intangible result of this change has been popular recognition that Canadian music is alive and well—a fact often drowned out in the past by the noise of U.S. imports.

The Canadians seem intent on applying a similar pattern to their broadcasting and cablecasting operations. They have already indicated their willingness to develop telecommunications regulations that will limit somewhat the impact of American broadcasting, including advertising, within Canada. However, this American impact remains a substantial one, if only because so many stations are within signal range of a large number of Canadian towns. In areas beyond normal signal strength, cable systems will continue to retransmit American stations.

It is doubtful that Canada's domestic satellite system—the first of its kind in the world—will be used to transmit signals from U.S. stations to the northern reaches of the country. The Anik satellite does transmit Canadian English and French language TV programs into isolated areas. Telesat, the Canadian satellite agency, is reported very much interested in plans for interconnecting Canadian cable systems in a national network. This could provide a strong boost for developing original programming on cable systems as well as limiting the impact of American broadcasting.

Whatever the final effect of the discriminatory regulations against American broadcasting, there is general agreement that the "Canadization" of the country's broadcasting and cable systems will depend largely on the degree to which quality local program materials are developed. The CBC, in particular, has made a major attempt in this direction. There is considerable discussion of proposals to increase Canadian TV program-production capabilities, along the lines of the support the government has given to strengthen the Canadian film industry.

Similar proposals are being circulated for providing greater support for raising the level of programs originated in cable systems. Canadian regulations on head-end origination are older and stricter than those adopted in this country. A considerable amount of innovative local programming has been done on Canadian cable systems. By and large, however, public service programming has been bedevilled by a lack of adequate funding.

The National Film Board has taken a strong lead in encouraging VTR experimentation for cable and for closed-circuit use. The Board's video publication, *Challenge for Change,* has been a gold-mine of documentation on imaginative use of VTR in local situations. In particular, VTR experimenters have addressed themselves to problems of Canada's multi-ethnic society. They have explored avenues of dialogue not only between English and French speaking communities, but also lesser known problems involving Indians, Eskimos and other minorities.

Canadians interested in public service cable programs are also looking into the structure of the present system to determine how it might better serve public needs. One of the more striking proposals in this area was put forward, in September, 1974, by the British Columbia Association of Public Broadcasting. The group proposed the conversion of all cable television systems in the province to public or cooperative ownership, utilizing the revenue to sustain what would, in effect, be a cable version of public television. The system would retransmit existing Canadian and American television stations. It would, however, also provide a strong schedule of locally-provincial government subsidies to underwrite its costs.

Late in 1974, it was reported that the British Columbia provincial government was seeking to purchase a Vancouver cable TV outlet owned by Western Broadcasting Co. for the specific purpose of providing public service broadcasting. There were political overtones to the move, following complaints by the provincial government that the Canadian Broadcasting Corporation was not adequately serving local needs. Similar proposals by provincial governments to sponsor local programming were also reported in Manitoba and Saskatchewan.

In March, 1975, the Canadian Radio-Television Commission (CRTC) issued a series of proposals which, if adopted, will have an important effect on the evolution of Canadian cable communications. One proposal is designed to limit further U.S. programming on Canadian cable channels. Its purpose is to insure that "in all but the most exceptional circumstances, Canadian services predominate." This would be accomplished by assigning priorities to various cable services, with re-transmission of programs from U.S. stations allocated a low priority.

The most immediately controversial of the CRTC proposals was one requiring that cable systems spend at least ten percent of their gross annual subscriber revenues on community programming. The proposal was challenged by the cable industry as unwarranted government interference ("the first corporate checkoff in Canada") and the expense which would require higher subscriber fees. However, the proposal received generally strong support from public interest groups in Commission hearings.

In a very real sense, cable in Canada faces the same questions as we do in this country. For the present, cable is looked upon as a system that retransmits over-the-air broadcasting. When and how it will provide quality services that will supplement many of the present broadcast services, as well as develop new ones, remains to be decided. We have a lot to learn from each other both in shaping the structure of cable communications and in experimenting with cable program services.

*　　*　　*　　*

Useful Resources

Beyond Babel: New Directions in Communications by Brenda Maddox, Simon & Shuster, New York, 1973. Good summary of British and American cable developments.

Cable: An Examination of Social and Political Implications of Cable Television Report of the November, 1973 conference on cable, London. Issued by the standing Conference on Broadcasting, London, 1973. Excellent papers from a November, 1973 conference on the future of cable, held in London.

L'Apres Television: Une Anti-Mythologie de L'Audiovisuel by Robert Wangernee and Hodle Lhoest, Hachette Literature, Paris, 1973. An inquiry into the role that cable and other new technologies can play in supplementing, and supplanting over-the-air television. Good case histories drawn from European, Canadian and American experiences.

Considerations for A European Communications Policy, Report of a symposium sponsored by the International Broadcast Institute, London, May, 1973.

Cable Television for Europe by Sharon K. Black, Report 74-28, Office of Telecommunications, U.S. Department of Commerce, Washington, D.C., 1974. Detailed survey of European CATV.

"Community Television: A New Hope," by Peter Lewis, New Society, London, March 31, 1972, pp. 490–493.

Cable Television Today: Policy and Practices in Europe, America and Japan, by Karen Dolmatch, Publication Number 12, Research Program on Communications Policy, The Center for International Studies, Massachusetts Institute of Technology, Cambridge, Massachusetts, 1974. An overview of cable developments in fifteen European countries, Japan, Canada and Mexico.

"Some features of CATV in Japan: 1973, Report by the Research Institute of Telecommunications and Economics, Tokyo, 1973.

"Canadian Broadcasting: A Single System," Canadian Radio-Television Commission. Ottowa, 1971.

"Cable Television in France: Experiments in video-animation," by Jean-Pierre Dubois-Dumee Council for Cultural Co-operation, Council of Europe, Strasbourg, 1973. Case histories of French experiments in closed-circuit VTR programming.

"Teledistribution and its Application in European Economic Community Countries report prepared by the "Innovation-Communication-Structure" planning group of Paris for the Director-General for Industrial and Technological Affairs, European Economic Commission, Brussels, 1973.

Saint Écran, by Henri Pigeat, Solar Editeur, Publishers, Paris, 1973. A wide-ranging look at the implications of cable and other new communications technologies, including a futuristic chapter on the wired world of the early 21st Century.

"La telédistribution," A special issue of the UNESCO-sponsored magazine, *Télévision et Education,* with articles on cultural and educational uses of cable systems in Europe and the U.S. Issue No. 32. April 1973. Paris.

Heinz-Dietrich Fischer:

The Contribution of Eurovision and Intervision
to Global Television

IT was as early as 1948 that the director of Radio Lausanne (Switzerland), Marcel Bezençon, got the basic idea to establish a so-called "Program Exchange" for all members of UIR (Union Internationale de Radio-diffusion) to prove the possibilities of transmitting TV programs from one country to others. But at this time there was almost no television on the European continent, and most of his colleagues did not feel an urgent need for such an institution.

When the successor of UIR was founded February 12, 1950, under the name UER (Union Européenne de Radiodiffusion) in Geneva (Switzerland) with a technical headquarters in Brussels (Belgium), the idea of international cooperation in the field of television came up again. In the meantime Marcel Bezençon had become head of the total radio networks of Switzerland, and so he had the chance to discuss his plan of 1948 once again in the gremiums of UER. On October 5, 1950, Bezençon sent his complete concept to the main office of UER, explaining the necessity of arranging TV program exchanges *before* the establishment of the television networks in the various European countries.

Bezençon's plan contained four main suggestions: (a) exchanges of films of different kinds, (b) live transmissions of main public events in the different countries, (c) exchanges of actual news, and (d) clearing of the copyrights for all over the world. The administrative headquarters of UER asked all the 21 member countries at that time to give reactions as soon as possible, but fewer than 10 answers arrived by mid-January, 1951.[1] But in the meantime there had already been a first step of TV program exchange between two countries *without* any activity of UER: On the 27th of August, 1950, the two most developed European TV countries, France and Great Britain, had a telecast across the sea from Calais to Dover, and they also worked together in research on technical problems of TV transmitting in different line systems. Between the 8th and 14th of July, 1952, they also arranged a real bilateral British-French so-called "Week of TV Telecasts" between Paris and London. These first steps encouraged the UER to evaluate the idea of international program exchange not only by Radio but also by Television Broadcast:[2]

▶ This is a revised original article done for this book by Dr. Heinz-Dietrich Fischer, Professor of Journalism and Mass Communication Research, Ruhr-University Bochum (Federal Republic of Germany).

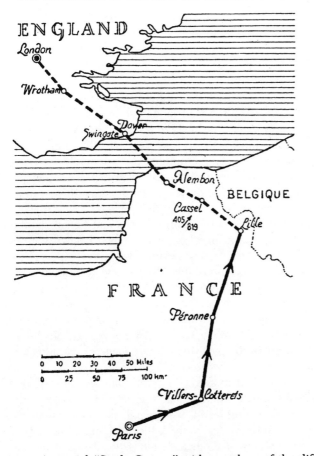

ENGLAND

London

Wrotham

Dover

Swingate

Alembon

BELGIQUE

Cassel
405/819

Lille

FRANCE

Péronne

0 10 20 30 40 50 Miles
0   25   50   75   100 km·

Villers-Cotterets

Paris

The link set up between Paris and London for the RTF/ BBC television programmes in July 1952

A special "Study Group," with members of the different UER countries, discussed many problems in this field during 1952 and 1953. At this time television had its early beginnings also in West Germany, Denmark, and in the Netherlands, and some of these countries tried to arrange an international TV transmission of the coronation of Queen Elizabeth II. When the coronation in London took place June 2, 1953, this event was transmitted not only by BBC in Great Britain, but also by a total of 12 TV Stations of France, the Netherlands, and the Federal Republic of Germany. During the coronation the combined radio and television programs were to last over six and one-half hours and ultimately to be translated into 41 languages besides English.[3] The result of this successful transmission encouraged many TV companies all over in West Europe to develop their technical equipment, especially their relay chains, enabling them to receive TV programs from other countries.

The most discussed problem at this time was how to transmit large parts of the World's Football (Soccer) Championship from Switzerland in the early summer of 1954. When this important sports event took place, there were already around four million TV sets with 60 to 65 million people in eight European countries receiving 31 hours of transmission. At the same time the British journalist George Campey came up with the term *Eurovision* that was used from then on for all kinds of international telecasts in Western Europe.[4]

Eurovision officially became effective on June 6, 1954, at first having a temporary network linking the TV networks of Belgium, Denmark, France, West Germany, Italy, the Netherlands, Switzerland, and the United Kingdom. For a short time the technical center was in Lille (France), but at the end of 1955 it moved to Brussels (Belgium), where it has been since that time.

Eurovision was established by linking a number of domestic TV services, rather than constructing a new and completely integrated network; it did not produce a separate program, but only coordinated it. By that time three distinct TV networks existed in Western Europe: (a) the BBC network using the 405 line system; (b) a chain of West German, Danish, Swiss and Italian stations using the 625 line system; and (c) a mixed-chain of French-Belgian stations using the 819 line system and Dutch-Belgian stations using 625 lines. There were some technical difficulties because of the different line systems, but the overall picture quality was pretty good. A partial solution to the problem of languages was achieved by sending commentators to the point of organization. The commentary mixed with the sound of the events was relayed over separate circuits to the receiving countries. Synthesized commentary was also employed: In this instance an announcer in the receiving country made his commentary while observing the picture on a monitor screen.

So the programs attempted to demonstrate how television services interpret local events, and thereby promote international understanding. Besides the World Football (Soccer) Championships in Switzerland, the programs in the early phase of *Eurovision* included: a Visit to the Vatican,[5] Queen Elizabeth II receiving units of the Royal Navy, a promenade along the Rhine River, St. Johannes' night at Tivoli Gardens in Copenhagen, the creation of a TV ballet in Brussels, and the illumination of Versailles Castle. A special series of programs was telecast during Christmas week, from December 23, 1954, to January 1, 1955. These programs included: Christmas carols from Kings College at Cambridge, Midnight Mass from Notre Dame at Paris, a "Rhythm on Ice" show from Switzerland, and a visit to Erasmus House in Brussels.[6]

Between the official start of *Eurovision* on June 6, 1954, until the end of that year, 55 different programs were relayed, covering 73 hours of transmissions.[7] By the end of 1955 most of Europe was able to participate in program exchanges without disrupting national domestic programs. Austria and some other countries inaugurated new television services and also joined the continental network. Highlights of programs broadcast during 1955 included the opening of the Four Power Conference and the Conference on the Peaceful Uses of Atomic Energy. The *Eurovision* telecasts of the 1956 Winter Olympic Games, held at Cortina d'Ampezzo in Italy, represented the most extensive operation undertaken thus far. Some fifty-four telecasts were made during the thirteen days of the games. Radio-Television Italiana (RAI) was the host organization, and extensive arrangements were made. It is interesting to note that two communist countries—East Germany and Czechoslovakia—were linked for the first time with the *Eurovision* network. Another event of interest televised during 1956 was the wedding of Prince Rainier III to Grace Kelly, transmitted by Radio Monte Carlo. The "Tour de France," perhaps the most famous of all cycle races, was also telecast to Western Europe in 1956 by Radiodiffusion Télévision Française. Another event was a Grand Prix d'Eurovision Competition. This represented the first program arising out of *Eurovision* itself: each nation entered a song in the contest.[8]

Luxembourg and Monaco became members of *Eurovision* in 1956, the Independent Television Authority (ITV) from Great Britain in 1957, Sweden in 1958, Norway in 1959, Finland and Yugoslavia in 1960, and in 1963 the

Year	Total number of programs transmitted	hours transmitted
1954	55	73
1955	91	115
1956 *	250	273
1957	207	261
1958	203	259
1959	292	339
1960 *	500	440
1961	679	606
1962	1427	586 **
1963	3110	3610
1964 *	3717	4497
1965	3115	4053
1966	3790	5212
1967	3387	4092
1968 *	6240	8251
1969	5363	6809
1970	4501	6582
1971	4573	7153
1972 *	7396	12189
1973	4028	6681
1974	5609	8312
21 Years	58533 (average of 2787 programs per annum)	80393 (average of 3828 hours per annum)

* = years of Olympic Games
** = until 1962: without newstransmissions

newly founded Second German TV network ZDF (Zweites Deutsches Fernsehen) got its membership. Early in 1964 *Eurovision* had 29 active members from 26 different countries and 28 associated members from all over the world; among them were the American television companies ABC (American Broadcasting Company), CBS (Columbia Broadcasting System, Inc.), NBC (National Broadcasting Company, Inc.), the Canadian CBC (Canadian Broadcasting Corporation), the Japanese NHK (Nippon Hoso Kyokai) and the SIA (Serviços de Imprensa, Rádio e Televisão Associados) from Brazil.[9]

The number of program exchanges among member countries of *Eurovision* climbed from year to year [10] (See chart p. 353).

When *Eurovision* started in 1954, in the eight member countries of that time there existed around 3,238 million TV viewers, but in 1961 this number had reached more than 28 million. In all those years the main problem for transmissions were the *different* European languages. So the main product of *Eurovision* was an international sports telecast. Between 1954 and 1961 nearly 55% of the total program contained sports of some kind.[11] But since the early 1960's, the percentage of non-sport-contents of the program grew regularly. At the end of May, 1961, a modest start was made with the relaying of news in pictures by means of the *Eurovision* network. This way of relaying news has rapidly developed into a comprehensive daily operation, involving nearly all the European members of the EBU. Other organizations outside Europe participate in the system, because they can pick up the images from the *Eurovision* network at a favorable point in Europe and relay them to their own country by air-freight or even by satellite.[12]

Since that time news and actuality programs together made up nearly 60% of all *Eurovision* activity. The value of this kind of operation was underlined by nearly all the member countries. Emphasizing that the *Eurovision* news transmissions had become "an essential source of news material," a special Study Group recommended that they should have priority over all other transmissions except live mutilateral programs and that they should be scheduled every day of the year including Sundays and public holidays.[13] The graph on page 355 demonstrates the quantitative importance of news transmissions in 1967 and 1968.[14]

In addition to *Eurovision* some of the Scandinavian countries tried to develop since October, 1959 the Nordvision [15] which—in its early stage—did not progress too well. The success of *Eurovision* in regional transmissions led the Communist-ruled countries of Eastern Europe to attempt a similar venture within their own borders. Early in 1956 some stations in East Germany and Czechoslovakia broadcast part of the *Eurovision* coverage of the Olympic hockey matches relayed from Italy, and in 1957 interconnections also were extended to Poland. The idea of an international television service of the East European countries was born in sessions of COMECON (the East European equivalent of the Common market). Since May, 1958, television experts from East Germany, Czechoslovakia, Hungary, and Poland discussed the different

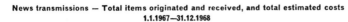

News transmissions — Total items originated and received, and total estimated costs
1.1.1967—31.12.1968

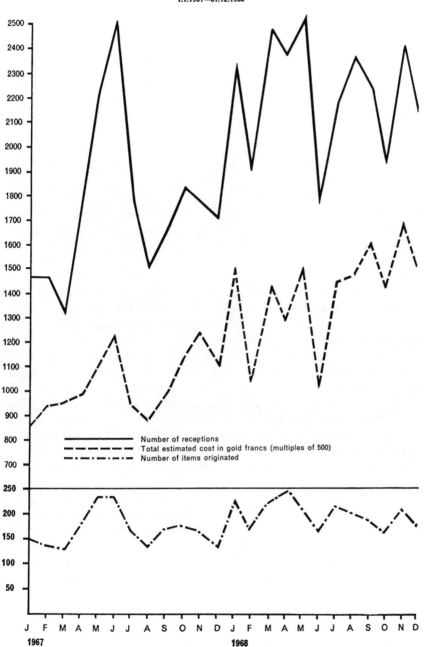

problems. The most developed TV system outside of East Germany was that of Czechoslovakia, and there was already a test transmission to Hungary on August 31, 1957.[16] In January, 1960, the Administration Council of OIRT (International Radio and Television Organization, usually referred by the initials of its French name, the Organisation Internationale de Radio et Télévision) decided to create the so-called *Intervision*. The foundation of this institution took place on January 31, 1960, in Budapest, and the first four members were the national TV networks of East Germany, Czhechoslovakia, Hungary, and Poland.[17] On February 6, 1960, in Geneva a contract was signed which dealt with a program exchange between *Eurovision* and *Intervision*.[18]

The formal inauguration of *Intervision* came on September 5, 1960, and the program aims of the organization were declared as follows: (a) actual information, live transmissions, (b) programs dealing with the economic, social, political and cultural life of the member countries, (c) artistic programs of classical and modern authors of the member countries, (d) programs for children and youth, (e) entertainment programs, (f) transmission of main national and international sport events.[19] Membership is open to "any television organization—not only O.I.R.T. members—which accepts the *Intervision* Statutes."[20] When links became available, the Soviet Union joined in 1961, and in 1963 Bulgaria and Romania became members of *Intervision*. The coordination center was established under the supervision of OIRT in its headquarters at Prague (Czechoslovakia). It is interesting to note that Finland, which already belonged to *Eurovision*, in 1965 became a member of *Intervision*, too. Very similar to this is the situation of the television organization from Yugoslavia which is a regular member of *Eurovision*, but also an associated one to the East European network system.[21]

Intervision in the later 1960's had together 14 active member organizations.[22] *Intervision* does not, however, service as many individual stations or as large an audience as its Western European counterpart. "The most important distinction between Intervision and Eurovision is, of course, their purposes," writes a researcher, and he continues: "Intervision is intended primarily to be a transmission belt for the propaganda of the Soviet Union and its European allies. It is international television in the service of Marxism-Leninism."[23] Between January, 1960, and January, 1965, more than 3700 programs were transmitted by the *Intervision* network. A Russian television executive classified the programs as follows: sports, 43.5%; topical, 30.5%; cultural, 9.8%; children's, 9.4%; and entertainment 6.7%.[24] These figures show that sports has nearly the same average percentage of the program of *Intervision* than it has on *Eurovision*.

After five years of *Intervision*, Aleš Suchý, Head of the Program Coordination Center at Prague, made this statement: "I think that it can be said in general that the five-year existence of Intervention has fully proved the necessity of establishment of this international organization which is, as testified by the daily life, needed by national television organizations; using it as their effective assistant in the mutual program exchange." [25] During the first five and one-half years of existence the *Intervision* center at Prague coordinated 4,941 programs, which makes 5,413 hours of transmissions. [26] A big event like a May Day parade in Moscow gets televised all over the bloc, and in certain cases these programs are transmitted to television stations outside of the *Intervision* networks. [27]

It was already mentioned that the first step of cooperation between TV networks of both members of *Eurovision* as well as of *Intervision* took place in 1956, when East Germany and Czechoslovakia broadcast some sports events from the Olympic Winter Games in Italy, transmitted by the *Eurovision* member RAI. Since 1960, when *Intervision* was founded, there has been certain annual program exchange: The figures for 1960 and for 1964 indicate the big interest in sports telecasts from the Olympic Summer Games in Rome (1960) and the Olympic Winter Games in Innsbruck/Austria (1964): Among the 74 program exchanges in 1960 there were 53 of sports events, and in 1964 there were 164 sports telecasts among the total of 246 transmissions from *Eurovision* to *Intervision*.

On the other hand, there have been regular program exchanges from *Intervision* to *Eurovision*, too. Most of these imports and exports have been cultural programs or sports events. The following statistics give an-incomplete-quantitative overview on the development of the exchange volume between *Eurovision* and *Intervision*: [28]

Year	Eurovision → Intervision		Intervision → Eurovision	
	telecasts	hours	telecasts	hours
1960	74	126	33	47
1961	54	57	17	30
1962	38	65	56	104
1963	87	128	49	88
1964	240	247	95	83
1965 *	124	36	128	61
1966	199	310	107	150
1967	174	274	76	131
1968	?		?	
1969	?		?	
1970	204	374	117	214
1971	253	475	82	153
1972	?		?	
1973	285	541	128	240

* only January–September

Beside of these mainly cultural or sports-oriented programs, *Eurovision* and *Intervision* started also regular newsfilm exchanges with each other. In 1972 a researcher from Finland proposed the idea of a joint study of *Eurovision* (EVN) and *Intervision* (IVN) news. There is no space here to discuss the theoretical basis for this research program which finally was undertaken between January and March, 1974, but here are some of the main results of that study: "The newscasts in Intervision countries contain a larger percentage of news items from western Europe (15–20%) than the newscasts in Eurovision countries from eastern Europe (5–10%). Intervision members show newsfilm received from EVN for 5–10% of their total newscast duration but Eurovision members take from IVN only 0–5%. The share of newsfilm taken from their own union's exchange is 10–20% for Intervision, 5–20% for Eurovision members." The following statistics show the contents of EVN, IVN and mutual EVN/IVN exchanges: [29]

Subject	EVN	%	EVN to IVN	%	IVN	%	IVN to EVN	%
Politics	579	53	379	52	297	32	35	60
Economic affairs	30	3	23	3	148	16	—	—
Security, war	76	7	56	8	28	3	—	—
Sport	200	18	136	19	120	13	18	31
Cultural, social, scientific	15	1	14	2	292	31	1	2
Disasters, etc.	168	15	107	14	37	4	4	7
Others	33	3	19	2	11	1	—	—
Total	1101	100	734	100	933	100	58	100

No country in Europe or anywhere in the world can expect to be self-sufficient in the TV field. An exciting new era began on July 23, 1962, when Europe and North America were linked by live television for the first time, through the Telstar-1 experimental communication satellite orbiting high over the Atlantic. An estimated 100 million Europeans witnessed 22 minutes of live pickups of everyday life in a dozen North American cities from Quebec to the Mexican border, during this memorable initial program. Later the same day, a North American audience of almost similar size became armchair tourists for 19 absorbing minutes as Eurovision cameras scanned from the Arctic Circle to the Mediterranean, and from the Danube to the Atlantic.[30] As a consequence of the Early Bird Satellite in 1965, the day-long transmission of live television across the Atlantic became technically possible at the very time there was increasing demand for news exchange. The new technical instruments made it possible that the number of 72 transmissions by satellites in 1964 [31] climbed to 186 in 1965. [32] The first transmission via Early Bird took place on May 2, 1965, when a two-way multiple-origin program was transmitted to mark the introduction of this new telecommunication facility. This program was rather similar in conception to the very first trans-Atlantic television program with which the satellite Telstar was inaugurated in 1962. [33] The following graph gives an overview on the trend of satellite telecasts with major events indicated (Atlantic region) from July 1965 through December 1968: [34]

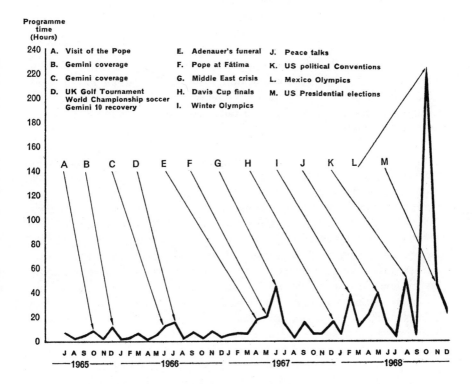

The various developments of international television made it necessary, that Marcel Bezençon, the "father of Eurovision," in 1966 came up with the question, how the future of *Eurovision* could look like: "Will Eurovision merge into Mondovision? Probably to the extent that Mondovision is no more than a network for direct relay gradually encircling the globe and enabling any television organization to give its viewers a show picked out from some other point in the world. At first sight, and ideally speaking, there does not seem to be any insuperable barrier to this fabulous expansion." [35]

One year after these remarks *Eurovision* made another step towards Mondovision. Television services from five continents worked together for a world-wide live program under the title "Our World" on Sunday, 25th of June, 1967. This telecast was the result of two years of intensive preparation, and it was the very first step to reach a global audience for two hours. Broadcast was between 8 and 10 p.m. Central European time, and its contents was comprised contributions of television stations in Africa, Australia, Canada, Europe, Japan, Mexico, and the United States. Because of the time zoning, viewers in the eastern United States watched it on Sunday afternoon, while in Australia and Japan it appeared on television screens early on Monday morning. This project was first put forward by the British Broadcasting Corporation in 1965 and since then developed by the EBU Television Program Committee with the assistance of the permanent staff in Geneva and Brussels.

The structure of the program was composed at a number of international conferences and technical planning commissions of 17 different broadcasting organizations. Nearly 10,000 broadcasting staff members all around the world were mobilized, and the equipment included more than a million miles of telephone line and 100,000 miles of micro-wave links. For the long-distance vision links there were four satellites over the Atlantic and Pacific, and sound circuits were also routed via the satellites; the transatlantic telephone cables provided a reserve path. The master control room and main switching center of the whole operation was located at the BBC Television Center's Studio in London. But there were set up also two regional zones for this telecast: The West Zone, with New York as sub-switching point, handled the items from Canada, the United States, Mexico, Australia and Japan, and the eastern zone, covered by the European Broadcasting Union with Brussels as switching-point, handled the sequences from Austria, Belgium, France, West Germany, Italy, Spain, Sweden und Tunisia. A system of simultaneous translation into English, French and German was set up in London, and a number of national commentators translated into their own languages where it was necessary. It was estimated that around 350 million viewers were watching this world-wide two hour program. Arrangements had also been made for a number of countries in Eastern Europe to take part in the program, but these were cancelled shortly before the start of the transmission.

The program started with a visit by television cameras to babies newly born in Japan, Canada, Denmark and Mexico. And when the transmission came to its end after two hours these babies were shown again how they looked after living for two hours in "Our World." The viewers were also shown for example scientists at work in different parts of the world in research to increase food supply, and housing development in Scotland, Canada and New York. The cameras of "Our World" were also able to show the global audience the Victorian mansion at Glassboro in the United States where at that same moment President Johnson and the Soviet Prime Minister Kosygin, were discussing the world situation. So it was really a historical day on this 25th of June, 1967, when an audience from great parts of the world was able to participate in events which happened at the same time in the various continents of "Our World." [36]

A few days after this successful event, Marcel Bezençon meditated on the future perspectives of international television: "Eurovision is no longer Eurovision. Its tight framework has been burst open by technology. Already it has Intervision as a travelling companion, and the satellites are pointing to the new paths it must follow. We are in transit between two eras . . . This process is not without its crises, its abrupt changes, fatigues, errors and thromboses. We cannot pass straight from the state of villager to that of universal man. Eurovision, Mondovision, the intensification of rapid news exchanges, and soon distribution satellites and perhaps broadcasting satellites, are going to lay bare massive and contradictory solidarities . . . One might wonder whether Eurovision in its present form will have any reason for existence in ten years' time, when broadcasting satellites will plunge their programs live into private receiving sets. . . ." [37]

On August 20, 1964, the International Telecommunications Satellite Consortium, better known as INTELSAT, was established. It started with a membership of 11 nations which climbed by 1969 to 68. [38] Since satellite transmissions in the early period were rather expansive, on February 1, 1969, shortly after the operational availability over the Atlantic Ocean a new satellite in the INTELSAT III series, the Communications Satellite Corporation (COMSAT) made a substantial general reduction in its rates for television service provided through the Atlantic satellites. On February 24, 1969, when the new INTELSAT III became operational over the Pacific Ocean, COMSAT made reductions of the same magnitude in its rates for television transmissions in that area. [39]

A leading representative of the Australian Broadcasting Commission, after establishment of that new satellite, made this statement: [40] "The transmission of programmes by communication satellite has meant as much to Australia in opening up new horizons of broadcasting as to any country in the world, and indeed more than to most other countries. This is so primarily because of the geographical isolation of Australia, literally 'down under' from the traditional centres of world power and newsmaking . . ." From there on this world-wide distribution of the Apollo II television material via three linked satellites was given. [41] (See map on p. 362).

As in earlier years, the program category which accounted for the longest global circuit-time in 1968 was sport. The main events were the Olympic Games: first the Winter Games at Grenoble (France) and in October, the Summer Games in Mexico. In both cases, a high proportion of the transmissions was already in color: about 56% in the case of Grenoble and about 85% in the case of Mexico City. [42] In spite of many difficulties, however, transmissions of the pictures via satellite (Intelsat III) during the Games went smoothly and reception quality was excellent. The EBU/OIRT Operations Group consisted of 160 staff members recruited from nearly all the European member organiza-

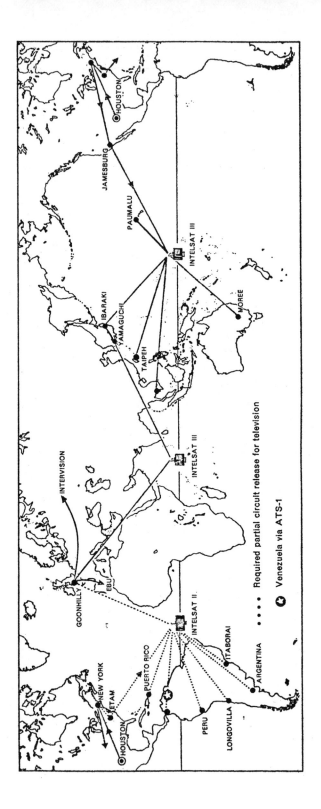

HOUSTON

JAMESBURG

PAUMALU

INTELSAT III

IBARAKI

YAMAGUCHI

TAIPEH

MOREE

INTERVISION

INTELSAT III

GOONHILLY

EBU

NEW YORK

ETAM

PUERTO RICO

HOUSTON

INTELSAT II

ITABORAI

ARGENTINA

PERU

LONGOVILLA

······ Required partial circuit release for television

✪ Venezuela via ATS-1

tions and in Mexico itself. The running of such a large multinational team, which had had no time to work together beforehand, was another experiment which worked satisfactorily. The European television organizations received, for selection and further distribution, 136 hours of sporting events from Mexico City. [43] An unique experiment in the television field was the cooperation of several major broadcasting organizations in running a common television production pool. The American Broadcasting Companies, Inc., EBU/OIRT and Nippon Hoso Kyokai (Japan) joined with Telesistema Mexicano in this project. [44] And this was the result of the Eurovision program during the Olympic year: [45]

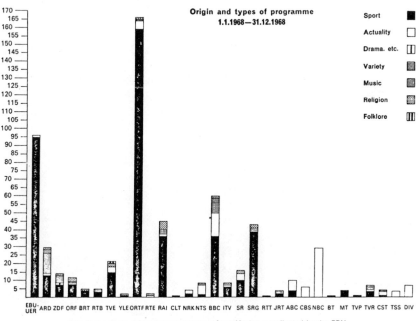

The first column refers to transmissions from Mexico coordinated by the EBU

The importance and functions of *Eurovision* grew steadily. So, for example, in 1969 Greece became member, and one year later the EBU opened a Television News Coordination Bureau in New York. This is the development of the memberships of the European Broadcasting Union during the first 25 years of existence. [46]

Apart from the progress of Eurovision, other steps of international television cooperation were undertaken. As noted above, the five Scandinavian countries—Denmark, Finland, Iceland, Norway, Sweden—founded the *Nordvision* in November 1969 at Copenhagen. "The general exchange of programmes between NV countries," an official says, "had as starting point the principle that each country should offer programmes from the current production and should itself—with the exception of some copyright items, and similar

year	active members	associate members
1950	23	4
1951	23	12
1952	24	11
1953	25	12
1954	25	13
1955	26	11
1956	27	15
1957	28	15
1958	26	16
1959	26	18
1960	28	16
1961	27	17
1962	27	26
1963	28	29
1964	28	40
1965	28	40
1966	28	39
1967	28	43
1968	28	49
1969	30	54
1970	33	54
1971	33	59
1972	33	65
1973	33	66
1974	34	64

matters—defray the extra expenditure involved in other countries. In other words, television programmes are not bought or sold between the Scandinavian broadcasting organizations. . . ." [47]

Another connection of similar intention shall be the planned *Arabvision*. The main reason for steps towards this direction was, that "Television stations in the Arab world are, with a few exceptions, still almost completely dependent on foreign non-Arab agencies both for fil coverage of each other and for the interchange of newsfilm between the Arab region and other areas of the world in both directions. . . ." [48]

These and other regional TV organizations cooperate with *Eurovision* and/or *Intervision* on an exchange basis. If one comes back to the *Eurovision* programs themselves one could raise the question, which kind of programmes there are exchanged. Besides the regular news-transmission here are the number and percentage of types of *Eurovision* programs for two years: [49]

Period	Actuality/* current affairs		Folklore		Religion		Sport		Light entertainment		Music Jazz		Total	
	No	%	No	%	No	%	No	%	No	%	No	%	No	%
1.1-30.6.73	37	10.7	1	0.3	7	2	277	79.8	22	6.3	3	0.9	347	100
1.7-31.12.73	30	9.5	2	0.6	8	2.5	258	81.7	14	4.4	4	1.3	316	100
Total	67	10.1	3	0.4	15	2.3	535	80.7	36	5.4	7	1.1	663	100
	No	%	No	%	No	%	No	%	No	%	No	%	No	%
1.1-30.6.74	25	5.5	2	0.4	6	1.3	409	89.7	12	2.7	2	0.4	456	100
1.7-31.12.74	26	8.6	3	1	5	1.6	251	83.1	15	5	2	0.7	302	100
Total	51	6.7	5	0.7	11	1.4	660	87.1	27	3.6	4	0.5	758	100

* as distinct from Eurovision news exchange

As can be noticed from these figures, the percentage of sports transmissions still is the highest of all—in most of the last years it was 75 to 80% of the total exchange program. In 1972, when the Olympic Summer Games at Munich took place, the total amount reached not more than an average of 78% of the annual *Eurovision* distributed programs,[50] but this was already a lot. Therefore, on the fourth Meeting of the Executive Group of the Television Program Committee of *Eurovision*, held in October 1973 in Geneva, the "ARD and ZDF (Fed. Rep. of Germany) and their consortium, DOZ (Deutsches Olympia Zentrum) were congratulated on the excellent coverage of the Munich Olympic Games, from which an impressive amount of material had been produced: 13,695 minutes of multilaterals and 7,349 minutes of unilaterals, without counting the transmissions from venues outside Munich."[51] At first glance it might be quite astonishing, that the percentage of sports transmissions in 1974 climbed to 87.1%. This can be explained by mentioning another world-televised sports competition: the World Football (Soccer) Championship in Germany.[52]

Among the internationally transmitted cultural or music programs, many European stations take part in the annual EBU-organized *Eurovision Song Contest*; in 1974 there were 17 television stations as participants of that transmission.[53] A British TV expert made this critical statement in behalf of the various competitions of this and similar kind: "Part and parcel of television's growth in Europe . . . has been the establishment of international festivals. For example, the *Prix Italia*, the *Golden Rose of Montreux*, the *Cannes CIRA*, and the more specialized *Festival du Prince* in Monaco and the *Golden Harp* in Dublin, as well as the two-yearly *Prix Jeunesse* and *Prix Futura* and now the *International Christian Television Festival* have all become fixed dates in our calendar. And there is the *Eurovision Song Contest!* . . . It is rather a question whether these European festivals can open their doors to overseas and so stimulate more *variety* of interchange."[54]

If one wants to get a certain overview on the quantitative changes and development of the total amount of *Eurovision* programs and news the following approximate figures give details on a five years' period: [55]

Programmes and news (approximate figures)

		1970	1971	1972	1973	1974
1	*(a)* Eurovision programmes originated	645	662	709	663	758
	(b) Intervision origins included in 1 *(a)* figures	73	40	58	72	57
	(c) Eurovision programmes cancelled, withdrawn by offering organization, no interest, interest cancelled	250	204	149	173	194
	(d) Programmes cancelled on the network (not included in 1 *(c)* figures) but sent in recorded form	43	42	35	45	21
	(e) Total number of programmes with performers (included in 1 *(a)*)	61	48	28	−	−
2	Relays of Eurovision programmes	4 500	4 573	7 396	4 028	5 609
3	Average number of relaying television services per programme originated	7	6.9	10.4	6.1	7.4
4	Regular Eurovision news exchanges and occasional transmissions of news items	746	749	861	981	1 057
5	*(a)* News items originated within the framework of transmissions under 4 (not including live actuality programmes)	3 800	4 278	4 564	5 423	5 085
	(b) News agency items included in 5 *(a)*	1 600	1 760	2 271	2 924	2 556
	(c) Intervision items included in 5 *(a)*	275	290	222	176	215
	(d) News items from Latin America included in 5 *(a)*	−	43	19	26	35
6	*(a)* News item relays	42 272	51 133	58 574	68 155	92 818
	(b) Items relayed by the news agencies not included in 6 *(a)*	100	93	70	327	295
	(c) Items relayed by Intervision included in 6 *(a)*	5 741	7 643	8 377	10 397	16 955
	(d) Items relayed by Latin American television services included in 6 *(a)*	−	1 578	6 349	6 733	8 566
7	Average number of relaying television services per item, including Intervision and Latin America	11.1	11.9	12.8	12.6	18.2

The international exchange of news programs especially seems to function pretty well. Encouraged by the success of this exchange service during the first three months of 1973 an extra daily multilateral news exchange was tried out on the *Eurovision* Network in reply to requests from several active member organizations. It was timed at midday in order to meet the early television news bulletins.[56] In the same year the EBU expressed its hopes to see an *Eurovision* program distribution satellite in operation before long. At the same time EBU examined the possibility of introducing, during the first half of 1974 and on an experimental basis, coordinated news transmissions from the United States to Europe (*Eurovision*). EBU also approved the introduction of a third daily multi-origin, multi-reception news exchange at noon.[57]

The Executive Group of EBU also recommended at that time that the existing news exchange with Latin America, through the intermediary of Spanish Television (TVE), should continue and that a new exchange with the Arab States Broadcasting Union (ASBU), based on the principle of reciprocity, should be started. Apart from that EBU also made this statement: [58] "There has, of course, been regular exchange of news between *Eurovision* and OIRT (*Intervision*), through the intermediary of Austrian Television (ORF), for many years now, as well as between *Eurovision* and North America, via the EBU Coordination Office in New York. But it is with the three U.S. networks that the EBU cooperates most actively, thus providing European viewers with full coverage of news events taking place in the United States. These include the space missions, the U.S. presidential elections and other political and public events normally covered by the U.S. Networks Pool, which the networks have agreed to place at the disposal of Eurovision in exchange for access to the Eurovision network for the transmission of television programmes and news to the United States. . . .". The charts on the following two pages give an excellent overview on the total *Eurovision* activities of a complete year.[59]

So the EBU and its subdivision *Eurovision* are really—according to the words of EBU's general secretary Henrik Hahr—"some kind of United Nations of Radio and Television Broadcasting."[60] But we have some indication that this UNO of TV is mainly a *Sports International*. In 1975 sports became that important, that "a special sports news conference has been held on the Permanent Sound Network every Tuesday to discuss the availability of news material on major sports events in the coming weeks . . . Sport, like news, took its usual large place on the Executive Group's agenda, especially in connection with preparations for coverage of the 1976 Olympic Games in Innsbruck and Montreal," and "it is expected that the Organizing Committees of the cities selected for the 1980 Olympic Games—Lake Placid and Moscow—will also avail themselves in due course of the broadcasters' advice, so it is felt that a good start has been made in this connection."[61] But the preparation of the transmissions of the 1976 Olympics brought big financial problems to EBU, and so a special *Eurovision* committee "discussed the difficulties being encountered over the purchase of television rights in the 1976 Montreal Olympic Games. . . . For the Innsbruck Games, on the other hand, there was happier news to report as the contract has been signed and arrangements for coverage are going ahead satisfactorily. . . ."[62]

Nobody really knows exactly if this program concept of *Eurovision* is really that which the viewers in Europe and abroad are wishing for. A German expert in international television expressed that problem as follows: "The market model means that the majority decides on the programming policy: programming by constant referendum. The consumer will indicate what program he would like to see more of and what program he does not find desirable. There will be ratings and the mounting silent terror of audience surveys. Anything that does not attract a majority among the viewers will be taken off the air. On the other hand, as soon as a program attracts a majority it will be beyond criticisms or any kind of discussion of its quality."[63]

Will this happen to international Television too—or is it already true?

Eurovision programmes (1.1.74—31.12.74)

Organization		Origin of programmes		Participation in exchanges	
		Total number of programmes originated	Total hours of transmission at point of origin	Total number of programmes received	Total hours received
Algeria	RTA	—	—	103	187 h 43
Austria	ORF	48	80 h 49	260	425 h 16
Belgium	BRT [1]	11	9 h 53	239	290 h 07
	RTB [1]	8	11 h 55	193	214 h 01
Denmark	DR	2	6 h 10	119	184 h 25
Finland	YLE	28	64 h 07	96	189 h 30
France	ORTF	97	88 h 48	189	315 h 32
Germany (FR)	ARD	32	62 h 39	118	185 h 04
	ZDF	31	28 h 01	92	152 h 40
	DOZ [2]	128	99 h 28	—	—
Greece	EIPT	—	—	35	83 h 51
Iceland	RUV	—	—	27	15 h 09
Ireland	RTE	7	8 h 26	132	216 h 26
Israel	IBA	—	—	48	44 h 56
Italy	RAI	68	89 h 45	180	223 h 02
Jordan	JTV	—	—	27	46 h
Libya	PRBC	—	—	25	49 h 06
Luxembourg	RTL	—	—	95	145 h 36
Monaco	RMC	1	1 h 46	14	25 h 53
Morocco	RTM	1	1 h 12	90	115 h 13
Netherlands	NOS	17	33 h 36	237	336 h 26
Norway	NRK	3	4 h 51	142	240 h 14
Portugal	RTP	—	—	173	218 h 24
Spain	TVE	12	25 h 18	195	262 h 44
Sweden	SR	18	44 h 39	127	187 h 10
Switzerland	SRG [1]	40	62 h 54	281	385 h 40
	SSR [1]	5	4 h 25	294	385 h 14
	TSI [1]	2	0 h 45	327	425 h 08
Tunisia	RTT	—	—	123	157 h 33
Turkey	TRT	6	10 h 17	107	139 h 43
United Kingdom	BBC	67	127 h 02	97	190 h 20
	ITV	10	17 h 34	86	153 h 41
Yugoslavia	JRT	43	89 h 59	202	301 h 24
Argentina	RPT	—	—	2	3 h 27
Brazil	TUPI	—	—	3	3 h 41
	TVG	—	—	5	7 h 41
Canada	CBC	8	17 h 14	—	—
	CTV	—	—	1	2 h 35
Colombia	IRV	—	—	1	0 h 58
Gabon	RTG	—	—	7	13 h 02
Iran	NIRT	—	—	4	7 h 02
Ivory Coast	RTI	—	—	19	35 h 26
Kuwait	KBTS	—	—	5	10 h 26
Mexico	TVA	—	—	5	7 h 45
New Zealand	NZBC	—	—	1	1 h 38
Senegal	RTS	—	—	9	16 h 32
United States	ABC	1	0 h 30	2	2 h 26
	CBS	4	5 h 38	3	4 h 07
	NBC	—	—	2	1 h 02
	USP [3]	1	0 h 24	—	—
Upper Volta	RTV	—	—	3	5 h 02
Venezuela	VV	—	—	1	0 h 58
Zaïre	VZ	—	—	9	14 h 26
Bulgaria	BT	13	33 h 58	108	147 h 33
Czechoslovakia	CT	6	10 h 27	174	287 h 20
Germany (DR)	DDR-F	28	38 h 27	173	291 h 10
Hungary	MT	4	9 h	157	255 h 44
Poland	TVP	2	2 h 11	195	254 h 31
Romania	TVR	—	—	64	104 h 36
USSR	TSS	4	8 h 03	160	292 h 32
Various		2	2 h 46	23	47 h 04
Total		758	1 102 h 57	5 609	8 311 h 55

Eurovision news exchange (excluding actuality/current affairs programmes)

Origin and reception tables (1.1.74—31.12.74)

	Organization	News items	
		Origins *	Receptions
I	RTA	45	2 437
	ORF	52	2 912
	BRT ¹	59	3 499
	RTB ¹	62	2 806
	CyBC	1	—
	DR	19	2 489
	YLE	18	2 523
	ORTF	391	2 250
	ARD	90	2 156
	ZDF	230	2 688
	EIPT	12	—
	RUV	1	—
	RTE	32	977
	IBA	11	1 723
	RAI	497	3 215
	JTV	9	1 761
	RTL	19	2 501
	RTM	23	1 909
	NOS	101	3 312
	NRK	29	2 620
	RTP	127	3 171
	TVE	92	3 753
	SR	54	2 547
	SRG	185	3 415
	RTT	35	3 235
	TRT	21	1 738
	BBC	1 434	922
	ITN	811	988
	JRT	50	3 527
	Total	4 510	65 074

	Organization	News items	
		Origins *	Receptions
II	ABC	5	59
	CBS	77	25
	NBC	21	26
	USP ³	8	15
	CBC	3	—
	UNTV	17	—
	Total	131	125
III	NIRT	2	2 080
IV	FTC	—	4
	NET	—	3
	NHK	2	4
	NTV	—	3
	TBS	—	4
	Total	2	18
V	Latin America	35	8 566
VI	Intervision	215	16 955
VII	ASBU	10	—
VIII	Various	180	—
	TOTAL (I to VIII)	5 085	92 818

* Including news agency material, with main originating points being BBC and ITN, the US networks and other services.

Key to names of organizations

EBU active member organizations participating in exchanges

ARD	Arbeitsgemeinschaft der öffentlich-rechtlichen Rundfunkanstalten der Bundesrepublik Deutschland, Germany (FR)
BBC	British Broadcasting Corporation, United Kingdom
{ BRT	Belgische Radio en Televisie, Belgium
{ RTB	Radiodiffusion-Télévision Belge, Belgium
CyBC	Cyprus Broadcasting Corporation, Cyprus
DR	Danmarks Radio, Denmark
EIPT	Ethnikon Idryma Radiophonias-Tileoraseos, Greece
IBA	Israel Broadcasting Authority, Israel
{ ITN	Independent Television News, United Kingdom
{ ITV	Independent Television, United Kingdom
JRT	Jugoslovenska Radiotelevizija, Yugoslavia
JTV	Jordan Television, Jordan
NOS	Nederlandse Omroep Stichting, Netherlands
NRK	Norsk Rikskringkasting, Norway
ORF	Österreichischer Rundfunk GmbH, Austria
ORTF	Office de Radiodiffusion-Télévision Française, France
PRBC	People's Revolution Broadcasting Corporation, Libyan Arab Republic
RAI	RAI-Radiotelevisione Italiana, Italy
RMC	Radio Monte-Carlo, Monaco
RTA	Radiodiffusion-Télévision Algérienne, Algeria
RTE	Radio Telefís Éireann, Ireland
RTL	Radio-Télé-Luxembourg, Luxembourg
RTM	Radiodiffusion-Télévision Marocaine, Morocco
RTP	Radiotelevisão Portuguesa SARL, Portugal
RTT	Radiodiffusion-Télévision Tunisienne, Tunisia
SR	Sveriges Radio, Sweden
{ SRG	Schweizerische Radio- und Fernsehgesellschaft, Switzerland
{ SSR	Société Suisse de Radiodiffusion et Télévision, Switzerland
{ TSI	Società Svizzera Radiotelevisione, Switzerland
TRT	Türkiye Radyo-Televizyon Kurumu, Turkey
TVE	Televisión Española, Spain
YLE	Oy Yleisradio Ab, Finland
ZDF	Zweites Deutsches Fernsehen, Germany (FR)

EBU associate member organizations participating in exchanges

ABC	American Broadcasting Companies Inc, United States
CBC	Canadian Broadcasting Corporation, Canada

CBS	CBS Inc, United States
CTV	CTV Television Network Ltd, Canada
FTC	Fuji Telecasting Company Ltd, Japan
IRV	Instituto Nacional de Radio y Televisión–Inravisión, Colombia
KBTS	Kuwait Broadcasting and Television Service, Kuwait
NBC	National Broadcasting Company Inc, United States
NET	Nippon Educational Television Company Ltd, Japan
NHK	Nippon Hoso Kyokai, Japan
NIRT	National Iranian Radio and Television, Iran
NTV	Nippon Television Network Corporation, Japan
NZBC	New Zealand Broadcasting Corporation, New Zealand
RTG	Radiodiffusion Télévision Gabonaise, Gabon
RTI	Radiodiffusion Télévision Ivoirienne, Ivory Coast
RTS	Radiodiffusion Télévision du Sénégal, Senegal
RTV	Radiodiffusion-Télévision Voltaïque, Upper Volta
RPT	Río de la Plata TV SA (Canal 13), Argentina
TBS	Tokyo Broadcasting System Inc, Japan
TUPI	Diários Associados Ltda, Brazil
TVA	Televisa SA, Mexico
TVG	TV Globo Ltda, Brazil
VV	Corporación Venezolana de Televisión CA, Venezuela
VZ	La Voix du Zaïre, Zaïre

OIRT/Intervision member organizations

BT	Bolgarskoe Radio i Televidenie, Bulgaria
CT	Ceskoslovenska Televize, Czechoslovakia
DDR-F	Deutscher Fernsehfunk, Germany (DR)
MT	Magyar Televizio, Hungary
TSS	Televidenie Sovetskoio Soiuza, USSR
TVP	Polska Telewizja, Poland
TVR	Radiodifuzlunea si Televiziunea Romina, Romania

ASBU   Arab States Broadcasting Union

UNTV   United Nations Television

¹ Separate figures for participation in the exchanges are given for each of the two Belgian and, in the programme table, for each of the three Swiss tv services, even though they constitute one EBU member organization in each country. As certain material was used by more than one tv service, the totals for Belgium and Switzerland are less than the simple addition of the figures for each individual service.

² DOZ indicates Deutsches Olympia Zentrum, an ARD/ZDF consortium set up for the 1972 Olympic Games and maintained for the 1974 World Football Cup.

³ USP—United States Networks Pool (occasionally in operation between the US networks).

NOTES

[1] Marcel Bezençon, "Eurovision—the Pattern of the Future," in: *EBU Bulletin* (Geneva), September/October 1954, p. 567, cf. also: Paul Bellac, "Die Vorgeschichte der Eurovision. Zum zehnjährigen Bestehen der Eurovision," *Rundfunk und Fernsehen* (Hamburg), Vol. 12/No. 1 (1964), pp. 26 ff.

[2] Cf. Donald K. Pollock and David Lyndon Woods, "A Study in International Communication: Eurovision," *Journal of Broadcasting* (Los Angeles), Vol. III/No. 2 (Spring 1959), pp. 101 ff.; source of the map is: *EBU Review* (Geneva), Vol. XXVI/No. 1 (January 1975), p. 12.

[3] Russell Brooks Butler Barber, *Eurovision as an Expression of International Cooperation in Western Europe*, Unpublished Ph.D. dissertation, Northwestern University, Evanston/Ill. 1963, p. 50.

[4] Paul Bellac, "Die Vorgeschichte der Eurovision," *Publizistik* (Bremen), Vol. 9/No. 1 (January-March 1964), p. 55.

[5] Cf. Alvise Horci, "Twenty years after. The Story of Italy's contribution to the first day of Eurovision programmes," *EBU Review* (Geneva), Vol. XXV/No. 3 (May 1974), p. 20 ff.

[6] Donald K. Pollock and David Lyndon Woods, *op. cit.*, pp. 104 ff.

[7] "Eurovision," *Internationales Handbuch für Rundfunk und Fernsehen 1967/68*, Hamburg: Verlag Hans-Bredow-Institut, 1967, p. E 46.

[8] Donald K. Pollock and David Lyndon Woods, *op. cit.*, p. 106 ff.

[9] *Internationales Handbuch für Rundfunk und Fernsehen 1967/68*, *op. cit.*, p. E 45 ff.

[10] From: *Internationales Handbuch für Rundfunk und Fernsehen 1973/75*, Hamburg: Verlag Hans-Bredow-Institut, 1974, p. E 104, and: *EBU Review* (Geneva), Vol. XXVI/No. 3 (May 1975), p. 69.

[11] Hans Brack, "Die Union Européenne de Radiodiffusion," *Rundfunk und Fernsehen* (Hamburg), Vol. 10/1962, p. 233.

[12] J. W. Rengelink, "Eurovision news—a first step to worldwide news," *EBU-Review* (Geneva), No. 90 B (April 1965), p. 10.

[13] N.C., "News overhauls sport in the Eurovision exchanges," *EBU Review* (Geneva), No. 90 B (April 1965), p. 12.

[14] From: *EBU Review* (Geneva), No. 115 B (May 1969), p. 29.

[15] W. Bauer-Heyd, " 'Nordvision' noch in Kinderschuhen. Die Entwicklung des Fernsehens in Skandinavien," *Kölnische Rundschau* (Cologne), Vol. 14/No. 241 (October 17, 1959); cf. also N.-B. Stormbom, "Nordvision—Television cooperation in the Scandinavian countries," *EBU Review* (Geneva), No. 129 (September 1971), p. 26 ff.

[16] Hermann Deml, "Osteuropäisches Fernsehen," *Publizistik* (Bremen), Vol. 4/No. 3 (May-June 1959), p. 168 ff.

[17] Cf. "Die Entwicklung der Intervision," *Hörfunk und Fernsehen* (Munich), Vol. 16/No. 2 (April 1965), pp. 13 ff.

[18] Hans Brack, "Die Union Européenne de Radiodiffusion," *op. cit.*, p. 233.

[19] OIRT, *Reglement der Intervision*. Prague: Organization Internationale de Radio et Télévision, 1964, p. 14.

[20] OIRT, *International Radio and Television Organization. General Information*. Prague: OIRT, undated, p. 3.

[21] Burton Paulu, *Radio and Television Broadcasting on the European Continent*. Minneapolis/Minnesota: University of Minnesota Press, 1967, p. 41.

[22] OIRT, International Radio and Television Organization. General Information, *op. cit.*, p. 3.

[23] Wilson P. Dizard, *Television—A World View*. Syracuse/New York: Syracuse University Press, 1966, p. 93.

[24] Cf. Burton Paulu, *Radio and Television Broadcasting on the European Continent*, p. 141 ff.

[25] Aleš Suchý, Intervision in 1965, in: *World Radio TV Handbook: Radio-Television 1966*, 20th ed., Hellerup/Denmark: World Radio-Television Handbook Co., 1965, p. 39.

[26] N. A. Skatschko, "Jahre der Entwicklung," *Rundfunk und Fernsehen—OIRT* (Prague), Vol. 1966/No. 2, p. 3.

[27] Cf. "Television in Eastern Europe," *Television Quarterly* (New York/N.Y.), Vol. 6/No. 3 (1967), p. 35.

[28] All figures are compiled by the author from: *Statistik des Programmaustausches zwischen Intervision und Eurovision*, unpublished material from the OIRT Center, Prague, undated (mimeographed).

[29] Yrjö Länsipuro, "Joint Eurovision/Intervision news study," *EBU Review* (Geneva), Vol. XXVI/No. 3 (May 1975), p. 37 ff.

[30] George Jacobs, "Global report on Television," *Television Age* (New York), Vol. XV/No. 24 (July 1, 1968), p. 22.

[31] "Eurovision program statistics," *EBU Review* (Geneva), No. 91 B (May 1965), p. 51.

[32] "Eurovision program statistics," *EBU Review* (Geneva), No. 98 B (July 1966), p. 26.

[33] J. Treeby Dickinson, "Eurovision in 1965," *World Radio TV Handbook. Radio Television 1966.* Hellerup/Denmark: World Radio-Television Handbook Co., 1966, p. 30.

[34] A. Bruce Matthews, "The history and philosophy of COMSAT's satellite television rates," *EBU Review* (Geneva), No. 116 B (July 1969), p. 14.

[35] Marcel Bezençon, "The destiny of Eurovision—Olympus above the clouds?" *EBU Review* (Geneva), No. 98 B (July 1966), p. 13.

[36] "Our World," *Report of Activities 1967—European Broadcasting Union.* Geneva: The European Broadcasting Union, 1968, p. 3 ff.

[37] Marcel Bezençon, "Mist veils an immense horizon," *EBU Review* (Geneva), No. 104 B (July 1967), p. 10.

[38] Richard R. Colino, "Use of the INTELSAT satellite system for Project Apollo," *EBU Review* (Geneva), No. 118 B (November 1969), p. 24.

[39] A. Bruce Matthews, op. cit., p. 10.

[40] W. S. Hamilton, "Australia's dwindling isolation—satellites bridge time and space," *EBU Review* (Geneva), No. 118 B (November 1969), p. 59.

[41] From: Piero Fanti, "European satellite rates for television service," *EBU Review* (Geneva), No. 118 b (November 1969), p. 49.

[42] J. Treeby Dickinson, "Eurovision in 1968," *World Radio TV Handbook. Radio Television 1969.* Hellerup/Denmark: World Radio-Television Handbook Co., 1969, p. 21.

[43] "EBU, Satellites: A Year of Transition," *Report of Activities 1968—European Broadcasting Union.* Geneva: The European Broadcasting Union, 1969, p. 7 f.

[44] Ernst P. Braun, "Mexiko 68: in retrospect," *EBU Review* (Geneva), No. 113 B (January 1969), p. 13.

[45] From: "Eurovision programme statistics," *EBU Review* (Geneva), No. 115 B (May 1969), p. 28.

[46] From: "25 years of the European Broadcasting Union—A Retrospect," *EBU Review* (Geneva), Vol. XXVI/No. 1 (January 1975), pp. 11–27.

[47] N. B. Stormbom, "Nordvision . . . ," op. cit., p. 29.

[48] Hamdy Kandil, "Towards Arabvision," *EBU Review* (Geneva), Vol. XXVI/No. 3 (May 1975), p. 59.

[49] Compiled from: *EBU Review* (Geneva), Vol. XXV/No. 3 (May 1974), p. 44, and Vol. XXVI/No. 3 (May 1975), p. 68.

[50] Cf. *EBU Review* (Geneva), Vol. XXIV/No. 3 (May 1973), p. 45.

[51] From: "EBU Activities," *EBU Review* (Geneva), Vol. XXIV/No. 1 (January 1973), p. 65; on details of the sports transmissions from Munich cf. also Robert E. Lembke, "Die Lokalrunde. Die Berichterstattung in Hörfunk und Fernsehen von den Olympischen Sommerspielen München/Kiel 1972," *ARD-Jahrbuch 72*, Hamburg: Verlag Hans-Bredow-Institut, 1972, pp. I–VII.

[52] Cf. Hans-Heinrich Isenbart, "51 Stunden Fußball. Die ARD und die Weltmeisterschaft," *ARD-Jahrbuch 74*, Hamburg: Verlag Hans-Bredow-Institut, 1974, pp. 74–76.

[53] Cf. C.R.B., "Eurovision Song Contest 1974," *EBU Review* (Geneva), Vol. XXV/No. 3 (May 1974), p. 47.

[54] Christopher Martin, "How international is international? And are our festivals sure?," *EBU Review* (Geneva), Vol. XXV/No. 4 (July 1974), p. 28 f.

[55] Compiled from: "Statistics of Eurovision programmes and news exchanges," *EBU Review* (Geneva), Vol. XXIV/No. 3 (May 1973), p. 45, and: Vol. XXVi/No. 3 (May 1975), p. 68.

[56] "EBU Activities," *EBU Review* (Geneva), Vol. XXIV/No. 4 (July 1973), p. 67.

[57] "EBU Activities," *EBU Review* (Geneva), Vol. XXV/No. 1 (January 1974), p. 60 f.

[58] *Ibid.*, p. 61.

[59] "Statistics of Eurovision programmes and news exchanges," *EBU Review* (Geneva), Vol. XXVI/No. 3 (May 1975), p. 69 f.

[60] Quoted from Horst Scharfenberg (ed.), Studienkreis Rundfunk und Geschichte e.V.-Protokoll der Gründungsversammlung am 10. Juni 1969 in Ludwigshafen/Rhein, Baden-Baden, 1969, p. 5.

[61] "EBU Activities," *EBU Review* (Geneva), Vol. XXVI/No. 1 (January 1975), p. 83.

[62] "EBU Activities," *EBU Review* (Geneva), Vol. XXVI/No. 4 (July 1975), p. 56 f.

[63] Richard Dill, "Television in the 1980s. A future signposted by question marks," *EBU Review* (Geneva), Vol. XXVI/No. 1 (January 1975), p. 39.

Kurt Koszyk:

The Development of the International Press Institute

IT began in a small way. With the consequences of cold war politics and Korean War fighting, which had begun in June 1950, impressed in their minds, 34 newspaper editors and publishers from 15 countries met in a conference room of Columbia University, New York, in October, 1950.[1] They discussed the foundation of an International Press Institute and elected an organising committee. After being granted 35,000 dollars by the Rockefeller Foundation and the Carnegie Endowment for International Peace, the nine members of this body reunited half a year later under Lester Markel of the *New York Times* in Paris and wrote the constitution of the I.P.I.

In the preamble they set out their aims and objectives: "World peace depends upon understanding between peoples and peoples. If people are to understand one another, it is essential that they have good information. Therefore, a fundamental step toward understanding among people is to bring about understanding among the journalists of the world."

The institute declared as its main objects:
1. The furtherance and safeguarding of freedom of the press.
2. The achievement of understanding among journalists and so among peoples.
3. The promotion of the free exchange of accurate and balanced news among nations.
4. The improvement of the practices of journalism.

According to the 1952 charter only representatives of newspaper publishers and responsible members of the newspaper staffs can become members of the institute.[2] They are elected by the Executive Board of 15 members which in turn is chosen by the general assembly. Also members of journalism faculties and free-lancers may become associate members of the IPI.

The First General Assembly took place in Paris in May 1952. At the same

---

[1] See: *IPI—The First Ten Years. The Story of the International Press Institute.* Zurich: IPI, 1962, pp. 12–13.
[2] *Ibid.*, pp. 18–19. Also the revised editions of the Charter of March 1955, May 1959, June 1963, June 1964, and June 1967.

▶ This is an original article done for this book by Dr. Kurt Koszyk, Director of the Institute of Newspaper Research at Dortmund and engaged in the journalism education at Dortmund Teachers' Training College.

time, the first issue of the "I.P.I. Report" was published in Zurich where the Secretariat of the Institute had been located and which had sponsored national committees in 29 countries and regions.

The Institute started work with a report on "Improvement of Information," based on a questionnaire entitled "What is Needed to Improve Information on World Affairs?". Replies were received from 248 editors in 41 countries. The second survey dealt with "The News from Russia" (1952) and was the result of inquiry in 16 countries. This report had as a result the continuous negative response from all communist governments and press institutions toward all IPI activities. On Sept. 3, 1968, East Berlin *Neues Deutschland*, the central organ of the East German Socialist Unity Party (SED), printed the latest vehement attack by Prof. Dr. Franz Knipping of Leipzig concerning the "hate chorus of international reaction against the assistance of five Socialist brother countries for the sake of the CSSR," a hate chorus in which there had been the voice of "an obscure institution called IPI." [3]

Knipping accused the director of the Institute, Per Monsen, of combining his "obligatory protest with the assertion that journalists of the CSSR had gained an honorary place in the annals of international journalism." The main aim of the IPI—in the words of Prof. Knipping—was now "to undermine Socialism from within" after a period of holding back national press systems in the developing countries. Another 150,000 dollars given by the Ford Foundation in 1967 made Prof. Knipping presume that the IPI was highly integrated in the anti-socialist conspiracy of capitalism. And he found it deeply disturbing that among the members of a seminar from 21 countries in Geneva in March 1968 there had also been, for the first time, journalists from socialist countries—especially Emil Sip (Prague) who was blamed for having sent a report on the situation of the Czechoslovakian press. Knipping called the report a "Guide to organising counter-revolution by mass media."

No doubt the organisers of the Institute will be very satisfied after such attacks, since they are still greatly influenced by the ideology of the cold war period.[4] The trouble is that on one side they find it rather easy to unveil the suppression of press freedom in communist countries which are obviously understood as natural enemies of Western democracies—and on the other hand they have to judge the press systems in countries like Portugal, Spain, South Africa, Brazil, Argentina, and the Philippines, which are deeply involved in the economic and military politics of the West.[5]

Although no description of the role of the IPI should overlook these problems, it is nevertheless important to state that IPI is one of the few institutions which tries to collect material on international press relations and thus make possible a comparative examination of different national press systems.

[3] *Neues Deutschland*, No. 244, Sept. 3, 1968, p. 5.
[4] See Basil Spiru, *Giftmischer*. Berlin, 1960, pp. 64–72.
[5] See Ahmed Emin Yalman (member of the Executive Board) in: *I.P.I. Rundschau*, No. 2/1954, p. 7.

No other private or university organisation so far has had the means to do similar research with greater efficiency.

The authority of the IPI mainly derives from its close connection with the newspaper trade. In fact, among its members there are the most widely respected names in Western journalism. The attraction of the Institute is shown by the steady growth of membership: 460 in 1952, over 560 and another 104 associated members in 1955. Today the IPI has more than 1900 members from 60 countries. As members pay fees (40 dollars from members, 20 dollars from assoc.) and publishers give extra amounts for special projects the budget, too, has steadily enlarged from year to year. The growing importance of IPI has been acknowledged by several American foundations which support special studies, seminars, and international conferences.[6]

Although it is not easy to get a clear picture of the sources and the amounts the IPI can rely on, it is obvious that the work of the Institute would have run down some years ago, if there had not been large grants from the Ford and Rockefeller Foundations. Both foundations gave increasing amounts starting with some 30,000 dollars in 1954 and reaching about 500,000 dollars in 1965. Since 1959, this income has not been mentioned in the ordinary budget of the IPI. The IPI's activities in Asia and in Africa are mainly based on the Ford and Rockefeller Funds. They reached 240,000 SFr in 1972.

The Asian programme started in 1965 and was based on the fact that a source of new readers had to be supplied with a new type of newspapers—a subject that had been discussed on the 1960 general assembly in Tokyo. Newspaper circulation had jumped in most Asiatic countries, [7] and by 1966 the IPI was actively collaborating with the National Press Institutes in Korea, Japan, India, and the Philippines. Furthermore, Pakistan, Thailand, Vietnam, and Malaysia were engaged in IPI seminars. About 200,000 dollars have been spent on these activities each year.

At first just one consultant and his secretary had been sent into the offices of each of 30 newspapers. But subsequently a group of six specialists toured the area from Pusan in Korea to Kottayam in India and gave instructions about how to develop editors' facilities and management methods.[8] Many additional courses and seminars were arranged to enlarge on the programme of intensive instruction. Priority was given to the development of new designs for the ideographic press in some of the Asiatic countries and here Japanese practices helped a great deal to make ideographic newspapers more readable. The Japanese publishers association Nihon—Shinbun—Kyokai took an active part in this work. The latest development is the Chinese-Language Press Institute

---

[6] The first Asian Conference of IPI in Tokyo 19.-23.3. 1956 was made possible by the Rockefeller Foundation.

[7] See Amitabha Chowdhury (IPI director for Asia), "Asiatische Ergebnisse," *IPI-Rundschau*, 7-1966, pp. 8–12.

[8] See *IPI in Asia*. Zurich, 1966.

which opened in Hongkong on Nov. 18, 1968. It is part of the Press Foundation of Asia which tries to develop new applied forms of journalism in Asia. A plan to found a national committee in Taiwan has just been accepted after a study on press freedom there. Programmes similar to those in Asia have been undertaken in Africa under the direction of Frank Burton and Tom Hopkinson. As a by-product much has been done in the respect of the emancipation of African women. In April 1966, for example, there were six female graduates of a course for journalists in Nairobi and Lagos.

The first culminating point of IPI's African work was the 1968 general assembly in Nairobi. It made obvious that the media situation in more than 50 African countries was still tremendously difficult. There are comparatively great differences between the technically and economically better developed regions and those that are less developed. IPI is prepared to collaborate with the new department of journalism at Nairobi university. A new African programme has been sponsored in 1971–72.

One of the deepest impressions which delegates took away from the 1968 Nairobi conference arose from the discussion on press freedom. Many of the European and American members of the IPI who had been ready to put forward very dogmatic idea of press independence had to learn that things cannot only be judged by traditional West European standards. Meetings of this kind have therefore helped to bring a more realistic attitude into the journalists' world.

In one of his many articles in the *IPI-Rundschau*, Per Monsen stated the gains and losses of press freedom.[9] IPI is not able to influence the development of press freedom in the countries without membership in the IPI, but the Institute's moral beliefs do influence journalists' and publishers' attitudes all over the world. Obviously it did not mean much that a Soviet journalist observed the 1973 conference in Jerusalem.

The 1967 conference in Geneva passed a resolution which defined the Institute's projects for the next five years. It said there would be further meetings of editors from different countries; a library and an information service would be built up in Zurich and press legislation would be one of the main subjects to be dealt with by the Institute. A first meeting sponsored by the Council of Europe in Salzburg in September 1968 resulted from an IPI initiative after a preliminary session of the International Jurists Commission in May 1968.

The new considerations arose from the dissatisfaction with the work IPI had done since its foundation. Again Lester Markel, the moving spirit of 1950, took the initiative. The report of his planning committee was delivered to the New Delhi general assembly in 1966 and formed the basis of the 1968 conclusions. It emphasized once more that the free flow of news between all countries remained the main problem of modern journalism. The preponderant interest

[9] See *IPI-Rundschau*, 4-1967, pp. 1–4.

of IPI in Africa and Asia as a result of the financial assistance given by American foundations was felt to be disproportionate in respect of the main task. To get a wider range of work, Markel's committee proposed:

1. research concerning the flow of news,[10] especially news exchange with the USSR.
2. seminars on the problems of news exchange.
3. a better presentation of international news.
4. studies in the origins of public opinion.
5. building up the IPI as a centre for sponsoring international news.

Although IPI work is actually co-operative and dependent on the activities of each member, the main burden is placed on the Executive Board and its president as well as on the director of the Zurich institute. The IPI Executive Board has had twelve presidents so far: Lester Markel (U.S.A.), Elja Erkko (died 1965, Finland), Oscar Pollak (died 1963, Austria), Urs Schwarz (Switzerland), Allan Hernelius (Sweden), Donald Tyerman (United Kingdom), Barry Bingham (U.S.A.), C. E. L. Wickremesinghe (Ceylon), Hans—Albert Kluthe (Germany, died 1970), Aw Sian (Hongkong), L. K. Fakande (Nigeria), Paul Ringler (U.S.A.) since 1974.

On Oct. 18th, 1968, the Executive Board elected Ernest Meyer (Paris) as the new director of the IPI. He followed E. J. B. Rose (1952–1962), Rohan Rivett (1963), Per Monsen (1964–1968), and Anthony Brock who have shaped and realised the Institute's programmes since 1952; new director, since 1975, is Peter Galliner. In his first report, shortly before the 1969 Ottawa general assembly, Meyer pointed out that the activities concerning press freedom were still the urgent interest of the IPI. Apart from continuous world wide studies in press freedom, single actions in favour of persecuted journalists and publishers have often been very successful. A study on journalism in the USSR has been published by the end of 1969 and almost at the same time a comparative study on "Slander by the Press." Earlier in 1969 Frank Burton's "African Assignment" had been delivered. *IPI Report, Les Cahiers de l'IPI,* and *IPI-Rundschau* are published monthly, *Press Topics* twice a month.

As the general assemblies in Hongkong (1970), Helsinki (1971), Munich (1972), Jerusalem (1973), Kyoto (1974), and Lagos (1975) showed, it is unlikely that IPI will turn to new fields. Press freedom remains a constant problem, and in the Western countries of Europe there are the questions of journalistic education and ethics as well. No doubt they will be topics of the general assembly in the remaining years of this century.

[10] See the IPI study: *The Flow of the News,* Zurich 1953.

Robert P. Knight:

UNESCO's Role in World Communication

"COMMUNICATION" is not part of the formal title of the United Nations Educational, Scientific and Cultural Organization. yet, since UNESCO's beginning in 1946, the organization has included the second "c" as one of its four major programmatic sectors, and this has been in a significant enough way to have had continuing impact on the communications picture around the world.

The preamble to the UNESCO constitution explains the idealistic rationale for the organization's involvement with communication, and at the same time, in nine words (italicized below), suggests a pragmatic goal easier of accomplishment:

> (S)ince wars begin in the minds of men, it is in the minds of men that the defences of peace must be constructed
>
> ....
>
> (T)he States Parties to this Constitution, believing in full and equal opportunities for education for all, in the unrestricted pursuit of objective truth, and in the free exchange of ideas and knowledge, are agreed and determined *to develop and to increase the means of communication* between their peoples and to employ these means for the purposes of mutual understanding and a truer and more perfect knowledge of each other's lives.
> . . .[Emphasis added] [1]

To what extent UNESCO's communication work actually has been anchored in the idealistic portion of the statement is hard to say. But it can be said UNESCO has had success in the pragmatic aspects of its communication mission. As an organization, UNESCO has fluctuated over the years from an idealistic to a pragmatic position and halfway back because of circumstances, changing world conditions and financial realities. [2] For example, it has had to meet such challenges as the Cold War, the emergence and rise of the Third World [3] and a less-accepting posture among receiving countries toward development aid. Each of these realities has impinged upon what UNESCO could do—or not do—in communications.

UNESCO has had to re-focus its communication activities as the world has changed, and the world has changed tremendously since representatives of 44

▶ This is an original article done for this new edition of the book by Dr. Robert P. Knight, School of Journalism University of Missouri, Columbia, 1976.

377

nations met in London in 1945 to form UNESCO.. Of the 135 nations which were members three decades later, more than 60 had not even existed as independent states when UNESCO was founded.

In communications, UNESCO spent its first decade in serving as a low-budget catalyst for post-World War II reconstruction of communications facilities and networks. In its second decade, UNESCO launched into fairly massive assistance to develop communications facilities and to train personnel in developing countries, including scores of newly independent countries emerging from colonialism (Substantial portions of the aid came from United Nations sources, which later merged into the U.N. Development Program; these moneys made the operational approach possible). In its third decade, UNESCO seemed ready to launch into heavy promotion of new media technology, especially communications satellites—only to discover, to some degree, that the obstacles were greater than anticipated and that it probably was making greater total communication gains with its promotion of one of the oldest media forms, books (The UNESCO-sponsored International Book Year in 1972 even more than expected set off a worldwide chain reaction in increase of books and the reading habit).[4]

Even from its earliest days, UNESCO had emphasized immediate and tangible communications goals, whether through intellectual stimulus or direct aid. Toward the end of the third decade, however, UNESCO's communication activities began to take on a new look, apparently for a number of reasons, e.g. worldwide economic problems which drastically were affecting the organization; an increasing reluctance among developing nations to take aid solely on someone else's terms; the increased muscle of a Third World bloc (especially Arabs and Africans); and perhaps the possibility that many nations were beyond a first level in communications development. Assistance in the fourth decade seemed to be shifting from a base of transmitters-and-journalists to one of national communication policies-and-other standards, that is, to more long-range goals emphasizing in-country planning for communication decision-making within a country (or region). UNESCO was returning to its catalytic mode of early days, but at a more sophisticated level, going beyond mere quantitative increase in communication facilities and networks. It was concentrating more than in the past on research and on helping countries and regions fashion communication infrastructures they felt were suited to their long-range needs, since their regions or nations would have to assume the major financial burden for further communications development.

Despite UNESCO's adaptability and its success in "handling," if not always solving, most of its problems, illustrations easily can be given of stalemates, hardly surprising in an organization whose members represent their governments. Many of the early stalemates were on an East-West basis, for example, in matters of free flow of information, and some of the later ones shifted more to a North-South basis, for example, in the degree to which governments should control communications (whether for "positive" purposes, such as to further development, or for "negative" reasons, such as to exclude certain communications).

A series of related examples can be drawn from the transitional mid-1970's—a period of ferment which included the problems and changed approaches already mentioned and which saw UNESCO get its first African Director-General, Senegal's Amadou Mahtar M'Bow, elevated to a six-year term, in late 1974, after five years as Assistant Director-General for Education. [5]

M'Bow characterized the 1974 session of the General Conference—UNESCO ruling body—as "one of the most disquieting" in UNESCO annals but one which also showed "the great hopes that Member States place in UNESCO." It showed, he said, "the difficulties to which certain problems may give rise within an international organization adhering strictly to the rules of democracy." [6] The "disquieting" issue, which was to have significant negative repercussions—at least in the short-term—on UNESCO's funding, its prestige in the world intellectual community and participation in its four program areas, involved Arab-led votes against Israel. One vote cut off UNESCO funds from Israel, for allegedly endangering Moslem monuments in Jerusalem excavations; another excluded Israel from the UNESCO European regional grouping with which it wished to be associated. Immediately a number of well-known intellectuals around the world withdrew from further collaboration with UNESCO in its projects, and the United States cut off its financial aid to UNESCO (about a third of the regular budget). (Note, however, that the regular budget comprises less than half of UNESCO's expenditures, the rest coming from various U.N. agencies and programs, especially the Development Program.)

At the same time another ideological dispute had been moving along in UNESCO channels and was soon to be enmeshed with the anti-Israeli issue. The Soviet Union in 1972 proposed what was to be a several-years UESCO effort for a declaration on "the use of the mass media in strengthening peace and international understanding and in combatting war propaganda, racism and apartheid."

UNESCO had declared itself against propaganda from its earliest days and it had begun a war against racism, with scientific studies on race and the like. It paralleled the efforts of the United Nations, which by the early 1960s had launched an anti-racism offensive.

The international bodies began moving on several fronts. When the role of mass media was brought into the picture, this brought into focus—whether intentionally or not—two communications issues with clear political overtones with which not only UNESCO but also the U.N. had struggled since earliest days, *with not much success*. Those matters are (1) the concept of freedom of information, and (2) the concept of responsibility of mass media. [7] At issue basically is the extent to which governments can or should shape and/or control

(1) and (2). It is only natural that in any international organization, *based on membership by governments*, such matters usually end either in stalemate or in non-adherence by states which disagree.

In the racism/apartheid matter, in early 1974 one meeting of experts, functioning as private individuals rather than government representatives, produced a "draft declaration." But the 18th UNESCO General Conference, late in the year, called for additional study, based on a variety of conflicting amendments offered by various governments. Another meeting of experts was called for late 1975—this time representing their governments—and charged with producing a revised declaration which could be put to a vote at the 19th General Conference in late 1976.

But because of an anti-Israeli move, the document which emerged was produced without direct input from Common Market and North American countries, and the result was said to be couched in terms primarily acceptable to countries which favor government control of media. (The anti-Israeli action which caused a walkout by 12 Western nations was the insertion, in the declaration, of reference to a controversial United Nations, November, 1975, vote equating Zionism with racism.)[8]

Serious as the division might sound, one delegate to the 1975 experts meeting noted that UNESCO was building additional quarters and that the organization would be around for a long time to come.[9]

For all the ferment and changes in direction, most of UNESCO's basic long-time, pragmatic programs continued. It is these, and not the politicized debates, which provide the backbone of UNESCO's international communication activities.

Communication Surveys

In its first years, the late 1940's, UNESCO set out to discover the technical, legislative and educational needs of the mass communications media, country by country, in a war-devastated world and this turned out to be a five-year project.[10] During those years, 29 UNESCO filed workers toured 126 countries and UNESCO officials corresponded with persons in 31 additional nations. Questionnaires with more than 1,500 items were used to obtain press data more comprehensive than ever before available.

This massive project seemed to set the pattern for UNESCO in the mass media field. It pinpointed shortages (especially of newsprint—a UNESCO concern in several post-war years and again in the mid-1970's when skyrocketing costs were added to a shortage problem); it showed the need for journalism education (a matter with which UNESCO was to become more involved beginning in the mid-1950's); it recognized educational possibilities of audio and visual media; it suggested cooperative international efforts; it recommended that governments recognize and help solve their own communications problems; it pointed toward the need for UNESCO to aid specific countries in developing their media systems; it produced numerous studies springing from the original documentation of the surveys (From 1949 to 1961 UNESCO published some 20 titles in a series called Press, Film and Radio in the World Today, with focus on education for journalism—notably Robert Desmond's *Professional Training of Journalists,* 1949—and on the role of radio and film in the educational process).

The surveys themselves continued, as one of the most important communications projects of UNESCO, although most of the data came to be provided by governments. New editions of *World Communications* appeared at ever-lengthening intervals (1951, 1956, 1964, 1975). A comparison of the amount of data covered—and the greatly increased number of countries to account for, thanks to the independence movements of the 1960's and 1970's—can be seen by noting that the 1956 edition contained only 263 pages, whereas the 1975 edition required more than twice that number (533). For the first time, the latter included information, for individual nations, on their situations in space communications and professional training and associations.

Between editions of *World Communications,* one can find abbreviated but more up-to-date UNESCO media statistics on countries and regions in the United Nations *Statistical Yearbook.* Data appear in even more detailed fashion in UNESCO *Statistical Yearbook.*

Copyright and "Neighboring Rights"

One of UNESCO's most notable achievements has been in the area of copyright and "neighboring rights." The thrust has been not simply to protect authors and performers but, more generally, to promote a free—and legal—flow of materials among countries.

In copyright, what UNESCO did was to offer a more liberal approach to copyright than that of the Berne Union (International Copyright Union), first drafted in 1886. It did so with the Universal Copyright Convention of 1952 (in effect since 1955), which, incidentally, introduced the circled "c" as a copyright symbol. At the end of 1974, 62 states had adhered to this convention; a majority of them also belonged to the Berne Union, but not the United States (Berne standards are higher than U.S. law provides).

On July 10, 1974, a Revised Universal Copyright Convention of 1971 took effect after ratification by a twelfth nation, Spain. It had been almost eight years since UNESCO had first considered revising the convention as a means of helping developing countries. Just compensation must be made to the author, as it is in industrial nations. However, the difference is that the non-industrialized nations can get compulsory translation rights and compulsory reproduction rights in much less time—for example, as little as one year for translation into a vernacular language (compared to the usual seven years after initial publication).[11]

A further step to aid developing countries came with the establishment of UNESCO's Copyright Information Center in 1971. Its purpose is to make it easier for developing nations to print needed books from other nations, by such means as letting them know about books whose rights can be obtained at favorable royalty rates (sometimes free of charge), providing model contracts and helping locate qualified translators. For example, one issue of the Center's mimeographed *Information Bulletin* listed offers made by publishers of first-year physics and chemistry textbooks.

General problems of copyright are treated in UNESCO's *Copyright Bulletin*, an annual volume until it became a quarterly periodical in 1967. *Copyright Laws and Treaties of the World* is updated annually with supplements.

Concern for rights similar to copyright (often called "neighboring rights" in UNESCO) has led to at least three conventions: the International Convention. for the Protection of Performers, Producers of Phonograms and Broadcasting Organizations (also called the Rome Convention) (dated 1961, ratified 1964); the Covention for the Protection of Producers of Phonograms Against Unauthorized Duplication of Their Phonograms (dated 1971, ratified 1973); and the Convention Relating to the Distribution of Program-Carrying Signals Transmitted by Satellite (dated 1974 and scheduled to enter into force three months after five nations had ratified it). The latter convention is explained as follows:

> Under the terms of the Convention, which does not concern direct broadcasting, every contracting State undertakes to take adequate measures to prevent the distribution on or from its territory of any programme-carrying signal by any distributor for whom the signal emitted or passing through the satellite, is not intended. [12]

Beginning in the late 1960's, UNESCO began to wrestle with copyright problems created by new technology, including photographic or reprographic reproduction and electronic computers, but found the problems so complex that decisions kept being deferred. [13] Also deferred, at least until the mid-1970's, was the extension of specific protection to translators for their works.

UNESCO's Free Flow Agreements

A significant and more direct step by UNESCO to insure free flow of materials came through two international agreements. Basically, these UNESCO agreements exempt from customs duties such items as books, newspapers, periodicals, audio-visual materials, works of arts, collectors' pieces and scientific equipment. One is the Florence Agreement on the "Importation of Educational, Scientific and Cultural Materials" (proposed 1950, ratified 1952) and the other is the Beirut Agreement for "Facilitating the International Circulation of Visual and Auditory Materials of an Educational, Scientific and Cultural Character" (proposed 1948, ratified 1954).

New technology and the interests of developing countries started a not-uncharacteristic movement in UNESCO for revision of the free flow agreements, and by the 1976 General Conference a draft protocol to the Florence Agreement was scheduled to be ready for a vote (experts had decided the Beirut Agreement was flexible enough to meet modern conditions; it has less than half the number of adherents of the other instrument). After noting that 1977 was the earliest that producers and users of import materials could expect the benefits of a revised Florence Agreement, the Director-General's annual report noted: "Even then conflicting interests may limit the scope of this protocol." [14]

One way in which UNESCO sought to extend the provision of its free flow agreements was by cooperation with and encouragement of other international groups, such as the International Air Transport Association (for lowered freight rates), the Universal Postal Union (for reduced postal rates) and the Customs Cooperation Council (which had adopted five conventions of its own at UNESCO's request). [15]

Still another way which UNESCO has used since its earliest days to encourage free flow is through research and publication. For example: *Getting the Message Across: An Inquiry Into Successes and Failures of Cross-Cultural Communication in the Contemporary World* 1975) *Television Traffic—A One-Way Street?*, 1974, by Kaarle Nordenstreng and Tapio Varis of Finland; *Removing Taxes on Knowledge*, 1969 (an up-date of the 1952 *Trade Barriers to Knowledge*), by F. K. Liebich of the General Agreement on Tariffs and Trade (GATT). Four seminal books from the 1950's are *Transmitting World News*, 1953, by Francis Williams; *One Week's News: Comparative Study of 17 Major Dailies for a Seven-Day Period*, 1953, by Jacques Kayser; *The Problems of Tranmitting Press Messages*, 1956, produced by UNESCO in cooperation with the International Telecommunications Union; and *Broadcasting Without Barriers*, 1959, by George A. Codding, Jr.

Book Development

An entire chapter or more could be written about UNESCO's efforts in book development, which began intensively in the mid-1960's, reached a peak with the International Book Year in 1972 and continued as a long-range program into UNESCO's fourth decade.

World book production had exploded by the late 1960's (a 70 per cent increase in 13 years) but a great imbalance existed:

> The wealth of books is, however, concentrated; Europe, which has only 13 per cent of the world's peoples, publishes more than 44 per cent of the books. Africa, which has 10 per cent of the population, publishes only 1.6 per cent, while even Asia, which contains 55.0 per cent of humanity, publishes only 20.5 per cent. [16]

Groundwork for the UNESCO efforts was laid in a series of regional book development meetings in the Third World; shortly thereafter regional book development centers were established in Tokyo, Karachi, Bogotá and Cairo and plans were made for an African center in Yaoundé, Cameroon (The centers emphasized training, e.g. in book production and distribution skills, and specific projects, e.g. the development of a Latin American common market for books and the establishment of a Tokyo program for publication of children's books); the book profession was encouraged to foster book development in the developing countries (They adopted a Charter of the Book in 1971 and formed an International Book Committee in 1973); research programs were launched at UNESCO, regional and national levels, e.g., in economic factors of publishing so as to lead to commercially sound ways to lower sale prices of books; relevant materials were published; [17] more than 75 book development projects were sponsored by UNESCO in almost that many countries; impetus was given to the educational and infrastructure-building activities of UNESCO's Department of Documentation, Libraries and Archives; and a new Division of Book Promotion and Development was established in 1973.

Reports and Papers Series

Most of UNESCO's communications concerns have been reflected at one time or another in a series of monographs entitled "Reports and Papers on Mass Communication," begun in 1952. By the mid-1970's, 75 titles had been published. An analysis of subject categories may give some idea of the organization's concerns during the period:

Subject	Number of Monographs	Number Which Include This Subject As Well As a Main Subject
Films and filmstrips	17	9
Mass media in rural and/or underdeveloped areas	15	2
Role of mass media in education	11	12
Education and research for journalism	9	2
Radio and television	6	13
Mass media and society	5	—
Surveys of communications	5	7
Space communications	4	1
Book development	3	—
	75	46

A majority of the monographs tend to be practical reports outlining successful models of communications media used for a given purpose—especially education and rural development—or detailing the needs in certain regions, particularly the developing areas. Many of them have been outgrowths of UNESCO-sponsored meetings or conferences.

Education for Journalism

UNESCO has helped establish regional and national training centers since the mid-1950's and has posted communications experts in various countries to offer seminars or cooperate with local institutions. The first regional center, the International Center for Higher Education in Journalism (CIESJ), opened in 1957 at the University of Strasbourg, France, a year-and-a-half after a UNESCO meeting of experts endorsed a new emphasis in journalism education by the organization. A similar meeting in Ecuador in 1958 set the stage for the International Center for Higher Studies in Journalism for Latin American (CIESPAL), which opened in Quito in 1959.

The Strasbourg center concentrated on four-week refresher seminars during its first years, changing its policy in 1963 to include round-table meetings on mass communications in today's world (The results are printed in CIESJ's infrequent periodical, *Journalisme*). It also offers diplomas and degrees at the university level. [18]

In Quito, some 700 journalism professors, journalists and other persons attended the annual two-month training course during the first 17 years of operation. An explosiion in journalism schools in the region caused the center to lead a crusade for journalism reform in Latin America after a CIESPAL area-wide study showed the existing curricula were not effective. CIESPAL prepared a plan for reform and issued a document entitled "The Teaching of Journalism and Mass Media," 1965, based on recommendations from four regional seminars attended by 400 teachers of journalism. [19]

UNESCO assisted in founding the Center for Studies in Mass Communication Sciences and Techniques (CESTI) in 1965 at the University of Dakar, Senegal, to train French-speaking journalists. Emphasis was placed on developing the rural press, then relatively nonexistent. In English-speaking Africa, UNESCO cooperated in the 1970's with the School of Journalism at the University of Nairobi, Kenya, and with the Institute of Mass Communication at the University of Lagos, Nigeria.

One of its main training efforts in Asia was through the Malaysian Center for Radio and Television Training in Kuala Lampur. More than 600 communications specialists already had been trained by the end of 1974, many of them on the spot in various countries of the region. [20]

In addition, UNESCO has aided in the creation of other schools and centers, some with regional and others only with national aspirations.

UNESCO and Development

It should be clear that UNESCO has devoted much of the effort of its communication sector to aiding development through communications. This has included assistance in introducing or building up the mass media in a country or region (ranging from rural mimeographed newspapers in Africa to a sophisticated communications satellite experiment in India); training personnel for the media; helping nations utilize the media for various development objectives, especially in education; and most recently in helping nations and regions to make communications policy decisions suited to their needs.

Something of a crisis in approaches to development began to develop in the United Nations' Second Development Decade—the 1970's—partly because of a world economic crisis but perhaps as much because of failure to modify development to changing realities, e.g. the ability to some Third World nations to contribute to development in other countries and the continuing image of international aid as "intervention by an alien will and an alien body" [21] rather than as a "joint undertaking for removing inequalities, with all due regard to the wishes of the nations involved." [22]

An example can be cited to show UNESCO's attempt to take into greater account the desires and needs of receiving countries and regions: In 1974 a feasibility project which had been under way five years in South America for a regional tele-education system produced a report favoring a microwave rather than a communications satellite approach for the system because that is what the countries wanted. The project had begun, however, with an expert mission sent specifically to foster a satellite approach. [23]

It was in 1962 that the United Nations General Assembly officially endorsed UNESCO's program for helping information media in less-developed nations. It had, by a 1958 resolution, called on UNESCO to formulate a concrete plan for development. In 1959 the Economic and Social Council had asked UNESCO to study assistance to underdeveloped countries in information media.

That study was conducted primarily through three meetings: Bangkok, January, 1960, for Asia; Santiago, Chile, February, 1961, for Latin America; and Paris, January, 1962, for Africa. Initially the results were published in monograph and document form and then were interpreted in a landmark volume by Wilbur Schramm, *Mass Media and National Development: The Role of Information in Developing Countries.* [24]

The reports accepted the UNESCO minimum standards for mass media—in themselves a significant publicity achievement—of 10 copies of daily newspaper, five radio receivers, two cinema seats and two television receivers for every 100 persons in a country. Using this as a base, Schramm pointed to a "band of Scarcity" circling the globe through the developing regions.

But publicizing the great lack of facilities and the time it would take to close the gaps formed only a preliminary part of a mounting UNESCO campaign to improve the communications situation in the world. A communication explosion was taking place, and during the first Development Decade:

. . . world circulations of newspapers increased by a quarter; the number of radio receivers increased by 100% in South America, 120% in Africa and 150% in Asia; television increased threefold in Asia, South America and Europe and fourfold in Africa. Technological advance introduced satellite transmitters, video-cassettes, photo-composition, computer typesetting and cable television, making communication more far reaching, faster and more flexible. [25]

The other part of the campaign and the one into which UNESCO thrust itself with some vigor concerned the use of the media in development, including education. By the mid-1960's UNESCO had been involved in enough media-supported educational projects that in 1965–66 it sent interdisciplinary teams to 17 countries around the globe to report ways in which the electronic media were being used for education. Three volumes of case studies and a summary were published.[26] Integration of media into educational projects continued into the 1970's, e.g. in Tobago, media were being used in functional education for women; in several African countries, a rural press was designed for new literates; in Thailand and Afghanistan, projects were under way to use electronic media in education.[27] An adult education project in Senegal had been completed and reported on earlier, and several universities were commissioned to study the role of modern communication techniques in promoting life-long education.[28] One of the most interesting media/education projects involved a satellite for India, about which more will be said later.

Another development program into which UNESCO integrated media was the population program. A regional communications adviser for population/family planning was posted in each of four areas, South East Asia, the Arab States, Africa and Latin America, concentrating efforts on meeting national requests and in furthering training.[29] Still another development example concerns the use of media to promote scientific understanding in the Arab States.[30]

UNESCO and Space Communications

UNESCO's program in space communication concerns itself with (1) the free flow issue, which is difficult to resolve especially since satellite technology virtually can obliterate barriers at national boundaries, and (2) the utilization of satellites for development purposes, usually through the dissemination of educational, scientific and cultural information.

The 17th General Conference of UNESCO in 1972 adopted a "Declaration of Guilding Principles on the Use of Satellite Broadcasting for the Free Flow of Information, the Spread of Education and Greater Cultural Exchange." Among those opposed to its adoption was the United States. As noted earlier, an intergovernmental conference called by UNESCO and the World Intellectual Property Organization unanimously adopted a "Convention Relating to the Distribution of Program-Carrying Signals Transmitted by Satellite" May 21, 1974, in Brussels and opened the convention for ratification by member states.[31] The convention specifically ignored the hard-to-resolve problems of direct satellites.

As a participant in space communications meetings at the international level—most of them originated by the United Nations or its agencies—during the 1960's and 1970's, UNESCO took the position that careful steps had to be taken in utilizing satellites for information dissemination.

Although UNESCO spent several years exploring the feasibility of regional satellites for the Arab States, South America and the sub-Sahara, it was in India that a communications satellite was first being tested as a means of reaching a massive segment of people with educational and development material. UNESCO and other agencies helped in the project, at first with several years of training for technical and production personnel. The Indian government contracted with the United States for the experimental use during one year of an ATS(F) satellite (originally launched so as to provide educational programs to isolated Appalachian and Alaskan communities and later re-positioned to serve India). Specially equipped community receivers in 2,000 Indian villages were to receive the satellite's educational programs—prepared in India—as were 3,000 villages served by ground television stations.[32] Meanwhile, educational methods and structures were being re-vamped to fit this new delivery method (India much earlier had been site of UNESCO-aided radio rural forums, utilizing local monitors to lead discussions on educational radio programs received by groups in the villages).

A Movement Toward Research and Policies

In UNESCO's history, projects offering concrete aid to individual countries abound, especially after 1955 when new budgetary and extra-budgetary resources were provided for that purpose (By the mid- 1970's, however, resources had started to shrink, relatively speaking). For example, UNESCO specialists helped develop broadcasting in Barbados and Israel; aided Colombian radio schools; counseled with persons in Liberia, Libya and Malaysia about the creation of national news agencies; provided training for personnel of the reorganized television service in Upper Volta; and helped establish a rural press in vernacular languages in Dahomey, Tanzania and other African countries.

Yet such projects often tended to operate in isolation from the overall communications and development needs of a country. As one UNESCO official noted:

> Communication planning which takes equal note of the priorities of society and the needs and preferences of the individual, of local requirements as well as national priorities, of private initiative as well as public policy, is non-existent in most countries.[33]

United Nations Secretary General Kurt Waldheim commented on possible results:

> Failure to assert the primacy of policy over technology is an alarming and increasingly dangerous phenomenon of the modern world . . . Unless that danger is removed, further developments in the field of communication may well produce consequences which were neither foreseen nor desired from a more comprehensive national or international perspective.[34]

Therefore, UNESCO's communication priorities increasingly have included communication research and national communication policies, both intended to help nations and regions in their long-range planning. In the case of research, the main aspect set by a meeting of experts and confirmed by Member States' reactions was "mass media and man's view of society." [35]

UNESCO has initiated an examination of policies toward the media, from governmental, institutional and professional levels. One study defines such policies as "sets of principles and norms established to guide the behavior of communication systems." [36] Studies of this type were commissioned in West Germany, Sweden, Yugoslavia, Hungary and Ireland and reports on them began to be published in 1974. These were to be followed by studies of Argentina, Brazil, Colombia, Costa Rica, Peru and Venezuela, then on selected Asian countries.

How UNESCO Operates in International Communications

A fairly consistent working pattern seems to emerge for UNESCO in regard to its international communication activities. First, several years before a topic becomes a major one for UNESCO, the organization begins to notice the matter, perhaps through the urging of the United Nations or one of its agencies. Structurally, the communications sector is headed by an Assistant Director-General for Communication. At least six major departments and offices are under his direction (Copyright comes under the Office of International Standards and Legal Affairs, connected to the Secretariat). [37] Through this network and through the communications field staff, who cooperate with regional groups and UNESCO National Commissions, UNESCO may begin paying attention to the matter through publications, small meetings or work in certain regions or countries.

Next, interest of a more urgent type is exhibited at some rather high level—the United Nations proper, UNESCO itself (often through the Director-General) or another agency—and some pilot projects may be launched. Then come "expert meetings," bringing together respected individuals in the field under study. The recommendations that come from such meetings are sent to Member States for reactions and usually lead to concrete action, such as the establishment of centers or the setting of programs and priorities. If an international convention or even a less binding "declaration of principles" is involved, the process is more detailed and includes meetings of governmental representatives.

Sometimes several years may elapse before a UNESCO idea comes to fruition, and during that period, conditions may change drastically. Still, when the need is there, UNESCO responds in such a way as to contribute to the improvement of the communications situation in the world.

NOTES

[1] *Looking at UNESCO* (Paris: Unesco, 1971), p. 101.

[2] T. V. Sathyamurthy, "Twenty Years of UNESCO: An Interpretation," *International Organization*, Vol. 21, No. 3 (1967), pp. 164–663, and *The Politics of International Cooperation: Contrasting Conceptions of U.N.E.S.C.O.* (Geneva: Librairie Droz, 1964).

[3] René Maheu (UNESCO Director-General from 1962–1974), "Serving the Mind as a Force in History," in *In the Minds of Men: UNESCO 1946 to 1971* (UNESCO: Paris 1972), pp. 281–319. Also, *Report of the Director-General on the Activities of the Organization in 1973* (Paris: UNESCO, 1974), pp. xxix–xxxiii. (Hereinafter *RDG* 1973. This format will be used for other volumes of the annual report. These volumes provide the best concise source of UNESCO information.)

[4] *Anatomy of an International Year: Book Year-1972*, No. 71 Reports and Papers on Mass Communication (Paris: UNESCO, 1974). Also *The Book Hunger* (Paris: UNESCO, 1973), a study of the world book situation.

[5] Pierre Kalfon, "Amadou Mahtar M'Bow: A Profile of the Sixth Director-General of UNESCO," *UNESCO Courier*, Vol. 28, No. 2 (February, 1975), pp. 14–18. For M'Bow's analysis of the situation facing UNESCO, see same issue, pp. 19–26, and *RDG* 1974, pp. xiii–liii.

[6] *RDG* 1974, p. xvi.

[7] *Preparation of a Draft Declaration: A Background Report by the UNESCO Secretariat* (Paris: UNESCO. COM-75/CONF. 201/4, 3 December 1975). Summarizes U.N., UNESCO actions and discussions on the two issues. For a look at non-progress in FOI in U.N., see William F. Buckley, Jr. *United Nations Journal: A Delegate's Odyssey* (New York: G. P. Putnam's Sons, 1974), pp. 195–203.

[8] *New York Times*, December 19, 1975, p. 3; *Washington Post*, December 19, 1975, pp. 1, 16j.

[9] Dean Roy M. Fisher, University of Missouri School of Journalism, member of the U.S. delegation to the meeting.

[10] *Report of the Commission on Technical Needs in Press, Radio, Film* (Paris: UNESCO, 1947, 1948, 1949); *World Communications: Press, Radio, Film* (Paris: UNESCO, 1950); *Press, Film, Radio* (Paris: UNESCO, 1952); *Television: A World Survey* (Paris: UNESCO, 1953). For concise history of surveys, see pp. 13–22 in 1952 book.

11 *UNESCO Chronicle*, Vol. 17, No. 10 (October, 1971), pp. 365–366; Marie-Claude Dock, "The Revised Universal Copyright Convention," *UNESCO Chronicle*, Vol. 18, No. 4 (April, 1972), pp. 175–185.

[12] *RDG* 1974, p. 188.

[13] Marie-Claude Dock, "UNESCO and Copyright," *UNESCO Chronicle*, Vol. 15, No. 3 (March, 1969), pp. 89–97, and copyright sections of *RDG*, 1968 on.

[14] *RDG* 1974, p. 165.

[15] *RDG* 1972, p. 187.

[16] *Looking at UNESCO*, pp. 74–75.

[17] Robert Escarpit, *The Book Revolution*, (Paris: UNESCO, 1969, second edition); Richard Bamberger, *Promoting the Reading Habit*, No. 72 Reports and Papers on Mass Communication (Paris: UNESCO, 1975). See also footnote 4.

[18] Hifzi Topuz, "UNESCO and the Training of Journalists," *UNESCO Chronicle*, Vol. 14, No. 11 (November, 1968), pp. 419–424.

[19] *Ibid.*, pp. 421–422. Also see J. Laurence Day, "How CIESPAL Seeks to Improve Latin American Journalism," *Journalism Quarterly*, Vol. 43, No. 3 (1966), pp. 525–530.

[20] *RDG* 1974, p. 170.

[21]. René Maheu, *RDG* 1973, p. xxix.

[22] Amadou-Mahtar M'Bow, *RDG* 1974, p. xxxi.

[23] *RDG* 1974, pp. 160, 166; *RDG* 1970, p. 129.

[24] *Developing Mass Media in Asia*, No. 30 Reports and Papers on Mass Communication (Paris: UNESCO, 1960); *Mass Media in the Developing Countries: A UNESCO Report to the United Nations*, No. 33 same series (Paris: UNESCO, 1961) (The Spanish edition includes a report on the Santiago meeting); *Developing Information Media in Africa: Press, Radio, Film, Television*, No. 37 same series (UNESCO: Paris, 1962); Schramm (Stanford: Stanford University Press, 1964).

[25] Gunnar Naesselund, "Communication in the Second Development Decade," *UNESCO Chronicle*, Vol. 18, No. 10 (October, 1972), p. 382.

[26] UNESCO-International Institute for Educational Planning, *New Educational Media in Action: Case Studies for Planners*, Vols. I, II, III, and Wilbur Schramm *et. al.*, *New Media: Memo to Educational Planners* (Paris: UNESCO, 1967).

[27] *RDG* 1974, p. 168.

[28] *Mass Media in an African Context: Evaluation of Senegal's Pilot Project*, No. 69 Reports on Mass Communication (Paris: UNESCO, 1973). The universities were Massachusetts Institute of Technology, Ontario (Canada) Institute for Studies in Education and the Open University and Middlesex Polytechnic, Great Britain: *RDG* 1974, p. 196.

[29] *RDG* 1974, pp. 170–171.

[30] *Ibid.*, p. 168.

[31] *Ibid.*, p. 188.

[32] Tor Gjesdal, "UNESCO's Programme in Space Communication," *UNESCO Chronicle*, Vol. 16, No. 11 (November, 1970), pp. 439–452. As Assistant Director-General for Communication until his 1970 retirement, Gjesdal was responsible for UNESCO's space communication program.

[33] Henry R. Cassirer, "The Role of the Communication Media in Rural Transformation," *UNESCO Chronicle*, Vol. 17, No. 4 (April, 1971), p. 143.

[34] Naesselund, p. 384.

[35] *RDG* 1973, p. 195.

[36] Walter A. Mahle and Rolf Richter, *Communication Policies in the Federal Republic of Germany* (Paris: UNESCO Press, 1974), p. 5.

[37] Department of Mass Communication, Office of Free Flow of Information and International Exchanges, Office of Public Information (which handles news releases, produces radio/TV programs and publishes UNESCO Courier and UNESCO Chronicle), Office of Statistics, Department of Documentation, Libraries and Archives and Division of Book Promotion and Development. Alberto Obligando Nazar of Argentina became Assistant Director-General for Communication in 1970.

Mary A. Gardner:

The Evolution of the Inter American Press Association

FEW organizations have been so vilified and few have received such unqualified praise as the Inter American Press Association.

Andrew Heiskell, chairman of the board of *Time*, once remarked that working with the IAPA had been one of his most fascinating, occasionally most irritating and, in the long run, one of the most rewarding experiences of his life.[1]

The late Demetrio Canelas, editor and publisher of *Los Tiempos*, Cochabamba, Bolivia, said simply, "I owe not only my freedom but my life to the Inter American Press Association."[2] And in 1963, Pedro Joaquin Chamorro of *La Prensa*, Managua, Nicaragua, and German Ornes of *El Caribe*, Dominican Republic, reiterated that they were among those who owed a similar debt to the association.[3]

Juan Perón and his bully-boys were more profuse in their homage. In 1951, when their efforts to take over the organization failed, they dedicated a 437-page book to denouncing the IAPA and its members. Among other things, the association was accused of defending the "imperialistic interests of Wall Street," and of "attacking national sovereignty with its aggressions, its excesses, its frauds and its lies; . . ."[4] It has been notable during IAPA's existence that such accusations by dictators of the right are markedly similar to those propounded by dictators and advocates of the left.

As an organization, the Inter American Press Association is an effort by private citizens in an area most often left to government or foundation funds.[5] It has been a pioneer in the formation of an independent, professional, financially self-sufficient, inter-American pressure group. Most of its members are publications whose dues are based on circulation, although provisions exist for

---

[1] *XVIII Annual Meeting*, October 1962 (Mexico: Inter American Press Association, 1963), p. 75.
[2] As quoted by James G. Stahlman at the annual meeting, Nov. 1, 1955. *XI Annual Meeting*, November 1955 (Mexico: Interamerican [*sic*] Press Association, 1956), p. 163.
[3] *XIX Annual Meeting*, November 1963 (Mexico: Inter American Press Association, 1964), p. 43.
[4] Cincuenta y Tres Periodistas Argentinos, *Libro Azul y Blanco de la Prensa Argentina* (Buenos Aires: Organización National del Periodismo Argentino, 1951), pp. 58–59.
[5] The International Press Institute has depended largely on foundation funds for its support. See *IPI Report*, August–September 1964, p. 5.

▶ From: *Journalism Quarterly*, Vol. 42, No. 4 (Spring 1965), pp. 547–556. Reprinted by permission of publisher and author, with certain updating by the author in November, 1975.

corporate and associate memberships. Monies from its members support the organization's operating costs.[6] By October 1975 membership was 946.[7]

The association traces its roots to the First Pan-American Congress of Journalists which convened in Washington, D.C., in April 1926 under auspices of the Pan American Union, and to later meetings in Mexico City (1942); Havana, Cuba (1943); Caracas, Venezuela (1945); Bogotá, Colombia (1946); Quito and Guayaquil, Ecuador (1949); and New York City (1950).[8]

IAPA's early meetings were often rowdy and disorganized affairs. Congresses were held at the convenience and the whims of governments. The expenses of delegates usually were paid by their governments. Government influence resulted in ambassadors, senators, typographers and others vaguely associated with the press being designated as delegates. Delegations sat and voted by countries, and heated arguments and nationalistic oratory occurred as delegates discussed political rather than press problems.

There were other difficulties also. Many Latin American editors and publishers were politically ambitious and saw no conflict in serving as a public official while still active in the newspaper business. They used their editorial columns to attack the opposition and to advance their own political causes. Then, once in power, "they would often go so far as to imprison editors of the opposition papers." [9]

Although the avowed purpose of the early congresses was to contribute to continental unity and to counteract pro-axis propaganda, the Communists attempted to manipulate the early meetings to their own advantage. There is considerable evidence that they wished to gain control of an international group whose membership would supply both the prestige and the organs for spreading communist propaganda. Two of the most active leaders in this movement were Carlos Rafael Rodríguez of Cuba and Genaro Carnero Checa of Peru.[10]

Rodríguez, then editor of the Cuban communist newspaper *Hoy*, has served as minister of agriculture in the Castro regime.[11] In 1960, Genaro Carnero Checa of Peru led a movement to take over the organizational meeting in Lima, Peru, of the Inter-American Federation of Working Newspapermen's Organization. His tactics were markedly similar to those used against the IAPA.[12]

Although it was the Mexicans who provided the impetus in 1942 for reviv-

[6] *Charter, By-Laws and Rules*, Inter American Press Association, pp. 4–8, 17–19.
[7] Letter from James B. Canel, general manager, Inter American Press Association, Nov. 13, 1975.
[8] Published volumes of the minutes of these meetings are available except for those held in Venezuela and Ecuador. The 1950 New York meeting minutes were published on newsprint by the *Trenton Times* of New Jersey.
[9] Letter from Hal Lee, executive secretary of the organizing committee, VI Inter-American Conference, March 18, 1959. (Mr. Lee died in December 1959).
[10] See the minutes of early meetings.
[11] *Hispanic American Report*, October 1964, (Vol. XVII, No. 8), p. 709.
[12] Interview with Nicolas Pentcheff, treasurer, Inter-American Federation of Working Newspapermen's Organizations, Panama City, Aug. 12, 1962.

ing the idea of inter-American press congresses, the Cubans eventually managed to have the secretariat located in their country. Leftist Cubans dominated the self-perpetuating executive committee and blocked other work by remaining in session throughout the Quito meeting of 1949. Its Treasurer, Carlos Rafael Rodríguez, never did present a report to the congresses. No dues were ever levied. The bills of the secretariat headquarters in Havana were covered by the Cuban government. [13]

A sturdy group of newspapermen from Latin America and the United States fought to make the congresses professional meetings and to wrest control of the organization from those who wanted to use it for their own political purposes.

It was Julio Garzón, then editor of *La Prensa* (New York), who proposed at the Bogotá (1946) meeting that a standing committee on freedom of the press be formed to report annually on the state of the press in the hemisphere. [14] The work of this committee under the chairmanship of Jules Dubois of the Chicago *Tribune* later proved to be the cohesive force which held the IAPA membership together in spite of sharp personal and ideological conflicts. Its reports became the focal point and the point of controversy at most subsequent meetings.

Delegates to the Bogotá meeting generally credit its presiding officer, Dr. Alberto Lleras Camargo, former president of Colombia, with maintaining the "general constructive spirit" which prevailed and which permitted the approval of the resolution forming the freedom of the press committee. [15]

Similarly, Farris Flint of Famous Features credits Carlos Mantilla Ortega, the presiding officer of the Ecuador meeting (1949), with making possible the Flint-sponsored resolution to change the organization into one made up of individual members [16] "without reference to nationalities and completely independent of government ties, sanction, or support." [17]

Flint called Mantilla's handling of the hot and noisy sessions "masterly." [18] Mantilla wryly observed that he often had to shout and once literally used force to maintain order. He stepped down from the chair and shook one Latin American delegate into silence. [19]

Thus the way was cleared for the tumultuous New York meeting in 1950 (an Argentine called the conference a "gangster meeting" because of the way the U.S. delegates ran it [20]) at which a small group of Latin American and

[13] "Background of Previous Inter-American Press Meetings," Confidential Memorandum prepared by Hal Lee, July 1, 1950.

[14] *Memoria del IV Congreso Panamericano de Prensa*, Noviembre 1946 (Bogotá: Editorial El Gráfico, 1946), p. 103.

[15] Julio Garzón, "Hemispheric Freedom Committee Appointed," *Editor & Publisher*, Dec. 14, 1946, p. 86.

[16] Interview with Farris A. Fling, Famous Features, New York, July 15, 1959.

[17] *New York Times*, July 15, 1949.

[18] Flint interview.

[19] Interview with Carlos Mantilla Ortega, Sub-director, *El Comercio* (Quito, Ecuador). Nov. 24, 1959.

[20] *Proceedings of the VI Inter-American Press Conference*, October 1950 (Trenton, N.J.: *Trenton Times*, n.d.), p. 15.

U.S. members rammed through a new constitution completely revamping the association.

The New York meeting was poorly organized, a fiasco financially (a number of members quietly bailed it out), but attracted outstanding editors and publishers.[21] The association was reorganized on a professional and independent basis with each member publication having one vote and supporting the organization by paying dues based on circulation. The New York meeting marked the end of government-sponsored inter-American press congresses, and since then the IAPA has depended on the yearly dues of its members to cover expenses.

There have been numerous rowdy meetings since 1950. Peronistas tried to take over the sessions in Montevideo (1951), and in the resulting noise and confusion Tom Wallace, the IAPA president, suffered a heart attack.[22]

During the 1953 meeting, a Dominican Republic delegate swatted a Peruvian with a 300-page, one-pound freedom of the press report for calling Trujillo's regime a "stomach turning" dictatorship.[23]

In 1956, dictator Rojas Pinilla of Colombia sent emissaries to sabotage the annual meeting in Havana. Three IAPA officers and its general manager had received threats and the hotel where the meeting took place was protected by armed guards and Cuban plain-clothes men. During the sessions, Jules Dubois was challenged to a duel by one of Trujillo's stooges, and the "Rojas Colombianos screamed themselves hoarse for a day and a half, but finally were fought down by the General Assembly."[24]

Recent meetings have not been without controversy, but disagreements generally have been expressed verbally rather than physically—perhaps an indication of IAPA's growing maturity.

Exiled Cuban members took offense to an editorial appearing in the New York Times during the New York meeting (1961), for which they blamed Herbert Matthews. A Cuban moved that the assembly "make a pronouncement on the attitude of Mr. Matthews. . . ."[25] The incongruous situation of an association advocating freedom of expression censuring its use was averted when cooler heads finally prevailed. The motion never came to vote.[26]

In Mexico City (1964), the IAPA Board of Directors in a joint meeting with the directors of the Inter American Educational Association discussed, among other things, the dangers of official textbooks being selected and required by the state. The two organizations adopted a resolution which said that "in a democratic society education on all levels should never be a state monopoly and that academic freedom as well as the economic independence of these institutions should always be guaranteed."[27] Citing Argentina's experi-

21 Interview with Joshua B. Powers, Joshua B. Powers Inc., New York, July 14, 1959.
22 Interview with Tom Wallace, editor emeritus, Louisville Times, Aug. 19, 1958.
23 Newsweek, Oct. 19, 1953.
24 Letter from James G. Stahlman, Nashville Banner, Oct. 22, 1958.
25 XVII Annual Meeting, October 1961 (Mexico: Inter American Press Association, 1962), p. 232.
26 Ibid.
27 English Document 14 (Mimeographed), XX General Assembly, October 1964, p. 1.

ence with Perón, Alberto Gainza Paz of *La Prensa* of Buenos Aires, vigorously supported the resolution.[28] This action precipitated a vitriolic editorial in the Mexican tabloid *ABC* which called Gainza Paz "the most hated man in Argentina."[29]

Indignant Argentine members voiced their objections to the editorial and called for a resolution expressing the association's "solidarity and its confidence" in Gainza Paz. A Mexican publisher dissented and violently shouted his disapproval when the presiding officer ruled him out of order. The vote of confidence passed.[30]

It could hardly be coincidental that the Mexican member who led the protest also had interests in the publication of official school texts.

These verbal barrages are rather tame when compared to the battles IAPA fought with the henchmen of Rojas Pinilla, Perón, Trujillo, Somoza and Pérez Jiménez.

Today, one of IAPA's principle targets is the Castro regime although the association continues to pinpoint aggressions wherever they may occur. It recently has reported suppression of press freedom in Brazil, Cuba, Chile, Haiti, Nicaragua, Panama, Paraguay and Uruguay.[31,32]

What tools of pressure did the IAPA use in its battles with Perón, Batista, Trujillo, Rojas Pinilla and other tyrants? Basically the tools of public opinion, of keeping aggressions against the press exposed to the glare of international publicity.

Foremost among these is the public arena in which the IAPA's annual freedom of the press report is documented, debated and presented. In the past, representatives of suspect nations have flocked to the assemblies, primed to attack and question the report. And member publications, nonmember publications and the wire services usually give the report extensive exposure throughout the hemisphere.

Firm but courteous cables generally are dispatched to the heads of states of the country in which abuses against the press have been noted. Not all replies are returned in the same vein. In 1953, when the IAPA protested the arbitrary closure of two newspapers and the imprisonment of an editor in Ecuador President Velasco Ibarra replied:

> Ignorant and insolent persons, such as yourselves, who speak without sufficient documentation, without the knowledge of foregoing events, without background of facts, merit only contemptuous silence.[33]

[28] Personal Notes, XX General Assembly, October 1964.
[29] ABC, Oct. 21, 1964, pp. 1, 7.
[30] Personal Notes, XX General Assembly.
[31] IAPA News, October–November 1974, pp. 1–2.
[32] Report of the Committee on Freedom of the Press, XXXI General Assembly, October 1975, English Document (Mimeographed).
[33] Press of the Americas, May 1, 1953.

Toward the end of his four years as constitutional president, the same Velasco Ibarra publicly praised the work of the IAPA.[34]

The association's headquarters also keeps the hemisphere informed of attacks against the press through news releases and through special bulletins on a country when the situation warrants it. Often some of the material used in the releases consists of information smuggled from the country under scrutiny.

Editorials from newspapers throughout the Americas are collected and made available to members. During the latter days of the Rojas Pinilla regime in Colombia, IAPA headquarters almost daily forwarded a packet of editorials to the dictator.[35]

The association has also sent envoys to conduct on-the-spot investigations of press conditions. Most often the envoy was Jules Dubois, but at times Latin American IAPA members have acted as special envoys at their own expense.

IAPA presidents also have traveled at their own expense to help a fellow member. In 1954 IAPA's president, the late Miguel Lanz Duret of Mexico, jumped through a window in the Costa Rican embassy in Managua, Nicaragua, to talk with a publisher who had taken refuge there.[36]

Like Perón, Castro fiercely condemned the IAPA and yet tried to infiltrate it, especially during the early days when he was consolidating power in Cuba. Now that he is solidly entrenched and in control of all media there, he appears to give relatively scant attention to the association's activities.

It was freedom of the press which first attracted most newspapers into the association, and which served as the cohesive force to hold them together. Yet IAPA members concerned themselves with other vital services even during the association's earliest and most difficult days.

Newsprint production, cost and availability have been discussed at almost every meeting since 1942. Newsprint supply became particularly critical for the Latin Americans after World War II and in 1951 they even proposed that U.S. publishers pledge 5% of their newsprint to Latin American members. One U.S. publisher pointedly suggested that instead of complaining, the Latin Americans do something positive about the situation.[37]

Under the leadership of Guillermo Martínez Marquez of Cuba, a permanent committee to study new sources of newsprint was appointed.[38] Sugar cane bagasse came under study as a possible raw material for newsprint, and other efforts to undertake newsprint production were studied. Although newsprint is now generally available, its cost and supply continue to concern IAPA members.

[34] XII Annual [sic] Meeting, October 1956 (Mexico: Interamerican [sic] Press Association, 1956), p. 95.
[35] XI Annual Meeting, November 1955 (Mexico: Interamerican [sic] Press Association, 1956), p. 15.
[36] Ibid., pp. 200, 202.
[37] Stenographic Minutes, IAPA Board of Directors' Meeting, March 1, 1951 (in IAPA files).
[38] Stenographic Minutes, IAPA Board of Directors' Meeting, Oct. 7, 1951 (in IAPA files).

IAPA's board of directors also decided that programs should be sponsored which would contribute to the financial stability and the professional stature of Latin American publications and perhaps make them less susceptible to political and governmental pressures.

Projects in three broad fields were considered: the education of journalists, the recognition of outstanding work by journalists, and technical aid to member publications in Latin America.

In 1952, the board of directors decided to investigate the possibilities of a scholarship program to encourage the exchange of journalists and journalism students. Under the leadership of William H. Cowles of the Spokane *Spokesman-Review* (Washington), the scholarship committee presented a comprehensive plan for such a program in 1953, and by 1955 the Scholarship Fund had been incorporated in New York State with the same board of directors as IAPA.[39]

Contributors to the fund come from both U.S. and Latin American IAPA members and donations by governments and commercial enterprises are politely rejected. By October 1975, a total of 233 scholarships for study in Latin America and the U.S. had been awarded at a cost of $686,824 from voluntary contributions.[40] The scholarships have been divided almost equally between North American and Latin American students.[41]

In 1952 the Mergenthaler Linotype Company offered IAPA funds to give $2,500 in prizes annually for 25 years to newspapermen of publications in the Western Hemisphere, excluding the United States.[42]

Designed as the Latin American counterpart of the Pulitzer Prizes, IAPA each year offers awards to a newspaper for outstanding service to the community, and to journalists for distinguished work in cartooning, photography, newswriting and reporting, features, columns and editorials, and for defense of press freedom.[43]

Candidates are nominated by editors or publishers. The IAPA has withheld awards when its committee felt there were no qualified nominees. The first Mergenthaler Awards were given in 1954, and, by 1975, 19 citations to publications and 96 to individuals had been presented.[44]

At the board of directors meeting in Buenos Aires (1958), Francisco A. Rizzuto h. of *Veritas* (Argentina) proposed that two prizes for North Americans, one for a newspaper and another for a journalist, be established. The resolutions committee regretfully decided that such prizes would be too costly.

Latin American members expressed a clear desire, however, to award

[39] *Editor & Publisher*, April 2, 1955.
[40] *Canel letter.*
[41] *Ibid.*
[42] *VIII Annual Meeting*, October 1952 (Mexico: Inter-American [sic] Press Association, 1953), p. 104.
[43] *Memoria de la Décima Asamblea General*, Octubre 1954 (México: Sociedad Interamericana de Prensa, 1955, pp. 178–180.
[44] IAPA Brochure, "Los Premios de SIP-Mergenthaler," 1975.

prizes in recognition of works furthering inter-American friendship. They quickly offered to finance them and by the time the general assembly passed the resolution, nine Latin Americans had already pledged financial support.[45] The Tom Wallace Awards, named after IAPA's first president, have been given since 1960, and perhaps the most rousing argument at the 1965 meeting involved whether an award should be withdrawn once its recipient had been designated.[46]

In 1952, IAPA members also began to look for ways to obtain more advertising for the Latin American newspapers. Carlos Mantilla of Ecuador noted in 1953 that Latin American newspapers were barely receiving one-tenth of the total publicity budget spent by the U.S. Industry in Latin America. This source of income, he maintained, was lost primarily because the Latin American newspapers and magazines failed to provide precise information concerning their circulations.[47]

The IAPA established the Office of Certified Circulation in 1954 and incorporated it under the laws of New York State in 1955. The IAPA directors felt that an enterprise which involved contractual and economic commitments should operate as an autonomous organization.[48]

International auditing firms agreed to lend their cooperation, and OCC's services were limited to IAPA members. The newspaper *El Espectador* and the magazine *Dominical*, both of Bogotá, Colombia, were the first to have their circulations certified.[49]

OCC, it should be noted, has never enjoyed the support from Latin American newspapers that its founders hoped it would. Many factors have mitigated against it. The Latin American publisher today is somewhat in the same position as the U.S. publisher of 40 to 80 years ago.[50] A newspaper's true circulation cannot be determined easily unless the owner desires to reveal it. Many Latin American newspaper publishers have tended to inflate their circulation figures. A true audit would be an embarrassing revelation of their deceit.

It is interesting to observe, for example, that the newspaper generally rated second in circulation in a country was more likely to subscribe to the audit service than the publication traditionally rated first. For example, *El Espectador* of Bogotá subscribed to the service before *El Tiempo* did. *La Prensa* of Lima, Peru, likewise submitted to audit while *El Comercio* did not.

Care must be taken, however, not to oversimplify the situation. There are other considerations. Deep-seated reasons exist why Latin American editors

---

[45] *XIV Annual Meeting*, October 1958 (Mexico: Inter American Press Association, 1959), pp. 30–31.
[46] Personal Notes, XXI General Assembly, October 1965.
[47] *IX Annual Meeting*, October 1953 (Mexico: Inter-America [sic] Press Association, 1954), pp. 82–88.
[48] *XI Annual Meeting*, pp. 51–52.
[49] *Memoria de la Décima Asamblea General*, pp. 62–66.
[50] *IX Annual Meeting*, pp. 92–93.

might not like to have outsiders poking into their books. Traditionally, they tend to look with suspicion upon this type of activity.

Fear that authoritarian governments might utilize legally or illegally such data to harass a publication is often quite real. Questions also might be raised concerning past income tax reports. Furthermore, an opposition newspaper might not want the government to realize how strong or weak it might be. Above all, many Latin American publishers are convinced that their national advertisers are well aware which newspaper reaches most of those who can read and who can afford to buy the advertisers' products.[51]

The cost of OCC's services also has been relatively high for Latin Americans. In 1956, John R. Reitemeyer, then chairman of the executive committee, told IAPA directors that one of the most important reasons OCC had not made rapid progress was because it was too expensive. He felt the costs of the service, which, "for a paper of 50,000 circulation might run to $1,200, are too high."[52]

After a special meeting in March 1957, OCC's board of directors revamped the organization. Voting control was transferred from publishers to a board composed of advertiser members, advertising agency members and publisher or publisher representative members.[53]

It has been observed that the one burning issue which has been greatly responsible for resolving the differences of IAPA members is freedom of the press. True, the freedom of press report has often roused the greatest controversy. Yet it has served as the common cause behind which members have rallied; in the long run it has apparently surmounted the barriers of nationalism, cultural differences and personal prejudices.

Should these reprehensible but sometimes colorful aggressions no longer occur with such regularity and the excitement of battle is replaced by the monotony of war, what can substitute for this stimulus which has been the welding force of the IAPA?

John R. Herbert, Quincy *Patriot Ledger* (Massachusetts), has long felt that a "technical center" would help fill such a need.[54] When he reported as chairman of the committee on exchange of information at the assembly in Mexico in 1953, he observed that one of the major requirements in a successful battle to maintain press freedom is strong newspapers—newspapers of technical excellence and efficient management. "You can never win the fight for press freedom," he said, "with newspapers financially unsound and weak in matters of policy."[55]

In January 1954, the Research and Information Center was established as a permanent agency of the IAPA to supply technical information to members

[51] Interview with Jorge Mantilla, subdirector, *El Comercio* (Ecuador), July 16, 1959.
[52] *XII Annual Meeting*, p. 24.
[53] Letter from Charles F. Rork, OCC managing director, July 28, 1965.
[54] Letter from John R. Herbert, Feb. 20, 1959.
[55] *IX Annual Meeting*, p. 157.

upon request. The center's members and advisers came principally from IAPA's associate members, specialists in such areas as printing, advertising and other technical aspects of journalism. Herbert was appointed president.[56]

From the beginning, however, the center's activities were fraught with problems. Attendance at its technical sessions during IAPA meetings was small and it was also beset with financial difficulties.

The center furnished services to IAPA members without charge and without a budget. IAPA policy did not permit it to accept contributions from outside sources, and the center existed through the good will and cooperation of its members and the help of Cranston Williams of the American Newspaper Publishers Association.[57]

In April 1957, the center was incorporated under the laws of New York State as an educational non-profit organization for the dissemination of technical information to IAPA members.[58] Incorporation, it was anticipated, would permit it to accept foundation funds to finance various projects. In line with IAPA policy, however, funds from governments and their agencies would not be accepted.[59]

Although the center arranged for the publication of the first English-Spanish dictionary of newspaper terms, convinced the American Press Institute to undertake another Latin American seminar, and continued with technical sessions at IAPA annual meetings, it was still without funds. In March 1958, its gross assets were $3.00. Very little money was available for a center which "could very well become the most important activity of the IAPA as it runs out of dictators."[60]

Largely through the persistent efforts of John R. Herbert, the Technical Center, Inc. received a $15,000 Ford Foundation grant in March 1960 to conduct a three-month survey of the technical needs of Latin American newspapers.[61] The study resulted in a $400,000 Ford grant in 1962 for five years of operation.[62]

Since that date, seminars and conferences have been held concerning such subjects as management, advertising and circulation. Harold Fitzgerald of the Pontiac *Press* (Michigan) also bolstered the center's budget by giving it eleven units of rotary press, five of which were sold to a Latin American newspaper and six to an Ohio newspaper for a total price of $97,000. Fitzgerald even helped further the center's profit by having his organization assume the cost of packing and shipping to the port of embarkation.[63]

[56] *Press of the Americas*, Feb. 1, 1954.
[57] *XI Annual Meeting*, p. 49.
[58] *Editor & Publisher*, Oct. 26, 1957.
[59] Records, IAPA Executive Committee Meetings, 1957 (in IAPA files).
[60] Stenographic Minutes, IAPA Board of Directors Meeting, March 1958 (in IAPA files).
[61] *Editor & Publisher*, March 26, 1960.
[62] Edición Especial de Centro Técnico de SIP, Ciudad de México, Octubre 1964, p. 3.
[63] Report of Guillermo Gutierrez V-M, general manager, IAPA Technical Center, XX General Assembly, October 1964, English Document 5 (Mimeographed).

Fitzgerald's donation precipitated additional offers of presses from the Allentown *Call & Chronicle* (Pennsylvania), the San Juan *Star* (Puerto Rico), Jack Howard of Scripps-Howard Newspapers and Andrew Heiskell of Time Inc.[64]

The center also has supplied technical bulletins and the services of a technical consultant and published books. In 1975, however, it severely curtailed its operations because of financial difficulties. Its major concern now is raising funds for its operations, and building a production and editorial training center on land granted by Biscayne College, Miami, with initial building funds from the Josephine Steddam Scripps Foundation.[65]

Herbert noted at the 1964 IAPA meeting that improvement in the news content of newspapers has been stressed at all IAPA seminars no matter what their official topic. "This," he said, "becomes our opening prayer whether the meeting is devoted to circulation or advertising or any other subject." [66]

It is notable that Latin American members had begun to share the costs of organizing technical seminars in their countries under the center's auspices and of paying the transportation, living expenses and token registration fees of their own representatives.[67] In addition, provincial newspapers were finally being encouraged to participate.

In 1960, this writer observed that the association tended to attract the larger and wealthier Latin American publications—newspapers whose prestige and financial stability helped make IAPA possible but which, relatively speaking, least needed IAPA's aid. Small provincial newspapers generally did not have access to IAPA's benefits because of the cost of membership and the expenses involved in attending annual meetings.[68] Furthermore, as a Latin American journalist once commented, when a small newspaper publisher is thrown in with the "dignified" owners he "feels like a humble priest in a cathedral." [69]

IAPA has since decreased dues for publications with less than 5,000 circulation and set up a promotion committee to help recruit new members. A short formal ceremony has been instituted during annual meetings to welcome new members and to provide them with special identification.[70]

The promotion committee also has produced and distributed literature about IAPA and Joshua B. Powers of Joshua B. Powers, Inc. reported in 1961

---

[64] Report by Guillermo Cespedes R., general manager, IAPA Technical Center, XXI General Assembly, October 1965, English Document 14 (Mimeographed).

[65] *IAPA News*, April–May 1974, p. 5, and Canel letter.

[66] Report by John R. Herbert to the Board of Directors of the IAPA Technical Center, XX General Assembly, October 1964, English Document 13 (Mimeographed).

[67] Report of Guillermo Gutiérrez V-M.

[68] Gardner, Mary A. *The Inter American Press Association and Its Fight for Freedom of the Press, 1926–1960* (Austin: University of Texas Press, 1967), p. 148.

[69] Interview with José María Navasal, coordinating secretary, *El Mercurio* (Chile), Dec. 14, 1959.

[70] *XVII Annual Meeting*, pp. 83–85.

that the committee had compiled a list of prospective members. About 900 eligible newspapers located in the United States and about 70 in South and Central America did not belong to the IAPA. The latter figure, as Powers noted, is surprisingly small.[71] This is particularly true if one accepts the figures submitted in 1960–1962 to UNESCO: Argentina listed 233 daily newspapers, Brazil 291, and Mexico 189.[72]

Nevertheless, IAPA's membership has increased steadily. Some members are dropped each year because of resignations, closings, retirements, deaths or delinquent dues. Almost twice as many Latin American publications become remiss in payment of dues as U.S. publications. Even so, the total number of delinquents annually is seldom more than 30.[73]

IAPA membership increased from 597 to 946 in 1975, and its annual operating costs rose from about $60,000 to $116,000 during the same period. In October 1975 the association comprised 527 U.S. members, 328 Latin American members, 76 Canadian members and 15 from the West Indies area.[74] No small feat for an organization which in 1951 had to extract $7,000 in pledges from U.S. and Latin American members to defray expenses.

Since its reorganization in 1950, the IAPA not only has snatched newsmen from jails, given scholarships and technical aid but also has influenced the formation and structure of other inter-American organizations.

There is evidence that the Inter-American Federation of Working Newspapermen's Organizations, although a union, benefited from IAPA's experiences, especially those concerning dissident Latin American elements. At its organizational meeting in Lima (1960), IAFWNO leaders astutely and democratically repelled a Communist attempt to take over their organization.[75]

The Inter American Education Association, established in 1962 by privately supported schools and associations, has received help from IAPA members and has scheduled some of its meetings to coincide with the IAPA's.

The IAPA and the Inter-American Association of Broadcasters also have long cooperated in the defense of their members. The Panama Doctrine, adopted by the organizations in 1952, provides that any aggression against either radio or the press will be considered an attack against both and will be resisted by all means possible. The two organizations have invoked the doctrine numerous times with varying degrees of success.

IAPA probably has been responsible indirectly for more extensive news coverage of Latin America in U.S. newspapers, especially during non-crisis periods. U.S. members become interested in the problems of their colleagues and tend to publish more news about their problems.

[71] Ibid., p. 225.
[72] UNESCO. World Communications (Amsterdam: Drukkerij Holland, N.V., 1964), pp. 177, 180, 155.
[73] See the yearly reports of the treasurer to the IAPA.
[74] "IAPA statement of income and disbursements, twelve months ending Sept. 30, 1975," and Canel letter.
[75] Nicolas Pentcheff interview. Also see IAFWNO's publications of the period.

IAPA members indicate that hemispheric solidarity and self protection are among the most pressing reasons they join the association. Nevertheless, they are finding it increasingly difficult to help each other. Repressive governments today are more sophisticated and subtle in their incursions against the press than in years past, and often use nationalism and the need for economic development as the rationale for whatever measures they take.

Such governments generally no longer find it necessary to use brute force and torture against editors and reporters to close a publication or bring it to its knees, although they still use these tactics when convenient. Instead, they merely squeeze a publication to death economically by controlling newsprint, advertising, and other means of production. And in the case of Peru in 1974, the government simply seized and expropriated major dailies after months of harassment.

The Inter American Press Association still stands, nevertheless, as the most effective inter-American force for the defense of freedom of the press in the hemisphere. Without it, many journalists indeed would stand alone.

8

INTERCULTURAL COMMUNICATION

Gerhard Maletzke
INTERCULTURAL AND INTERNATIONAL COMMUNICATION

Michael H. Prosser
THE CULTURAL COMMUNICATOR

L. John Martin
THE CONTRADICTION OF CROSS-CULTURAL
    COMMUNICATION

Godwin C. Chu
PROBLEMS OF CROSS-CULTURAL COMMUNICATION
    RESEARCH

8

INTERCULTURAL COMMUNICATION

INTERCULTURAL communication has gone a long way toward merging with international communication in academic programs in the last several decades. Communications departments of all kinds in colleges and universities are increasingly stressing the theoretical and practical dimensions of communicating across cultures. Certainly as communication crosses cultures, it also frequently crosses national borders: hence the close relationship between intercultural and international communication.

Dr. Gerhard Maletzke, long-time teacher and researcher at Berlin's Deutsches Institut für Entwicklungspolitik and now at the Asian Mass Communication Research and Information Center, Singapore, begins the section with an illuminating article on the similarities and differences in intercultural and international communication. This is followed by a survey of the special problems of the communicator attempting to send messages across cultures; this article is by Dr. Michael Prosser of the University of Virginia's Department of Speech Communication.

Next, L. John Martin, of the University of Maryland, offers a fascinating, and controversial, view of cross-cultural communication, in which he challenges some traditional definitions of culture. And, finally, Dr. Godwin Chu, of Hawaii's East-West Center, summarizes many basic problems connected with cross-cultural communication research.

* * * *

Related Reading

Applebaum, Richard P. *Theories of Social Change.* Chicago: Markham Publishing Co., 1970.
Buchanan, W. and H. Cantril. *How Nations See Each Other.* Urbana, University of Illinois Press, 1953.
Davidson, Henry. *Barriers to Effective Communication at the Frontiers of Culture.* London: Guild of Pastoral Psychology, 1965.

Deutsch, Karl W. *Nationalism and Social Communication.* Cambridge: M.I.T. Press, 1966.

Hall, E. T. *The Silent Language.* New York: Doubleday, 1959.

Herskovits, Melville J. *Cultural Relativism.* New York: Random House (Vintage Books), 1972.

Hoggart, Richard. *On Culture and Communication.* New York: Oxford University Press, 1972.

Nisbet, Robert A. *Social Change and History.* London: Oxford University Press, 1969.

Oliver, Robert T. *Culture and Communication: The Problem of Penetrating National and Cultural Boundaries.* Springfield, Ill.: Charles C. Thomas, 1962.

Prosser, Michael H., ed. *Intercommunication Among Nations and Peoples.* New York: Harper & Row, 1973.

Rogers, Everett M. and F. Floyd Shoemaker. *Communication of Innovations: A Cross-Cultural Approach.* New York: The Free Press, 1971.

Samovar, L. A. and Richard Porter, eds. *Intercultural Communication: A Reader.* Belmont, Calif.: Wadsworth Publishing Co., 1972.

Gerhard Maletzke:

Intercultural and International Communication

BY VERBAL definition, intercultural communication is communication between human beings of different cultures. This, of course, does beg the question a bit as to just what a "culture" is. It is not our task here to go into the deeper philosophy of the meaning of culture. Sufficient for our purposes is the general and rather simplified anthropological sense that "culture systems" are groups or populations of humans who share a variety of things in common.

" 'A culture' refers to the distinctive way of life of a group of people, their designs for living." [1]

This is a concept that can either be restricted or enlarged depending on just which perspective the observer may adopt. Observed from close up, relatively small groups of people show signs of their own "culture" which sets them apart from their neighbors; but in such instances it is really better to speak of "sub-cultures." Seen from a broader perspective, these smaller groups tend to amalgamate into a larger cultural group in the usual sense, a group which, despite many inner diversities, nonetheless reveals a substantial unity in basic beliefs and forms of experience—in customs, norms, and behavioral characteristics, and almost invariably has a common language.

Thus intercultural communication is the process of the exchange of thoughts and meaning between people of differing cultures in the sense just defined. Here the situation very soon becomes rather complicated, since we must bear in mind that the communication takes place not only between individuals as such, but also that "systems" begin to emerge here as communicating partners—even when they may, in fact, be represented by individuals. Very often these individuals are quite conscious of their "roles" as representatives of "systems" in intercultural communication.

Very often, in the American literature in particular, the phrase *international* communication is frequently used, and one can never be sure whether the authors intend to differentiate as between international and intercultural. This may not be necessary in very general and basic approaches, indeed, not

[1] Clyde Kluckhohn, "The Study of Culture," in: Daniel Lerner and Harold D. Lasswell, eds., *The Policy Sciences*, Stanford, Calif.: Stanford University Press, 1951, p. 86.

▶ This is an original article done for this book by Dr. Gerhard Maletzke, Asian Mass Communication Research and Information Center, Singapore. It is actually a shortened version of a very long (42 pp.) paper entitled "Intercultural and International Communication: An Introduction."

even possible. But there are other cases where the distinction is not only quite possible, but very useful, and as follows:

Whereas *intercultural* communication is an exchange of meaning between *cultures, international* communication takes place on the level of countries or nations, which is to say across frontiers. This means: *Intercultural* and *international* communication can, on occasion, be identical; but this is not always so. Very often people who belong to a common culture are separated by a state frontier, with the effect that international communication is taking place within a single culture. And, the contrary case, humans of quite differing cultures can be united in the same state, so that within this single state intercultural communication can take place. It is thus that one tends to use the word *international* when speaking of communication on the purely political level, whereas the concept of *intercultural* communication corresponds more to sociological and anthropological realities.

In conclusion, note should be made here of the fact that research in the fields of either intercultural or international communication is not to be regarded as the same thing as research in the field of comparative communication. Although there is no absolutely clear line of distinction,[2] one difference is this: at the center of all research in the intercultural communications processes stand the relation and contacts between peoples of different cultures or nations; research in the field of comparative communications studies and compares the communications system of varying cultures or countries as such, in order then to draw comparisons.

Whenever in the field of scientific research an attempt is made to study such a concrete object as intercultural communication in its full complexity, a difficulty soon arises in defining categories, arising out of the subject itself, which can be used as measuring-sticks for a scientific approach. The very complexity of the matter under study implies that it may be studied under any of several varying categories. It becomes thus the task of the researcher to adopt an analytic approach to these dimensions and categories, and then to decide which system is best, which system is fairest to the matter under study, and promises to yield the most fruitful scientific results. It is in this aspect of the matter that we must now inquire what dimensions of classification seem best for a scientific analysis of intercultural communication.

Very provisionally, and by no means pretending to be complete, there seem to be four large dimensions that can be easily distinguished and differentiated. Intercultural communication can be broken down for study purposes under:

1. Scientific Disciplines,
2. Areas of Life,

[2] Here above all: Charles Y. Glock, "The Comparative Study of Communications and Opinion Formation," *Public Opinion Quarterly* (Princeton, New Jersey), Vol. 16/No. 2 (Winter 1952/53), especially Note 2.

3. Means and Forms,
4. Varieties of Cultures, Nations, States.

In what follows, each of these dimensions will be briefly defined—in order to locate the specific standpoint of each of the individual contributors to the Berlin Symposium on Intercultural Communication between Industrial Nations and the Developing Countries. But we should admit here that in some cases not all studies can be too neatly classified under one dimension or the other. They cannot all be pidgeon-holed.

Modern communications research, including that in the field of intercultural communication, belongs in the category of "Scientific Integration," [3] in which the approach, perspectives and methods derive from several separate disciplines—sociology, psychology, anthropology, political science, et cetera. It was precisely in this field of the comparative study of complex cultures that the old-fashioned "disciplines" proved inadequate to the task at hand, and had to make way for an "interdisciplinary" or, better, still, "integrative" approach. And this is why only very few of the contributions to this symposium can be too neatly labelled as belonging to this or that specific discipline.

It becomes apparent, too, that the traditional academic disciplines are no longer enough to serve in themselves as a framework for study, or for an ordering of the material in the field of intercultural communication. The deeper reason for this is that today many of the practitioners of the traditional disciplines no longer feel satisfied with them as the ideal means to approach and integrate the new material in this field. This is the situation today which has led to the demand for interdisciplinary research and to the development of modern "Integration Sciences."

Intercultural communication takes place today in almost every sector of human activity. The most important of these would seem to be (1) Politics, (2) Science, (3) Art and Culture, (4) Economics, (5) Journalism, (6) Tourism, (7) Technics, (8) Church and Charity affairs, (9) Sport, (10) the Military Sector, (11) Institutions, Organizations etc., (12) the Personal, Private Sector.

As in every field of human endeavor, it is not always correct to try to make too absolute distinctions; indeed, because of the complexity of human life, it would be quite false to do so.

The basic psychological problem [4] in intercultural communication becomes apparent when one poses the question of understanding, non-understanding and mis-understanding as it takes place between cultures. In order to come to grips with this problem, we have had recourse to a concept which psychologists have been using for some time, with much success, to solve certain

[3] Cf. Werner Schöllgen, "Integrierende Wissenschaften als neuer Typ von Wissenschaft," *Publizistik* (Bremen, West Germany), Vol. 5/No. 4 (July/August, 1960), pp. 195–204.
[4] Cf. Gerhard Maletzke, *Psychologie der Massenkommunikation: Theorie und Systematik*, Hamburg: Hans Bredow Institut, 1963.

special problems of Psychology. It is the concept of mankind's World View or "Weltsicht."

With the mature individual, a quite specific manner and method both of apprehending and dealing with the world has already developed, which enables him to interpret and evaluate it. This relatively constant and stable World View is the product of a few inherited traits and a larger variety of living experiences in his concrete, social and cultural surroundings. The psychologists have quite a variety of concepts to deal with this situation, which may not always be quite synonymous, but in principle tend to be describing the same phenomenon, namely the fact of a definite structuring and evaluating of human experience within its environment. The various concepts for this are called either "World View" or "Cognitive Structure," "Cognitive Style" or "Private World," "Subjective Experience World," "Frame of Reference," "Subjective Value System," "Value Constellation," "Thinking Style" and other such terminology. It cannot be our task here to compare and analyse these various concepts, to find out just how they relate to one another and what shades of difference in meaning they may have, or in which psychic field they may have their special relevance.

Most social groups of humans, populations and cultures show themselves to be, or are so constituted, that they consist of people with a similar realm of experience, with the same frames-of-reference and value-systems. Moreover, these common groups or culture-specific World Views are very closely linked with the language. The common language is both an expression of the *Weltanschauung* and a determinant of it. Here we come to a series of very complicated inter-dependencies, which we can however simplify into the formula that, on the one hand, the art and manner in which one understands the world is determined to a large extent by language; but language, at the same time, is an expression of a specific group-experiencing of the world, and therefore may itself be shaped by the *Weltanschauung* as well as the wishes, expectancies and motivations of the group using it. It is from this frame of reference that we get the hypothesis that, by language-analysis, one can arrive at a direct approach to the cognitive and affective structure of the group or population which speaks this language.

From these psychological facts communications research learns the following: The extent to which individuals or groups understand one another, fail to understand, or misunderstand, is determined by the degree to which the World Views and frames of reference of the partners in communication overlap. The larger the common ground of *Weltanschauung* is, the more likely and more simple it is that there will be an adequate meeting-of-minds. The less common ground there is, the fewer frames of reference, then the more likely it is that there will be serious misunderstandings and non-comprehension. And yet, while mentioning all these things, we must also not lose sight of the fact that total understanding is never possible since, as psychoanalysis has shown, there does not exist a total and perfect self-understanding.

Since, by definition, international communication is something that takes place between people belonging to different cultures, and who in many respects live within different frames of-reference, then it follows at first that in intercultural communication there will be much narrower bounds drawn than in communications between people or groups within the same culture. Ignoring for a moment the exceptions, we can say with certainty: the extent of intercultural understanding, misunderstanding or non-understanding is determined by the extent of likenesses and differences in frames-of-reference, value systems, or World Views of the cultures involved, from their cognitive and affective distance from each other.

This concept of the psychological background of intercultural communication indicates what it really means to understand a foreign culture, and to conform to it when this is desired. It means comprehension of the foreign manner of seeing, experiencing and judging, an accommodating to the alien cognitive structure, and adopting of a foreign frame of reference. We can here only note in passing that such a process of understanding and accommodation brings with it a plethora of problems and difficulties; that, to mention only one aspect, it calls for a very high degree of empathy, and empathy is a quality that varies markedly in individuals; that there are whole cultures with greater or lesser desire and readiness to show empathy; that intercultural understanding can never be perfect in itself, and that intercultural understanding and accommodation are often a very difficult and even painful process, which can often lead to a kind of culture-shock.

It is thus that, because of the differences in frames-of-references, vertical barriers are erected between cultures, barriers which make difficult mutual comprehension or hinder it completely, and the height of which is determined by the distance between the cognitive structures of the cultures involved.

One factor that plays a role not only in international communications, but also in the development process, is the creation of conceptions or images, attitudes, prejudices and stereotypes, which develop within a given culture in reference to another.[5] These images tend to concentrate themselves on a very few marked traits, they tend to run very uniformly throughout the population, are relatively constant, and almost invariably take on a derogatory nature.[6]

Every process of communication in the intercultural realm has to deal with these pre-dispositions. Images and attitudes play a decisive role in modifying the content and form of dialogues, they determine the process of acclimatization or comprehension, the content and form of diplomatic, journalistic or private reports on foreign countries, and many other aspects of the intercultural dialogue. It is not only among individuals, but also whole groups and even nations and populations, that one can detect two types, the xenophiles and the

---

[5] Cf. Herbert C. Kelman, ed., *International Behavior*, New York: Holt, Rinehart and Winston, 1965. Cf. also: William Buchanan and Hadley Cantril, *How Nations See Each Other*, Urbana: University of Illinois Press, 1953.
[6] See William A. Scott, "Psychological and social correlates of International Images," in: Herbert C. Kelman, ed., *op. cit.*, p. 72 *et seq.*

xenophobes, those who have an open and those who have a closed approach to foreign peoples and groups.

In the last decades there have been numerous studies in the field of social psychology concerning national images, prejudices and stereotypes, so that here we are standing on ground that has been well-researched.

International attitudes and images taken on special weight in the realm of foreign policy, which is to say in the decisions that can lead to war or peace. These decisions and their consequences are very much dependent on whether one has correctly or falsely judged the attitudes, intentions and perspectives of the other side.

If we inquire now after the functions which these images, above all in the form of stereotypes, have for people, if we ask after the drives and motives that correspond to these images, then they reveal themselves to be relievers of pressure on the ego, as means or instruments for making the world simpler, comprehensible, and without nagging questions. The differentiation and complexity of existence is subjectively eliminated, and what remain are only a few superficial, governable features. This relieving or unburdening tendency expresses itself in two psychological facts which are also most important for comprehending intercultural communication—in "self-evident truths" and in the over-estimation of one's own and the underestimation of the opponent's position.

In our previous considerations, we made the assumption that nations or cultures are separated from each other by various viewpoints and experiences, by differing frames-of-reference. We must now, however, both modify and elaborate on this model of "vertical barriers" between cultures.

International communication in general takes place not between countries *in toto*, but rather between single individuals or groups of two cultures. Thus intercultural communication does not come about haphazardly between certain people and groups, but, in by far the great majority of instances, it takes place between communications-partners who share several things in common—for example, a similar level of education, common interests, a common profession, similar motivations, et cetera. The scientists in a foreign cultural environment will invariably seek out contact with the resident scientists there, the artist with fellow-artists, the athlete with other athletes; politicians, business-men, technicians, journalists, soldiers and tourists tend, when they are in foreign environments, to seek out fellow-humans with similar professions, interests, status; in short, with partners whose viewpoints and way-of-thinking will parallel theirs at least in fields of common interest. Because of this fact, there develops, right across the vertical barriers a kind of horizontal field of communication. And, without doubt, these common interests can very often be stronger and more binding than other loyalties that have been built up in various strata within the culture itself. A German scientist will very often feel more at home with a fellow-scientist from France, Nigeria, India or Venezuela than with a German farm-laborer; and technicians and businessmen from different cultures have a broader basis of understanding each other than, let us say, a Bavarian and a Holsteiner.

"Intercultures" or "Third Cultures" have thus been built up along the lines of these intercultural, horizontal, common interests. But as yet we do not have many studies about the extent, structure, or dynamics of these cultures which extend out beyond the bounds of a given culture. *Flack* in his Symposium contribution [7] does look closely at this particular problem of the type and significance of these Intercultures.

It is a wide-open question, how binding these Intercultures might turn out to be under serious stress—for example, during an international crisis or in time of war.

It must be reserved for subsequent research to think through the psychological and sociological aspects of intercultural communication in the special case of communication between developed and developing nations. Assuredly this can be a wide and fruitful field of research, along the following lines:

—reciprocal identification and projection;
—the roles and status relationships between developed and developing nations, which is to say the social-psychological relationships which, for example, come into play in negotiations over development aid or voting in the UNO or other international organizations;
—the question of confidence and mutual trust between the communicating partners;
—research into the psychological functions which the partners in communication may be fulfilling, as in such cases when aggressive instincts are deflected toward an external foe, or when major powers or former colonial powers are made into scapegoats in the developing nations.

"*Intercultures*" also without doubt grow up between developed and developing nations. Yet it is nonetheless quite obvious that this form of social contact takes place much more often on the level of the "élites" than in the broad masses of the people.[8] As welcome as such intercultures may be as bridges between cultures otherwise not in contact, there is a danger that should not be overlooked, particularly in developing countries. When members of the élite in developing countries join such intercultures, then the danger exists that they are only increasing that process of alienation from their own culture which in turn only strengthens the dubious dualism already noted.

After all that has already been said, it would be superfluous to go into detail about the extraordinary practical significance that attaches to research in intercultural communication between developed and developing nations. Devel-

[7] Cf. George N. Gordon, Irving Falk and William Hodapp, *The Idea of Invaders*, New York: Hastings House, 1963.
[8] Cf. Charles A. Wright, "Functional Analysis and Mass Communication," *Public Opinion Quarterly* (Princeton, N.J.), Vol. 24/No. 4 (1960), pp. 605–620.

opment aid, diplomatic negotiations, economic contacts, the exchange of students and scientists, mutual cultural and information work, will all be less testy and more successful when we know more about the situations and questions which have been raised in this study.

Michael H. Prosser:

The Cultural Communicator

COMMUNICATION and culture are so closely bound together that virtually all communication engaged in by humans is culturally linked. Even when we engage in intrapersonal communication, that communication which takes place unconsciously or consciously within each of us, our own cultural background affects all of our actions and reactions. Communication and culture are ongoing processes without precise beginnings or endings. Much of our communication, whether intrapersonally, or interpersonally, occurs whether or not we wish it. We really have no choice except to communicate. It is an aspect of being animate. Similarly, we have relatively little choice about much of our cultural background and heritage. Biologically, we inherit certain traits which have a bearing on our cultural development. Tendencies or weaknesses toward certain illnesses can now be traced back several generations through heredity.

Recent studies demonstrate that pregnant mothers who are alcoholics, or who use drugs heavily, or who smoke excessively, or who have poor diets pass on these quasi-cultural problems directly to their unborn children. We now know that no one is a totally blank slate or *tabula rasa* at birth to be written on as John Locke once believed. Since a major aspect of cultural transmittal includes the traditions, language, attitudes, beliefs, values, non-verbal patterns, and thought orientations passed down from generation to generation, it is clear that many of these contributions are part of the unconscious cultural development of the individual.

At the same time that much communication and culture are entirely developed by happenstance and without regard to the wishes of the individual, it is also true that parts of the individual's communicative and cultural development are consciously planned or intended. A major feature of humanness is the symbol-building, symbol-manipulating, symbol-using function which we all share together. Although we are not often conscious of all that allows us to communicate or all that has helped to develop us as specific cultural beings, we do have the power to choose consciously various goals when we communicate and frequently we intend to influence others in our own distinctly cultural way. We also have various symbols which can be used in such conscious and planned communication that demonstrate our own individual cultural identity

▶ This article by Dr. Prosser, chairman of the Department of Speech Communication at the University of Virginia, is from a paper presented by the author at the International Communication Association Convention, Chicago, April 23–26, 1975.

as we desire. We are always both unconsciously and consciously cultural communicators.

While it is a given fact that all humans possess similar potential for complementary communicative and cultural development, these developments are always affected by a multitude of factors. Culture transcends time and space, but it is also affected by variations of time and space. The age in which a person lives, the locality, the climate, the geography, and many other factors deeply influence the way that person communicates and develops as a cultural being. The rich variety of the human character as it has evolved in different time sequences and localities is a feature which both unites and pulls us apart from each other. Many studies have attempted to illustrate that the more that persons have in common with others, the less likely they are to suffer serious breakdowns in communication or cultural distortion. Unfortunately, despite the closest cultural affinities, communication breakdowns and cultural distortions are still more frequent than exceptions. It seems to be in the nature of man to seek unity and disorder simultaneously. Conflict and struggle appear to be major components of the human condition. When a mature person is eulogized after death as having never spoken a cross word to anyone, it suggests a plastic saint, and not the stuff that real human beings are made of. The increasingly alarming violence which occurs among friends and relatives, and the continuing breakup of major societal institutions such as marriage and the family, are indicative of the problems faced as cultural communicators even when persons share the same intimate similarities. It is no wonder that the more dissimilar members of two cultures are, the more likely there will be serious communication breakdowns and cultural distortions which aggravate tensions.

SIMILARITIES & DIFFERENCES IN VIEWING CULTURAL COMMUNICATORS

Edward Stewart argues that the major reason that we ought to be vitally concerned about the communication which takes place between members of different cultures is this very aspect of the significance of dissimilarity (Stewart, 1974, 4, 5). The more that our patterns of language, non-verbal cues, attitudes, beliefs, stereotypes, prejudices, values, and thought orientations differ the more likely that we are to communicate ineffectively or at cross purposes and the more likely that we are to engage in serious cultural distortions. For the sake of appearing to seek unity, the impact of cultural distinctions is often blurred. Stewart believes that although in some societies differences may be assumed necessary for communication to take place, other societies hold as sort of a mental set that it is more important to find similarities between people rather than differences. He contends that "it is on this issue of differences, either naturally or by acquisition, that intercultural communication rests its claim for identity." (Stewart, 1974, 4–5).

If differences do not matter, and do not matter in a most significant way, as communicative and cultural barriers and causes of breakdowns, then there is little reason either to study the interrelationships between communication and culture, or to attempt to overcome the breakdowns which are likely to affect us as cultural communicators. The inseparability of communication and culture and the problem of cultural differences and conflict between people are such basic principles to the understanding of human communication that they serve as the *sine qua non* or fundamental reason for undertaking such study. Nevertheless, as there is a great danger in believing that cultural differences are of no significance, so too, is it dangerous to believe that cultural differences are insurmountable and that effective intercultural communication can never take place.

It is probably true as Condon and Youseff suggest that there is no real universal communicator, or one who can always communicate effectively no matter what the cultural time or place (Condon and Youseff, 1975, 252), and such a person would again represent the plastic saint, but it is also inherent in the study of intercultural communication, that we seek to learn enough about cultural similarities and differences, so that we can actually operate as effectively as possible in whatever cultural setting we find ourselves. . . .

Cultural Pluralism Versus Cultural Homogenization

At one end of the spectrum, there is the danger of so much cultural factionalism and pluralism that scarcely anyone can communicate successfully with anyone else. In such a case, the divisions are so pronounced that within a single society, state, or region, there is virtually no sharing of language, traditions, customs, values, or thought-orientations. For all the evils imposed by colonialists on suppressed peoples, from the early Romans to the more recent British and French exploitations in Asia and Africa, such major colonial masters have generally aided the conquered peoples by the imposition of a common major language, allowing them to advance as part of the world community in terms of trade, diplomacy, education, literacy, and modernization. This policy has not proven entirely successful sometimes because a developing nation wishes to discard all reminders of their colonial past, as is the case of Uganda whose leaders are trying to eliminate the colonial language as an official language. In India, though English has been retained as one of the official languages, there are so many official and non-official language groups and dialects that successful language interchange is difficult a very few miles from a person's usual home. The same example can be multiplied in many parts of the world. While recognizing the importance of cultural pluralism, however, many countries have taken the initiative to retain a dominant Western language as a major unifying force within their countries and with other nations.

Canada's movement toward cultural pluralism and its adoption recently of English *and* French as its two official languages have resulted in mixed benefits and problems in terms of the harmonious working of the French and English Canadians. The French Canadians, often categorized in the past as the "niggers of Canada" by English-speaking Canadians can take pride that there is now no officially sanctioned discrimination in their country on the basis of language and that they are now eligible for various federal and provincial jobs which were previously open only to English-speaking Canadians. Still, the problems of being an officially bi-lingual country have been substantial, with other minority groups pressing their claims for additional official languages; in providing bi-lingual employees for all federal and provincial offices, including, for example, small rural post offices; in printing all official documents in both languages; and with the continuing intense hostilities between French and English-speaking groups. These problems are relatively simple in contrast to similar problems in the multi-language countries but still cause the most serious intercultural and intracultural communication breakdowns. When we add to these problems the fact that value orientations even within regions of these countries have no common basis, the problems become staggering.

At the opposite end of the spectrum, there is the danger that so much homogenization of culture will take place that no cultural diversity will exist at all. Colin Cherry writes so poignantly:

> One of the great dangers into which these post-War developments of world communication can lead us is the delusion that, as the global network expands, so the walls of our mental villages are being pushed back: the delusion that increased powers of communication will bring us all closer together into better understanding and a sense of human compassion. There is no function whatsoever for such an emotional belief. . . .
>
> The ever-mounting volume of news that presses upon us requires us at least to adopt some personal attitudes towards millions of different people. We cannot know them individually as persons, but read about them only as names and activities. We can see them only as classes and types, as institutions, as abstracts, and speak of *the* Biafrans, *the* Chinese, *the* Arabs, as though such populations varied little among themselves as persons! We sometimes need to speak of *the* Americans, as though every one were alike, or worse, of *teenagers*, the *black races*, *students* . . . . a host of gross generalizations in increasing numbers, as world affairs come to interest and concern more people. . . . The sight of a single foreign face on the television screen or a single ugly incident in a vast crowd, picked out by the newsthirsty cameraman, may create symbols falsely representing something "typical" of whole populations or crowds. (Cherry, 1971, 8–9).

Cherry writes of various attempts to promote international unity both through real and through artificial language systems. Among the artificial language or sign systems, he includes those which require users in any part of the world to accept precisely the same sign systems—for example, the language of mathematics, scientific inquiry, geographical measurement, the measurement of time, international road symbols, and as a substitute for real language, Esperanto. These sign systems have fixed rules and are static. They are cross-cultural and international as their usages are strictly restricted and formally defined, with some sort of penalty attached for breaking the rules, such as being shortchanged in the market place, missing appointments, having extra chances of road accidents, etc.

Esperanto works far less well than all of the other artificial language systems as it seeks to imitate real languages which are in a constant state of evolvement and flux both in terms of their grammar and their vocabulary. Cherry comments: "There is no universal, worldwide *culture* whose changes and development might sustain such languages and continually modify and adapt them consistently everywhere. A universal artificial language may have undoubted value for specific and limited purposes, but the difficulty is that people of different cultures live in very different circumstances and don't always want to talk about the same things!" (Cherry, 1971, 15).

Within the United States, there has been a recent heated debate about the values of cultural pluralism versus cultural homogenization. For most of our recent history, we have accepted, in John Kennedy's phrase, in a nation of immigrants the concept of "Americanization," an idea which not only causes all of our citizens to be forced to learn a common language and a sort of common culture, but also a commitment to American ideals and goals which have made us a great country. (Rosenfeld, September 27, 1974, A18).

In the mid 1960's, the value of placing all Americans in precisely the same language and cultural mold began to come under sharp attack. Blacks were searching for their own cultural identity and awareness. Spanish-speaking Americans, who had long lived under the handicap of utilizing one language at home and another at school without consideration for the original language, were beginning to insist upon the ability to utilize Spanish without being shamed for their ignorance of English. Puerto Ricans, American Indians, and other cultural groups or areas under United States control and flag have been caught in a bureaucratic struggle about whether the administering authority intended to allow them to use their native language was to be eliminated for all educational and official purposes. With the struggle about the language, there was always a simultaneous struggle about cultural values and norms. . . .

WE ARE CULTURAL COMMUNICATORS

Arguments about making us all similar or all culturally diverse continue with increasing tension and intensity. We cannot escape them. Despite mainline America's attempt to homogenize all of its citizens, and the citizens of many other countries as well, total elimination of all individualistic and group cultural traits would leave us as dreary 1984 Orwellian carbon copies of each other. Such a loss would be incalculable in terms of the most important dimensions of our humanness which allows us to build and utilize symbols through a vast and rich variety of linguistic and non-linguistic codes, verbal and non-verbal patterns, perceptional, attitudinal, value-laden, and thought-oriented constructs.

If we were all precisely similar, one set of patterns at every level would suffice for all of us. The great questions of "who am I?"; "what is the meaning of life?"; "where are we going?" and "why?" would not need to be raised or reanswered from age to age and in different locales and settings. If we were all precisely the same, our art could be completed with a single stroke, our literature and history with a single pen, our laws and guidelines for living by a single lawmaker, and our cultural, religious, and moral value system by a simple and unchanging edict.

Certainly it is true that cultural norms and values have been established which are serviceable to all men as exemplified in our great human documents, the Ten Commandments, the Old and New Testaments, the Torah, the Twelve Tables of the Romans, the Koran, the Magna Carta, the American Declaration of Independence, the American Constitution and its Bill of Rights, the Universal Declaration of Human Rights, the Declaration Granting Independence to All Colonial Countries, and many other moral, religious, literary, and philosophical landmarks of human history. Without such fundamental values and norms to guide men's lives, civilization itself would be in perpetual chaos and could not have survived as long as it has. If such similarities in the conduct of men, and in relation to biologically similar characteristics, did not exist, the expected lifespan of the human race would be perilously short. Even so, with the potential threat to the environment and because of the nuclear capacity, many of our great philosophers and doomsday prophets have been long predicting the end of human life as we know it.

Despite the necessary unifying factors keeping mankind from total chaos, it is also true, as Suzanne Langer (1942) suggests that humans cannot live with total order or total chaos, but must seek a measure of existence somewhere in between. It is this in-between stage that identifies us as cultural communicators. We are affected culturally by our civilization and history, by our national and societal institutions such as church, education, and labor in our lives, by the influences of technology in our lives, by geographical boundaries, by our cities and our towns, by our family ties, and finally by our own individual growth and development.

In some ways, everyone in the world is the same, but at the same time, no two persons in the world are the same. Thus, each of us is a cultural communicator. Each of us communicates interculturally all the time at many levels. Obviously, the more alike we are with those whom we communicate with, the more we ideally ought to be able to communicate effectively. Generally speaking, the more dissimilar we are, the more likely our intercultural communication will stress conflict and communication breakdown. The conflict and communication breakdown may occur at a variety of levels because of misperceptions related to our linguistic and non-linguistic codes, our attitudes, perceptions, values, and thought-patternings.

The causes of such conflicts and communication breakdowns and their remedies make the study of intercultural communication among the most significant subjects which we might consider and requires careful attention by all of us. The practical result may be that while it isn't probable that we will become universal communicators, we will at least learn to become the most effective cultural communicators possible and will come to know better who we are in the context of human life and culture.

*   *   *   *

Sources

Cherry, Colin.
1971. *World Communication: Threat or Promise?* London.
Condon, John C., and Yousef, Fathi S.
1975. *An Introduction to Intercultural Communication.* Indianapolis.
Langer, Suzanne.
1942. *Philosophy in a New Key.* New York.
Stewart, Edward.
1974. "Outline of Intercultural Communication." mimeographed and supplied by the author.

L. John Martin:

The Contradiction of Cross-Cultural Communication

COMMUNICATION has been defined in a variety of ways and the list of qualities and capabilities attributed to it is necessarily a function of the particular definition subscribed to. Among the most common uses of the term is the definition that equates communication with "encoding"—written or oral: "Written communication is not a perfect means of communication. . . . But it is the fastest reliable means when large groups of people are concerned" (Vance 1966, p. 282). A related definition is "the transmission of a message," as in "One may favor uninhibited communication of government business to 'the people' through the media" (Bobrow 1973–1974. p. 551). Then there is the definition that implies the two-way exchange of messages: "The communication between the farmer and his labourers on agricultural innovations can be an important topic for research" (Van den Ban 1973, p. 389); or, "When an American of Mexican origin talks with a fellow American of Japanese ancestry . . . the type of communication that takes place is interethnic communication" (Sitaram 1972, p. 22).

Theroetical definitions are concerned less with the process than with the effect of communication. They speak of communication as an interactive process, a give-and-take, the transmission of a message with feedback; "it is on-going, dynamic, without starting and stopping points" (Berlo 1960, p. 106).* A unidirectional, though theoretical definition is that of Gerald R. Miller: "In the main, communication has as its central interest those behavioral situations in which a source transmits a message to a receiver(s) *with conscious intent to affect the latter's behaviors*" (1966, p. 92). This is a hypodermic definition that concentrates on the effect or outcome of the process from the viewpoint of the communicator. It involves a purposive act by a communicator, and it implies that the purpose is persuasion. Some have defined conmunication as a purposive act that has some effect on an audience, although the effect may be

---

* Yet Berlo also relapses to more prosaic, strictly process-oriented definitions, as when he says: "There is research evidence to indicate that the average American spends about 70 per cent of his active hours communicating verbally—listening, speaking, reading and writing, in that order." *Ibid.*, p. 1.

▶ From: A paper read by Dr. Martin, University of Maryland, at the Seminar on Mass Communication, Mexico City, March 14, 1974. Reprinted here with permission of the author.

merely to alert the audience to the presence of the communicator (see Herb and Thompson 1968, pp. 738–9).

Other theoretical definitions, while they concentrate on the effect of the process, do so from the point of view of the receiver or audience. Communication in terms of these definitions may be either intentional or unintentional, since what matters is not what is transmitted and by whom, but what is received and how. Lee Thayer speaks of "a more advantageous view of communication as something which occurs in the receiver" (1968, p. 39). George Gerbner says that "we are inquiring into a communication act which has consequences. To reduce the range of observation to those acts, aspects, or consequences which may have been 'intended' as parts of a conscious communication effort is to place blinders on the researcher" (1966, p. 101).

Finally, there are theoretical definitions that ignore the dynamics of the process, the initiator or the assignee, the medium or the message, and limit communication to the "*sharing* of elements of behavior, or modes of life, by the existence of sets of rules" (Cherry 1957, p. 6). Charles Morris defines communication as the establishment of "a commonage or signification" through the use of signs. (1946, p. 118).

The present discussion is concerned with this last definition of communication. Communication is viewed as an event—which the dictionary defines as a happening, outcome or result—and the event is the successful sharing of meaning by two or more individuals—an "isomorphism in construct" I shall call it later. Communication is not any act that precedes this sharing, such as talking, writing, symboling, transmitting, encoding; or any act that may follow these activities, such as listening, reading, receiving, decoding. Nor is communication a consequent of the sharing, such as the activities that are referred to as feedback, reaction, ego-defensive or tension-reducing behavior, information-seeking, and so forth. Communication is no more and no less than the concidence of constructs (to be defined below). Everything else has some other name.

Why define communication so narrowly? For the same reason that we avoid asking two-part questions in survey questionnaires when we expect a single answer. Ambiguity in the question merely leads to ambiguity in the response. To say that there are barriers to cross-cultural communication, when by communication we mean any or all of the following activities: encoding, transmitting, receiving, consummating, decoding, influencing, and reacting, is to be guilty of very fuzzy thinking. There may be barriers to one or more of these activities and not to others, but who knows which activities the speaker has in mind, or the listener for that matter?

The Communication Process

In their excellent model of the communication process, Bruce Westley and Malcolm MacLean show that in addition to the sender, receiver, channel and message, there also are certain "objects of orientation" (1957), without which no communication can occur, since there would be nothing to talk about.* These objects or events in the world outside of the mind of an individual are the stimuli that imprint and trigger an ideational storage system. How this happens is central to the feasibility of communication, including cross-cultural communication which is merely a special case of communication.

Referents: The stimuli or objects of orientation are the referents of a person's physical and spiritual environment. They are the things about which he attempts to communicate and they may be concrete objects such as trees, tables and people or concepts and attributes such as intelligence, beauty and redness.

Referents are culturally defined. The determination of what constitutes a particular referent in terms of size, color, texture, location, appearance, function, number, and variety of attributes, and so forth is arbitrary and follows the rules of a culture. Thus, where one color begins and ends is not the same in all cultures, as Brown and Lenneberg have demonstrated (1954, pp. 454–462). In Chinese, fruit and nuts are a single concept. Eskimos don't consider snow or seals as a single referent but a number of different ones.

Referents are rarely objects-in-isolation: they are almost invariably objects-in-situations, and generally an individual experiences them not as an object-in-being but as an object-in-action. While man has the unique ability among animals of thinking of an object in the abstract, divorced from its situation and action, he must speedily record the abstraction before it assimilates situation and action tendencies.

To illustrate, it is hard to think of a "boy" in abstraction without locating him in a given time and place, doing something, if only standing or sitting. This fact is important in cross-cultural communication, because even if the referent is familiar in abstraction, for communication to occur it must also be familiar in a given situation and action. This is immediately evident if we think of the sentence, "The man flies." A Pacific islander who has never seen an airplane is familiar with each of the referents in other contexts, but would fail to understand the message.

Wars have been fought and people killed over classifications and definitions of referents. Definitions of race, for example—who is a black or a Jew—have led to lynchings and genocide.

Constructs: Throughout life, a person comes into contact with many different versions of a referent, no two of which are identical. No two apples are alike, no two petunias, to say nothing of flowers. Referents are unique, and, besides, they occur in unique situations and are involved in unique actions. Culturally, they may be defined as one and the same referent: but morphologically they are discrete, and it is next to impossible to store all the variants of a referent separately. One is forced to conceptualize an "average referent," which I have called a *construct.*

---

* I do not consider this or any of the other so-called information or communication process models *communication models* since they do not depict what I term communication but rather the transmission or reception of symbols or information. These, too, are important activities, however, and I find the models useful.

A construct is the result of experience with all the variants of a referent. It may be stereotyped or caricatured or an extreme version of the referent; but more often it is a composite of most of the referent experiences of the individual—a central tendency.

A construct is not fixed and inflexible but subject to change and development, since it is sensitive to every new experience with the referent. Constructs also are subject to assimilation and contrast effects that Muzafer Sherif and Carl Hovland have shown exist in social judgment (1961, chap. 3).* A version of the referent that differs slightly from the construct (with which it is compared upon any new experience with the referent) is assimilated and seen as more similar to the construct than it actually is, or is contrasted, if the difference between the referent and the construct is seen as great. In the former case, the attributes of the new version modify or expand the construct; in the latter case its attributes are associated with a contrasting construct.

An example would be the view that people have of the system of government of a friendly and of an unfriendly nation. If the nation is friendly, the system is more likely to be seen as like one's own and assimilated to the relevant referent, e.g., a democratic government; if unfriendly, it is likely to be contrasted and its attributes are associated with the contrasting form of government, e.g., dictatorial. These are not necessarily polar forms of government in a technical sense, but they may be perceived as polar constructs. It is fairly obvious how assimilation and contrast can lead to reduced effectiveness in communication.

Symbols: The vehicle through which constructs are brought to the conscious level in the minds of communicants is the symbol. A symbol may be a word or a gesture or an article of clothing or any act or artifact that represents some other act, artifact, natural phenomenon or concept by common agreement within a culture.

When two or more individuals use or manipulate symbols, they evoke in each other's minds a series of constructs. Constructs are, therefore, the sensations or the pictures in the mind that correspond to an individual's experiences with the referents being mentioned. Since referents are never experienced in the same way by any two individuals, the constructs developed and later evoked through the manipulation of symbols by two individuals are never identical, or isomorphic.

That people develop constructs was shown by Edna Heidbreder in her study of concept formation (1946). Her subjects abstracted certain recurrent attributes inherent in referents with which they came into contact. These attributes they then generalized to all cases that contained similar attributes and associated them with a symbol. Heidbreder concluded that this is how language is learned, i.e., symbols are associated with concepts. But while the symbol is a useful mnemonic device—one that helps in classifying and storing concepts—

* See Roger Brown, *Social Psychology*. New York: The Free Press, 1965, pp. 322–328, for a discussion of the studies of Vigotsky, Piaget and Inhelder, and Bruner and Olver, all of which indicate that this is probably true.

the relationship between the referent and the concept or construct is equally important.

The fact that referents are associated with constructs and vice versa in the absence of symbols is illustrated by Helen Keller's story of how she was first exposed to language (White 1949, p. 38). Becoming deaf and blind before she had learned to speak, she was tutored by a Miss Sullivan. This is how she describes her first encounter with words:

> As the cool stream gushed over one hand she [Miss Sullivan] spelled into the other the word *water*, first slowly, then rapidly. I stood still, my whole attention fixed upon the motion of her fingers. Suddenly I felt a misty consciousness as of something forgotten—a thrill of returning thought; and somehow *the mystery of language was revealed to me*. I knew then that w-a-t-e-r' meant that wonderful cool something that was flowing over my hand. That living word awakened my soul, gave it light, hope, joy, set it free!

That constructs vary from one person to another even within the same culture, has been shown by a number of researchers using a variety of techniques. Osgood, Suci and Tannenbaum used the Semantic Differential, which they developed, to locate a concept in semantic space by means of a series of differentiating judgments (1957). Even by this crude measure, few people place concepts in identical positions semantically, although it has been shown that there is higher consistency within cultures than between cultures (Tanaka and Osgood 1965). Concepts have also been defined by free verbal association or by a similarity judgment method in which the subjects are asked to match concepts with words in a list presented to them (Szalay and Brent 1967). These methods, too, indicate that there are greater similarities in constructs within cultures than between cultures, but that there are wide divergences among subjects within a culture.

Communication would be impossible if it depended on perfect isomorphism in construct. Fortunately, we tolerate deviations from our constructs because these represent central tendencies of referent experiences, with appropriate confidence limits. Tolerance makes communication possible, while at the same time making it more ambiguous. The development of tolerance is well illustrated by studies of concept formation, such as Heidbreder's mentioned above, or of how children learn to speak. Lewis watched his son from age 16 months through age 23 months learn to understand the concept "flower," by learning to tolerate variations in kinds, locations and even pictorial representations of flowers (1959). Man also tolerates an incomplete message and learns to complete a construct contextually, as David Krech and Richard Crutchfield point out (1971), and as Wilson Taylor demonstrates with his "cloze procedure" (1953).

An example may help. The symbol "house" retrieves my construct of house from storage in my brain. It certainly would not correspond to anyone else's construct of house. If I were shown a picture of a house, I would probably agree that while it did not look anything like my personal construct, it was essentially what I had in mind. Culturally imposed tolerances would probably permit me to accept the deviation from my construct; but it might not. If two individuals were raised in different cultures, their constructs may be dissimilar beyond tolerable deviations. It can easily be seen that the point must be reached when there is no isomorphism in constructs, i.e., no communication.

This suggests that there are degrees of communication and that communication is always less than fully effective. The point may be reached where there is no communication at all through a given transmitted message. This is in one direction of a continuum. In the other direction is ever increasing improvement in communication, tending toward isomorphism in construct.

The Nature of Culture

Now let us look at what we mean by culture. Melville Herskovits defines culture as "the man-made part of the environment" (1948, p. 17). George Murdock says that culture consists of habits and tendencies to act in a certain way, not the action itself (1956, p. 249). And Ward Goodenough says culture is whatever people have to know to operate acceptably in society. "It does not consist of things, people, behavior, or emotions. It is rather an organization of these things. It is the forms of things that people have in mind, their models for perceiving, relating, and otherwise interpreting them" (1964, p. 36).

Benjamin Whorf has said that language functions not only to communicate thought but (by implication) it serves as a vehicle of culture (1964, p. 139). Sapir, Whorf and others have suggested that one's entire world view depends on the language he speaks, *since language* defines and structures our experiences for us (Henle 1966, p. 1). While people acquire most of their culture in the process of learning their language (Goodenough 1964, p. 39), and some have said that if cultures were grouped they would coincide with language areas (Hoijer 1964, p. 455), it is not necessarily true that people speaking the same language have the same culture. British and American cultures differ, and the culture of English-speaking India differs even more from that of the two Western countries.

Yet, undeniably, language is one of the most important factors in creating similarity in culture. Harry Triandis asserts that other factors are values, ideals, attitudes, geographic location, race (physical type), social class, occupation, religion, nationality, age, sex, and roles. He says, "similarity in any of the characteristics listed above may produce similarities in culture between two groups" (1964, p. 2). Furthermore, "subjects employing a particular set of categories [imposed by language] experience difficulties in communicating with subjects employing another set" (pp. 9–10). Conversely, Clyde Kluckhohn says that "when people from two groups, despite perceptible variation in the details of their life-ways, nevertheless share enough basic assumptions so that they can communicate in the broadest sense of that term—comfortably, then their cultures are only variants of a single culture" (1962, p. 65).

Communication, therefore, occurs only within a culture, since culture defines and patterns our experiences, and these, in turn, control the development of our constructs.

If that were the whole story, we might as well say farewell to the prospects of cross-cultural communication. But most of us would say, "Nonsense. I have personally experienced talking to people with manifestly different cultures, and we had little or no problem communicating." This is true, and it seems to negate the proposition that communication is possible only *within* cultures, not between them.

The problem lies in the ambiguity and breadth of meaning of the term "culture." we have said that culture may be defined as the rules of behavior of a given group or society and that a variety of demographic and attitudinal factors may be the constitutive base of these groups. Every one of us belongs to a number of groups and shares the cultural norms of those groups. The term "culture" is sometimes used metonymically, however, and in this sense a characteristic of a society—for example, its language or geographic location—is permitted to represent the society as a whole. When we speak of "French culture," we mean either the group of people who speak the French language or the group of people who live in France. "Culture," in this sense, suggests a closed and discrete society whose cultural norms are unique to itself as contrasted with the cultural norms of other societies.

This, of course, is not the case, and it is one of the p problems of equating culture with language areas. Kluckhohn argues that "every man is, in certain respects, (a) like all other men, (b) like some other men, and (c) like no other man" (1962, p. 26). This suggests that culture, like communication, may be thought of in terms of a continuum. Culture ranges from an individual's unique patterned ways of behaving, feeling and reacting to certain universal norms that are rooted in the common biological needs of mankind. The further one goes in the direction of cultural universals, the greater the chances of communication. In the opposite direction, of course, lies ever decreasing chances of isomorphism in constructs.

Clark Wissler and others have argued that cultural universals stop at biological needs or drives. "It seems reasonable to suppose," he says, "that what all men have in common is inherited" (Herskovits 1948, p. 234; also White 1949, pp. 121–123). The only thing one might term cultural, these anthropologists say, is man's response to his innate drives. Thus, eating is biological, but how one satisfies one's hunger is cultural (White 1949, p. 152). And in this respect, people are dissimilar in different parts of the world. The Chinese, for example, hate milk and cheese; Navajos won't eat fish; Americans won't eat dogs. An Arizona hostess served rattlesnake in sandwiches and caused her guests to vomit when they were told what it was. Until then they had enjoyed it (Kluckhohn 1957, p. 22). Sex, too, is biological; but with whom and how it is permitted is cultural (White 1949, p. 154). Culture, in fact, is defined in terms of these very differences. People tend to think their cultural traits are human nature, but, says White, "there is no custom or belief that can be said to express 'human' nature more than any other" (White 1949, p. 287).

There are some anthropologists, however, who present equally cogent arguments for cultural, as opposed to biological, universals. In a paper, "Looking Backward," A. V. Kidder in 1940 pointed out that man has universally used stone tools, cultivated plants, created pottery, spun fibers out of wool and woven them into cloth, domesticated animals, fashioned tools out of metals, developed writing systems. In the spiritual realm, man has universally worshiped gods, recognized priesthoods, established governments, and created paintings and sculptures (Moore 1961, pp. 94–95n). These are examples in which not only the underlying need is universal but also the method for satisfying that need.

Closer examination quite plainly shows why anthropologists disagree. Cultural conformity is manifested not only in a continuum of common institutions, beliefs and artifacts—that is, an increasing or decreasing *amount* or *number* of similarities—but it is also measurable hierarchically—that is, in terms of *degrees* of similarity. Thus, priesthood may be at one level of the hierarchy, the type of priesthood at another, down to the specific priest, who is unique, of course, at the lower end of the hierarchy. There is cultural homogeneity between two societies that resolve the unpredictabilities of life by recourse to priesthoods; there is greater homogeneity between societies that select their priests, train them and organize them in a specific way. Societies that share a common priesthood (such as the Roman Catholic church) are obviously even more homogeneous. One cannot, therefore, argue, as some have, that two societies are either culturally discrete or culturally homogeneous. There are only degrees of homogeneity, with universal biological homogeneity at one end of the spectrum being generally conceded.

In other words, it is not physical contiguity, it is not language, it is not even a common heritage that creates common culture—although all these things help; it is simply the intentional or unintentional decision to follow certain common rules of social interaction, of perceiving things in the same way, of organizing one's environment similarly that produces cultural resemblances.

Secondly, people may be culturally similar without being identical. In fact, close examination will show that there is no perfect cultural identity between any two individuals, there are only degrees of similarity.

Thirdly, cultural norms exist for all human behavior. While one often speaks of a particular culture and thinks of a group of individuals who "possess" that culture, this is a totally misleading use of the term. To say that one person belongs to the Western culture and another to the Oriental culture suggests mutual exclusivity that certainly does not exist. Two individuals belonging to the so-called Western culture (thinking in terms of their habitat, ethnic origin or language) may be more different in many of their cultural traits than one of those individuals is from someone belonging to the so-called Oriental culture. In other words, people do not belong to a culture, but a variety of cultural traits belong to people, and two individuals even from the same family may differ in a large number of these cultural traits.

The Contradiction

Not only is all communication—regardless of who the communicants are—of necessity less than 100 per cent effective, but communication must also be thought of as existing between individuals who are less than 100 per cent culturally homogeneous. Communication is always approximate, at best. Nevertheless, because human beings are programed for construct tolerance, communication can be made adequately precise for almost all purposes.

Since individuals may differ not only in the number of cultural traits they share in common but the degree to which each of these traits are similar, the number of possible cultural characteristic combinations is infinite. Variables such as language, geographical origin, age, sex, class, education, race, religion, personality and general attitudes will affect cultural consanguinity so that two individuals who are culturally diverse on one topic or at one time, may be culturally homogeneous under different circumstances. Communication effectiveness between them will, therefore, fluctuate even during a single contact. Over a period of time, communication will improve because constructs will converge, tolerance will increase, and cultural norms will tend toward homogeneity.

It has never been claimed that the building of the Tower of Babel resulted in the confounding of cultures, only the confounding of language. But even if humankind had started out with totally different cultures, and there were no cultural universals—not even biological—there has been so much economic, political and social intercourse among people down the ages that they cannot help but have developed numerous common cultural traits. To the extent and in the areas that these have evolved, communication is not cross-cultural but intra-cultural and relatively effective. To the extent that cultural traits have diverged or remained divergent, communication is correspondingly less effective since cultural characteristics are disparate.

This is another way of saying that there is no such thing as cross-cultural communication, although there may be much relatively effective communication between people and peoples, most of whose cultural characteristics may seem hopelessly different.

* * * *

RERERENCES

Berlo, David K., *The Process of Communication.* New York: Holt, Rinehart and Winston, 1960.

Bobrow, Davis B., "Mass Communication and the Political System," *Public Opinion Quarterly*, Vol. 37 (Winter 1973–74), pp. 551–565.

Brown, R. W. and E. H. Lenneberg, "A Study in Language and Cognition," *Journal of Abnormal Social Psychology*, Vol. 59 (1954), pp. 454–462.

Cherry, Colin, *On Human Communication*. New York: Science Editions, 1961.

Gerbner, George, "On Defining Communication: Still Another View," *Journal of Communication*, Vol. 16 (1966), pp. 99–103.

Goodenough, Ward H., "Cultural Anthropology and Linguistics," in *Language in Culture and Society*, ed. Dell Hymes. New York: Harper & Row, 1964.

Heidbreder, Edna, "The Attainment of Concepts: Terminology and Methodology," *Journal of General Psychology*, Vol. 35 (1946), pp. 173–189.

Henle, Paul, ed., *Language, Thought and Culture*. Ann Arbor: University of Michigan Press, 1966.

Herb, D. O. and W. R. Thompson, "The Social Language of Animal Studies," in *The Handbook of Social Psychology*, ed. Gardner Lindzey and Elliot Aronson, 2nd edition. Reading: Addison-Wesley Publishing Co., 1968.

Herskovits, Melville J. *Man and His Works*. New York: Alfred A. Knopf, 1948.

Hoijer, Harry, "Linguistic and Cultural Change," in *Language in Culture and Society*, ed. Dell Humes. New York: Harper & Row, 1964.

Kluckhohn, Clyde, *Culture and Behavior* (edited by Richard Kluckhohn). New York: The Free Press, 1962.

———, *Mirror for Man*. Greenwich, Conn.: Fawcett Publications, 1957.

Krech, David and Richard S. Crutchfield, "Perceiving the World," in *The Process and Effects of Mass Communication*, ed. Wilbur Schramm and Donald F. Roberts, 2nd edition. Urbana: University of Illinois Press, 1971.

Lewis, M. M, *How Children Learn to Speak*. New York: Basic Books, 1959.

Miller, Gerald R., "On Defining Communication: Another Stab," *Journal of Communication*, Vol. 16 (1966), pp. 88–98.

Moore, Frank W., ed., *Readings in Cross-Cultural Methodology*. New Haven: HRAF Press, 1961.

Morris, Charles, *Signs, Language and Behavior*. New York: Prentice-Hall, 1946.

Murdock, George Peter, "How Culture Changes," in *Man, Culture, and Society*, ed. Harry L. Shapiro. New York: Oxford University Press, 1956.

Osgood, Charles E., George J. Suci and Percy H. Tannenbaum, *The Measurement of Meaning*. Urbana: The University of Illinois Press, 1957.

Sherif, Muzafer and Carl I. Hovland, *Social Judgment*. New Haven: Yale University Press, 1961.

Sitaram, K. S., "What Is Intercultural Communication?" in *Intercultural Communication: A Reader*, ed. Larry A. Samovar and Richard E. Porter. Belmont: Wadsworth Publishing Co., 1972.

Szalay, Lorand B. and Jack E. Brent, "The Analysis of Cultural Meanings Through Free Verbal Associations," *Journal of Social Psychology*, Vol. 72 (1967), pp. 161–187

Tanaka, Yasumasa and C. E. Asgood, "Cross-Culture, Cross-Concept, and Cross-Subject Generality of Affecting Meaning Systems," *Journal of Personality and Social Psychology*, Vol. 2 (August 1965), pp. 143–153.

Taylor, Wilson L., " 'Cloze Procedure': A New Tool for Measuring Readability," *Journalism Quarterly*, Vol. 30 (Fall 1953), pp. 415–433.

Thayer, Lee, *Communication and Communication Systems*. Homewood: Richard D. Irwin, 1968.

Triandis, Harry C., "Cultural Influences Upon Cognitive Processes," in *Advances in Experimental Social Psychology*, ed. Leonard Berkowitz, Vol. I. New York: Academic Press, 1964.

Vance, John W., "In Defense of the Mossback," in *Perspectives in Public Relations*, ed. Raymond Simon. Norman: University of Oklahoma Press, 1966.

Van den Ban, A. W., "Interpersonal Communication and the Diffusion of Innovations," in *Intercommunication Among Nations and Peoples*, ed. Michael H. Prosser. New York: Harper & Row, 1973.

Westley, Bruce H. and Malcolm S. MacLean, Jr., "A Conceptual Model for Communications Research," *Journalism Quarterly*, Vol. 34 (Winter 1957), pp. 31–38.

White, Leslie A., *The Science of Culture*. New York: Farrar, Straus and Cudahy, 1949.

Whorf, Benjamin Lee, "A Linguistic Consideration of Thinking in Primitive Communities," in *Language in Culture and Society*, ed. Dell Hymes. New York: Harper & Row, 1964.

Godwin C. Chu:

Problems of Cross-Cultural Communication Research

IN THE post-war era considerable research in mass communication has cumulated a sizable amount of empirical knowledge. Most of the experimental studies, however, were carried out against the western cultural background. We have now come face to face with the question of whether our knowledge about communication behavior can be employed with enough generality beyond the boundaries of western societies.

This question can only be answered by testing our empirical knowledge in other cultures. Findings from such cross-cultural studies will, it is hoped, provide further empirical support to our knowledge and furthermore, redefine the scope within which our current knowledge may be applied. The findings from one side will supplement the findings from the other, and at the same time generate problems to which research on the other side may provide answers. The present discussion will be limited to three technical problems: strategy of cross-cultural studies, conceptualization of research problems and methodology of cross-cultural research.

Strategy of Cross-Cultural Studies

The strategy of cross-cultural communication research is essentially one of hypothesis testing and exploratory theory building. The former provides an additional test of a previously corroborated hypothesis in a different culture. For instance, we might want to know whether the findings about one-sided versus two-sided communications (Hovland, Janis and Kelley, 1953) [1] also holds in an Oriental culture. Cross-cultural confirmation of the original hypothesis will widen the scope of its generality.

But if we fail to replicate the original findings in another culture, we would want to know what cultural factors are responsible for this failure. So, in addition to testing the original hypothesis, it will often be fruitful to explore additional propositions concerning certain important cultural variables. For instance, it may be argued that in a culture which stresses authoritarian submission, people will tend to be overly dependent and have a high need for cognitive clarity. Therefore a persuasive communication presenting a clear-cut

---

[1] Hovland, C. I., Janis, I. L., and Kelley, H. H. (1953), *Communication and Persuasion.* Yale University Press.

▶ From: *Journalism Quarterly* (Iowa City, Iowa), Vol. 41/No. 4 (Autumn 1964), pp. 55–562. Reprinted by permission of the publisher and of the author.

one-sided argument will likely be accepted, while a two-sided argument may cause confusion and doubt. It can then be hypothesized that in this type of culture, one-sided communications will be consistently more effective than two-sided communications.

In cross-cultural hypothesis testing, we sometimes adopt the straight replication approach. We would use exactly the same procedure and same materials, except for translation, and retest the hypothesis in another culture. By holding everything else constant, we can be sure within reasonable limits that whatever differences occur in the findings cannot be attributed to differences in methodology, but rather reflect cross-cultural diversities. If the replication comes up with essentially the same findings, then we will have evidence that the specific hypothesis we are testing has cross-cultural validity.

This approach, however, is likely to encounter procedural difficulties in communication research. Usually a straight replication in another culture will be feasible with psychophysical and certain other psychological experiments where culturally-based ideas, perceptions and attitudes do not constitute essential variables. For instance, it may be possible to replicate the autokinetic test (Sherif, 1937) [2] and the judgment of lines for testing group pressure (Asch, 1951) [3] in another culture without essential changes in the procedures. But if our research problem involves values, ideologies, social patterns, and experience, which may differ from culture to culture, then a straight replication is hardly feasible.

In communication research, the questionnaires and communications may not convey the same meanings when applied to a different culture. Take the fear-arousing experiments by Janis and Feshbach (1953), [4] for instance. Some of the fears employed in the communications had to do with "ugly or discolored teeth." These will become effective "fear-arousing" appeals only in the sense that the subjects are worried about having ugly or discolored teeth. In a society where people do not regard sparkling white teeth as something of a social value, having ugly or discolored teeth will not likely cause worry or fear. This is to suggest that in communication research where the original materials are phrased against one cultural background and reflect its values and beliefs, it is not at all possible to do a straight replication in another culture.

These limitations, both procedural and theoretical, make it advisable to take a different approach. Instead of replicating the same materials and procedures, this approach calls for testing the hypothesis in another culture by use of new materials, new operational definitions, and even different procedures whenever necessary. This approach is concerned not so much with keeping the

[2] Sherif, M. (1937), "An Experimental Approach to the Study of Attitudes," in *Sociometry*, Vol. I, pp. 90–98.
[3] Asch, S. E. (1951), "Effects of Group Pressure Upon the Modification and Distortion of Judgments," in *Groups, Leadership and Men*, ed. by Harold Guetzkow. Pittsburgh, Carneigie Press.
[4] Janis, I. L., and Feshbach, S. (1953), "Effects of Fear-Arousing Communications," *Journal of Abnormal and Social Psychology*, Vol. 48, pp. 78–92.

same materials and same procedures as with making the meanings of the situation and materials comparable.

This exploratory approach has one drawback. If the findings confirm the hypothesis, we shall have evidence that the generality holds not only in another culture, but also for another experiment. But if the findings fail to support the hypothesis, then we do not know whether it is because of cultural differences or because of change of procedures or measurements, which may lack reliability and validity. This is a risk the cross-cultural communication researcher will have to face. In general, the pitfalls in cross-cultural communication research are no different from those in any social studies, namely, the problems of conceptualization and measurement, in addition to the researcher's limitation of knowledge about the specific culture itself.

Conceptualization of Research Problems

We now consider the conceptualization of research problems. Let us start with a few basic assumptions about mass communication research. We wish to delimit our discussion to the investigation of the effects of communication, as reflected in changes of behavior as well as attitudes. We are interested in attitudes because they are predispositions of behavior. Also, we regard exposure to communications, the acceptance thereof, and change of one's attitudes as a type of behavior.

We assume that human behavior is goal-oriented, the goal being gratification seeking and deprivation avoidance. Acceptance of communication and change of behavior or attitudes may be due to either seeking gratification, e.g., the fulfilment of some personal needs, or avoidance of deprivation, e.g., conforming to norms to avoid sanctions.

Starting with these assumptions we can then study response to mass communications from a behavioral approach. The following analysis of communication behavior is based on the general conceptualization of Parsons (1951),[5] as well as the Lewinian concept of situational forces (Lewin, 1951).[6]

We treat response to communication as a unit of behavior, and analyze it in terms of the self, which is the audience; significant others, including the communicator; and the situation, which consists of cultural values, goals and norms—forces that may affect the reception and acceptance of the communication. This analysis suggests that in cross-cultural communication research, our choice of research topics will be guided by three broad concepts: the self, the others and the situation. Miller (1961),[7] in discussing cross-cultural study of personality within the framework of interaction, uses similar concepts.

---

[5] Parson, T., Shils, E., et al. (1951), *Toward a General Theory of Action*. Harvard University Press.

[6] Lewin, K. (1951), *Field Theory in Social Science*. New York, Harper.

[7] Miller, D. R. (1961), "Personality and Social Interaction," in *Studying Personality Cross-Culturally*, ed. by B. Kaplan. Evanston, Ill., Row, Peterson (pp. 271–98).

In Lewinian terms, situation is defined in terms of the forces that prompt an individual to move in various directions, resulting in tensions, goals and goal achievement. We need data on the forces, goals and barriers.

Significant others, which Parsons calls alter, include parents, siblings, spouses, associates, friends and other members of a social hierarchy. A person in this hierarchy is identified by his social roles and the specific behavior patterns required of these roles.

The self develops through interaction with others. Through interaction, a person becomes oriented to the values and norms of others and forms standards for evaluating himself. He develops stable interpersonal behavior patterns.

It is assumed that cross-cultural diversities exist with respect to these three broad concepts. Furthermore, assuming an invariant human nature, we may postulate that these cross-cultural diversities are mainly the results of differences in the situation, which also exert influence on the self and the others. All this is saying that in cross-cultural communication research, we shall keep our attention on the three broad concepts of self, others and situation, while bearing in mind that it is the situational differences underlying the three concepts that we are mainly interested in.

Take the situation first. How would the situation of receiving a communication differ from one culture to another? In terms of goals, what are the motivations for receiving a message from the mass media, for accepting the message? What forces, if any, are prompting an individual toward the mass media? What barriers exist in the culture that would tend to keep the audience away from the media and mass communication? In this category we may include such specific problems as the basic cultural values, norms and beliefs, economic activities, modes of social control, and their influences on communication effects.

About the significant others, we want to know in what social roles the communicators are perceived by the audience. How are the mass media related to the authority structure of the native culture? Are the media recognized as a potential source capable of meting out reward or inflicting punishment or both? Subsumed under this category are such familiar problems as communicator prestige, the criteria of credibility, the image of media, the roles of opinion leaders, interpersonal influence versus media influence, and social structure.

Finally we need to take a look at the self. What are the specific interpersonal response traits resultant from certain particular situational influences in that culture? How would these response traits influence the audience behavior toward persuasive communication? How would certain dimensions of self-identity that are characteristic of this culture affect people's susceptibility to communication? These are mainly problems having to do with personality and persuasibility in different cultures (Janis and Field, 1959,[8] Chu, 1964).[9]

---

[8] Janis, I. L., and Field, P. B. (1959), "A Behavioral Assessment of Persuasibility: Consistency of Individual Differences; and Sex Differences and Personality Factors Related to Persuasibility," in

Also, cultural differences in modal personality may necessitate reconsidering certain problems concerning the effects of communications. It may be hypothesized that in a culture where the virtue of modesty is eulogized, people will be more reserved, and attempts to change attitudes through group discussion and participation not only may be a waste of time because people are reluctant to participate, but may even boomerang because of resentment if they are forced to participate.

Methodology of Cross-Cultural Research

The methods of cross-cultural research in general have been discussed by Kluckhohn (1940),[10] Paul (1953),[11] Whiting (1954),[12] Maccoby and Maccoby (1954)[13] and Lindzey (1961).[14] Here we are mainly interested in methods of cross-cultural communication research. We may either be testing a hypothesis in one culture for comparison with data collected from another culture, or gathering data from a number of cultures to see whether empirical laws can be formulated between certain cultural variables and communication behavior. In either case we need to consider the problems of sampling and data collection.

In a cross-cultural research requiring controlled experiments, sampling will involve no more difficulty than in a western society if students are available to serve as subjects. Arrangements can usually be made with local schools.

If the research requires a survey, then sampling is likely to post a serious problem because of incomplete or out-dated census data, inaccurate maps and transportation difficulties. Take the Asian regions for instance. With the exception of Japan and a few other areas where considerable facilities are available, surveys on a national basis would probably be extremely difficult and expensive, if not impossible. An example to follow is Deming's design of a national sample in Greece (Deming, 1950).[15] Another method worth considering is a combination of area sampling and quota sampling. This was used in a radio audience survey in Taiwan in 1960. In several cities the only data available were city maps showing the main streets. First all the blocks on the map were

Personality and Persuasibility, ed. by C. I. Hovland and I. L. Janis. Yale University Press (pp. 29–68).

[9] Chu, G. C. (1964), "Culture, Personality and Persuasibility." Unpublished doctoral dissertation, Stanford University.

[10] Kluckhohn, Florence R. (1940), "The Participant-Observer Techniques in Small Communities," *American Journal of Sociology*, Vol. 46, pp. 331–43.

[11] Paul, B. D. (1953), "Interview Techniques and Field Relationships," *Anthropology Today*, ed. by A. L. Kroeber. University of Chicago Press (pp. 430–51).

[12] Whiting, J. W. M. (1954), "The Cross-Cultural Method," in *Handbook of Social Psychology*, ed. by G. Lindzey. Reading, Mass., Addison-Wesley (pp. 523–31).

[13] Maccoby, E. E., and Maccoby, N. (1954), "The Interview: A Tool of Social Science," in *Handbook of Social Psychology*, ed. by G. Lindzey. Reading, Mass., Addison-Wesley Publishing Co. (pp. 449–87).

[14] Lindzey, G. (1961), *Projective Techniques and Cross-Cultural Research*. New York, Appleton-Century Crofts.

[15] Deming, W. E. (1950), *Some Theory of Sampling*. New York, Wiley & Sons.

numbered, with no consideration to the possible differences in size. A number of blocks were then drawn at random. The interviewer was allowed to choose a designated number of respondents within a chosen block on the basis of two quota controls: sex and age. Although this was not a probability sample, and people with better education and higher economic status were likely over-represented, yet the interviewer was unable to seek out his friends and acquaintances. Such a sample is likely to eliminate this serious source of bias mentioned by Cantril (1947).[16] Depending on the purpose of the research, we may introduce other quota controls like education, economic status in addition to sex and age.

Data collection poses another problem. In a group experiment, paper and pencil tests will ordinarily be usable although the problem of validity can be serious. Caution needs to be taken to make both the questionnaire and communications meaningful in the native culture. Materials that may violate the basic cultural mores have to be discarded.

Data collection by survey will present additional problems, mainly those of overcoming resistance and improving rapport. In most non-western societies the idea of enquiring about other's opinions is completely alien to the natives.

But various attempts have been made to increase rapport in communication research in Taiwan. In a 1960 radio audience survey, it was found that tandem interviewing by a male and female interviewer met with better reception. This was possibly because the presence of a female made the interview situation less formal. However, this would mean doubling the cost of interview. In a comparative study of social effects of communications in three villages in Taiwan, it was found that courtesy calls on the farmers by the interviewer and the village elder made it easier to interview them later on.

After the interviewer has been received, there is the problem of presenting a legitimate reason for the interview. If the interviewer fails to offer a plausible explanation, then the respondent himself is likely to seek an answer of his own, which might structure his perception of the situation in such a way as to seriously impair rapport. The explanation offered should be one that is understandable to the respondent. To say that the interviewer is collecting data for research, or measuring public opinions, usually doesn't mean much to the natives. Also sociometric questions intended to reconstruct the patterns of friendship and the flow of communications in the villages failed entirely. The village people simply would not give any names. Saying things about others was regarded as gossip, and the traditional Chinese belief is: Gossip breeds trouble.

The lack of interest in things not directly concerning the natives themselves adds to the difficulties in communication research. Typically, we measure the effects of communications in terms of opinion or attitude change in a before-and-after study, where communications serve as the experimental ma-

---

[16] Cantril, H. (1947), *Gauging Public Opinion*. Princeton University Press.

nipulation. In a non-western society with a low literacy rate, this procedure is likely to be inapplicable because the natives usually are not aware of social issues and do not have opinions.

Generally, depending on the circumstances, the researcher may adopt either the cross-sectional or the longitudinal approach. If we can locate two communities comparable in all other respects except that one has radio, we can compare these two communities for behavioral differences and see if we can trace such differences to the use of communications. For instance, does the radio-village have a higher voting rate than the non-radio-village? If so, how is decision to vote related to having heard certain messages over the radio? This is the cross-sectional, comparative approach. The longitudinal approach is applicable where it is possible to observe a community for a lengthy period while it is being exposed to communications. For instance, what would happen when we install a television set in a secluded village? Do the villages become more conscious about personal hygiene? Do they go to the city more often? Do they adopt some of the farm methods presented on the television?

The measuring instrument in cross-cultural communication research needs reconsideration. On the one hand we need refined instruments in order to detect true differences under a false surface of indifference. This would call for the use of scales with structured response categories. On the other hand, the low literacy rate would render the Likert or Guttman type scaling technique inapplicable. Usually respondents with little education are unable to make the fine distinction between "strongly agree" and "moderately agree." A solution to this dilemma may lie in the use of judgment type scaling techniques like Thurstone's equal appearing interval scale but with fewer intervals. Instead of the usual attitude scale items to which the respondent is asked to indicate agreement or disagreement, behavioral items might be used. Even people with no education will be able to report whether they have engaged in certain kinds of behavior. For instance, instead of presenting a statement like "Religious discrimination is something bad" and then asking a Buddhist farmer to indicate his agreement or disagreement, we might ask "Do you have any friends who worship Jesus Christ?" or "Have you entertained anyone who goes to church?"

The use of behavioral items instead of the typical attitude items is suggested for several reasons. First, attitudes are abstract concepts which the natives may not be able to grasp. Even though people in an Asian village all worship their own heavenly lord, they may not be able to understand the term "religion." A term like "discrimination" is perhaps even more difficult to grasp. Secondly, the natives probably have not clearly formed their attitudes—even if they have such attitudes—and are therefore unable to verbalize them.

The use of fewer scale intervals is suggested for two reasons. First there may be the practical difficulty of sorting a number of behavioral items into say eleven scale intervals. Using five or seven scale intervals is likely to achieve higher agreement among the judges, in the relative sense of comparing the obtained spread with the possible maximum variation of a flat-topped distribution. Of course this question can be settled by empirical data. Secondly, asking eleven behavioral questions on one single topic would be tiresome to the respondent, even if eleven items of different scale scores could be constructed on the same dimension. Five or seven questions would work better.

9

THEORY AND RESEARCH IN INTERNATIONAL COMMUNICATION

9

THEORY AND RESEARCH IN INTERNATIONAL COMMUNICATION

In recent years there has been a tremendous amount of theorizing and researching in the expanding area of international communication. Many scholars feel that research has far outrun theory; other scholars take the opposite position. At any rate, articles and scholarly papers delving into almost every conceivable aspect of international communication have poured forth from numerous journals and from numerous participants at communications conferences and conventions. There is much uncertainty in the academic community as to the value of much of this material, but there is no doubt but that increasing battalions of theoreticians and researchers feel that their contributions are needed.

Countless papers and articles were available for this section, and we have tried to select a few that we believe to be well-written, substantive, and provocative at the same time. And this, of course, made our job of selection somewhat easier. We think that these six articles which follow do, indeed, make a significant contribution to the serious literature for those who would theorize and research in the field of international communication.

L. John Martin, University of Maryland, opens the section by merging practical questions with theoretical questions and research propositions—all aimed at trying to get at the prospective state of international communication. This article is followed by offerings from two outstanding European communications scholars—Kaarle Nordenstreng of the University of Tampere (Finland), who writes about recent European developments in communication theory, and Henk Prakke, now in retirement in the Netherlands after a long career at the University of Münster (Germany), who deals with a new approach to communications on the Continent called "Publicistics."

In the fourth article, Hamid Mowlana (American University, Washington, D.C.) presents a new conceptual framework for analyzing mass media systems. This is followed by an old (1953), but still relevant, article by Columbia University's outstanding sociologist (emeritus professor), Paul Lazarsfeld, on international communications research. Finally, in what is believed an appropriate conclusion to this section and the entire book, we are presenting an article by Robert Lindsay, of the University of Minnesota, suggesting new priorities of concern and causing our eyes to turn even from earthly dimensions of communication to frontiers among the planets.

*   *   *   *

RELATED READING

(Excellent readings on theory and research in mass communication abound in several languages, and it seems unnecessary to list a few here. Please note the references listed by the authors of the articles which follow in this section.)

L. John Martin:

Prospects for International Communication

SEVERAL YEARS AGO, many students at the University of Maryland participated in a glorious revolution to redress a number of wrongs, both domestic and foreign. Among these wrongs was a parochial one: the lack of communication between students and the administration of the university. Communication is a very "in" concept these days and the lack of it ranks with pollution and the absence of relevance among the deadliest sins of the Establishment and its way of doing things. I assume that it is relevant, therefore, to examine the state and the prospective state of *international communication* and to speculate about whether there is to be or not to be communication. No one at the University of Maryland seemed the least concerned that communication might pollute the atmosphere, a fear that worried the world greatly in regard to international communication following World War I—certainly between the wars if not since World War II—far more than its complete absence.

What then are the prospects? This immediately raises a myriad of questions. Do we mean, "Will there be more communications (in the sense of messages)?" "Will more people communicate?" "Will more people understand one another?" "Will more people agree with one another?" "Will there be more transmitters?" "More receivers?" "Will communication be more necessary?" "Will it be easier?" "Will it be faster?" "Will there be different, better media?" "Will we have more communication problems?" "Will we have more quarrels over communications?" "Will we be friendlier as a result of communication?" "Will there be more friction for the same reason?"

Actually, providing an answer is much easier than formulating the questions. It is simply "yes." Obviously!

What I would like to demonstrate is that communication is a regenerative process that improves in effectiveness through use; that this is as true across cultures as it is within a culture; that international intercourse is increasing inexorably, and that, with equal certainty, international communication is improving and will continue to improve exponentially, regardless of whether or not we learn to love one another in the process.

Views of international communication have ranged from the universalist, which exhorts the world to communicate for all it is worth because its only salvation lies in communication,[1] to the particularist, which bemoans our Babelic

▶ This is an article written for this book by Dr. Martin, College of Journalism, University of Maryland.

lot that has condemned us to everlasting mutual unintelligibility.[2] I will expound an optimistic, evolutionist paradigm that eschews any purposiveness in "improving" international communication—since "improvement" depends on a subjective definition of goals, and communication per se will as often as not lead to negative results.

Conceptual Propositions

In developing my model, I will suggest a number of propositions, some of which may be supported empirically while others are heuristic assumptions. My first proposition may be stated as follows:

Proposition I: At any point in time, communication, if it is continual, is less effective than it will be and more effective than it was.

Communication is its own regulator. In use, it adjusts itself to the needs of its users in a constant, self-refining and regenerative process.

As we know, the communicative act occurs at different levels. A communicator decides to communicate about a referent. He stereotypes and reduces the referent, which may be an object or an abstraction, to a construct. This construct evolves from a central tendency of all the referents in his experience. The construct, in turn, is communicated through a symbol, which may be a word.[3]

Let us look at one or two examples. The word "kin" is a symbol that means "relative" in English, "gold" in Japanese, "chin" (when spelled "Kinn") in German. The construct or meaning that a person gives it in English is based on the varied experiences he has had with relatives—the referent. Both the cognitive and affective components of "relative" vary according to a person's "unique reality world," as Hadley Cantril called it.[4] Each person, therefore, has a different referent or set of referents and a different construct. The symbol is the only common factor. (I will, hereinafter, refer to symbols, constructs and referents as SCRs.)

Let us take another word. "Table" is a symbol. It could be "Tisch" or "mesa" or "asztal"—depending on the language you are speaking. When I say the word "table," everyone who is familiar with the symbol has a picture of a table in his mind. Now if we asked everyone in this room to draw this picture, we would probably get pretty much the same picture with a few permissible variations. Some may be large, some small, some rectangular, some round, some square. If we asked a Near Easterner or an African to draw a table, we might get a few more variations. We would tolerate these variations because our construct of "table" is a functional one—it is one of "tableness." Anything that we recognize as having "tableness" we would be willing to assign the symbol of "table" to.

The referent is the particular table—the concrete image—that we had in mind. Since each of us has a different image of a table, the refrent, paradoxically, is subjective, whereas the construct is objective. The construct is the meaning of the symbol, and without a common meaning there would be no communication.

Another example may further clarify the various levels. "Beautiful" is an adjective symbol that conveys a comparative construct tied to a particular referent that will obviously vary within a culture and even more so between cultures. Its concomitant is highly personal, of course.

This analysis of the elements of language is similar to the referent-thought-symbol triangle of Ogden and Richards, or the three-factor approach of Hungarian linguist Låszlő Antal—sentence form, sentence meaning and sentence content.[5] The construct-referent dyad in my model is not too dissimilar from Richard F. Carter's object-attribute model, except that Carter's detail in indicating the steps in construct formation is irrelevant for my purposes.[6]

Proposition II: Isomorphism in construct—i.e., comprehension—is always approximate. Meaning approaches but never attains identity.

Since a construct evolves from a mean of referents, and since the universe of referents is never identical for any two persons, the construct that is associated with a particular symbol is only approximately similar for any two individuals. Obviously, the more similar the referents in the cognitive systems of communicants, the closer will be the constructs symbolized by words in their language, or by their non-verbal communication symbols.

Meaning may be derived structurally or contextually as well as referentially, i.e., relating the symbol to a particular referent. I may never have seen a surgeon and may not know what he does, but it is possible for me to develop from the context a conceptual referent by tying his function to referents in my real world.

While communication never achieves perfection, even in the same family, there is no reason to despair. We can tolerate a great deal of inexactness in human intercourse without being completely isolated from one another. Which suggests

Proposition III: As communication continues, a communicator-receiver dyad develops increasing tolerance for variation in SCRs. Acceptable tolerance varies according to topic and intent.

We all have experienced trying to understand a person speaking English with a foreign accent. One study we did in India when I was in USIA found that while 91 per cent of Indian college students said they understood an Indian lecturing in English, only 31 per cent said they understood an Englishman and 19 per cent said they understood an American.[7] Some of these students had obviously had more contacts with British speakers than with American and had learned to tolerate aberrations in symbol formation, usage and possibly in constructs. We did not probe into meaning variations but we assumed a certain amount of heteromorphism.

Tolerance is often built into a computer program.[8] It is useful in communication in that it is a "reaching out" and meeting someone part of the way. Starting anywhere from zero base and beyond, communicants progress toward an ever-growing number of common SCRs and toward increasingly effective communication. Communication improves in inverse wave formation, i.e., it starts at the outside extreme of the concentric circle of ripples and gains in comprehensiion centripetally, contextually dragging with it further waves of comprehension. Like the computer, we are programmed for a certain amount of tolerance as to symbols (we will accept variations in pronunciation and spelling), constructs (we manage to communicate in spite of certain variations in meaning), and referents.[9]

Useful tolerance has both an upper and a lower limit. If tolerance is too low, some people and some topics are excluded from communication. If it is too high, tolerance makes communication fuzzy and weakens its effectiveness.

Procedural Propositions

SCR tolerance, as we have suggested, is the grappling hook of communication and works centripetally toward, without ever really attaining, isomorphism in meaning. Now let us turn to the communication process itself.

> **Proposition IV: Communication is a symbiotic process that is purposive both on the part of the communicator and of the receiver.**

There is no such thing as fortuitous or unintentional communication. That would be a contradiction in terms. Since there is no *transfer* of meaning in communication, merely isomorphism in constructs generated in the minds of the communicants by symbols, one might well wonder in what sense communication can be considered dyadic. Is the receiver at the other end actually necessary? And if he were not there—say, if someone were writing something in his diary—would communication not exist? The answer is that communication exists whenever a human being encodes a message, the receiver being the communicator himself if he merely encodes it in his mind for future storage.

I do not want to enter the debate on whether a person's world view depends on the structure and characteritics of his language. I think that Whorf, Sapir, Henle and others have a good *a priori* case in suggesting that language and world view are interrelated, while George A. Miller, Charles E. Osgood and others have argued just as forcefully that empirical evidence points to cross-cultural uniformities of thought unrelated to language. I merely want to suggest that to the extent that thought draws on language, it does so as the result of and in response to some paradigm which controls the selection process of the language/thought bits. If this implies that thought begets thought, I am willing to accept the dilemma.

Now if a paradigm or thought-program precedes the encoding process, communication must be purposive. Similarly, receiving, decoding and storing a message requires a paradigm or thought-program that instructs the receiver on the reading of the message. This, too, must be purposive rather than unstructured and haphazard.

Since there is a symbiotic relationship between communicator and receiver, yet both are encoding or thinking purposively, what if they are operating from different paradigms, a virtual certainty, unless communicator and receiver happen to be the same person? The Chaffee-McLeod coorientation model suggests that accuracy and understanding (my isomorphism in construct) increase with communication without necessarily affecting congruency and agreement.[10] My hypothesis, as I indicated in Proposition I, is that, in the long run, communication improves not only comprehension but, by increasing the number of common referents, it lays the groundwork for common opinions-attitudes-beliefs and values, hence agreement.[11] Zajonc suggests on the basis of experiments on the affective connotations of words following repeated exposure to them that "mere repeated exposure of an individual to a stimulus object enhances his attitude toward it."[12] Berelson and Steiner found evidence that

> The more interaction or overlap there is between related groups, the more similar they become in their norms and values; the less communication or interaction between them, the more tendency there is for conflict to arise between them.[13]

Furthermore, they say that "connotations are remarkably similar among similar people."[14]

It may, of course, be objected that Berelson and Steiner are talking about "related groups" and "similar people." And that is true. But, under what circumstances do groups become related and people become similar? Kumata and Schramm did a cross-cultural semantic study back in 1956 in which they came to the conclusion that "The remarkable correspondence across cultures tempts one to say that perhaps there is a pervasive semantic frame of reference used by humans."[15] Their study involved Japanese, Korean and American students, and they hastened to add that "It must be remembered that all subjects were tested in the American culture." This may cause some to throw up their hands and exclaim "Ah, so!" But it makes my point. These Japanese, Korean and American students were not similar to begin with; they did not come from related groups. Communication made them similar.[16] And if it is objected that they were in physical rather than just communication contact, let me once again quote Berelson and Steiner:

Human beings can think about things that are not present at the moment as well as things they have never actually experienced. Man can represent and manipulate objects, events and relationships vicariously or internally—that is, symbolically—and not only through direct physical experience with them. [17]

In other words, while physical experience may be faster, communication is just as certain.

Substantive Propositions

Having expounded my evolutionary hypothesis of communication, it remains for me to show that the desiderata for increasing international communication exist, since this will, in keeping with my model, inevitably lead to ever more effective communication. I will go a step further. Not only is communication itself regenerative, but

Proposition V: World economic development is leading to universal economic values, preferences and demands, which in turn will result in more effective communication.

Peter F. Drucker contends that underlying the world's common economic behavior is a community of information. This being the case, people all over the world are accumulating a wealth of common referents. This has led not only to the use of common artifacts, so that the country markets in the most underdeveloped areas are peddling the mass productions of the most advanced economies, often complete with the foreign name that symbolizes them, but to a marked development toward common constructs and abstractions. [18]

Proposition VI: As greater proportions of the populations of all countries become educated, cultural homogeneity will increase and variations will become less pronounced.

The substance and method of education are becoming increasingly similar as countries borrow from one another. The mass media have contributed greatly to educational homogeneity, although formal education has always had a cosmopolitan tinge. Despite the rapid growth of human knowledge, it has never been so superabundant that anyone could long ignore advances in it, no matter what culture happened to spawn it. What is new is the increasing universality of education. In poorer countries this often leads to the need to learn one or more foreign languages along with some substantive field. The wealthier countries, such a the United States, can afford to pay translators and publishers to translate human knowledge into their own language. But while the symbols may be relatively easy to translate, the need soon develops to approximate and learn new constructs and to experience new referents. [19]

I do not bemoan the increasing cultural homogeneity that is engulfing us any more than I regret the passing of the genteel life that slavery and other human bondage made possible for some. And there is not a shadow of doubt that it is bearing in on us. Says Herbert I. Schiller (one of the moaners), "The cultural homogenization that has been underway for years in the United States now threatens to overtake the globe." [20] Anyone who has traveled around the world periodically will have noticed the trend toward uniformity and conformity in almost all countries even over as short a period as two or three years.

Instrumental Propositions

If the airplane and radio extended our horizons in the first half of the twentieth century, the jet and television brought humanity much closer together in the second half. The distinction is an important one since it involves a reaching out and a pulling in. For the first time in history, man has been capable in this century of making "real time" [21] contacts with his fellow man anywhere in the world. Furthermore, since about the middle of the century, television, jet travel and other technological advances, plus increasing affluence which liberated man from the immediate environment of his birth, have brought man into an intimate frame of reference with other cultures all over the world. [22]

Unquestionably, the mass media have been the major factor in this paradoxical expansion-contraction process—a process that at first greatly increased the number of participants in international communication by giving them a radio and airplane link but in a relatively distant frame of reference, and 50 years later drew them in with the help of television and the jet in a much more intimate frame of reference.

> **Proposition VII: The near monopoly over the collection and distribution of world news by the five or six international wire services is producing conformity in news judgment, is narrowing the areas of attention in the world's press, and is contributing to the number of common SCRs of people all over the world.**

While I have no empirical evidence, it is my impression from personal observation of the press of a large number of countries over the years since World War II that the world's press is becoming very similar in both content and format. In large measure this is due to the ever increasing monopoly over the collection and dissemination of international news by the six international wire services. These are the Associated Press and United Press International in the United States, Reuters in Britain, Agence France Press, the Soviet Union's TASS, and Mainland China's New China News Agency.

Although there are some 85 countries that have domestic wire services of their own, with a very few exceptions these do not have their own correspondents outside the country or, at best, outside the immediate region. Those domestic news agencies that have foreign correspondents or stringers normally locate them in New York, Washington, London, Paris or in countries of great importance to domestic politics. Countries other than the Big Five (who happen to coincide with the permanent members of the United Nations Security Council) get their world news in one of two ways: their domestic wire services, in some cases, have an exchange agreement with one or more of the international news agencies; or else their news media subscribe directly to the major news agencies. Frequently, both these arrangements exist.

> **Proposition VIII: The broad cultural equalization begun by motion pictures will be given a quantum boost as relay satellites beam world events in the intimate frame of reference of television into homes all over the world.**

Experts believe that it will be possible to broadcast television programs directly from satellite to receiver within the decade. They also predict that miniaturization and other sophisticated advances in technology will put television receivers in the poorest homes both in urban centers and in the hinterland. "Every village in Pakistan or the Sudan will be drawn into direct contact with all other centers of mankind," writes Bernard Rubin.[23]

The ability to receive information from still or motion pictures is not innate, as many have pointed out,[24] but it can be learned without too much difficulty. Young people, especially, learn to read pictures fairly fast. Another difficulty that has been mentioned in connection with piture communication is that pictures are pre-selected symbol complexes and unless a person is properly programmed to receive the message—in other words, had the right preconceptions about what he is seeing—he may find it difficult to process the information being conveyed.

*   *   *   *

What then, after all this has been said, are the prospects for international communication? The inevitable conclusion is that they are excellent. It has been said that the mass media and the Great American Railroad made it possible for the United States to be one nation under God with liberty and conformity for all. It has been suggested that the BBC gave the British people their common accent, if not their common language. Technological advances and the means of communication—both physical and symbolic—have since the turn of this century put us on a course that must unfailingly lead to increasingly effective world communication. Will this also lead to agreement and to reduced world tensions? Maybe in the long run, although it probably takes more than communication to produce agreement. There is no doubt that policy decisions—such as, for instance, the extent to which we are willing to share resources that are in short supply—without communication are as meaningless as communication without policy decisions. Whether policy is real or imagined, it is symbiotically tied to communication.

But, you may object, this writer's model completely ignores balance theory and cultural variations in cognitive structures, he makes no mention of information-seeking and the pros and cons of selectivity, he appears to thumb his nose at source credibility, message permutations and persuasibility. I don't deny it. These are complicating or facilitating factors, as the case may be. They do not negate my basic paradigm.

In first thinking about a title for this article, I considered "If cultures cross can communication be far behind?" My message is that cultures have crossed.

NOTES

[1] Carl Rowan, "The Challenge of Cultural Communication," in Heinz-Dietrich Fischer and John C. Merrill, *International Communication*, New York, Hastings House, 1970, pp. 392–399; Robert T. Oliver, "Culture and Communication," *Vital Speeches of the Day*, Vol. 29, No. 23 (September 15, 1963), pp. 721–724; Lee Loevinger, "Cooperation in International Communications," *Department of State Bulletin*, November 27, 1965, pp. 828–834.

[2] Yasumasa Tanaka, "Cross-Cultural Compatibility of the Affective Meaning Systems (Measured by Means of Multilingual Semantic Differentials)," *Journal of Social Issues*, Vol. 23, No. 1 (1967), pp. 27–45; Michael J. Flack, "Communicable and Uncommunicable Aspects in Personal International Relationships," *Journal of Communication*, Vol. 16, No. 4 (December, 1966), pp. 283–290.

[3] I will not here develop a fourth level, the concomitant, which is an associative, purely affective factor. A vulgar equivalent of a clinical term may (or may not) be based on the same referents and have the same construct. Its concomitant adds a communicational level.

[4] Hadley Cantril, *The Pattern of Human Concerns*, Rutgers University Press, 1965, chaps. 1, 2, 16.

[5] C. K. Ogden and I. A. Richards, *The Meaning of Meaning*, London, Routledge and Kegan Paul, Ltd., 1949; László Antal, *Content, Meaning and Understanding*, The Hague, Mouton and Co., 1964.

[6] See Steven H. Chaffee, Keith R. Stamm, Jose L. Guerrero and Leonard P. Tipton, "Experiments on Cognitive Discrepancies and Communication," *Journalism Monographs*, No. 14, December, 1969.

[7] *Indian Student-Faculty Survey*, January, 1963, Research and Reference Service, USIA. Unpublished report.

[8] The State Department has stored several million names of visa applicants, their date and place of birth, and the disposition of their visa applications. The program tolerates certain deviations in the spelling of names—a necessity when dealing with transliterations from other alphabets or laxity in the spelling of names in some cultures—and the computer will report approximations. Thus it may report that it has no "Smith, Joseph Alonzo" but it has a "Psmith, Josef Alonzo."

[9] An example is the riddle, popular in Women's Lib circles, of the girl and her famous surgeon father who are both seriously hurt in a car accident. When the girl is wheeled into the operating room, the surgeon is shocked to see her and says, "I can't operate on this girl. She is my daughter." Obviously, the surgeon is the girl's mother, but in a male-oriented world, "surgeon" has a male referent, even though the meaning, or construct, is clear.

[10] Steven H. Chaffee and Jack M. McLeod, "Sensitization in Panel Design: A Coorientational Experiment," *Journalism Quarterly*, Vol. 45, No. 4 (Winter, 1968), pp. 661–669.

[11] There are certain situations that do not lend themselves to agreement, regardless of how much comprehension there is. The most obvious of these involves conflict over a desideratum that is in short supply.

[12] Robert B. Zajonc, "Attitudinal Effects of Mere Exposure," *Journal of Personality and Social Psychology (Monograph Supplement)*, Vol. 9, No. 2, Part 2 (June, 1968), pp. 1–27.

[13] Bernard Berelson and Gary A. Steiner, *Human Behavior: An Inventory of Scientific Findings*, New York, Harcourt, Brace and World, 1964, p. 331.

[14] *Ibid.*, p. 200.

[15] Hideya Kumata and Wilbur Schramm, "A Pilot Study of Cross-Cultural Meaning," *Public Opinion Quarterly*, Vol. 20, No. 3 (1956), pp. 229–238.

[16] Two semantic studies done by the same author under different circumstances make this point even more strongly. The first was an experiment with 32 American and 36 Japanese students at the University of Illinois. The Japanese students had spent an average of 27 months in the United States.—Yasumasa Tanaka, "A Cross-Cultural Study of National Stereotypes Held by American and Japanese College Graduate Subjects," *Japanese Psychological Research*, Vol. 4, No. 2 (1962), pp. 65–78. The author was much more optimistic about cross-cultural similarities in this study than he was in a later experiment with Japanese students at Tokyo University, whose responses he compared with those of American students. Here he concluded that "incompatible semantic systems could . . . become another critical obstacle for cooperation, reducing the opportunities of mutual understanding, or even producing high emotional hostilities among different language/culture communities."—*Loc. cit.*, see note 2 above, pp. 44–45.

[17] Berelson and Steiner, *op. cit.*, p. 44.

[18] Cf. Joshua A. Fishman, Charles A. Ferguson and Jyotirindra Das Gupta, eds., *Language Problems of Developing Nations*, New York, John Wiley and Sons, 1968, *passim*.

[19] See Pierre Alexandre, "Some Linguistic Problems of Nation-Building in Negro Africa," in Fishman et al., *op. cit.*, pp. 119–127.

[20] Herbert I. Schiller, "National Development Requires Some Social Distance," *The Antioch Review*, Vol. 29, No. 1 (Spring, 1967), pp. 63–67.

[21] "Real time" in information processing systems may be defined as providing computer outputs in time to be usable for subsequently needed inputs.

[22] For an interesting view of the role of television in bringing humanity into an intimate frame of reference for the televiewer, see Gerhart D. Wiebe, "A New Dimension in Journalism," *Journalism Quarterly*, Vol. 31, No. 4 (Fall, 1954), pp. 411–420.

[23] Bernard Rubin, "International Film and Television Propaganda: The Campaigns of Assistance," *The Annals*, Vol. 398 (November, 1971), p. 82.

[24] See Leonard W. Doob, *Communication in Africa*, New Haven, Yale University Press, 1966, pp. 269–275; John Wilson, "Film Illiteracy in Africa," *Canadian Communications*, Vol. 1, No. 4 (Summer, 1961), pp. 7–14; John H. Humphrey, "Experiences in Production for Film Illiterates," Project in Educational Communication, Teachers College, Columbia University, 1961.

Kaarle Nordenstreng:

Recent Developments in European Communications Theory

COMMUNICATIONS research and theory has its origins in the development of the media of communication, particularly mass media. In the beginning, starting around the shift of the century, studies of mass communication were occasional exercises carried out from the traditional bases of history, law, etc. But as the social importance of mass communication increased with mass-circulated commercial press and particularly after the introduction of radio broadcasting in the 'twenties, this field of social communications research began to grow and take shape. First it was usually associated with particular media, like German *Zeitungswissenschaft* ("Newspaper science") or American "radio research." The latter was strongly stimulated by the market needs of rapidly expanding commercial broadcasting which in this form of audience research at the same time served as the main force to develop general public opinion surveys.[1] Gradually, however, media-bound approaches were replaced by a more general view of the mass media; in the German area this development led between the wars to the emergence of *Publizistik* ("Science of public communication") while the concept of "communication research" broke through in the American arena towards the end of the 'forties (significantly enough, Paul Lazarsfeld and his colleagues even changed the title of their series "Radio Research" into "Communication Research").

During the three decades that have been passed after the last war, mass communication research in Europe has constantly increased. This increase, however, is far from the boom which has taken place in the United States. In fact, compared with the rise of social sciences in general and sociology in particular, the field of mass communication research has in only a few countries become an especially popular area of study (one of the rare exceptions is the country of this author, Finland).

Consequently, the European arena of mass communication research is not a very abundant source of intellectual exercise: usually there are only one or two significant bases of communication research in a country. And yet, even if it may be easily accessible as far as quantity is concerned, qualitatively it pro-

[1] See e.g. Herbert I. Schiller, "Waiting for Orders—Some Current Trends in Mass Communications Research in the United States," *Gazette*, 1974, pp. 11-21.

▶ This article is a public lecture given by the author at Simon Fraser University in Canada (March 19, 1975). Reprinted here with permission of Dr. Nordenstreng, professor at the University of Tampere, Finland.

vides a most varied spectrum of activities, approaches and traditions. They extend from routine audience research carried out for the press and broadcasting organizations to experimental studies of media effects, content analyses of media output and various kinds of journalism research. And besides this research activity, which is more or less repeating American patterns, there is much such research which might be characterized as genuinely European: for instance, semiotic and structuralist schools particularly in France and Italy, studies of contemporary culture particularly in Great Britain, and Marxistic orientations in Eastern Europe but increasingly also in the West, particularly in the Federal Republic of Germany. Right now it is a fascinating field which seems to be in a state of rapid expansion (mainly because of increased interest in communication policies) and also in a state of "identity crisis." Accordingly, speaking of intellectual exercise, the American arena, despite its abundance, might well turn out to be relatively poor compared with the European arena with all its qualitative variation.

Given this variety, a fair and balanced reporting of the whole European arena—especially if Europe is considered (as it should be) to include the socialist countries—is therefore impossible in this presentation. What I shall try to do instead is an overview of current trends in the more basic theoretical orientations, i.e., in the conceptual framework in which European communications research is being carried out. I shall limit my review to the Western part of Europe because the socialist countries would deserve a completely separate treatment.

It is typical of current European orientation in communication research to expand the focus of attention beyond the media, their messages and the psychological reception process of the messages to the social and material living conditions of the people. As I once put it, in listing factors that determine the reception of adult education programs, "however good the timing policy, however dominant the channel, however close to real-life experiences the programs may be, however easy the language, and however much promotional information and even organizational mobilization may be exercised, nothing helps if a person is seriously deprived in his objective and physical surroundings, and consequently if he is psychologically so apathetic and alienated that the total motivation for improvement and change in his socio-economic situation is missing." [2] Manifestations of this way of thinking are the Scandinavian projects started in the early 'seventies and called in Finland "citizens' informational needs" and in Sweden "information gaps in society." Both were initiated and are mainly being carried out within the broadcasting organizations, which incidentally is an indication of the social and informational commitment of these mass communication institutions.

The points of departure of the Swedish project are stated by the researchers as follows:

[2] Kaarle Nordenstreng, "Definition of the Audience and How to Increase It," *Adult Education by Television* (Geneva: European Broadcasting Union, 1973), pp. 31–38.

Marked differences among social groups with respect to access to and utilization of essential information constitute a problem in our society. ("Essential" information is tentatively defined as information that enables the individual to survey and understand the society he lives in, and allows him actively to influence the conditions of his daily life.) These differences are primarily functions of factors outside the control of mass media, factors such as the structure of society, the social and economic status of various groups and individuals, their personal capabilities, etc.

Even so, the roles and potential roles of mass media should not be considered *a priori* to lack significance. Depending on how they are controlled and utilized—in terms of policy, on planning and production levels—the media may doubtless contribute either to the broadening or to the closing of information gaps.[3]

The Finnish project on citizens' informational needs shares these points and stresses the socio-economically determined mechanisms which accumulate on the one hand material and mental wealth accompanied by informational activity and material and mental poverty accompanied by informational passivity on the other. The project refers to a governmental committee on the quality of life in Finland which found that due to the accumulation process differences in the overall standard of living become greater than differences with regard to any single component of the standard of living. In analyzing mechanism of social inequality the committee had further pointed out the functions of segregation in society: minimization of contacts between the privileged and underprivileged reduces the informational and social fields of operation of both groups, leaving the privileged to enjoy their benefits with good conscience and the underprivileged to remain satisfied with their lot. It was also noted that social studies and official statistics had until recent years largely supported these same overall tendencies.

Empirical results of a nationwide survey carried out for this project further verified the presence of this vicious circle: those who were already well informed were most open to new knowledge and most capable of finding relevant knowledge, whereas the ill-informed, i.e., socio-economically underprivileged, were passive and unable to tell where to find relevant knowledge; furthermore the latter group did not regard information and knowledge as particularly important.

An essential theoretical distinction applied in the project is between subjective and objective informational needs. It was not found sufficient just to carry out an opinion survey and register subjectively perceived informational needs and wishes; besides these it was necessary to construct an all-round picture of the respondent's objective living conditions and his possibilities for social action. The aim was to see an individual's informational behavior (sub-

---

[3] Sveriges Radio (Swedish Broadcasting Corporation), Audience and Programme Research Bulletin No. 3, 1973.

jective needs) as an integral part of his total living conditions and social environment (objective needs). Expressed in these terms it is evident that objective informational needs are least satisfied among the underprivileged sections of the population and that the greatest difference between the subjective and objective levels of informational need is to be found in the same groups which are left outside the positive accumulation of material and informational wealth in society. The "haves" do not objectively have many informational needs unsatisfied and yet they subjectively have more informational hunger than the "have-nots," whose objective informational needs are burning.

Besides social segregation referred to above the socio-economic system is seen to employ various mechanisms which tend to keep the level of subjective informational needs low. One central concept in this connection is the (bourgeois) hegemony which may be understood as a filter extending to the personal world-view of an individual and biasing or blocking his process of perceiving reality. The de facto function of the bulk of mass media is taken to be an overall support of this hegemony, e.g., by means of a long-term indoctrination of certain implicit values and a fragmentation of message supply which prevents rather than helps an individual to construct a holistic view of objective reality.

The Finnish project—as well as the corresponding Swedish one—might equally well be classified as an exercise in political science or in general sociology as a piece of communication research: the problem is to study the actual and potential conditions for social equality and participatory democracy. Consequently, there is a tendency to avoid a narrow communicologist's point of view and instead take a fairly broad perspective with a wide range of socio-economic (objective) factors to interplay with (subjective) communication phenomena. In this context media of mass communication are studied as a dependent rather than independent variable.

It may be said that such an approach is no innovation in the tradition of communication research. However, a close look will reveal that the theoretical framework used in these studies usually differs from those applied in earlier research into the same problems. The social factors employed go far beyond the primary group considerations which used to dominate earlier receiver studies; now it is the economic structure of society—the "total system"—that is taken as the point of departure, instead of some more or less loosely defined groups in society.

In fact, after having left the stage of media-boundedness and becoming an overall mass communication research the field may be seen to advance to another stage: from a still narrow approach centered around the media (as separated from society) to a wider approach with the media as no more than integral parts of an overall ideological machinery in society, often called "ideological apparatuses." And it is usually understood that this machinery, which is seen as an integrated function of all social and cultural institutions with potential effects on people's consciousness, has a hegemonistic character, i.e., it impinges upon the individual consciousness such elements which would not spontaneously prevail there but which will also not be rejected by consciousness as they are so commonly shared by the cultural community. Thus the concept of "mass consciousness," introduced along with the traditional concept "public opinion," is seen not only as a sum or average of a number of individual pieces of consciousness (a phenomenon at the micro level) but also as a social phenomenon (at the macro level) relatively independent of individuals. One might even say that the field, after only recently gaining its identity, has with this orientation started to move from mass communication research towards a general social science, i.e., political economy of society on the one hand and an overall study of culture on the other.

At this point one might observe a dilemma in the theoretical orientation I have been describing: on the one hand it is the material living conditions of people and the socio-economic structures that are seen as vital in describing and explaining communication phenomena, and on the other hand there seems to be a strong emphasis on the ideological and manipulative processes taking place at the level of mass consciousness or generally speaking at the level of the contemporary culture. Serious questions may be raised concerning the philosophical origins of these levels and their methodological compatibility.

And indeed, a vivid debate is currently taking place in Europe around the relative importance of material and ideological factors in communications theory. Not surprisingly, this debate is taking place in the wider context of the social sciences in general: nothing less is at issue than the very nature of society.

As is well known, the western orientation in sociology has largely avoided a materialistic concept of society with structural factors in a central position and has instead constructed a model of society with individual and group interaction, i.e., basically communication processes, as the critical factor. Such an orientation has facilitated, among other things, a conceptual confusion of power relations with the relations of communication—so popular in the dominant western thinking, which tends to reduce the objective power antagonisms to plain linguistic complications. It is not difficult to note how such a notion of society is politically useful in the context of capitalist economy, for instance when disturbances in industrial relations may be explained by notions like "semantic noise" and pressures towards industrial democracy met by measures to "facilitate the flow of information." In this tradition, the political democracy is de facto reduced as a phenomenon to be placed mainly at the ideological level: politics is being played usually in the consciousness of the people and only exceptionally—in revolutionary situations—in the more fundamental power relations of society.

This approach in social sciences has increasingly been faced with a strictly materialistic approach inspired by the classics of Marxism and Leninism which not only introduces the materialistic socio-economic structures in addition to interaction processes and related phenomena of (mass) consciousness but also claims that they must be taken as primary factors in explaining individual and social behavior. The socio-economic structures are seen to be composed of the material arrangements of production in society, i.e., the productive forces and the relations of production, with the corresponding social and economic institutions determining relations between individuals (e.g., ownership conditions). The nature of these structures is materialistic, although in practice they may mostly operate by means or symbolic (and in that sense immaterial) communication.

Consequently, the rise of modern communication research advocating a societal approach and equipped with new concepts of non-material social communication processes has taken place within a very delicate context—we might say in an explosive situation. Paradoxically, many of those who have sincerely thought they had advanced a wide approach with a concept of mass communication as a social process and mass media as social institutions are often finding themselves among the traditional "interactionists" being accused by more orthodox materialists of just being modernised versions of old "psychologizers" and "ideologizers" of social phenomena. In fact, the same criticism is being directed towards some of the most outstanding representatives of the current leftist schools in France and Germany, names such as Louis Althusser and Jürgen Habermas. And as is typical of social scientific debates in Europe, criticism and counter-criticism are coupled with statements of political positions in which many of those communication researchers who consider themselves "progressive"—and who certainly by North American standards would be classified "leftists" if not "ultra-Marxists"—have been labeled by the critics as "right-wing deviants."

This debate, as hot and bitter as it may be to those concerned, will certainly prove to be a very useful medicine for the field—and not only for communications research but for the study of social and cultural phenomena in general. First of all, it serves as a guarantee that the field does not fall back into the era of narrow communicology but continues to be socially oriented. Secondly, such a climate of scientific debate will eliminate what might be called a *"petit-bourgeois* reform" of the field, i.e., a superficial reorientation without questioning the fundamental theoretical conceptions. Examples of this type of risky "half-way approach" are studies of the economic structure of the media industry and critical appraisals of media contents (often ambitiously calling themselves exercises "in the political economy of mass communication") *not* accompanied by a conceptually comprehensive theory of socio-economic processes. Thirdly, the debate compels research in this traditionally quite eclectic field to undertake an explicit analysis of its basic theoretical and philosophical propositions. And, finally the debate on the nature of communication and communication research is a welcome phenomenon because there seems to be a tendency in several traditional social and even humanistic sciences to "find" the concept of communication and consequently to recapitulate their own theories in terms of human communication.

Naturally there is nothing wrong as such in attempts of the traditional fields to incorporate concepts and findings of communications research and information theory in their (often quite poor) theoretical frameworks. But in Western tradition there is a potential risk of communication becoming another magic phenomenon which would easily occupy a dominant position in many fields of arts and sciences (from literature to economics) and rather mask and obscure than clarify and advance the state of the art in these fields. A German participant in the debate on the nature of communication and its research has directed the following bitter words to both modern communication researchers who are overlooking material elements in the process and to those outsiders who have become so fascinated by the concept of communication that it is understood as *the* element of human nature and is thereby mystified: "The general tendency to explain everything from communication . . . is not science but *ideology*. As not a single one of the objects of communication research is essentially composed of communication, communication becomes a *fetish* which not only explains nothing but even largely disturbs." [4]

As has become clear by now, all these developments and debates are certainly not isolated from the general trends in social and humanistic sciences or from the changing patterns of the overall socio-politico-economic system. I should like to conclude my presentation by discussing not only European but more universal tendencies of the field. I am in fact suggesting that the reorientation taking place in the field of mass communication research more or less everywhere in the western (i.e., capitalist) world is characterized by precisely the same tendencies as the current European thinking. Significant global tendencies may just become more visible in European (and particularly Scandinavian) circumstances.

The global trends in the field of mass communication research can be summarized in terms of two interrelated tendencies on change: (1) a tendency towards a more *holistic framework*, and (2) a tendency towards *policy orientation*. [5] The holistic approach, for its part, may be seen to imply two sub-aspects, namely, (a) a stressing of the *processual approach* covering simultaneously various stages of the communication process, and, (b) a stressing of the *contextual approach* tying the particular communication phenomena into wider socio-politico-economic settings.

It is not difficult to trace in these tendencies a rebellion against the positivist-behaviorist tradition. In terms of the philosophy of science it is exactly this shift from positivism towards anti-positivism that may be seen as crucial in the present reorientation of communication research—as well as in the so-called crisis of western social sciences in general.

In the present context it is particularly important to note the implications

[4] Karl Held, *Kommunikationsforschung—Wissenschaft oder Ideologie? Materialen zur Kritik einer neuen Wissenschaft* (Munich: Carl Hanser Verlag, 1973), p. 184.
[5] Cf. UNESCO, Proposals for an International Programme of Communication Research (COM/MD/20, 1971), p. 6.

of positivism for policy considerations. The crucial notion of positivism—called in philosophical debate the "Humean guillotine"—argues that one cannot infer from "how things are" "how they should be." Goals of social activity are understood as something voluntary and subjective; value-bound choices are placed by definition outside the scope of objective knowledge. Consequently, research and politics are sharply separated from each other, and there prevails a relativism of values. Anti-positivism, for its part, claims that a study of the objective laws of social processes, in their widest sense, can be derived from social goals grounded on objective facts. These social goals—the "how things should be"—can be inferred, at least to a great extent, from the laws followed by goal-directed social processes, once the latter have been discovered. Consequently, research and politics cannot and should not be sharply separated.

At this point one might ask why such a reorientation in the social sciences in general and mass communication research in particular has begun to take place. What are the cultural and social determinants behind this "movement"? In the present analysis only one overall factor will be singled out which, however, seems to the present author to be of crucial importance.

The suggested significant factor is the historical development in western industrialized societies, in consequence of which ideological control over the mass consciousness has become increasingly difficult—and hence ever more vital for the socio-economic system to handle. In spite of the indoctrination influencing individuals through all established institutions in society—not least by the mechanism of fragmentation in education and mass communication—large segments of the population remain dissatisfied, and what is also significant, new elements such as students have become involved in this refusal to digest what is centrally fed to them through socializing institutions, including the mass media. This is not a proper context to discuss the reasons for this surveillance of spontaneity and protest amid the manipulative mechanism of society (including the falsification of the theory of "repressive intolerance"); it suffices here to note that there is something in the concrete social reality which "breaks through" all manipulation.

Accordingly, since the traditional methods of ideological control have proved inadequate one has been urged forward to search for more effective means to touch the minds of the masses. This is why so much is said today of "comprehension of messages," "audience passivity," etc.; these kinds of new looks into the mass communication process (including the activitists of "citizen participation") is a must for the established social order if it is going to maintain in the long run its mental and material control over the bulk of the population. Similarly, at the level of the social sciences it has been an objective need of social forces to turn the positivistic tradition into a more holistic approach. It was no longer sufficient to contribute to the manipulative mechanisms by piecemeal studies and theories which by-pass many significant features in social developments, particularly those generating dissonance and revolutionary potential.

By and large, it simply became vitally important to assess the social reality, including the process of mass communication, more truthfully and in a macro perspective. And this assessment was not to be made for academic convenience but for an emerging, socially determined concern for communication policies.[6] As is well known, systematic policies and long-range planning are another vital response to the objective development of the socio-economic system ("state-monopoly capitalism" in industrialised countries and the process of "modernization" in developing countries). Consequently, a need for policies and planning in the communication field of society derives not only from the motives for ideological control but also from a general tendency towards more coherent socio-economic processes. All these pressures have caused a bankruptcy for the positivist tendency to define policy-related goals and objectives as "non-scientific." Western social sciences, including communications research, have moved closer to the Marxist concept of social science.

But the philosophical and political situation is far from a simple one. In terms of the present analysis, the new approach in communication research as well as boosting interest in communication policies can be seen to reflect the same basic tendency of having the mechanism of the prevailing social order brought up-to-date, and thus supporting the basic tendencies of the status quo. Accordingly, a "progressive" communication researcher finds himself in a paradoxical situation: no matter what he subjectively might advocate, his services are largely channeled in the given socio-economic context for the benefit of the existing social order. However, this certainly is no deterministic process—to become a defaitist would be another form of "ultra-leftism"—and there always remains a certain scope of movement within the scientific tradition as well as in social development in general.

[6] See e.g. UNESCO, Meeting of Experts on Communication Policies and Planning (COM/MD/24, 1972), and Ithiel de Sola Pool, "The Rise of Communications Policy Research," *Journal of Communication*, 1974, pp. 31–42.

Henk Prakke:

Towards a Philosophy of Publicistics

IN TRYING to find an approach toward a philosophy of publicistics I am talking as a representative of the German-Dutch discipline of "publicistics," which has been defined by Walter Hagemann in a rather short form as the theory of public diffusion of messages with topical contents.[1] The discipline involves more than this definition, however, and its latest expansion to a theory of *functional* publicistics indicates the need for a broader definition. For the moment, however, and while dealing with the phenomenon of applied publicistics, Hagemann's formula of "public diffusion of messages with topical contents" may suffice.

Just as individual newspapers keep a diary of current events and register the thoughts and feelings of society, the aggregate of publicistic documentation, both in its historical and contemporary dimensions, constitutes the annals of mankind, which tell in word, picture and sound of the transactions of mankind and testify in various ways to the truth of the saying: *Tempora muntiantur nos et mutamur in illis.* (Times are changing and we are changing with them.)

Does publicistics mean only the registration of past and present events by an objective observer? Have not thinkers about public activities since Aristotle been predominantly interested in persuasive publicistic activities of individuals, since many contemporary scholars of publicistics still feel more closely related to the publicist than to the field of publicistics? And again: Does publicistics actually influence events; does it really change public opinion; does it determine opinions, attitudes and behavior, and, thus, ultimately influence the course of history; and did public opinion exist, perhaps, at the time when the concept became a slogan, or has it been an illusion, a professional myth of politicians and journalists from the very beginning? Publicistics describes what happens, in reports and comments, but many times also simply in fictional accounts. But does it, in this manner, also produce a lasting effect on the course of the world, and contribute to its historical evolution?

---

[1] Walter Hagemann's definiton of publicistics: "Publizistik ist die Lehre von der öffentlichen Aussage aktueller Bewusstseinsinhalte," is discussed in his book, *Grundzüge der Publizistik,* 2nd ed., (Münster, 1966), 37.

▶ *From:* "Towards a Philosophy of Publicistics," by Henk Prakke, in: Occasional Paper, Center for the Advanced Study of Communication, The University of Iowa, No. 1, 1971. Dr. Prakke, former head of the Institut für Publizistik, University of Münster (Germany) is now professor emeritus and lives in the Netherlands; this article is reprinted here, with certain changes by the author.

As long as man in his philosophizing has given thought to the nature and the essence of his earthly existence, the ceaseless revolution of all that is has occupied his mind. *Panta rhei*—"all is in flux"—describes movement as the principle of life; it constitutes the essence of the philosophy of Heraclitus. Also, the wisdom of the Old Testament has been preserved for us in a proverb expressing a similar attitude: "To every thing there is a season, and a time to every purpose under the heaven" (Eccl., 3:1). In short, publicistics owes its existence to this dynamic principle: where something happens, where something is flowing, *in actu*, there is its element. In a state of equilibrium and absolute tranquility, no one needs information and no one is able to report on anything new. Where no difference is known about some *thing* or some *one*, no questions are asked. There is no discussion, no need for comparison, and, thus, no comment.

To a new citizen of the world, the order and the style of life of the society into which he is born constitute his first frame of reference for thoughts and actions. Growing up, he soon observes that his frame of reference is in a state of flux and liable to change. Every society has its own order and its own style of life. These two components constitute its culture, which I would describe, with Pieter Bouman and Bronislav Malinowski, as its organization, beliefs and knowledge, tools and consumer goods.[2] While the order is expressed in the relation of these elements to each other, the style of life is determined by the specific manner of their application. A change of these elements of culture, partially or completely, may be an evolutionary or a revolutionary process. The consciousness of change, the recognition of cultural evolution, begot the historical consciousness of man.

Historical thinking led to the division of cultural history into distinct periods of civilization, and to the realization that in each of the successive epochs a specific pervading Spirit of the Time (*Zeitgeist*) and a specific Sense of Life (*Lebensgefühl*) become manifest. Since human thinking and feeling change in the course of time and from one epoch to another, the assertion is supported that man as cultural beings can change collectively in the course of time as well as along with their times.

The pervading spirit of the Enlightenment was different from that of medieval times and a comparison of the publicistics of each period yields a picture of these changes. In the same way, the idea of life varies from one epoch to another.

However, it is by no means rare for changes to become apparent through the re-introduction of earlier elements, a phenomenon that could be described as an echo-effect. For instance, motifs of the songs of Anakreon (fifth century B.C.), full of the joy of life, reappear during the periods of Hellenism, Renaissance and Rococo; in each of these epochs the *Zeitgeist* led to concepts of life that were more or less similar. On the other hand, should one ask whether it

---

[2] For Bouman's and Malinowski's influences see: Bronislav Malinowski, *A Scientific Theory of Culture and Other Essays*, Chapel Hill, 1944, and *The Dynamics of Culture Change*, New Haven, 1946; and Pieter Bouman, *Sociologie, Begrippen en Problemen*, Antwerpen, 1940.

was a new *Lebensgefühl* that induced a change in the spirit of that time? After all, these two principles of cultural change are not of a causal, but of a functional nature.

Great cultural changes, however, such as the influences of Christianity upon the Roman Empire, the rebirth of Greek culture during the Renaissance, or the emancipation of non-white peoples, share at least one characteristic: they are peak periods of publicistics.

Furthermore, the concept of change embraces not only a temporal but also a spatial dimension in every epoch; change is indicated by the co-existence of several cultural cycles. Each of them has its own image of the world (*Weltbild*) and its own evaluation of the world (*Weltwertung*). Similarities as well as differences of men of different social orders, and what separates men as well as what unites them, are factors that have always been an inexhaustible source of publicistic activity.

It was Cicero who called Herodotus (fifth century B.C.) the "father of history"; in his time, however, he was no more than a traveling reporter who visited the most important centers of the old world. He recorded his observations and experiences. For instance, as a contemporary and as an eye-witness he described the successful Greek campaign against the Persians just like the common *logopoioi*, the storytellers of Greece. Herodotus, however, wrote down everything and called this account of his travels through the old world "investigations" (Ionic-Greek: *historie*). This word contains the meanings of reconnoitering, recognition through the sense of sight, and direct evidence; hence, reporting. From separate reports Herodotus then created a contemporary review of Greek encounters with the barbarians. Out of single stories he created *history*.

Voltaire and Montesquieu present examples of the principle of motion during an entirely different epoch. Their intellectual horizons, and consequently their publicistic activities in France, were influenced greatly by two years of residence in England that provided a "different" experience. Information about historical change enriches the image of the world. Comparisons with one's neighbors and with the past lead to comment and, thus, to affirmation or correction of one's own world evaluation.

Therefore, the inquiry into the meaning of history is closely bound up with the inquiry into the sense of publicistics. Our thinking about the nature of history has been deeply affected by the considerations of the role played by man in the changes of history. Publicistics inquires about those elements of this role that are marked by public activity.

The Greek way of feeling and thinking was static, that is, historical change meant a temporary deviation from the Ideal. On this point Plato and Aristotle expressed similar ideas. Deviations from the ideal government were meant to last only a short time. The course of humanity was symbolized by a circle, in which the revolutions of time returned the same phenomena.

In contrast, Christianity promoted a new concept of man as well as of time. It was Augustine who opposed that "Godless doctrine of useless circulation" in his *De Civitate Dei*. (From a point of publicistics this treatise represents the last great polemical attack of Christianity on the heathens.) Augustine attributed all occurrences to the Heavenly City; according to him, all that happens becomes manifest in a continuous struggle between two invisible kingdoms: the *Civitas Dei* and the *Civitas Terrena*. The actor is God, and it is only through their faith that men can participate. There have been innumerable publicistic testimonies in favor of this proposition in the course of the centuries.

Consequently, extremely important religious movements arose and contributed a particularly effective statement of Christian eschatological doctrine which included pragmatic hopes of rescue from earthly distress. The publicistics of these movements often consisted of utopian novels. The seventeenth-century French preacher Jacques Benigne Bossuet demonstrated that the history of Christian salvation was completely interwoven with the history of this world. And not until the era of Enlightenment was the idea of an infinite, divine Providence discarded and replaced by the conception of a finite, world-immanent development according to rational and identifiable laws based on the knowledge of life and matter in nature.

The philosophy of history after the French Revolution contains a number of systems, characterized especially by their consideration of the future as a higher standard of the present state of affairs. For example, the planning of social order for the future, according to Iring Fetscher,[3] should involve a consideration of three types: must-be (*gemusste*), wished-for (*gewollte*), or should-be (*gesollte*) futures, expressing inevitability, freedom of decision-making, and moral or ethical requirements, respectively. These categories become more visible in some cases than in others. But even when people believe in the inevitability of a particular development as if it were a law of nature, this development is, as a rule, justified on moral grounds.[4] They see no contradiction in calling upon others to further this development despite its recognized inevitability. For this reason even those movements that are based upon a doctrine of predestination rarely renounce missionary and propagandist publicistics.

Thus it was argued against Marxism that an appeal for direct action ("Proletarians of all countries, unite!") was a contradiction, since, according to its doctrine and in agreement with its laws of history, the classless society was bound to materialize. The Marxists, however, countered this attack by saying that, while the ultimate goal of the development was, indeed, fixed, the exact time of its realization was left to mankind. Metaphorically, they suggested that the pangs of parturition introducing the New Age be cut short to render the transition as painless as possible. In doing so, they also proposed not to shrink

[3] Iring Fetscher, "Geschichtsphilosophie," in Alwin Diemer and Ivo Frenzel (eds.), *Philosophie*, Frankfurt, 1958.
[4] Karl Popper discusses this historical phenomenon in his books, particularly, *The Open Society and its Enemies*, London, 1945, and *The Poverty of Historicism*, London, 1957.

from the use of violence, which under certain circumstances might even be required. Interesting in this connection is the opinion of the young Georg Lukacs who shared with others the belief that the goal of the progressing historical process was, indeed, a classless society, but that the world might possibly relapse into barbarism if the proletarian revolution should not take place or should fail.[5] It is clear that in this instance, too, people trusted persuasive publicistics as a force that would support or even bring about the predicted historical event. Therefore, it may be concluded that in an ideological system active intervention might become a theoretical necessity.

Thus, on the ruins of Carthage, I once tried to find an answer to the apparently unanswerable question: word or deed? It was the native guide's abridged version of the colorful history of Tunisia that made me reflect on "ups and downs" of events, conquest and annihilation, reconstruction and prosperity, rise and fall of society. According to his story, the use of power determined the succession of cultural epochs. And the question remains, did the word actually play an essential role , if, after all, it was alwyas violent action that brought about the decisive changes of culture? [6]

A culture is identified by the *Weltbild* and *Weltwertung* of its bearers. Our world image is the result of manifold information, our world evaluation the fruit of manifold comment. We stated that this dichotomy refers exclusively to legitimate publicistic phenomena. If, however, at the historically decisive moment, world image and world evaluation are fixed by the conqueror and consequently by his rules ("*Cuius regio eius est religio*"), we may wonder what remains of the publicistic postulates of a free flow of information and comment and their interplay in the form of discussions which result in a public consciousness or a public opinion. Is it perhaps only the violent act ("propaganda for action") and not the publicistic word that constitutes the basis of real power? Is the word merely a concurrent and inconsequential phenomenon, and does the publicistic approach to such a situation consist only of what Emil Dovifat called "publicistics of action"? Dr. Martin Luther King, for instance, once remarked: "Lacking sufficient access to television, publications and broad forums, Negroes have had to write their most persuasive essays with the blunt pen of marching ranks."

In a way the Roman Senator Cato Major may provide an answer to these questions. Both as an exponent of culture and as a politician, he was feared and praised in Rome for his rhetorical powers; he was undoubtedly a gifted publicist. With a keen sense for public effect he used the publicistic form of the slogan and employed the publicistic technique of repetition in his personal fight against the Carthaginians, whome he considered the greatest menace to Rome. Invariably he reduced the expression of his opinion about Carthage at the end of each of his senate speeches to "*Ceterum csenseo Carthaginem esse*

---

[5] I am using Fetscher's example here.
[6] A discussion of these ideas can be found in Henk Prakke, "Als Publizist auf den Ruinen Karthagos," *Publizistik,* 8:4 (Juli-August, 1963), 329–36.

delendam." The succinctness and the striking character of this unmistakable slogan combined with the technique of pounding repetition publicistically, without any doubt, made a decisive contribution to the fall of the North-African city. Thus, for once at least, violent action was preceded by the rhetorical power of the word; this is an instance of a form of publicistic communication that led to a change of culture.

Another example is provided by the Arab conquest of the Roman provinces of Africa. Behind brute force operated the flaming words of Mohammed in whose name the Islamites fought their holy war with fire and sword. (The crescent in the green flag of the Prophet defeated the cross of Christianity and the scepter of the Byzantine emperor, to express it in a symbolic-publicistic manner.)

The role of publicistics from the earlier phase of North-African culture to the recent changes in Tunisia under Habib Bourguiba, furthermore, confirms that its effects are apparent in gradual as well as in radical changes of culture (*Kulturwandel* and *Kulturwende* respectively). In both, word and action accompany each other continuously. The deed generates the word, and words inspire action.

It might be objected that the charisma of great publicistic personalities is altogether a different issue and merits a separate discussion, while, on the other hand, there is no strong indication of the influence of editorial writers and radio commentators or reporters and editors all over the world. This objection becomes less convincing, however, if one considers that the great and "influential" publicists were young at one time and also had to learn their trade. In this connection it is always very interesting to ask what their parents used to read and to find out about their own readings during their years of training and peregrination. The answers may yield some information about the influences of friends and teachers during their years of greatest receptivity. A research project concerning the Dutch political elite showed, for instance, that for those without university training, newspapers and periodicals frequently were the friends and teachers that effectively determined their political rise.[7] Also, the history of ideas (*Geistesgeschichte*) proposes that a great idea never arises suddenly and fully developed; on the contrary, an impressive new stream or idea is only comprehensible if the whole area surrounding this stream is thoroughly investigated.

In its process of growth and in its essence, every great idea that moves the world originates from a variety of dialogs and is the result of a polyphonic colloquium.

The noted German historian Leopold von Ranke (nineteenth century) believed that careful investigation enabled the historian to present actual relationships and to reach an objectively valid type of historiography, but the realization that human pronouncements are historically determined has led instead

---

[7] Henk Prakke, *Pers en politieke elite*, Assen, 1954.

to the conviction that every new cultural epoch is bound to require new interpretations of the past and a new self-image.

During this century, which began with a cultural crisis, publicists have attempted to give a particular epithet to the epoch, to master its uncertainty and to fathom its consciousness of this crisis. We talk about the "age of industrialism," "the time of mass society," and recently about the "atomic age." Who among us, poor sorcer's apprentices (*Zauberlehrlinge*), is able to act and function properly *vis-a-vis* the robots of our own creation and who succeeds in mastering them because he understands their purpose and meaning?

In the field of publicistics these robots are called "mass media." They are part of a significant communication explosion, and their effects have stimulated interesting interpretations and criticisms in the areas of cultural criticism (e.g., Marshall McLuhan), philosophy (e.g., Karl Jaspers) and modern sociological theory (e.g., Helmut Schlesky).[8] There is a trend of thinking in terms of modern organized mass audiences as *the* actors in the publicistic process. Of course a student of publicistics must consider the significance of the social setting for any publicistic process and acknowledge the power of collectivism in this highly industrialized mass society, apart from practical economic and political factors. But he will not cease to reckon with the impact of the individual, his mental abilities and their particular effects upon publicistics. It is impossible to think only of collective minds and deeds when the mental and spiritual impressions of the individual constitute the basis of all experience and knowledge. "An event has to enter into an individual's realm of perception before it can be put into words. It is only via the individual that it finds its way to the public and here it can only be received separately by each individual."[9] Hagemann deduced the following theorem from this chain of thoughts: "Communication begins with the individual and proceeds to the individual." The history of the mind is evidence of the extent to which spiritual factors influence the course of mankind. Ideas have governed epochs. In this connection the history of publicistics has recorded the names of many individuals who courageously said "no" to developments around them (Max Scheler called them *Nein-sagenkönner*).

In the stream of time, however, man as a cultural being subjects his thoughts and feelings to collective changes. Who or what ultimately brings about and provides guidance for this collective change of *Zeitgeist* and *Lebensgefühl* is a matter of creed, regardless of how strongly some people believe that the ultimate mystery of the world can be reduced to a scientific system. (Christian Morgenstern once said: "He who has a keen 'second ear' for the

---

[8] For a discussion of these interpretations see: Marshall McLuhan, *The Gutenberg Galaxy*, Toronto, 1962; and *Understanding Media*, New York, 1964; also W. J. M. Evers, "De Wereld van Marshall McLuhan," in *Communicatie Cahiers*, 1 (1967), 6–25. Karl Jaspers, *Die Atombombe und die Zukunft des Menschen*, München, 1958. Helmut Schelsky, "Gedanken zur Rolle der Publizistik in der Modernen Gesellschaft," in Fritz Hodeige and Carl Rothe (eds.), *Atlantische Begegnungen*, Freiburg, 1964.

[9] Hagemann, 47.

prompter, gets a different view of the history of mankind.") Publicistics, however, always plays its part—reporting, persuading, and entertaining man.

Finally, every human activity can be deduced from a world image and a world evaluation. No world image, however, exists without information and no world evaluation without comment. The publicist formulates and disseminates messages continuously in changing words, pictures and sounds and in old as well as new plots, motives and ideas. Publicistics accompanies cultural change; it frequently achieves it, not only in terms of gradual changes but also in terms of large-scale revolutionary changes.

My epilog may consist of my personal conviction that the notions of reporting, persuading, and entertaining form a triad of publicistic objectives in which publicistics finds its highest realization when, and only to the extent to which, publicistics recognizes its obligations to historical truth in reporting, ideological truth in persuasion, and poetical truth in fiction.

Hamid Mowlana:

A Paradigm for Comparative Mass Media Analysis

IF THE students of mass communication are to generate a body of theory and concentrate their efforts on making the theory more general and valid, comparative and cross-cultural mass media research is absolutely essential. The concepts that are used in such comparative studies—for example, comparison of the broadcasting systems of two countries—must not be culture-bound, at least insofar as the concepts will be applicable to cultures embraced by generalizations which grow out of the original empirical research.

The need for a new conceptual framework stems from the explicit recognition that the old mass communication field (or the "press study") was concerned primarily with Western democratic systems—a parochialism reflected in the concepts employed. Such concepts as press freedom, social responsibility, libertarian practices, and authoritarinan methods have proved inadequate for understanding new mass communication technology that has come into being during the last two decades; they are even less appropriate for the study of mass media systems in new nations.

COMPARATIVE STUDIES OF MASS MEDIA SYSTEMS

In the comparative study of mass media, the tendency in the United States has been to categorize the communication systems of various societies into Western, Communist, and non-Communist developing models (Pool, 1963), or to see them in the tradition-transition-modernity continuum (Lerner, 1958). For over a generation, the prescriptive and normative framework of mass communication systems formulated by a group of American scholars (Siebert, Peterson, and Schramm, 1956) has been the backgbone and common denominator of analysis of national communication models by students of the press and mass communication.

Their four categories of communication systems include: (1) authoritarianism from the birth of modern communication in 1450 to development of authoritarian society; (2 libertarianism, born through struggles in the sixteenth and seventeenth centuries; (3) the Soviet Communist system developed by Marx and Lenin; and (4) the social responsibility model newly developed in the current century as a response to criticisms on the performance of libertarinan

▶ This is a shortened version of a paper by Dr. Hamid Mowlana of the School of International Service, The American University, Washington, D.C. Used in this book by permission of the author.

press, all of which have their roots in political and ideological philosophies.

In Western Europe, similar theories have been expressed in a neat descending order of control of communication channels: authoritarian, paternal, commercial, and democratic (Williams, 1962).

When compared with the American models, two interesting features of the European concepts seem to stand out. They are the concept of paternalism, as a halfway house between the authoritarian control and the *laissez faire* approach, and the emphasis on the weaknesses of the commercial system, which are discussed far less comprehensively by the Americans, with their presentation of the system emphasizing self control and responsibility. These features obviously reflect the West European socialist approach to socio-economic organization, which is different from the mainstream of American ideology that stresses self-control and autonomy rather than public control in any discussion of abuses of freedom by mass media.

As has been observed, there is a tendency to generalize the problems and situations of developing or communist nations at the cost of a careful consideration of their diversity. When all the varied difficulties and pitfalls in development efforts are lumped together, regardless of the obvious variety in the cultural, social, economic, and political backgrounds, the resultant weight of the problems appears no doubt appalling and unbearable. There are many countries, for example, where authoritarian, paternal, commercial, and democratic modes are *all* to some extent active. It may be easy to see the differences between libertarian and authoritarian systems, but a model like the social responsibility theory is unclear at best. Practically any media system in the world could justify its behavior as socially responsible to its people and polity (Merrill, 1974).

The problem has moved into sharper focus in recent years as the students of mass communication have sought to operationalize and compare press freedom (Nixon, 1960, 1965; Lowenstein, 1967, 1970), and national development (Farace, 1966), and as political scientists have used such a measure as an index and adjunct of political development (Almond and Powell, 1966) and integration (Russett, 1965). In some instances, the comparative study of communication systems has been linked with democracy—raising further difficulties, since even the attempts to operationalize democracy have resulted in separate sets of indicators which are not highly correlated.

For example, in cross-national studies of press freedom, researchers have not used a standard set of criteria for each country, nor have they considered factors other than those of obvious governmental interference. Comparative mass media systems research has been concerned mostly with variables dealing with the relationship of the media and government. There are, however, a multitude of other factors which can inhibit press freedom.

In one study there is such excessive reliance on legal and/or government factors that with the exception of the United States and several European countries, the rest of the world is at a disadvantage: 17 of the 23 factors used in measuring press freedom are either directly or indirectly related to government regulation (Lowenstein, 1967). In many countries, government is the *only* social entity with sufficient resources to maintain any form of communication network.

There also is a tendency among researchers to separate the press—predominately newspapers—from other media such as magazines and broadcasting (Nixon, 1960, 1965). In making this analytical distinction, one necessarily limits the applicability of his measure of free press, or on a broader scale, freedom of information. If one encounters a situation in which government control over media varies in different areas, he may find a free press alongside a severely restricted broadcast system.

The lack of an analytical framework within which comparative media research can be conducted should not imply that no attempts have been made to fill that gap empirically. The plethora of study and research in mass media systems, despite its lack of coordination as to approaches and methods, offers a significant body of information.

It concentrates mostly on the description of a single system on a country-by-country basis (mainly historical in nature), or on a media basis. Examples include studies on broadcasting systems of the world (Emery, 1969; Dizard, 1966), the press surveys of various countries (Merrill, Bryan, and Alisky, 1970; Sommerlad, 1966), the development of newspaper press in Europe (Olson, 1966), and description of mass media channels in Africa (Hachten, 1971; Mowlana, 1969), Asia (Lent, 1971), the Middle East (Lerner, 1958; Mowlana, 1971), and the Soviet Union and China (Inkeles, 1956; Markham, 1967; Yu, 1964; Liu, 1971; Hopkins, 1970).

Most of the studies give insights to the extent of government censorship, multitude of media, and pattern of ownership and readership, but are not functional analyses in the sense of focusing on the media system of the country or the region as a whole. Some studies attempt to do this in part by relating the media system to certain aspects of the society, such as national integration and national development (Schramm, 1965; Pye, 1963), but do not offer an all-encompassing, integrated view of the mass communication systems.

A recent review of studies on mass communication in the United States has demonstrated the uneven nature of international mass communication research and the lack of comparative mass media studies on a cross-national basis (Mowlana, 1973, 1974). . . .

A Paradigm for Whole Media Systems

The functional process approach to mass media systems analysis may be envisaged in terms of the following schema:

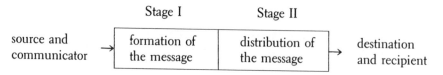

	Stage I	Stage II	
source and communicator →	formation of the message	distribution of the message	→ destination and recipient

The paradigm proposed here embraces eight broad areas pertinent to both stages of the communication process: the formation, and the distribution of messages through the media in any given mass media system. The principal influencing factors include: (1) types of ownership; (2) types of control; (3) sources of operation; (4) disposition of income and capital; (5) complexity of media bureaucracy; (6) perceived purpose; (7) messages; (8) types of content. Some of these factors may seem obvious, while others may require further elaboration.

(1) *Types of ownership.* In the search for non-culture-bound concepts and operational definitions, each stage of formation and distribution of a given mass media system is divided into three broad areas of *public, private,* and *mixed* sectors, with further suitable categories for data gathering.

For example, looking at the ownership of the newspaper press in India, one finds that the papers are privately owned by single companies, families, or a single individual. The government has some specialized and technical journals at both the metropolitan and provincial levels; but it has no daily newspapers. Some papers have mixed ownership, private citizens and government forming a corporation; government officials are on the board to which the paper must show its accounts. There are a few small party presses.

Ownership of distribution agencies of a given mass media system varies from country to country, and the type of ownership may influence the message. Government-owned media facilitate researchers' analysis of the respective government position. It must be stressed that in most cases, even when ownership is completely private, governments have some degree of control over the distribution of the message (especially through licensing and legal control).

A relatively new phenomenon is the extensive ownership of media in one country by (predominantly private) interests in another country. The five television stations comprising the Central American TV Network (South America) are 51 per cent owned subsidiaries of the American ABC network. This same company owns the American Television International Network Organization, which operates in six countries. Both the American television networks, CBS and NBC, also operate internationally. The British Lord Thomson owns close to 400 media networks, predominantly newspapers, including some major elite papers from around the world.

(2) *Types of control.* In the formation and distribution of stages of a given mass media system, the control aspect is by far one of the most significant variables in its complexity and measurement. Control over the system can take many forms: it comes from within the structure of a given mass media system, as well as being exerted from the outside. Some controls are actual, others are perceived. (Control here is the process of deleting or limiting the content or distribution of any of the media of communication.)

Although the process of perceived control has become more organized and consciously applied during the past four centuries, it has existed as an informal check in all societies. This control of the media system is applied not only by authoritarian, legal, or economic restrictions, but also by the individual's and

A PARADIGM FOR COMPARATIVE MASS MEDIA SYSTEM ANALYSIS

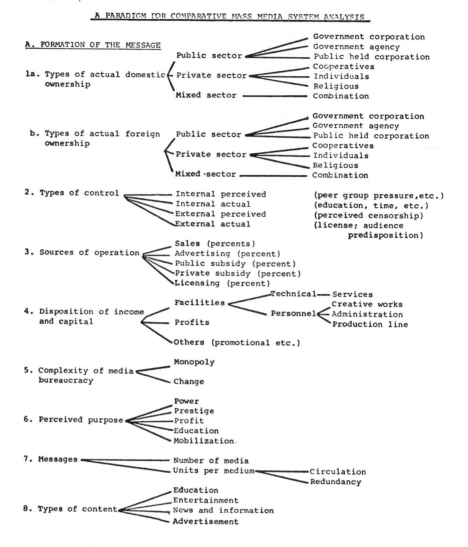

A. FORMATION OF THE MESSAGE

1a. Types of actual domestic ownership
- Public sector
  - Government corporation
  - Government agency
  - Public held corporation
- Private sector
  - Cooperatives
  - Individuals
  - Religious
- Mixed sector — Combination

b. Types of actual foreign ownership
- Public sector
  - Government corporation
  - Government agency
  - Public held corporation
- Private sector
  - Cooperatives
  - Individuals
  - Religious
- Mixed sector — Combination

2. Types of control
- Internal perceived (peer group pressure,etc.)
- Internal actual (education, time, etc.)
- External perceived (perceived censorship)
- External actual (license; audience predisposition)

3. Sources of operation
- Sales (percents)
- Advertising (percent)
- Public subsidy (percent)
- Private subsidy (percent)
- Licensing (percent)

4. Disposition of income and capital
- Facilities
  - Technical — Services
  - Creative works
- Personnel
  - Administration
  - Production line
- Profits
- Others (promotional etc.)

5. Complexity of media bureaucracy
- Monopoly
- Change

6. Perceived purpose
- Power
- Prestige
- Profit
- Education
- Mobilization

7. Messages
- Number of media
- Units per medium
  - Circulation
  - Redundancy

8. Types of content
- Education
- Entertainment
- News and information
- Advertisement

the organization's mental processes. In psychoanalysis, of course, the idea of thought control has been developed whereby the dominant consciousness limits the admission of certain materials to conscious attention. In individual development, standards and values are learned from the general culture, and also developed in a way that are individually unique.

These standards, existing in the conscious mind, reject alien and dangerous subjects. For example, a newspaper reporter or a broadcaster, having observed the standard of his employer or organization or culture, limits his observation to what he should do, see, and write, and after a time may be quite unaware of the limitations upon his observation. This informal or perceived

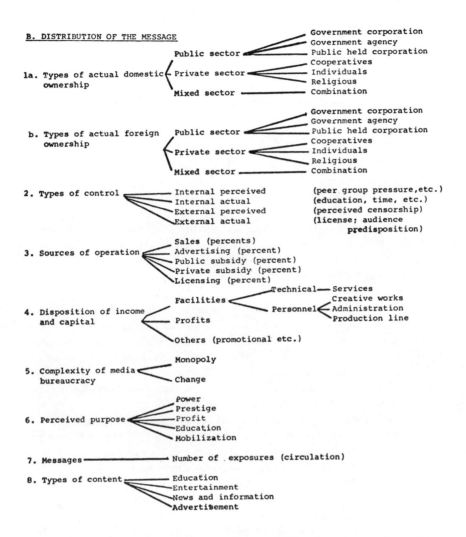

B. DISTRIBUTION OF THE MESSAGE

1a. Types of actual domestic ownership
- Public sector
  - Government corporation
  - Government agency
  - Public held corporation
- Private sector
  - Cooperatives
  - Individuals
  - Religious
- Mixed sector ——— Combination

b. Types of actual foreign ownership
- Public sector
  - Government corporation
  - Government agency
  - Public held corporation
- Private sector
  - Cooperatives
  - Individuals
  - Religious
- Mixed sector ——— Combination

2. Types of control
- Internal perceived (peer group pressure, etc.)
- Internal actual (education, time, etc.)
- External perceived (perceived censorship)
- External actual (license; audience predisposition)

3. Sources of operation
- Sales (percents)
- Advertising (percent)
- Public subsidy (percent)
- Private subsidy (percent)
- Licensing (percent)

4. Disposition of income and capital
- Facilities
  - Technical — Services
  - Personnel
    - Creative works
    - Administration
    - Production line
- Profits
- Others (promotional etc.)

5. Complexity of media bureaucracy
- Monopoly
- Change

6. Perceived purpose
- Power
- Prestige
- Profit
- Education
- Mobilization

7. Messages ——— Number of exposures (circulation)

8. Types of content
- Education
- Entertainment
- News and information
- Advertisement

control in the interest of the social system or of folk values is pervasive and insidious. In many countries and societies this form of control is usually far more effective than the formal control of a ruler or a hierarchy. Thus, in the paradigm we distinguish four types of control for any mass media system.

(a) *Internal actual control.* These are specific rules and regulations such as education, professional qualification, internal rules, and hierarchy created and institutionalized formally by the mass media system itself, to which members in a media system subject themselves;

(b) *Internal perceived control.* Social control in the newsroom, peer group pressure, perceived gatekeeping functions, and unwritten but understood rules of the internal conditions of the organization are examples of perceived control. These are the so-called "rules of the game," and consist of all those arrangements that regulate the way members of the mass media system must behave within the perceived institutional boundaries of the unit they work;

(c) *External actual control.* Direct censorship, licensing and any other external legal, professional, governmental, or external institutionalized factors form this category. Further sub-categories can be established here to divide external actual control into such areas as constitutional, legal, economic and political sectors;

(d) *External perceived control.* In every society we have such systems as culture, personality, social structure, and economic and political elites. Each of these can constitute a major set of variables in the process of demands entering a mass media system. Not all demands and influencing factors have their major locus inside the institutional system of mass communication. Important factors in determining the outcome of both the production and distribution stages of a media system stem from constraints and unwritten rules of the environment. Predispositions and wants of readers and audiences, reactions to perceived political preferences and idiosyncrasies, and pressures exercised by elites and organizations in the society are examples of this type of control.

(3) *Sources of operation.* Primarily an index on the media's dependence upon capital and income, this variable is at times inversely proportional to the size of a given medium or a mass media system as a whole. The five categories of *sale, advertising, public subsidy, private subsidy,* and *licensing* are described here to accommodate the variety of income sources in different systems and media under study. For example, in many systems radio and television may receive their revenues from advertising, and from licenses.

In other cases the costs are supplemented by government subsidies, To boost exports, as well as to stimulate the local production of film, governments of many countries give huge tax incentives and subsidies to film production or distribution companies. Private subsidies may come from labor unions, religious institutions, or even from abroad. For example, in Finland and several Scandinavian countries, public subsidy of the media extends even to support of political parties and their newspapers.

(4) *Disposition of income and capital.* Fiscal policies and priorities as they affect the ways in which income and capital are spent and invested are influencing factors in both the formation and distribution stages of the message. The fierce competition among the media and the high cost of technology and labor, make it almost imperative to invest in the continuing improvement of the product. The *facilities* category here refers to all the technical and personnel matters in a mass media system. In the *technical* sub-category, we can gather data on machinery and hardware, such as number of printing presses, number of transmission stations, and number of trucks and transportation facilities in a given media unit of analysis.

The *personnel* category accounts for salaries in creative work (writers, artists, editors, etc.) or *administrative* (secretaries, managers, other personnel categories), and *production* includes labor involved in printing, typography, and maintenance.

Profits and other categories, such as promotional activities of the system, are self-explanatory. The subcategories listed in the paradigm are not meant to be definitive, but to suggest the type of operationalization needed for the researcher in dealing with the disposition of income variable.

(5) *Complexity of media bureaucracy.* A bureaucracy of the mass media system can be defined as "a hierarchy of non-hereditary positions subject to the authority of the executive." In organizations in which dependence upon the government is rather extensive, a study of the bureaucracy is requisite to proper evaluation of the degree of autonomy or even reliability of newsgathering and distributing levels of the institution. Distribution of correspondents, organization of the media, and concentration of ownership in the mass media will be elements of the bureaucracy of that system.

Monopoly refers to the network or the organization as a whole, its subsidiaries, its subdivisions, its sister organizations, its organization chart and the concentration of ownership. *Change* is the capacity of the system to adapt itself to internal and external environments. Job mobility, the degree of turnover, promotional policies, the movement of information in the system itself—in short, the infrastructure of bureaucracy—are important elements to ensure efficient and timely output in the formation and distribution of messages.

(6) *Perceived purpose.* In different countries and in different political economies, a newspaper, a broadcasting station, or a mass media system as a whole may define and perceive its role and purpose in different ways. Here we are concerned with the perceived purpose of a medium or the mass media system as a larger unit in both the formation and distribution stages. The five subcategories outlined in the paradigm—*power, prestige, profit, education,* and *mobilization*—may be at times illusive and overlapping. But the overwhelming importance of one or two of these factors in the operation of the mass media system cannot be denied. In fact, the perceived purpose of production and distribution of messages varies from one medium to another, from newspaper to television, even under the same political and economic system.

(7) *Messages.* By messages we mean the *number of media* in the system under analysis and comparison. *Units per medium* in the formation stage stands for the number of newspapers, in the case of the press, and for the number of radio and television stations, in the case of broadcasting. In the distribution stage we have only the number of *exposures,* the frequency with which the same message is distributed and repeated over time. In the formation stages of the message this is indicated by *redundancy.* Here the researcher can gather data on such aspects of the media as uniformity and group reading, readership and audience data.

Within the more common orbit of communication research, let us assume that the comparativist is interested in developing a cross-cultural or cross-national index of readership and he toys with the idea of using statistics on newspaper or magazine circulation. Obviously, this would not be a valid index in countries where group readership is common or in a political system where the population is exposed to intensive pressures by the authorities or the party to subscribe to newspapers or other publications. In the case of broadcasting, in addition to group listening the matter of exposure takes further dimension by the fact that the number of radio sets will not indicate the range of exposure unless we have data on the number of FM, AM, and shortwave receivers.

(8) *Types of content.* This last category is an obvious variable. By proposing the four kinds of content—*education, entertainment, news and information,* and *advertisement*—we have not made an attempt to provide an exhaustive or definitive set of categories of content. Nor do we claim that the proposed set is acceptable cross-culturally. What may be considered entertainment in one system can be educational and news in another. Advertisement can have both educational and/or cultural and informational value. The suggestion here is that the first categories of this section of the paradigm must be broad enough to provide some guidelines for further classification and operationalization. The tendency in the past has been to start from specific categories with a definite cultural bias.

Data Basis in Comparative Media Research

It has been shown that comparative study of mass media systems, like that of any other social process, requires that the researcher concerns himself with questions concerning the adequacy and validity of the concepts he will employ, the variables he will include in his investigation, and the data and measurement he will utilize. Although these and other methodological questions are important, they are often left unanswered, and comparative mass media analysis has had its share of poorly defined terms, vague and ambiguous concepts, and culture-bound variables, which have made the task of analysis, data gathering and theory-building difficult.

The paradigm proposed here is a modest attempt to remedy this situation by taking the attention of the researcher to some of the most critical factors in comparative studies. It is realized that the type of taxonomic research schema discussed here poses some restrictions on the user and necessitates the exploration of a rather exhaustive set of categories. But the problem of theory in comparative mass communication will not be solved if we continue with the grand and general heuristic models. There is a whole host of basic technical and methodological problems involving cross-cultural research that will have to be dealt with before we are in a position to solve any interesting puzzles.

To identify certain factors in a mass media system is not, of course, to trace their influence. Nevertheless, to uncover certain processes that affect communication behavior and to explain why and how these operate under the prevailing conditions in the specific system under analysis, we must have a set of empirically workable categories that is applicable to *all* political systems.

There has been a tendency in comparative communication and national development processes to look to aggregate statistics of societies and mass media systems as a basis for comparison. But such data tell us little about the intrinsic characteristics of the mass media systems enumerated. Such statistics as the number of radio sets per thousand, average per capita income, and educational level of the population give us information about environmental variables, and their usefulness arises in the context of explanation and not of comparison. They tell us little about the mass media system itself. As we identify, by structural and functional criteria, some varieties of mass media systems, then we can use environmental statistics to test hypotheses about relationships between the mass media and the national development process.

The proposed paradigm demands different types of data some of which may be readily available, while a substantial portion may require various research techniques to obtain. It is recognized, of course, that some of the data suggested may not be easily accessible, or may not be available to the researcher at all. However, the socio-cultural, economic, political, and technological categories of variables suggested in the paradigm can be summarized under four kinds of data. The first are *aggregative data*, the kind of statistical data on ownership, number of media, budget, and economics of production and distribution. The second type are *sample survey data* giving the researcher evidence on aspects of control of the media and such factors as audience analysis and readership. The third type of data stems from *content analysis* describing the messages. Finally there are the *cultural data* which cultural anthropologists and other scholars can uncover and can be a major tool for closing the gaps in the aggregate and survey data.

Comparative methods have been adopted in a number of the human and social sciences including political science and the field of comparative politics (Merritt and Rokkan, 1966; Holt and Turner, 1970). In the field of mass communication non-ethnocentric comparative research is needed. We may not be able to eliminate all the culture-bound variables at hand but we learn how to minimize and manage them better.

*　*　*　*

REFERENCES

Almond, Gabriel A., and Bingham G. Powell. *Comparative Politics: A Development Approach* (Boston: Little, Brown, 1966).

Hachten, William. *Muffled Drums: The News Media in Africa* (Ames, Iowa: Iowa State University Press, 1971).

Holt, Robert T. and John E. Turner (eds). *The Methodology of Comparative Research* (New York: The Free Press, 1970).

Hopkins, Mark W. *Mass Media in the Soviet Union* (New York: Pegasus, 1970).

Inkeles, Alex. *Public Opinion in Soviet Russia: A Study in Mass Persuasion* (Cambridge: Harvard University Press, 1956).

Lent, John A. *The Asian Newspapers, Reluctant Revolution* (Ames, Iowa: Iowa State University Press, 1971).

Lerner, Daniel. *The Passing of Traditional Society: Modernizing the Middle East* (New York: The Free Press, 1958).

Liu, Alan P. L. *Communications and National Integration in Communist China* (Berkeley: University of California Press, 1971).

Lowenstein, Ralph L. "Measuring World Press Freedom as a Political Indicator," Unpublished Ph.D. dissertation (Columbia, Missouri: University of Missouri, 1967). "Press Freedom as a Political Indicator," *International Communication: Media, Channels, Functions*, eds. by Heinz-Dietrich Fischer and John C. Merrill (New York: Hastings House, 1970), 129–40.

Markham, James W. *Voices of the Red Giants: Communications in Russia and China* (Ames, Iowa: Iowa State University Press, 1967).

Merrill, John C. *The Imperative of Freedom* (New York: Hastings House, 1974). *The Foreign Press* (Baton Rouge: LSU Press, 1970)—with Carter Bryan and Marvin Alisky.

Merritt, Richard L. and Stein Rokkan. (eds.) *Comparing Nations: The Use of Quantitative Data in Cross-National Research* (New Haven: Yale University Press, 1966).

Mowlana, Hamid. "Communications Media in Africa," *Expanding Horizons in African Studies*, eds. by Gwendolen M. Carter and Ann Paden (Evanston, Illinois: Northwestern University Press, 1969), 259–274.
"Mass Media Systems and Communication Behavior," *The Middle East: A Handbook*, ed. by Michael Adams (London: Anthony Blond Ltd. 1971), 584–598.
"Trends in Research on International Communication in the United States," *Gazette: International Journal for Mass Communication Studies* XIX, 1973. 79–90.
"The Communication Dimension of International Studies in the United States: A Quantitative Assessment," *International Journal for Communication Research*, 1974. (Köln, Germany) 2, 1–19.

Nixon, Raymond B. "Factors Related to Freedom in National Press Systems," *Journalism Quarterly* 37, 1960. 13–28.
"Freedom in the World's Press: A Fresh Appraisal With Data," *Journalism Quarterly* 42, 1965. 3–14.

Pool, Ithiel de Sola. "The Mass Media and Politics in the Modernization Process," *Communication and Political Development* ed. by Lucian W. Pye (Princeton, New Jersey: Princeton University Press, 1963), 234–253.

Pye, Lucian W. *Communication and Political Development* (Princeton: Princeton University Press, 1963).

Russett, Bruce M. and others. *World Handbook of Political and Social Indicators* (New Haven: Yale University Press, 1965).

Schiller, Herbert I. *The Mind Managers* (Boston: Beacon Press, 1973).

Schramm, Wilbur. *Mass Media and National Development* (Stanford: Stanford University Press, 1964).

Siebert, Fred S., Theodore Peterson, and Wilbur Schramm. *Four Theories of the Press* (Urbana, Illinois: University of Illinois Press, 1956).

Williams, Raymond. *Communications* (Baltimore, Maryland: Penguin Books, Inc. 1962).

Yu, Frederick T. C. *Mass Persuasion in Communist China* (New York: Praeger, 1964).

Paul F. Lazarsfeld:

The Prognosis for International Communications Research

SOMETIME during the interval between the two World Wars, communications research became a fairly well defined and well organized sub-division of social research, with a sizeable program of teaching, research and publication. At least three origins for this development can be discerned. The first was the considerable concern with the problem of propaganda that followed in the wake of the First World War. Lasswell's study of allied propaganda during the First World War [1] was a major factor in directing this concern into systematic thinking, and the Institute for Propaganda Analysis was its first institutional result. A second mainspring lay in the cultural concern with the effect of the rapidly growing mass media. The Payne Fund studies, started in the late twenties, investigated the effect of movies on children's morals, attitudes and behavior. Subsequently, the interest of the Rockefeller Foundation in the cultural effects of radio as a mass medium led to the establishment of two more permanent institutions: the Princeton Office of Radio Research and the Institute for Educational Radio at Ohio State University.

In addition to the political and cultural roots, there was a third source of stimulation, namely the commercial. As long as newspapers were the main advertising medium not much research was needed, because circulation data provided sufficient evidence of the existence and size of an audience. But the situation changed with the coming of radio. The new medium naturally led to rather fierce inter-media competition. Radio had nothing comparable to sales figures and box office receipts by which to count its audience, so it was forced to use research to find out who listened to radio programs. Research on commercial radio, in turn, led to competitive developments, especially in the magazine field; soon commercial audience research became a dominant feature of the communications research field, recruiting the aid of academicians in most of the social sciences. [2]

During the Second World War most government agencies made extensive

---

[1] Lasswell, Harold D., *Propaganda Technique in the World War*, New York: Alfred Knopf, 1927.
[2] It is worthwhile noting that each of the three main threads in the history of communications research is connected with one major technique: in the political sphere content analysis was prevalent; in the moral and cultural spheres most of the efforts toward effects analysis originated; the bulk of commercial research was audience analysis.

▶ From: *Public Opinion Quarterly* (Princeton/New Jersey), Vol. 16/No. 4 (Winter 1952–53), pp. 482–490. Reprinted by permission of the publisher and of the author.

486 | *Paul F. Lazarsfeld*

use of domestic communications research. This led to a multiplication of established activities rather than to a search for new problems and new methods, a kind of freezing at the pre-war level. At the same time, international communications research made its beginning. The concern with shortwave propaganda, especially from the German side, stimulated most of the early research and writing.[3] Toward the end of the war, interest in international organization as a means of preserving peace became very strong and the possible role of communications research in the service of international cooperation was discussed. Linton published a volume on the role of the social sciences in a time of crisis,[4] including a section on the role of mass media in the building of an international authority. This article, however, was largely a re-statement of the standard Lasswell formula (Who says what to whom, and with what effect?), with examples from the international field substituted for those which had become customary in lectures and writings in the domestic field.

After World War II not much that was new happened in domestic communications research. The foundations evidently felt that they had done their part, and that from then on the new social science should be left to grow at its own pace. There were few developments in the commercial sphere because the coming of television had an upsetting effect on the financial structure of the whole communications industry, with the result that the problems of content and audiences remained minor. Furthermore, the commercial effectiveness of television was so obvious that it did not seem necessary to conduct the refined studies which were undertaken when radio was in its infancy. In short, in the domestic field the time seemed to have come for solidification and codification. The new research organizations which were established followed well-known patterns, and the textbooks were sent to press. But for a few new ideas, which will be mentioned later in this article, a period of near-stagnation might have developed. We should be grateful for the sudden upsurge of interest in international communications.

Opportunities of International Communications Research

There is no need to explain at this point where the interest comes from. It, however, seems important to clarify the special opportunities and responsibilities of international communications research as a major new development within the social sciences. These opportunities and responsibilities can probably best be explored within the framework of three major premises. First, it can be assumed that international communications research will have most of the talent, funds and interest which domestic communications research has commanded for the past twenty years. Consequently, since the domestic area will

[3] See Harwood Childs and John B. Whitton. *Propaganda by Short Wave*. Princeton: Princeton University Press, 1942 and Ernst Kris and Hans Speier. *German Radio Propaganda*. New York: Oxford University Press, 1944.
[4] Linton, Ralph (ed.), *The Science of Man in the World Crisis*, New York: Columbia University Press, 1945.

not have many opportunities in the years to come, the new ideas in communications research which made their appearance after the end of World War II will have to be picked up and developed in the international field if they are not to be neglected altogether. Secondly, there are certain comparative possibilities in the sphere of international communications research which will open up new and rather exciting subjects for investigation. So long as communications research struggled in one country only, to wit, in the United States, it was difficult for it to "bracket out" the pervasive features of American culture. Now, in the international field, where comparative studies between various countries will be made, these cultural variables and their role can better be discerned. Finally, there are a number of methodological problems, left relatively unsolved in the domestic field, which might be more expeditiously explored internationally.

The first premise can be somewhat reformulated along the following lines. The new groups which work in the international field are expected to redeem us from the neglects and oversights which were part of the domestic development. A few examples may serve to bring many more to the mind of the reader. Because we were partly influenced by commercial problems, there was a tendency, in domestic research, to look at audiences as a rather homogeneous mass and the emphasis, therefore, was on large-scale statistical analysis. Only in the 1940's did notable interest develop in finer differentiations. Because everyone in this country has a radio, it seems to have been assumed that except for program tastes there is not much difference between one listener and another. But listening goes on in a social context. Some people, for example, undoubtedly play the role of brokers in the field of mass media; they listen a great deal, they read a great deal and then they pass the material on to others. There are such small-scale opinion leaders in every social stratum, people who are asked by others for their advice and help. Thus, the audience to every medium is structured, with its members playing certain active or passive roles beyond the medium as it were, but also as a result of it. In the domestic field, then, it became clear that one cannot really understand the impact of mass media if one does not study how their influence is reflected and spread by the small group organizations of the whole audience—groups which may be either of a formal or informal character.

In the international field there was no such time lag in recognizing the importance of this point. In Arabic countries, for example, there are very few radios, and in entire villages there may be just one individual with a radio and only a few people who can read a newspaper. In such a situation, one cannot speak of the audience as a homogeneous group; we have to think of a kind of two-step flow in which people who get the content of the mass media directly and those who get it indirectly, through brokers of all kinds, must be distinguished. It is not enough that these different audiences and manifold processes be carefully described and studied in their implications. The problem calls for completely new statistical approaches, once we have a larger body of data.

Previously, we were content to analyze the size of the total audience. Then we became interested in differences among broad social groups, noting that rich people listened to or read different things from poor people; that the old and the young, or men and women, were different in their listening, reading or viewing habits. In a third stage, the search began for psychological characteristics. Were there, for example, differences between media habits of extroverts and introverts, between isolated women and women who had many friends, etc.? International communications research requires a further step; we must now explore the sociological characteritics of the audiences. In the small towns we may ask: What is the relationship between social position and listening habits? Inversely, how does the ownership of a radio affect a man's status in the community? How should we take into account, in a country like Lebanon, the differences among the various sects which play such a role in Lebanon's political structure? What will be the relationship between the Indian caste system and the conception and reception of mass media?

The omissions of the past, incidentally, were in no way from one side only. Other disciplines committed the same sins, and it is interesting to speculate on the potentialities of international communications research for filling gaps in other social sciences as well. A striking example comes from anthropology. In the wake of the last war there developed an interest in what is called area research. The Social Science Research Council has published a monograph [5] on efforts to study certain parts of the world through a concerted effort by all branches of the social scientists. The author of this monograph, the anthropologist Julian Steward, describes in great detail how these disciplines work together to analyze the social trends of an area with special reference to problems of the United States. In the entire 200 pages of Steward's work, however, there is not a single reference to work done by communications or opinion research specialists. The terms information, public opinion, or any of the concepts with which we have become so concerned in the last twenty years are not mentioned. While he worries gratly about the relationships among the sociologist, the psychologist, and the anthropologist, he seems to be unaware that communications research exists. However, this is not a deliberate avoidance, nor is it really as surprising as it looks at first glance. The anthropological tradition has not been primarily interested in the processes by which cultural phenomena come about. The studies which have been done on inter-cultural contact and acculturization have been mainly concerned with what one might call general morphological laws. What happens to the primitive culture, if, for example, a primitive culture and a more industrialized culture come into contact? Through what phases does it go? What changes in form does this contact bring about? The emphasis was on the changes themselves and not on the mechanisms by which they came about, while communications research, if

---

[5] Steward, Julian H., "Area Research: Theory and Practice," *Social Science Research Council,* Bulletin No. 63, 1950.

viewed as part of the study of cultural change, would focus its attention on one of the mechanisms by which cultural changes occur. In fact, one might almost say that international communications research is a part of anthropology which has so far been neglected: the study of the processes by which the various cultures influence each other.

Comparative Research Opportunities

Now to the second point, namely that the "international" nature of the new field will probably open up a great number of new intellectual opportunities. They fall roughly into two classes: first, the possibility of studying the same social phenomena in different cultural contexts; secondly, the possibility of studying topics so unique to particular countries that they are not generally available to the social scientist.

The comparative possibilities are obvious and numerous. We take it for granted, for example, that we know what news means to people. But even in this country we have found that that is not wholly true. At the time of a newspaper strike, Bernard Berelson observed what people did when they could not get a newspaper.[6] The general expectation was that they would get their news from the radio. Actually, many people read an old newspaper. This means that they were really not concerned with the content of the day's news, but rather they wanted to engage in the nerve-soothing activity of reading small bits and pieces of stories. There can be little doubt that the meaning of news will be very different from one culture to another, and that we cannot know in advance what these variations will be. Charles Glock, in an article in this issue, elaborates on how any international information service needs to have a clearer picture of what news is, what it means to people and how it fits in with their images of themselves and others.

In addition to the possibility for cross-country comparisons, there is that of selecting problems which can be studied only in certain countries and not in others. For instance, we did not learn from American research anything about the public effect of government ownership of mass media. There is no doubt that, in general, radio under government ownership in countries such as England has a greater proportion of what one might call sophisticated or educational features. But we do not know whether this is because such programs have been imposed by an enlightened elite or whether they have been, at least partly, demanded by the people. If imposed, it may well be that cultural tastes are more malleable than we think; perhaps, as a result of these more serious programs, people's tastes improve. Take, as another example, the Scandinavian countries, where there coexist two principles which we generally consider quite contradictory: stringent economic controls and complete political freedom. In

[6] Berelson, Bernard, "What 'Missing the Newspaper' Means" in *Communications Research*, 1948-1949, edited by P. F. Lazarsfeld and F. N. Stanton, New York: Harper & Brothers, 1949. See also a very systematic discussion of "The Nature of News" by Wilbur Schramm in *Mass Communications*, Urbana, Ill.: University of Illinois Press, 1949.

America, we tend to assume that economic laissez-faire and political liberty go together. So let us study the formation of opinion and attitudes in countries where the two principles have developed independently and where economic state control has apparently not interfered with political freedom.

The use of various countries as research laboratories on specific problems bears a close relationship to some of the ideas which Harold Lasswell expresses. . . . His concept of the function of social research resembles, on a social level, the functions which, on an individual level, we have come to expect from psychoanalysis. It shows people possibilities of conduct other than the ones to which they have become accustomed. The neurotic pwerson is unaware of other possibilities of conduct; the function of the therapist is that of bringing such other possibilities to the awareness of the individual. In the same sense, the social scientist could have a great therapeutic effect if he were to call attention to the possibilities for other solutions to social problems than the ones to which we have become accustomed. International communications research should be looked to for a large share of such contributions.

Methodological Contributions

Our third and final point combines, in a way, the two previous ones, repeating both in methodological terms. Domestic communications research has fallen short on certain technical problems. The international field permits us to experiment with methods more productively than was possible on the national scene. We usually do communications research by systematic interviewing, while the community research people rely much more on observation or participant observation. What we really need to know is the relation between the interviewing and observation techniques. What kinds of data are more easily obtained in one way, and for what kinds of information is the other technique in order? How should data collected by direct interviewing and by observation be related to each other? It is significant that even in these early days of international communications research, such problems have alrady entered general discussion. At a meeting of the Viking Fund in 1951, an entire day was given to the exchange of experiences between anthropologists and what was then called "survey" people. While opinions were still fairly diffuse, and often confused, there is no doubt that international communications research will necessarily lead to some clarification. There are many problems such as the relation of information obtained from informants about other people and the information obtained directly. Sociometric methods will also enter the field, since the singling out of opinion leaders and news brokers will require methods which so far have only been used in the small group studies of the sociometrists.

One especially baffling methods problem should be mentioned here. There has been a great deal of talk in social research to the effect that, in order to do really good survey work, one needs to know the background of the community, its history, its mores, and so on. Whoever has attempted to combine this informal and general background information with formal tabulations obtained from surveys, has generally encountered serious difficulties in bringing the two together. In the international field the need for the area specialist seems especially obvious and, as this volume indicates, everyone concerned seems to stress this. However, we do not know what actually is the relation between the historical and intuitive knowledge of the area specialist who has traveled in, or lived in a community, and the precise data gathered in systematic field studies? Obviously, one of the area specialist's functions is to lead us to the right problems; in other cases he will help us to interpret our data. But this is all still quite vague. The actual potential relation between modern, precise research procedures and the more traditional, broad approaches of historical and, if you please, journalistic appraisal of a country, presents a very pressing methodological problem. Any progress on this question would have very healthy repercussions on domestic social research as well.

There is another point on which the extension of communiations research to the international field should make a methodological contribution. The weakest sector of domestic communiations research has always been in the field of evaluation. The effectiveness of educational programs, of efforts to promote racial understanding, and so on, has always been open to question. In a survey by Klapper [7] on our present knowledge of the effects of mass media on cultural activities, it was shown how little our literature contributes to any real knowledge, and the reasons for this deficiency were discussed. One is that so many outside stimuli impinge upon audiences that any single stimulus can have only a very small effect. There was negative feedback here; research problems were difficult, few students had the courage to engage in such work, and as a result no progress in methods was made. In the international field, we can hope that things will be different. We can expect that in a fairly stable situation such as we might find among one or two countries of the East, the Point Four program, for example, may have noticeable and rather speedy effects. After all, the introduction of a new way of plowing, or the coming of the first movie to a village, is an event of considerable importance and the research situation a fairly clear-cut one. Studies of effects under such circumstances should therefore be less discouraging, and students in the international field may be more disposed to follow them up. As the international communications research field becomes organized, one of its tasks will be to keep in close contact with all other agencies which are new to a particular country. It should not be forgotten that the Point Four activities or Mutual Security aid are also communications activities, except that in this case communication is not by exchange of symbols

[7] Klapper, Joseph T., *The Effects of Mass Media: A Report to the Director of the Public Library Inquiry*, New York: Bureau of Applied Social Research, October, 1950. Since the war, Carl Hovland has started a systematic series of experiments on attitude change; they might lead to a real psychological foundation of communications theory, but it is too early to appraise the Yale contribution. For an interesting programmatic statement, see Carl L. Hovland, "Changes in Attitude through Communication," *Journal of Abnormal and Social Psychology*, V. 46, July, 1951, pp. 424–437.

but by exchange of activities or objects. A combination of evaluation research methods with the activities of agencies which actually introduce new habits or new institutions into more remote countries should open up a wide area for social research experimentation. Even in the United States we know that one of the most fruitful research fields is one where a new social situation (a housing project, for example) is established. It is quite likely that the near future will bring about considerable numbers of such new situations abroad. Certainly the international communications research people should not conceive their role as involving only their traditional media. It is their task to be the evaluation officers of all contacts between the new, more industrialized countries and the older ones.

Conclusions

It is on this note that our remarks should be closed. We social scientists usually consider ourselves stepchildren on the scientific scene. We feel that we have more to contribute than we are permitted to contribute at the moment. This may or may not be the case, and the future will show what we are able to produce. Still, it should not be forgotten that the relationship between practical policy and social science should be a two-way relationship. It is not only that we should contribute to the policymaking of the United States; we should expect the policymakers also to make sure that their work contributes to the social sciences. This is imperative not merely for academic reasons but because, to a considerable extent, the national and international welfare of the country, as Lasswell points out, is tied up with the techniques of social research. The policymakers should be joined by social scientists, not only because we can help them, but because the exclusion of the social sciences from the social events of the day impoverishes the social scientists who are themselves an important resource in a country. It is very much to be hoped that, in this sense, international communications research, because it is working in an exposed area, will contribute to the improvement of the relation between the social sciences and those groups and institutions who are the actors on the social scene.

Robert Lindsay:

International Communication: A Need for New Priorities

CONCEPTUALIZING the future of international communication no doubt is an intrinsically rewarding academic exercise. There are in this country alone enough conceptualists anxious for publication to assure the enterprise.

Even so, it can be argued that these proceedings have the taint of obsolescence.

Interplanetary travel is imminent, and intergalactic communication nearly so. At Jackass Flats, we have already had a successful testing of a nuclear-powered rocket. The distance from Jackass Flats to Alpha Centauri is only 4.4 light years, and from our nearest star to, say, Alpha Crucis it's another 225 light years; laser-borne motes of information will make the trip in due time, and in close to real-time. Thereafter, the problem may become interesting: astronomers analyzing the reports from OAO-II say it appears that "the universe may be several times larger than previously believed"—whatever that means.

The point is that Man soon will be trekking to the stars; why bother with pontification about international communication? Perhaps we can profit from studious examination of the near-future of world communications. Good minds are at work on this, as we have seen. Still, for some of us, there is challenge and reward in contemplating the humane implications of deep-future communications. Besides, to be free of the earth-bound research-cult is to be free of a great deal. As Dr. Herbert Friedman has expressed it: "Space development, besides meaning the opening of a new astrophysical age wherein man can unravel the mysteries of heavenly bodies free from the retrictions of the earth, has a great significance in that it widens man's vision without such restrictions."

On the other hand, how wide can man's vision become? It has been less than 200 years since Keats became, we are told, the first poet to rag the disparity between art and life. Even now, talk of a pill to enhance human intelligence is serious; we shall have one within 15 years, according to one scientist. At Yale, ESB—electrical stimulation of the brain—is under intensive investigation. Somewhere out there, in my "deep-future" of human communications, we must be prepared for the Age of Psycho-Civilization. That's what Dr. José M. R. Delgado calls it, the next step in human evolution.

▶ This is a paper presented by Dr. Lindsay, professor in the School of Journalism and Mass Communication, University of Minnesota, on April 16, 1971, at a symposium in honor of Dr. Raymond Nixon on the occasion of his retirement. Used in this book with permission of the author.

"Our conduct," he says, "is burdened by a lag of 50,000 years between emotional and technological evolution." And so it is. But we still don't know which is life, which art. Perhaps it won't matter far from now, if science will have enabled humans to make mood-inspired choices by pressing a button implanted on their wrists.

There is little science-fiction available today. Twenty years ago we read about the all-purpose brain, encased in infinitely renewable sustaining fluid. This was the human being of the far future. But that "future" is at this moment being sculpted in laboratories. Twelve years ago I was one of very few academics writing about satellite communications; today, the literature of the field is weighed by the long-ton. Yesterday, unisex was silly stuff; it still is, perhaps, despite being dignified by mention in *Encounter* articles and selling well as Pop-cult fashion and song. It's defined in standard dictionaries, too, which for contemporary American educationists is tantamount to sanctification.

Let me propose a candidate for admission to the next revised editions of the dictionaries: "uniculture." This is the residuum found when ideology has been terminated with extreme prejudice. It suggests an equation: international communication plus anticulture equals uniculture. (Or maybe it should be "unicommunication".) We shall have it, when the time comes that intercultural communication is so much like what communication scholars declare it ought to be like that communication scholars will no longer be necessary. Something like this does seem to be the ultimate goal envisioned by many of my more didactic colleagues in this academic meadow.

Much of the research in mass communication, as in international mass communication, distills out to reports on how or why communications output and input seems under various circumstances to be the same or not the same compared with communication under other, not necessarily comparable, circumstances. In many of these reports, or anyway the comprehensible ones, I sense an impression that the investigators harbor a deep-seated wish for neatly-configured, quantifiable congruency in all human communication. I detect strong trace elements of this cultural death wish increasingly, in fact, in the literature and conferential discourse of communication scholars everywhere in the world. For my taste, this is repellent. (I find unisex repellent, too, and for approximately the same reasons, although my age and this climate are further factors.)

The eminent Canadian communicator, Alphonse Ouimet, has urged that we must work now "so that we may hope that some day it will be possible for us to let go of our technological tail." He was speaking of the communications revolution, or explosion, as the trendy expression has it. We have all spoken of this awesome happenstance of our lifetime, and understandably, since we know it so well, like an earthquake experienced.

Yet who in our schools of journalism and mass communication is teaching and learning about the imminent *implosion* of communication?

People-to-people communication and research thereon is sometimes interesting, even important. It can also be described as quaint. Brain-to-brain communication and research thereon is at least as significant for the future of human communication. (Dr. Delgado and his associates have already linked an animal's brain and a computer in a message-feedback loop.) One need not travel down so lonely a road as that followed by Chomsky, of course, to find oneself arguing—let alone "teaching"—that it's what humans are *capable* of saying, as opposed to what they in fact say, that deserves our attention. Yet Cartesian innate-idea theory needn't be all that unfamiliar to a mass communication student, either.

Nor should we, in seeking to conceptualize the future of international communication, fail to pay close attention to such other (literally) inner-directed research as that on the autonomic nervous apparatus as communication system. Instrumental training is used at the Baltimore Gerontology Research Center to treat heartbeat disorders. That is, visceral responses can, in effect, be harnessed, made voluntary. Related research has demonstrated that human beings can control their blood-pressure and heart-rates through instrumental learning. Such findings would indeed seem to "have profound significance for theories of learning and the biological basis of learning," as suggested in a recent report on this research. And, it could be, for the proper study and understanding of intercultural communication, as well.

Communication, in fact, might conquer *everything* you and I internalize as being of highest priority for vanquishment. Death, for instance. In old age, the human body dodders; equilibrium is lost. As the British zoologist, Alex Comfort, puts it, it's "the failure of information, the inability to maintain the living state against the laws of entropy." If "interference" (the familiar "noise in the channels") is responsible for bodily breakdown—"a loss of coded information"—this could be reduced, perhaps eliminated, and the aging process controlled. There would seem to be opportunity here for cross-disciplinary team research involving doctors-medical and -philosophical.

What I am postulating is a prescription to recast our concept of international communication, *per se.* This is neither to say nor to imply that we ought substantially to reduce our concern with demographics and descriptive inventorying as preliminaries to the full-flight study of global mass communication. As a matter of unfortunate fact, we remain grossly handicapped in our endeavor by the lamentable paucity of data and statitical verities in most of the world. We are obliged to retain, I believe, a measure of the comparative and cross-cultural approach to the study of internalitional communication and its systems. And surely there is no question about the crucial importance to human progress of the attention we are lavishing on communication in programs of development.

I do find it easy to suggest, however, that we could with benefit dispense with much of the overripe research generously, if in the main automatically, funded and endlessly replicated among the tuber farmers of the Third World and the college sophomores of America. The time, money and talent expended on this feckless game of academic jackstraws are desperately needed out among the cow pies and rice paddies.

This plea for a fresh formulation of our conceptual approach to international communication, especially the study thereof, is founded on the premise that we ought first to capitalize upon the best of what our mentors with foresight established in our behalf. But building therefrom we ought, I should think, be willing to move forward as well as laterally in freeing up the parameters of our scholarship and service.

I propose, therefore, a reordering of concerns and priorities in this field, and for two reasons, essentially. The first is that it is torch-passing time. This occasion is a glittering benchmark for all scholars, throughout the world, professionally involved in international communication studies. And of course several of us here stand in person and symbolically in tribute to the trail-blazing enterprise of Raymond B. Nixon in exploring and mapping the very field of international communication studies. He showed us the way, and shaped our carers, and enriched beyond measure the first and most difficult efforts to establish this field in universities and multi-national organizations throughout the world. This country pioneered the concept of sytematic, university-level study and research in journalism; Raymond B. Nixon ensured that international mass communication should be an integral part of that concept. He advocated and practiced responsiveness ad adaptability to change and innovation, in communications studies as in international communication itself. He lived and taught and inculcated an attitude indispensable to detached, objectively critical scholarship. And I know with gratitude that this attitude includes approval of the requirement that improvement of international communication—as discipline and as process—can be realized only through determination by the succeeding waves of scholars to carry on in accordance with their own insights and instincts.

My second suggested reason for a recasting of our conceptualization of this field is that we are now well into a critical era of technological change which for human communication, alone, contains challenges, and hazards, as urgent as they are formidable. I am concerned that we are, if not inadequately prepared, psychologially unprepared for the planetary communiations situation immediately ahead.

I believe, therefore, that it might be profitable if we could accept something like the following agenda for restructuring our concerns and priorities in international communication.

1. *Disestablish irrelevant concepts, research and conventional wisdom.*

Not much, or not enough, of what for the past quarter-century has been sanctified through publication as mass communication research seems to me especially useful for preparing the planet for the communications conditions likely to obtain in the near, far and deep future. Tidy constructs and schematic models laced with impenetrable ant-tracks about ephemeral audience-samples in East Lansing or university classrooms in the 1950s no doubt have much statistical significance, for the media and their audiences in those American sites and in those times. In context, these studies and hypotheses and published doodlings served, conceivably, worthwhile purposes. Now, however, it would seem prudent to re-examine our *prima facie* acceptance of these laborious efforts to produce communications research presumed requisite for contemporary mass communications conditions. Effects studies, still glaringly imperfect, are in any case marginally relevant to the wired city, whose Year One this is. I know of no research in progress or considered in schools of mass communication anywhere on the role of the professional communicator and his present media in the era of the wired brain, whose Year One is in the near-future. The dominant demographic characteristic of most developing countries is rapidly-increasing urbanization; American communications research and aid programs continue to emphasize rural and agricultural concerns. It is time, too, to question the methods as well as the concepts of various of the international agencies more or less dedicated to improved international communication. No few of these bodies are the object of scorn in countries where they purport to operate, and recently have been scored in dispassionate studies commissioned by their parent organizations. It seems to me we should at the least consider jettisoning such superfluous or obsolescent verities as typified by those cited here.

2. *Embrace a futurological attitude toward international mass communication.*

In rural India two years ago, a village elder smashed a television receiving set intended for communal use. He was and will remain unprepared for the visible manifestations of communications innovation. But Daniel Lerner, in India last year to tout "Sesame Street" before educators and broadcasters, found viewers of village square television sets turned on by old movies, turned off by government-supplied educational programs. Next year, or the one following, India will become the first nation to utilize a direct broadcast satellite for non-military purposes. There is the acute problem of diverse languages and dialects, of course, but the Japan Broadcasting Corporation is experimenting with a scale model of twin satellites to enable simultaneous telecasts in different languages. For the color blind, an American has invented a "translator" device to obviate their handicap in viewing color television. Laserfax, utilizing both a laser beam and holograms, could render obsolete present printing processes; it was patented three years ago. When man lands on Mars, live television coverage on Earth will be provided by laser. About all of this, as for numerous other examples one could parade, there need be said only that it is by no means "futurological"—it is in fact contemporary or within contemporary capabilities. But consider that the transistor was given to us less than 25 years ago; the laser, a decade ago. The student who wrote in an examination bluebook for me that "mouth-to-mouth communication is the most important form of communication" no doubt knew whereof he spoke. As for the future, who knows?

It is at least possible that most, perhaps all, of what we conceive as the future (however defined) of international communication in our present planning and thinking is inept because conventional. Our minimal obligation in Academe, I suggest, is to infuse our conceptualizing with an appreciation of the need to think "futurologically," to be receptive to ideas, however esoteric or novel, having implications, however remote, for communication on and beyond the planet we know best.

3. *Acknowledge the future of planetary communication, as in the past and present, as imperfect, and desirably so.*

A headline over an article in IPI *Report* several years ago, a quotation from a speech by Edward Barrett, read, "Almost anything is going to be technically feasible." The qualifying hedge, "almost," suggests Ed is a conservative in these matters. *Technically,* I am convinced, there neither are nor can be communication impossibilities. What bothers me is a gnawing conviction that neither technological innovation nor humane planning is likely to ameliorate the human propensity for imperfectibility. Communication has never healed a broken heart, nor opened a closed mind. And never will, this humanist assumes. We must strive to be *au courant* in our ruminating about the future of communication, of course. I agree with Daniel Bell, chairman of the Commission on the Year 2000, when he says in this general regard that a hallmark "of modernity is the awareness of change and the struggling effort to control the direction and pace of change." This is utterly significant for communication specialists, who certainly will play major roles in the configuration as well as the direction of future planetary society. I invoke here James W. Carey and John J. Quirk, in their extraordinarily illuminating articles in *The American Scholar:*

> The first task is to demythologize the rhetoric of the electronic sublime. Electronics is neither the arrival of apocalypse nor the dispensation of grace. Technology is technology; it is a means for communication and transportation over space, and nothing more. As we demythologize, we might also begin to dismantle the fetishes of communication for the sake of communication, and decentralization and participation without reference to content or context.

The "future" of our thematic title has for me, then, a somewhat different meaning than it may for my colleagues. I am interested to consider the quantifiable dimensions and the projective scope of international mass communication in the next two or three decades, but not deeply so. I doubt that there will be many striking changes in the quality and purposes of communication flowing through the world communications grid in the next 10 or 20 years.

I do foresee, however, an acceleration, somewhat slow in its initial stages, in the rates at which purposive communication in the international channels will achieve significant results. I would suppose, for example, that introduction of the new devices—satellites, cassettes, electronic video recorders, and others—into the world markets will in fairly short order reverse the current upward trend in illiteracy rates. At the same time, incidentally, proliferation of these devices and their refinements seem destined to have unexpectedly forceful impact on vulnerable sectors of the global social system. Facsimile, for one: What is to become of the newspaper as we know it and still are prone to laud for its intrinsic indispensability? Or of the journalist, who likewise may be obsolescent, as well. And there is the Really Big Question certain to arise before the end of this century: What is to be done about the advent of the laser as replacement for virtually all the capital items and carrier channels of the present world telecommunications systems?

And by the middle of the 21st Century, surely, there will be need of international communication specialists equal to the task of resolving problems which today can be predicted only as intuitive insights. Mine calls for a planet and a time of exceedingly limited social interaction of the sort human society so far has assumed normal and necessary. The wired city of the late 20th Century will lead to a planetary communications grid of symbiotically linked humans, computers and ancillary communications machines, with laser providing real-time communication with orbiting habitations, communities, and nuclear-powered, interplanetary commercial and pleasure craft. Humans, on or far from Earth, likely will lead largely sequestered lives, affiliating only briefly and sporadically with small, fluid social units. Kinship and friendship bonds will be on the way toward becoming vestigial until, as Cooley decided long ago, the only "cement" holding all of us together is communication.

But *what* "communication"?

BIBLIOGRAPHY OF BIBLIOGRAPHIES

T HIS BOOK could only touch on a few of the principal aspects of the very broad area generally understood as "international and intercultural communication." A great many fascinating subjects relative to this very broad area are missing; many of them are included in the brief "Related Readings" list at the end of each introduction for the nine sections of this volume.

The editors feel, however, that they should give the reader further help in ascertaining the extremely wide scope of literature in the field of international and intercultural communication. This could be done by presenting an extensive bibliography here. Instead, the editors have decided to provide the reader with a "bibliography of bibliographies" in this field. Some of the bibliographies which follow may not seem to have a supranational appeal if one looks only at the titles. But most bibliographies listed are concerned with international problems, also. Many bibliographic aids are in English, but several are from other language countries.

In the broad field of the different communication sciences there does not as yet exist an overview of bibliographic aids—a kind of Master Bibliography of Bibliographies—and although the editors realize that all the possible titles are not listed here, they feel that the following list is at least a first step toward a full-scale bibliography of bibliographies.

AAPOR (ed.) *Public Opinion Quarterly. Cumulative Index to Volumes 1–31, 1937–1967.* New York: Columbia University Press, 1970.

Adkins, Gale R. *Books on Radio—Television—Film. A Collection of Recommendations.* Lawrence/Kansas: The University of Kansas, 1962.

Advertising Research Foundation. *A Bibliography of Theory and Research Techniques in the Field of Human Motivations.* New York: Advertising Research Foundation, 1956.

AEJ (ed.). *Journalism Abstracts,* Chapel Hill: Association for Education in Journalism, 1963 ff. (annually).

Alisky, Marvin. *Latin American Journalism Bibliography.* Mexico, D.F.: Fondo de Publicidad Interamericana, 1958.

Barcus, Francis E. "A Bibliography of Studies of Radio and Television Program Content, 1928–1958," *Journal of Broadcasting,* Vol. IV/No. 4 (Fall 1960), pp. 355–369.

Barcus, Francis Earle. *Communications Content: Analysis of the Research, 1900–1958. A Content Analysis of Content Analysis.* Urbana/Illinois: Graduate College of the University of Illinois, 1960 (unpublished).

Barrow, Lionel C./Westley, Bruce *Television Effects: A Summary of Literature and Proposed General Theory.* Madison/Wisconsin: University of Wisconsin, 1958.

BBC (ed.). *British Broadcasting—A Bibliography.* London: British Broadcasting Corporation, 1954, revised ed. 1958.

Beall Hamill, Patricia. *Radio and Television. A Selected Bibliography.* Washington, D.C.: Government Printing Office, 1960.

Behn, Hans Ulrich. *Presse—Rundfunk—Fernsehen in Asien und Afrika. Eine Bibliographie in- und ausländischer Fachliteratur.* Bonn: Forschungsinstitut der Friedrich-Ebert-Stiftung, 1965.

Berkmann, Dave. "Undergraduate Broadcasting Curricula: An Annotated Bibliography," *Journal of Broadcasting*, Vol. VI/No. 3 (Summer 1962), pp. 269–278.

Beuick, Marshall. *Bibliography of Public Relations.* New York: M. Beuick, 1947.

Beuick, Marshall. *Bibliography of Radio Broadcasting.* New York: M. Beuick, 1947.

Bird, Charles. "Suggestion and Suggestibility: A Bibliography," *Psychological Bulletin*, 36:264–83, April 1939.

Bishop, R. L., *Public Relations: A Comprehensive Bibliography*, 1974 (3rd. ed.). Ann Arbor: U. of Michigan Press.

Blaser, Fritz. *Bibliographie der Schweizer Presse / Bibliographie de la Presse Suisse*, 2 Vols., Basel: Birkhäuser Verlag, 1956–1958.

Blum, Eleanor. *Basic Books in the Mass Media. An annotated, selected Booklist covering General Communications, Book Publishing, Broadcasting, Film, Magazines, Newspapers, Advertising, Indexes, and Scholarly and Professional Periodicals.* Urbana—Chicago—London: University of Illinois Press, 1972.

Bömer, Karl. *Internationale Bibliographie des Zeitungswesens.* Leipzig: Otto Harrassowitz, 1932.

Bolle de Bal, Françoise et al. *Bibliographie Belge des ouvrages et articles sur les Techniques de Diffusion Collective (presse, cinéma, radio, télévision), 1944–1961*, 3 Vols. Brussels: Centre National d'Etudes des Techniques de Diffusion Collective, 1965–1967 (mimeographed).

Bouman, Jan C. *Bibliography on Filmology—As Related to the Social Sciences.* Paris: UNESCO, 1954.

Broderick, Gertrude G. *Radio and Television Bibliography.* Washington: Government Printing Office, 1949.

Brown, D. "Radio and Television: An annotated Bibliography," *Journalism Quarterly*, Vol. 34/1957, pp. 378–386.

Bucharchiv München (ed.). *Bibliographie des gesamten Rechts der Presse, des Buchhandels, des Rundfunks und des Fernsehens.* Berlin—Neuwied: Herman Luchterhand Verlag, 1957.

Cannon, Carl L. *Journalism: A Bibliography.* New York: New York Public Library, 1924.

CBS (ed.). *Radio and Television Bibliography*, 4th. ed. New York: Columbia Broadcasting System Reference Library, 1941.

Clyde, Robert W./Jaberg, Eugene C.. *The Use of Mass Media in Religiously Motivated Adult Education. A Review of the Literature.* Syracuse, N.Y.: University College, Syracuse University, 1971.

Cole, Barry G. and Al Paul Klose. "A Selected Bibliography on the History of Broadcasting," in: *Journal of Broadcasting*, Vol. VIII/No. 3 (Summer 1963), pp. 247–268.

Committee for National Morale. *German Psychological Warfare: A Critical, Annotated and Comprehensive Survey and Bibliography.* New York: 1941.

Cooney, Stuart. "Analysis of Broadcast Literature—The Quarterly Journal of Speech," *Journal of Broadcasting,* Vol. 1/No. 1 (Winter 1957), pp. 91–92.

Cooper, Isabella M. *Bibliography of Education Broadcasting.* Chicago: University of Chicago Press, 1942.

Cutlip, Scott M. *A Public Relations Bibliography, and Reference and Film Guides.* Madison/Wisc.: University of Wisconsin Press, 1957.

——— *A Public Relations Bibliography,* 2nd ed., Madison—Milwaukee: The University of Wisconsin Press, 1965.

Danielson, Wayne A. and G. C. Wilhoit Jr. *A Computerized Bibliography of Mass Communication Research.* New York: Magazine Publishers Association, 1967.

Davis, E. E. *Attitude Change. A Review and Bibliography of Selected Research,* Paris: UNESCO, 1964.

Denney, Reul/Meyersohn, M. L. "A Preliminary Bibliography on Leisure," *American Journal of Sociology,* Vol. 62/1957, pp. 602–615.

Dick, Donald. "Religious Broadcasting 1920–1965. A Bibliography," *Journal of Broadcasting,* Vol. IX/No. 3 (Summer 1965), pp. 249–279.

Dill, Richard. *Bildung und Fernsehen. Eine einführende Bibliographie.* Munich: Bayerischer Rundfunk, 1961 (mimeographed).

Disch, Wolfgang K. A. *Bibliographie zur Marktforschung / Bibliography on Marketing Research.* Hamburg: Hamburgisches Welt-Wirtschafts-Archiv, 1964.

Draper, Benjamin. *Television—Terminology—Bibliography.* San Francisco: California Academy of Sciences, 1953.

Drewry, J. "Magazine Journalism: a Selected Bibliography," *Journalism Quarterly,* Vol. 25/1948, pp. 260–277.

Eapen, K. E. *Annotated Bibliography on the Mass Media of India.* New York: Foreign Area Materials Center, State University of New York, 1967.

EBU. *Selected Bibliography:* Part 1: Broadcasting in education, Part 2: Broadcasting in Society, Geneva: European Broadcasting Union, 1967 ff.

Fearing, F./Rogge, G. "A Selected and Annotated Bibliography in Communications Research," *Quarterly of Film, Radio and Television,* Vol. 6/1952, pp. 283 ff.

Fielding, Raymond. "Broadcast Literature in Motion Picture Periodicals: A Bibliography," *Journal of Broadcasting,* Vol. III/No. 2 (Spring 1959), pp. 172–192.

Filmbuchhandlung Hans Rohr. *Filmlagerkatalog 1966/67,* Zürich: 1966, *Filmlagerkatalog 1967/68,* Zürich: 1967, *Filmlagerkatalog 1968/69,* Zürich: Verlag Hans Rohr, 1968.

Fischer, Erika J./Fischer, Heinz-Dietrich. *50 Years of Communication Research. A Bibliography of M.A. theses and Ph.D. dissertations from the School of Journalism, University of Missouri, Columbia, 1921–1971.* Columbia, Mo.: School of Journalism, 1973.

Fischer, Heinz-Dietrich. "Bibliographie zur Publizistik im Ersten Weltkrieg," in: Heinz-Dietrich Fischer (ed.). *Pressekonzentration und Zensurpraxis im Ersten Weltkrieg,* Berlin: Verlag Volker Spiess, 1973, pp. 276–301.

Franzmeyer, Fr(itz). *Presse-Dissertationen an deutschen Hochschulen, 1885–1938.* Leipzig: Verlag des Börsenvereins der Deutschen Buchhändler, 1940, 1. Suppl. 1939 o.J. (1941).

Geiger, Kent. *National Development: An Annotated, Evaluated Bibliography of the*

Most Important Articles on National Development. Metuchen, New Jersey: Scarecrow Press, 1969.

Gilburt, S. G. "Selected Bibliography on Radio and Television for Teachers," *English Journal*, Vol. XXXVIII/May 1949, pp. 295–297.

Golter, Bob J. *Bibliography of Theses and Dissertations Relating to Audio-Visuals and Broadcasting.* Nashville/Tenn.: Methodist Publishing House, 1958.

Graham, Robert X. *A Bibliography in the History and Background of Journalism*, Pittsburgh: University of Pittsburgh, 1940.

Greb, Gordon. "Analysis of Broadcast Literature—The Journalism Quarterly 1948–1958," *Journal of Broadcasting*, Vol. III/No. 3 (Summer 1959), pp. 244–251.

GWA (ed.). *Aus dem Schrifttum über Werbung.* Frankfurt a.M. (Germany): Gesellschaft der Werbeagenturen, 1963, 1965.

Haacke, Wilmont. "Public-relations-Bibliographie," in: *Jahrbuch der Absatz-und Verbrauchsforschung* (Kallmünz/Germany), Vol. 3/No. 2 (1957), pp. 149–153.

Hamill, Patricia Beall. *Radio and Television—A Selected Bibliography.* Washington/D.C.: Government Printing Office, 1960.

Hansen, Donald A., and Parsons, J. Herschel. *Mass Communication, A Research Bibliography.* Santa Barbara/Calif.: The Glendessary Press, 1968.

Harris, Dale B. *Children and Television: An annotated Bibliography Assembled for the National Association of Educational Broadcasters.* Urba na/Illinois: National Association of Educational Broadcasters, 1959.

Harwood, Kenneth. *A World Bibliography of Selected Periodicals on Broadcasting*, Los Angeles: University of Southern California, 1961.

Haverfield, Robert W. *100 Books on Advertising.* 9th ed., Columbia/Mo.: University of Missouri, School of Journalism, 1969.

Heath, Harry/Wolfson, Joel. "Analysis of Broadcast Literature: Broadcast Journalism in 'Education on the Air' 1930–1953," *Journal of Broadcasting*, Vol. VI/No. 4 (Fall 1962), pp. 363–368.

Heinrich, Karl. *Film and Youth—Film und Jugend—Le film et le jeunesse. Deutsche und ausländische Bibliographie.* Frankfurt/Main: Hochschule für Internationale Pädagogische Forschung, 1959.

Herzog zu Mecklenburg, Carl Gregor. *International Jazz Bibliography—Jazz Books from 1919 to 1968.* Baden-Baden: Librairie Heitz, 1968.

Hesse, Marlies. *Literatur und Fernsehen. Eine Bibliographie.* Marl—Dortmund (Germany): Wulff, 1963.

Husain, Asad. *Bibliography of a Century of Indian Journalism 1858–1958.* Minneapolis/Minnesota: University of Minneapolis, School of Journalism, 1959.

Hyde, Stuart W. "Graduate Theses and Dissertations on Broadcasting: A Topical Index," *Journal of Broadcasting*, Vol. II/No. 1 (Winter 1957/58), pp. 55–90.

Institut für Publizistik der Freien Universität Berlin. *prd—Publizistikwissenschaftlicher Referate-Dienst.* Köln und Opladen: Westdeutscher Verlag, 1966–1967; Munich: Verlag Dokumentation, 1968 ff. (quarterly).

Institut für Publizistik der Universität Münster (ed.). *Handbuch der Weltpresse*, 2 Vols., Cologne—Opladen: Westdeutscher Verlag, 1970.

Institut für Zeitungsforschung der Stadt Dormund. "Dokumentation für Presse, Rundfunk und Film," in: *Zeitungs-Verlag und Zeitschriften-Verlag* (Bad Godesberg), Vol. 57/1960 ff. (quarterly Supplement).

Internationales Zentralinstitut für das Jugend—und Bildungsfernsehen (ed.). *Bibliographie Fernsehen und Jugend/Television and Youth/Télévision et Jeunesse*. Munich: Internationales Zentralinstitut für das Jugend—und Bildungsfernsehen, 1969.

Internationales Zentralinstitut für das Jugend-und Bildungsfernsehen (ed.). *Bibliographie Schulfernsehen/Instructional Television/Télévision Scolaire*. Munich: Internationales Zentralinstitut für das Jugend-und Bildungsfernsehen, 1968.

Jaryc, Marc. "Studies of 1935–42 on the History of the Periodical Press: Bibliographical Article," *Journal of Modern History*, 15:127–41, 1943.

Kempkes, Wolfgang. *International Bibliography of Comics Literature*. Detroit—Munich: Gale Research Company/Verlag Dokumentation, 1971.

Knödler-Bunte, Eberhard et. al. *Bibliographie der Massenkommunikation*. Frankfurt—Ulm (Germany): Deutsches Seminar an der Universität Frankfurt/Institut für Filmgestaltung an der Hochschule für Gestaltung, 1970 (mimeographed).

Knower, Franklin H. "Bibliography of Communications Dissertations in American Schools of Theology," *Speech Monographs*, Vol. 30/No. 2 (June 1963), pp. 108–136.

Knower, Franklin H. "Graduate Theses and Dissertations on Broadcasting (1956–1958), (1959–1960), (1961–1962)," *Journal of Broadcasting*, Vol. IV/No. 1 (Winter 1959/60), pp. 77–87; Vol. V/No. 4 (Fall 1961), pp. 355–370; Vol. VII/No. 3 (Summer 1963), pp. 269–282.

Koszyk, Kurt/Eisfeld, Gerhard. *Die Presse der deutschen Sozialdemokratie. Eine Bibliographie*, Hannover: Verlag für Literatur und Zeitgeschehen, 1966.

Koszyk, Kurt/Pruys, Karl H. "Bibliographie zur Publizistik," in: Kurt Koszyk/Karl H. Pruys (eds.): *Wörterbuch zur Publizistik*. Munich—Berlin: Verlag Dokumentation, 1970, pp. 435–539.

Lasswell, Harold D./Casey, Ralph D. and Smith, Bruce L. *Propaganda and Promotional Activities. An Annotated Bibliography*. Minneapolis/Minn.: The University of Minnesota Press 1935, reprinted Chicago—London: The University of Chicago Press, 1969.

Lent, John A. *Asian Mass Communications: A Comprehensive Bibliography*. Philadelphia: Temple Univ. School of Communications and Theater, 1975.

Library of Congress, *Freedom of Information. A Selective Report on Recent Writings*. Washington, D.C.: Library of Congress, 1949.

Lobscheid, Dieter. *Das Fernsehen unter soziologischem, psychologischem und pädagogischem Aspekt. Eine Zusammenstellung der deutschsprachigen Literatur seit 1958*. Cologne: 1963.

Lowenthal, Rudolf. "Western Literature on Chinese Journalism: A Bibliography," *Nankai Social and Economic Quarterly*, 9:1007–66, 1937.

Manz, H(ans) P(eter). *Internationale Filmbibliographie 1952–1962*. Zürich: Verlag Hans Rohr, 1963. Supplement I (1963–1964). Zürich: Verlag Hans Rohr, 1964. Supplement II (1965), Zürich: Verlag Hans Rohr, 1965.

McCoy, Ralph E. *Freedom of the Press: An Annotated Bibliography*. Carbondale: Southern Illinois University Press, 1968.

Meyersohn, Rolf. *Television Research: An Annotated Bibliography*. New York: Columbia University, Bureau of Applied Social Research, 1954.

Mitry, Jean. *Bibliographie Internationale du Cinema et de la Télévision*. Vols., Paris: Institut des Hautes Etudes Cinematographiques, 1966 ff.

Moldstad, John. "Doctoral Dissertations in Audio-Visual Education," *Audio-Visual Communication Review*, Vol. IV/No. 4, pp. 291–333; Vol. VI/No. 1, pp. 33–48; Vol. VII/No. 2, pp. 142–153; Vol. IX/No. 4, pp. 220–229.

Mowlana, Hamid. *International Communication: A Selected Bibliography*. Dubuque/Iowa: Kendall/Hunt Publishing Company, 1971.

Myers, Lawrence, Jr. "Doctoral Dissertations in Radio and Television." *Journal of Broadcasting*, Vol. 1/No. 4 (Fall 1952), pp. 377–383.

Nafziger, Ralph O. *Foreign News Sources and the Foreign Press. A Bibliography*. Minneapolis/Minnesota: Burgess Publishing Co., 1937.

———. *International News and the Press. Communications, Organization of News-Gathering, International Affairs and the Foreign Press. An Annotated Bibliography*. New York: The H. W. Wilson Company, 1940.

National Education Association (ed.). *Short Bibliography on New Media and Instructional Technology*. Washington, D.C.: National Education Association, Department of Audio-Visual Instruction, 1961.

Nelson, R.U./Rubsamen, W. H. "Bibliography on Music in Film and Radio." *Hinrichsen's Musical Yearbook* 1949–50, pp. 318–330.

Nielander, William A. *A Selected and Annotated Bibliography of Public Relations*. Austin: Bureau of Business Research, University of Texas, 1956.

Niemi, John A./Anderson, Darrell V. *Television: A variable Channel for Educating Adults in Culturally different Poverty Groups? A Literature Review*, Syracuse, N.Y.: Clearinghouse on Adult Education, 1971.

Nixon, Raymond B. (ed.). *Journalism Quarterly*. Cumulative Index Volumes 1–40, 1924–1963. Minneapolis/Minn.: The Association for Education in Journalism, 1964.

NORDICOM. *Bibliography of Works on Mass Communication Published by Scandinavian Scholars in English*. Tampere/Finland: Nordic Documentation Center for Mass Communication Research, 1975.

Obunbi, Adebayo. *A Select Bibliography on Mass Communication in Africa*. East Lansing: Mich. State Univ. Dept. of Radio & Television, 1972.

Paulu, Burton. *A Radio and Television Bibliography*. Urbana/Illinois: National Association of Educational Broadcasters, 1952.

Peet, Hubert W. *A Bibliography of Journalism; a Guide to the books about the Press and the Pressmen*. London: Sells Ltd., 1915.

Peterson, Wilbur. *Organizations, Publications and Directories in the Mass Media of Communications*. Iowa City/Iowa: School of Journalism, The University of Iowa, 3rd. ed., 1965.

Pötter, Günter. Bibliographie zur Wissenschaft von der Publizistik, in: Wilmont Haacke; *Publizistik: Elemente und Probleme*. Essen: Stamm-Verlag, 1962, pp. 289–369.

Pool, Ithiel de Sola et al. (eds.). *Handbook of Communication*. Chicago: Rand McNally Publishing Company, 1973.

Power, Hilton M. *Mass Media in Public Affairs Adult Education: A Review of the Literature*. Syracuse, N.Y.: Clearinghouse on Adult Education, 1970.

Price, Warren C. *The Literature of Journalism. An Annotated Bibliography*. Minneapolis/Minnesota: The University of Minnesota Press, 1959.

Price, Warren C./Pickett, Calder M. *An Annotated Journalism Bibliography 1958–1968*. Minneapolis/Minnesota: University of Minnesota Press, 1970.

Proehl, Friedrich-Karl. *Verzeichnis ausgewählter Hochschulschriften, 1945–1966.* Hamburg: Stiftung Wissenschaft und Presse, 1967.

Reichs-Rundfunk-Gesellschaft (ed.). *Deutsches Rundfunk-Schrifttum.* Berlin RRG 1930–1935. Continued from May 1936 as supplement of *Archiv für Funkrecht,* and from 1938–1943 as appendix of *Rundfunk-Archiv.*

Rivers, William L. *Finding Facts: A Research Manual for Journalists.* New York: Magazine Publishers Association, Inc., 1966.

Rogers, E. M. *Bibliography of Research on the Diffusion of Innovation.* East Lansing/ Michigan: Michigan State University, Department of Communication, 1964.

Rogers, Everett M. *Bibliography on the Diffusion of Innovations.* July 1967, 144 pp,; and *Supplement to the Bibliography on the Diffusion of Innovations.* September 1968, 36 pp. E. Lansing, Michigan: Michigan State University.

Rose, Oscar. *Radio Broadcasting and Television: An Annotated Bibliography.* New York: H. W. Wilson Co., 1947.

Ross, Albion and Heenan, Yvonne. *English-Language Bibliography on Foreign Press and Comparative Journalism.* Milwaukee/Wisconsin: Marquette University, Center for the Study of the American Press, 1966.

Saunders, James G. "Analysis of Broadcasting Literature: Periodical Publications in Psychology 1950–1960. An annotated Bibliography," *Journal of Broadcasting,* Vol. VI/No. 1 (Winter 1961–62), pp. 75–91.

Saur, Karl Otto jr. *Internationale Bibliographie der Fachzeitschriften/World Guide to Periodicals,* 3 Vols., 5th ed., Munich: Verlag Dokumentation, 1967.

Schacht, John H. *A Bibliography for the Study of Magazines,* 2nd ed. Urbana/Illinois: University of Illinois, College of Communications, 1968.

Schramm, Wilbur. *The effects of Television on children and adolescents. An annotated bibliography with an introductory overview on research results.* Paris: UNESCO, 1964.

Schroeder, Theodore. *The Free Speech Bibliography.* New York—London: The H. W. Wilson Company, 1922.

Smith, Bruce Lannes, Lasswell, Harold D., and Casey, Ralph D. *Propaganda, Communication, and Public Opinion. A Comprehensive Reference Guide.* Princeton/N.J.: Princeton University Press, 1946.

Smith, Bruce Lannes, and Smith, Chitra M. *International Communication and Political Opinion. A Guide to the Literature.* Princeton/N.J.: Princeton University Press, 1956.

Sparks, Kenneth R. *A Bibliography of Doctoral Dissertations in Television and Radio.* Syracuse/New York: Newhouse Communications Center, 3. ed., 1971.

Spiess, Volker. *Bibliographie zu Rundfunk und Fernsehen,* Hamburg: Verlag Hans-Bredow-Institut, 1966.

———. *Verzeichnis deutschsprachiger Hochschulschriften zur Publizistik, 1885–1967.* Berlin-München: Verlag Volker Spiess and Verlag Dokumentation, 1969.

Sternberg, Beno/Sullerot, Evelyne. *Aspects Sociaux de la Radio et de la Télévision. Revue des Recherches 1950–1964.* Paris-La Haye: Mouton & Co., 1966.

Swindler, William F. *Bibliography of Law on Journalism.* New York: Columbia University Press, 1947.

Taft, William H. *200 Books on American Journalism.* Columbia/Missouri: University of Missouri, School of Journalism, 1969.

Topuz, Hifzi. "Selected Bibliography of News Agencies," in: '*Bulletin de l'A.I.E.R.J.*' (Prague), Vol. 1966/No. 5–6, pp. 105–111.

Traub, Hans/Lavies, Hans-Wilhelm. *Das deutsche Filmschrifttum. Eine Bibliographie der Bücher und Zeitschriften über das Filmwesen.* Leipzig: Verlag Karl W. Hiersemann, 1940.

Tuber, Richard. "Broadcast Rights: A Bibliography. An Annotated Bibliography of Articles published in Legal Literature from 1920–1955," *Journal of Broadcasting* Vol. II/No. 3 (Summer 1958), pp. 263–272.

Ubbens, Wilbert. *Presse-Rundfunk-Fernsehen-Film. Ein Verzeichnis deutschsprachiger Literatur zur Massenkommunikation 1968–1971.* Berlin: Verlag Volker Spiess, 1971.

UNESCO. *Current Mass Communication Research—I. Register of Mass Communication Research Projects in Progress and in Plan. Bibliography of Books and Articles on Mass Communication, Published since 1 January, 1955.* Paris: UNESCO, 1957.

UNESCO. *Tentative International Bibliography of Works Dealing with Press Problems (1900–1952).* Paris: UNESCO, 1954. (Reports and Papers on Mass Communications no. 13.)

UNESCO. *The Influence of the Cinema on Children and Adolescents. An Annotated International Bibliography.* Paris: UNESCO, 1961. (Reports and Papers on Mass Communication no. 31.)

(Various editors). "Articles on Mass Communications in U.S. and Foreign Journals. A Selected Annotated Bibliography," in: *Journalism Quarterly* (Iowa City), Vol. 7/No. 2 (1930) ff.

(Various editors). "Bibliography," in: *Gazette—International Journal for Mass Communication Studies* (Leyden/The Netherlands), Vol. 1/1955 ff. (quarterly).

(Various editors). "Blick in die ausländische Fachpresse," in *Publizistik* (Bremen), Vol. 2/1957 ff. (annually in last edition).

Vincent, Carl. *Bibliografia generale del cinema—Bibliographie générale du cinéma—General Bibliography of Motion Pictures.* Rome: Edizioni dell' Ateneo, 1953.

Voyenne, Bernard. *Guide bibliographique de la presse.* Paris: Centre de Formation des Journalistes, 1958.

Wales, Hugh G./Ferber, Robert. *A Basic Bibliography on Marketing Research.* Chicago: American Marketing Association, 1963.

Weed, Katharine Kirtley and Bond, Richmond Pugh. *Studies of British Newspapers and Periodicals from their Beginning to 1800. A Bibliography.* Chapel Hill: The University of North Carolina Press, 1946.

Werhahn, Jürgen W., and Maiwald, Joachim W. *Bibliographie des Film- und Fernsehrechts, 1896–1962.* Baden-Baden: Verlag für angewandte Wissenschaft, 1963.

Wersig, Gernot. *Inhaltsanalyse. Einführung in ihre Systematik und Literatur,* 3rd. ed. Berlin: Verlag Volker Spiess, 1974.

White, D. *The Comic Strip in America: A Bibliography.* Boston: Boston University Press, 1961.

Wolseley, Roland E. *The Journalist's Bookshelf. An Annotated and Selected Bibliography of United States Journalism.* 7th ed., Philadelphia—New York: Chilton Company—Book Division, Publishers, 1961.

Wright, Charles R. "Television and Radio Program Ratings and Measurements: A Selected and Annotated Bibliography," *Journal of Broadcasting,* Vol. V/No. 2 (Spring 1961), pp. 165–186.

Yamamoto, T. "A List of Books and Articles on Journalism Published in Japan," *Gazette,* 4:197–8, 1958.

INDEX